SELL UP
AND SAIL

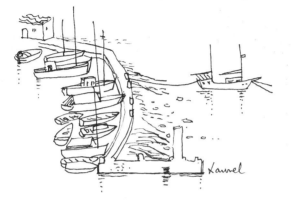

Laurel

SELL UP
& Sail

FIFTH EDITION

Bill and Laurel Cooper

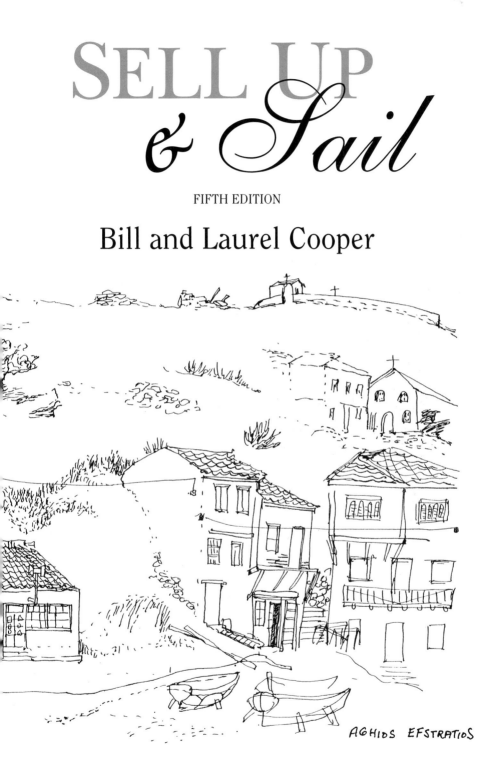

AGHIOS EFSTRATIOS

ADLARD COLES NAUTICAL
LONDON

Published by Adlard Coles Nautical
an imprint of A & C Black (Publishers) Ltd
36 Soho Square, London W1D 3QY
www.adlardcoles.com

First edition published by Stanford Maritime 1986
Reprinted 1987
Second edition published by Nautical Books 1990
Paperback edition with amendments published by
Adlard Coles Nautical 1994
Reprinted 1995, 1996
Third edition 1998
Reprinted 2000
Fourth edition 2001
Fifth edition 2005
Reprinted 2011

ISBN: 978-0-7136-7403-3

A CIP catalogue record for this book is available from the British Library.

This book is produced using paper that is made from wood grown in managed,
sustainable forests. It is natural, renewable and recyclable. The logging and
manufacturing processes conform to the environmental regulations of
the country of origin.

Typeset in 10½/13pt Clearface by
Falcon Oast Graphic Art Ltd.
Printed and bound in Spain
by GraphyCems.

Note: While all reasonable care has been taken in the production of this
publication, the publisher takes no responsibility for the use of the
methods or products described in the book.

All quotations at chapter headings and elsewhere
are either by Laurel Cooper, or Captain John Smith from *A Sea Grammar*,
published in 1627, unless otherwise attributed.

Contents

Dedicated
~ to our parents and children ~
who let us go

Introduction

Living and travelling aboard a cruising boat has become such a popular and widespread way of life that most seafarers, and even many landlubbers nowadays are well aware of it. In the last couple of years, the number of live-aboards has increased phenomenally and it is a wonder that it has escaped the attention of sociologists; not much else does. We, with the waters of the wide world for our homeland, are an increasing constituency: footloose, disenfranchised (not too unhappy about that), and currently with little responsibility for anything much except our own lives. That's the way we want it.

- We don't want rules, regulations, forms and bureaucracy.
- We do not want to be labelled and classified.
- We don't want to be tied to one place.
- We do not need counselling.
- We like travelling, but don't want the waiting, the strikes, the discomfort and expense of air travel, nor the noise, pollution and parking problems of a car, and worst of all, the surrender of one's destiny to people whose main agenda is NOT that of the comfort and timely arrival of their passengers.
- We don't want the Health and Safety Police breathing down our necks when we've been living aboard successfully for probably 30 years longer than they have been alive.

In the first four editions of *Sell Up and Sail*, we reprinted all the introductions of previous editions to illustrate the way this mode of life has developed. In this edition, after a brief introduction we will move straight on to deal with the historic, social and practical aspects of this way of life in the text.

We'll try to show what makes us all tick, but as it's a laid-back life, our clock runs slowly.

This is not a book on technique: seamanship, how to sail, how to maintain engines, though we do indulge ourselves from time to time. It is about attitudes, about mindset (avoidance of), and about ways of ordering your existence on the move.

We are not concerned with obsessive achievers speeding round the world almost without touching land except to have their Round the World ticket punched at the more spectacular blue-water stopping places. We have done huge distances and long ocean crossings, but without timetables or deadlines, and have had time to enjoy people and places on the way.

Our live-aboard world has changed noticeably in the last five years. When we started this life, and when we first wrote about it, the majority of our fellow travellers had visions of world cruising, the trade-winds, flying fish, palm trees and coral atolls. This is no longer the case, though the number of those chasing the flying fish to the nearest palm tree has probably not decreased. What we have seen (partially by observation, and partly from the sharply increased sales of this book) is a very large number content to sail and settle in warm seas, and an even larger number of part-timers who wish to spend the summer living aboard (we call them the Swallows). All are welcome: this is no life for the purist or the prejudiced. You do not have to be a latter-day Captain Birdseye, or rich, or a member of a Royal Yacht Club. We take each other as we find us; and mutual support and help is our creed.

This book is written by two sailors who have each sailed for over 70 years. We have lived afloat for over 30 years, cruising almost 100,000 miles into 45 different countries, over-wintering in nine of them. But it comes with a word of warning. We long-distance cruising yachtsmen are being legislated out of existence. Over-watched, over-regulated, and over-protected by bureaucrats. As our numbers increase annually, so do theirs, and so does the resulting flood of regulation and restriction. We can recall the complete absence of regulation when we first started sailing, and we find the volume and scope of the rules and undemocratic jurisdiction of the bureaucrats frightening. They limit our freedom to design and build good boats as we wish, to travel as and where and how we want to, and add greatly to the expense of doing it.

If you want to sail away in the perfect freedom we enjoyed 30 years ago, you are already too late, but we and many others think it is still worth doing.

SO DO IT, before you are compelled (for your own safety, of course) to join a supervised and inspected convoy in order to cross even the Channel, let alone the Atlantic. And the Pacific and Round the World? Well, that might come to be out of bounds to European yachtsmen. For our own safety, of course.

HEALTH WARNING. CAUTION!

This book contains:
- Personal opinions; some shocking to sensitive people, whether of a die-hard or cutting edge turn of mind.
- Political incorrectitudes, the sort where elaborate avoidance of offence can be more offensive than a friendly acceptance of a fact we think readers need to know. Spades remain spades, not that there's much use for them in a boat.
- Seductive words and beguiling images that may lead you to seriously alter your lifestyle.

UNITS OF MEASUREMENT

Well over 50% of yachts registered in English-speaking countries belong to people who use the old Imperial system. Of the remainder, most mature people will have used the Imperial earlier on in their lives and will be familiar with it.

Of the two major chart publishers, the largest prints in Imperial measure and, though the other is changing to metric, there are still many older charts in use with the Imperial system.

It seems to us, therefore, that we should use the Imperial system as the principal one for this edition. But we hope this book will be useful for a long time, and because there is no doubt that the metric system has gained ground, some of the more significant units have been converted. Now you know why.

1 • Why Do We Do It?

'What a greate matter it is to saile a shyppe or goe to sea.'

In 1976 we sold our house, waved goodbye to the family, and took to the sea in a boat we had built ourselves. We became long-distance, live-aboard cruisers, for whom no very accurate generic term has yet been established; 'Sell-up-and-Sailors' begins to be heard, and perhaps 'Yachties', though this latter is too broad a description, comprising weekenders as well as long-term. We long-term sailors abandoned brick walls and gardens, property taxes, and interference from authorities who continually tried to order what we might or might not do, we took on the less comfortable but much more invigorating life: taking responsibility for our own actions, health, welfare and safety, and through this self-reliance achieved contentment.

Since then, especially latterly, the interest shown in our way of life has increased to a point where the number of people who wish to emulate us, and others like us, has become almost a social phenomenon. The idea of a life afloat seems endlessly appealing. Although it is the antithesis to the collective responsibility of the Welfare State, that may be a perverse explanation for its attraction. It may also be why some people find they cannot handle the idea, since there is no doubt that great exchanges have to be made (we prefer not to call them sacrifices).

Sudden change is not good for the system. The idea should grow on you slowly. The beauty of a boat is that you can usually choose to change slowly, to stay a while or go on as the mood takes you. An Atlantic crossing under sail is slow travelling these days, giving you time to get used to the changing time and climate, and hurling no insults at your biological clock.

Have we not, some people ask, merely exchanged one set of problems for another? Yes, in a sense. We have exchanged the insoluble problems of politics, the fast pace of modern life, the battles with bureaucracy, and the appalling proliferation of paper which push one to the edge of madness, for problems of wind and wave and how and where to go next, which we *can* solve. That alone does wonders for your wellbeing.

When the wanderbug bites you, the symptoms vary from person to person. The aching boredom and frustration of many of today's jobs – or the lack of any job at all – produce understandable feelings of restlessness, and in some people a desire to chuck it in and go elsewhere. Many people in middle life feel that travelling is something they wish to do before they get too old. (I first wrote this 20 years ago, I know now that I shall never be too old to want to travel.) The young feel they would like to do it now, before family responsibilities and education become too great a burden. Many feel that it would be a great way to retire. All have differing requirements and expectations. With some, the idea of travel comes at the head of the list; with others, the escape vehicle comes first and travelling in it second. There is a third category to whom the building of the boat is a sufficient release. They dream of going, but remain at home, quite content. Bill was born restless, and there was no doubt in his mind that he wanted to build his own boat, and travel in it. There was a great deal he wanted to get away from: a very stressful 9–6 job, complications of property and officialdom, winters of ill health, the speed of life, and the trauma of too much change too quickly and for no good reason. I could see his point.

Why a yacht? Because it is a romantic dream that has a chance of coming true: you can build it yourself. And when you've built it, you can travel in it, which is another romantic dream. Building a boat, or acquiring one and refitting it to your own requirements seems to appeal to something very ancient and necessary in man. Your life, and that of your family, depends on how well you build the boat and how carefully you plan the voyage. In a world where someone else is always to blame for any misfortune (and where, with luck, you can sue), to take responsibility for your lives firmly on your own shoulders and find out that the burden is bearable, brings feelings of worth and confidence.

A yacht has a freedom of travel that no other vehicle enjoys. The sea is, by and large, still free to all to cross from one side to the other, starting and finishing where you please, or to stitch your way round its shores. There are still not too many restrictions and regulations specifically affecting yachts on the move. Close to land and in harbour, and on inland waterways, you will find the only restrictions you are likely to meet. In or near big commercial ports you will find one-way systems, parking regulations and choked traffic just as on the busy roads of any city. Away from the big ports, restrictions dwindle until they disappear altogether. A yacht marina is merely a specialised commercial port, and you can expect the same sort of restrictions; added to those of a caravan camp (no rubbish, no barbecues). We avoid them if we can, though this is getting less easy.

God help us if the day ever comes when we are all directed into marinas because commercial interests or overcrowding demand it, or indeed for any other reason. That will be the day when Bill and Laurel start building their kit-form space capsule. (Well, it's got to come, hasn't it?)

Until then, if your aim is carefree mobility, then a yacht is the ideal vehicle. Some people may find eventually that cruising is merely an interval between long stops in one place. Some find a place they love so much they never leave it. Would a caravan have been a better choice? It is certainly cheaper. To use a yacht to stay in one place means that you are not using to the full the expensive and specially designed equipment that was intended to give you mobility: like using a Rolls-Royce as a chicken shed.

If you find, after doing the UQ test which follows, that neither sailing nor travelling are really what you want, but that you would like to drop out of the Stress Layer for a while, or forever, and sink down to the quieter levels of the world, afloat or ashore, then it would make sense to search for your place in the sun by land cruising.

This involves driving at an average of 50 miles an hour instead of five knots. You need registration, insurance and a driving licence, but nowadays most yachts need these too. (Though we don't get done for speeding and there's no MOT. Yet. Keep a wary eye on Brussels.) In most places where you would feel like staying, caravans are strictly regulated into campsites. If you are not in a campsite, water and sanitation can be a problem. You cannot carry much fuel, and yet cannot move without it. You have to stick to roads, of more or less good quality. You are dependent on ferry services to get you across water, and filling stations for fuel, therefore you are at the mercy of strikes and industrial policy. But, yes, it is cheaper. Still, find your ideal small village, town or island, and you will, in some ways, be less isolated than in a bed-sit in outer London.

We find that during a stay of one month in a tiny port we can, even if not accepted as part of the village, at least lose our tourist status. It takes care and tact, however. (The following was written in the first edition, and it is slightly embarrassing to realise how tourism has changed both people and places in 20 years, usually for the worse. We have to give the following encouragement to culture tolerance much more loudly and strongly than once we did, in the days when we half expected everyone to understand.) These strictures no longer apply in those well frequented and notorious places, already ruined, where the punters can order what they want and behave pretty well as they like until the police arrive. For quiet little places, which we hope will stay so, here are the guidelines:

- Try to change nothing. Watch before you join in. Does Baba Iannis always sit in the same chair in the taverna? Then don't pinch his chair. Do the old men like to cluster in one corner of the porch and gaze out over the bay? Then don't block their view with a table full of strangers.
- If the village turns in at half past nine, don't keep them up with noisy chat and laughter, ordering strange drinks that the taverna has not got. Try to talk a little in their language to assuage the inhabitants' natural curiosity as to your age, marital status, and number and age of children. Don't go on too long, though; they have the whole world to run in their deliberations, don't forget, and if they missed an evening who knows what could happen? Catastrophe.
- If Selene brings out her distaff to spin a little in the evening, I go and sit near her with my knitting, and we can exchange wordless admiration without making many waves.
- Sense the mood, so that you do not behave inappropriately. One day, on a small island when the ferry came in, everybody stopped smiling. We, too, put on grave expressions. The men ran down to the ship and came forth

bearing a coffin. The women came down to meet it and fell in behind. It was taken up the little alley beside the taverna to a courtyard where three old ladies had been wont to sit on the warm stones in the evening. Now only two remained: Eleni had been whisked off to hospital on the mainland the day before, and had died there. She was very old, so faces were grave, but not tearful. 'Poor lady,' said the baker, 'I gave her half a loaf of bread many times. She was too poor to pay me, so I forget always to ask for the money.' Everyone came to her funeral, as she had no relatives left. The village cared for her in death, as they had done in life. Can one ask more?

Some people can. They want to go and spend another month at a different place, learn to understand another kind of village and another sort of people, drinking rum punch on a coral beach or rough red wine in a bodega, or 'island tea' in a Turkish tea house, or cook their stew in fumeroles in the Azores and eat lobster-in-the-rough off paper plates in New England. I cannot think of a better way of doing this than to go with your house on your back like a sea snail, at a speed where your surroundings change slowly and without shock to the system, and where your passing leaves no crashing waves behind you.

> *What is this life, if on our cruise*
> *We have no time to sit and booze?*
> *Conversely what, if full of booze*
> *We never get to sea and cruise?*
> *What is this life, I'd like to know*
> *If I am always down below?*
> *And if, upon the starboard tack,*
> *The loo is always out of whack?*
> *And what if I am ill at ease*
> *With not a ripple on the seas?*
> *What is this life? It suits us well.*
> *It's mostly heaven, rarely hell.*

To have built your boat, or at least lovingly altered and equipped her for such a voyage, is a process which brings in itself many rewards. For us, the real reward was the travelling. We held on to this aim through many black days during the building period. Oh, yes, there will be some of those.

This is a book for dreamers, but especially for those who would like to achieve the dream. We would like to take the stars out of your eyes, and use them to illuminate practicalities.

While anyone contemplating long-term cruising would be foolhardy to embark without some nautical ability, the effort of acquiring it can be eased by planning and dreaming. Indeed, dreaming may be one of the most enjoyable aspects of the whole enterprise. If you never get beyond the stage of catalogues and cruising yarns by the Sunday fire, enjoy the book. Just before we sailed, the Lifeboat cox'n said to us, 'A lot of people want to do what you're doing. Difference is: you've done it.'

We were dreamers once. Dreams can become a reality. It is hard work, rather than magic, that gets it done.

2 • Crucial Questions

'Make voyages! Attempt them! There's nothing else.'
Tennessee Williams – *Camino Real*

It was the insidiousness of it that got me.

From the day he retired from the Royal Navy, Bill began the 'one day we'll have a boat and sail away to sea' gambit. Over the years, punctuated by annual visits to the Boat Show (I always went with him – I almost always got migraine), the subliminal mention became less subliminal, and during his next two careers became friendly persuasion, then gentle insistence, and finally downright intransigence.

Not that I disliked either the sea or sailing; far from it, though my experience, while considerable, was largely on inland waters. I even liked the Boat Show. But I was entrenched in a comfortable little life and saw no reason to abandon it in order to get wet, cold and seasick away from my books, cats and children.

It became clear that if I was not to be shanghaied to sea willy-nilly, I should have to take certain steps. These were all backwards, and included countering every stated assumption that I would go with him by good-humoured negatives and careful references to '*your* boat' and '*your* voyage' and 'when you go, I'll have a cottage somewhere for you to come back to'.

After some years of this it dawned on my husband that I meant it, and that I did have good reasons for doubting my capacity at sea. With a sigh, he began to design singlehanded yachts. At this point I realised that he too meant what he said. My bluff called, negotiations began with frank and free discussions, and meaningful dialogues; and the next few designs were very different. If I was going, I wanted a say in the sort of boat I would live in.

• *The inevitable compromise* •

Bill says now that he built *Fare Well* round my books and my bath. For the next few years he worked on my sense of adventure and I worked on his sense of responsibility. We had two children whom we could not leave until it seemed they could do without us. We had cats (one horrid and one super) and a dog. How could Bill leave his tiresome, but very lucrative job? We had a large house that I adored. My life was busy and interesting, and I loved the work I was doing. It was going to be very hard to sell up and go.

However, we made a start. Bill's design took steel shape, and the building began.

• *Departure* •

In the end, as so often happens, some decisions were made for us by events. Bill became very ill for a year or two, able only to potter about the half-completed boat; and there was no longer any problem about breaking away from the job – he'd chucked it and the firm had already filled the vacancy. The children grew up suddenly and moved out, leaving us in a house far too big and expensive on our own. The horrid cat died, and we decided to take the other with us – one of our more brilliant decisions, as was the idea of giving the dog to Bill's widowed father, leading to one of those man-dog relationships worthy of letters of flame.

It began to look as if the sooner we sold up and sailed, the sooner Bill would regain his health. There was the little matter of finishing a 55-foot ketch, and getting it to sea, but we had been working on that for some time anyway. (It took five years altogether and is quite another story.) Gradually the people who had been saying 'you'll never finish it' began to realise that we damn well would, and that we were damn well going.

Don't kid yourselves, it was hard. Morale was sometimes very low. It was as hard as I had thought it would be to sell the house, part with the dog, and say goodbyes to family and friends. On the plus side, our son Ben decided to accompany us for a while. A sense of excitement began to grow as we worked, planned and stored ship; and found some pleasant people to share our maiden voyage to Gibraltar. This being (apart from trials) our first trip, and nearly my first ocean trip, Bill had decided to be prudent and take some extra muscle.

When we finally set sail from Lowestoft: six people and the cat Nelson, a burden rolled off my shoulders that I had never been aware of. I smelt the sea, saw the first of many ocean sunsets, and felt a freedom I'd never known before.

I wouldn't have changed places with anyone.

• *Looking back* •

I had always loved the sea in rather a romantic and sentimental way. I was born and brought up by the sea, and dipped my toes in it nearly every day of my childhood summers, or sat in the shallows and let the little waves bounce in my lap. You could pee in it without anyone knowing. You could watch the storms from the cliffs and be amazed by the crashing noise of the breakers, the cold hiss and rattle and roar of grating pebbles; even at that distance you must shout to be heard. In bed you could hear the waves above the fitful pelt and spatter of the winter rain. How blissful to be warm in bed, and not out in the dark on the wild sea.

As I grew up I learned to sail, on the Broads of course, as did the young Nelson, but I was 17 before I even crossed the Channel in a ferry, and the sea was still magic, and dangerous and attractive like an elder brother's motorbike.

That attitude was not very helpful when faced with a life at sea in one's mid forties. How would I cope with storms? How would I handle seasickness and exhaustion when we were short-handed? Could I stand my companions (let alone my husband) at close quarters and under stress? It seemed a good idea to find out about this sort of thing while the boat was still a-building. I do not advise anyone less dedicated to leave it as late as this. It is far better to do all this and more before you embark on a project that has a momentum as inevitable as the birth of a child, and to abort which is just as painful and a good deal more expensive.

• *Getting some sea-time in* •

My only real sea experience at that time (I discount dinghy racing where you are home and dry after a couple of hours) was a four-week cruise in 1954 with Bill, our six-month-old daughter and my brother. The yacht was a 5-tonner, *Phoenix*, without motor or loo. I felt that there was some basis for confidence here, as although it was July in the Mediterranean we had had one of those unseasonable summer storms, and a thick fog in the Sicilian Channel shipping lanes to boot. I had by no means disgraced myself; I had cooked, washed nappies, kept watch,

Our first cruising experience, back in 1954, was in Phoenix, *a little 5-tonner which, as you can see, was very compact and had little in the way of creature comforts and safety features such as guardrails and netting. But we enjoyed our four-week cruise and the baby loved it!*

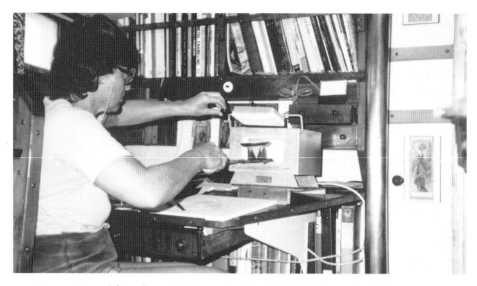

Laurel found a quiet corner on Fare Well *for her enamelling.*

steered and been useful. The baby enjoyed every minute. I enjoyed most of it. So far, so good.

I had the great advantage of faith in my captain. Bill is an experienced deep-sea yachtsman, and an ex-professional navigator. He is also a seaman of the old-fashioned kind, which he describes as managing without what you haven't got, and which leads to some amazingly ingenious ways of achieving the aim. I felt I should have confidence in the boat, too; she was strongly built and looked sea-worthy, and I was getting to know her by building her. I had had a lot to say about the design, and not just in the galley. The guardrails were to be very strong in case my congenitally dislocated hip failed me. (It didn't seem to worry Bill that his life-long cruising companion was what had been successively known as crippled (1930s) handicapped ('40s and '50s) disabled ('60s and '70s) and differently-abled ('80s and '90s) and back to disabled in 2000. What will the next term be we wonder?) On the foredeck we had strong netting to prevent a body slipping through the guardrails. Below, the furniture was built strongly enough to fall against in a seaway without damaging it, the corollary being that such solidity can cause a lot of mayhem to bodies bouncing off it. Despite the numerous handholds that we put everywhere, strong enough to Tarzan around the boat on, I still some-times ping-ponged off the furniture. Gazing at my doleful bruises, I insisted on more cushions, in the cockpit as well. Bill hates them, but they do cut down injuries, not only mine.

We have mentioned the bath. For anyone with bone-aches like mine, a hot bath is a solace greater than any medicine. Salt water can be used. Since it is now believed that more yachtsmen die of hypothermia than drowning, and a recommended remedy for the former is a warm bath, maybe it's less of a luxury than we thought.

I wanted a corner for drawing, and I refused to share the chart table, as I knew it would cause friction. I got it, a neat solution that was flexible enough to become a workbench when I started enamelling.

Double bunks were unusual in the late 1960s, when practically all cruises were a fortnight in the summer, and a few weekends. Long-term was different, you spend a lot of your life in bed, you might as well be happy there: we designed the first double bunk we'd seen that could be got at from three sides, instead of being shoved against the ship's side. I heard of someone who had an arm broken by a heavy bunkmate crawling over her in such a bunk, answering a night call. Twice. Of course, Bill's design is commonplace now, as are many of the features on *Fare Well* that were entirely new at the time.

• *Gaining experience* •

To get more confidence in myself, I went to the National Sailing Centre at Cowes (now alas no more) to learn some navigation (the coastal part of the Yachtmaster® qualification). Bill normally does all this, and to compete with him seemed foolish: if someone can play the Moonlight Sonata should you join in on a penny whistle? But I felt a lot better for knowing something, and it might have become vital.

I gained more experience. When we could we helped friends who were new to sailing by doing short trips round the coast or across the Channel. I began to realise I was not the first in the crew to succumb to seasickness, that pills and sensible precautions to prevent overtiredness and chilling were better than being frightfully brave, and that I was so hungry I had to cook something. I found that a little yacht flying down-Channel before a stiff breeze was great. I discovered that I did not much like going to windward. We remained on speaking terms with our friends. It looked as if things were going to be all right.

The house was sold. I still writhe with pain when I recall this period. Although planning and forethought went into everything we did, it turned out there was still a lot to learn. Much of it, thirty years on, we are still learning by pleasurable stages, a little of it the hard way.

Thirty happy years of cruising are witness to the fact that we did our home-work, and that by the end of our maiden voyage, a romantic dreamer had become something of a practical sea-person, and Nelson had enthusiastically embarked on the life of a one-eyed sea-cat.

Having described the process whereby I came to accept and enjoy living at sea, there are some relevant questions *you* should answer.

PART TWO: TEST YOUR UQ

'Too little thought before you go,
And you'll be back before you know'

We have devised a test to measure what we shall call your 'Ulysses Quotient' or UQ. While it should not be taken desperately seriously, it will nevertheless give you plenty to think about. You and your mate may even have your first disagreement over the first question. Ulysses, it will be remembered, roamed the seas for about ten years, looking for his homeland, the island of Ithaca. UQ can be described as a tendency to wander off for years in a small boat without actually getting anywhere much. (Though he was probably the worst navigator in history, he did, it is pointed out to us, suffer under the handicap of having an all-male crew!)

The desire, the will, to go cruising is paramount. We realise that nothing we say will stop you if you are determined; whether you are an unskilled, penniless tyro, incapacitated by alcohol and agues, embarking in an unseaworthy boat with a sack of lentils and aiming to be the first member of Depressives Anonymous to round Cape Horn; or a thrifty couple with a small but well-found boat, making well-planned voyages that are triumphs of ingenuity, courage and dedication.

However, we want you to enjoy your cruising; and time spent now on thinking and planning will save you money and misery later on. We cannot say this often enough.

You and your spouse, or mate, or lifelong companion, whatever (living at sea we have come across every combination of all four sexes), should do the test separately, in private, and *without discussions or comparisons* until all the scoring is finished. If you would like your children to do it, the same conditions apply: certainly they should join in the discussions which follow. Incidentally, I had better make it clear that I use the word 'Mate' throughout this book to cover: wife, husband, son, daughter, companion, friend, crew, lover, consenting adult – whoever is going with you to be your team mate.

You each (or all) have a lot of decisions to make, and you might as well know what your sticking points are now. They may prove to be immovable, they may need hard work and compromise to find a way round them, they may in time vanish like smoke, but at least you will know what you are up against. Name your enemy and the battle begins.

Despite the fact that we have somewhere called it a quiz, note that your scores are nothing to do with winning or losing, or with being right or wrong. It's not a contest. It is an attempt to assess: (1) your present situation, which may of course change, (2) practical considerations which may have a bearing on your future, (3) your abilities and capabilities, and (4) your attitude to mobility and change. The scoring comes under three different headings: Alpha (A); Kappa (K); and Sigma ($\sum$). Their significance will become apparent later.

If you cheat, have fun, and carry on dreaming. If you are really keen on the idea, take a good look at yourself, answer honestly, and this could be the first step in your voyage.

'Courage, my hearts!'

THE ULYSSES QUOTIENT

SECTION ONE – BASIC QUESTIONS: DO YOU REALLY WANT TO GO?

1 Do you like sailing?
   (a) Yes, very much.
   (b) Keen to try.
   (c) Not sure, I think I shan't enjoy it.
   (d) Done it. Don't like it.
   If (a) score A4, if (b) score A2, if (c) score $\sum 5$. If (d) score $\sum 15$, and go to question Q3.

2 You are faced with a rough sea and a rising wind on a long beat into harbour. Do you:
   (a) Grin and bear it?
   (b) Say 'This is what it's all about chaps,' and call for eggs and bacon?
   (c) Get sick and miserable, and let the others get on with it?
   (d) Get sick and miserable, but try to produce the eggs and bacon?
   If (a) score A2, if (b) score A1, if (c) score $\sum 1$. If (d) score A1.

3 Do you like travelling abroad? If Yes, continue. If No, score $\sum 4$ and go to Q7.

4 If you have never been abroad score $\sum 4$ and go to Q7.

5 When you are abroad, do you prefer to go to or with:
   (a) A *pension*?
   (b) A campsite?
   (c) A hotel?
   (d) Bareboat charter?
   (e) Flotilla?
   If (a) score 0, if (b) score K1, if (c) score $\sum 2$, if (d) score K2, if (e) score KI.

6 When you are abroad, do you:
   (a) Like eating local dishes?
   (b) Go for snake soup and the honeybees coated in chocolate?
   (c) Prefer your normal diet?
   If (a) score K1, if (b) score K2, if (c) score $\sum 2$.

7 Do you speak any language other than your own (enough to be polite and do some shopping)? Score A1 for one foreign language, A2 for two foreign languages and so on.

8 Can you afford this venture?
   (a) Yes.
   (b) In time, and with care.
   (c) No.
   (d) I've just won the Lottery.
   If (a) score A2, if (b) score 0, if (c) score $\sum 3$, if (d) score what you like!

• Discussion on Section One •

Questions (1) and (2) are germane. If you are unsure, you had better find out the answers for certain, for your own sake and the rest of the crew. Do this by sailing with friends, in as many different boats and situations as possible. If you ultimately intend to go singlehanded, skip the next paragraphs and go to (3). If you are going to sail with a mate, and your answers to Questions (1) and (2) differ widely from your partner's, the battle lines could be already drawn.

If you like ear'oling (sailing with the lee rail under) and spray in your face, and your mate prefers to go over on the ferry, you have a compatibility problem which needs to be resolved. How much can (and will) Salty Sam or Sue throttle back to accommodate the natural fears of less adventurous members of the crew? We

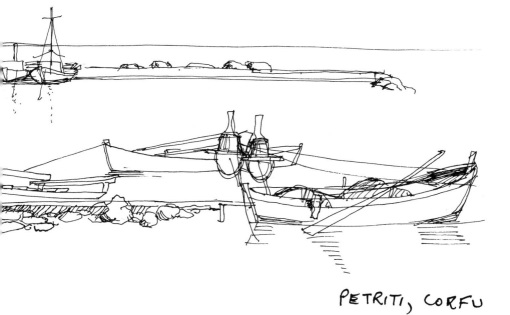

PETRITI, CORFU

have known voyages founder on the fact that the skipper was too harsh, hard-driving and self-punishing. This is fine for racing weekends but unbearable for a long cruise, which ought to be a pleasant experience; and feeble crews do not contribute to this either.

Be assured that if you go, and stick to it, you will both, or all, change, perhaps in unexpected ways. We have known people find strength and health and self confidence. We have known tough looking characters fall apart. When push comes to shove, there are surprises in store.

Willingness is all, however, and much may be learned and achieved with determination. We have mentioned sailing with friends. Some might consider that a flotilla holiday would be the ideal way to do this. We do not. It makes a marvellous holiday and may tempt you into thinking you like cruising; but it is an artificial set-up. You will learn little that is of any use for your purpose, since flotilla sailing has less to do with long-distance cruising than the child licking the basin has to do with making the cake. It also suffers the curse of the ticking clock (must get to the airport), that destroyer of relaxed cruises. Plus, you never meet the locals.

While many people get bitten by the cruising bug on a flotilla holiday, you will need a lot of practice in situations where you must get out of trouble on your own. That said, bareboating (ie chartering a boat to sail without professional assistance and as you wish) is probably a happy medium. You will learn a lot, and help should not be far away.

For Absolute Beginners there is a starter pack in Chapter 7 which will help you to be useful even on your first sail.

Questions 3–6: Do you really like 'abroad'?

We all love the thought of the palm trees, soft breezes, and swaying hula hula girls. But do you enjoy new tastes and smells, or would you rather have your joint and two veg and tea like mother made (for Brits), or biscuits and red eye gravy (for Americans)? You can get McDonalds, French fries and Foster's lager almost anywhere.

Do you find it all interesting and exciting, or do you worry about the drinking water and the loos? Are you happy in a *pension*, eating with the family and making a stab at the language, or do you prefer a coach tour or hotel where a courier takes care of all the hassle? Are you, in other words, a self-reliant traveller?

Question 7: Languages

If you are not good at languages, you can always go West, where most of the continent of North America and a good many of the West Indian islands, plus the Bahamas and Bermuda, are populated by people who speak English of a sort. You can also go down to the Antipodes. If you go to the Mediterranean, and many other seas where the language is strange, you will have to cope with foreigners on entry to a new country; and you will have to store ship, get water and fuel, and deal with spares and repairs. This will be stressful if you are impatient with people who speak little or no English. The other side of the coin is the fun of it. When I was much younger and prettier, I left our yacht *Phoenix* in Syracuse harbour and went looking for a fishhook with my Italian Dictionary. 'Amo?' I said hopefully to the proprietor of the fishing tackle shop. His eyes lit up. 'I love you too!' he said. It was a while before I could get him back to the subject of fishhooks. When Nelson had a skin problem that I suspected to be a fungus, a young German came over to help. 'I hear your cat suffers from the mushrooms,' he said. And I have never forgotten the phrase written in our visitor's book by a Turk, wishing us 'Mary Christmas'.

Question 8: Can you afford this venture?

What is enough? Selling your house, or your business, if you own it, will provide enough money for a reasonable boat. But it has to be maintained, as you do; you will need to fit her out and store before you go, and you need reserves for contingencies – which may be drastic. Don't count on being able to find work on the way. The next chapter on Finance will give you some idea of probable costs, but a lot depends on whether you are in the champagne and nightclub, or local wine and festival bracket. Perhaps you need more time to work and save, in order to sail with debts paid, mortgages discharged, some reserves and a light heart.

SECTION TWO – YOUR JOB: CAN YOU LEAVE IT?

1 Do you own your own business? If Yes, go to Q4. If No, continue.

2 Are you unemployed or retired? If unemployed score K2, if retired score K2. In either case proceed to Q7, otherwise continue.

3 How do you feel about the job you are doing now? Choose any of the following:
   (a) I have a strong vocation.
   (b) I really like my job.
   (c) It's just a job.
   (d) I'm in line for promotion.
   (e) I'll be glad to leave.
   (f) I'm ready for a change.
   (g) I've embezzled the tea fund and I'd better go.
   If (a) score $\Sigma3$, if (b) score $\Sigma2$, if (c) score 0. If (d) score $\Sigma1$, if (e) score K1, if (f) score K2, if (g) score K10. Proceed to Q5.

4 Which of the following statements is nearest to how you feel? (Choose one.)
   (a) I can't let my work force down.
   (b) It's a family business: I have obligations.
   (c) I work all the hours God sends, and love every minute of it.
   (d) I used to enjoy it, but it's getting me down.
   (e) It's a good living and I'm content.
   (f) I'd sell if I could find a buyer.
   (g) I'd be glad to be shot of it.
   If (a) score $\Sigma2$, if (b) score $\Sigma3$, if (c) score $\Sigma1$, if (d) score 0, if (e) score $\Sigma1$, if (f) score K1, if (g) score K3.

5 Are you worried that you might lose skills and/or seniority while you are away?
   (a) No problem.
   (b) I'll catch up later.
   (c) Yes.
   If (a) score K2, if (b) score K1, if (c) score $\Sigma4$.

6 If you are a member of an occupational pension scheme, what happens if you give up your job now?
   (a) I get a reduced secure pension on retirement.
   (b) I get a return of contributions but no pension.
   (c) I have no protected rights.
   If (a) score K1, if (b) score 0, if (c) score $\Sigma1$.

7 Can you use your skills abroad? (A skilled craftsman is welcome almost anywhere, but the Professions often erect barriers against foreign practitioners. See chapter on Finance.)
   (a) Yes.
   (b) To a certain extent.
   (c) No.
   If (a) score K2 A2, if (b) score K1 A1, if (c) score $\Sigma2$.

8 If in Section One (Basic Questions) you scored: A's: more than 6, score a further K1. K's: more than 5, score a further K1. ∑'s: more than 6, score a further ∑2.

9 Are you any of these, or do you hold similar posts: Justice of the Peace, President of the Women's Institute or Townswomen's Guild, Provincial Grand Officer in the Buffs or Freemasons, chairperson or officer of any Clubs or Societies, Mayor, Councillor etc? Score ∑2 for each post you hold. If you hold more than three, score a bonus of ∑3. NB: If you are dying to resign from them all, score K3.

10 Do you spend more than two nights a week at meetings which are nothing to do with your job? (Here only, your job means what you are paid to do. In all other questions 'job' includes unpaid work such as housewifery, parenthood, voluntary work etc.) If Yes, score ∑4, but see NB above.

11 Do you spend more than two nights a week at meetings which are to do with your job? If Yes, score ∑3.

12 Can you give up the interests in Q 9?
   (a) Easily.
   (b) With regret.
   (c) No.
   If (a) score K1, if (b) score ∑1, if (c) score ∑3.

• *Discussion on Section Two* •

Question 1: Can you leave your job?
If you are unemployed, now could be your chance to go until the job situation changes, especially if your skills are such as to enable you to pick up work here and there on the trip. 'Job mobility' is much in everyone's minds, 'serial professions' as envisaged by Alvin Toffler in his book *Future Shock* are already with us: that is, a series of occupations where you will change jobs at around five-year intervals. Such flexibility will make leaves of absence or sabbaticals between jobs a much more feasible proposition, and probably improve the mental and physical health of all concerned. On the other hand there are signs that insecurity of tenure of jobs is causing increased tension; frequent changes are with us, but they are not always so beneficent as Toffler anticipated.

Questions 3–5
If yours are technical skills in a fast-changing field, it will be hard to keep up while you are away. Technical journals are heavy: trusting them to foreign mails is expensive and chancy. Once we used to ask friends to bring them when they visit us, and were smitten with guilt when their heaviest piece of luggage turned out to be full of yachting magazines, a pilot book, the Sunday papers, 'and a few paperbacks' plus several Royal Institute of Navigation Journals. Total weight 10 kilos. Publications are profligate with paper these days.

If you want to keep your options open, then leave of absence, while you find out if you really enjoy the life, is the best answer. Otherwise you face a refresher course of some kind on your return, if there is one. This also applies if by leaving your job you lose status and seniority. It could be hard.

So we wrote in the mid-eighties.

The above two paragraphs were still true for the last edition, but the internet has changed everything, and now keeping up with events, news and communication gets easier every day, *if that is what you want.* Some people manage to continue to work via the internet and e-mail while living aboard. Paradoxically, this has not become easier with new developments unless you are well-off. The internet has developed and websites etc have become more complex. People are more verbose in e-mail. Downloading now takes ages unless you are on a shore line at least – preferably broadband. The whole laptop thing can be a drag on a relaxed and carefree existence. Nevertheless it's hard to find a yacht without one these days.

If leave of absence is not possible and you cannot take your job with you on your laptop, you should look on your voyage as early retirement, with the possibility that you might have to return to work later. If your skills are really rare and valuable you should have no trouble finding a job when you come back, and your employer will not care where you have been, so long as it wasn't in gaol. If your skills are less useful, you could face re-training for a new career. In either case, we don't need to tell you that your curriculum vitae (resumé, to Americans) would need to be carefully worded. You will clearly be able to provide adequate, not to say impressive, reasons for your absence. The usual pack of lies, in fact. At least your health and vigour should have improved, and you might have acquired a whole new set of skills, but in the present climate you may face great difficulties getting back into the labour market after a certain age.

Questions 6–8

If you are used to being a person of consequence, consider whether you will be satisfied with being 'just a yachtie'. We tend to come a bit lower on the social scale than some of you are accustomed to. If you sell your house you will be 'of no fixed abode', and won't get a credit rating (just try it with no fixed abode – just try it, that's all!). In some countries you will end up classed with gypsies, travellers, beggars, tramps and chicken-stealers. There are many compensating and pleasurable feelings of achievement and satisfaction, but these do not scintillate outwardly in Rolls-Royce and Rolexes; rather in an air of contentment and relaxation.

And once having tasted real freedom, could you ever again settle to a 9–5 existence? We think we could if the devil drove – but he'd need a big whip. And who'd give us a job at our age?

SECTION THREE – YOUR HEALTH: ARE YOU FIT TO GO?

1　Do you feel unwell a lot of the time? If No, continue. If Yes, score $\sum 4$.
2　Do you have a condition for which you regularly seek medical advice? If No, continue. If Yes, score $\sum 5$.
3　Do you have a condition which worries you and for which you have not sought medical advice? If Yes, score $\sum 4$. If the answers to the last three questions were all No, score K3 and go on to Section 4. Otherwise continue.
4　Do you remember your condition:
　(a) Hardly ever?
　(b) Some of the time?
　(c) All the time?
　If (a) score K1, if (b) score $\sum 1$, if (c) score $\sum 3$.
5　Would your doctor allow you long periods of self-medication?
　(a) Yes.
　(b) No.
　(c) He doesn't give a toss.
　If (a) score K1, if (b) score $\sum 4$, if (c) score 0 and change your doctor.
6　Could your condition:
　(a) Prevent your standing a watch, night or day?
　(b) Endanger the boat or fellow crew members?
　(c) Necessitate expensive and/or time-consuming medical attention while on voyage?
　(d) Cause over-tiredness or require a rigid regime or schedule?
　If your answer to Q6 is No to all four, score K1. If your answer is Yes to (a), (b) or (c), score $\sum 2$ for each Yes. If (d) score $\sum 1$.

• *Discussion on Section Three* •

Questions 1–4: Are you fit to go?

There is no doubt that we go to sea with the most amazing handicaps. We have met unbelievably courageous long-distance cruisers with diabetes, cancer, heart conditions and stroke, amputees, people with imperfect limbs and paralysis; not to mention those souls (perhaps more foolhardy than courageous) who were obese or alcoholic or addicted; to which list we should add several who were clearly bonkers. Nothing short of coma seems to stop us, as long as we are willing and able to 'manage' our disability with long-range advice.

A positive mental attitude will assist one's fellows to make a few (oh, very few) allowances, as will a determination to excel in the things one can do, while not shirking those tasks which will cause discomfort but not damage. Realism is of the utmost importance here, and the quality of enjoyment one can expect must be considered as carefully as physical well-being. A long talk with a doctor who understands exactly what long-distance cruising is all about will be necessary. (See below.) If you have not already consulted on anything that worries you, ask yourself why.

Question 5

At sea you will have to care for yourself. This requires more sense than bravado. A golfing doctor who doesn't understand what is involved will merely tell you not to go: professional people must be cautious about giving advice in unusual circumstances, as they feel they could be held liable for the consequences. Find yourself a yachting doctor to consult. Where do you find him? Offshore at the Yacht Club, of course, where his patients can't get at him! If you are in luck you should get a realistic answer; pointing out dangers to avoid, how to monitor your condition, what drugs or medication to take with you, how to inject yourself safely, what situations you really must beware of, and what to exercise and how. See later discussion on First Aid at Sea courses.

Question 6

Consider carefully whether you are a danger to the boat or crew. Red-green colour blindness, for instance, is a strong contra-indication for singlehanded sailing since it is of vital significance on a lone night watch to be able to distinguish red and green lights on shore and on other vessels. (Get round this by sailing with others and volunteering for extra day watches. You can still help change sails at night.) A condition that causes you to tire easily, or requires a rigid regime or time schedule, should give you pause; since one of the great benefits of the life is being able to forget time and rigidity. Most of us long-term cruisers don't even know what day it is, and find that getting friends to airports on a particular day, let alone a particular time, is an unwelcome return to a scheduled world. That said, a little structuring of the day to accommodate your condition, whatever it is, ought not to upset your fellows if your presence brings compensating advantages. (A courageous yachtsman we heard of recently commuted from Mexico to Vancouver every two weeks for essential treatment – not many of us would have the stamina or the cash.)

A word on drinking. Most of us do this with great gusto – the rum or wine being cheap and the company enjoyable. But note that air pilots are forbidden to drink before and during flying. Naval navigating officers are not so forbidden, but nevertheless have a long-standing tradition of not drinking at sea. (Of course when let off the hook you'll find them sinking a gin while alongside; but that's better than drinking at sea and sinking the ship.) Make up your own mind, but the sea is no place for alcoholics. We know of at least one yacht that was lost with all hands, where drink was a contributing cause, and a good many drownings from dinghies on the way back from the pub.

Don't forget that alcohol in the bloodstream increases seasickness. Not a few wild farewell parties have caused a sensible postponement of the sailing day. Nor is it unknown for a yacht, after the gongs, bells and cannons have wished them

Bon Voyage, to creep into a bay round the very first headland and drop anchor till their headaches improved.

Now the good news. On a well-organised voyage your general health will improve, as the outdoor life and the lack of stress seep into your body and mind. You will probably be cured of your migraine (as I was), your asthma or your hayfever, tummy cramps, eczema, PMT – anything with its true origins in tension and stress.

PORTE DE PECHE
BEAULIEU.

Laurel Nov 85

SECTION FOUR – YOUR FAMILY: HOW STRONG IS THE PULL?

1 Have you parents, children, or near relatives living?
   If No, score K1 and go to Q4. If Yes, score Σ1 and continue.

2 Are you worried about any of them?
   If No, score 0. If Yes, score Σ3 for each one.

3 Are you the only child? If No, score 0. If Yes, score Σ2.

4 Has your mate (if any) parents, children or near relatives living? If No, score K1
   and END THIS SECTION. If Yes, score Σ1 and continue.

5 Is he/she worried about any of them? If No, score 0 and END THIS SECTION. If
   Yes, score Σ3 for each one and continue.

6 Is he/she an only child? If No, score 0. If Yes, score Σ2.

7 What age will your child (children), both yours and your mate's, be when you
   sail? Will you take them with you? Score as follows:

Age	Taking them	Leaving them
0–5 years	0	Σ5
6–12 years	Σ1	Σ4
12–18 years	Σ2	Σ4
over 18 and/or independent	Σ2	Σ1
over 18 and dependent	Σ2	Σ4

   (The score is additive, thus if taking a baby and toddler with you score 0; and if
   you are taking one four-year-old and leaving two of 13 and 15 years respectively, score Σ8.)

8 Is there someone reliable to care for children remaining at home? If Yes, score
   K2. If No, score Σ4.

9 Do you have children of school age?
   If No, END THIS SECTION. If Yes,
   (a) Will you teach them yourself?
   (b) Will you use a correspondence course?
   (c) Will you send them to boarding school at home?
   (d) Will you send them to local schools as you travel? And stay long enough to
   benefit?
   If (a) score K2, if (b) score K2, if (c) score K1. If (d) score 0.

Note Q8 There is a wide range of possibilities here. Boarding schools fill the bill in
term time, but usually other arrangements must be made in the holidays if they
cannot join you. Compliant relatives may take your child on for a while; this was a
common thing in wartime, and most of us did not seem to suffer from being parked
on aunts and grandparents and changing schools at frequent intervals. The criterion
has to be that the arrangement is satisfactory to all parties.

• *Discussion on Section Four* •

Questions 1–6

You will not enjoy your cruise if family responsibilities lie heavily upon you. It makes sense, therefore, to solve as many problems as you can before you leave, so that on sailing you know that the situation is as stable as can be expected. Good communications after your departure are important; apron strings pull in both directions, and your family will sometimes be as anxious about you as you may be about them. Forwarding snailmail can be rather a chore. And you do get to a stage where receiving it is a chore as well. Some member of the family usually takes it on, sometimes quite gladly. Make sure they are reimbursed for any postage, and that they clearly understand what is junk mail to you and what is not, otherwise you might get the bulb catalogues and *You May Have Already Won* (date of competition expired, of course) instead of a sought-after spare parts list and the OCC Journal. Mobile phones are universal now, but roaming charges are still costly. E-mail, both a blessing and a curse, is now the answer. There are internet cafés in the most surprising places these days, under a roof of banana leaves or halfway up an icy mountain.

Get the Social Services off your back and on the ball

If you have elderly relatives that you have been in the habit of visiting, it is well worth going along to the DHSS and pointing out that you will not be available after such-and-such a date. The Social Services can often help a great deal, and will do more if prodded: a talk with them may produce Home Help, meals on wheels, and a regular health visit, for instance. Your absence will precipitate mild panic, and quite right too, but the concern will not be for either you or your 'rello' (as our Aussie friends call them).

If you think more help is needed, Age Concern can tell you what might be available. A good neighbour can be your communication link in case of need. The more people who know the situation the better: doctor, lawyer, fellow club members, fellow church members, and reliable neighbours: anyone who could help to hold the fort if need be. Don't forget great-nephews and nieces, and grandchildren, all of whom should be concerned, and encouraged to visit and give what assistance they can. However, they will all expect you (if you are female) to reappear and wave a magic wand if anything goes wrong, and this can be tricky if you are one donkey, two ferryboats and a bus away from an air terminal, as I was on one occasion. Let alone the expense.

If you are male, then it is considered that you have an excellent reason for whatever crazy thing you are doing, usually connected with the sacred word *business* which excuses everything, and far less pressure is applied. So that's all right then. You may, however, be the only son and your relative may be isolated and friendless. The Social Services and Age Concern will be vital in this case, especially if the idea of moving to sheltered accommodation (for example with a warden) is met with resistance or is not possible for other reasons.

What if, after all your efforts, your obstinate 90-year-old tells the meals on wheels lady where to put her gammon and mashed, and slams the door on the Health Visitor as if she were the double glazing man? What if your old person, in fact, insists on self-sufficiency and independence, in a mountain shack or the middle of Dartmoor? Presumably they do this from choice. You are a chip off the old block, aren't you? You'll be doing the same thing when you're their age. In the meantime you wish them good luck, and sail; also from choice. Only you can decide, but if things are unstable at home, it is particularly necessary for your peace of mind to have frequent communications, and a reserve of cash to travel home; and this will affect your choice of cruising ground.

Make sure the old ducks know how to use a computer, or know a man who does. The second best thing we two old ducks did when we reached 60 was to go on a computer course. This is now known as 'silver surfing'. (The best thing we did, of course, was to continue sailing.)

Some years ago the majority of live-aboards 'Went Home' only rarely. In the last few years, the cost of flying has decreased considerably and you can see more of the 'rellos'. Since the advent of Ryanair or Easyjet, visits are easier and cheaper, but this may not last, recent cut-throat price wars have put some airlines out of business. Prices are rising again. The last time we flew between the UK and Greece we got a better price with BA. And more leg-room and better service too.

Children

Take 'em or leave 'em? Many people have taken their children to sea, from birth to 13 or 14, and few have regretted it. Books written by survivors of wrecks can frighten you off, but note that the children DO survive. Read the many articles written for cruising magazines by parents who find, in the main, that cruising with their children has been an enriching experience. Their tales of sailing to new lands, meeting new people, and how the children develop self-reliance and confidence, and better yet, a stronger family bond, will be an inspiration for you. We also have a feeling that crews with children on board take more care.

SECTION FIVE – BOAT SKILLS: HOW ABLE A SEAMAN ARE YOU?

1 Do you own, or part-own, a boat? Or have you in the past? If Yes, score A2. If No, score Σ1.
2 Do you maintain, or help to maintain, a boat? (Hands-on, not just paying for it.) If Yes, score A2. If No, score Σ2.
3 Are you a qualified Master Mariner with a lifetime of experience and over 30,000 miles under sail in your log? If Yes, score A30, and go to Q17.
4 Do you potter about in boats? If Yes, score A1. If No, score 0.
5 Are you a weekend dinghy or small-boat sailor? If Yes, score A1. If No, score 0.

---

6   Have you cruised locally at home or abroad in a yacht for more than 14 days? If Yes, score A2. If No, score 0.

7   Have you made a passage to a foreign country? If Yes, score A2. If No, score 0.

8   Have you kept a night watch by yourself at sea? If Yes, score A2. If No, score 0.

9   Can you take a compass bearing? If Yes, score A1. If No, score 0.

10 Can you make any of the following: bowline, clove hitch, rolling hitch, fisherman's bend, figure-of-eight knot, sheet bend? If you can do them all NOW score A2. If you can do three of them score A1.

11 If your car goes wrong do you:
    (a) Call in the garage?
    (b) Have a go at mending it?
    (c) Read the manual and then have a go at mending it?
    If (a) score $\sum 2$, if (b) score A1, if (c) score A2.

12 Can you cook:
    (a) Under difficult circumstances?
    (b) With unfamiliar and limited ingredients?
    (c) Without getting seasick?
    If (a) score A1, if (b) score A1, if (c) score A1. If Yes to all three, score a bonus of A2.

13 Do you suffer from seasickness?
    If No, score A4 and go to Q17. If Yes, continue.

14 Is your seasickness controllable or reducible by drugs?
    If Yes, score A1 and go to Q16. If No, continue.

15 Do you recover after 24 hours or so at sea?
    If Yes, score A1. If No, continue.

16 Are you prepared to suffer the occasional day of misery?
    If Yes, score A1. If No, score $\sum 10$.

17 Do you have a smattering of any of the following skills? Carpentry, compass adjusting, computer technology, diesel and petrol engineering, electrics (AC or DC), electronics, firefighting, fishing, food preservation, haircutting, how to move heavy loads, laundering (by hand), metalworking, meteorology, musical instrument (small), paramedical skills, painting, plumbing, refrigeration engineering, radio, rigging, sail repair, scuba diving, sewing, soldering, swimming, upholstery. Score A1 for each skill you claim.

• Discussion on Section Five •

'If there be more learners than saylors all the worke to save ship, goodes and lives must be on them especially in foule weather.'

It seems to us that anyone who wishes to go in for the cruising life will have acquired some skills. Such is the availability of experience these days that failure to have done anything so far could indicate a lukewarmth: or maybe you are just dreaming.

Some definitions might be useful. In Questions 1–3 we clearly infer a sailing boat, though if for perfectly valid reasons you are thinking of going in a motor yacht, then adapt the question accordingly. Question 4, on the other hand, could mean any type of boat, which is clearly better than none at all. Questions 5–9 involve many conditions which might be borderline: you must use your common sense. If you haven't any common sense, subtract A20!

Question 10 is a fundamental. At first we thought it should score very high; then we reasoned that we are not testing seamanship, but a kind of nautical wanderlust of which ability is only a part. Bill would not like anyone to go to sea without being able to do all these knots in the dark, or to drive even a motorboat away from its moorings without knowing the bowline at least.

If you are a novice and learn to tie these knots (or make these bends, or bend these hitches: what a rabbit warren old nautical jargon can get you into), then you will be already useful. We have come across many yachtmasters who make their yachts fast with snowball hitches that melt in the sun.

In Question 11 we are after your willingness to get stuck into a dirty problem with some chance of solving it effectively. Too many of us dash at a problem without thinking first. Always start with the simplest explanation, because that is often the case. And emulate John Guzzwell who was crewing for the Smeetons when their yacht capsized and was badly damaged rounding Cape Horn. His first re-constructive action was to sit down and sharpen his saw. There are rites of passage in all crafts: preparation before deciding what form the work will take is good thinking time. There's a standard acronym for this: RTFM. Guess what it means. (Read the ******* manual.)

Cooking (Question 12) is one of the basic skills of cruising. Skippers are not entitled to hide behind wifey's apron all the time. Poor food is as demoralising as bad weather and bad temper. What's more, good cooking saves a lot of money.

Seasickness (Questions 13–16) must be taken seriously, since it can affect the morale and capability of everyone who suffers. A determined effort should be made to discover whether you start to recover after about 18 hours at sea and then are immune for the rest of the voyage, as the majority are; whether pills help you; or whether yours is the truly resistant kind, in which case you will probably hate the sea for ever.

The list of skills in Question 17 are those that we have needed (or lacked) in more than a quarter of a century at sea in a yacht. (It is not definitive: if we have missed out your special expertise, sorry.) We intend the level of competence to be that of a conscientious amateur. Being a Pro does not score extra, but might improve your earning capacity. Moving heavy weights is an art worth studying if you don't want to get a hernia.

SECTION SIX – GOODS AND GARDENS: CAN YOU LEAVE THEM?

1 How many homes have you lived in during the last 6 years?
   (a) 5. Score K5
   (b) 3. Score K3
   (c) 2. Score K1
   (d) 1. Score nothing.
   If you love your house, score (a) $\Sigma 2$, (b) $\Sigma 3$, (c) $\Sigma 4$, (d) $\Sigma 6$. If you are ready for a change, score (a) 0, (b) 0, (c) $\Sigma 1$, (d) $\Sigma 1$.

2 Do you like gardening? If No, score K1. If Yes, score A4.

3 Do you like horses and riding? If No, score 0. If Yes, score $\Sigma 2$.

4 Do you own antique furniture or fine pictures?
   If No, score K1. If Yes, are you prepared to sell it, or give it to parents/children?
   If Yes, score 0. If No, score $\Sigma 2$.

5 Do you have a fine collection of anything too big or fragile to take with you:
   old cars, steam engines, carousels, mangles, Ming china, 13th century armour,
   books, bird's eggs? If No, score K1. If Yes, are you prepared to sell it, or give it
   to parents/children? If Yes, score 0. If No, score $\Sigma 2$.

6 Do you have a sport or hobby that you cannot take with you, eg billiards,
   model railways, pottery, hang-gliding, monumental sculpture or mink breeding?
   If Yes, score $\Sigma 2$. If No, score 0.

7 Can you manage without the local library?
   (a) Yes.
   (b) With difficulty.
   (c) No.
   If (a) score K1, if (b) score 0, if (c) score $\Sigma 2$.

8 Is there life without TV? Do you watch, per week,
   (a) 6 hours?
   (b) 6 to 12 hours?
   (c) more than 12?
   If (a) score $\Sigma 1$, if (b) score $\Sigma 3$, if (c) score $\Sigma 5$.

• Discussion on Section Six •

To some people, possessions are status. It is important to them to have a quality car, a house in the right part of town, and the latest gadget. They get a lot of fun out of their things, and are not likely to be reading this unless escape by yacht becomes frightfully fashionable one year, when they will buy a frightfully fashionable yacht to do it in, and have a lot of frightfully good fun doing it for a short time before wanting to get back to their other gadgets. In our world, some people travel as light as a soul to heaven: Dan was one of these, he crewed for us from Antigua to Bermuda on his way to Europe and seemed to possess what he stood up in, and what was in its pockets, a tracksuit, some running shoes and a tooth-brush.

Between these two extremes lie most of us, with a heap of rubbish that we could gladly say goodbye to, some useful odds and ends whose passing we might regret, and a further pile of junk that we cling to fiercely and beyond all persuasion. The more of it you can get rid of, the less hassle you will have on your voyage.

Question 1: Houses

If you are going on a long voyage, your house back home will be a nuisance. Besides, you are probably buying your boat from the proceeds of selling it. Renting it in case you want to return can cause a lot of headaches: the Hiscocks tried this at first but eventually sold the house as the tenants caused so many problems. We have this spring met a French couple whose summer cruise to Greece had already ended in Fiumicino near Rome: they had to return and sort out some legal difficulty with their house. Another yachtie we know was summoned urgently back to England by the police as their tenant was using their house as a full-scale brothel. And they weren't even getting a cut.

We sold our house. It was a wrench at the time, but the wound heals.

Questions 2–6: Possessions

Those possessions that we could not bear to part with we left with various members of the family to mind for us. Funny, I can't remember what some of them are now. A few we took with us. So, we find, did other people; and it is surprising what a variety of objects mean enough to someone for them to find room and make a safe stowage for. We saw a cello on the 26-foot *New Life*, lovingly cradled on the forward berth (the second best cello, to keep in practice), an icemaking machine which worked by burning camel dung or any other solid fuel on *Northern Light*, an electronic keyboard for writing songs on *Clarity*. We carry Laurel's enamelling kiln. Eight-year-old Ben Lucas on *Tientos* had a most impressive Lego set. *Snow Goose* was the first yacht we met with a PC aboard, the full start-of-the-80s television-sized works before laptops existed. TVs, guitars, bicycles, laptops and mobile phones are run-of-the-mill; golf clubs and tennis rackets rather less so. A dentist we know keeps a neat case of the tools of his trade on board, so do most doctors; indeed anyone with skills might want the wherewithal to use them, with the possible exception of lion tamers and nuclear physicists. *The Sell up and Sail* Collection-Riddance Award goes at present to the couple who sold a collection of more than 20 British World War Two armoured vehicles and a field gun before setting off on their cruise.

Beware of Grandsons, Goods and Gardens:
Here your wife's resistance hardens.

Question 7: Reading
Book swaps occur all the time between passing ships, and more and more marinas and yacht 'clubs' have quite numerous collections.

Question 8: Television
The satellite dish appears all over Europe these days. (See Chapter 17.)

SECTION SEVEN – ATTITUDES: YOU'VE GOT TO BE CRAZY

1   Is your dreamboat taking shape? Are you (or your mate) currently:
   (a) Buying or building her?
   (b) Planning or designing or choosing her?
   (c) Still looking for the right one after ten years?
   (d) Designing for the tenth time in ten years?
   (e) Still building after fifteen years?
   If (a) score K4, if (b) score K1, if (c) score 0, if (d) score $\sum 1$, and if (e) score $\sum 3$.

2   All of us have fears and uncertainties about such a voyage. Let's look them in the eye. Which one of the following statements is most true for you, concerning:
   Keeping a night watch alone
   (a) I'll be OK.
   (b) I'm a bit nervous
   (c) I'm rather nervous.
   (d) I'm not keen on the dark.
   If (a) score 0, if (b) $\sum 2$, if (c) $\sum 4$, and if (d) $\sum 7$.
   Becoming ill on the voyage (you or your mate)
   (a) We'll cope somehow.
   (b) I don't know what I'd do.
   (c) I'm going to first aid classes.
   (d) We'll have a check up before we go.
   (e) He/she would be helpless without me.
   If (a) score K1, if (b) $\sum 1$, if (c) 0, if (d) 0, if (e) score $\sum 2$.
   Bad weather
   (a) I'm used to it.
   (b) I think I'll be OK.
   (c) I'm a bit nervous.
   (d) I'm very nervous.
   (e) I'm scared stiff.
   If (a) score K2, if (b) K1, if (c) 0, if (d) $\sum 1$, if (e) score $\sum 4$.

3   Pick whichever of the following best expresses your situation:
   (a) I'm determined to go.
   (b) I'm looking forward to it.
   (c) I can't wait, but I don't think he/she wants to come.
   (d) If he/she won't come, that's the end of it.

(e) I love planning, but I'm nervous about going.

(f) If he/she really wants to go, I suppose I shall have to.

(g) If we go for a year, he/she might get it out of their system.

(h) The idea is great, but I can't leave my grandchildren/dogs/ cats/garden just now.

(i) I don't think he/she has enough experience yet.

(j) My friends seem dubious about my going.

For (a) score K4, if (b) K2, if (c) 0, if (d) Σ3, if (e) Σ1, if (f) 0, if (g) 0, if (h) Σ5, if (i) Σ4, and if (j) Σ2.

4   How long do you envisage doing this?

(a) For the rest of your life?

(b) For a year or two?

(c) For several years?

(d) Until you get too old?

(e) For the foreseeable future?

If (a) score K4, if (b) K1, if (c) K2, if (d) or (e) score K3.

5   If you are not yet committed to going, how long before you do commit yourself?

(a) This year?

(b) Next year?

(c) Sometime?

(d) Never?

If (a) score K3, if (b) K2, if (c) 0, and if (d) Σ5.

6   Why haven't you already gone?

(a) I'm really just dreaming.

(b) For reasons I don't wish to reveal, or am not sure about.

(c) I have.

If (a) score Σ5, if (b) Σ4, and if (c) you are fouling up the system! Behave yourself. If your score in this section is more than K15, you are somewhat imprudent: subtract A4.

• *Discussion on Section Seven* •

In terms of partnership, one person is usually the instigator and prime mover of the Ulysses plan and the other (or others) the more or less willing follower. Usually the man is the instigator, and is going to be Captain. Usually the women and children are followers, and are going to be mate and crew. To the discussion which follows, it does not really matter which way round it is, but in order to avoid saying he/she too often we will go with the majority.

Trouble is clearly going to arise if the views of the partners are too divergent. Now, before you go to great expense and disruption, is the time to find out: if you disagree fundamentally about whether to go at all; or less radically about the kind of boat, the amount of time and money to be spent, what areas you will travel to, and the standard of comfort required.

Women have been home-makers ever since the first cave-wife hung a skin on the wall of her cave, instead of wearing it or lying on it. The habit, after 5000 years, dies hard, and it is too much to expect your wife to live in a production boat, stark as a railway station gents (and probably smelling rather similar), without letting her cosify it, within reason. The happiest boats we meet seem to be the ones with the homely touches. I have seen the sideways look in a woman's eyes when her man boasts that 'We haven't altered or added a thing since we got her at the Boat Show: keeps up the resale value, you know.' I am far more inclined to Hal Roth's view:

'the layout and detailing of the little ship on which a man lives and travels ought to be as personal as his fingerprints.'

I cannot see that curtains, covers, cushions and décor ruin the resale price. Nor has any production boat designer thought of all the extra gear you need to live aboard: indeed in many production boats it is hard to find space for the oilskins and seaboots for every crew member. I shall say more about this later when we talk about storage.

If you embark on this life with any hope at all, you have to trust and have faith in each other. It follows that there should be some basis for this trust, and that you should set out to acquire skills and experience that will justify it. It's no good sailing out into the sunset, Captain, with your manly hand on the tiller and your manly pipe clenched between your teeth, if your mate quickly concludes that you do not really know what you are doing or where you are. No good, Lady, posing like the yachtimag ads, in immaculate whites holding a rope that obviously goes nowhere, when your Captain needs knowledgeable help. You owe it to each other to learn as much as you can by sailing together and separately, with friends or by answering 'crew wanted' ads, for long or short journeys, in different kinds of boat with different kinds of skipper.

If you have both been living the 9–5 life, you will be used to speaking to each other about five to six hours a day: less if you are silent breakfasters, TV addicts or in the darts team. How will you cope with being in each other's company 24 hours a day, barring night watches? When in such close quarters, a seventh sense needs to be developed. You should know when another person's space and privacy should be respected, and words that can wait half an hour be left unsaid. Long companionable silences should be easily achieved, and just as easily broken at the right moment. When we have friends on board we find that siestas are a great idea. Everyone separates to their own patch of space, and quiet activities, rest or sleep prevail for a blissful couple of hours. On meeting again later the chat is all the livelier, and the wit keener, for having had a break.

Fears and fancies we all have, and they need dragging out into the light where they can be more carefully examined. It is no good saying 'Cheer up, it won't happen!' because it probably will; no cruise is without incident. If you are aware of danger you have already taken the first step to prevent it; but be sure that you are guarding against realities, and not bogies under the bunk. You will reduce unnecessary worry to a minimum if you develop confidence in your boat, your

Captain or crew, and yourself. Fear is allayed by encountering, and coping successfully, with trouble; this is what experience means. From the statistics, one ought to be far more terrified of crossing the High Street than keeping a night watch, but the first is a known and familiar danger and the second an unknown one. Eventually it becomes as ordinary as crossing the road, and rather less dangerous, though never to be taken lightly.

Illness on the voyage (either oneself or one's partner) is one of the thoughts that perturb us. Why do we not worry as much over becoming ill in our ordinary life at home? Because help would be available, in the form of doctors, hospitals, and friends. We have only to seek advice, and the burden is straight away on other shoulders: all we have to do then is follow instructions. If you wish to have the freedom that the cruising life brings, you have also to accept that you are going back to the pioneer days of being self-reliant.

Having said that, you will certainly be a lot healthier than if you'd stayed at home; and it's surprising how often there is a doctor in the next boat just when you need one. We have come to no serious harm in 30 years of cruising, some of it in very remote places. (See Chapter 15 for further comment on prevention of illness and accidents.)

I suppose most of us are afraid of bad weather, though some of us are reluctant to admit it. It's no fun at all to have your house bucketing about at all angles, and the corners of your galley attacking you when you cook; and when the cat burrowing on to your lap under your oilskin while you steer is the only bit of companionable warmth you'll get till the weather improves. But if your boat is strong and your Captain capable and prudent, and perhaps above all you have got your sea legs, then it's possibly a little better than two hours in a packed commuter train, especially nowadays.

No blame attaches to people who are afraid to go to sea, any more than those who would fear mountain climbing or motor racing, or (in my case) pot-holing: I'm already not too happy on the Underground. Some people do these things precisely because they are afraid, and singlehanded too. To such brave hearts we give our admiration, but this book is not for them. Cruising is a game that two or more should play: no sane person goes mountain climbing or deep diving alone, and people who go off on journeys which they mentally label 'One Man against the Elements' or 'Alone in the Southern Ocean' are taking greater risks than we would care to. There is no need to be that crazy.

Nevertheless, if you want to undertake the life, you must develop a self-reliance that is unusual these days. We yachties are felt to be eccentric, a curious cross between hermits, voluntary exiles and adventurers. We feel very normal, of course; and only at gatherings of landspeople do we realise that we are perhaps a bit peculiar – when our answer to the inevitable question 'And where do you live?' is followed by an odd little silence, or a rush of enthusiastic clichés covering extreme social embarrassment. If you can't be classified, you are too alien to converse with. If they don't know where to put you in the social order you naturally go to the bottom. It's quite comfortable down there, there's no competition!

So, you do have to be a bit crazy. But at least do it with planning, forethought and prudence.

If you scored all (a)s in Section One, you have crossed the first barrier with ease. If you scored all (c)s someone probably gave you this book as a present. Tough. Enjoy reading it, however. If you came somewhere in the middle, you have some thinking to do.

SUMMARY			
Now, write down your scores:	A	K	Σ
Section One	. .	. .	. .
Section Two	. .	. .	. .
Section Three	. .	. .	. .
Section Four	. .	. .	. .
Section Five	. .	. .	. .
Section Six	. .	. .	. .
Section Seven	. .	. .	. .
Totals for each type of score:			

Now add up the totals for A and K, and multiply by 100. Divide this figure by your total Σ score: this gives your ULYSSES QUOTIENT, ie:

$$UQ = 100 \times (A + K) \text{ divided by } \Sigma$$

- A represents your APTITUDE and ABILITY for cruising.

- K represents KINESIS which is the mobility force in your personality.

- Σ (SIGMA) represents STASIS which is the inertia in your personality.

  - UQ below 100: you are a static person from a cruising point of view.

  - UQ between 100 and 200: you are moderately kinetic: go with someone who has a higher one.

  - UQ between 200 and 300: you are kinetic: you'll get by.

  - UQ over 300: you have marked kinesis.

  - UQ over 1000: you are a bit weird; why haven't you already gone?

There is a possibility of obtaining a total Σ score of zero, which would lead to a UQ of infinity. This is only possible if you are already following the life of a Ulysses, and are thoroughly content. Go on and enjoy it in good health.

PS: If you can't do the arithmetic, you probably wouldn't be able to load the tidal prediction programme on the laptop, especially on XP. Dream on.

3 • Finance

'For now no good thing's gotten without money'

There has to be a chapter on money because everybody worries about it. The trouble is that the word means different things to different people.

We see the subject as divisible into strategy (the overall picture) and tactics (the detail). Strategy covers everything and has to be considered carefully because it is long-term and therefore difficult and perhaps costly to change. It represents, let us say, the asset part of your balance sheet.

FINANCE: STRATEGY

Let's look at strategy first. Some people who have experienced the volatility of the housing market and also the stock market will query the exhortation contained in this book's title. Tough. It's a good title and it stays. It is aimed at people such as ourselves, who wish to commit themselves to living in a yacht for the rest of their lives. They will leave their boat only if physically dragged off to the old-folk's penitentiary (sorry, I mean home) or perhaps by taking a long walk on a short ship. For such folk, the state of the markets is not a strategic matter. One of the major cares of life is removed. They need to think of finance only in terms of tactics.

But we sense that most readers will not come into this category. Many are more cautious, or are willing to commit only to a longish break and wish to resume the cares and worries of shore-side life one day. These people need to consider the first two words of the title more carefully.

The first thing to say is that there abound numerous firms offering advice (for a fee) to persons moving abroad for a short or long time, which is what you would be doing.

I've never publicly stated my credentials in this subject. Perhaps it's time I did. When I signed the forms for joining, the Royal Navy had 52 aircraft carriers, 9 battleships and countless cruisers and destroyers. It was still bigger than the US Navy. The Royal Navy seemed like the Rock of Gibraltar. Immutable. There for ever as a major force in the world. I signed on to a job I loved for life.

Within 15 years, the Home Fleet had been reduced to five ships and they stayed in harbour because there was no fuel for them. I went to London to get a new job as navigator of a cruiser and I was told that it would be my last sea-going appointment. I submitted my resignation. I was offered early retirement to take effect two years later with a pension as compensation for the loss of the promised career, and I started on the Actuarial Tuition Service correspondence course.

By the time I left the Navy I had several good passes, and was offered a studentship with the Norwich Union. I passed the Fellowship exam in advanced Finance and Investment, and was made an assistant to the Investment Manager. Three years later I was head-hunted for a partnership in a leading stockbroking firm specialising in government stock (gilts) in the money market, and I moved to London, where my work, apart from the usual dealing, was to forecast changes in interest rates. This I did using harmonic analysis of the type I had learned for predicting tides. Hence my reputation as the idiot who foretold economic changes by studying the phases of the moon. Well, it got me known. The truth was that I knew as much as anyone else, which was very little but I could make it sound good.

Before taking any of my advice, you should know that I was one of the special advisers to Harold Wilson, probably the worst Prime Minister of the last century. He would not listen, did not take any, let alone my, advice; devaluation ensued as I had forecast, and I got so fed up with the strife that I quit and returned to a simple life at sea. This, I've enjoyed ever since. Though prosperous, I was not at all happy in the City.

People nowadays see the present prosperity as enduring as the Rock of Gibraltar, when it is probably far more like my naval career. They think, as I did, that it is a permanent feature of life. Everything will last for ever. But it doesn't.

My memory is longer. I was too young to have direct experience of the 1929 crash but it was talked about by my unemployed relatives in my presence and I recall the way of thought of those living through the ensuing depression. I was directly involved in the massive crash in the Wilson era – when the share index fell to 150 (it is about 7500 now) and house prices dropped. What caused this?

- Enormous hire-purchase debt.
- Horrifying balance of payment deficits.
- Marginal tax rates of 91%.
- Massive government spending.
- Wage demands in excess of inflation.
- Government borrowing had driven gilt-edged interest rates up to 16%.
- Intransigent and powerful trade unions.

At present, not *all* those problems exist, but we have others:

- Personal debts now exceed £1,000,000,000,000, and restraints on building society lending and bank liquidity have been removed or eased.
- The balance of payments deficits are quasi-permanent.
- Government spending is increasing.

- Wage demands are growing, though not yet dangerous.
- Government borrowing is increasing and forecast to increase still further soon.

In addition, we have:

- A post-war military occupation that appears to be becoming a running sore.
- The unions, freed from Thatcher restraints, flexing their muscles again.

Six worries out of the old seven, plus one new one. Admittedly things are not nearly as bad as in 1973, with the exception of consumer debt, which is terrifying. And again we have a Prime Minister who won't listen. (Did any of them, ever?)

I think the economy is unstable and will move towards a turning point again. But then, I'm just a grumpy, grotty old yachtie now, Bah, humbug! Harrumph! Out of touch, quasi-senile, don't pay any attention to my views. Sort some out for yourself.

Seriously, if you have assets, including property, think very hard. Property prices have risen outrageously and, surprisingly, the house price inflation has spread abroad for the first time. So many Brits are buying houses in Greece, for example, that prices of property there have risen by 50% in the last 18 months. In one small island, new building for foreigners rose to 60 starts per month last year. Where is all the money coming from?

This is not the place to go on about the follies of international banking practices except to say that too much of the money being used to finance the consumer boom is money that does not really exist, and that its velocity of circulation is getting ever faster.

Now, a word about financial advisers. Because of the fees that they charge, these mostly work for rich people, and as a consequence they tend to think in terms of income tax and inheritance tax. Of trusts, and offshore devices. I've played around with these in my time. It was vital with a tax rate of 91%.

If you feel inclined to consult advisers, then use a British-based one who is properly registered. Not only is he less likely to be dishonest, but also his fees will be lower and you have redress in the event of negligence or misconduct. Check the fees before committing yourself. Then check them again.

The August 2001 edition of *Practical Boat Owner* had a commendable article (entitled 'Raising the Wind') on this subject, one which other yachtimags have largely ignored. I do not agree with everything in it, or even with the emphasis, but it was a very good attempt to lay out the factors in making a difficult decision. I will try to persuade the editor to re-run it in updated form, and then it will be up-to-the-minute. You ask him, too. Or is he a her now? These editors change so.

============ FINANCE: TACTICS ============

Now for tactics. Tactics are more flexible. They can be divided into nautical and domestic, which together constitute the profit and loss part of your accounts. This is the Micawber outlook: spending less than you receive equals happiness, spending more than you get equals misery. So cut your coat according to your cloth.

In April 2003 *Yachting Monthly* published an article by Mary and Richard Neate with a short title of 'The Med For Less' which provoked a lively and largely disbelieving correspondence. (Nowadays the yachtimags have much more on living aboard than they used to years ago. They have realised that it is an important and popular branch of yachting. The RYA have still not taken this in, nor have yacht designers and builders. More fools they, they are missing a large and growing market.)

Before Laurel, who watches over our housekeeping like a chartered accountant threatened with redundancy, deals with the cost of living in detail, here is a word to back up the Neate family, who wrote that they had lived in the Med on £100 a week. There is nothing impossible about this, most of us cruisers have lived on similar amounts for limited periods. This life costs far less than you think, though you might need to pick up a few wrinkles, and alter a few old habits to achieve the economies. It costs so much less that we advise the British government to muster all pensioners on the quayside, shove the lot of them into yachts and sail them off to the Med or the Caribbean. The national pensions problems would be solved overnight.

• *Pensions* •

In passing, if you are not yet of pensionable age, do not neglect to keep up your voluntary payments under National Insurance. This can only be done while you are resident, but it can be done with one lump sum and is a good investment, or has been up to now. We know that the politicians are in a sixpenny panic about the national old-age pension, mainly because successive governments have not saved the contributions of the population (as they were supposed to do under the 1948 Act) but have squandered them. However, the geriatric vote grows, and will grow, ever larger, and no government will dare give the elder constituency a raw deal. (Would they? Let's hope not.) Up to now the state pension has been a wonderful bargain and you should not jeopardise your share.

• *Cheaper living* •

As a principle, shipping pensioners off by boat is not as daft as it might appear at first sight. Obviously it could not suit everybody; we exaggerate. There are always exceptions. But consider life wintering in a small Eastern Mediterranean port with about 10,000 habitants. Average winter temperature 12 to 18°C compared with 3 to 8° in England. In England, deaths among old folk increase dramatically in winter. Here, they rise a little but not nearly as much. Keeping warm is simpler and costs less. A large Camping Gaz bottle is currently €5.50 (£3.85) instead of €22 (£12.15) in France. One can walk to all the shops, including four supermarkets. The hospital is within walking distance: do you need an X-ray? Walk there, wait for a few minutes only and it is done for a modest payment, 3€ (£2) for the doctor, and 8€ (£5.50) for the X-ray. The social life is within yards: take it or leave it alone. A 3-course meal out, with a bottle of wine, costs us from €17 to €24 for the two of us (£12–£17). A light meal for two with beer or wine can be had for €8 (£5.50). You do not spend nearly as much on daily living, no newspapers and magazines, no luxury foods, and very little clothes shopping. Probably the only increased dangers are cirrhosis of the liver and, if you are a non-smoker, the effects of passive smoking. (The EU subsidises tobacco in Greece to the extent of about 500 million Euros per annum, and nobody understands why.)

• *So what does it cost to run the boat?* •

In previous editions we gave an analytical estimation process that must have seemed like statistical alchemy and probably made as much sense. Seriously, it was not far out, but things have changed and we do not think it would be as useful now. So farewell formalised figures and let's start on the back of an envelope.

Thirty years ago there were dozens of different types and designs of boats built of many different materials. No longer! Fewer of us live in nautical oddities as we, ourselves, do. A walk round the marina found 108 yachts built of glass-fibre and only 7 of wood, aluminium or steel (including our own conversion from a commercial ship) and two self-built boats. If you have owned a glass-fibre yacht already, you will know what is involved in looking after her. If not, there is a mass of literature and articles in yachtimags. The cost is less than most think, but still my advice would be not to stint. It is easy to get complacent with glass-fibre and think that it is everlasting without any maintenance. And anyway, there are rigging, engines, and a host of comfort fittings that were uncommon 30 years ago, but are quasi-universal now. For instance, 100% of yachts here have refrigeration. Some have air-conditioning, since self-contained 220 volt air/con units can be bought in the local supermarket for €180.

But as regards total expenditure, be reassured. Laurel and I live on a modest naval pension (I retired in 1959, for heaven's sake, so it's obviously not much), plus the state pension, and the income from some savings, augmented by an average of about 6% of the sales of this book. Our income is well below the national average. On this meagre sum, we have for 20 years run an 87-foot three-masted schooner-rigged barge yacht which is still in good order, we eat out two or three times a week, drink a fair amount of wine, eat well, sometimes run an old car, make (on average) one flight per year back to England to see the kids, we clothe and feed ourselves and we actually SAVE. Not much, but we gradually build up a contingency reserve, and never need to buy anything on credit.

We could not lead nearly such a good life living in a small house in England.

Having said that, I would not like to try to live *permanently* on the sum given in the *Yachting Monthly* article. It's pushing it if the yacht is to be maintained over a longish period, but we know it is quite possible to lead a frugal, happy life like that, *for a year or two*.

Consider our lifestyle on an income reckoned to be below the American poverty-line (though in Britain we are spared that undignified pigeonhole). The secret is to have modest expectations.

COMPARISONS WITH A UK HOUSEHOLDER

We pay nothing for:
- *Mortgage*
- *Debts*
- *Health insurance*
- *TV licence*
- *Council tax*
- *Car* (Not necessary)
- *Garden equipment*
- *Holidays* (Not necessary)
- *Health and beauty treatments* Fresh air, exercise, a little sunshine and swimming, absence of speed and stress, all come free with the package
- *Luxury goods* (No temptation because unobtainable)
- *Anchoring*
- *Magazines and newspapers*

We pay much the same for:
- *Marine insurance (comprehensive)* This costs about the same as domestic house plus car.
- *Our income tax* It is deducted at source.
- *Our phone bills* Though our roaming calls each cost more, we make less of them. We get a local card for local calls.
- *TV and radio reception by satellite* (Optional for yachts)

We pay less for:
- *Club subscriptions* (Lower for non-residents)
- *Heating costs* These are either lower or non existent; though shore-power and fresh water both cost more, a boat uses far less than a household.
- *A haircut and shampoo* This costs for Laurel € 12 now and then; Bill often gets his cut on deck by the mate.
- *Dentistry*
- *Food and drink*
- *Entertainment* (Mostly self-generated among yachties)

We pay more for:
- *E-mail and internet* Usage can be more expensive, though we use it less

profligately than those with a landline. In our case only for essential messages, not for pleasure or chat.

- *VAT* In most countries this is higher and on more goods than in Britain.
- *Some kinds of medical treatment*
- *Prescription drugs* Free for pensioners in UK, not necessarily so abroad.

Required for yachts but not householders:
- *Ship radio licence*
- *Liferaft, annual check*
- *Occasional haul out, and maintenance costs and repairs* (But compare house maintenance, plumbing repairs etc)
- *Antifouling, and marine paint*
- *Marina and harbour dues* (Optional)

• *Marine insurance* •

As the world gets more litigious, and people take more and more a motorist's view of minor knocks and damages, and as there seems to be more and more nautical idiots about, insurance rates have risen. So much so that some are tempted to voyage without insurance. This has led to some Mediterranean countries making third party insurance compulsory. Grin and bear it.

Generally, it is not difficult to arrange insurance cover in the Med, or for Europe's inland waters. Ocean voyaging, however, and any unusual proposition can be tricky.

Some insurers impose restrictions on ocean passages. Do not assume that because one does, all will – certainly not.

You should always check your insurance policy carefully and check that you are covered for storm damage, especially if you are cruising in the hurricane zone.

STONINGTON, CONNECTICUT.

Many yachtsmen who do their own maintenance and repairs want third-party cover only. This can be hard to find.

Try Bishop Skinner at www.bishopskinner.com for European waters. They may cover transatlantic voyages, too, but I do not have this in writing. I understand that the Navigators and General will also consider writing (or re-insuring for another company) third party only policies.

Scrutinise the policy. Check the terms of use of the vessel. These vary from company to company. Some exclude single-handers, for instance. You can always find yourself on your own for a few days and you might face the prospect that it would be wise to change berth or port for safety reasons because of a bad forecast. Make sure you would not be doing it uninsured, get a policy that is as flexible as possible if living aboard. Insurance can be anomalous when you are prevented from acting prudently because of arbitrary restrictions.

There is some sort of 'arrangement' (I will not call it a racket) between old world and new world insurers that seems to prevent them from insuring boats registered in each other's territory. I don't know why. To me it is collusion in restraint of trade and ought to be illegal.

• *A word about medical treatment* •

Though there are reciprocal arrangements between Britain and other EU countries, sometimes certain conditions apply and small payments are due. We have

no health insurance. Instead, over 30 years we have paid for the usual small accidents, visits to surgery and dentists, and two major operations. We are still ahead of the game, and healthy for our age.

As people in Britain have no idea what their health or their drugs cost, it's worth knowing that a visit to a doctor in France costs €17, and for that he will do minor surgery, stitch a cut, or lance a boil for example. This is about £12, and is not very much, as we pointed out to a doctor in France, having just taken the cat to the vet and been charged twice that.

If success is the penalty for aiming too low, then happiness is the penalty for not asking too much of life. The secret, we repeat, is to have modest expectations.

That doesn't prevent one enjoying a damned good grumble now and then, but that is one of life's cheaper pleasures.

Now for a few technicalities.

• *Getting money? No problem* •

We wrote at length about the difficulties of getting money while overseas in previous editions. As long as you already have the money in a proper bank, accessing it is no longer a problem. The ubiquitous ATMs have changed that. We were suspicious at first, but experience has shown that the service is all it should be. Some folk complain about the charges, but these are reasonable when compared with the expense and awkwardness of transferring money from place to place that we had to endure years ago. You will still find old practices obtaining in some of the eastern European countries that we have cruised in. Once we were really in difficulty in Romania and were held to ransom with a charge of over 25% by the Romanian bank. A recent visit to Serbia showed that things are improving. There were ATMs in Belgrade, but we cannot comment about the smaller towns. We do not think there is any need to worry much about cash transfer, and travellers' cheques are no longer necessary. Nonetheless, we advise carrying a small reserve in low denomination US dollar bills when cruising in primitive countries.

If you plan to stay in any one country for a few years then opening a bank account in that country can be worth while. Beware though: banking practices in various countries are not the same. British banks are much more flexible and there are sometimes legal obligations that seem unduly restrictive to us. In France, one sometimes needs a sort of bank reference before being able to deal with various quasi-bureaucratic institutions. These come automatically with a current account.

In America we found that the cheques we proudly presented from the 1st Washington Bank of Westerly, Rhode Island were not cashable in the next *town*, let alone the next State.

Credit and/or debit cards are much less use in the rest of Europe than in Britain and the USA. France accepts them in all supermarkets, but Germany is surprisingly difficult. In Greece, we hardly ever use a credit card. Be aware that in much of Europe, shops and restaurants supplement the bill if you offer a card in payment.

• *Taxation* •

There is no longer any noteworthy benefit in trying to second guess the UK Inland Revenue with smart schemes unless you have so much income that you are prepared to present a fair dollop of it to tax specialists. There used to be many tax loopholes, but gradually most of them have closed. I do not think fancy, complicated schemes for tax-wriggling are that important with the present income tax rates, especially with the income levels enjoyed by most live-aboard yachties. My experience is that complicated schemes can become counter-productive with a change in the law, and that all too often annual fees soak up the benefits unless these are substantial. The highest marginal rate of tax while I was working was 91% (for over £35,000), and the standard rate was 37%. Tax rates like that encourage jiggery-pokery. Now the highest tax rate is 40% and the tax threshold has been raised until most live-aboards are not even bothered by it.

• *VAT* •

VAT is difficult to avoid and you pay an enormous amount of VAT each year. Britain has a lower rate than most EU countries so it is worth considering buying expensive spare parts (and books) in England. Balance the VAT saving against the cost of freighting.

If you winter in a country outside the EU, and these are growing fewer (soon there may be more countries in the EU than there are in the United Nations), then you might need a friendly arrangement with a native so as to be able to get a rebate on any VAT you pay on goods that you buy in Britain and take to that country. (The important criterion is a convincing address.) Take into account that such countries often have import duties that nullify any advantage. We have heard of those wintering in Turkey who personally export items from Britain by car, say, and take them free of all duty into Greece. They then sail their yacht to Greece, install the items on board as fittings, and then return to Turkey to await the arrival of the VAT cheque. This practice is illegal.

VAT is not payable in the Channel Islands. Provided your yacht is VAT paid-up (see below) then, if embarking on a world cruise in a new yacht, it might pay to postpone the installation of certain expensive items (radar, nav-systems, radio etc for examples) and then call in at Jersey, say, to install them. This practice is not illegal. See Appendix.

Do not overlook the essential pre-requirement to navigate safely to Jersey.

VAT on yachts

This is a subject that catches some people out. Basically the rule is that VAT must be paid on all yachts built in and based in the EU unless built before 1985. Proof may be required. This is enforced with vigour almost everywhere. You get lumbered by:

- Buying a yacht from a non-EU citizen.
- A non-EU citizen staying in Europe longer than allowed in the regulations. This period varies from country to country. Might be as little as 3 months, usually six. It is advisable for them to make periodic visits to a non-EU country from time to time and get something stamped so as to re-establish a starting base. This gets less easy as the EU grows and grows.
- Buying a yacht which has previously been kept in a non-EU country (watch out for Cyprus; there used to be lots of rackets centred on Cyprus) and then trying to bring it to an EU country.

Keep your VAT documents safe, and keep a certified photocopy, too. Even so, we have heard of some officials who will not consider photocopies.

If your boat is self-built, then keep all receipts showing VAT payments. Yes, all three million of them.

• *Earning your keep as you go* •

Earning a living locally is theoretically possible but in many cases not wholly practicable. Even if local unemployment is not a problem, elaborate precautions are often taken to protect locals from foreign competition. The question needs looking at in three ways:

- How can you earn in a way that does not upset the locals, wherever you are?
- What jobs, trades, or professions are generally welcome anywhere?
- What about the European Union?

Don't upset the locals

- Be discreet
- Bring skills that are not available locally
- Don't be too successful

There are various occupations that can be carried out aboard, especially if your income is not being obtained locally.

Artists come under this category, provided they are not seen to sell in direct competition with the locals, though even here there is often a degree of tolerance not evident in most fields. The keynote is discretion; it does not seem to matter how much you make, it is the degree of ostentation involved which is important. We have personal knowledge of this field. Artists in general are very tolerant of one another, respecting genuine talent in any form. The chief source of possible objection comes from the local art gallery or souvenir shop, but sales direct to other foreigners excite little attention. Bermuda has really restrictive laws, be careful there. Places where the artist can make a little something are the West Indies and the Bahamas, where the locals do not do much towards providing a souvenir industry, and where the majority of tourists are comparatively wealthy Americans dying to spend on something local.

Writing is not an easy way to earn. It wins a little respect in some countries, and best-seller novel writers live like kings, but a couple of well-known novelists living afloat in the West Indies do so modestly. Writing for yachting magazines is hard work, and a very poor return for the time spent. One would need to produce a very large volume of words to make much of a living. Magazine writing has to be seen as a way of making an occasional bonus, especially as there has been a growing tendency for the magazines to become more glossily professional. Which means that they tend to prefer articles written by full-time professional journalists who have little time to sail, rather than by experienced amateur yachtsmen or women.

Craftworkers We know a yachtswoman who makes very high quality bikinis for the boutique trade. She is now well known, and hers is a good example of a well-planned, suitable home industry, carried on in winter in order to sail in the summer. We know people who bake, or make preserves. We know woodcarvers, and craft jewellers and scrimshankers, any craft worker should be able to make a bit where there are tourists to buy their work.

Skills and services There are other services you can carry out for foreign yachtsmen – for example, I have made some pocket money adjusting compasses. Some people sail all summer but spend the winter working in a local boatyard. Electronics used to be a fruitful field, but it is becoming less so as more and more equipment follows the 'do not repair – fit the spare' policy. However, competent IT people who can recover computers when they crash will probably be busy. Several people we know design web-sites for locals. Greek companies, for example, are at a big disadvantage if they want a web-site in English.

The massive expansion of air-conditioning and deep-freezers in yachts, as well as ashore, demands increasing services from competent refrigeration engineers. They should get enough work anywhere to prevent them enjoying life. So would sailmakers and upholsterers. In Greece, it is difficult to get good welding work done. The few competent local craftsmen are overwhelmed with work.

Those skills which are universally welcome are not so numerous. *Trained nurses* are in demand world-wide, but *doctors* definitely are not; the latter seem to have devised some very nasty restrictive practices against their fellows in other lands. *Mechanics* can do well in some parts, though often it is a question of a direct job for another yachtie, but really skilled men are almost always needed, especially in some West Indian islands. *Shipwrighting jobs* can be found, though these are usually in the busy season which is when the dedicated cruiser wants to be doing his own boat. This applies also to casual labour; even if found it is likely to be when one would rather be sailing. Qualified *teachers* can sometimes get work, especially those with a certificate to teach English as a foreign language.

• *Working in the European Union* •

Persons from one member country are supposedly allowed to work in the others. I am only aware of the situation round the Mediterranean coasts. Not unreasonably, the various countries demand that any foreigner working there should pay local taxes and social service dues; however, the bureaucracy is a wilderness for the foreigner to get lost in, and it is necessary to take care. In general, I have found French authorities are sympathetic, and fair about unintentional breaches of regulations, but they do not take kindly to attempts to pull a fast one. Keep in the open; they suspect anything of a clandestine nature.

If French bureaucracy is difficult, the system in Italy is a complete enigma that even the natives do not try to solve. I get the impression that everyone lives illegally, and pays up when, or if, caught! It is a completely undisciplined society, and the illegal work going on is widespread. Italians, however, are the most tolerant and least chauvinist people in Europe.

Greece is settling into the EU slowly and with much grumbling, now the money shower has ended and it's time to pay back. They were quick to exploit the handouts, which they originally called Delors' Drachmas, trading in last year's donkey for this year's BMW. Conformity to EU rules is taking much longer, and is disagreeably painful. The rules for working, starting businesses, etc, now seem to be being honoured in law, even if in practice the process is not so easy. Greece is a Levantine country and West European methods and business ethics are foreign to the Greek culture. But we do believe that they are trying to adapt. In the meantime be very wary of doing anything that could be wrongly construed: the Greeks are among the most hospitable people in the world provided they do not think their hospitality is being abused. Then they can become quite annoyed. A Greek who is quite annoyed is about equivalent to an Englishman who has gone ballistic.

There is a growing tendency for some live-aboards to find a quasi-permanent mooring and take a full-time, legal job in something connected to either the tourist or construction industry. Very often they end up moving ashore and selling their boat. (This is a good source of cheap boats.) It is not only boat people who are opting out of Britain. The problem for us is that gradually the nice informal little tavernas are being taken over by resident ex-pat cliques. Some of them are even opening their own tavernas and starting to serve egg and chips. Worse, some of the Greek tavernas are serving egg and chips.

• *Syndicates* •

'The Purser doth keepe an Account of all that is received and delivered'

The majority of craft we come across are manned by a married couple (the word 'married' being interpreted a little loosely), but there are a number of boats being sailed by syndicates, and as these are essentially financial arrangements this is perhaps the place for some comment. There are two broad kinds of syndicate, but it is possible to have a combination of both sorts:

Running a syndicate
The expenses of running the boat and living aboard are shared, but the boat herself belongs to only a part of the syndicate, perhaps to just one person.

There is no question of ownership of assets, thus the syndicate is comparatively easy to start, break up or alter as it goes along. Many running syndicates have no formal agreement; they run happily on a shared interest and good fellowship. Given goodwill all round, a break can be just as easy: the person who wishes to leave just packs up and goes. Cautious people might like to have a more positive agreement; I would, but few actually do.

It has to be recognised that the boatowner(s) have the right to withdraw their vessel. But they cannot reasonably exercise this right suddenly in a completely isolated port and thus leave the rest of the syndicate stranded. Likewise, members must not leave the owners stranded, supposing the boat needs a crew to sail. A period of notice needs to be agreed, and it should be expressed in two ways, both in time and in geography; ie there should be a minimum notice of, say, two weeks, but that the break shall only take place in a reasonably accessible port, to which the vessel should be taken as soon as possible. New members can be added at any time, but I know of problems, where, for example, one member wishes to bring in a marvellous girl he met last night, and the others just do not see eye to eye with him about her value to the syndicate as a whole.

The loose agreement might at least define what types of expenditure are covered, eg housekeeping, ship's stores, fuel, repairs, replacements and so on. It should certainly appoint a book-keeper. It should ideally set up a contingency fund to help meet accidents or disaster; the decision to use the fund has to be a majority one, and it should be used only for an item too large to be met out of two (say) months' total contributions. Most people would accept simple provisions like that otherwise there is no point in starting. If disagreement becomes serious, expulsion or dissolution has to follow, even if a somewhat different syndicate re-forms.

In these circumstances the major problem is often the distribution of the contingency fund, especially if it is long standing and/or substantial. In theory it is possible to work out the refunds arithmetically, but a lot of syndicates have fairly frequent changes, and the mathematics might be daunting. One terminating syndicate I knew (a German one), threw a fantastic party, inviting all yachtsmen in the port to drink the fund which was eventually done. The real problem is that goodwill is often thinned on a dissolution.

A running syndicate problem occurred when an aggrieved party considered that a major repair that became necessary arose from neglect by the owner before the formation of the syndicate, and that the repair could enhance the value of the vessel after the syndicate broke up. He felt this was a capital matter, not maintenance; the owner thought otherwise. Such arguments cannot be pre-defined, or pre-determined. They are questions that have to be answered as and when they occur. All parties to a running syndicate must accept the vessel 'as is, where is', and they have to use their judgement as to future liabilities. Of course, an arbitration agreement would help.

Property syndicate

All the members have shares in the boat, though not necessarily equal shares. This type is concerned not only with running a boat from day to day, but also with the ownership of, and responsibility for, a very valuable piece of property. In these circumstances an agreement MUST be made in proper legal form, for though there will be no problems if goodwill prevails, the scope for bitterness, anger and nastiness when tempers become frayed after some real, or imagined, injustice or slight is so immense that the exercise can turn into a lawyers' benefit. Better a small fee for legal advice at the start. The syndicate agreement must, therefore, lay down clearly:

- Who is the skipper for purposes of running the ship (there can be only one).
- How decisions, other than navigational ones, are reached.
- Procedure for changes in the syndicate.
- How unforeseen liabilities will be paid, eg reconstruction due to previous neglect or hidden defects.
- Procedure for final dissolution.
- Arrangements for arbitration.

No syndication agreement should ever give one person a right of general veto. When all goes well, such a right is exercised with tolerance. But if one person gets disaffected, or has a breakdown perhaps, then such a bloody-minded partner can ruin everyone's life. For similar reasons, agreements should contain a clause that in the event of a death the remaining syndicate members have the right to buy out the deceased partner's equity at a valuation arrived at by a stated method. Though all the partners might be the best of friends, this happy relationship may not extend to an executor, or to a legatee of one of these friends. If the capital values are substantial, and exercising the right is liable to cause embarrassment to one or more of the partners, then it is possible to obtain a temporary, contingency insurance on a number of lives payable to the survivors on the death of one of them, though full-scale tontines are illegal.

I do not think the concept of *time-sharing* has any relevance to the type of cruising we are considering. Come to think of it, I do not think it is much good for anyone except the organising entrepreneur.

• *Marine mortgages* •

Though vessels can be bought with marine mortgages, it would need a lot of careful weighing up before sailing off with such a burden. The finance companies would not be overjoyed to see their security, mobile as it is, disappearing to parts of the world where they could have great difficulty and expense exercising any rights in the event of a default. Even if they granted a loan, it would have to be considered less secure than a loan on a boat owned by a man in a steady job, and who never left the country in her, and this would probably lead to a higher rate of interest.

And how would you pay the regular, very large, instalments? Out of a substantial pension, perhaps, if you are lucky enough to have one. You are very unlikely to earn the level of income needed to pay a mortgage while actually cruising. Another method of providing finance is to invest a large sum in property and use the net rental of the property to meet the mortgage payments on the yacht, but this presupposes that the former is greater than the latter. Remember that the finance company is in the investment business too, and in my experience (one of my careers) it would be a very special investment opportunity that would make that sort of deal profitable after taking into account all the on-costs of the various arrangements.

To try to earn enough as you go along to meet mortgage payments is crazy, other than for best-selling novelists, artists who can regularly sell a load of rubbish to the Tate Gallery or hard drug smugglers. The latter will assuredly have their yacht confiscated when they are caught, so the less equity they have in her the better. *They* should mortgage to the hilt.

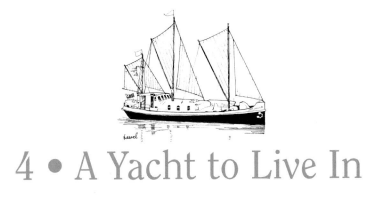

4 • A Yacht to Live In

'Were I to chuse a shippe for myselfe I would have her sail well yet stronglye built, her decks flush and flat, and so roomy that men might pass with ease.'

In the first edition of this book, we went into details of the sort of yacht that would be most suitable for living in. The idea was that you do not need to give yourself a handicap right at the start by trying to make a go of living in a yacht that does not give you a fair chance. She is not just a vehicle, she has to be a home, and many people have said to us: 'We started in a boat that was too small.'

In the mid 1980s there were plenty of one-off yachts about for the number of potential live-aboards. Not so now. The number of live-aboards has risen dramatically; whether or not it is our doing (we still get hailed by passing yachts(wo)men with the cry 'It's all your fault I'm here'). In the Ionian, where we wrote the first edition 20 years ago, and where we are now writing once again, the increase has been certainly five-fold, perhaps ten. At the same time the mass-produced yacht has come to dominate the market because, like the old Ford Anglia did, it is cheaper. The supply of good one-off yachts has decreased; the older ones are getting a bit long in the tooth, and the cheaper mass-produced yacht has not – and was never intended to have – the lasting qualities that in our young days meant that you sailed Grandad's boat and eventually passed it on to your children.

Now there is another problem affecting the supply of good new boats. Currently we are contemplating selling *Hosanna* and having a smaller boat built for our old age. We are finding small boatbuilders reluctant to build us a one-off because of the bureaucracy of the Recreational Craft Directive, an imposition from Brussels. One builder said that it was not the extra cost of compliance with the Directive (which might be as high as £6000) so much as the exasperating expenditure of his time, which could be far better spent in more rewarding ways. Yes, we've said that before, but it's getting me down. I need to let off steam.

'Yet I have knowne a ship built (that) hath sailed to and againe over the Maine Ocean, which had not so much as a naile of iron in her,(being built of Cedar,) but onely one bolt in her keele'

Old boats, if you can find one, need extra maintenance (don't we know it! *Hosanna* was built in 1931). Many more people are now living aboard new production boats of the most extraordinary type and apparently it does not worry most of them much, at least in the first few years, though we have heard a few horror stories. So we are less dogmatic nowadays about the type of boat you should have.

What we can discuss frankly are the features you should look for if you want live-aboard comfort together with short-handed sailing. Many of you will be well aware of these features, even if only at the back of your minds, but to set them out may help those in the planning stage. Every boat is a compromise; just know what you are compromising about.

Do not place too much emphasis on the boat's performance. Many boats that are a joy to sail would make abominable homes, and vice versa. From reading accounts written by famous ocean voyagers, it is apparent that few, if any, spend more than 40% of their time at sea. In our case, over 30 years of full-time, year-round cruising; the average number of days when we were at sea was 85 days per year: about one day in four. In our busiest year with three ocean passages, it was only 118 days at sea. After a 20-odd day voyage without seeing land, one tends to dwell a pause.

Many others spend less time at sea, especially those who stay in the Mediterranean where seagoing in winter is not always congenial and sometimes downright dangerous.

It must also be borne in mind that even at sea one is *living* aboard the yacht, and that is a different thing from doing a holiday cruise. A degree of discomfort acceptable for a week or two rapidly becomes intolerable over a long period, especially in bad conditions.

SIZE AND TYPE OF BOAT

The reader has to balance the amount of boat to the amount of money and to the size and capabilities of the available crew. It is a mistake to try to live in too small a boat. Small size admittedly requires less energy to handle and to maintain, but the extra difficulty of moving about, the unavoidable close intimacy, and the obtrusiveness of all those stores for which there is no locker, make a breeding ground for irritation. We know a couple still living aboard a 25-footer after crossing the Atlantic in her, but they are young and very much in love, as well as being short of personal possessions. A German couple lived in a 24-foot boat with an Alsatian dog. Next year we met them in a 68-foot converted Baltic trader.

A yacht that is too big can be a liability, of course. A physically fit, experienced couple cruising carefully and prudently could expect to cope fairly easily with 75 feet or even more, as we have done ourselves for the past 18 years, but one has also to think of mooring fees and maintenance. Surprisingly, gear does not always cost more in the bigger sizes; often chandlery for yachts is fancy, made of materials chosen for looks rather than strength, and the ability to use fittings made for small tugs, fishing boats or barges can save money in some cases. And do remember that, to your astonishment, you will inevitably and inexorably get older.

Fare Well is a 55-foot ketch of about 30 tons displacement. We sailed her long distances over 11 years, and Laurel, my wife and mate, and usually sole crew, is a

Fare Well, a 55-foot, steel-hulled ketch, was our cruising home for over 11 years, and suited us well. Before you start looking for your cruiser, do the Cooper Yacht Evaluator questionnaire to help you decide on your priorities.

lightweight five-footer with a congenitally dislocated hip. Since then we have motor-sailed our 70-tonne sailing barge *Hosanna*, and though we have been less adventurous, we are beginning to find her a bit more tiring than we used to. Our boats are fine, but sometimes we age faster than they do.

We wrote in the first edition of *Sell Up and Sail* that the ideal monohull for any age would have a waterline length of 33 to 37 feet, a beam of just over a third of that, and not too V-shaped in cross-section. That would provide a home that can be comfortable, have enough storage space, be easy enough to manage even when years advance, and be reasonably economical to moor and slip.

Since then the average cruising yacht has increased in size, gear is better designed and easier to manage, expected standards of living have risen by a huge factor, and by 2005 the ideal size could be a tad more than the higher figure we originally gave. If you decide on a little ship that is outside this range, be very sure your decision is soundly based on reason and experience, rather than emotion. Our own decision to go for a barge yacht of 87 feet turned out to be a good one, possibly because Bill is professionally used to handling big ships, but now that we reach the age of 77, we cannot expect to be able to manage her for much longer. We could, though, reasonably expect to handle a smaller craft for some time. Alan Prince spends most of each summer aboard 30-footer Nauticat *Philos*. He is 90 years old, capable and prudent, and recently coped magnificently in a strong blow that had many skippers half his age caught on the hop. Many younger yachties could learn a thing or two by watching him. There is more to sailing than trimming sails. Avoiding trouble is a major part of good seamanship.

• *Multihulls* •

Multihulls give more boat for the money, and are usually faster, but they have disadvantages. When heavily loaded, and in our cruising life they *always* would be, they seem to lose proportionately more performance than a monohull. Some even become dangerous. It is also necessary to go up in size to get enough headroom in the living accommodation. One can get by with an overall length about 25% shorter than a monohull to get equivalent accommodation. But again there is a disadvantage: berthing becomes more difficult, and when it has to be paid for, much more expensive, the loading being 50 to 100%. This is a big factor in the increasingly crowded ports of the Mediterranean; it is less significant in the West Indies where you will spend a lot more time swinging to a single anchor. It is even less significant in the Bahamas where many of the best harbours are closed to the deeper-draughted monohulls. It's horses for courses.

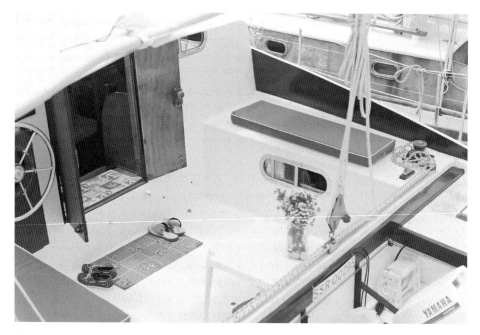

As you can see, the twin hulls of a catamaran give you lots of extra space in the cockpit.

• *Motor yachts* •

It is not easy to be a long-term deep-water cruiser in a pure motor yacht, partly because long passages are virtually impossible, and also because one must be much more cautious about the weather. And the well-head price of oil, once $13 a barrel, was $66 last night. We do know of several long-distance motor yachts (we are not talking here about the millionaire's 150-foot job, but sensibly sized 40-foot vessels) split between the Mediterranean and the USA Intra-Coastal. In the former they have access to the attractive European canal system, and in the latter there is much scope for short sheltered passages. The Intra-Coastal Waterway is rather a special case as, apart from a few Canadians, most yachts there are in their home waters. The European inland waters are another popular cruising ground, especially for those who get seasick.

As Laurel and I are unwilling to give up this life, it looks as if motoring will be our eventual mode. Certainly in *Hosanna*, we have been motoring more as we get older. A motor yacht provides considerably more living comfort than a sailing yacht of the same length. We are actively considering whether or not to make *Hosanna*'s replacement a motor yacht and reluctantly forget the sticks and string.

Will we miss them? Yes. But think what changes have taken place since we first got our love for sailing.

Sixty years ago, when we began sailing, it was uncomfortable and actually quite difficult. It was a serious challenge coping with miles of string and acres of cotton canvas. The work aboard was non-stop: when not actually sailing or bailing, there were ropes' ends to whip; common blocks needed new grommets (there were no sheet winches and everything was done by tackles); galvanised rigging needed more lanolin and then re-parcelling and serving. The work was endless but we were young and strong and enjoyed it, and when we finally got the jackyard top-sail to set properly there was a massive sense of achievement. Now, by winding the mainsail out of its in-mast roller, I don't get that buzz and worse, I get breathless. I gave *Hosanna* an old-fashioned rig with over half a mile of string to play with and it has been fun, but enough is enough. I don't want any old boat. Whatever we build next will probably not appeal to many, but she will appeal to us. That's what matters.

Would we be changing class and making a pact with the devil? True, motor craft can be driven inconsiderately and be a downright pest, but that is not necessary at all. The fault lies with the owner, not with the boat. Nowadays the demon sailing yachtsman has arrived, the bareboat charterers who've done a few night-classes and know it all or do not care if they do not. Motor yachtsmen often conform to cruising etiquette much better than this. It is a different matter regarding those in planing or semi-planing craft. These latter are almost all *de facto* inconsiderate or incompetent, even if their owners hope and imagine they are not. They should look behind them occasionally and cringe at the mayhem they have left astern in their wake. Long-term cruising is an attitude of mind and is not logically compatible with speed.

WHERE TO BUY SECOND-HAND

If you are trying to buy second-hand, do not expect very much help from yacht brokers. They are not dishonest (they cannot all be, can they?) but are blinkered. They come to believe that what sells easiest must be better than a yacht that needs a discerning buyer (in brokerage terms this latter expression means a blasted nuisance).

Even if you itemise carefully exactly what you are looking for, the office boy will send you, for a time, details of craft that are manifestly unsuitable for your purpose, and then shortly you will be sent nothing further. We have yet to meet a broker with the first idea what long-term living aboard is all about. We have met one recently who patronisingly claimed to understand, but as he expounded what he considered our important needs to be, the bullshit meter went up beyond the red line. Well, he's a professional salesman, isn't he? Selling second-hand boats is no different from selling second-hand cars.

Britain is not the only place to look for a boat, though beware of VAT complications if buying out of Europe. There are many people who start on this cruising life, who for one reason or another do not get very far. Perhaps they have not done their homework. In any event there are often bargains to be picked up in Gibraltar, the Canary Islands, southern Spain or Portugal, where perfectly good

This Dutch motor sailer is a good example of a live-aboard. She has a sturdy wheelhouse and is well-equipped with a rigid dinghy (carried on davits at the stern) and has substantial guardrails.

yachts have been abandoned by a disillusioned crew, a split in the relationship, sickness in the family, or the need to go home and earn some cash.

There are many suitable yachts to be found in the live-aboard areas. We discuss these areas later on.

English language magazines where suitable boats may be advertised are *Cruising World* (Newport, RI), *Sailing Today* (England) and *Yachting Monthly* (England). *Yachting World* (England) for the larger, ritzier boats, and *Practical Boat Owner* (England) is useful for the smaller sizes. *Boats and Planes for Sale* (England) is a good source. *Fluvial* (France) has many advertisements for barges and river-craft on the Continental waterways.

BUYING A BARE HULL

If the extent of alterations required is large, or one's requirements are very eso-teric, one should consider buying a hull and then finishing it. This is basically what we have twice done, though I did have some say in the design of *Fare Well's* hull too. It is possible we will do it again.

Completing a hull is not as difficult as may be imagined. Generally, the cost of the bare shell itself is a surprisingly small fraction of the total cost of a profes-sionally built boat, often about one sixth. This means that there is much work in finishing it, and it is a long, time-consuming project. *Fare Well* took 4000 logged man-hours of amateur work, and *Hosanna* took even longer. A few jobs have to be done by professionals, but be careful: good free-lance professionals are hard to find these days, and you may end up as we sometimes did, having to re-do 'pro-fessional' work ourselves. An intelligent and manually competent person with motivation and access to a good reference library can easily out-perform some of the ham-fisted part-timers often found doing casual boatwork.

> *'I will arise and go now, and go where the wind is free,*
> *And a fine keelboat build there, Of wood and metal made.*
> *Nine summers will I sail her, With a cat for the company;*
> *And live content in the awning's shade.'*

WHAT FACTORS AFFECT THE CHOICE OF BOAT?

• *Cooper's Law* •

Any boat being lived in will float about six inches deeper in the water than her designer thought desirable.

Well, that screws performance yachts for a start. It's the extra gear, stupid (to misquote Clinton).

Since we first wrote the above we have been interested to read a paper by Hugo du Plessis, an experienced naval architect and ocean cruiser, pointing out the dangers of lightweight boats for long-distance cruising. To sum up his contentions (with which we heartily agree) he says that lightweight boats cannot carry the loads necessary to support a crew over long distances, and that when they are, inevitably, overloaded they can become dangerous. When loading a boat for a four-week (say) passage, the increase in weight (about a tonne) for a lightweight boat is proportionately much more, and her sailing characteristics would be much more seriously affected than for a boat that is intrinsically heavy. His arguments are convincing. We are surprised that his article has not been reprinted by a yachting magazine for wider circulation; it should be, even at the risk of offending advertisers.

The vast majority of so-called cruising yachts being marketed these days, particularly by Continental builders, could reasonably be said to be lightweight. When at the Boat Show, ask the salesman for the TPI of the yacht. Probably he won't know what these letters mean. It is very doubtful he will know the figure they represent. This is Tons Per Inch, and is the amount of weight necessary to increase the draught by one inch. No design is finished without this calculation and it is VITALLY IMPORTANT for the live-aboard. (I suppose these poor Continentals work in metric.)

One needs a boat where less attention is paid to fashion, rating rules and high performance, leading to more attention being paid to load carrying and stowage, ease of handling under both sail and power, crew comfort and a handsome appearance. Oh! and she should be economical to berth. This is of growing importance as expensive marinas come to replace those quaint little public ports we once used for almost nothing, and anchorages fill up with fish farms. Of course, if you buy a one-off second-hand, you will have to calculate TPI for yourself. It's not difficult. Let's go metric, just to show we can. Calculate the waterplane area in square metres using Simpson's rule. Multiply this by 0.01 and you will get the volume in cubic metres of a horizontal slice of boat at the waterline. A cubic metre of water is one metric tonne, so you will get, thereby, the tonnes per centimetre of immersion. I did it for *Hosanna*, and the figure is 0.98. Clever dicks will notice that the figure changes as the boat gets deeper or lighter because the area of the waterplane changes. You can go on enjoying arithmetic all night like this and never go sailing at all.

• *Weatherliness* •

'A well bowed shippe so swiftly presseth the water as that it foameth, and in the dark night sparkleth like fire. If the Bow bee too narrow . . . she pitcheth her head into the sea; so that the meane is the best, if her after way be answerable.'

I have already referred to the yacht that is a joy to sail but hell to live in. Understandably, most dreamers and planners contemplate a boat with good performance; yachting journalists write endlessly about the perfect performance yacht, recalling with enthusiasm the drenching they got batting to windward for a few hours last weekend. A glorious exhilarating sail! Then they went home afterwards for a hot bath, a decent meal, and a change of clothes.

It's a bit different slogging for days on end, trying meanwhile to prepare and cook good meals, to do the maintenance and repairs, and to keep your clothing dry. Many dedicated cruisers never beat to windward at all. Our own motto is 'if you have to beat, you're going to the wrong place'. *Gentlemen do not tack*, was a motto heard in the first half of the 19th century, though it may have been because the boatmen (who were not considered gentlemen) did all that for you. Most live-aboards are not used to being treated like gentlemen either. On a long passage it is occasionally necessary to compromise, and beat to windward, but we have been known to heave-to in mid-ocean when confronted by an unseasonable heading force 6 and wait for it to change. Do not trust ocean sailors who bang on about windward ability: suspect them of masochism or worse.

It is a question of enjoying life and having all the time in the world to do it. Generally, in *Fare Well*, we did not approach closer to the wind than 55°. If we did it was usually for a short leg or to keep a better offing, and even then we tended to run the engine at half revs, which contributes some ever-welcome amps as well as thrust and gets the unfortunate episode over sooner. In *Hosanna*, we motor much more. She had eight sails in all but now we carry only six. In the Med we are often too lazy to set them all for a comparatively short voyage, and setting only a few is not enough to maintain a fair speed. You will often see us with the upside down black triangle in the rigging forward, indicating that we are motor-sailing. She is heavy to steer, and with an engine ticking over we get power-assisted steering, and *hot water*!

• *High performance* •

You sometimes hear the opinion that high sailing performance is a potential safety factor. Let us examine this hypothesis. In over 40,000 miles of cruising in *Fare Well*, and over 35,000 in *Hosanna*, extending over 30 years, the following were our 'dangerous situations':

- A fire at sea.
- A hurricane.
- Damage from a heavy squall (perhaps a waterspout?), in the Gulf Stream.
- A lightning strike.
- Disintegration of a shaft coupling, leaving a big leak.
- A fall and resultant injury in a gale off Cap Corse.
- An improperly secured forehatch led to the forepeak filling with water.
- Failure of the genoa furling gear. At the same time I allowed the trailing sheet to foul the screw while approaching a crowded anchorage. (Classic!)
- Loss of the foremast in a near gale in the southern North Sea, with a lee shore not far away.
- Going hard aground in a ship canal.

In addition we have endured 11 other gales of force 8 or over, with no worries other than understandable apprehension.

At no other time in 75,000 miles over 30 years were we in danger of our lives; we have only once needed assistance, the canal grounding (see *Yachting Monthly* Dec 2003) and at no time at all would high performance on the wind have been of any benefit whatsoever. Nor any other high performance for that matter.

Let us contrast that with the racing fleet, which we suppose to be the exemplars of high performance. In the Fastnet Race of 1979 the fleet met a short summer gale of admittedly above average severity, but the racing yachts with their large, fit crews dropped out like 80-year-olds in a polka. We do know that a small American cruising yacht sailed through the worst of that storm with the owner, his wife, and two children under four on board, and wrote home merely that they had 'had a rough passage'.

Since then the Sydney to Hobart race has experienced similar tragedies among the generously crewed, expensively equipped and supervised racing fleet; while cruising yachts going through the same conditions survived unharmed.

In the 1996/7 Vendée Globe Round the World Race, the yachts were heavily sponsored and designed by leaders of their profession. They were built and fitted out at enormous expense using state-of-the-art materials. Their keels fell off, their rudders broke, their masts fell down, and several of them capsized and sank. Worse, there was loss of life. These boats, sailed by competent, experienced sailors, were built to win races, not to survive bad conditions. Do ocean racing stars feel no shame at the way the world's rescue services are being exploited to the tune of millions of pounds to help satisfy a craving for personal glory and/or commercial publicity *at any cost*? Yes, it's rough down there in the Southern Ocean, but the designers know that, don't they? So why send brave men and women out in dodgy racing yachts? Well, it's sport, I suppose.

For reliably safe cruising one should seek well-tried and proven dispositions of sail, with everything much stronger than computer models suggest. Use of new materials should include a generous safety margin to take care of factor x, the great unknown. In our world of small family crews, any sail should be able to be furled or trimmed by one person without recourse to power assistance.

In Mediterranean conditions, where winds are often light and the seas can be unexpectedly, and uncomfortably, short and steep, we find that we have always used the engine much more than we first expected to. (Our first ever Med cruise of a month in 1954 was in a boat without an engine. It was fun.) The number of engine hours per year remained fairly constant for a time, but has started to increase a little as we age. In any case, with fridge, running lights and other domestic conveniences (and their use has much increased over the years) some battery charging is needed. In the Med, many passages are of 30 to 50 miles and if the wind changes or drops as it often does in the evening there is a strong incentive to set the iron topsail for an hour or so to ensure timely arrival in a good berth before the whole port is full of flotillas and Sunseekers.

In the Bahamas and West Indies, things are somewhat different. Winds are more reliable, it is easier to sail to an anchorage and/or weigh under sail, and the line of the Windward Islands runs as their name tells you conveniently across the wind, generally giving a comfortable reach in both directions. Your engine is not so crucial.

• *Sails, ease of handling and the rig* •

I do not propose to write much about choice of rig. I have my own preferences (if I were to build a 40-foot cruising yacht now, I would choose a wishbone ketch) but that would not be everybody's choice, perhaps because they have no experience of the rig.

Sailing, as we discussed already, has got much easier to do. So the fact that we are all contemplating a small crew, usually two persons, is no longer the strange phenomenon it once was.

One question that suggests itself is to choose the ideal roller-furling/reefing gear. It is impossible to recommend any particular gear because new ones come and go frequently. It is not advisable to seek sailmakers' advice, as most sailmakers either have their own gear or are agents for one or two, and objective advice

Fare Well *had a Bermudan rig, which I originally thought was the most suitable for long-distance cruising. Through experience, however, my views have changed as a period of short-tacking with this rig can be exhausting for a crew of two.*

is difficult to get. Few people, and I am not among them, have experience of more than one or two different makes, deep-sea experience I mean. Experienced delivery skippers probably have – perhaps one of these could write an article for a yachtimag comparing makes. It's not a subject for a magazine in-house comparison article because this sort of trial cannot fully cover a subject like this. You just have to use whatever advice you can get and apply your own judgement. Fortunately, the technique of rolling has advanced considerably in recent years and some of the early dodgy gears have disappeared.

Mainsails that roll inside the mast are commonplace now. I have no intimate knowledge of them. Problems are probably not too significant now that experience has ironed most of them out. Some gears have a serious social problem in harbour, when with strong winds the mast slot turns itself into a gigantic organ pipe, and the whole place is disturbed with the hooting of a demented owl. Makers once notorious for this defect now claim to have solved the problem. They lie. (Or one eminent maker does.) Two new charter boats fitted from that stable lie close to us as we write. They do not even moan in harmony with each other, let alone the same note. It's worse than tapping halyards.

We have mixed reports of in-boom rolling. It involves having a rather over-size boom and a rigid kicking strap or martingale. Personally I would prefer it to in-mast gear because it is more accessible. I do not like climbing masts at sea.

Whatever rig you have, make sure that you can furl all of the sails single-handed, and quickly. In these circumstances the divided rig makes a lot of sense, but remember that one cannot furl or reef all the sails simultaneously. Standing rigging should not be the flimsy affair of the racing fleet: it must be able to support full canvas in gale-strength squalls, then as sail is reduced things will get better. My father's view, which I endorse, was that the standing rigging all together should be able to hoist a weight of three times that of the boat.

There is one case to watch which I have found little appreciated nowadays: in gaff-rigged craft when the main is furled or close-reefed before reducing the headsails, there is still great compression in the mast and without the pull of the mainsail hoops to dampen vibration, it is possible to lose the mast. In spite of knowing all about this we still managed to lose *Hosanna's* solid wooden foremast off the Kentish Knock, but it had been weakened by a soft spot round a small knot. We had known about that and were on our way to look for a suitable tree.

One now sees yachts with a permanently fitted sailbag on the mainboom, accompanied by lazyjacks. After lowering the sail, there is a zip on top to cover all. Looks neat in harbour, but a bit untidy otherwise.

Being somewhat conservative, we think that all booms, but especially main booms, should have a stout gallows, not only for stowing in harbour but also with slots in the outboard ends so that the boom can be easily bowsed down to leeward to be worked on. It is far easier and safer to hold onto a rigidly fixed boom than to cling to one that is allowed even a little movement. If the gallows is fitted about two-thirds of the length of the boom from the mast it is possible to arrange a slot on the outboard end of the gallows, so that the extreme end of the boom, when

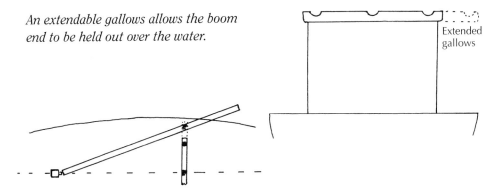

An extendable gallows allows the boom end to be held out over the water.

Extended gallows

stowed in it, is a foot or so outboard of the ship's side. This provides a good lifting point for bringing heavy weights on board, or recovering people from the sea. Production boats never seem to have gallows.

With roller furling, if heavy weather is expected, then over-roll a furled sail by a few turns. I once left our 8oz genoa loosely rolled, with perhaps a square foot or so still off the roll. When a Gulf Stream squall hit us in the middle of the night the force was enough to pull all taut and effectively unroll a few feet of sail, which disintegrated into ribbons in seconds. An 11oz sail that was set survived in usable state but a conventionally, though hastily, furled 12oz mainsail was ripped out of its gaskets and was lost too. One cannot go about continually taking precautions against squalls of this extreme violence, but where their occurrence is possible or likely, then one should.

Roller reefing/furling does partially solve a problem of stowage, for sails so set remain above deck and one needs fewer separate sails. Space below in a long-cruising boat is so valuable that many stow their sails on deck. It is possible to have a sailbag such that a headsail can be put in it while it is still hanked on its stay. It does not look very elegant, making the average yacht look as if she has a nosebag on. It is quite important that all sails should be covered when not in use. Simple light covers will do: all that is necessary is to stop ultraviolet light damaging the synthetic cloth. I have seen no evidence that this ultraviolet problem has so far been solved (2005). Incidentally, elegance is not a feature of the average live-aboard boat. We like to think it is, but we delude ourselves.

• Hull shape •

A full keel is desirable for passage-making, but in areas such as the Bahamas Banks there are innumerable bays and anchorages out of reach of deeper boats but where shallow draught yachts can find wonderful peace (provided the wet-bikes stay away). Moderate draught also gives opportunities for exploring canals and rivers, especially those of France, or the lovely Intra-Coastal Waterway of the US east coast. These factors point the need for a compromise, so consider a mono-hull draught of 1m 60cm or less.

Fare Well was designed for 1m 85cm and for her size that is quite modest, but she did not end up that way, and cruising yachts never do, because no one can ever believe the incredible weight of things that they need to carry on long voyages, or when living on board. We repeat the Two Golden Rules:

- In every case, when cruising with full living load, the draught will be at least 6 inches more than expected.
- There are no exceptions.

Centreboards are not an ideal answer. When the Bollay family took their Rhodes-designed centreboard sloop *Snowgoose* into the French canals they eventually exported a good part of the mineral wealth of the country, which had got itself jammed up the trunking, and it took a lot of getting out. Centreboards can be awkward to manage in larger boats because they have to be heavy to be strong enough to take the big lateral cantilever strains. In smaller boats the draught need not be so very deep anyway, so that centreboards are perhaps an unnecessary complication.

It is worth mentioning that *Fare Well*, while drawing 6ft 7in (say 2 metres), cruised the Bahamas and the full length of the Intra-Coastal Waterway without any serious problems. We found the bottom a few times; once we stuck on a coral head in the Bahamas for a tide, but got off unaided by laying out two bower anchors.

Long overhangs have a sporty look, but are expensive in mooring and construction; they add to the maintenance and contribute little to usable boat. I do not think they are an advantage for our purpose. Now that more and more harbours are being converted into expensive marinas, the overall length of the boat is an economic factor militating against overhangs. Our research shows that 99% of live-aboards have to watch their pennies carefully. Some sacrifices have to be made and perhaps the elegant long yachts with handsome sheer-lines are among them. Pity!

Other contributions to economic mooring are retractable bowsprits, and folding stern platforms, the latter leading logically to the sugar-scoop or retroussé stern and spade rudder hung right aft. These pose problems for a cruising yacht. Not only do you lose a commodious locker and some valuable deck space without any corresponding saving on mooring fees, but if you berth stern-to, as in most Mediterranean ports, this configuration can be a positive hazard. Lying bows-to is an alternative that has its own disadvantages, which I will refer to under both anchoring and misadventures. The problem with a deep rudder right aft is that quays in primitive ports seldom have vertical faces to their full apparent depth. Often they are ballasted to just below water level, and odd rocks together with the assorted detritus of centuries extend some distance from the quay. We have some pictures and a drawing to illustrate.

However, the scoop stern does have compensations. Many yachts are now to be found that are completely open aft so that one may more easily walk aboard when

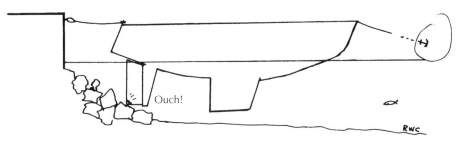

A deep rudder hung well aft near the transom is vulnerable when mooring stern-to.

moored stern-to a low quay. Sometimes this accessibility is eased further by twin steering wheels. A bit of an affectation, this; it looks racy. Joystick steering is far easier and the helmsman's position then has no limitations.

The sloping transom is a good site for a permanent bathing or boarding ladder, and a little platform there forms a safe(ish) place to stow a can of petrol (gasoline) for the outboard motor.

Twin screws are an unnecessary luxury for sailing yachts in the sizes we are contemplating, but for the pure motor yacht they would make a lot of sense. Although undoubtedly vulnerable in canals, there will be occasions in less frequented parts where the ability to limp home might be a blessing. Away from the

The open platform of a sloping transom is a relatively safe place to store fuel cans and provides good access for swimming.

British or US coasts, help is not so readily available, or even not at all. In some parts we have visited, VHF channel 16 may be of more use for ordering a taxi than asking for assistance.

• *Paint* •

Maintenance is heavier with steel, but it is unskilled labour for the most part, and the dedicated cruiser is there all the time to do it. If the hull is initially shot-blasted to an even grey (S3), then instantly coated with epoxy-based cover to a thickness of half a millimetre, you have a good basis, but it is important to touch up damage to this film as soon as possible.

Fare Well's initial paint job lasted eight years, and even then only needed re-doing near the waterline. Some people like zinc or aluminium spraying, but I believe this actually weakens the bond of the epoxy to the steel, though there may be some merit in epoxy-zinc as a paint. I think one can get too clever over this problem. The vital thing is to get the strongest possible skin to adhere in the strongest possible way, and any minor damage to the coating below the waterline ought to be taken care of by fitting good sacrificial anodes, whose life and effectiveness can be periodically checked. Choice and place of anodes is a matter of skill. Get professional advice. MG Duff advised us well.

HULL CONSTRUCTION AND MATERIALS

• *Steel* •

The banning of TBT antifouling has undoubtedly worsened the case for the steel boat. I, personally, think that, given the comparatively minute proportion of steel and aluminium yachts compared with wood or glass-fibre (about 1% of the total), that a 'grandfather' exception could have been made for existing vessels, many of which were built with the expectation of having non-reactive antifouling available to them. Such an exception has been made in some countries. Only in nanny-state Britain are our laws governed by self-appointed pressure groups with deficient detailed knowledge of anything. But the Greens are like the Roman Church in the Middle Ages: any criticism of them is a heresy and clearly I would be burned at the stake if it were not that it would damage the ozone layer.

It is in craft over 12m waterline that steel becomes an economical material. Then it becomes possible to have a hull of plate thickness sufficient to stand a variety of abuses, including abrasion and impact. In fact the only short-term danger to a steel hull is the tin-opener effect typified by striking a sharp rocky pinnacle or an iceberg. It is the most effectively resistant material to pack-ice, though that rarely concerns us.

Once the plate thickness rises above 4mm, this danger recedes for the speeds we are likely to reach. The bottom of *Fare Well*'s keel is 1in armour-plate Royal Dockyard surplus, rounded up at the forefoot, and when we sledded up 60cm out

A convincing argument for keeping your boat well-fended – this damage to a glass-fibre hull occurred in just a few seconds.

of the water after striking a coral head at 7 knots, the resultant scratches on the steel were less than a millimetre deep.

• *Glass-fibre* •

Steel hulls do not leak, except through contrived openings. Similarly, glass-fibre hulls ought not to leak, but strength and reliability depends on the quality of the materials and also on the conscientiousness of the laminators; factors which are difficult to assess in a second-hand boat later on in its life.

Hulls of this material have been known to crack, particularly where skegs or keels adjoin the hull, and this seems to happen irrespective of the reputation of the yard, and particularly with light-construction boats from weight-conscious designers. The material abrades easily, which is an important consideration if one visits non-yachty harbours where there are fishing boats with sharp steel projections, like metallic porcupines. GRP burns, and is a poor conductor of electricity which can cause it to disintegrate in lightning strikes, which are much more common in tropical climes. Like steel, it is not habitually eaten by any known animal (except Greek goats), but it does have its equivalent to corrosion osmosis, which can be difficult to deal with. Glass-fibre is expensive on a one-off basis but this can be ameliorated by using the sandwich method, which has the great advantage of insulating the skin and is therefore an appreciated method of building for the hotter climates.

• *Ferro-cement* •

These boats have a bad reputation, which is not fully deserved. The well-built hull is very good indeed, but poor technique gives rise to nautical disasters. (Buried somewhere in the Medway marshes is a hull constructed by a professor of building technology, which fell to pieces.) I would consider a hull made by the Wroxham firm of Windboats to be worth a second look, as I have seen some good work of theirs, and some good boats have come from New Zealand builders. New Zealand seems to be the skill centre for this technique. As for the material, abrasion resistance is poor compared to metal, though better than GRP. Impact resistance is good for boats with a heavy steel reinforcement, but chicken wire, often used by amateurs because it is cheaper, lighter and easier to shape, is vulnerable. Maintenance is a lot less of a problem than with steel. Ferro is thought of as being the cheapest material for a one-off amateur built hull, but so much depends on standards. In any case the cost of the hull is likely to be between one sixth and one fifth of the total cost of building. Resale of these boats is supposed to be difficult, but those with experience tell me they are much like any one-off: it depends on the quality.

• *Wood* •

Timber has a lovely feel about it, but it presents many problems. All sorts of things eat it, and it rots and grows fungi, problems which are all worse in warm climates. Hulls built traditionally are subject to leaks. It can be easily repaired, though often good hardwoods are hard to come by, and this is a worsening situation as the Greens gain ground. Abrasion resistance is moderate, and whereas impact is unlikely to penetrate because of wood's elasticity, it can lead to planks springing, or to distortion with multiple small leaks that can be hell to stem.

I now have some knowledge (though not an expertise) of the more recent wood techniques. Boats built in the West System (a sort of epoxy-saturated wood method, which seems to combine the advantages of GRP with the advantages of wood) have impressed me and their owners all seem satisfied. I have recently watched at Bure Marine Ltd, Great Yarmouth, a boat built in this system being expertly repaired after being damaged and sunk (she had impaled herself on a submerged pile on a falling tide; an interesting salvage job). She was double diagonally planked and seemed to have much to commend her. Her heavy epoxy coating would proof her against insect attack.

• *Aluminium* •

A hull of this material has some of the properties of steel, but is lighter and not nearly so resistant to damage, a fact that is apparent in many a large repair yard. One of its principal problems is that it is softer than steel and dents very easily. It is vulnerable to electrolytic problems if great care is not taken over the selection of alloys and fittings, and it is by no means unknown for the wrong alloy to creep in because the right one is temporarily unavailable at the yard. It is expensive to build and extremely difficult, not to say impossible, to get repaired neatly outside the major sophisticated yachting venues. For a cautionary tale, read up the history of one of the first aluminium boats, *Gulvain*.

• *Steel-aluminium* •

It is now possible to have hulls built of steel with superstructure of high-grade aluminium alloys, without all the bother of bolting, insulating (to prevent electrolysis), and worrying if it is all going to hold together. Aero-Spatiale of Toulouse has invented a way of welding aluminium to steel. It cannot be done on site, but they sell strips in the form of a sandwich of aluminium and steel with a filler of thin titanium, the three 'welded' together by the pressure of detonating explosives. This strip can be conventionally welded to steel on the one side and to aluminium on the other, and seems not to suffer from electrolytic action. It is easy to use, but expensive.

• *Decks* •

These should be made of sheet material and should never rely on caulking for their watertightness. If they do, they will leak, which is a catalyst for rot and marital discord.

LONG-TERM VALUE

Whether a particular yacht will retain or lose pecuniary value depends on many factors. Investment analysts have a lot of trouble accurately forecasting future prices of quite simple things; it seems to me very dangerous to base decisions on projected future assumptions about prices of one second-hand yacht against another. Some points are worth bearing in mind:

- A long-cruising yacht will get much more wear and tear than a similar yacht that is seldom out of its shed, or off moorings. On the other hand it will be better looked after.
- A strongly built boat which is unfashionable today may well be a 'character' boat when today's fashionable trade-in models are in the scrapyard, provided hull, engine and gear are in good condition and she's not too massive.
- Resale prices are heavily dependent on fashion.
- Are you buying a boat for life? If not, how long do you envisage cruising? If over seven years, it seems to me that resale worries should not be allowed to cause sleepless nights. Almost everything I worried about seven years ago seems to have solved itself in the meantime.

The most important thing is to buy a boat that suits you well. You would not buy a car that was a bastard to drive just because someone suggested it had a good resale value. We once knew a couple who had started out to live aboard, and thinking that they might not like it they had chosen a Finnish production boat with a good reputation for being easy to sell. A moment's thought would have shown its complete unsuitability for long-term living aboard. Of course they did not enjoy the life; they had ruined their prospects by forgetting what was the principal purpose of the boat and instead basing their choice on other criteria. Still, they got a good price for it when they sold the dream.

If you are not going long-cruising as a completely new way of life, but as a short break of perhaps two years in a working career, your attitude to resale prices will be somewhat different. You will still need to consider your aims carefully in order to live reasonably well, but you would be a hostage to financial fortune to ignore the likely proceeds from the sale of the yacht, which you are unlikely to want to keep forever. It is quite reasonable to forecast two years ahead, and a good broker's advice might be valuable in this respect. Do not, however, pay much attention to his advice on what sort of yacht to cruise in unless you are really sure he knows what living aboard is about; I have never met one who does. Your aim may be different from the aim of a long-term cruiser, but you will still have an aim that is not entirely centred on resale. You make the compromise.

A YACHT TO GROW OLD IN

'The saylers are the antient men . . . and nothing but experience can poffibly teach it.'

This is a difficult subject to find a name for, mostly because we have all got into the habit of using euphemisms for 'old-age'. My preference for calling spades spades has not changed much since becoming a pensioner, but I discarded the word geriatric because my elementary knowledge of Greek suggests to me that the word really means an old doctor.

When we originated the first ever cruising symposium on the 'Sell Up and Sail' concept, we were very impressed by the strong interest in the subject shown by people who had retired. We were in process of changing to a boat more suitable to our own increasing years, and were somewhat shamed by the ambitions of some of our fellow symposers. It became evident to us that there is a positive demand for boats suitable for retired people to do a lot of sailing in, even if not to live aboard full-time.

This is the time of life when living aboard becomes especially attractive. No more worries about careers, children growing up, and income, because you should have seen to all that by now. The only problems are to do with one's physical capability, and the fact that it can be expected to decline as the years go by. (You can also go bonkers, but many of us are quite a long way down that road already.)

Improvisation is the key to comfortable cruising. Here a plastic chair has been customised to provide comfort in the cockpit.

If you are buying a boat to retire into, it is important to project ahead what you can cope with. Certainly your skills will improve to offset failing strength, but there will come a time when skills reach a plateau and strength goes on declining.

It would be unwise to contemplate frequent changes of boat. God knows, it is hard enough to find one super-boat in a lifetime without giving yourself the task of finding several, and every change is expensive and traumatic. Like marriages. Nevertheless it requires quite a lot of self-discipline to buy a boat that will not perform to the full extent of your present capabilities. If you are not ready to face this prospect yet, come back to the subject in a few years' time.

We wrote in a past edition that we thought production boats were not very suitable for the live-aboard. In this we found ourselves at odds with some yachting journalists, who are no fools and not inexperienced. It just goes to show that opinions can differ. But note that when a former editor of *Yachting World* retired, he wrote that he found the production boat not exactly ideal for old-age, and he had his retirement yacht specially designed to suit him. I didn't like this boat either, but that is beside the point. We note with amusement that a later editor who once disagreed with us has now sold his production boat and taken delivery of a one-off. Anticipating retirement, perhaps?

We faced the problem of changing boats 20 years ago. We do not pretend that our personal solution would be the best for other people, but we feel it might help some folk if we described the arguments that led to our decision.

Firstly, prospective old salts should consider their personal qualities. For example Laurel is small, and somewhat lame. Her disability will not improve;

Hosanna, *the converted Dutch barge which has been our comfortable cruising home for the last 19 years. She has three engines, three screws and a bow-thruster – and probably three tons of books.*

rather the opposite. Bill is big and very strong in the short-term sense, but short-ness of breath prevents him exerting himself for long periods without resting. None of our problems will improve.

If we were each at 90% of our best-ever capacity when we first set sail as live-aboards in 1976, we were probably at about 65% at change-over time in 1986, which represents a decline of about 2% per annum. This had to be projected for-ward. We had owned *Fare Well* for about 15 years, this meant that our new ship *Hosanna* might be our ultimate if she would last us another 15. What would be our physical capacity then? Probably not good.

We have known and met a fair number of yachtsmen who have gone on cruis-ing far and wide into old-age, and we have become aware of some of their difficulties. We have helped some with their problems, for example, diabetes, and colostomy which is only one of the possible scourges of the elderly. Many of these problems can be coped with, at least until they become debilitating. Some old salts we can think of clearly went on far too long. It is one thing to rely on other people's help in an occasional crisis, but when one can no longer cope without frequent and almost regular assistance, it becomes time to think about swallow-ing the anchor, however much it sticks in your throat.

With regard to the boat, the obvious solution to the problem is to settle for a smaller boat than would the younger person. I say obvious because it seems to be everyone's instinctive answer. I don't think it is necessarily the right one. A lot

A cheap and ingenious solution to both protecting the bow for bow-to mooring and giving a secure foot-hold for boarding.

depends on what you think you will be able to handle. Surprisingly, size is not as important as, for example, whether the boat itself acts like a gentleman or a hooligan. Some boats are intractable yobs.

The process of adapting to decreasing faculties can be approached in two ways. One is to have a boat that will be easily coped with until death us do part, come hell or high water. The other is to have a boat that is comfortable and reasonably sea-worthy, but which will both require and allow one to modify one's cruising range when that becomes necessary. We chose the latter course, but let us consider the other option first.

Maintenance is not so much of a problem because it can be undertaken in slow time. Clearly it is unwise to take on an impossible burden, but apart from that, maintenance should not figure too largely in the argument.

Assuming one is going to come down in size, what is the right size? We have to have good living conditions, so the boat cannot be too small. Small sporty boats need quick physical reactions, something we tend to lose as we get older. Space is needed for personal things: souvenirs, photographs, small treasures and so on.

On the other hand it is desirable that the boat should be of a size that can be pushed or pulled short distances in harbour by old-man power without gut-busting effort, and that her gear should be light enough to be handled without causing hernias.

These two opposing factors indicate a boat of up to 15 gross registered tons, and sails that do not exceed 35 square metres each. To get good living

The open pulpit facilitates boarding over the bowsprit.

comfort in this range you are going to have to sacrifice some speed and sportiness. Good fat lockers lead to good fat boats, and contented old skippers.

• *Down below* •

Inside, the accommodation should be arranged so that tired people do not have to step over things, so that a person falling does not fall far, so that edges and corners are rounded and padded, and there are innumerable handholds. It is a sad fact that you sometimes fail to pick up your feet in old age, and you are thus far more likely to trip. Unless there is a deck-house configuration, which has its points, the whole accommodation should be on a level, thus avoiding those irritating little three-inch steps that naval architects find essential, and which even able crews are always falling over. Much better to have two or three standard sized steps, which keep you in practice, than a host of tiny trip-you-ups.

There should be a good seat at the galley, and bunks that are not too difficult to make. Many problems down below become the woman's problems; she may stay fit longer than her old man (she may well be younger into the bargain), but how many yacht designers have been deeply into the ergonomics of an old lady at sea? Going to the loo in a small yacht arguably produces more broken bones than any other nautical accident, strong handholds in the head and a sit-down shower are essential. Even such a simple thing as bed-making can be difficult with awkward enclosed bunks; fitted bottom sheets and a duvet can help here. And, it should not be necessary to demount the table in order to have a restorative nap.

• *Above decks* •

On deck we come to the real difficulties. Admiral Goldsmith was one of the earliest dedicated live-aboards. I had tried to talk him into having electrics in his boat, but he was adamant. 'Ampères are the curse of mankind' he bellowed at me from a distance of about three feet. Admirals tend to do that. He died in his 80s while hauling up his anchor.

I am torn while writing this bit because if I had the chance to choose a way of dying, this would be it, except for the awful problems it would leave my devoted crew. But isn't it better for many reasons to have an electric windlass and a self-stowing anchor? Heart attacks apart, there are times when, caught perhaps by a squall in an anchorage, one is obliged to work cables and anchors under trying conditions. Getting exhausted doesn't help.

Nowadays there are some excellent little windlasses on the market. They use a lot of amps, but not for long; most of them pull in at over 20 feet a minute, so weighing would not normally take more than three minutes. Forty amps for three minutes is two ampere/hours, not very much is it? Especially as one would almost certainly have the engine running at the time.

Sheet winches do come with electric motors, but the prices are prohibitive as you need a fair number of them. It is better to have geared winches with plenty of power. When getting on it is easier to give six gentle turns than three hard ones; it takes longer, but so little extra in cruising terms. Winches should be just above waist height if worked standing up, which is the best position for the effort. If you have to work them sitting down, then even more power is required. Don't risk straining the back.

The steering position should be in a wheelhouse. There is positive evidence that old people can be distressingly unaware of the onset of hypothermia. I know that the evidence applies strictly to very old persons, but I do not suppose that the condition jumps suddenly to danger level overnight: its development is almost certainly spread over quite a period; its onset probably arrives with your bus pass. Do not suppose that hypothermia is unknown in the tropics. Of course on a star-lit night with a gentle force 3 blowing from the quarter there is no problem, but during Hurricane Alberto I was wearing a thick sweater down below. (I didn't go on deck; I was too scared.) And remember you don't always stay in the hot climates. In the Med from November to March it can get quite chilly. We lit our wood-burning stove on 15 May close to the Mediterranean coast.

The wheelhouse should have opening windows for fine weather, and a good chair to rest in. In *Hosanna* we have seats from which both of us can see around at the same time, and why not? It is still essential to have somewhere to sit outside, and even to entertain on a small scale, but do not place too much emphasis on sun-bathing; one gets tanned well enough under the awning without ever going into the direct sun. The process takes a little longer but the tan lasts. Many people who have spent long periods in direct sun now have skin problems.

Sail plans must be arranged for ease of handling rather than sailing efficiency.

All sheets should come to a cockpit; all halyards or roller furling lines too. It should be possible to douse a sail without having to put on an act like a chimpanzee in a circus. In my view this makes roller sails virtually essential, and means either leaving the spinnaker behind or saving it for when junior pays a visit.

Have really big cleats. Hands and fingers get less agile, and fumbling with irritatingly miniature fittings is bad for one's frame of mind.

Give a lot of attention to lifelines. The aged do not pick their feet up as easily as the young, and we have seen so many people of all ages tripping over deck fittings; the average deck-level lifeline is a perfect tripwire. It needs some experimenting but a lifeline at waist height may be the best. One tends to crouch a bit in bad conditions, and it might be easier to duck under than clamber over.

• *Mooring* •

Mooring is a pastime which can tax old bones. Though Old Tom will undoubtedly be more experienced than Young Fred, his reaction time will be slower. Ensure that the boat is responsive under power and steers well at slow speed. Even if the boat is less than 15 tons, a miniature bow-thruster is probably a better buy than a lot of electronic navigating equipment (though I do not discount the value of anything which takes some of the physical burden off a small crew).

A boat with a substantial motor is probably the best type of craft. One will need a good engine. Consider how you could manage if one of you had to cope on their own. I could have sailed *Fare Well* back to the harbour by myself (I did once), but Laurel would not have had the strength. If the event had arisen then she would have had to motor back, and it is essential that the boat has enough engine power to make headway in a rough sea. I have even sailed *Hosanna* on my own, but it was for a challenge. Not for real.

• *Finding the ideal boat* •

This isn't by any means all there is to say about choice of the ideal boat. It will be a recurring theme throughout the book, and also throughout your cruising life.

Do not feel guilty if you use the engine more as you age. There is nothing wrong in this: a prudent mariner uses all or any of his resources to the best advantage. We have written about this subject at greater length in *Sail Into the Sunset*.

So how have we solved our problem of the 'old man's boat'?

First of all Bill designed a steel boat in accordance with all that we have said above. We never built it. We approached the basic problem by considering the cruising grounds we enjoyed the most, and those we had not yet cruised but wished to. Some would require more nautical effort than others; quite clearly some are getting too much to contemplate unless done soon.

Having graded these by degree of ambitiousness we found we had more than a lifetime's cruising ahead of us, and we decided to cut down by removing those areas such as the China Sea, which are unlikely to become congenial to the casual yachtie for some time.

It was about now that Laurel indicated that she wanted to bring more of her library this time, so we threw away our lists and Bill proposed putting in a bid for the *Queen Elizabeth II*.

When the argument settled down again we both went to look over the market in sea-going Dutch barges in their raw, unconverted state. Bill had seen several conversions in the West Indies and in the USA which had sailed there on their own bottoms, and it seemed to him that one of modest size might suit us well. When sea sailing got too difficult we would have all those European canals and rivers to potter about in. In the meantime we would be limited to the fine weather zones in their more reliable periods, but our list was mostly that anyway. We tend towards a quieter life.

When we found a beautiful little barge available for what was virtually the price of her engine, we dealt. It was our intention to cut out 4 metres of length and make a full motor sailer of her. After the two of us had driven her in ballast across the North Sea in February in quite rough conditions we became very impressed with what we had bought. Bill looked again at the pile of books. He decided we could cope with the Little Dutch Barge under power under all but survival sea states, once one or two things were improved. The cost of cutting out 4 metres, if invested, would produce enough income to maintain said 4 metres.

So *Hosanna* has ended up entire and whole and perfect, a token of our love, with three fixed keels and a sail plan divided into three low masts, and all sails rolling. She has three engines, three screws and a bow-thruster. And probably three tonnes of books.

Since writing the above we have circumnavigated Europe, cruised *Hosanna* over the North Sea, the Med, the Ionian, the Aegean, and the Black Sea, as well as various canals and major European rivers, including the Rhine and Danube. Navigationally speaking, her size has caused us little anxiety. Occasionally in bad weather, the two of us have found her a bit exhausting: the worst case was the dis-masting at 0400 in a rough North Sea (where we are proud to say the two of us coped on our own), though the most tiring experiences generally have been in the great rivers. Now 20 years on we have to contemplate another change because she shows signs of becoming too much for us. We do not want to allow *Hosanna*'s 70 tonnes to deteriorate as we have sometimes observed in old people's boats. One has to be sensible. A couple 10 or 15 years younger than us could easily cope. We now need time to think, though we expect you will be able to see the likely direction of our thoughts. Pity about Laurel's books though; there will have to be a compromise.

NAMING YOUR BOAT

When we came to registering our new home (*Hosanna*) we had to face up to the problem of naming her. We would have liked to keep her existing Dutch name, *De Tijd zal 'tLeren IV*, which means 'Time will teach you', but we do not like names which have numbers after them, and we had found it impossible to cope with the Dutch name outside Holland. Almost unpronounceable to the English, it would be completely so to the French, Italians and Greeks; it promised us a lifetime devoted to spelling it out in full and having radio messages garbled out of recognition. *Hosanna* she became. It is a word that is reasonably common to all languages, it is cheerful, and it doesn't tread on anyone's toes. These are things which have to be thought of, or should be, if one is off to foreign cruising grounds. Also it is one of the traditional Lowestoft fishing boat names; names with a ring to them like Kipling's trawler-minesweepers:

'Call up Unity, Clarabell, Assyrian,
Stormcock and Golden Gain'

If you intend to do long-distance cruising it is as well not to give your boat names like *Ploughboy of Loughborough*, or *Pwllhelly Phyllis*. Make up your own little list of impossibles. We once came across an Italian yacht called *Titty*. And off the coast of the USA we overheard a distress call from a boat called *Sexy Lady*. It was very difficult to take it seriously, and who wants ribaldry if in trouble.

In the West Indies, where all the local traders keep watch on VHF, we heard an English 'county' voice calling *'Scuba Shop*, this is *Darling Two'*. Eventually a deep bass Paul Robeson voice answered 'Hallooo Darling!'

Even our beloved old *Fare Well*, which you might have thought was straightforward enough, was written down sometimes as 'Fairly Well', or 'Fairy Well', and on one never to be forgotten document in Turkey as 'Fart Well'. So name your yacht with care.

5 • ABOVE DECKS

'For a man of warre a well ordered taunt-mast is best, but for a long voyage a short mast will bear more canvasse and is less subject to beare by the boord.'

NAUTICAL TERMS

Neither Laurel nor I are sticklers for using too much nautical jargon. We are both inclined to talk of our bedroom, windows or ceilings, to give three examples. But there are items or doings which are peculiar to the sea, which are well described by sea terms, and for which no other words are adequate. Sometimes these terms have been debased by yachtsmen using them wrongly; it is my intention, when discussing equipment, to be precise and to go back to the right ones. Of course *you* know the right words, don't you? So that's all right then. This chapter consists of a few words about bits and pieces on deck. It probably wanders about a bit. So do I. That is what live-aboards do.

MASTS

Shorter masts make a lot of sense when cruising, especially when off to distant parts, but one does need to keep a fair area of sail up aloft where the wind is stronger. I could like Mr Hoyt's cat-rigged Freedom boats but for the necessity of stepping heavy masts through the deck, which has never appealed to me. I favour the tabernacle; perhaps it is my East Anglian breeding. It is so convenient to be able to raise and lower masts using on-board gear. It baffles me why the tabernacle is not more common. It makes life much easier.

If one does have a shorter mast, then standing rigging is much simplified. It is possible to save a lot of money from this simplicity, and some of this will come with the sailmaker's bill. Sails made very simply for a rig that is not state-of-the-art (whatever that really means) generally last twice as long and cost half as much as those from fashionable sailmakers with gimmicks, big advertising accounts and rubber plants in the outer office.

Mast steps are seen on many long-distance cruisers; along with astrodomes (the latter as a result of Moitessier's invigorating experiences in the Southern Ocean, perhaps). They became for a time a status symbol of sorts, but are less seen nowadays. The Perspex in astrodomes tends to scratch and craze. *Fare Well* had mast steps, but I would not waste money on them again. *Hosanna* has none. Age tells.

Although regarded as something of a status symbol by long-distance cruisers, the Perspex of astrodomes tends to scratch and craze.

COOPER'S LAW OF MAST CLIMBING:

Let the prospective height of mast in metres be h.
Let life expectancy at birth be x and one's present age be t. Then one should no longer contemplate climbing masts when $t > (x-h)$.
Isn't science wonderful?

This formula inevitably means that the master will stop climbing masts before his wife, who will have a longer life expectancy as well as (very likely) less present age. Tough! Get her used to the idea. Anyway, male or female, one does not want to go up a mast that often; and at sea, when rolling, one's moment of inertia at that radius is more than most mature adults can cope with and still do a job. If you have to go up, use a re-inforced cloth bag type of boatswain's chair. Nonetheless, a pair of steps conveniently placed about a metre or so below the cap or wherever work is likely to be needed would enable a person to steady himself, frap himself down, and thus leave both hands free to work.

• *Collecting rainwater* •

With a boomed conventional mainsail it is possible to have a hollow aluminium boom made with a simple 'fairing' riveted on either side of the track to collect rainwater that falls down the sail and allow it to pass into the boom. A 1 inch BSP

Catching rainwater with the mainsail.
The fairing strips trap water next to the
sail track where it runs into the boom
through holes (A) and drains away to the
tanks via an outlet (B) near the gooseneck.

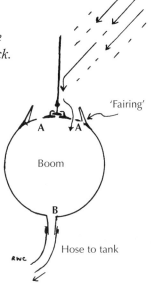

hole tapped underneath, close to the gooseneck, allows a hose to be connected and the water fed straight into a tank. You can collect many gallons during a squall and it's cheaper than osmotic water-makers. Let the first couple of gallons wash the salt off the sail. Also, if you have awnings, and you must have, fasten them so they collect rainwater and can decant it via a length of hose. If you leave rainwater standing in an awning, it will stretch out of shape.

RUNNING RIGGING: CORDAGE OR WIRE?

'. . . spread the shrouds (the wider the better) to succour the masts'.

This is a great expense, and I prefer cordage. Wires are tolerable if turned on to a reel winch, but they have disadvantages. First, they have a tendency to spring into kinks which if inadvertently pulled taut, in the dark, say, will seriously weaken the wire and also stop it passing easily through blocks or eyes. Second, when minor damage occurs, some of the small wires break and the ends project. The discovery of one of these can be painful and even disabling. Third, it is apparently impossible to find sheaves properly designed for wire rope. I once took part in some elaborate Admiralty tests to discover the best size and section of sheave for modern wire. It turned out to be a question not of finding the best, but of finding the least worse (passing over a sheave seriously weakens the wire), but the trials did show a requirement for very large diameter sheaves (12 times the diameter of the rope was decided upon), and a deep narrow groove of roughly semi-circular section.

Cordage, on the other hand, chafes. It also stretches, but in lengths up to 20 metres or so I have never found this much of a problem with pre-stretched poly-ester. It cannot be conveniently wound on self-stowing reel winches, and thus it can leave one with lengthy snakes about the deck. These can have their ends washed overboard where they will surely find the propeller; even if it is only trailing, it is doing enough revs to wind wool. (Someone defined a screw propeller as the perfect self-tailing winch.)

• *Winches* •

This leads on to winches. I believe in the self-tailing type, and have found those little blue rubber gadgets that can be added to existing winches to be less than perfect. This is a department where the money should be found for the proper job. It is not necessary to go for the metallurgically perfect, every part turned by a master-craftsman, models that cost more than the boat. For cruising, a sturdy well-made job with simple bearings that can be kept clear of salt and well-lubricated without having to dismantle them into a kit of parts every few days, is what is needed. But do fit big enough ones: you'll be glad of them when you get older. Under-sized winches cause accidents in squalls or emergencies. We fitted Gibb winches, but they are not made any more. Probably too simple.

STEERING, SAFETY AND COMFORT

The chore of steering a boat for long periods is usually eased by self-steering vane gear or autopilots, which I will discuss later. One finds that they are in use for 99% of the time, but the occasion will arise when hand steering becomes unavoidable and a comfortable position is essential.

• *Awnings v wheelhouses* •

'An awning . . . spread over their heads . . . especially in hot countreys to keep men from the extremity of heat or wet, which is very oft infectious.'

I am all for a wheelhouse. The convertible car syndrome becomes less relevant as you mature. For my part, I no longer fancy a wet shirt and a flowing sea. A first-class permanent awning is necessary over the conning position if there is no wheelhouse.

The Americans have long had the Bimini awning, which is excellent, and can be fitted to allow for it being spread under the boom and therefore valuable while sailing. European sailmakers are getting good at making these; for smaller boats they are the best.

Without an awning, the sun will boil your brains or else the rain will drown you. As the rain can also come at you horizontally, we are back to wheelhouses again. Of course the windows should open, the glass should be triplex or safety glass of some strength, and one of them have a substantial water-shedding device.

Awnings can be a simple canvas stretched over the boom as below or a more sophisticated, purpose-built awning with its own tubular frame such as the one illustrated above

The Kent Clearview Screen is good, though in the smaller sizes the clear area is not big enough. There are also some very powerful windscreen wipers on the market which work well, though they have a tendency to scratch the glass. Even if the side windows are polycarbonate or Perspex, the window through which you look ahead MUST be real glass. Salt crystals soon scratch plastic windows. In which case you must polish out the scratches. There is a special polish you can buy at great expense, but to save money try using toothpaste. It takes longer, but is a fraction of the price.

• *Guardrails and harnesses* •

If a wheelhouse is impossible, make sure the cockpit is well fenced in. If the cockpit is large, it must have big drains. Some nowadays are open at the stern. Not a bad idea in principle because it eases access in harbour, but have a washboard with a large hinged scupper-drain for fitting in bad weather at sea. Guardrails become even more important when short-handed or family cruising. In the early days of offshore racing we did not have them all round, and I went overboard one night, so I have intimate knowledge of this; not many of us survive to be able to discuss it. Don't let it happen to you.

From 10m LOA upwards, the minimum height of the top rail should be 75cm and the maximum vertical gap 30cm. Anything else is a perfect trip-wire. They need to be strong enough to arrest the progress of 100kg of body falling across the beam of the boat, assisted by flowing water – that exerts a very large force indeed. This is not an area to take chances about: consider the extreme case, and remember that disasters are rarely caused by something being too strong, only by being not strong enough.

Another aspect of guardrails is their vulnerability when mooring. Novices have an irresistible urge to push boats about by heaving on their stanchions, and given the apparent numbers of novices, it is desirable that the rails withstand this deplorable but widespread practice. Modern motor yachts are designed with high freeboard and considerable flare at the deck edge: for the comparatively low-freeboard sailing yacht, these features make mutual fendering very difficult. The ability to fender against one's guardrails is an asset. *Fare Well*'s guardrails are 80cm high, that is 55cm above the gunwale. The stanchions are 40mm x 40mm

Guardrails are an important safety feature on any cruising yacht and secure netting is even more important when children are on board. Note the sturdy mechanical anchor winch – another consideration when fitting out a boat for short-handed sailing.

x 4mm RHS steel welded on at 120mm intervals, the intermediate rail is welded and the top rail is 75 x 25mm teak. They are sufficiently strong to allow the unbraced top of a stanchion to take the sheet lead block of the 67 square metre genoa, and I feel happy about them. Up forward there is a different arrangement with netting, as the foredeck has less impedimenta to interrupt a fall, and netting is nicer to fall into than steel bars. Laurel has dodgy hips and needs protection from falls. Don't we all.

Harness is very important on deck in rough weather. My opinion is that, given good strong guardrails as a back-up, one can move about better without clipping on to lifelines, but instead use two clips and move from one ringbolt to another. However in small yachts with light guardrails, narrow side decks, and the necessity to do a lot of work on the coachroof, some forms of stout wire lifeline are required. One should extend from cockpit to mast on each side, and another from mast to headsail tack. Wire of 8mm diameter is about right, but must be made fast to strong fittings. I fear that a falling body could pull the mooring cleats out of some of the production boats I have seen, let alone the lifeline seating.

There is something to be said for a fair-sized yacht having a folding davit by her midship gangway rail-break. It would not only be of great help recovering heavy weights from the sea, but would be good in harbour for doing the same from the dinghy.

MAN OVERBOARD

One of the useful things to have on deck during a man overboard emergency is a moderate length (50m, say) of light floating rope, about 8mm diameter. This will not get in the screw, and given two circumstances: that manoeuvring is difficult and the victim is conscious, it is possible to come close enough and turn so that the rope is brought across the victim. If the yacht can be stopped, it is possible to haul him alongside (gently, he may be weakened, in which case keep the line hand taut while manoeuvring the yacht closer). The rope should have a metre-long loop at the end, but the person should not normally be towed by the yacht. If you have too much way on, it is better to let the rope go from on board, and to pick it up again. There are some commercial 'kits' which perform the above function; they are not expensive and have the right sort of fittings.

I believe in use of engine in recovery. My experience is that even when running under spinnaker, the engine at full astern will not destroy steerage way and will save valuable yards while the sail is being furled: a point of importance for short-handed crews. But beware of trailing cordage when furling. In my actual experience, it is difficult when short-handed or solo, to recover a man overboard while you still have sails set.

WINDVANES AND AUTOPILOTS

When we commissioned *Fare Well* there was no windvane steering gear strong enough, so we had a Sharp Mate autopilot which was the simplest I could find. In consequence I know little about pure windvanes, except that the Mediterranean's variable winds cause problems for them. The Sharp was a good companion; it let us down only once (on the first day out on an Atlantic crossing!) when a diode failed. One little peculiarity of this autopilot (and others) is that it occasionally went barmy and took us round in a 360° circle before resuming the previous course on its own. We had trouble running before a big quartering sea, and I believe some vanes are not so good on this point; it certainly is a difficult point of sailing. Nowadays, things have changed somewhat. Electronics are no longer get-attable for amateur repair with a soldering iron. I used to say that the only gear suitable for a boat was the sort that you could repair with a hammer and screwdriver.

So, in *Hosanna*, because Sharp had gone out of business and electronic hammers are hard to come by, we fitted a Cetrek, which is a much more complicated, all-singing-all-dancing affair with an 'intelligence' which measures weather helm and trim and automatically allows for them. After a measuring time, of course. For a sailing boat this is a big snag for it cannot be made to anticipate a gybe, so that you have to steer by hand for a time, just when you should be tweaking sheets and things. Try to find an autopilot that permits you to pre-adjust it with knobs so that, as you set the alteration of course on it, you can also change the side of the trim. Proper knobs, not dainty little fairy buttons that gloved fingers cannot feel, and preferably with dials in Light-Emitting-Diodes, which can actually be seen in tropical sunlight. Normally, LCDs cannot.

Knobs! They get smaller and smaller! Buttons were all right when you could feel them with cold wet fingers, but now the beastly little things are hidden behind a sheet of smooth plastic looking like a Picasso painting, and often the best one can manage with a large fat masculine finger is to press about four at once. If only manufacturers were aware of BFS, the Big Finger Syndrome.

LIFERAFTS AND TENDERS

I suppose most people contemplating long cruises have read with interest, if not alarm, the accounts of yachts lost and the experiences of survivors. One feature that is worth stressing is that an inflatable liferaft is not designed for long-term survival, while there are several cases where persons have been recovered from rigid dinghies after astoundingly long periods adrift. I have moved back to the view that the best liferaft for an ocean or well-offshore cruising yacht in the tropics or temperate zones is a good rigid dinghy, even in the severest storm where survival needs an element of luck anyway. This might not hold good in Arctic conditions or the North Atlantic in winter, but I'm not writing about that sort of sailing. We do not sail as a punishment for past sins.

The dinghy must have first-class inherent buoyancy, and a stout cover or at least a partial one, and rope-loop handholds below the gunwales. The Panic Bag should be kept in it at sea, and it is the best place for the vegetable locker in any case. It requires no annual service, which is very expensive plus VAT (for God's

We prefer to use a rigid dinghy which we feel is both safer, easier to row and can also be fun to sail up secluded creeks and waterways. This little lugsail dinghy is ideal for teaching your children or grandchildren to sail.

sake), and is often inconvenient to arrange and check. It is also virtually impossible to verify that the work charged for has actually been done, and in too many cases it has not, or not properly at any rate. A rigid dinghy has many other uses.

The British Maritime and Coastguard Agency has made liferafts obligatory. This, as I have said, is probably justifiable for cold-water sailing, and it may be justifiable (barely) for coastal sailing where the availability of early helicopter rescue is a likelihood, but the regulation is downright stupid for ocean cruising. The trouble is that bureaucrats need to demonstrate that they are *doing something* and particularly doing something about *safety*. As most of them have little practical knowledge of the subject they are supposedly supervising we get ludicrous legislation. Yes, I know the senior MCA people have nautical qualifications, but they have long since stopped using them in practice and the nautical world has changed and will go on changing faster and faster. Extra Master Mariners working ashore, navigating mahogany desks across rough parquet seas should be obliged to re-train in small boats at intervals; they are desperately out of touch with long-distance yacht cruising. And so is the RYA, which seems to my dismay to be complicit in all these silly rules.

Which, somehow, leads us to tenders. Once we had a rigid dinghy *and* an Avon, but we found that we used the rigid one for choice; and when we met a fellow traveller whose Avon had perished in the sun, we contemplated the inevitable deterioration of this asset and sold him ours. We have not missed it.

Our dinghy is a small Norfolk lugsail dinghy, good for pottering up creeks and by-waters, but it is not a heavy load carrier. In *Fare Well* we hoisted it on side davits which I made myself. We had stern davits too, but a stern-hung dinghy is a nuisance in the Med, though a stern-hung inflatable makes a good emergency fender when lying stern-to a quay. The advantage of the side davits is that the dinghy can be turned in and stowed on deck in rough weather or when manoeuvring, where it is much safer and makes an extra locker. We still have the Norfolk dinghy (a super one built for us by Leslie Landamore of Wroxham).

Now, in 2005, inflatable dinghies have improved a little.

We got rid of our 2hp Evinrude outboard. We used it very seldom, it was noisy,

You may prefer to use an inflatable dinghy with an outboard as your tender. *This one is secured on davits at the stern.*

always giving trouble, and in our view had more potential as an anchor than as a propulsion unit. Our dinghy sails and rows very well, and for when we were tired we had a very cheap Sears Roebuck electric outboard that ghosted us about at slow speed, needing no maintenance and not waking the neighbours. In the end we disposed of that too, because we find it fun to sail, and the exercise of rowing ashore is good for us: helping to remove the results of too much Greek food and wine at the tavernas.

On the other hand, our American friends have a large Zodiac with a powerful outboard, and they tend to zip into some harbours for a little shopping without berthing the yacht. Unless the harbour is very encumbered I feel berthing is rather less trouble than fiddling about with dinghies and outboards. Once we returned to Gouvia very late at night, formally dressed: Laurel in long skirt and so on. The chap who was taking his dog for a walk and took our lines for us as we berthed asked where we had been in formal dress. 'To the theatre', we said. 'What?' he said, 'In a 50-foot yacht?'

Another form of tender is a wheeled vehicle. Many dedicated cruisers are advertised by a bicycle on deck; larger boats sometimes have a mini-motorbike, which, if under 50cc, does not require licensing in most desirable countries. In some it requires insurance (France is one) but no driving licences. Now we contemplate one of those Methusalalagonda buggies in which OAPs terrorise the shopping

Once on shore, a folding mini-motorbike is a handy vehicle for exploring and light shopping.

precincts. The obligation of a crash helmet for mini-bikes is spreading; France and Tunisia insist and there may be others. Crash helmets are obligatory in Greece but you hardly ever see one. That's Greece! Motorbikes should have a painted sign 'Tender to . . .' instead of a number plate. This seems to work everywhere except the UK.

Hosanna, being a barge, is able to carry a small car: a Mini or a Fiat 600 on deck (there we go, one up on the Jones's that is!). In the canals it is worth it on occasions, but on the whole it was more trouble than asset, and the practice has been discontinued. The Mini rusted before our eyes in the salt spray and turned into a little heap of brown powder. For anyone living aboard a barge that is committed to the canals, it should be considered, but it must have its own loading crane. Second-hand hydraulic cranes can sometimes be obtained from truck-breakers.

ANCHORS

The long-term cruiser will have to take more thought to his anchors than the marina-based animal who probably never anchors at all. During 1982 we spent 134 nights riding to single anchor, and a further nine moored with two. In 1995/6 we spent 410 consecutive nights riding to anchors in one way or another. We dragged once or twice. *Fare Well* was fitted with two 75lb (34kg) CQR bower anchors which self-stow over rollers close either side of the stem. To port we had 45 fathoms (100m) of ⁹⁄₁₆in (14mm) chain, and to starboard 40 fathoms (110m) of ½in (12mm), both handled by a Simpson-Lawrence 521 electric windlass. This layout owes a lot to big-ship experience, and it meant that Laurel, the vertically and orthopaedically challenged cable officer, could manage anchors and cables in all normal circumstances without any help. Foul anchors are another thing altogether.

The size of bower anchors is very important. Most published tables of recommended anchor sizes seem to have in mind the marina denizen or the ocean racer, and not the real sea-going yacht. For example, I followed the advice of Simpson-Lawrence who were not noticeably incautious as a rule (sadly, they are no more), but wish I had fitted larger anchors. Their table:

Waterline length	Displacement in tons	CQR anchor weight
40ft (12m)	25	60lb (27kg)
45ft (13m)	30	75lb (34kg)

In my view, to enjoy peace of mind, you should have bower anchors larger than this. My table, in metric this time, just to confuse you (which is what the European Commission is always doing to me):

Waterline length	Displacement in tonnes	CQR or Bruce anchor	Chain cable links
10m	17	25kg	10mm
12m	25	30kg	11mm
13m	30	40kg	12mm
15m	35	50kg	15mm

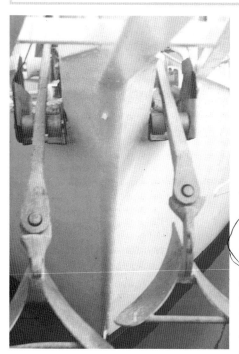

We fitted two self-stowing bower CQR anchors on either side of the stem of Fare Well.

When moored bow or stern to a quay (Med mooring), use as much scope of anchor cable as possible. Anchor cable does you no good at all when in the locker. Use the lot if you can, the more the better. Use an angel with nylon anchor cable (see page 95).

Remember that, with an anchor out, the wind on the beam has a sort of sweating-up effect on the anchor cable, which in a strong wind can multiply the tension in it several times. Add to this the fact that a wind on the beam acts on a larger area of boat than a wind from ahead, and it is not surprising that anchors of apparently adequate size come home. If you expect to spend much time in the Mediterranean consider an increase in size of both anchor and cable. The alternative, which we follow, is to have two bower anchors and use both if a strong wind is expected. The practice of waiting until

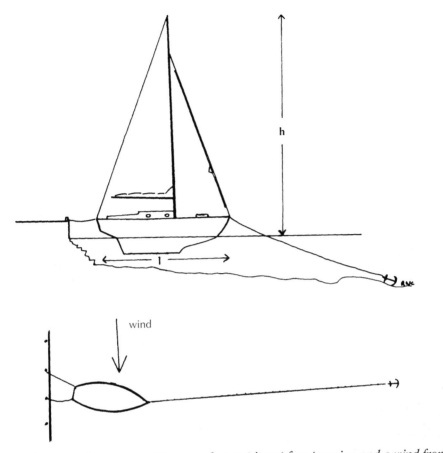

A yacht moored to a quay with an anchor out is not free to swing and a wind from the side has more windage to act upon and causes far more strain on the cable and upwind mooring lines.

the wind gets up and then laying out a second anchor by dinghy, upwind, may provide much-needed exercise and be very satisfying (it's not always easy), but it inconveniences those across whose cables the second anchor is laid, who may justifiably moan a bit. Indeed we have seen this gambit not only fail to secure the yacht in question, but trip the anchors of several others, leading to drag acts quite as dramatic as anything on stage. We discuss the problems of lying to single anchor in the chapter on Navigation. It may seem odd to divide this up, but we have our reasons. At least, I think I do.

If I had thought further ahead I would have fitted *Fare Well* with a self-stowing stream (stern) anchor with its own capstan or windlass. It would have been useful on several occasions, especially in restricted tideways such as the Intracoastal Waterway. *Fare Well* had no kedge, and I saw no need for one as there is little point using a lighter, less secure anchor when the heavier, safer bowers could be managed more easily. She had a spare 75lb Danforth which we never

You need to regularly check the condition of your ground tackle. Here Bill is adjusting the shackle on the main anchor.

used. If the need arises to send away an anchor in a boat (after a grounding, say) I have always used a bower with enough chain cable; one does not need a lot if it is shallow enough to run aground.

For *Hosanna* we have adopted a different approach to berthing end-on. We use a stern anchor that is twice the weight of the bower. We go ahead into the berth with a stem fender over the bows, and nudge the quay with our stem. No matter what the wind, we can leave the boat pressing end-on against the quay, leaning on Greece you might say, with the centreline engine going slow ahead and the rudder adjusted to allow for any cross wind. In this condition we have all the time in the world to put out head ropes, set taut the stern anchor cable and get out gangways. Of course this is only possible in straight-stemmed steel boats, but it enables us to berth a very big boat with just two people. However nothing comes free, and leaving the quay and weighing the big stern anchor while the bows quest in all directions can be a bit nerve-wracking in strong winds. You cannot just back out fast and weigh anchor at leisure, because you are liable to get the anchor cable tangled in screw or rudder.

Choice of anchor type is a personal matter. They are mostly difficult to stow, other than as described above. But the criterion of choice should not be a tabulated holding strength in one or two particular conditions, but a good all-round security in most conditions where sea sense indicates anchoring is worth considering. No anchor holds on smooth marble as we discovered at Xania in Crete.

Taken overall I have found the CQR satisfactory, but respect that some friends prefer Danforth, Bruce or Fortress, though I would approve the latter very cautiously. It's their choice. All these anchors were very carefully designed. Avoid imitations. The CQR and Bruce anchors will stow over rollers. I have an idea that the Bruce is not so good in the smaller sizes as it is in the larger; perhaps this is another case where one should read the next line in the table. It is worth noting that the Bruce was designed for positioning oil rigs in deep water. Here, security is paramount, but absolute holding power is achieved with the help of very, very long cables which have a pull in a constant direction: ie the oil rig is not sheering about. It is this latter which is the Bruce's weak point. The Danforth will hang conveniently over the guardrails in a smallish yacht. Admiralty Pattern and Fisherman's anchors are really not worth it, except as rock picks or in thick weed, while ship anchors, such as the Hall's pattern, only come into their own over 100kg.

CABLE

I favour chain cable, though with frequent use the galvanising does wear off and begins to look dreadful. When this happens (as re-galvanising is not only very expensive outside the UK, and often very badly done too, turn the cable end for end, wire-brush it and keep it soaked in boiled linseed oil) which is the only suitable oil without a nasty smell (it smells of old cricket bats). You can get stainless chain – at a price. Nylon cable has advantages, and for the lightweight yacht, which is normally in a marina and does not often anchor, it is a good choice. There is on the market a coil of flat-braid polyester which I do not like. Though the principle of rolling up a flat braid is excellent and practical, the material should be of nylon, which is highly elastic and not of polyester, which is meant to be non-elastic. The importance of elasticity in an anchor cable cannot be overestimated. I once had a fascinating job navigating *HMS Cumberland* which had dozens of scientists on board and spent her time carefully testing all sorts of

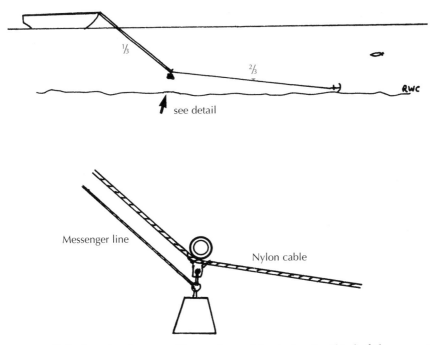

An 'angel' designed to hang on the anchor cable at about a third of the scope out from the bows, with its own light messenger line to lower and retrieve it. The weight should ideally be half that of the anchor.

equipment. (The Admiralty doesn't test any more. Tells you something, doesn't it?) We tested all sorts of anchors to find the best for a new class of minesweeper. I found that anchors were easily caused to drag by a series of jerks; they would not move for a much greater steady tension in the cable. It is the weight of the chain cable in catenary that acts as a spring, and if you do want to use the polyester braid I would recommend lowering a weight (the angel, mentioned above), which should be about half the weight of the anchor, down the cable to about one-third of the scope from the bows.

Interruption over. Back to cables. One sees reference to nylon being subject to chafe or cut over coral, but I have no personal knowledge of this happening, probably because my friends are sensible enough not to lay out a nylon cable over sharp coral heads, which in any event are not good holding ground. More important is the fact that nylon will abrade over sand and in fairleads, especially when strong winds have the ship sheering about. Nylon is more awkward to stow coming in than chain, especially as you need double the scope, and another consideration, especially in the Med, is the question of security in crowded harbours when other boats are manoeuvring. Nylon cables lead at longer stay than chain, and thus enter the water much further away from the bows, and are easily cut by another vessel manoeuvring with difficulty.

It is the ease of handling self-stowing bower anchors with a good windlass that makes berthing stern-to a quay the best proposition for craft needing an anchor

When mooring in the Med, you need plenty of scope; the rope cable from the yacht in the foreground is a hazard for passing vessels.

of about 20kilos or more, even though skippers will find it simpler to manoeuvre ahead, rather than astern. If one had a self-stowing stream anchor the case might be altered, but a bowsprit does make boarding difficult and larger boats with normal sheer find the stemhead a little high.

There will be more on anchoring in the chapter on Navigation, because it is such an important feature of live-aboard cruising. We also discuss the dangers attached to berthing bows-on to a quay. See chapter on Misadventures.

BOW-THRUSTERS

A recent development has been the introduction of moderately priced bow-thrusters. Quite strong ones can be purchased for less than £2000. For short-handed single-screw yachts above, say, 12m such a device might be a good investment if you are planning to moor in popular harbours. Hydraulic ones are best, but electric is not bad in small yachts, preferably 24 volts.

BITTS AND CLEATS

For serious cruising it is essential to have very strong bitts or cleats, because you are occasionally obliged to berth in harbours where the shelter is not perfect, and a swell or scend will have boats constantly dancing in their berths. Most deck fittings seen on production boats are criminally inadequate. The main centreline bitts forward should be strong enough to take the weight of the boat, and one needs two shoulder cleats or bitts fit to spring on. Two midship cleats ditto and two substantial bitts aft, strong enough for towing. Spring bitts or cleats should be on the gunwale, thus avoiding the need for fairleads which are seldom as good as their name. For fairleads read 'chocks' in the western hemisphere. The reason for this apparent over-strength is that the cleats will inevitably have to cope with sudden shock-loads which can have much more destructive effect than a steady

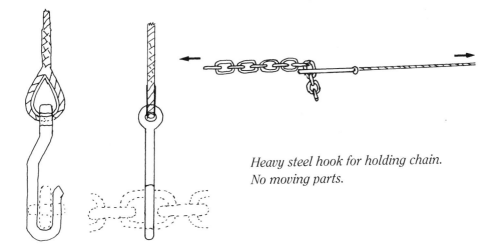

Heavy steel hook for holding chain.
No moving parts.

A typical Dan Leno shackle, very useful for joining small chain to large rings, etc but hard to find. Chandlers that supply fishing and commercial craft may be a source.

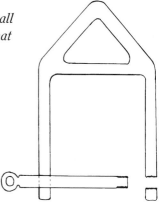

pull. We have often witnessed cleats that have been pulled out of the decks of glass-fibre yachts. On expensive yachts, too.

In many primitive harbours, the chafing of ropes on quay copings is a nuisance. A common Med practice is to have a loop of chain at the end of the rope, sometimes with a carbine hook. Unfortunately the size of chain equivalent to the strength of the nylon would be impossible to heave. In any event, stand clear of people throwing chain about. A nylon rope of 16mm diameter has a breakload of 4000kg, which is much more than that of a 13mm chain and more than twice that of the biggest carbine hook. One suggested solution to this problem is to use a soft wire eye at the end of the nylon, or if you wish to use chain, first use a picking-up rope of lighter nylon and afterwards substitute the main berthing chain and/or rope which can be quite short.

Chain is more secure against the obnoxious hooligan practice of cutting boats adrift during the night. This has happened to us thrice, once in Germany, once in Savannah, and once in France. We usually have one chain or wire mooring if in a port with a military presence or where there are signs of civil disorder.

FENDERS

These are expensive; and do not stand up to hard wear alongside rough concrete or chipped stone quays. Most people use air-filled plastic fenders, and for light-

A well-fendered Greek fishing boat recorded by Laurel's skilful pen. Tyres used as fenders on yachts are often frowned upon but they can be given a coat of white rubber paint to protect the gelcoat of your neighbours' boats.

ness and convenience a few of these are more or less essential. But they are not ideal. Hot sun decomposes the plastic material of which they are made and they turn into sticky, grit-covered, abrasive puddings.

A couple of small motor tyres are advisable for bad conditions against rough quaysides, though it is not nice to use them against someone else's topsides. We do have several, but most are painted white with rubber paint. We have found that plastic fenders are cheapest in Greece. Don't ask why.

Remember that all boats are a compromise, and that you will never find the perfect boat. All you can do is to find one that is good enough to love, then you can ignore her faults.

6 • Below Decks

'On each side of the Stearage roome are divers Cabins . . . with many convenient seates or lockers to put any thing in, as in little Cupberts.'

KEEPING WATER OUT

Though there is a natural emphasis on comfort in a long-term cruising boat, it is essential not to lose sight of the requirement that the comfort should extend to comfort at sea, otherwise we will end up with something like a Chelsea houseboat. So important is the ability to maintain efficiency and safety at sea, that the question of comfort, whether in harbour or offshore, has to be fitted round the requirement to survive such rare testing moments that the yacht might encounter. Important factors in keeping going at sea are minimising both physical and mental strain; and minimising the possibility of water entering the accommodation, which in effect will comprise most of the hull.

In our view, watertightness is a vital part of living in a boat. Inevitably one has more possessions on board than the holidaymaker, some of which are perhaps precious even if only for sentimental reasons. Seawater is the great destroyer, and it has allies. Dampness breeds mildew, mould and rot. And bad temper. Avoid it. It may not always be possible to stop every whit of water entering the bottom, but do get a watertight deck and windows. (It surprises us that in this day and age this still needs saying.) The aim is to be able to clean the bilges with a vacuum cleaner, and it is perfectly achievable.

But water WILL get in. Spray flies, waves do wash over the deck; a moment's inattention when tired and there goes the seawater, slopping down the hatch or skylight. Only a paragon can maintain eternal vigilance. We once had a terrible night beating down the Ionian Sea toward Kephalonia into a rising force 6 to 7; the spray flying the length of the ship as her head ploughed into each short sea, making us duck rhythmically behind the sprayshield to avoid the worst of it. Then, worried because she seemed to be diving a little more deeply than usual, Bill misjudged a duck and, through the spray was able to see the forehatch lift, only an inch or so but enough to swallow a gallon or two from the water swilling about the deck. We bore away instantly, foregoing the pleasure of mutual recriminations, and investigated the forepeak which is fortunately separated from the accommodation by a watertight bulkhead. Bill later calculated that there must have been four tons of water in it, and all because we each thought the other had screwed down the bad-weather fastenings. And that was not all: it was a night when Professor Murphy drove home several points. (This is a phenomenon known as the cascade effect: any mishap gleefully passes on the baton to another, or even two and so on ad infinitum. If you can't get on top of the situation before mishap breeding gets out of control, you have a disaster.)

Detritus and mud from the anchor cables had blocked the pump intake, but then, they say there has never been a pump as fast as a frightened man with a bucket. And you cannot trace the problem if it is several feet under water.

You could not enjoy living in a yacht with the watertight integrity of a submarine, though there are rare times when it would be useful. There is a mean, and how far one goes in either direction depends on the chosen voyages, the chosen times, the chosen crew.

One way water can get below, even in harbour, is on the crew's clothing. A surprising dampness can build up this way over a period of prolonged rain or spray. I make fun of Laurel's bath, but at sea it is an invaluable temporary drop for wet oilskins. Another source of damp is condensation, something that yacht designers have yet to appreciate fully, or perhaps yet to master. Aboard a production yacht in which a young couple were wintering in Corfu they were unable to use two of the bunks because of condensation dripping from the aluminium window frames. Now this is bad design and outrageously common. It is something to look out for when buying a boat. Older ships used to have 'save-alls' under scuttles and portholes to gather the overnight condensation or the odd leaky drops. With plastics why are not save-alls moulded under all window holes? A palliative is to cover the aluminium with the adhesive foam strip sold for stopping draughts round door frames in houses or a few layers of masking tape, but it doesn't look all that nice. If you are building from scratch, ensure that no bunk has a hatch over it, then it can't leak over your bedding.

INSULATION

Wooden boats are composed of material with its own insulating properties though often not enough, but all other constructions need massive insulation, and as steel or aluminium are the worst from this aspect, let us consider these.

The best steel hull insulation is to cover the interior above the waterline with four or five centimetres of sprayed-on, closed-cell polyurethane foam, which is also an excellent protective coating for steel.

Some years ago, this used to be flammable and gave off toxic smoke if it ignited. While insulating *Hosanna*, we discovered that this foam is now available in a highly fire-resistant form. We used this and found it good, so much so that it was possible to make small welds on the opposite side of the steel plate without igniting the foam. We even cut a hole with oxy-propane, and the foam melted and blackened, but did not burst into flame. Of course, we drenched the area with water immediately. In these circumstances, and with care, this foam is ideal for boats that are going to be lived in. We plead with chemical companies to produce a foam which contains insect repellent. Perhaps they do though we haven't found one.

Other insulation methods are to line with glass-fibre wool (Rockwool), which does nothing to protect the steel. I have seen an old steel ship with hardpacked natural straw and another (Dutch built) with scrumpled-up newspapers packed behind the linings (and she was A1+ at Lloyd's, which gives one pause for thought). In my opinion, the sprayed foam is far and away best.

How to protect the steel behind the insulation? The foam will adhere well to an epoxy-based holding primer which should be sprayed on immediately after sand-blasting. New steel which is inconvenient to sandblast is best treated with a 20% solution of ortho-phosphoric acid to remove mill-scale, the surplus acid neu-tralised with industrial alcohol (>75% is best), and then painted with a good quality primer, but the foam will then adhere only to the paint skin. Foam is really effective only on sandblasted steel. *Hosanna* is an old ship and the after accom-modation (the *roef* in Dutch) was in excellent condition after 55 years untouched (we could tell by the dates of the newspapers). She had been coated there, behind the panelling, with a mixture of old engine oil and paraffin wax. We tried to sand-blast, but the mixture had penetrated into the steel itself, and as there was no sign of rust, we slapped on another coat of the same greasy mush. The Dutch know a few things about steel boats, and they do not like spending money.

Ventilation alone will not cure condensation when dewpoint conditions are really ripe. In fact, ventilation can import dampness when the air outside becomes saturated, so some means of closing off ventilators is desirable.

Designers might well reply to my criticisms of them, that they do not attempt to design boats for living aboard in winter. This is probably true, but why not? A yacht should be capable of use whenever its owner wants, unless its unsuitability for a particular use is openly stated.

SEAGOING CITADEL VERSUS OPEN-PLAN

Our own solution of the comfort/seaworthiness dilemma was eased by *Fare Well*'s size, but I believe the principle is adaptable further down the scale. It is to recog-nise those bits of boat that are vital to the navigation, those that are desirable for harbour comfort in winter or summer, and then those that are common to both, such as galley and heads. Then design a layout with a seagoing 'citadel' separated from the rest of the boat, not completely, but so that in bad weather especially there is no need to go beyond it. In our citadel, mostly in the deckhouse which is at half-deck level, we had the galley, chart table, radio, refrigerator, switchboards, a sea bunk, a small table, tool chests, big oilskin locker (21 × 24in × full height), and close by but down a ladder: the bathroom. (This actually contains a bath, essential in our case for therapeutic purposes and, as we said above, it also makes a first-class place to dump soaking-wet clothes.) The deckhouse is also the access to the engine-room, which is beneath it.

In the ends of the yacht (excepting the forepeak and the lazarette) are the saloon

As you can see from this comfortable stylish saloon on Hosanna, *life afloat doesn't have to echo the conditions of a cramped caravan.*

forward, a small guest cabin and our own double bedroom aft. This latter is not a cabin; we use the word 'bedroom' deliberately to emphasise the comfort and peace of the place, which is the biggest single space in the ship. I do not say that our conception of the best (there is no perfect) layout is the only one, or even the right one for another couple. It has worked well for us, for a long time, for deep- and short-sea cruising and winter living. The only substantial improvement we would have made would be to have had a wheelhouse instead of the then shelter, which we subsequently did when we converted *Hosanna*.

Others we know have an open-plan layout, one enormous airy space. It's nice for a party, and it suits the smaller yacht. It does suffer from 'one place wet-all places wet', and there is a lack of privacy when one has guests. Some have a small, separate after cabin as guest accommodation. These are very good for children, but having once been a guest in a Seadog ketch where I needed a shoehorn to get myself into bed, I suspect their long-term use for the grown man is a question of hope rather than reality.

A more conventional use for the half-deck deckhouse is to make it the saloon. This certainly looks better on demonstration models at the Boat Show. It does feel nice to have a light and airy saloon, but in Laurel's view it is also nice to have a light and airy galley. Certainly the catering tends to improve if the cook is not condemned to working in an ill-lit, ill-ventilated dungeon, conducive to seasickness. In the climate we aspire to, most of the living is on deck, which is the ultimate in light and airy. In a Mediterranean winter our saloon does have its disadvantages because our side ports are often blocked by neighbouring craft, but we use it mostly in the evenings and it gets dark early.

We are not really able to talk about *Hosanna* in these terms. Even a small barge like ours is almost big enough to hold a village dance. We have in fact as much space as a small flat and are in danger of becoming spoilt. But we are getting on now, and will have to move to a smaller boat soon, so the subject is very much in our minds.

FUEL

This subject has to be approached in conjunction with the heating. There are many good arguments for having only one fuel aboard: one that is easily and universally available, and easy to load. The commonest fuel, and one that most of us are obliged to have in any event, for propulsion, is diesel oil, so let us consider that as a sole fuel.

• *Diesel* •

It not only drives the main engine but it can also drive an auxiliary generator if you want one. It will drive an outboard; unfortunately these are heavy though powerful, and not very convenient. In the low power range one can have a battery-run electric outboard, thus using diesel oil at one remove.

There are very good diesel heaters on the market. At the simple end I like the Danish made Refleks heater which requires no fan and is therefore silent, but of course it heats only the compartment in which it is mounted. English-manufactured Taylor's are similar, and actually look a little neater, as do the Kabola. There are American and Dutch heaters too, all having gravity feed and dependent on a sort of carburettor made in the USA. Some of these heaters have a back-boiler which can be used for hot water and/or a syphonic radiator. There is a good but very expensive tiny water-circulating pump available for central heating.

I am not so happy with blown-air oil heaters, having seen a serious fire in Antibes which happened when the crew were ashore for a very short time. It is possible in a bigger boat to have proper central heating with a normal oil-fired boiler. There are very good boilers working on the same gravity feed system we mentioned above. The basic boiler is quite small, but it can be installed in multiples. Very clever.

Cooking can also be done by diesel. There is a Canadian stove, the Dickenson, it not only cooks but provides hot water and central heating too. Bulky and heavy, and expensive too.

• *Gas* •

There is no other single-fuel alternative to diesel. Bottled gas for cooking will, however, save considerable initial cost and a certain amount of weight, some of which will be lost because of the price, size and weight of the necessary number of cylinders required for reasonable independence from the shore. It will bring problems apart from its propensity to explode, which can be controlled: practically every major country has its own size and design of gas bottles, very often with differently threaded connections. To change bottles at a retail supplier it is necessary to hand in a local bottle. Odd-sized gas bottles can sometimes be refilled at depots, but then there is the problem of transport, for the depots are seldom conveniently placed for yachts. I remember helping another boat take their bottles to a depot in Greece, and beating a hasty retreat as I observed the workman pouring liquid gas into an open cylinder through a funnel while he was smoking a cigarette. Possibly the mixture was too rich to explode, and the fumes did not rise. I wonder if he is still alive.

If only Brussels would devise the European standard gas bottle . . . but that would be doing something useful.

One problem with gas in the present nanny-state environment is that installations must be made by specialists who consider themselves on an intellectual and financial par with brain surgeons. Perhaps they are.

Think hard before opting for gas as the sole method of cooking, except in a small boat when I would agree that it is the only solution. If the boat is big enough to have a powerful separate 240v generator, then one can maintain the one-fuel principle by cooking with electricity. We do this in *Hosanna*. It can mean a lot of generating, even in the evening, when it can cause bad feeling among neighbours in a quiet harbour. It is becoming more and more common especially among charter yachts. Generators have become much quieter and more tolerable recently. We have a four plate hob, one of which is electric and three gas, and using the gas below and the barbecue on deck is a good way of solving the noise problem if too close to neighbours, the amount of gas required for this occasional use being very small. *Hosanna* has on deck a little sheltered summer kitchen with a single miniature gas ring for brewing up late at night. We do tend to swing at anchor rather than moor cramped up in harbours, and it's more peaceful for us too. We use Camping Gaz, and though this is about three times the price of normal methane, the cylinders are exchangeable almost everywhere.

• *Paraffin (kerosene)* •

This is not suitable for the ordinarily hedonistic live-aboard. We have small oil lamps in gimbals which we keep lit at night at sea, turned low, when they provide a faint glimmer which allows us to move about without switching on electric lights and spoiling night vision. We have recently seen a Canadian yacht with tiny, low-powered floor lights such as aircraft have along the walkways; this is an excellent idea while at sea by night. Coarse, cheap paraffin is getting hard to find because rural communities are changing to liquid gas, while the refined, treated anti-pong variety is available in miniature bottles at very high prices.

• *Cooking with alcohol* •

This is a menace. It surprises me that the Americans have tolerated it for so long, and I am happy to note a trend away from it at last. In some popular Caribbean anchorages you can sit enjoying a Planter's Punch after sunset while watching neighbouring Americans tossing overboard their flaming alcohol cookers. Some keep them on the end of a wire so they can easily haul them back inboard.

• *Solid fuel* •

The lovely old sloop *Diotima* in which the late Admiral Goldsmith lived the life of a dedicated singlehander (and, as previously mentioned, on the foredeck of which he died, weighing anchor at Monemvasia) had a solid fuel stove which was lovely in winter but noticeably warm in summer. Fuel was never a problem for him, he just gathered it from the beach. What a lovely little yacht! We last saw her in Hydra, now owned by a Greek sculptor who cares for her. *Hosanna* has two wood-burning stoves for winter evenings; we can sometimes find enough driftwood to feed them for free. We have a derrick, and finding a full-sized eucalyptus tree floating offshore in the Ionian, we hoisted it aboard, acquiring fuel and at the same time removing a danger to navigation. We then landed it to cut it up with a chain saw. We were told off by the Port Captain for making too much mess, but we swept up the sawdust which made good firelighters when soaked in old engine oil. The cruising life teaches you to use any resource you come across, usually this is better than the latest gadgets.

ELECTRICITY

Even if you do not have a 240v generator it is worth considering a circuit powered from the DC batteries by either a rotary converter or an electronic one. Electronic inverters have greatly improved recently and the newer ones have something like 95% efficiency. One can also get them with continuous ratings of over 3000 watts, and these can be used for a food mixer as well as electric drills, sanders, blow-dryers, vacuum cleaners, soldering irons and many other things that ease the chores for permanent residents. Usually this type of appliance is on for a few minutes only, so the battery drain is small. In any event, a 240-volt AC circuit is desirable if one is going to spend a Mediterranean winter on shore power. We will bring this subject up again when talking about refrigerators and power.

Do not rely on all countries having the same wiring practice. The UK system of Earth, Live and Neutral is a good system in principle, but foreign electricians often do not wire up three-pin sockets in a consistent way. It is a good idea to have twin fast circuit-breakers, one on each load-carrying wire of your shore power connection, and to have a certain means of completely isolating the ship's AC generator when connected to shore supply. Also, do not rely on the third pin in shore connection being connected to earth; use a two-wire shore power cable and bond the earth connections of all your shipboard outlets to your own earth. It is possible to buy elaborate gadgets offering protection against esoteric wiring practices, and these also protect against stray currents causing electrolytic corrosion. This is not my expertise.

Some professional electricians recommend the use of an AC to AC transformer when on shore power abroad. This provides all the power you need, without any direct connection with shore terminals, and can be made to step up the continental voltage which is very slightly lower than the British 240v. Sometimes, at the outer end of a long marina pontoon the Continental voltage falls as low as 180v, which is not good for your appliances. Of course, this transformer is safer, but I wonder whether the increase is cost-effective. I think our method, with reasonable vigilance, is 99%: to improve that to 99.5% is of dubious significance.

In Europe generally, the supply is 220v 50Hz, but, as we said above, voltage at the dockside sometimes falls as low as 180v, especially in Italy where we know that a lot of people tap into the domestic supply illegally with crocodile clips. In the USA the supply is generally 110v 60Hz, but it is possible with some shore sockets to get 220v by connecting up the pins in a particular way. Local knowledge is necessary, as the pilot books say, but Americans are very obliging. We found that all our 50Hz equipment worked without any noticeable ill effect on 60Hz, and I suspect that there is considerable tolerance in the design. Motors and clocks go faster. Most things do in America.

REFRIGERATION

This is the biggest energy user in the boat, apart from propulsion. Nowadays there are virtually no families cruising without refrigeration, even in small boats.

In *Fare Well* we had a top-opening refrigerator of about 3 cubic feet, and beneath and accessible through it a storage freezer of 2 cubic feet. This was a good installation, driven by a Grunert compressor unit, with a large holdover tank. The control was manual with an externally reading thermometer. The compressor was driven by 24v DC from the battery. It was mainly switched on during the daily battery charge. It was a robust system, as strong as a brick privy and was the equivalent of a steam engine compared to the modern ones. It worked without fail for 10 years!

For *Hosanna* we could not get an American installation and had to fit one made in Italy (Frigoboat). The system works from time to time, but needs a lot of expensive attention, and the service agents (apart, we must say, from the one in England) have not proved noticeably co-operative or effective. Even with English maintenance we have never had the thing going satisfactorily for more than a few months until recently. In Greece, a hot summer loomed, and in desperation, we asked Apostoli to fix it. He tutted a bit, pulled out all the specially designed Italian tubing, threw it away and replaced it with copper pipes soldered at the joints. (The compressor (Danforth) and evaporator were OK.) Since Apostoli took us back to

Laurel .

Calvi,
Corsica

first principles and ditched the Frigoboat flexible piping, we have had three years of first class refrigeration. Simplicity is best.

For smaller boats the 12v units working on the Peltier system are very simple though not highly efficient, technically. They are unlikely to make ice, but they will keep a small amount of food cool using two miniature fans; take spare fan units as these do not last for ever.

There is now on the market a range of normal-looking refrigerators, some of which have limited freezer space, which can work on 230v AC, or 12 or 24v (110v 60– is also available) according to the current. Two larger, made by Engel and sold by AquaMarine Ltd, and a smaller marketed by Penguin Engineering Ltd (addresses in Appendix) are known to us. This is a great advance in boat refrigeration. They use a powerful lot of DC current and need to be run either when the generator is going, or by a good solar or wind-driven generator. These fridges are not as cheap as ordinary domestic models, which can occasionally fit the bill, but probably represent the best solution for a boat too small to have a custom built job.

An alternative is to buy a bog-standard fridge from a High Street shop for very little money and run it through one of the bigger inverters. This will necessitate having big batteries so the saving in cost will not be all that marvellous. Face it: you pay a lot for cold beer. See the chapter on Power.

The custom-built fridge is probably more energy-economical as its insulation is usually better, and the refrigerant is usually cooled by sea water. (The standard domestic system cools by air, which can heat up the accommodation if not ducted out.) And household fridges are not very well insulated, the makers rely on your need for compact housing and not noticing how much current you use. See how you can improve the insulation with extra sprayed-on foam at the back and sides. We think we doubled the insulation, but of course we have invalidated any warranty. Not that warranties are much use in our wandering life. In the event of major breakdown the bog-standard domestic fridge is much easier and cheaper to replace than the marine model, though deceased fridges can be difficult to get rid of. We are not allowed to recommend ditching them at sea.

If you have an old boat with an existing fridge using Freon gas, note that this gas is now virtually unobtainable. It can be replaced by R49 gas which will keep the Greens happy until they find something wrong with that too.

There are refrigerators working on the absorption method, getting energy from a gas or paraffin flame. In 1953, we tried the latter, and though quite pleased at the time, there is no doubt that the present system is much better. The absorption system can be troublesome at sea because tilting and movement inhibits its operation. I am told that the use of naked flames in absorption-type refrigerators is now forbidden in boats in the UK.

WATER SYSTEMS

In small yachts, water is usually manually pumped; the larger boats normally have a pressure system. The best I know of was made by Godwin but alas they have ceased to make them. As in most things, the Rolls Royce job is getting hard to find and we have to make do with Mickey Mouse gear. Power consumption is negligible, and in *Fare Well* we had running hot and cold via the Perkins cooker. In *Hosanna*, the generator or the main engine heats the water.

I know of some boats which use a header tank. One has a tall, narrow 5-gal cylinder inside the mainmast with a visual sight glass. The skipper pumps water up each morning and has a very exact check on consumption. Knowing him, I bet he has a lock on the pump! Usually live-aboards use more water than holiday-makers; again it is a question of wanting a higher standard of living for long stays.

I would make sure that the yacht has capacious fresh-water tanks. Most production boats, being dedicated to weekend use, are poorly fitted in this respect. *Fare Well* carried 400 Imperial gallons and without any drastic economy measures we used about 10 per day. With two extra guests, this rose to about 13. For an ocean voyage we exercised a little economy and used 5 on average, laundry day was always an upset to the calculations. Probably tankage of 200 gallons, or 1000 litres, is the minimum for comfortable living and water security.

Water-makers are becoming a practical proposition at last. We once wrote that they converted a gallon of diesel into a gallon of barely usable water, but the ratio has improved. They now turn a gallon of diesel into two gallons of water. They should be investigated if cruising to some awkward parts of the world, but they are not necessary in the Med.

Having a good awning with a hose connection leading to a bucket is effective, but there are areas where rain is occasionally scarce. See our mainboom rain-collecting arrangement (illustration on page 83).

PROVISION OF STOWAGE

One of the major factors in the accommodation aboard a long-term cruiser is the relationship between bunks and stowage. Ocean racers can get by on half a cubic foot per man, but such an allowance would make for marital discord, and in time a pretty smelly crew.

In tropical conditions, when humidity can be high (and the same applies during a scirocco in the Med), the best way of stowing clothes is the hanging cupboard or wardrobe. Though women's clothes are smaller and lighter, the female needs (and demands, and usually gets) rather more space than a man. If we were to decide on a requirement of 1m 20cm of wardrobe bar for a couple (and this is a bit on the mean side) it would indicate 70cm for her, and 50cm for him. Generally, summer guests need only about 15cm each.

The problem is that while living afloat you have to carry on board full outfits of hot weather decent, hot weather casual, the same for temperate climes, and finally winter garments for both sea and shore, which are very bulky. Whereas a man is moderately content to put on a shapeless old sweater to do the winter shopping, most ladies prefer to look a little less like an itinerant scarecrow.

Each person living on board ought to have about 12 cubic feet of locker or drawers for clothing, quite apart from the wardrobe and any oilskin stowage. I like to provide a guest with 2 cubic feet, enough for a two to three week stay.

Food stowage is not such a problem in most EU countries, where one is seldom far from a good open-air market, but in the oceans, the West Indies or Bahamas, a fair bit of fridge/freezer or tin space is needed. We've already discussed refrigeration. The bilges are traditionally used for tins. Without leaks, you need not go through the old ritual of marking tins with a chinagraph pencil: we never have. Also, with dry bilges, tins keep for very long periods. We did once have a labelling problem by stowing tins in the bilge just above the prop. The vibration made the tins rotate slowly and wore off the labels, leaving the tins brightly polished and anonymous. It took some time to trace the cause for we didn't go down there while motoring.

• *Stowage for tools and spare parts* •

Tools are very important, and by keeping the boat dry, I have had few bad rust problems. You need to keep some tools very handy. *Fare Well* had five large shallow drawers, each one sub-divided, in the deckhouse close to the main hatch. There is seldom a hardware store round the corner at sea.

By the same token, spare parts are a problem. Most of the spares we started with are still intact in their wrappers: it has always been something else that has gone wrong. So the quantity carried has grown, and the ship has settled deeper and deeper into the water. It is necessary to make a list of all spares to carry.

- Class A spares, the lack of which would cause severe problems.
- Class B spares are from those suppliers who are so bad: slow or unreliable, that one is obliged to carry them on board.
- Class C is for those companies who can be relied on to help you out of a hole if their product goes wrong, by sending a spare by a fast and convenient carrier.

Make a policy of buying the products of companies in class C: they deserve every encouragement. Unfortunately there are occasions where you have to patronise a mediocre outfit, and the more you do, the more spares you have to carry.

• *Chart stowage* •

Designers seldom give sensible thought to chart stowage. I have seen a claim for a boat to be well endowed in this respect with space under the chart table for 25 charts, a height of about 12mm. A yacht's outfit (a full one would be much larger) of charts for the UK to the Med, the Med itself, Black and Red Seas, the Middle Atlantic, the West Indies, Bahamas and the USA makes a stack 24cm high, and is probably the heaviest movable item on board. And quite possibly one of the most expensive, too. This problem will be eased by electronic charts but not completely eliminated.

Navigational publications for the same areas, ie pilot books, tables, almanacs etc, occupy three metres of bookshelf; and while it is true that I have one or two old chums among these which are no longer of practical use any more, the figure is not far out. There are 16 Admiralty Pilots alone. Space must be found for catalogues, a few books giving advice on problems, multi-language nautical dictionaries, and instruction books for equipment. To the suggestion that one does not need all these charts or books at once, the answer is that they have to be on board because the ship is your home. There is no other place: no shed at the bottom of the garden, no convenient storage at Grandma's that you can easily get to.

Other books can be a problem too. People who have been brought up to read seem to need books to keep in practice, and books abhor damp. The worst are those printed on glossy paper, whose pages tend to stick together. (Yachting magazines are bad offenders; I suppose their editors never take them to sea.) Thank heaven Penguin and others publish a good list of paperback reference books.

VENTILATION

The frequent mention of dampness leads naturally to ventilation and light. We have already referred to the possibility of moisture coming in through the ventilator, but unfortunately other things can get in too. A good wire mesh (which should be of bronze because rats eat plastic) is desirable, to exclude mosquitoes, rats and mice. Laurel will take up this point later.

In really hot weather, it is nice to have windows that open, though our steel boat is often cooler down below than on deck, largely because she is well insulated. The problem with windows that open is that they are seldom completely watertight, whatever the type. Our fixed windows have aluminium frames, as do the skylights. They all give a little trouble from time to time because after 18 years the sun has perished the rubber-like compound in which the glass or acrylic is bedded, and we came to the conclusion that aluminium framed openings or windows are not really good enough for the long term. Replacing seals is a tedious job, and I cannot recommend an alternative system, though we all badly need a better one. We have poor experience with Houdini hatches. We have nine. They are inexpensive and look good, but when their sealing compound started to perish (after about five tropical years) all except one leaked like sieves.

It is not strictly necessary to have windows of the miniature mousehole size so often counselled by the old salts in the magazines. I have heard tell of Messrs Camper & Nicholson selling a large yacht to an American who, to demonstrate that he thought their windows were not strong enough, hit them and broke them with a hammer, telling the builders that that was the type of force that they would need to withstand at sea. As if Camper and Nicholson had no experience. While having every sympathy with an owner in quest of confidence in his vessel, I feel also for the builders, who had already fitted extra strong glass which was almost certainly adequate.

Don't forget that the windows have to be very well fastened into the surrounding hull. We have had a couple of very severe storms, and been knocked down until the deckhouse was submerged, but our hull and deckhouse windows (considered too large by some) did well. (A few squirts got through, but they were not particularly noticeable in the ensuing disorder.) The 10mm toughened glass in the deckhouse windows measured 37 × 19 inches, while that in the biggest hull window is 17 × 12. It is possible to build the boat like an armoured submarine: the best thing for the nervous is to have removable deadlights of 5mm aluminium plate, and enjoy the pleasure of good windows during 99 per cent of the time.

As peviously mentioned, though it may be very nice to contemplate a cooling breeze coming down a skylight or ventilator over your bunk, do not do it. Sooner or later the breeze will come with water. It takes just one second to get your bedding wet; it takes ages at sea to get it even tolerably dry. One can tell the boats with this design fault as they arrive in Barbados or the Azores: their drying mattresses are slung across the main boom, and the telltale banners of their shame are drying in the rigging. Surprising how often these boats have been well reviewed in the magazines.

We have seen a lot of boats with miniature fans. We have an exhaust fan built in above the galley stove. For years, we had no other, but recently we have succumbed. Perhaps it is due to global warming or something. Anyway, they use little power but make a noise. One significant use I have found for it is to juice up the barbecue. I can get it as hot as a blacksmith's forge now that I no longer have to fan it with an old pilot book.

HEADS

'The Beak-head is . . . of great use as well for the grace and countenance of the ship, as a place for men to ease themselves in' [This is the derivation of the sailor's term head.]

Two heads are better than one, for sooner or later one will become a blocked head, usually while guests are on board. This is not always due to items being put down without being eaten first (watch out for people who swallow their cherry stones, that can be the trigger). The underlying cause is usually scale owing to the salinity of the water. It is necessary to dismantle the flexible tubing every six months or so and beat it against the quay, preferably when there are few people about, and when wearing a hat. An alternative method is to flush the loo a few times with a 10% solution of hydrochloric acid, which can be bought over the counter in most Med countries for just this purpose. It is not a way endorsed by the manufacturers, but it works.

We changed the heads on board to Lavac because this loo has a separate pump away from the basin. We carry a spare pump so if a loo pump becomes blocked it is a comparatively simple task to fit the spare, leaving the unpleasant servicing job to a more convenient time.

More recently, with one of us complaining about the work involved in flushing, we have invested in a Superflush™, a French machine marketed by Lee Sanitation of Banbury (a firm which gives excellent service). Unfortunately, the Superflush, an all-electric loo, does not. It did not work on arrival, and after much angst we found it had a red wire on the negative and black on the positive as fitted in the factory, and this took some sorting out as we did not think any manufacturer could be that daft. Well, one can. After that, all went well for three months and then the timing mechanism failed. This consisted of three nylon cams operating switches. Of course the nylon had quickly abraded away. We flushed with a bucket for a time. The replacement (electronic) timing unit did not work either. Lesson: the more expensive an item is, the more likely it is to go wrong. It is a good loo when it works – it still doesn't.

HOLDING TANKS

We originally (30 years ago) fitted a holding tank head because it looked as if everywhere was going ecology mad, but well-meaning attempts to control yacht heads and make discharge illegal generally ended in an administrative shambles. In the USA 20 years ago, the legislation was discreetly ignored as nobody had provided pump-out facilities, except on certain waterways with locks. This is still the case in many places on the European side of the Atlantic.

Since then, the ecology war has hotted up. Turkey has become most aggressive, its pump-out laws include ALL waste from yachts. It seems that both the informer and the magistrate get a proportion of the fine levied for infractions; there must be some inducement for the local peasantry to be so eager to shop foreign offenders even for emptying the washing up basin over the side, and the fines are disproportionate. We accept that in certain marinas, such as Marmaris, where the enclosed, virtually land-locked marina is itself in a virtually land-locked bay with little water movement, control is necessary. Even so, we have found the regulation being rigidly enforced in other, quasi-open ports where the town's sewage system already drains untreated into the sea.

We anchored in a bay in Grenada (West Indies) where it was forbidden to use the ship's heads. There were five other boats there, in a water plane of about 5000 square metres. With a tidal range of a metre, that bay was flushed twice daily by 5000 tonnes of water. Just how sensible or necessary are some of the restrictions that the more barmy ecologists so enthusiastically impose?

Now, in *Hosanna*, we have two 140-litre galvanised soil tanks which will cope with a fairly long stay in port, especially with only two of us on board. And NO, we have never yet been accused of pollution: we are not by nature polluters, we just exercise common sense. Before World War Two, the seas absorbed all the sewage waste from almost every seaside town and I do not recall anyone being upset about it, nor of any outbreaks of illness in these towns. I know that modern sewage has other nasty things in it besides excreta, but yachts' heads are dealing specifically with human waste which the sea efficiently deals with except in enclosed ports. After all, fish crap too.

Most authorities recommend that sullage tanks, to take drainage from sinks, showers and washbasins below the waterline, should be enclosed. Our experience is the opposite. *Fare Well* had an open sump in the keel in which was a submersible pump, and an automatic switch operated by air pressure as the water level in the sump rose. (Float switches are unreliable.) Received opinion is that this is supposed to be smelly and nasty. It was situated in the engine-room, which was well ventilated, and it did not seem to smell at all, or at least not as much as the engine, and it had the big advantage that any gunge could be easily observed and readily dealt with. In *Hosanna* we use two plastic rubbish bins with plastic plumbing. Every year or so, we dismantle them and clean out the black gunge at the bottom with a pressure washer.

WASHING MACHINES

If the electrical situation will stand it, it is worth having some sort of washing machine; laundries ashore are often inconvenient and expensive, and the launderette has not penetrated everywhere. In the larger boats, where the machine is usually plumbed in, take care that the whole system has some sort of drip tray

Eddie and Anneke with Misty Two's neat little plastic washing machine (above) which may save you quite a lot of effort but when it comes to wringing out, this mangle (left) may take a bit more muscle. Note Misty Two's substantial stern boarding ladder.

under it, for almost all machines spill a little water, and even if your hull will not rust, the soapy mush will soon expand and fight you for possession of your ship. There are some good miniature washing machines which could be carried in a small boat and used on the pontoon in a marina (see also page 232).

ACCOMMODATION

Some yachts equip themselves with guest cabins in the hope that they can do the occasional charter to help pay their way. I am in two minds about this. Chartering is getting ever more professional and customers demand more and more fancy facilities. In these conditions, agencies are not too keen on the casual charter, which in any event is never as lucrative as the professional. Charters can also be hard to find just when the owner wants them. The alternative is to devote that space to more comfortable living. Of course, when friends come to visit they have no super cabin, but our friends are the sort who would holiday with us in a 5-tonner, and we can accommodate them better than that. However, it does not solve any financial problems for the owner. Double bunks are now accepted but it is as well to have a method of dividing them, even for non-marital reasons. Part of our padded headboard in *Fare Well* could be lifted out and slotted fore and aft to make two very comfortable sea berths.

All in all, do not over-concentrate on the boat as a boat. Think of her as living space for a good deal of the time. Sit aboard and use your imagination – before buying her if you can.

HOW TO COMPARE CRUISING BOATS

'Considerations for a Sea Captain in the choise of his ship'

It is comparatively easy to contemplate a yacht which you are going to use for a purpose which is already thoroughly familiar. However, not many people will be familiar with the complete dedication to the way of life required of a confirmed live-aboard, long-distance cruiser. If they are, then they are unlikely to need any help choosing a boat, but for those who would like to consider another person's outlook, I have devised the following rough assessment system. I do not expect it to stand rigorously when applied to any and every boat, but it might be used to give an idea of whether a yacht is a genuine or suitable design for long-term cruising. You can then eliminate a lot of the attractive rubbish at the Boat Show and end up by choosing on personal taste and that feeling of attraction to a craft that is the foundation of a true boat marriage.

For my part, I like to say something is lousy if there is good reason for saying so. You could probably say it about this evaluation scheme: I know it's not perfect, but it does contribute something to the debate.

• *Cooper's Yacht Evaluator* •

To be taken lightly salted.

Then for the Captain's cabben or great Cabben, the Stearage, the halfe Decke, the Round house, the Forecastle . . .

Take a piece of paper and a pen. Draw two columns, head one *Sea* and the other *Comfort*. The questions are arranged so that an affirmative answer will score as indicated in one column or the other (sometimes in both), while a negative answer will not score. Where a question is complicated there will probably be a few words of clarification immediately following. I'm sorry but I have insufficient knowledge of multi-hulls to make an intelligent contribution. So, mono-hulls only.

QUESTIONNAIRE

		Sea	Comfort
1	Length overall of ship: is it under 30ft	0	–2
	30–35ft	1	1
	35–40ft	2	3
	40–50ft	2	4
	over 50ft	1	5
2	Draught: is it under 6ft	0	4
	6<6ft 6in	2	2
	6ft 6in<7ft	2	0
	over 7ft	2	–4
3	Is the length of the keel bottom more than half the waterline length?	1	0
4	Is the after lower tip of the rudder less than ⅕ of the length overall from the stern?	–3	–1
5	Is there a retroussé transom?	–2	0
6	Is the keel bottom horizontal, or nearly so?	1	1
7	Is there clear standing headroom throughout at least 50% of the accommodation?	0	5
8	Is there a wheelhouse?	1	3
	Or if not, is the conning position well protected?	2	1
9	Deck integrity. Is the area of cockpit (including seats) below the level of the main watertight deck:		
	nil	5	0
	less than 24sq ft	3	0
	between 24 and 40sq ft	0	0
	over 40sq ft	–4	1
10	For each hatch or skylight score	–1	1
11	For each Dorade type ventilator over 4in dia. score	0	1

		Sea	Comfort
12	For each hatch or skylight over a bunk	0	−4
13	Is the mast(s) in tabernacle(s)?	0	1
14	Is there room for a bicycle on deck?	−1	1
15	Can a rigid tender be carried aboard?	1	2
16	Is it easy to get aboard from the water?	1	1
17	Easy access from shore by either bow or stern?	0	2
18	Are there more than four openings below waterline?	−2	0
19	Add together the breaking strain of all standing rigging that reaches the deck (see table at end). If the total is greater than:		
	7 x displacement in tons	10	0
	6 x	7	0
	5 x	4	0
	less than 5 x	0	0
	less than 4 x	−6	0
20	Mast compression: if greater than:		
	2 x displacement in tons	10	0
	if greater than 1.5 x	5	0
	if less than 1.5 x	−10	0

Calculation of compression strain is somewhat complex; there are yacht designers who have never heard of Euler's formula. If you can find out from a mast maker, well and good; or you could try the approximation given in Skene's Elements of Yacht Design; or omit this question.

21	We define the foretriangle as the distance from the foot of the forestay to the foreside of the mast at deck, times half the height of the mast as far as the highest foresail halyard sheave.		
	If this is greater than 40% of area of all plain sail	−4	−2
	if greater than 50%	−6	−3
22	Are there running backstays?	−2	0
23	Is there a permanent gallows for the main boom?	1	1
24	Are there internal halyards?	−2	0
25	Is there roller reefing/furling on headsail?	4	3
26	Is there roller gear on main	4	2
	and mizzen?	1	0
27	For each sail over 400sq ft (40 m²)	−3	0
28	For a yacht over 10 tons displ. are there two or more geared sheet winches?	2	0

		Sea	Comfort
	ANCHORS ETC		
29	Is the bower (main) anchor self-stowing?	5	1
30	If the bower is over 40lbs, is there a power windlass?	2	3
31	Bower anchor cable. Is it chain, more than 150ft?	4	0
	less than 150ft?	1	0
	part chain	0	0
	all nylon?	–2	–1
32	Bower anchor size. Calculate frontal area of craft: multiply mast height from waterline by beam of hull, both in feet. (I know the boat is not that wide at the top of the mast, but the wind is a lot stronger up there and this is a good approximation.) Divide this area by 8. This gives desirable anchor weight in pounds, and applies to Danforth, CQR and Bruce anchors. Anchors of other types score nothing, and that includes imitations of above.		
	If no anchor of above size	–5	0
	If one anchor of above size	4	0
	If two	6	0
	If three	7	0
	(One might reasonably have one or two additional anchors at about three-quarters this size for use as a kedge or lunch-hook.) Q 32 applies only to conventional sailing yachts.		
33	Chain cable size. Take one quarter of anchor weight in kilos, add 2, and this gives cable dia in mm. Minimum 6mm.		
	If chain diameter over or equal to above size	4	0
	If chain smaller	–4	0
34	Does fuel tankage in litres exceed 12 x engine hp?	1	4
35	Is there a second means of generating electricity?	0	3
36	Are deck and hull skin well insulated?	0	4
37	Are there two separate batteries?	1	2
38	Fresh-water tanks.		
	At least two, with total capacity in litres more than 40 x displacement in tonnes?	0	4
	Two tanks but more than 10 x	0	0
	One tank only (ignore rubber tanks)	–1	–6
39	Can you sit down on all four sides of the engine?	0	2
40	Do you have access to the engine without dismantling half the accommodation?	0	1
41	Is the heating system independent of electricity?	0	2
42	Is cooking by either diesel, paraffin or bottled gas?	0	1
43	Is the cooker either gimballed or fully fiddled?	0	1
44	Is there a fiddled drainer or putting-down space?	0	1
45	Is there a refrigerator?	0	1

		Sea	Comfort
46	Does total dry locker space for clothes exceed 6cu ft (160 litres) per permanent bunk?	0	2
47	Number of permanent berths. Divide displacement in tons by number of berths:		
	if over 5	0	6
	under 5 but over 4	0	3
	under 4 but over 3	0	1
	under 2	0	–5
48	Is there separate saloon and sleeping accommodation?	0	3
49	Is there a WC compartment with shower?	0	2
50	Non-clothing stowage, above the cabin sole: is there more than 1.5cu ft (40 litres) per ton displacement?	0	2
51	Is there a good clear area of deck for lounging?	0	1
52	Is there an autopilot?	2	4
53	If no autopilot, is there a windvane?	2	2
54	Is an echosounder fitted?	1	0
55	Are there at least two deck cleats, eyes or bitts each capable of taking a lateral pull of half the weight of the boat without pulling out? (How to	4	0

tell? Well, it's a bit difficult to provide a complete answer: such a fitting will probably look too big, but won't be. If in any doubt, it's not big enough.)

TABLE OF APPROXIMATE BREAKLOADS

for 1 x 19 stainless steel wire, for use with the above Questionnaire:

Circumference (in)	Approx. diameter (mm)	Breakload (lb)
5/8	4	4,700
3/4	6	8,000
1	8	12,000
1 1/4	10	17,500
1 1/2	12	30,000
1 3/4	14	46,000

To evaluate the boat, add the scores of each column separately. The Sea column is meant to give some estimate of whether the yacht is fit to go to sea at all as a cruising boat. Do not expect the score to be conclusive; I am quite sure that there could well be exceptions, but most really worthwhile cruising boats should score well over 50 points.

The Comfort column has a broad coverage of those factors which affect one's standard of living; the idea is not to provide sybarism to a grand standard but to try to achieve a living above the 'grotty squalor' level, the sort of compromise between comfortable existence at sea and relaxed life in port. A good score in the Comfort column would be 60, but 50 might be treated as a minimum.

We have inevitably leaned heavily on our own preferences and opinions but have tried to allow for other points of view. If you have a strong opinion on some factor that differs from ours, then give it your own weighting; the important thing is to use common criteria for all vessels surveyed.

For interest, we reckon *Fare Well* scores 58 + 65. Bearing in mind that all boats are something of a compromise between sea-keeping and comfort, it might be as well, after first making sure that there is an adequate score under each heading, to compare totals.

A problem with this 'evaluator' is that it takes quite a time to assess each yacht; it is a very detailed examination giving a weighting of some sort to most things worthwhile in a live-aboard yacht. To save time one should have a means of quickly discarding unsuitable craft by drawing up a shortlist. Keep the two broad criteria, seaworthiness and comfort. I suggest the following are seriously on the debit side in assessing seaworthiness in the context of this book:

- Deep fin keel which tends to directional instability and limits harbour access.
- Spade rudder hung right aft, fragile in big seas and which is vulnerable to damage when berthing in the Med.
- Large foretriangle with Bermudan rig is tough on small crews.
- Main shroud chainplates well inside deck edge (leads to higher tension in shrouds and greater compression in mast).
- Anchors not self-stowing.
- Running backstays are a pain in the transom.
- Bendy masts. They can bend too far.
- Two or more sails over 400sq ft. Tough on small crews.
- Steeply cambered decks are a poor foothold. In theory OK on one side when heeled. In practice one is never at a constant angle at sea.
- Guardrails less than 30in high are tripwires.
- Cockpit that is not self-drained, and adequately so.

All things are a compromise, but I think I would not like to trust my life in a yacht with more than five of the above debit points.

Items that detract seriously from the joy of living in a yacht are more idiosyncratic. Make your own list, but consider:

- Lack of good shelter at the steering position.
- Lack of separate sleeping/daytime accommodation.
- Cockpit that is uncomfortable to lounge about in.
- Lack of a simple heating system.
- Insufficient fresh water (less than 1000 litres).

- Poor hanging lockers.
- Poor ventilation.
- Engine access in living space.
- Pokey galley, ill-lit or ill-ventilated, badly designed.
- Less than 6 metres of bookshelves.

I would not be very comfortable in a yacht with many of these points. Set your own limit: five perhaps.

In the end, whether you are looking at the short assessment or the more detailed, you have to face the fact that logic often plays second fiddle to love in the choice of both spouses and boats. Did you really go through all this sort of thing before choosing your wife? Minus three for a long nose, plus two for good puddings? Of course you didn't (I hope). And you probably won't choose your yacht this way either, but you might have fun looking at a few. Boats, not wives.

7 • People, Pets and Pests

'There are so many young Captaines and those that desire to be Captaines, who know very little, or nothing at all to any purpose'

A great many preconceived notions can be left on the quay on departure, along with the cardboard boxes, empty beer crates, broken gadgets bought at the Boat Show and other cruising detritus. Among these could be stereotypes long overdue for discard, such as: old ladies cannot be expected to climb on board boats, girls can't row, children are not useful, and pets are a nuisance at sea.

You now enter a world where many a nippy Grannie leaps lightly into a dinghy and trims it without being asked as others follow. She has probably been sailing since before you were born, and steered a yacht in a gale on an Atlantic crossing. Yon lovely girl, so slim and ethereal, can probably get the starboard jibsheet to the winch and hove in while you are still thinking about it, let alone row you a mile ashore. The rope you have just thrown to a likely-looking native, who is standing there looking perplexed while the wind carries you rapidly away from the quay, is apt to be seized by a tow-headed eight-year-old, who makes a bowline in the wink of an eye, drops it over the upwind bollard and disappears down the companionway of that little Dutch sloop. As for pets, my ideal crew has a vacancy for a cat.

Without too much prejudice, then, let us look at who can do what on board, and how to avoid unnecessary conflict.

It is many years since the concept of 'Captain' equals 'male'. Many girls and women are Skippers these days, so when I speak of Captains please believe that they can be of either sex. I am more familiar with a male Skipper, and being told what to do as regards navigation and ship handling. Other areas are my concern: the feeding, health and welfare of the crew are in my charge. In case of bodily accidents, I take over; not because I know more than Bill, but because in that situation I have a cool head and don't mind the blood. Much.

Also, Bill still has to sail the boat. (Ah! you say, but what if the Skipper has the accident? We'll come to that in Chapter 11.) I am also in charge of victualling and storing for long voyages, which is as it should be since I am usually also the shopper and cook. In these days of IT I am also the troubleshooter for the computer, as Bill likes to kick things that don't work.

HOW TO BE CAPTAIN

'The Captaine's charge is to command all.'

Our good Captain Smith once again says it all in a nutshell. The one person who need not worry about his status is the Captain: it is never in doubt. No company president, managing director, or even eminent surgeon on his rounds tailed by milling underlings, can know the power of being Master Under God (as the Lloyd's policy puts it) of a ship, however small. The rest of us, according to another well-known source, are a little lower than the angels, which presumably puts the Captain slightly above them. This gives him a natural authority instantly recognised by landsmen, which is not surprising. What is perhaps surprising is that the quiet authority of a good Captain is recognised even when he is in bare feet and ragged shorts, and by his/her spouse.

No ship can ever run satisfactorily as a commune: the job of a Captain is to be Captain. I have never been Captain (except for a few hours entering the Turkish port of Datça, when Bill had a bad attack of Saladin's Revenge), so of course I have every right to comment on the subject, especially from the point of view of the crew. I use the word 'Capting' to signify Bossiness without leadership, so if I answer my spouse, 'Yes, Capting,' he knows I consider he is merely throwing his weight about and not giving sensible orders. He does not do it often.

A good Captain:

- Explains a manoeuvre in advance, and thus does not need to shout complicated instructions at a bewildered crew at the last minute.
- Gives orders that are clear and unambiguous so he does not need to repeat them with rising hysteria and ever-increasing decibels.
- Wastes no time cursing if his crew make a mess of it. He says 'All right, folks: we go round and do it again.' (He is allowed to grit his teeth, however.) Always start from NOW!
- Accepts without fuss if he makes an error of judgement, and does not blame his crew for it.
- Does not get too excited if the anchor cable comes in slowly, when it always does come in slowly.
- Shouts only when ambient noise at the crew's end makes it necessary.

Having said that:

- Captains are the ultimate authority on everything connected with the ship and crew. Wise mates and knowledgeable crew may help him to make the decisions, but he is the arbiter.
- He should make sure all on board know his policy on certain important mishaps and events, such as fire, shipwreck and man-overboard.
- The Captain is able to delegate many tasks, but it must be clear whose responsibility they are, and he should be prepared to back up his delegate with authority.
- He should be loyal to his crew, as they are to him.

A good Captain is recognisable not by his autocracy and didacticism, but by the respect in which he is held by his crew. It is not necessary for him to be the best qualified one on board, since it is possible for highly qualified people to be bad Captains. This is not to say that experience and knowledge are not to be acquired wherever possible; but courses of instruction should be carefully selected by recommendation rather than picked with a pin from alluring ads in the Yachting Press. Thus you will avoid those courses run by old and bold military men who are nutty about semaphore, and patronise your wife: 'This the little woman?' they roar, 'Soon make a good cabin boy out of her, eh? Can she cook?'

The Yachtmaster Certificate®, for example, is all useful knowledge and updated at intervals; but to have gained it is not the be-all and end-all, nor is the Coast Guard Captain's Licence in the USA. There is a danger, in fact, that such certificates entrain dubious feelings of an all-powerful super-knowledge of the sea. Bill has occasionally had to be very tactful (which doesn't come easily), when given shouted and peremptory advice by Yachtmasters off their home patch, advice which would have been inappropriate at best, and dangerous at worst.

Both the admirable qualifications above mentioned tend to be oriented towards local waters and conditions, and should be regarded as forming merely a basis for a great deal of further experience: there will be much to learn about sailing in more distant parts, and much nautical wisdom yet to be acquired. After 60 years at sea, one thing we have learned is to give advice only when it is asked for, or when a real and unnoticed danger threatens. We, too, are still learning.

A good Captain conducts an orchestra in which he may not play the bassoon too well, but he knows its function as part of the whole and all the players look to him for direction. Or to her, since both conductors and Captains may well be women these days. This causes no bother to most people, as she is usually in this position because her crew feels comfortable about her being there. It is again a question of respect. If certain bigoted and reactionary people find it intolerable to take orders from a woman, they must go and find a bigoted and reactionary male Captain who will suit them better.

I had thought all this sexism was in the past in the new millennium, but have just heard from a woman captain whose skill and experience I deeply respect that she had trouble of this kind with a macho crew member very recently. In the end he got so bolshie that after warning him twice Sue dumped him in Cuba. So watch it, guys.

Every Captain will make mistakes, and sometimes they will be serious. Apportioning blame may be balm to the wounded spirit, but it is unproductive. After disasters, start from NOW. He may find himself in dire straits through no fault of his own, or indeed anyone's, and he will still blame himself. We left Bermuda with an excellent weather forecast, heading north with the expectation of leaving the West Indies well before the hurricane season: June, the rhyme goes, is too soon (for the hurricanes to come). On the eighteenth of June, two days out, we got warning of a tropical storm, which had rapidly deepened into Hurricane Alberto. After the vortex had passed us, with a lot of discomfort and terror but no great damage, we were struck by a violent squall and a flash of lightning, early in the morning.

Bill's only crime was being on watch when it happened, but the shock of it, and the despair at seeing our sails in ribbons, laid him very low for an hour or two. We were three on board. The watch below, Nora and I, were precipitated up on deck by the noise and the knockdown. Even if richly deserved, recriminations are unaffordable luxuries at such times, and this squall had been far too sudden for any action to be effective. Nora and I made comforting and reassuring noises to our stricken Captain, and as soon as I could get the stove going we fed him on quantities of scrambled egg, since we were in no immediate danger and all had headaches from the lightning strike. Then we took a deep breath, and under his direction began to restore the ship to order. We were still 400 miles from land and it was going to be a slow and uncomfortable voyage, but it had to be faced. We arrived in Newport Rhode Island 11 days overdue, with considerable material damage, but no bodily harm. A successful voyage in that we arrived where we headed for. Neither Master nor crew can say in the middle of a difficult passage, 'I don't want to play any more.'

A year or two back we watched a TV programme which features Lennie Henry crossing the Atlantic in company with an eminent sailor. It made good television, but be aware of the difference. Poor Lennie, like an ordinary human, was sick, uncomfortable, afraid, and missing his family. There the resemblance to any voyage we make stops. Lennie's yacht was never, in such a high profile voyage, going to be run down by a rogue tanker, capsize, or sustain a medical emergency out of reach of help; as might happen to you and us. Not with a million quids' worth of support vessel never more than a mile away: they were even able to replenish the teabags when they ran out in mid-Atlantic, for God's sake. When they ran out of time, however, nothing could be done, and Lennie was lifted off by the high speed support vessel, voyage unfinished, to catch the plane back to the UK and fulfil another film contract.

We cannot say it too often: NEVER put restrictions on time. An orderly voyage takes as long as it takes. With no clock or calendar to worry you, there is no stress beyond wind and waves and the task of arriving in good shape.

What if the Captain and crew really don't get on at all? Suppose your Skipper, at the Yacht Club bar so smooth and full of salty tales of successful voyages and dangers overcome, turns out to be sufficiently bogus to be a menace to both his ship and crew? Suppose he retires to his bunk at times of stress, abdicating to his crew decisions which he should make, and for which he will later blame them? The following is a true story, and happened to a friend of ours who is a very experienced crew, on passage from the Azores to Gibraltar. They reached Europe at a point that the cataleptic skipper insisted was Gibraltar, and though our friend instantly recognised that it was Setubal, on the coast of Portugal some 600 miles to the north, she said nothing. The Skipper left the yacht at once, claiming urgent business, and ordered the crew to sail on and he would meet them in Majorca in a couple of days. They said, 'Well, we'd like a few days to see Gibraltar first, give

A happy crew: Bill and Laurel looking very relaxed in the cockpit. One of the important questions you need to ask before you contemplate living afloat is 'Will it suit both of you long-term and will you both enjoy it?'

us a week.' There's support from a tactful crew. No physical hurt or damage occurred, probably due to a good crew on the watch for trouble.

Suppose the apparently athletic girl taken on for crossing the Atlantic screams when the boat heels, or is afraid of the dark and won't keep night watches? Or the strong lad turns out to be impossible to live with? (All true instances.)

Most incompatibilities of this kind can be avoided by a shakedown cruise, with no commitment on either side. Living aboard is about long-term tolerance, so a series of weekends or holidays afloat are not really the answer, though they may reveal intolerably irritating habits or personality aspects. You need to fight your way through a few situations to find out how you are going to get on under stress. To be able to duck out of trouble too easily, as you mostly can on weekend and holiday cruising, negates the point of the exercise. Most of all, you need time to work together and evolve an everyday smoothness of running, so that routine tasks become second nature, and there is more time and energy to cope with unexpected surprises. Thus, while no one is perfect, you will not set off on a long cruise with someone who rubs you up the wrong way. I have said elsewhere that marriages may not survive the strains imposed on them by the cruising life (this goes for friendships and Captain/crew relationships too), but marital breakdown, mutiny, mid-Atlantic mayhem and murder are outside the scope of this book. Not far outside, though.

As you will have noticed, a great many observations that can be made about Captains are inextricably entangled with those about crew, since they are two sides of the same coin.

There is a little handbook called *Reeds Skipper's Handbook* by Malcolm Pearson (Adlard Coles Nautical) which we advise carrying. It is 99.9% accurate (a high rating on Bill's scale), and well laid out for the inexperienced. It could be useful for settling arguments, and the Skipper will always be able to creep sneakily below to check up on something he has forgotten. It happens to us all.

THE PIERHEAD JUMP

Should a short-handed Captain take on a 'pierhead jump' (an unknown crew who joins at the last moment)? It is a desperate measure, fraught with risk and uncertainty. Only the Captain can weigh need against risk. In the West Indies, such a crew must possess an air ticket outward before being allowed to sign off the crew list of any vessel. It is the Captain's responsibility to ensure that such a ticket exists, or he risks being landed with the person indefinitely. We have sometimes taken on someone at short notice: all but one were a great success; all but one came with recommendations from people we knew and trusted. Many couples we know have had a very different experience, however, even resulting in vowing never to take crew again however short-handed they were. The sins of the said crew varied from drug abuse, smuggling, theft and laziness, to actually taking command of the yacht in mid-Atlantic, from a rather elderly couple who were powerless to stop them.

The only time we took a crew who had not been personally recommended by someone who had actually sailed with them and knew them well, but only by a man they had done some boat painting for, we regretted it all the way from Gibraltar to the Azores. (Our insurers had sprung on us, at the last minute, a requirement to have more than two persons on board for ocean sailing, a requirement they have since modified, thank goodness.)

Be aware that if drugs are found on your boat, the boat is liable to confiscation, even if you were unaware of the existence of the drugs. It is not necessarily the hippier-looking people who take or deal in drugs. Which takes us back to reliable references, living with prospective crew for a few days, and discovering their attitudes and habits, with these days, alas, a certain amount of healthy suspicion of anything that does not quite add up. At close quarters, one has a better chance of finding out before it is too late. We come, inevitably, to:

HOW TO BE CREW

'These are to take their turn at the Helme, trim sailes, pumpe, and doe all duties for eight glasses or four hours, which is a watch.'

There is no task in a boat that is sexually exclusive. Some jobs require brawn, and there are women who can do them and have enough breath left to whistle at the same time. Others of us are rather less muscular, but perhaps good at fiddly jobs requiring great patience. Apart from being helpful, tolerant, humorous at the right moment and tactful, it helps to have a little knowledge.

For *absolute beginners* and a few others we could name, we include a 'Starter Pack' on one or two essentials, see further on. While unlikely to prove the definitive work on the subject (indeed, this book is not about seamanship), *no one who has taken in the full import of this section is useless*. Anyone who can make a bowline, and has learnt the intelligent use of fenders without bumping into the rest of the crew is already of considerable help; I particularly address myself to those windblown lovelies who are so disrespectfully called 'crew's comforts' by their companions.

• *Laurel and Bill's starter pack for would-be cruisers* •

'Here mayst thou learn the names of all ship's gear'

No one should embark on a long voyage or a life afloat without having acquired a minimum competence, which should be got not only by study but also partly by doing some boatwork. It is all very well to plan that the Skipper will sail the boat to all intents and purposes as if singlehanded, and that his chosen crew will be entitled to consider themselves solely for catering and/or decorative purposes. It never turns out that way.

Circumstances will arise when it is a case of 'all hands to the something-or-other' and a certain basic knowledge of somethings-or-other would be no bad idea. Likely areas of difficulty are when berthing, or when others are berthing on you. There are occasions when sails will not do as they should, and no Skipper, however brilliant, can see to both ends of a rope at once. People do fall overboard, even in harbour, especially from dinghies, and things do break or part.

Let us look at a checklist for the absolute novice so that he or she has, at the least, a basis on which experience can build.

WHAT A CREW MEMBER SHOULD KNOW

- Learn the names of important bits of boat or gear, so that you know what the Skipper is talking about especially if he is excited or overwrought. Examples: bows, stern, jib, genoa, mainsail, mizzen, sheets, halyards, topping lift, forward, aft, port and starboard. Know what he means when he says take a turn (or whatever term your own Skipper uses to indicate bringing a rope to a cleat or winch), turn up, make fast, fend off, check or ease sheets, luff or bear away, haul, veer, cast off. Concentrate on the phraseology of your own Skipper: it is more important to have certain and accurate communication than the precisely correct nautical jargon.
- Learn to tie a few nautical knots. We suggest the bowline is very important. Then comes the rolling hitch, the round turn with two

half-hitches, the clove hitch, the sheet bend and the figure of eight. The reef (square) knot may be better than a granny, but it is a bad knot except for tying reef points, and perhaps also for tying two Boy Scouts together.

- Learn well that in boats over 10 tons, on no account try to stop them moving with hands or feet unless you have an amputation impulse. A fender is built for the job and does it very well if you play your part.
- Learn that when boats move towards a quay or each other there will be little or no damage if someone (why not you?) interposes a fat soft object (no, NOT you) so that the impact is absorbed.
- Learn that these fenders can be pre-positioned as a precaution and to save time, but that does not remove the need to see that in the event they are in the right position (ie where the impact takes place) and not too high or low.
- Learn to heave a line. Most yachts in the sizes we are writing about can be controlled by rope light enough to be thrown quite a long distance. Remember to hold on to one end of it. (Oh yes! we've let go both ends in our time.) If berthing, when you have thrown your rope to the quay and some kind soul has made it fast there, adjust your end so that the rope has no slack and take one full turn round the cleat and back it up. There is more to it than this, but that is a basically useful thing to do: if the Skipper wants the rope hauled or veered (tightened or let out), or made fast, he will say so.
- Learn about riding turns. If you should be so unlucky as to make one (a turn that binds and cannot be undone while the strain is on it, and sometimes welds the rope inextricably even when the strain is off) your Captain will ensure that you learn rather quickly what it is, how to avoid it, and never to do it again.
- Learn to steer a compass course. It is not difficult and it gets easier with practice. It is a lovely feeling when you master the art, and on long passages can give the autopilot a rest and prevent seasickness.

When you are able to cope with the above you will be very useful on board if you keep alert and use your loaf. Your typical Able Seaman is no great genius. He has a few basic skills, some basic knowledge but most comes as he sails. A lot of the mystique is pure bullshit.

With even this small amount of knowledge, you would be welcome in all yachts. Such happy beginners are far more use than the theoretical know-all we once had on board, who while on watch and unbeknownst to the Skipper, devised and executed a splendid new lead for the genoa sheet, which carried away the starboard rail when he tested it. He'd been to Evening Classes.

WHAT A WATCHKEEPER SHOULD KNOW

'The saylors are the elder men, for hoising the sailes, haling the bowlings, and stearing the shippe.'

Next step: To be of real use as a trusted watchkeeper, a crew member should know:

- Where everything to do with the sailing is kept, and what it is called.
- How to switch on the engine and use it for simple manoeuvres.
- What the normal reading should be for all dials and meters.
- How to lower and row the dinghy.
- The Rule of the Road at Sea (part B first, then C and D).
- Enough navigation to put a GPS fix on the chart.
- Basic sail and shiphandling.
- How to steer a compass course.
- The first steps to take in several various emergencies (MOB, fire, taking in water, collision, grounding etc).
- How to use the VHF or other radio.
- How to use the GPS to steer a course, and KNOW WHEN IT'S NOT WORKING.
- Use the GPS to key in the Man Overboard Position (MOB).
- How to identify echoes on the radar, switch on the variable bearing marker and read off their ranges on the right scale.

The RYA publish brochures which list recognised sailing schools, with details and prices of the courses run. Go on one, or go to evening classes, there's nothing wrong with them, as long as you regard them as the beginning, and not the end, of your nautical education. You will learn some basics that will help you to understand a very rich craft and words of the vocabulary you will need in this new language.

We now have to recall that the crew and Captain are likely to be members of one family, or friends (long may they be so), and there is a lot to be said for everyone learning everything. In *Freya*, whom we met in the Chesapeake and the Bahamas, the family, with two young daughters, changed tasks daily so they all had their turn at engine bleeding, navigating, cooking and so on. This system might suit you very well. Diffident crew members also appreciate being given an area of personal concern, and time to research and study it. Such areas could be meteorology, cooking and victualling, radio, engines or first aid. The Captain does not have to be the navigator.

Bill and I use the 'specialist and backup' system. He is such a good navigator that it is hard for me to compete; but it would be obviously stupid for me not to know my coastal navigation. In the old days I could take a sun sight and work it out, however slowly and painfully, but satellite navigation has changed all that. Our GPS (Global Positioning System) has taught me so much about navigation

Sometimes all crew are needed on watch – including the ship's cat Bograt.

that I am probably almost as dangerous as someone who has been to two evening classes. I can feed in waypoints, but get Bill to check that I've fed in the right points, with their correct latitude and longitude. It never does any harm for a second person to check these things. As with all computer based programs (but with potentially lethal results if you are driving at sea in earnest and not from 4 Dagmar Terrace), if error goes in, error comes out. Errors at sea can mean rock, wreck and ruin.

I am a far better cook than the Skipper is so I do most of it, but when he has to do it for a while we do not starve. When Bill is upside-down in the engine-room on a rough day at sea I am guiltily aware that I would far rather be steering, cooking, sail trimming and piloting (all at once) plus handing him his tools, tissues and tea, and receiving in exchange bad language, bad temper and blame. The 'dirty bits' of the boat are not for me, unless I am required to wriggle into some small corner that Bill is too big to get into. This gets me the job of packing grease into the shaft tunnel greasebox, and painting inaccessible holes and corners. In fact, I do most of the painting, after Bill has done the preparation. The miserable job of antifouling, so called because it IS foul and most people are Anti (the work, not the paint-scheme), must be shared.

We are well aware that most cruising crews consist of one man and one woman, most of the time. It behoves both of you to be capable. Running a yacht properly requires teamwork of operating theatre calibre.

ΚΑΦΕΟΥΖΕΡΙ
Η ΑΝΑΓΕΝΝΗΣΙΣ
ΒΑΣΙΛΕΟΣΜΠΑΛΗΣ

SYMI (Aegean Sea)

TOLERANCE

Whether your crew is large or small, we will suppose that they have been chosen after a shakedown cruise, and you have weeded out (or selected, according to preference) smokers, vegetarians, flat-earthers and bridge fiends. Even when the crew has been tailored, as it were, to fit, irritating habits should be curbed. In a small space the utmost tact and tolerance is essential. Snoring, nail clippings, washing (either too much or too little), black hole filing systems and food fads are all annoying; make your own nasty little list. If the crew is the basic man/woman one, there should be room for you to sulk (as we do) at opposite ends of the boat till tempers are recovered. At sea, this is hardly necessary, since the days are busy, and we hardly meet at night except to hand over the watch and are usually pleased to see each other by breakfast time.

We have a little rhyme that describes the sort of crew we do not want to take with us. It goes:

> *No no-hopers, no topers,*
> *No one round the bend,*
> *No no-soapers, no gropers,*
> *No windbags (either end).*

Practical opportunities for crewing can be found in the ads of Yachting magazines (be wary), the notice board or journal of most Yacht Clubs, and the Cruising Association's Crewing Service (see Appendix).

CHILDREN AND BABIES

The children we meet who live aboard yachts are almost invariably courteous, at home in any company, pleasant to talk to, willing and reliable. They are integrated with their family in a way that is fast being forgotten when children no longer work alongside their parents at any demanding task; especially against time and the elements. Children in general now do not help with the harvest, mend the nets, help launch the lifeboat, or dig for victory as used to be the case; and so do not share with their parents the satisfaction of a difficult job well done. A sea voyage, however, is something that is achieved by the whole family; and the pride in it shines out of the children's eyes.

On *Maplin Bird*, Cecily and Morgan are a good example, just the children any parents would be proud of, on their way back to England to resume regular schooling after a year's sabbatical. Parents Stephen and Marina explain what the appeal is:

'The ability to choose a different "front garden". As a family we sit down together every meal time, sheer delight in experiencing new places, people and foods. Enjoying the challenge of sailing in spite of the scary bits and our relatively recent introduction to sailing.'

Morgan says:

'I feel the most useful thing I've gained is my confidence with talking to adults. I also like the fact that I'm seeing what's new in the world as well as meeting new people, good and bad.'

Cecily says:

'What I've enjoyed is spending time with Mum and Dad and Morgan every day, enjoying simple activities like badminton, swimming off the boat in warm water in quiet bays where you can see the sea bed through the clear water, and discovering new shops.'

If the child or children accompanying you are of school age, you have to deal with their education. Whether you do this alone, or with help from their teachers, or by correspondence course, you are in for a tough time. In Australia, France and the USA, correspondence courses are quite usual. Ten-year-old Ben Lucas on *Tientos* was working on an Australian course, which needed assistance from his mother Pat. The parents of Grant Dawson on *Iolanthe* had tried both the Calvert system (USA) and the British PNEU course. They preferred the latter as being more of a challenge, though the Calvert system needed no assistance from parents since everything was provided down to the last pencil and rubber and the child could be left to tackle it alone. Most parents prefer to be more actively involved, however, though it costs many hours of work.

One British couple we met had had remarkable co-operation from the state school that their child had attended: a stack of about 20 books was provided and

Special care must be taken when fitting out if you are cruising with children: strong rails and stanchions, netting, secure hatch covers and an eye to fittings that might trap little fingers. Babies are relatively easy to care for on board – until they start crawling.

a syllabus of work covering the next two years – which must have taken some dedicated teacher a lot of time and trouble to prepare.

However you go about it, it is no joke having to cope with lessons when you would rather be swimming; and this is as hard for the supervising parent as it is for the child; if you are temporarily in a yachtie community it can help to run 'the school' on one boat in rotation: the children benefit from interaction and competition even if they are doing different courses, and only one parent need supervise the gang. Mornings are best for the heavy work, while the minds are fresh (you will notice that a good school timetable puts the maths before the first break if they can), leaving the more pleasurable side of things till later. (Who says maths isn't pleasurable, demands Bill, passim.) At sea a single child often misses the company of other children, and plenty of opportunity should be found for mixing, since it is too easy in an adult environment where responsibility is the watchword, for the child to forget how to be a child, and to find difficulty in relating to his own age group when the time comes.

Thank goodness, there is the other side of the coin. Great delight and interest can be found in visits ashore, studying people and places, the local museums, the customs and culture of many lands; and some of the language does not come amiss either. There is also a wealth of sea and shore life: fish, birds, plants, dwellers in rock pools and in sand holes, shells, trees and flowers. Recognition books for all these things should be part of the 'school library'. A scrapbook will find a place for exotic bus tickets, postcards, programmes, labels and so on.

A well-kept log by each child combines many disciplines: writing, drawing, recording things seen, self-expression and observation are only a few of them. A rough notebook would help the preliminary layout of an attractive page. Since such a log will one day be a treasured reminder of the voyage, it would be worth presenting the child with a really important-looking hardcover book, such as are now available with unlined pages and attractive leather-type bindings, to encourage best efforts and the production of something to be immensely proud of.

If you carry a laptop, then CD-Roms for Encyclopaediae and other educational material take very little space, though in our experience they do not tell you a lot about, say, the island of Samos. Think of the effect on children to discover from what they see and hear ashore, and even from brochures at the Tourist Office, they are writing things in their log *that the encyclopaedia does not know*! It goes without saying that computer skills will stand any child in good stead on their return to formal schooling. Computer games that all the family will enjoy might be good in bad weather, but on the whole, shipboard life is too full and busy to need them, or indeed the TV, and it's such a relief to leave them behind.

• *Sea babies* •

Small babies pose few problems at sea. In a basic small yacht with a lack of gear that would raise eyebrows today (the Health and Safety people would have had a fit) my six-month-old required only feeding, a change of nappies (no disposables then) and a safe place to sleep; nothing else. She did not seem to be at all worried by even quite violent motion, and was certainly not seasick: this seems to come with the toddler stage. At times of stress (ours, not hers) we put her in a carry-cot wedged between the two forward bunks where, to our amazement, she learnt to stand up briefly, before sitting down suddenly when we hit a wave.

As for feeding: battling with baby bottles and a Primus on a stormy night is a very good way to get scalded, as I discovered. Bottled milk is not nearly so convenient as draught, especially at sea: I have yet to hear of anyone coming to any grief through breastfeeding. You certainly don't get scalded. Nowadays I should probably use a cold-water method such as Milton for sterilisation of the bottles, and think of a foolproof way of warming the milk.

Baby food, in jars or tins, is widely available in the western Mediterranean, the States and the bigger West Indian islands, but stock up if you are venturing farther, or to Eastern Europe (especially the old Communist bloc).

When my mother took me sailing at six weeks old (a daring thing to do in those days) she put me in a box of bran with a muslin square under me, and tossed out the damp bran as necessary. I have heard of sawdust, sand and seaweed being used in the same way. Kitty Litter is feasible, but a little lumpy, it is great in a bucket for adults when the head gets blocked, but is not available in the wilds. Nowadays we have disposable napkins (diapers to the US cousins) and you would think that washing nappies was a thing of the past. So it is, in many parts of Europe and the USA where disposables are readily available. If you are going to remote places, however, they will be hard to find and even more expensive. They are too bulky to store many on board. Remember that disposal is getting more difficult as marinas and non-tidal basins get more and more fussy about what you throw, drain, drop, discharge, put, pee or spit into the water. You may have to revert to the terrycloth or muslin squares of Grandma's day – at least some of the time.

Mark and Felicity on *Scout* used a mixture of disposables and terry nappies for young Teresa. The terry ones were given a preliminary cleaning by towing astern, a watch being kept for dolphins who enjoy stealing them to play with. The nappies needed a thorough final rinse in fresh water, or terrible chafing and soreness would result. At 18 months, Teresa loved the shipboard life. She was used to being dunked in the water (many yachtie babies can swim at six months) so she had no fear of going underwater, but she could not quite swim yet without her inflatable armbands.

Yachts with small children on board usually reinforce the guardrails with netting, to fill in the gap down to the toerail that a small child might slip through. We had netting on the foredeck of *Fare Well* as we felt it was just as well to stop adults and sails falling through.

It has to be remembered that toddlers are all little Paganinis: great fiddlers. I watched recently, fascinated but unable to intervene, as three-year-old Suzanne on the neighbouring boat unpegged her mother's bikini from the guardrail and, chuckling, dropped it over the far side. We lent them our shrimping net, always handy for such events. Teresa loses tools and other objects by posting them into the rubbish bin. Sea mothers need even sharper eyes than their shore counter-parts, since there are so many knobs, switches, buttons and hand pumps on a yacht; and they cannot all be put out of the reach of an active and curious toddler. I have seen a variety of ingenious devices to protect vital switches: shockcord, wedges, Perspex lids over a whole bank of them: necessity (nay, desperation) is the mother of invention.

In times of activity or crisis, babies are plonked in a safe place. This is essential for parents to get any peace at all. It takes the form of a playpen, or a well-wedged carrycot or 'padded cell'. The best idea, which I have seen many variations of, is the pilot berth transformed into a miniature nursery, well cushioned, with a strong net that snaps in place over the front. The baby comes to consider this as 'his', it is comfortable, full of his soft toys and comfort blankets or pillows, and he seldom objects to being put there for a spell. And even if he wimps a bit, you know he's safe and can be ignored till the rush is over or you have had your siesta. We have recently seen a toddler's car seat firmly fixed in the cockpit with the toddler happily strapped in, part of the family but safe in times of crisis or activity.

Children are people too, and while their skills are yet few they can be helped to feel valuable. They should join in all the activities they are capable of, and be taught the right way to do them. They should be given definite jobs to do, such as care of the fishing gear, teach them how to stick the hooks into a cork for safety. On long passages, they can be asked to read the speedlog or the GPS at intervals and record the result. It can be their job to identify and record birds, fish and sea creatures seen. The tasks must be seen to be genuinely useful or reward-ing, and take them to the limit of their capabilities, so that they are not shrugged off when they are not in the mood: responsibility starts early at sea. It all helps to prevent boredom. (Yes, long passages can be very boring.)

HOW TO BE NAVIGATOR

'The Master is to see to the conning of the shippe.'

Traditionally a man's task, this is changing fast. There is no foundation for believ-ing that women are less numerate than men are: many of us were very badly taught. We can, however, learn. A female navigator is a threat only to very old-fashioned Captains who have forgotten that centuries ago no Captain, usually a moneyed aristocrat, would have been able to *'see to the conning of the shippe'* since that was a well-protected mystery known only to the Master, a mere profes-sional. The wealth of published pilot books, tables and charts that we had when we were young did not exist 300 years ago. Only much later did the job of the Shippe man and the Captain merge, when it was realised that a practical seaman made a better Captain than the aristocrat who knew nothing.

Navigation is a practical skill. The theoretical side can be learned on courses (see the yachting press for ads) and there are also Evening Classes, usually asso-ciated with various Certificates.

To acquire the practical knowledge, there is no substitute for doing it. Like driving, it is a skill that is probably *not* best imparted by one's spouse if peace is to reign. The practical courses at the National Sailing School at Cowes were excellent, what a pity they no longer exist. Similar courses are widely available and ensure that you do not remain an eternal student, without confidence in your convictions, but return with a self-assurance born of knowledge, coupled with a respectful wariness for those who have done it for longer and further.

A good navigator:

- Tries to be always aware of his ship's position in space.
- Is always checking the instruments that tell him where he is.
- Checks his compass daily: in coastal waters against known transits, at sea against the rising or setting of the sun or moon (Amplitudes).
- Will not rest until he has solved the problem if something puzzles him or does not add up; he pays regard to a strong feeling that something is wrong.
- Is rigid about keeping his DR going (DEDuced reckoning, DED not DEAD reckoning) and expects you to do the same when it is your watch. He will be very unhappy if you fib about the course and speed, whether because you nodded off and did not pay attention, or because you would prefer your helming performance to seem rather better than it was.
- Checks his sextant for index error in case someone has fiddled with it.
- Notices and jots down what time the electronic log failed, and remembers to allow for the half hour you spent going round in circles when the jib furling gear jammed.
- Never leaves anything to chance. You do not hear him say 'Yes, I think that's Cape Krio, we can alter course now.' He checks till he knows that it *is* Cape Krio.

Otherwise, you end up like the honeymoon couple we met in the West Indies, who mistook the radio mast on Union Island for that on Mayreau Island, and instead of (as they thought) entering harbour ran their boat on the reef off Carriacou.

The advent of GPS changes little of this: you still have to spot when it's lying, only you now have to be really creative in explaining to the Captain why the boat is in the wrong place after you've been steering for an hour. ('Well, there's a current, isn't there? We've been SET,' doesn't work these days, your cross track error should have told you that.)

Harmony can be maintained at the chart table by not getting ink, coffee and cocoa rings, gravy, chewing gum etc on the charts. Pencils should not be allowed to drop, otherwise the lead breaks at half-inch intervals all the way through, causing terrible anguish as pencils are always sharpened when the Master doesn't know where he is, and the irritation effect is cumulative. In the old days we used to warn you to practise with a cheap plastic sextant, and so you wouldn't be worrying about damaging that gorgeous brass and varnish antique that your spouse was so dotty about, but we rather doubt if anyone learns to use one these days. Avoid using the Navigating notebook for shopping lists, and the dividers for opening tins, and perhaps the Cook's wooden spoon might not get used for stirring bilge paint.

HOW TO BE THE WEATHER-MAN

'It overcasts. We shall have winde, foule weather.'

I don't think it is chauvinistic to say that women are (by my observation) much better at languages than men. It may be that we are more willing to try. Perhaps it is to do with having to make sense of what the very young and the very old are saying to us: we seem to have a greatly enhanced aural perception. That is to say, we can listen to a toothless old biddy in the marketplace speaking a thick dialect in a language we don't understand; then turn to our astonished menfolk and say, 'It's four and a half Filas for a Katlo, and please will we bring the container back.'

This leads to the women getting the job of listening to foreign language weather forecasts, which at times of bad reception sound far worse than the market lady and there are no nods, gestures and mime to assist comprehension. Thus, we get to be the meteorologist, too.

If you have previously studied nothing more weighty, weatherwise, than aching joints portending rain, it is time to find out why you can't break Buys Ballot's Law, why weather systems have fronts but no backs, and why:

> *When in port you choose to stay*
> *The Goddam gale will go away,*
> *But when to sea you choose to go,*
> *The Goddam wind comes on to blow.*

Courses in Meteorology for Yachtsmen in the UK are run mostly in conjunction with the Yachtmaster's Certificate®. They are a subject that can be taken as evening classes (see your Local Education Authority list, which usually comes out in August for classes beginning in September) or as practical weeks or weekends as part of a Cruising School Course, with emphasis on meteorological and practical forecasting according to students' needs, as well as the usual navigation, seamanship etc. UK courses tend to concentrate on UK weather. Conditions can be very different elsewhere.

You can learn by CD-ROM if you have a computer, an excellent one is Meteorology CD in the Tomorrow's Yachtmaster series by PC Maritime, address in Appendix (www.pcmaritime.co.uk).

Since most weather forecasts are read at normal speed, you need shorthand of some kind. While there are international symbols for weather phenomena, they are not adequate even if you know them by heart, and you will need to supplement them with your own. Do not believe the RYA booklet *Weather Forecasts* when it blithely tells you that the international symbols 'will enable you to appreciate at a glance the information which is contained on any weather map which you may see displayed in Clubs or Ports of call'. This applies only to Great Britain. Elsewhere in Europe, the Mediterranean, the West Indies and America (except for some huge and expensive marinas, which rarely concern the cruising yachtie), the weather reports are in words, on teleprinter or standard form in the local language and often the local handwriting. A few years or so ago a very few Port Captains were beginning to post grey-on-grey Weatherfax reproductions, which were so appallingly smudgy and hard to read that they always put the plain word teleprint form up as well. Even in a foreign language, it was easier to read. Both the RYA handbook and various Almanacs have weather vocabularies in several languages, which are very useful. Most weather handbooks explain weather symbols, and tell you how to take down broadcast information, link it to your own observations, and construct and understand weather maps.

• *Radio weather reports* •

Most of the European radio reports are good, and Greek Radio translates them into English after their early morning bulletin. Nowadays radios with an inbuilt recording facility save a lot of trouble, since you can replay the forecast for words you might have missed at first hearing, and worry it out at leisure. Best of all, you don't have to stay up till 1 am or rise yawning in the grey dawn to 'Get the Weather'. You will get used to the orderly progression of the forecast, and the sound of the words in a foreign language, and soon be able to take it down direct.

• *TV weather reports* •

At first sight this is an excellent way of getting the weather, the pictures being easily understood in most languages. Alas, some of them insult our intelligence, and many of the TV weather forecasts in Europe are scanty with information about wind speed and direction, which we sailors are more interested in than the rain belt or the temperature.

Italy used to get the Gold Sou'wester for the best TV weather report in the Med, on RAI Uno (Radiotelevisione Italiana Channel 1), but the senior Airforce chap who did it with proper synoptic charts has been supplanted by pictograms and the usual bimbo standing in front of the map. France (TF1) has a good forecast, after the eight-o-clock news, though the presenter's gimmick is to talk as fast as he can, and that is *fast*.

• *Navtex* •

Nowadays almost every yacht has Navtex for weather and shipping notices, whether the one that prints out and fills the boat with paper, or the one with a miniature screen. We find it useful, not only because I no longer have to get up at an unearthly hour to 'Get the Forecast'. The cheaper Navtex receivers that display on a LCD screen (such as NASA) do not have enough scroll space to take the amount of guff that is put out nowadays. We have limited ours to weather and gale warnings only and still it gets filled and difficult to sort out before it starts overwriting itself. If we left in navwarnings as well, it wouldn't cope with an hour's input, for the US Navy keep broadcasting that they will sink on sight any vessel acting suspiciously *in their opinion*. We get the message. The Americans are specialists in friendly fire. Do not approach.

The only weather services which reach right across the Atlantic in either direction used to be in Morse, now phased out. The *Admiralty List of Radio Signals, Vol. 3* is certainly the most comprehensive book of weather broadcasts in the world, but it is usually out of date by the time it is published and is laid out like a Chinese puzzle.

Big ships are mostly happy to pass the time of day with you in mid-ocean and give you a weather forecast: they get bored on long passages too. Do not expect to see more than two or three ships, big or small, on an entire ocean crossing (unless you stumble across the ARC), and do not try calling up US warships, as we did in mid-Atlantic. At first, they would not even admit that they were there at all, reminding us of a large Newfoundland puppy trying to hide in a daisy patch. Then they told us that the weather forecast was a classified piece of information. After much delay and seeking of permission they gave us a cautious description of the weather we were actually experiencing at the time. The Russian 'trawler' shadowing them was much more helpful. That said, the long-distance cruising yacht is very much on its own and must be self-sufficient.

We act at all times as if there were no such thing as rescue services, which indeed is the case in mid-ocean, unless you are a racing yacht or a media celebrity. We are proud of 30 years of deep-sea cruising with no calls for assistance; if we got into trouble, we coped with our own resources. Judging what the weather was going to do next if you could get no forecast is an important and normal part of that resource.

If you ever need detailed weather forecasting in home waters – if you are looking for a weather 'window' to start a particular voyage for example – you can get expert forecasts tailor-made for your boat, your crew and your voyage, over the period of a month, from the British Meteorological Office at a cost. If you speak good enough French, Météo Consult by telephone in France puts you in touch with the professional forecasters, who will advise you directly.

There are now far too many forecasts which is a change in the right direction because 30 years ago there were not enough. Most of the improvements are receivable via the internet which is much better than Weatherfax.

• *Weather on the NET* •

If you carry a laptop, and are used to the Web, there is a great deal of weather information on the internet. Some websites will be found in the Appendix, but here are some short comments on a few, based on our experience:

- Meteo France's shipping forecast is splendidly bells and whistles.
- The German one (Dusseldorf) is often said to be good but we are not that impressed. It seems to be often out of date and to over-estimate the wind force.
- Lastly the GRIB forecasts. These are received by e-mail and you have to set up the system in advance. They are based on NOAA data and have been 'passed' by Frank Singleton, a retired British metman. The service is highly recommended by RCC members but we have not yet used it. Try www.franksingleton.clara.net.

HOW TO BE COOK

'The cooke is to dresse and deliver out the victual.'

It is a poor cook who is not also a psychologist. This comes fairly easily to most women who, knowing how to cook on shore, have a head start at sea, and therefore get landed (not the most apt word here) with the job. Notwithstanding centuries of professional contempt thrown at the historical sea cook, and the extensive list of rude names for his dishes and his person (Q. who called the cook a ****? A. Who called the **** a cook?), his contribution was vital and his lack of skill often lethal. It is a job of immeasurable importance. Preserving morale in bad weather or other adverse conditions may rest heavily on the cook. 'Fate cannot harm me, I have dined today' said Sidney Smith. There is something unbelievably heartening about hot food and drink, and anyone who can rustle up an appetising one-pan dish in hell-and-high-water conditions is more to be prized than a Cordon Bleu. I've not noticed that men are any better at this than women: I have a strong feeling that it depends sometimes on who is hungriest. But the young male still tends to give cooking a low priority, and will stuff himself with anything that costs him no trouble rather than remembering the welfare of others, as a true cook should. I remember with gritted teeth the wally who was only 'vegetarian' when I was doing the cooking. Left to himself, he couldn't be bothered, and opened tins of corned beef.

Practical help on cooking and victualling will be found in chapter nine, but before you embark be sure to take a few books to help you cope with the odder products of nature. You may not actually have to eviscerate a duck-billed platypus, or lightly kill an armour-plated turtle that is looking you straight in the eye; but you can see the way my mind is working. You may be leaving the fish fingers and pre-packed drumsticks far behind, and encountering unfamiliar fruits and vegetables as well. Asking the market women's advice on how to prepare and cook their produce is very rewarding, if you can understand the replies.

Be sure you learn to make bread, in all its varieties. Fresh hot bread is as good for the spirits as the sight of land after a long voyage.

HOW TO STEER AND KEEP A NIGHT WATCH

*'He that keepes the shippe most from yawing doth commonly use the least
motion with the Helme, and those steare the best.'*

*Bograt finds a captive lap as Laurel takes
her turn at the helm.*

Steering looks so easy. To some people, it is: they fall into the way of it immediately. Others find it hard. They wrestle and wrench the wheel; they oversteer and the ship hunts this way and that like a dog after truffles. The compass confuses them and the watch below groan as the ship's motion deteriorates. These hapless helmsmen chase the lubber's line, spinning the compass card till they are dizzy, and seem to have no tenderness or coaxing in them, to sense the ship's needs. Naval Officers of the Watch of Bill's day had an order to deal with this phenomenon. They bellowed wrathfully down the speaking tube: 'STEER SMALL, BLAST YOU!' (use less rudder).

Fortunately, most of us learn to be at least adequate helmsmen. In bad weather, half an hour may be quite enough at the wheel or tiller. It is hard work; you are likely to be steering because it has become more than the autopilot can cope with, however excellently it can perform in calmer seas (better than most of us, rot it), and your concentration quickly tires. A certain mad exhilaration can set in with a force 7 behind you; you think you are doing very well indeed, like a drunken driver. It took quite a bit of persuasion to pry me loose from the wheel on one such occasion when it could be seen that I was tired, losing control of the ship, and likely to gybe all standing. I was soaking wet, singing loudly, drunk on the weather and indignant when firmly removed. They led me, babbling, below; and quelled me with porridge.

Steering is more than just fooling about with the wheel. Unless told otherwise, the helmsman 'has the con'. This means that he is currently in charge. As well as steering the correct course, he should have an eye to the following:

- Are the sails flapping, or setting correctly? Has the wind or weather changed?
- If the engine is in use, are the revs, the fuel gauge, the oil pressure and temperature all reading normal?

- Other ships in the vicinity, the lights they carry, their probable course, speed and distance away. (Both by eye through open windows if you are in a wheelhouse, as well as the radar.)
- The sea: is it getting rougher, or a swell developing? Is the visibility getting worse?
- Can you see any shore lights or lighthouses?
- Odd noises or smells repay investigation: we have often prevented something dire by due attention to these.
- If the log fails, the time and reading should be logged at once, and thereafter you must estimate the speed as best you can. You will also have to be honest about the course you actually succeeded in steering, however reluctant you might be to admit less than perfection, since the DR (deduced reckoning) depends upon it.
- Check your GPS is really working properly, and if it has lost power, or its satellites, note the time.
- Finally, the ideal watchkeeper will know when to call the Captain for something he really needs to deal with, and when he can be left to sleep.

All this probably seems a lot to pay attention to. It is just as well that it seldom happens all at once, and that a night watch can be a period of great peace or even paralysing boredom. The autopilot takes some of the strain, but conversely if nothing much is happening it can be a good idea to switch it off and steer by hand for half an hour, to keep you on your toes. If there is a moon and stars, and enough wind to carry you gently along: that is dreamstuff, and happens often enough. If you are in a nasty sea left by the last storm and slatting about with no wind, it can be exasperating. To pass the time some mentally write books, some listen to the personal stereo (what a boon this is: no more do the loud-music freaks, whether adherents of Bach or Blur, Shostakovich or Massive Attack, disturb the sleep of the watch below). Bill invents things, plans *coups d'etat* and generally puts the world to rights. I have imaginary conversations with the Great, write poems and songs, which I sing (quietly).

'Steer steady and keep your course so you go well'

It can be a long night.

HOW TO BE A DECKHAND

'The younkers, or common saylors, for furling the sayles, bousing or trising, and taking their turn at the helm.'

If you are a team of two, it pays to do nothing in a hurry. Whether changing sails, or berthing, or any other bit of seamanship, take a little time to think. If you are entering a new harbour, the crew should check through the binoculars where any other yachts are, whether the mooring is likely to be stern-to or alongside, and whether the quay is provided with bollards or rings; or (as sometimes happens in remote Greek islands) a park bench and a lamp post.

It is also important to note where the ferry berths, and whether there is an irate little harbour official blowing a whistle and waving you off your chosen spot because that big freighter that you have only just noticed is coming in there and you are badly in the way. Having avoided these things, and the shallow end where all the little fishing boats are, you now get out what mooring ropes you need and place your fenders where they will do some good. If there are bollards, it is often a good idea to put a good sized bowline in your line before you even throw it, especially if there are no obvious sailors on the quay. Wait till everything is ready, and untangled. There is usually *time*.

This avoids the panicky hurling of tangled ropes at the last minute, which inevitably fall short; we see this happen countless times every summer. Since there is so often a rapt audience, it is nice to do these things well. It is sad to see a headrope thrown towards the shore too soon, so that it stops short and falls in the water. Skippers should not expect a 40-foot line to reach across a 50-foot gap just because they say 'Now!' and deckhands would do well to practise (on a quiet quay out of sight of mockers) coiling and throwing a line that is at least 40 feet long. A good able seaman can throw an unweighted line 80 feet on the level. Bill recalls an AB aboard *HMS Loch Quoich* who threw 109 feet, a record.

A few good practice heaves will kill two birds with one stone (perhaps literally if you use that nasty ferryboat trick of having a weighted monkey's fist at the rope's end). One, you learn to heave the line with your whole arm; and two, you learn to judge the distance. Thus you avoid throwing too soon, and having the line snake out beautifully to its end, only to fall short into the sea; or that movement akin to closing a chest-high filing cabinet that gives the same result, the rope slithers into the (inevitably) oily water and heads like a homing pigeon for the screw. There should be no need, given the necessary forethought, to go through that rib-tickling performance that has all the other yachts in stitches: the last-minute disinterment of what seems to be a doormat knitted in 12mm nylon, heaved despairingly ashore for the dock committee to wipe its feet on, before the entire mat is dragged back into the water by the rapidly receding yacht attached to its other end. To bring the house down, the line has only to catch in the prop as the yacht circles.

Anchoring also stands a bit of secret practice before your public debut. You will still occasionally drop your anchor neatly into the dinghy (thoughtfully brought to the bow as you knew you were going stern-to, and subsequently forgotten) or get the chain caught in the hawse pipe, or fetch up a snarl which jams in the fair-lead. But you will get it right nine times out of ten, and avoid the really calamitous things like failing to make fast the end or, as I did once, pulling an extra metre of chain cable up through the navel pipe, absentmindedly allowing it to slip off the gypsy that controls the links and onto the smooth warping drum. Since there was no longer anything to stop it, I watched aghast as, with a thunderous roar, the entire 45 fathoms of chain cable ran out into deep water. Right to the bitter end. Which fortunately was properly made fast and fetched *Fare Well* up with the sort of jerk you give the lead when your puppy is about to eat something disgusting. Bill achieved new heights, both in jumping up and down and creative language, while we slowly got it all back in again. Note that I did not try to stop it running out, otherwise serious injury could have resulted.

PETS AND PESTS

'Hale the Cat!' – Captain John Smith

Of course he does not mean cat like our Nelson, or any of our subsequent cats. Our egregious Captain, from whom we quote so much, lists the following on a man-o-war in 1627: *the Cat, the Hounds, the Falcon* (a kind of cannon) *the Crab* (a launching device), *the Crow's nest, the Crow's feet, the Fish block, a Goosewing, Hogsheads, Marlin, Ratlines, Monkey, Sheeps' feet, Sheepshanks and Whelps*.

Apart from these, many and various are the living birds and animals we have met at sea. Their company is comforting, not only to singlehanders (who can still end a three-week voyage talking non-stop for hours to the first person they meet) but to any crew who are not averse to animals. People will put up with a lot to have their pets with them; we have known a tiny yacht weighed nose-down with two enormous and beloved dogs, stowed forward like a couple of bower anchors. They had to be rowed ashore every few hours. Their owners got a bigger boat the next year. We met a Dane in Spain who swore he had rowed his dog ashore twice a day all the way from Denmark.

We have met parrots, large and small. Nelson is very fond of birds. So are we, but not to eat. The first parrot we met was a huge scarlet Macaw on the island of Minorca which came up our gangway on its owner's shoulder. On confronting Nelson: black, alert, chops a-slaver, it squawked and committed an indignity on its owner's shirt, and had to be shut in his car in hysterics. That was the start of a great friendship. Moored next to us in Aegina, near Athens, a young circumnavigating family in *Active Light* had a tiny green parrot. Nelson was not hungry, but even a sleepy cat was enough to frighten poor Birdie across the street and onto the awning of the taverna opposite, where she had to be coaxed and climbed for. We met them again in Grenada in the West Indies, where we were all at anchor, and were able to exchange pleasant visits with bird and cat safely apart.

While birds are easy to look after, dogs are a horse of another colour, to mix metaphors. If you are doggy-minded you will take your dog with you and care for it like an extra child: which it will be, not being as self-sufficient as a cat or with the simple needs of a bird. A dog produces large turds, which (unlike the cat) it does not know what to do with. It is theoretically possible to get your dog to use the scuppers, or to home in on a short length of tree attached to a stanchion, or a square of artificial grass. We have heard of all these being tried, with or without tempting bottles of 'Do it here, Doggy' perfume. In the cold real world, however, we observe that all dog owners have to use a shovel and hose the deck down pretty frequently; or row the culprit ashore at intervals that interfere with one's beer-time. Dogs do not like being left. It takes only one of them, howling because its Dad and Mum have gone ashore, to turn a quiet anchorage into Banshee night in the Wolf forest. On the other hand they are a good deterrent for thieves (though our Nelson could be a bit frightening, with the eldritch shriek she used to fend off unwanted toms, and the moonlight glancing off her one eye, an emerald as large as a saucer). At least dogs are Faithful Pals. Cats are anybody's: if you upset them (by hoovering or varnishing, for instance) they go and live with someone else for a few hours, whereas a dog will grin miserably and put up with it.

Cats are better in rough weather, it seems to me. They seem to be like humans as regards seasickness: some are and some are not. We know of one kitten that had to be found a shore home because it was very seasick, but we also know a very large number of contented ship's cats. Till recently, we had one of each kind, one insouciant up to force 5; the other hibernated in the lifeboat the minute the motor went on. As a matter of record, Nelson was with us at sea for ten years and upwards of 40,000 miles, and the recent cats clocked up seven years and 14,000 miles. I have heard that Keeshonds (Dutch barge dogs) were trained to leap ashore with a headrope in their teeth and drop a bight over a bollard. We never managed to get our Keeshond to do this in the days when we took children, dog and all, out for the Sunday cruiser race. Ours was a good dog in a boat, so breeding helps a bit; he kept out of the way and did not moan, and when we were

Our much loved one-eyed cat Nelson took such a liking to this bundled up staysail on a transatlantic passage that we let it lie, unused, until we reached the Azores.

tacking up the narrow rivers of the Broads he would leap ashore on one tack, use a tree, wait until we tacked back again, usually having made only a few yards in two tacks, and jump back on board. He was so much a part of our racing crew that if we crossed the finishing line without him we were threatened with disqualification. For long-term cruising, however, cats take a lot of beating. They are neat in their habits, and when you run out of Kitty Litter, they tolerate sand or pebbles. (This once led to a misunderstanding when a young pebble-trained cat, who was my guest while his people went home for a week or two, decided that my Christmas bowl of walnuts was The Right Place.) They are philosophical about bad weather; an example to humans, in fact. They find the warmest, driest spot on board (on your lap under your oilskin for example, or the airing cupboard, or the lifeboat) and hole up for as long as possible. When it's all over they emerge, all smiles and hungry. Nelson could suspend all bodily functions for about 36 hours when necessary: if only we humans could too. If she had to go and her tray was awash, she would come and tell you so, complaining indignantly until you put it right. Braced, intent and swaying with the ship's motion she then did her housework rather more rapidly than usual, skipping with relief back into her chosen hideout. Sometimes this was her box behind the compass (cats are not magnetic) but sometimes she liked to wriggle well down into some folded canvas; a bundled-up staysail became such a haven for her when on a transatlantic passage that we let it be unused until we reached the Azores.

• *Pet vaccination* •

It used to be a difficult task to get your cat or dog vaccinated against rabies in England. In 1976 at first I was told that it was impossible, but with a little persistence I got a bit higher up the chain of command and asked how, as we were going to sea, to get Nelson vaccinated. 'Oh, a Ship's cat' said the man. 'That's all right.' So Nelson became a Ship's cat and was duly vaccinated. The vaccine was not normally used in Britain because the country, being rabies-free, insisted on 6 months' quarantine for incoming animals, and tests at once revealed if such animals were infected. These tests are much more equivocal on vaccinated animals and uncertainty would have set in. When the inevitable happens and someone smuggles in a rabid cat or dog, or quite likely brings in a horse (yes, *horse*: they are allowed to enter and leave the country freely to go to race meetings, with no rabies quarantine restrictions) – and rabies comes to Britain, the rules will change and vaccination will become normal. So said I in 1985, and by the 1998 edition it seemed we were on the brink of change.

• *Pet passports at last* •

Vaccination against rabies has improved to the state of being trustworthy, as long as the animal is clearly identified by tattooing or microchip, and pet passports are now available in the UK, thanks to the Pet Travel Scheme run by the Department for Environment Food and Rural Affairs (DEFRA). Before you get too excited, however, understand that it is as yet a pilot scheme, and there is no question of fetching up in Falmouth after a round-the-world trip with dog or mog and expecting to get away without quarantine. Not for some years, anyway. A restricted trial is in progress, and could suit you if you go no farther than Europe, and bring the animal back (with required documents) not in your yacht, but by train, air or ferry, and then only to certain designated ports. Installing the microchip and getting ancillary certificates will cost about £150–£200 on the British side. On the French side the appropriate flea and tick certificates are available at the Channel ports, the process costing between €10 to €80.

To qualify for the Pet passport scheme in a nutshell (Pets means cats or dogs, nothing else at present):

- Countries from which your pet may arrive are limited.
- Services on which you may travel are limited.
- Ports of entry that operate the Pets scheme are limited.
- Your pet must be fitted with a microchip.
- Your pet must be vaccinated against rabies, and six months later have a blood test to ensure that the vaccination has succeeded.
- 24 to 48 hours before you enter the UK with your pet, it must have treatment against ticks and tapeworm, with an appropriate certificate.

So you have to think about it in plenty of time, the first stages should be completed before you start your cruise.

There are circumstances in which your pet, if complying mainly with the rules, could get quarantine time reduced. If you require more detailed information look on the official website: www.defra.gov.uk.

In the meantime, the veterinary headquarters of your county should be able to assist you with rabies vaccination if you are leaving Britain for good. Make sure you say it's a ship's cat as this cuts through a lot of red tape.

Up till now, I have for 30 years or more carried documents attesting to vaccination against rabies for any ship's cat or cats on board. No authority in *any* country has ever asked to look at them. In Gibraltar, Nelson was vaccinated willy nilly; British rules then prevailed about bringing in animals, a bit odd considering that any squirrel or fox can trot over the border to or from Spain when it feels like it. Cats and dogs were confined to the yacht. Gibraltar has recently relaxed this rule: now if you are a resident of Europe visiting Gibraltar and your pet has a valid certificate of rabies vaccination dated not less than 28 days before your arrival, and providing you do not arrive from North Africa, it will be allowed ashore.

Malta still has the British regulations. Being an island, it makes some sense. However, they have no quarantine facilities and do not allow your animal even to be confined to the yacht. They used to employ the draconian solution of shooting them. This led to a high rate of pet smuggling in Malta, which defeats the aim of the regulations. I recall a lady who gave both her small dogs sleeping pills to get them into Malta in her yacht. One woke up too soon and was duly destroyed, but she succeeded in smuggling in the other. She was not British, but Brits are not all blameless in this matter either.

• *Pets in the Pacific* •

If you intend to cross the Pacific with pets, on most islands your boat will not be allowed alongside, you will have to anchor off, as pets are not allowed on shore.

• *Rats and mice* •

Cats eat mice and kill rats. Until you have had one of these pests on board you have no idea what good things cats are. We met a yacht in Corfu in a state of siege after one month of Spanish Rat: they could buy only enough food for one day, which had to be kept in the oven, which was the only rat-proof place they had, as it had eaten through clothes, flags, Tupperware, and even teak lockers. They had already tried traps and poison and they were ready to sell their lovely little yacht for a song, rat and all, but they acquired a small cat and had no further trouble.

We have had no cats for a while, and did acquire a rat that got on board while we were away for a month a couple of winters ago. It ate into a great deal in our absence, bags of rice and sugar, the woolly drawer, the knitting basket, it had no trouble getting at certain flours, pasta and cereals that had been stored in thin plastic containers, just chomped a hole in them. I had a miserable week or two cleaning up after it, keeping fresh food in the oven as above, going through every-thing with my specs on, and throwing stuff out. Wouldn't you know the wretch would take a nibble at four different packets of sugar instead of contenting itself with one? I put the uncontaminated stores into the heavy plastic or tin contain-ers with screw-down lids that you can buy in the Med to keep your olives in and laid down pink bait in the rat's floury tracks with murder in my heart to hasten the thing's demise. Not till a native told me 'Oh, rats love that pink stuff, you need the Big Blue Ones.' I hunted down these things, the size of gob stoppers – lay them out one per day, three or four should be enough. It took seven before the chewing and scratching that kept us awake at night stopped. The body was never found.

In some parts of the world, you are still required to sign a document concern-ing the health of any shipboard rats, in case you are carrying the plague. We found one of these in St Thomas's in the Virgin Islands, but rather piquantly rephrased: they wished to know 'if there was any unusual morality among the rates on board' (sic). We were also required to state the health of our rats as we entered Turkish waters in the Bosphorus.

Mice are almost as destructive as rats; it just takes them a little longer to chew through your Tupperware. They are also fond of other varieties of plastics. We once had the saloon lights fused by a mouse that bit through the electric cable.

This was one of Nelson's failures: she went through a phase of posting lizards and beetles down the forward ventilator into the roof space. Once, when she wasn't hungry, she posted a live mouse. It couldn't get out again and the roof space was only an inch or so high: too small to feed the cat into it.

Calling Nelson many unpopular names, we removed a panel and tried some Italian Mouse Glue, a substance that you spread on a piece of card which you then lay in the mouse's path. You then sit back and wait, hoping that the mouse is stupid enough to walk across it and stick. After some days the stuff slumped off the card and began to drip down the cabin wall. The regular scrotch, scrotch, of chewing mouse went on. We took the panel off again and threw the card, now dusty and ineffective, away. The drips down the wall remained sticky for weeks and appeared to have no solvent known to man. I was relieved when the mouse, tiring of polyfoam, bit through the electric cable and fried itself.

This one shameful incident apart, however, Nelson was all that one could hope for: she never allowed a wharf rat on board unless she personally accompanied it. Some people, especially in the States, have neat-looking metal ratguards on all their mooring lines, usually an aluminium disc about 30cm across. Sorry, but to circumvent a determined rat, they should be at least a metre in diameter. It is hard to find stowage for four or five of those. I prefer a ratguard that purrs. The purr of a cat is also a great tranquilliser, and has no side effects.

• *Insects* •

Sooner or later you will have insect trouble: flies in the galley or midges round the barbecue.

Mosquitoes
In a few places, the mosquitoes are large enough to make life a misery. You will know where, because you will notice on shore the screened verandas, and the eerie blue light and sudden sputter of the electric bug frier. A very promising party of ours in Calabria broke up in disorder when, at dusk, swarms of mosquitoes drove us below decks. An hour later they were all gone, and we were able to reassemble.

On entering the Intra-Coastal Waterway in America, we asked the advice of a weathered waterman about mosquito screens. 'Well,' he drawled, 'ya might put one on yo door there; but our mosquitoes are too big for yo windas.' As we did the trip in winter and spring, mosquitoes were absent and we had no trouble.

Where mosquitoes abound we have tried anti-mosquito candles, and nearly burnt the boat. We have tried Off and Autan and Oil of Lemongrass; Boots' Jungle Formula has been highly recommended. The bugs don't come near you but nor do your friends. A vicious little breed of mosquito is found in the Eastern Mediterranean. We went ashore to have a barbecue and noticed what appeared to be a shepherd's bed in the branches of a tree, about 2 metres off the ground. While our supper cooked we made many jokes about savage beasts that couldn't climb trees (we couldn't think of many), and became more and more uneasy as the sun set. Then, in the space of about one minute, we learnt the reason for the tree bed: we were set upon by millions of tiny but savage little beasts, kinky about ankles, none attacking above the knee. After the quickest clean-up and evacuation ever, we rowed back out to *Fare Well*, our tingling ankles peppered with bites as close together as the dots on a smocking transfer.

One gadget that seems to work in a small space is the mini electrical hotplate on which venomous pastilles are warmed till they give off fumes noxious to insects. The warmer did not suit our electrical system, so Bill contrived one in a Kit-e-Kat tin which worked well. Then *White Whisper* told us of their simple and effective solution: put the pastille on some copper gauze above the oil lamp. Turned down to the absolute minimum, it makes the pastille fume nicely.

There is a pocket battery device which is said to scare bugs away with ultra-sound. I used to worry about people who carry vibrating objects in their pockets but now we have mobile phones.

If you are in an area where malaria is rife, then take no chances and sleep under a mosquito net. This at least does not smell, cause fires, or make your friends look at you oddly.

We are collecting more and more evidence that shows that taking tablets of Brewer's Yeast alters the taste of your blood to the point where mosquitoes cease to bite you. Though presumably each mosquito needs its own test bite.

Cockroaches

When we built the boat, we wrote to Shell asking them to recommend a long-term insecticide. We sprayed two coats of it on the foam that covered the interior of the steel hull, on top of the fire-retarding paint and inside the linings where no one was likely to touch it. It was obviously lethal, as it kept *Fare Well* insect-free for six years. Not until we were coming back from the West Indies did we finally 'catch' cockroaches: not (luckily) the 'Mahogany Mice' of the Caribbean but a smaller breed.

We took steps. Nelson ate some (they were crunchy). I took out the loose Formica linings from the galley drawers and sprayed them with Baygon (the Greek anti-katsarida kind which bears very little relation to the lily-livered stuff of the same name which is all they will allow you to have in the Western Med).

As a precaution, I had bought in the USA a trap called a Roach Motel, and I dug it out for use. It was well named: it seemed to invite them in for a hamburger and a night's sleep, and then let them go with me picking up the bill for their entertainment, which was not cheap as I had bought two of them. I found only one cockroach in it, and that was slightly bent as if Nelson had chewed it a bit and it had gone in there for a dry Martini and counselling.

When we came to the conversion of *Hosanna* ten years later, we found that the attitude to insecticides had greened and hardened, it was very difficult to get a long-term insecticide. Some of them (Dioxin and DDT) have been completely banned, and the use of the remainder is restricted to industry, who are supposed

CLOCKWISE FROM RIGHT:

- Bill in safety harness after a trip up the mast during a Transatlantic crossing.
- An aerial view of *Fare Well* and some of our family in the Ionian islands.
- Our mark at Horta, in the Azores. It is the custom for visiting yachts (all of whom have sailed 600 miles or more to get there) to paint their name on the breakwater. Hundreds of yachts have left their mark over the years.
- A Transatlantic sail-change.

FARE WELL

1983   1986

Laurel and Bill Cooper

Fare Well (LEFT) ends another Transat at Portimao, Portugal.
ABOVE LEFT AND RIGHT: Nelson relaxes off watch. On watch, Nelson oversees the Captain.
BELOW: Enjoying a 'pot luck' supper night whilst wintering in Levkas, Greece.

RIGHT: Laurel sketches at Port Leone in the Ionian.

Hosanna in Angistri, Greece (BELOW). We were only a few miles from Athens but all alone. INSET: *Hosanna*'s spacious saloon.

LEFT: Marketing in Corfu Old Town.
Laurel (ABOVE) sailing the dinghy in Abelaki
Bay, Meganisi.

CLOCKWISE FROM ABOVE:

- Teamwork: 14 yachtsmen, wintering at Levkas, help to shift the mast of *Aqua Domus*.
- Bill in *Hosanna*'s roomy, well-equipped wheelhouse.
- A fine winter's day in Levkas sees Laurel painting.
- Characteristic live-aboard clutter on the Swedish yacht *La Vie de Råå*, Liyia.
- *Råå*'s wide bowsprit makes for safe and easy boarding and anchor work. This boat is well designed for Mediterranean living.
- *Fare Well* sailing in the Balearics.

ABOVE: Skyport marina on the East River, New York.
RIGHT: Bill and Laurel on board *Hosanna* in Levkas, Greece.
BELOW: *Fare Well* wintering in Caper Island anchorage on the Intracoastal Waterway, USA. Whilst anchored here, we harvested a feast of oysters.

to be more responsible about the use of such dangerous substances than we poor mortals with only our cats and our children to think about. (Since industry has given us the blessings of BSE and antibiotic resistant bacteria, it makes you wonder.) It required great persistence then to get a killer insecticide, and now in the 21st century will, we think, be impossible. It will be necessary to use physical prevention (traps, cats, netting, smoke candles and pastilles and creams), and the watered down sprays with biokindly propellant that are all you can get now. We must consider keeping insect-eating pets, chameleons perhaps, or a cuddly little toad. Encourage spiders.

Stop press: the increase of malaria since these substances were banned is now so terrifying that DDT is being allowed back in Africa to fight it. Well, well. At last the Green Loonies are on the retreat!

We tried a secret anti-cockroach mixture imparted to us by the German skipper of a charter yacht, alongside whom we had berthed in St Lucia.

'Haf you cockroaches?' he asked us. 'No,' we said proudly. 'Now I am alongside you vil haf,' he said, and gave us his recipe, Jorge's Revenge: sweetened condensed milk and powdered boric acid. (Now wash your hands please.) The cockroaches yaffle the mixture, and the boric acid concretes up their insides till it's like treading on plum stones. (No, don't try it as a remedy for the runs. It is cumulative and dangerous, so prevent the puss from eating doctored cockroaches.) I found that Jorge's mixture dried solid and was ineffective after a few days, so I mixed icing sugar with it instead. Hal Roth in *After 50,000 Miles* quotes entomologists at the University of California as saying that any additives to the boric acid are unnecessary and counter-effective. Well, my mixture, put in a flat tin and wedged where children and cats couldn't get at it, must have got up the cockroaches' noses and choked them. Something worked, we have no cockroaches at present.

It must be the size and obviousness of cockroaches which upset people and cause a disproportionate amount of hysteria, since in fact they are not known to be the carriers of any disease.

Flies

These are infinitely more dangerous, but do not cause the same reaction. A fly alighting on the table to lick up a beer spill elicits a half-hearted wave of the hand, instead of the panic and recourse to major artillery in the shape of slippers, pilot books and even winch handles that characterises the appearance of a cockroach. And yet, friends:

> *The fly that on your bread has wiped its feet,*
> *Has also been and wiped them on the meat.*
> *But worse than that, this morning (for a treat)*
> *It trod in something nasty in the street.*

Whether buzzing round the galley, or groggily dive-bombing your nose in the bunk, they have got to go. I keep the galley noticeably cleaner in warm weather to discourage them, covering any exposed food or fruit and leaving no water in the sink (flies too have to drink). We have a fly swat, disgusting but non-pollutant. We also have a flyshooter, a perforated disk attached to a plastic pistol which gives visitors endless harmless amusement and even kills a few flies. If desperate, we use an aerosol spray. No need to gun down individual flies: this is total war. Shut the windows, spray the area and go up on deck for a while. Then come back when it's all over, like the politicians. As the sprays get more and more useless (like the politicians) fly papers are in the British shops again, I notice – I bought some at once. In Greece, every household keeps a pot of basil to keep the flies away. This is the little-leafed basil, not the one with large leaves grown in Italy to go with tomatoes. The Greeks tuck a sprig behind one ear or carry some in their hands; you will see the pots on their caiques and yachts as well, to brush a hand across and release the aroma.

Wasps

These arrive in September unless you are well out to sea and stay there. This leads to breaks in the conversation while you or your guests perform Kung Fu, ending with a wham on the table that makes the glasses rattle. Eating on the poop becomes a little less than perfect, and bare feet are inadvisable as wasps are dying all over the deck.

You can rig up a diversion in the shape of a tin containing enough soda pop, Sprite, or 7-Up for them to drown in: they seem very fond of it, but there will still be a few left to zzzz round the salad. After one especially efficient attack with the fly swat we watched the stretcher-bearers arrive in the shape of hornets, come to carry away the dead. One tried to carry two corpses at once and ditched slowly into the sea, like a crippled Lancaster with two bombs slung under it. It made nearly as much noise, too. The less ambitious hornets cleared our decks of dead and dying wasps in no time at all.

Ticks

We knew a yacht that took on board a pathetic little Greek kitten, only to find that it was infested with pathetic little Greek ticks. Their bedding burst forth from below like spinnakers on the downwind run, and clothing bloomed in the rigging, scented with pyrethrum. I've seldom seen a gayer sight, even at Carnival. Frying ticks with a cigarette end is nauseating but effective. You can also use ether on cotton wool, but mind you don't anaesthetise the pet, or yourself. I found a tick on my neck once in the French canals, it took a lot of ether on cotton wool before I could persuade it to drop off, by which time I was as tight as the tick.

Food invaders

Pests that come into the boat on fruit and vegetables, apart from those already dealt with above, can be reduced by discarding all cardboard boxes on the quay. Salt in the washing water deals with slugs and caterpillars (always make the fussiest person on board responsible for the chore of washing fruit and salads, and see that they wear their glasses).

Weevils are rare in well-packaged goods these days, but they will occur in the West Indies and the Mediterranean when buying pulses, cereals or rice from the sack or in paper bags. If you can put the stuff in somebody's deep freeze for twenty-four hours, in a plastic bag, this will kill any eggs, and you can then transfer it to beetle-proof containers. Watch things like instant mashed potato and dry dog and cat food, which are very prone to attack. If you find a few beetles in something, you need not throw it out as they are not in themselves harmful; but never add coarsely ground black pepper to your risotto until you are sure there are no weevils in the rice: they look too similar. If there are more than a few it becomes psychologically unappetising and is better thrown away.

• *Other pests* •

Worms

In the early days of 'abroad', when we were in our teens, both Bill and I caught roundworms, Bill from a Spanish paella and I in Morocco from heaven knows what. This caused a lot of excitement; passing a creature about 9 inches long and quite firm in texture is a startling event. My doctor reverted to alchemy and prescribed extract of male fernseed. It was not surprising, therefore, that I tried to find some remedies to take with me before we left on the Great Cruise.

When the chemist came out of his little white stillroom to find out what hophead was buying 12 packets each of Stugeron and Kwells, and decided that maybe this little sailing woman was not hooked on seasick pills, I began to ask him about worms. He backed off and disclaimed all knowledge. Fortunately, in 30 years of cruising, not all of it in civilised places, we have not had occasion to use any remedy, but see below.

All the baby books mention threadworms, but not the round or tape variety, which in Britain seem to attack only dogs and cats. It is easy to get multi-worm tablets for your pets, and you should take some, as infestations are often picked up on shore. Roundworm eggs are carried on fruit and vegetables, and tapeworm eggs in undercooked meat. The eggs are not visible to the eye, but heat kills both types. Since we do not like to forgo our salads and raw fruit, we wash them well, in water (you can use clean sea water) with a little potassium permanganate (a few crystals, enough to pinken the water). Since these days one does not know what chemicals it has been sprayed with, I'm even more thorough about washing raw food.

There is no great cause for panic if you do acquire one of the above internal guests, as those mentioned are more upsetting than harmful, unlike hookworm and other tropical murderers. For remedies see Chapter 16.

Wet-bikes

A new pest has appeared since we first wrote. It is very dangerous to swimmers and wildlife, aggressive, and extremely noisy, shattering the peace of anchorages wherever it appears. It goes under the generic name of a wet-bike, can be ridden uninsured and unrestricted by anyone of any age and at 60mph. At present there is no remedy that will not land you in gaol, but the *Sunday Times* ran a campaign for safe waters which includes a ban on wet-bikes. If you are a wet-bike fan, roar about where there is already high ambient noise, so you will be seen and not heard.

> *Anchored in a quiet bay.*
>   *Watching birds and fish at play*
> *Hush of evening rent asunder*
>   *Wet-bike whines, a chainsaw thunder*
> *Decibels near ultra-sonic*
>   *Overturn our gin and tonic*
> *Yell aloud and shake your fist – I'll*
>   *Go below and fetch the pistol.*

Monkeys

We were berthed close to a rather theatrical family in a small yacht in Sicily. They had two young children, and two monkeys. They were bad-tempered, noisy and ill disciplined. (The children, however, were charming.) The parents ego-tripped up and down the quay with the monkeys on a lead, getting lots of attention. Nelson watched from her top-of-the-gangway sentry post, with distaste. Next day the parents were bored with their pets and sent the children to walk the monkeys. They got a little too far from their boat and were cut off by a large friendly dog, who barked at them playfully. The monkeys' reaction was instantaneous: with shrieks they shot up to the children's heads, where they loosed their bowels ready for further flight. For the next hour the dock committee watched with suppressed glee as the parents, tight-lipped and grim of mien, scrubbed their hapless children under the dockside hose with magnums of shampoo.

Other people's unwanted pets, whether roaming toms after your maiden moggie's virtue or those rangy pooches who seem to be able to pee for half an hour on your freshly washed mooring ropes, are discouraged by the handgun in the form of a water pistol, or (the heavier artillery) a Squeezy bottle of water, if possible iced, directed at the active member.

I'm told that goldfish get seasick.

8 • Maintenance and Repairs

'. . . Decayed by weeds or Barnacles . . . which will eat thorow all the planks if she be not sheathed.'

There is a class of yachtsman who says 'Get it fixed', and Lo! it is fixed, and he signs a cheque. He is usually one of the racing fleet, or he keeps his boat on the Riviera. He is unlikely to be a dedicated live-aboard for we are fairly firmly in the do-it-yourself class. Nevertheless, at either end of the economic scale there are those who occasionally employ a little casual help, or who actually provide that help. There is no difference in their respective social status because none of us has any social status. That is left behind as you plot your departure fix. We give and accept help and advice to and from each other with no embarrassment but acknowledge that this can be of a measure that some recompense is appropriate. In any case we are all watching pennies to a greater or lesser extent.

Once we would winter in primitive places where life was cheap and relaxed. Our boats, often self-built or self-amended, could be maintained by ourselves with primitive, on-board means. Often it was difficult to get hauled out or to get technical support. Sadly (in a way), this is no longer the case. There are now many more marinas than there were, and the number of live-aboards has increased and, as we have discussed earlier, more and more are living in production boats. The modern production boat, lightly built with fin and skeg, does not lend itself to rough handling over a shingle beach. Marinas have travel-lifts and nowadays more people organise their annual refit on a marina hardstanding. Also, modern production boats often require specialist work and it is in or around marinas where people claiming to be craftsmen can be found. It is all more expensive than it used to be, but we all seem to want a higher standard of everything and it has to be paid for. With most equipment now based on 'do not repair, fit the spare', you have to be where the spares can be obtained.

We want to consider how the live-aboard can minimise expense and problems by appropriate action before starting out.

SPARS, SAIL AND RIGGING

First, a story. We met a modern yacht that had been dismasted off the Canary Islands. They were still there ten months after their mishap, waiting for a replacement aluminium spar. By contrast, an old schooner discovered rot in the heel of the foremast while cruising Turkish waters. A new heel was scarphed in ten days, the labour cost then being around one pound per hour.

Now, new masts are not needed that often and one may cruise a lifetime without the necessity, but those stories illustrate a general rather than a particular point. Sooner or later repairs will be necessary to something, and if those repairs can be effected from local resources, then one gets sailing again cheaper and sooner. The lesson applies, though with less force, even when cruising to sophisticated countries where certain basic standards differ. For example, electrical replacements following our lightning strike in the USA were more difficult and expensive to obtain because our equipment was 24 volt, which is not common over there.

A good solid spar can be got almost anywhere trees grow, except in sophisticated countries. I have heard of an impecunious French owner who stole a telegraph pole for the purpose; though this displays initiative, it is not likely to enhance the reputation of yachtsmen. In the port of Gravelines, there are some most attractive, tall, tapering aluminium lamp standards. Mmmm!

Going together with a wooden mast will probably be a lower sail plan, cheaper galvanised wire rigging, and cheaper sails. Some people chop and change their sailmaker, looking for an advantage here, or a bargain there. My family have used Jeckells for several generations, and though we might get a sail that is less than perfect on rare occasions, I do get excellent service. This would probably apply to a regular customer of any other old firm such as Cranfields. For cruising, one does not need 'state of the art' sails. A good heavy-weight cruising sail, if protected from the sun when not in use, should last ten years.

That does not apply so surely to roller jibs, which somehow seem to get more unfair wear. Sacrificial strips along leech and foot are a nuisance. I designed our

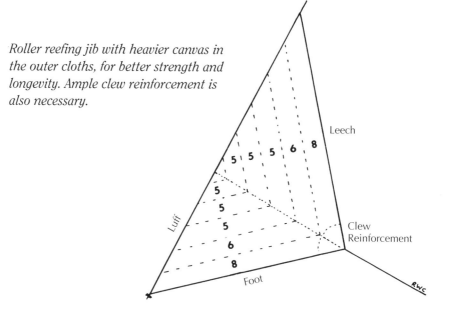

Roller reefing jib with heavier canvas in the outer cloths, for better strength and longevity. Ample clew reinforcement is also necessary.

No, Bill is not on his knees scrubbing the pontoon, he is sail-cleaning at Sibari, Calabria.

replacement genoa to be mitre cut with the cloths parallel to leech and foot, and with the outer cloths of stronger material (see illustration). I have always found cloth to be stronger lengthwise, and old smacksmen knew this too, for it is the way they cut their 'tow foresails', which were the forerunners of the modern genoas. If the leech or foot deteriorates in the sun, it is comparatively easy to replace the affected parts.

Do not leave jibs rolled up when out of use for a long time or over winter. This is a common practice to be observed in marinas and a temptation with roller headsail gear.

Generally, sail and rigging maintenance is a continual process, mainly because it is one of the more pleasant chores. But once a year at least all sail seams should be checked, because they are the weak points. We have a modern Singer sewing machine capable of zigzag stitching, but it will not sew several layers of heavy cloth very well. Neither will our friend's Reads, which is sold as a sailmaking machine. I have a deep feeling that an old-fashioned hand-driven Singer would be best. Sew one's 'homeward-bounders' (temporary repairs) in straight stitches (we have been known to glue a patch on) and later get the job re-done professionally.

PAINT AND PROTECTION

If one is living aboard and cruising continuously it is sometimes easy to overlook passing time and the need for annual checks. In the Med these are done over the winter, but even then you have to allow for quite a bit of bad weather when work is impossible or inconvenient. In the Ionian it rains a lot in winter. At Bodrum, we had gales and even snow. One winter at Rome we had snow on several occasions and even ice on the deck. Painting in these conditions is not really a good idea.

Painting is important in a yacht. I have a feeling that a lot of fibre-glass boats could have done with it from time to time, but for wood or steel it becomes essential. We try to keep a little paint in a small glass jar to touch up instantly any damage, and some is bound to happen. This way the annual chore, for that is what it is, is eased. GRP boats should have two-part filler and gelcoat on board. The big paint job is so purgatorial that it has to be carefully planned. Part of it will be on the slip or hard, but upperworks can be done afloat, though we were dismayed in Porto Xeli in Greece to be arrested by the Port Police for painting our guardrails. As a Greek boat nearby was doing the same thing, it was clearly a bit of xenophobia, and vigorous argument solved the problem.

The chief purgatory is the preparation. Whether sanding, wire-brushing, descaling or whatever, bits fly about and doors and hatches left open to receive the debris soon leads to marital disharmony. With sand-blasting it is even worse, and it is evident that when doing messy work, you should respect your neighbours.

Glass Reinforced Plastic (Polyester)

Once the topsides had been given a fresh coat of paint, Laurel got busy repainting Fare Well's *name on her stern.*

I am going to interject a word on behalf of the mate here. It is necessary to work hard and long at this chore to get it over sooner, and if 'sir' expects 'madam' also to do a full ten-hour day with sander or brush, then it is unfair to expect her to cook the evening meal afterwards. If you don't share the cooking, we see as essential to the cost of the exercise having baths and a dinner, however simple, at a local hostelry each evening. This does not cost a lot in places where the live-aboards foregather.

Preparation, somehow or other, is the key. I have been concerned with painting steel ships for a lot of my life and have become disenchanted with paint companies. Apart from doing the job under laboratory conditions, the paint industry has made no real advance in protecting steel at sea since the First World War. Apart from the initial paint job, applied under ideal conditions, the chipping hammer, red lead and oil paint routine I knew when I first went to sea lasted just as well as the latest advice and products of the industry from a maintenance aspect.

I really want to emphasise that paint companies make paint for use only in ideal conditions, and write their specifications sitting in an office. All too often conditions at the sharp end of life involve a worsening weather forecast and an obligation to be off the slip by tomorrow, inevitably leading to the decision to slap it on and hope for the best. Nobody makes paint for the real sailing world.

With *Hosanna* (a steel boat), chlorinated rubber paints have been successful. Their remarkably short overcoating time, 15 minutes in a Mediterranean summer, means the job can be done quickly, largely overcoming weather changing problems. You would not call it a 'super yacht finish', though it is effective enough. It does not fully cure in 15 minutes, of course, but it is touch dry, reasonably stable, and can be overcoated.

We suspected the Greens of trying to get this paint banned, but on this occasion we apparently maligned them. It has not been banned, however, but most paint companies no longer manufacture it. Apparently it is carcinogenic, not to the customers who would get comparatively little exposure to its dangers, but to their staff who have to make and can it. Fair enough! It is now difficult to find. There is a fairly good substitute available.

Varnish is not compatible with our existence, at least not on the upper deck. Beautiful Italian yachts gleam from the attentions of vast crews of nautical char-women (this is how they solve their unemployment problem; they are all cleaning the rich men's yachts). Sometimes one has pangs of envy and this leads to a token bit of varnish in the cockpit, but it is not really a practical affair in hot sun. So-called ultra-violet screening is hopeful rather than effective.

Antifouling becomes a problem as you move from one area to another. Do not fall for International Paints' sales pitch that their paints are available world-wide. While I think their paints sold in Britain are good, and paints with the International label are found elsewhere, they are not to the same specification in every country, different rules apply and one can come badly unstuck (and so can the paint). In the USA they print a full analysis of the paint on the tin, and this is very helpful. One wonders why there is no obligation to state the same valuable information in other countries.

Since the ban on Tri-butyl-tin (TBT) antifoulings for pleasure craft has become virtually worldwide, owners of steel boats are in a fix. Paint companies are now advising us to use products they previously said were totally unsuitable! We do not have an answer, except that a boat over 25 metres is exempt from the ban. Considering how few small steel and aluminium boats there are, exemption for existing boats could have been sought (a sort of grandfather clause) if the RYA had been alert to the problem. In 1993 in various Greek ports there was a flourishing black market in merchant ship antifouling, to be delivered after dark. Presumably it had fallen off the backs of lorries. We have heard that some countries, notably the Netherlands, have banned ALL forms of antifouling on pleasure boats. Of course we do not want to poison the water, but evidence that antifouling causes poisoning in any but busy closed port areas is not convincing.

HAULING OUT

The place where you haul out needs selecting with some care. In general, the more primitive the equipment the more it costs, an example where sophistication seems to have its benefits for the yachtie. There are far more marinas in the western Med than the east, and hauling out in the west does seem to be cheaper. More marinas are planned for Greece and Turkey, so this differential may disappear. It is difficult to envisage more marinas in the western Med which seems already to consist of one gigantic marina running from Gibraltar to Messina, interspersed with small sandy bits of beach.

Yachts with a long straight keel can be hauled out on the old-fashioned ways, or on a proper marine railway. We have been out on the municipal slip at Barcelona, and at the de Gasperi yard at Porto Santo Stefano (surely one of the best yards in the world, now under different management but still excellent). At both of these the care and competence were of the very highest. We came out on an old cradle over a shingle beach at Erol Ayan's yard near Bodrum in Turkey, one of the high experiences of our lives; a wonderful place, but the whole thing was hair-raising and not at all cheap. We have recently done the same thing at Nidri in the Ionian Sea.

In the Western Hemisphere, we hauled out at Hazzard's slipway in Georgetown, South Carolina, a lovely family boatyard and cheaper than Greece or Turkey. We had planned to haul again, but found that the high cost of antifouling paint made it pay to wait until we got to Spain. I found the lift operators at the Club Nautico in Palma and also at Trehard's in Antibes to be good, and at both places the charges were reasonable. Facilities are not good in the West Indies. There is a slip at Grenada and another at English Harbour; there may well be others, but I did not see them at that time. There is, however, a 3-foot tide in some parts and it is possible to do something of a job between tides. The big problem there is the long grass-like weed that grows close to the waterline, but it is no great chore to drop over the side and remove it every few weeks. I found a home-made scraper like a butter pat made out of 6 mm ply very effective. You can do the same thing between tides round the coast of Britain and elsewhere, but the water is pretty cold.

In the USA, travel-lifts are frequent, though as most Americans own boats of a similar size to those in northern Europe, most lifts have a maximum load of 20 tons (bigger ones do exist). Some American yards tolerate DIY, though most of them demand that you buy paint through them. In most of the Med DIY is considered normal, but this is changing at the more up-market marinas in the western Med. In Turkey, labour was so cheap that I employed jobbing painters who worked very hard but used about 30% more paint than I did. Conditions are changing in Turkey; the marinas are now well-equipped.

Keep a few photographs of the yacht's underwater profile and section to help lift and slipway operators. They cannot always read lines drawings, though in a good yard these are a help when slipping. Clearly mark the strength bulkheads on the hull. If you do not want a permanent mark, identify them with chalk or tape when necessary, so that props and shores are wedged into the right places underneath. It is a good thing to mark the gunwale permanently with the positions of the log impeller and any other sensitive device or projection. There is no reason why a steel boat cannot have lifting eyes welded to the gunwales, then you can dispense with slings which often scrape off quite a lot of the paint that you have laboured so hard to put on. Do NOT use oil drums to shore up the boat. Oil drums have two expansion ridges round each drum so that, when full, the contents can

Hosanna *out on the slip at Nidri, Greece, for a much-needed bottom clean.*

expand or contract without bursting the drum. When the drum is compressed, these give a little. A high wind can cause the yacht to lean on one side more than the other, the drums move, the wedges fall out and over goes the yacht. The photo on page 43 shows a flotilla fleet that had been shored on oil drums. They were the only ones to go over in this particular storm: about force 10. Also check that shores are on firm ground so that the load is spread, and that they are up against bulkheads or stringers. If against unsupported shell plating, the shell can flex, the shore will loosen and the yacht gets a dent.

REPAIRS AND FAILURES

Quality of repairs varies enormously from place to place. The more primitive the place the more ready are the local craftsmen to undertake anything, usually with tolerable results. You do not buy spare parts, you have them made at half the price. It is only when you rediscover the village blacksmith that you see what Western sophistication has lost: the Mr Fixit, par excellence. In the West Indies, however, the development and education of the local people is such that there are very few local craftsmen. Exceptions occur: there are some good wooden boat-builders at Bequia, and they get some good wood up from South America.

Nowadays, one can find most repair and service skills available throughout the Med. Do bear in mind that repairability is an important factor in choice of boat. Insurance underwriters ought to take more note of the repairability of the craft they insure, bearing in mind that the majority of claims are for damage rather than total loss.

If one tried, one could have a very pleasant Mediterranean boat that would reduce or cut out a lot of the payments the owner has to make to others. She would have shoal draught, a reinforced cutaway stem and a powerful stream anchor. She would avoid marinas: just drop anchor and put her bows to the beach, and rig the passarella over the bows. Have four 5-ton screw jacks vertically in tubes through the hull next to the bulkheads and at refit time choose your weather carefully and just jack her up clear of the water. I would not think the installation would cost more than a couple of haulouts, and from then it would pay for itself. Simple strong masts, simple strong rigging, lead to easy repairs. Have basic electronics and electrics only. (Electric navigation lights are essential: no others are remotely adequate. Electric engine starting is also desirable. And see the chapter on navigation.)

We find it convenient to fix (temporarily) sail repairs of seams with strong parcel tape and then to sew over the taped seams. This makes the job much easier, the stitching perforates the tape, making it simple to rip off afterwards. We have also had success with a temporary repair by glueing a patch on both sides with Evostik contact adhesive.

If travelling far afield, take plenty of spare cordage. Not only is it a consumable item that must be replaced, but it is also an attractive commodity in less prosperous communities; the theft of all of a yacht's running rigging is by no means unknown and one should be able to replace the more vital items at least.

Always use anhydrous lanolin for greasing shackles, rigging screws and other deck fittings. It is not only more waterproof than grease, it does not wash off easily, and it is cheaper and less messy. After all, you do not come across sheep that are full of water. Never use graphite grease in a steel or aluminium ship's fittings because it can produce local galvanic corrosion problems.

MAINTENANCE REMINDERS AND THE LOG

As a logbook we use an A5 page-to-a-day diary. Those sold by High Street stationers are often glued together and do not last too well, but on the Continent it is possible to get old-fashioned sewn and bound diaries. (These will have the added advantage of giving Mediterranean holidays, and local phone numbers, but will omit the metric conversion tables.)

These diaries or logs become also maintenance reminders. Insert items that are time-critical on their expected days. Normally it will be highly inconvenient to do that job when the day comes round, and when the page is turned, the job gets forgotten. This likelihood can be reduced (though not eliminated) by having a cardboard bookmark. When an item crops up which cannot be done at once it is added to the list on the bookmark, eventually to be crossed off when done. I have a very large bookmark.

If you have no engine hour meter, then whenever you use engine or generator note the time run in the log and keep a cumulative total. I record it only to the nearest half-hour, trying to be consistent about rounding up or down as appropriate.

Even in the tropics, use antifreeze in the cooling water because it has good corrosion inhibiting properties though it can be understandably hard to find in hot climates.

Do not forget to keep your sextant and compass gimbals lightly oiled. (Oh, and please pronounce gimbal with a soft g.) If you have an old-fashioned magnetic needle compass, swing the compass yourself once a year to check for alterations in the deviation. If it is only a degree or so different, just make a note on the card, but if there are some large differences, or if the differences are clustered in the same quadrant, then check to see if you have left anything magnetic about or have moved or fitted something significant. If there is no simple explanation get a professional adjustment done. Note that after passing through a violent thunderstorm or if the ship is on a cardinal heading for a long period, the magnetic characteristics of a steel vessel can be altered quite a bit. Take an early opportunity of checking. (But you do that daily while cruising, in any event. Don't you?) Such changes are normally not permanent. You can also find significant changes in deviation and/or heeling error if on a long voyage, especially a north/south voyage. Keep checking. And also remember that variation changes on a long voyage.

If one of the crew is contemplating having a replacement hip or knee joint, make sure to specify to the surgeon that the metal parts must be non-magnetic. No joke! The Charnley type are OK.

GET-YOU-HOME TIPS

To repeat, repair problems are best avoided by keeping things simple. What you cannot repair yourself with on-board materials and facilities is probably going to cause trouble sometime. Things do go wrong; even well-designed, well-made items break or fail for no apparent reason. Murphy's Law being certain in its effect, you can bet your life things will fail just when you need them. Here are a few examples of preplanned jury-rigs that can be used to manage temporarily:

- Bulldog clips for rigging: keep quite a lot of the right sizes stowed in lanolin to keep them usable, and a few lengths of wire rope or short chain to bridge a gap. If a wire parts and you have no spare wire, make eyes with the clips and close the gap with a lot of turns of small cordage, which is better than one or two of larger.
- Carry a little impeller pump of the sort that can be used on an electric drill. I have used one when the cooling water pump on the generator failed, and for other less important jobs.
- Holes in rubber exhaust hose can be fixed with a short length (an inch or two is enough) of the right size steel pipe. Cut the hose, insert pipe and secure with hose clips. Holes in a rigid exhaust are best closed by a hose clip over a soft leather patch (if wet exhaust), or over a 'Fearnought' pad (if dry). On wet exhausts, heavy cloth and rubber are usable. Hose clips have a variety of unofficial uses – they do not merely stay round, they can be used to bind all sorts of things together.

Various advisory or regulatory bodies approve copper tube for diesel fuel lines. I think this is dangerous in a boat that gets a lot of use; copper not only work-hardens by having its shape changed repeatedly, but also time-hardens when liquid is flowing through it. In either case it becomes brittle and breaks when it will cause the most trouble. Bronze pipe would be fine, but I prefer the flexible woven metal-covered type, which are not overly expensive. Metal-clad plastic will only protect against accidental physical damage, but it does not proof the tube against fire. But when your copper (approved) tube breaks, and it certainly will before the plastic, that can lead to fire, too. For this eventuality (the break, that is):

- Keep some strong plastic tube and clips. If using the metal-covered flexible piping, make sure that the metal cover is in contact at each end to eliminate static electricity build-up.
  In the year 2000, we came across approved flexible tubing for diesel oil. This will solve the problem (we have fitted it in *Hosanna*), but many boats will not be so fitted. There is a lot of rubbish in the Recreational Craft Directive (a nauseous bit of Brusselcratic nonsense).
- A frequent failure spot is a metal elbow in a wet exhaust system. Spares are very heavy, and the darn things fail so often that you can get caught out.

- Look around lorry agencies for rubber cooling water elbows, which can be the right size. Indeed, they might be cheaper, lighter and better fitted from the kick-off.
- Steering gear fails from time to time, this problem is mostly solvable by using the emergency tiller which you will have in the locker. It is not unknown for the rudder shaft itself to break, leaving the rudder intact but swinging freely. As a precaution against this horrible event:
- Arrange a small V-shaped notch (open downwards) near the top after-edge of the rudder. It is easy to lower over the stern a bight of rope with a few overhand knots in it, or with a length of light chain (6mm section, say) in the middle. With one end either side of the boat, pull gently up and the knots or the chain can be jammed into the V, thus getting the rudder under some sort of control without having to go over the side to do it (see diagram).

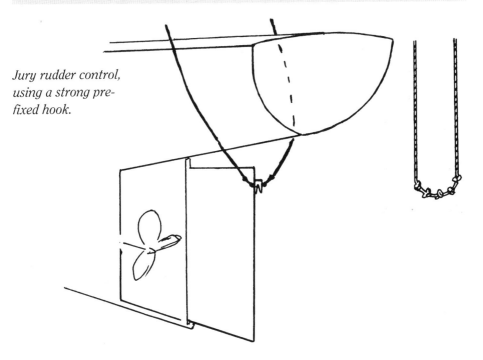

Jury rudder control, using a strong pre-fixed hook.

SPARES AND TOOLS

Finally, here is a list of the spare parts I have needed over the past 30 years, which must indicate something. The tool list is somewhat longer than for normal cruising. If you become able to use all of these tools competently before you start, you will be better off than I was at that point, for a lot of these have had to be added to my original outfit. Do not let the chores spoil the sailing.

SPARES USED IN BOTH *FARE WELL* AND *HOSANNA*

These were used in more than 30 years of continuous cruising. The number in parentheses is the number used where this is more than one.

ON DECK

Oil seals renewed on SL521 windlass (2).

Shockcord, various sizes, over 50 yards.

Cordage for sheets and lashings.

Shackles: I mostly use galvanised, and replace them when they rust. But stainless ones do fail, and of course the pins I lose never match the bows I drop at other times.

SL hatch stays (3).

Hatch handle.

Various hinges with brass pins (these are never strong enough).

Hatch sealing round the acrylic.

Winch handle.

Deck caulking. Rotator for towing log (dropped overboard).

IN THE ENGINE ROOM

Submersible bilge pumps (3); switches (1) for same.

Water Puppy washdown pump (2).

Godwin fresh-water pump shaft seal and bearing. Also a new motor for same.

Float switches (7).

Air-pressure pump switches.

Sight-glass plastic tubing on FW and oil fuel tanks (2).

Fuel-oil tubing, olives, cocks, bits and pieces.

Exhaust rubber tubing, exhaust elbows.

Dozens of hoseclips, all sizes.

Water pump on refrigerator (2)

Refrigerator filters (4)

ON THE MAIN ENGINE

Flexible lube oil pipe, set of cooling water hoses, numerous filters, shaft gland packing.

ON THE GENERATOR PRIME MOVER

The Farymann generator needed: injector, water pumps (2), set of flexible mountings, fuel pipes, valves and valve gear.

The Petter generator needed: new cylinder heads (2), valve springs (7), new lube oil piping, water pumps (2), water pump impellers (3), set of flexible mountings, bleed screw on injection pump, injector, corrosion inhibiting anodes (22) and a great deal of blasphemy.

The Perkins needed impellers for raw water pump (2).

ELECTRICAL

Lucas AC5A alternator (3).

Lucas 440 regulator (6). *(voltage)*

Lucas indicator bulb for above circuit (2).

Bosch alternator.

Auto voltage control for G&M 3kVA 230V alternator.

Transformer (1), rheostat, and bridge rectifiers (2) for G&M alternator.

Brushes for all motors.

Diodes in charger rectifier (5).

Main batteries: Obviously, these will need changing from time to time.

Battery isolating switches (3).

Japanese battery changeover switches (2).

A large-scale rewiring following lightning strike.

Diodes for Sharp Autopilot (2).

Solenoid spool valve in Cetrek hydraulic pump.

Ammeter.

Many switches, sockets and plugs of all types. Fuses.

Dry batteries by the dozen. New torches.

Fluorescent tubes

Bulbs – dozens, but especially the 24V 6W.

NAVIGATION INSTRUMENTS

Impeller assemblies for Walker Trident Mk 3 log (14!), and major repairs (3).

Wind instrument: complete due to lightning strike.

Photo-transistor in anemometer. Vane blown off wind direction instrument – twice.

Rotator and flywheel for Walker Cherub log.

Echosounders: various small repairs, 1 new instrument and 1 transducer (Seafarer) and one co-ax plug.

Radio receivers (2).

Pencil sharpener.

Magnets for compass correction; they rust away in time. (Watch this carefully if they are encased.)

DOMESTIC

Weights for pressure-cooker valve, and seal.

Sewing machine driving belt.

Tap washers.

Photo-electric cell for Perkins Mate cooker.

Sealing strip for hob of cooker.

Fire-cement for cooker furnace.

Fire extinguishers

Lavac WC: spare seat seals (2), flap valves (2), joker valves (5). Tubing for WC installation. Lavac WC bowl: (the aluminium casting disintegrated, but they don't make that type any more, sensible people).

A SPARES LIST FOR CONSIDERATION
FOR (EACH) ENGINE

Water hoses.

Pump impellers.

Any flexible pipe.

Complete exhaust run.

Filters.

Pipe couplings and olives.

Gaskets and seals.

Mountings, if flexible.

Valve springs.

Plastic fuel pipe and clips.

Hose clips – dozens all sizes.

HP fuel pipes (from pump to injectors).

Spare belts.

Duplicate flanges for hoses.

Coupling bolts.

ELECTRICAL

Terminal strip.
Crimp terminals.
Alternator regulator warning lamps.
Circuit breakers, fuses.
Switches, sockets, plugs, light bulbs.
L E D's

Assorted resistors, capacitors, diodes, transistors – you may not be able to use them, but someone else might on your behalf.
Lucar connectors.
Cable of all sizes.
Motor brushes.

OTHER

Spares kit for all pumps.
Piece of rubber sheet (2mm).
Gasket material for water, oil, and dry heat (exhaust).
Paint, brushes etc.
Soft aluminium sheet (3mm), or copper in wooden boat.

Threaded rod, nuts to fit.
Bits of plywood, timber.
Sealing compound.
Caulking.
Stainless sheet (about 1.5mm).
Duct, and self-amalgamating tapes.

ON DECK

Drive belt for windlass.
Bolts, nuts for spreader roots.
Shackles, thimbles etc.
Canvas and thread.
Cordage.
Bulldog clips.
Lanolin.
Oar for dinghy (plus oarlocks, if of the loose type).
Flags and ensigns.

Eyebolts.
Clevis and cotter pins.
Whipping twine.
Shockcord and terminals.
20ft of largest wire.
20ft of smallest wire.
Winch handle.
Wooden plugs, assorted.
Spare sail battens (if foolish enough to have them).

TOOL LIST

I did not start out with all these. A lot have had to be added on the way, which tells one something.

SAWS

A general-purpose, medium tooth.
Large hack and small hack.
Coping (if jigsaw not carried).
Spare blades.

HAMMERS

Large ball-peen.
Claw.
Chipping.

SCREWDRIVERS

For no. 4, 6, 8, slot-screws.

Dumpy for no. 8 slot-screws.
Small and large crosshead.
Dumpy crosshead.
Very large slot, angled slot, and crosshead (preferably ratchet percussion).

CHISELS

¼ and ¾in firmer.

Hard chisels.

FILES

Small triangular.

Round and half-round large, round and half-round, half-round wood rasp (the wood-butcher's *vade mecum*).

Thread-restoring files.

CLAMPS

Assorted, including adjustable opening vice, or a Black & Decker Jobber or Workmate.

ASSORTED TOOLS

Bradawl.

Bevel gauge.

Square.

Small smoothing plane, rebating plane.

Pliers: large, small pointed, and circlip.

Spanners: ring or open tube according to choice.

Socket set. Large and small adjustable. Pipe wrench.

Large and small Mole wrench or Visegrip.

Nut splitter.

Stud removers.

Taps and dies.

Hand drill.

Steel rule, calipers.

Allen keys.

Punches, drifts.

A gasket making kit.

Sheet metal shears.

Oilstone, rough and smooth each side.

Dentist's probe.

Long angled, surgeon's forceps (the best dropped-item recovery tool).

Funnels.

ELECTRIC TOOLS, AND TOOLS FOR ELECTRICAL WORK

Two-speed drill up to 10mm.

Jigsaw orbital sander.

Small angle grinder (steel boats).

Soldering iron.

Wire clippers and strippers.

Insulated screwdrivers (lots).

Pointed-nose small pliers.

Multi-test meter to read:

0–25V DC

0–250V AC

0–10 ohms

0–100 ohms

0–1000 ohms.

Crimping tool.

Long jump leads (lorry type, say about 20ft).

Short jump leads.

Plenty of screws, bolts, nuts, washers, o-rings, friction washers, self-taps, tacks, panel pins and nails to choice.

Aboard *Hosanna*, which followed *Fare Well*, our needs have been rather different. We fitted out *Hosanna* while living on board, and even while cruising, so we carried vastly more tools than one would need for maintenance. This did not matter much for *Hosanna* is the size of a small factory; there is a wealth of difference in maintaining a small yacht and a large barge. Most of it is a matter of strength, not only of the barge, but also of the crew.

Watch out you do not get a boat so large and heavy that she is beyond your resources, financial and physical. Laurel and I are twenty years older than when we bought *Hosanna*, and they are significant years. We are starting to find the maintenance hard going. Maintaining *Hosanna* (26 metres LOA, and displacing 60-odd tonnes) has been hard but rewarding work, but we feel repaid by having lived and cruised widely in a damned good boat in which we are completely and literally at home. We could not wholeheartedly recommend such an undertaking to anyone who has not had some experience of big boats, though they would soon get it if they survived.

Financially, the difference is not in proportion to her size because one can buy chandlery second-hand, or from commercial suppliers who do not demand the same mark-ups as the yacht-chandlery trade, but that too suggests knowing where to look, experience that takes time to acquire. One will use different tools and the work will be on a different scale, often involving far more physical strength, lifting things for instance.

The most important criteria are to marry comfort to financial circumstances, to knowledge, to physical ability, and lastly to bring to the enterprise a sense of joyous improvisation, problem solving, and being undaunted. The latter we still have.

If, however, you lack practical hands-on experience, gain it on something handier in size, and then work up.

And after all that hard maintenance work . . . Bill enjoys a cold beer.

9 • Power

'. . . some onely will burne and fume out a most stinking poyson smoake . . .'

There have been references to engines and power sources in various chapters, but I would like to pull some of this together to consider the question as a whole.

We once made a long cruise with a six-month-old baby in a wooden yacht with no engine and no electricity. There was no water tank, wash-basin, or galley come to that, nor were there any guardrails, lifelines, radio, or lavatory. Instead of the latter there was a bucket marked 'For sanitary purposes only' in red paint. When we lent the boat to a foreigner, we were dismayed to find he had used this bucket for fresh water. He had read the bucket's legend and reasoned that the loo bucket would be marked 'for INsanitary purposes only'. We thought it kinder not to disillusion him, but have wondered ever since about the claim that English is the most easily understood of languages.

That cruise was wildly successful: three adults and a baby enjoyed it immensely, but it was almost 50 years ago; expectations were not that high, and you could sail (literally) into any Mediterranean harbour and never meet another yacht. The late Geoff Pack, a splendid sailor, was a great advocate of the simple life afloat: KISS, or Keep It Simple, Stupid, but even he expected a slightly higher standard of living when we discussed this with him in the 1990s.

An engine of some sort has become a necessity. Before yacht harbours or marinas existed, a yacht would enter commercial harbours under sail and warp herself into a convenient berth with little effort, as we have done even 30 years ago. Nowadays many commercial harbours are closed to yachts altogether because there is a marina next door where they are supposed to berth and pay for the privilege. And marinas tend to have rules forbidding yachts to meander about under sail because there are not only too many yachts, but too many yachtsmen who have never learnt to manoeuvre in a constricted space under sail.

Even those that have can get it wrong. Hal Roth, a renowned sailor who has sailed many times round the world, liked to berth engine-less. We were in the Yacht Club in Seville when he arrived. We watched him as he jilled about waiting for the huge road bridge to swing open and close off traffic on the four-lane main highway. When it did, he tried to sail through, but found that he had to pass in the lee of the bridge piers against a contrary current. As he was blanketed, he lost way. He remained poised motionless between the bridge abutments while half Spain fumed and hooted on the roads above. Finally, after about a quarter of an hour, he made it through, to resounding cheers, sounding of car horns and possibly a firework display as well. He reached the berth near to us, the usual stern-to affair.

He must have been un-nerved by the bridge business. In the end it took more than half an hour for the massed crews of several yachts already in place to man-handle him bodily into the intended gap. Not a pretty manoeuvre! If sailors like him can make such a horlicks, what chance have lesser mortals?

So, take advice: an auxiliary engine is now essential, and the sense to use it.

ENGINES

If there is an engine already fitted in a yacht you are thinking of buying, then in addition to the broad views I have given, view with suspicion any product of a small company that is the wholly-owned subsidiary of a major conglomerate holding company. The small company's managers may be competent and conscientious (though not necessarily: many of them are now run by accountants in suits) but in any case they are completely at the mercy of the management of their parent company, whose decisions will pay little attention to the interests of customers at the far end of an attenuated chain, but they will certainly affect such matters as spares availability and their overseas distribution.

Might I please appeal for someone to produce a range of marine diesels with all adjustments, controls and service points on one side and/or the top? It's not impossible.

In the year 2005, engines have changed. Perkins seem not to be as good as it was, though now being in the Caterpillar stable and having access to increased development capital, they can be expected to regain some of their old reliability. Sadly, they have decided to hive off their marine engines for adaptation by another company, and thus marine engine service has deteriorated in some parts of the world. They have also decided to produce small engines based on castings, etc from other companies, though these appear to be very good.

We, ourselves, in our big boat, have had a disaster with a Cummins engine. Though the French Cummins agent was excellent, I have to add this engine to Volvo on my personal avoid list, not because it is badly made or because the service is not good, but because it is far too complicated an engine for amateurs to self-maintain, and unless meticulously looked after it goes wrong stealthily. I want an engine I can abuse. Not seriously, you understand, but tolerant of a little incompetence. I also want spares to be easily obtainable, at reasonable cost, and with luck to be able to fit them myself.

There are fewer small slow-running diesel engines about now. The industry seems to think we are all obsessed by power/weight ratios, so they produce engines that deliver horse-power by means of revolving at an ever-increasing rate. I am unhappy about this. My experience is that slow-running diesels are the more tolerant, and easier to self-repair, and they do not give off that irritating high-pitched whine that characterises anything revolving at 3000 rpm or over. For me the diesel is epitomised by those old engines like the Kromhaut, the sort that revolved at 100 rpm, gave off a reassuring *thonk, thonk thonk*, sound and blew smoke rings out of the exhaust. Simple (though energetic) starting and almost impossible to stop. Would run on anything including wheat flour and fine sawdust.

Diesel fuel in the back of beyond, one reads, is often contaminated. I have never found it so, and suspect that such water-in-the-fuel complaints are the result of on-board sources, as it was on the only occasion when we suffered from this problem – probably condensation. Supply pipes should have good water-trap type filters, preferably mounted in parallel, and each separated by cocks so that you can change one filter while the engine is running on the other. Other filters are needed in line, of course, preferably two. Carry a fair stock of filter elements, but change them frequently and in rotation, because most have metal in them somewhere and are liable to rust while in storage, thus rendering the filter element useless. Racor fuel filters are expensive but much better than any others we have come across, and fishermen swear by them.

If you have conventional filters, obtain a world-wide list of equivalent elements and lubricating oils from your engine's makers. Manufacturers do not like supplying such a list, on the grounds that only their own products are good enough for their engines. This is rubbish; they want to charge up to three times the proper price for an item with their name on, which does not differ from the part manufacturer's basic model. Engine dealers like to sell, so if you are buying a new engine, get the list before you deal. They'll say they don't have the information: they lie. *Get it before you deal*. It is in any event impossible to obtain well known brands in many places, you will need the generic part.

Some people in the UK report biological degradation in diesel tanks. These seem to be uncommon in the eastern Med and nobody I know has had problems. Danger of hubris here, of course. Maybe it is caused by the red dye?

Make sure the fuel tank has a draw-off point above and clear of a sump. It should have an access big enough for a clenched fist, to enable the sump to be cleaned out. There should be a drain cock at the lowest point to drain off condensation accumulating under the fuel in a cold spell.

I do not like outboard motors. Generally I find they make excellent anchors. I believe they are getting more reliable. They need to. From observation, it seems to me that the 4-stroke, such as Honda, have advantages over 2-stroke motors without being that much more expensive. The chief thing I have learned is to flush out with fresh water at the end of the season and to put a few drops of 3-in-1 oil into the cylinder and turn it over. Then stow it below in the dry. You could even share a bunk with the beastly thing if you want to.

If possible, have all machinery in one compartment that you can get your body into. It is no joke having a diesel engine in pieces all over the living room floor, and it ought not to be necessary except perhaps in the smallest yachts. (We hear

GIORGO'S TAVERNA, MEGANISI

of a boat for sale because the wife objected to this. She fell down the hole into the engine compartment, and she has a loving husband.) Nor should the machinery be fitted in like a three-dimensional jigsaw puzzle for this is a poor inducement to do maintenance. Ideally one should not have to remove A to work on B or vice versa. The engine space should be well ventilated for hot climates.

I don't think it necessary to discuss engine exhausts. More people nowadays buy production or second-hand boats and they take what they get. Those who undertake self-build will generally have enough experience to have their own opinions. All we would say is that for inland waters, it pays to consider keel-cooling because of the junk and silt that can be sucked into water intakes.

Even at sea, jellyfish sucked in can cause some minor grief, as can plastic bags. It was in the canals, however, that we met a dead furry animal that even the World Wildlife Fund could not persuade me to love.

A problem arises from the fact that the cooling water you blow out over the side is sea water. It is not desirable to cool engines with sea water because so many of them contain dissimilar metals which corrode electrolytically in sea water. It is essential to cool marine engines with fresh water containing corrosion inhibitors such as diesel anti-freeze and then cool that fresh water with the sea water in a heat exchanger. (Anti-freeze in the tropics? Yes, it is a good idea for rust prevention.)

You will find various small diesels on the market cooled by sea water, a system known as direct cooling. Their makers will try to persuade you that sacrificial anodes solve the problem. They do not. They are sacrificed very much faster in warmer sea water, you do not have any ready means of checking what sacrifice they have made, they sometimes become difficult to extract when corroded, and often the right ones are impossible to obtain. If you buy a yacht with a directly cooled engine, it is quite possible to modify it to indirect cooling. Do so for heaven's sake, and your own peace of mind.

In *Hosanna* we have piping leading to the calorifier to give us hot water, but be careful: engine cooling water comes out at about 180°F, which is much too hot to wash your hands in. A mixer tap at the point of delivery helps.

The other alternative: a dry exhaust and air-cooling, whether directly or via a water circulation and radiator, is not wholly suitable for a boat bound for hot climates.

All the above considerations apply equally to diesel generator exhausts and cooling.

Hosanna does have a small air-cooled diesel generator for use on those occasions when we take the mud. Derisory remarks are uncalled for; we do it voluntarily from time to time, but occasionally in much the same way that hunters are known to dismount on the opposite side of the fence to their horse. We got the air-cooled diesel generator at half-price in Castorama's (France) annual sale. Probably nobody else wanted it. It makes a noise to waken the dead, and is fitted in the bows. Fortunately, we have a long ship.

Hand cranking a diesel engine is not for the middle aged and breathless, let alone the old and tired. It is heart-attack stuff. We once did that sort of thing to cars and lawn-mowers (Remember?) but modern cars do not even have starting handles and we have all got used to that. So our boat engines have electric starting, too, because it is easier.

BATTERIES

Nickel-alkaline batteries are by far the best, but their virtues are bought at a price. We have used many of the nickel-alkaline ones, second-hand from various government surplus sources which, sadly, are now drying up. A 20-year life is normal so they repay their very high cost. A big one aboard *Hosanna* has just died after 21 years. We feel bereaved and ought to get counselling. They take any amount of bad treatment and normally seem to resurrect themselves, with a little help. The electrolyte (potassium hydroxide) needed for their life-support is safe to store in a steel boat. (It is a superb grease solvent, but it is caustic and should be treated with care.) The cost of providing the ampere-hours that many fairly sophisticated boats need these days would be astronomical, for they would be more than six times the cost of lead-acid batteries.

Lead-acid batteries come in different types. Starting batteries for engines are not suitable for running domestic electrical circuits, except in the very smallest of boats where having two separate batteries would be inconvenient. For most modern boats, it is best to have separate batteries for starting and domestic use, and these would be of two distinct types. The latter should be of the deep-cycle variety that withstand frequent discharging and charging. These are the type fitted to milk-floats and town delivery vans, and the batteries last much longer than starting batteries. *Hosanna* has a bank of them (they come in separate cells) made by Exide, that are now 15 years old and on their last legs. Like the nickel

The galley on Hosanna *was well equipped with a gas hob and microwave oven. Note our indispensable Bamix on a bracket and the excellent runs of walnut shelving for bottles and jars.*

batteries, they do not come that cheap, but over time are a bargain. They cost (new) two or three times as much as a starting battery of the same power. There are other batteries marketed as having 'deep-cycle characteristics' and they cost about twice as much as a starting battery for the same nominal power. They are not bad, but cannot compete with the real thing. Batteries' power used to be measured in ampere-hours, and I knew what I wanted this way. This was obviously too simple for the public to be allowed to know. Now batteries have mystic numbers that appear to have no real meaning unless it is a secret lottery. Bad luck Mr Smith, this month all batteries whose numbers end with a seven are duds.

I do not propose to go into details about how much battery power you need. There are excellent books on the market (or in the library) on direct current wiring for boats and it is a business that should be overseen by experts more proficient than I am. All I will say is that modern domestic and navigational equipment can need substantial battery power, and it is false economy to underpower a cruising boat.

• *Charging* •

The process of keeping batteries healthy in a sophisticated boat has changed dramatically. Once one ran the engine for an hour or two per day and that was that. No longer. We are investigating a new (to us) system which sits at the centre of a spider's web of cables that interconnect all the different gadgets on board whether they are 12 volt, 24 volt DC, or 230 volt AC, together with shore power of varying voltages and cycles per second, batteries, inverters, chargers, alternators, and the occasional divine intervention. It probably plays Rule Britannia on October 21st as well.

The one we are looking at has the trade name Phoenix. It all sounds fantastic but I am worried that it might need someone with a PhD in astro-physics not only to set it up, but also to keep it in a subservient mode. We don't want it calling itself 'Hal' and taking over the boat. In any case, it will not be operational before this goes to print.

Most boats now have separate AC circuits for use in marinas. We do. But if the above system really works it may become more convenient and less costly to install ordinary commercial or domestic appliances rather than items 'specially made for the marine environment' which always cost ten times as much.

Inverters that convert DC to 230 volt AC have become cheaper and much more efficient, 95% is now normal. They can tolerate starting loads on induction motors (such as domestic fridges). The point is that special 12 volt fridges cost hundreds of pounds more than the standard equivalent from the out-of-town warehouse. Household appliances (cleaners, microwaves, mixers etc) in 12 volt are also much more expensive, and what you save goes to finance a big inverter and bigger batteries. Twelve years ago our super-special yacht fridge expired and we were hard up at the time. We bought an ordinary domestic fridge-freezer in a sale at a French *hypermarché* and have been running it on inverters and the generator ever since. When not on shore power, we stack part of the freezer compartment with two-litre jerricans of mildly salt water that act as a cool bank for overnights and other longish periods when we do not want to feed it with real amps.

Windvanes are good wherever there is wind, especially in tradewind zones. We have written elsewhere about Bill's accident with a windvane (the idiot!), and we will spare him the shame of repeating it. They are dangerous beasts and need mounting high up and well out of reach of idiots and others – higher up than heavy gear like this should be on a small yacht. *Fare Well* had an Ampair, and it was excellent. It gave 5 amps at 24 volts in a force 4 wind. Its main problem was that it made too much power in winds of force 5 or above, when it would 'cut out' and then free-wheel. With no power to generate, the blades accelerated and whizzed round like aeroplane propellers, and made a hell of a din, a variable noise that it was difficult to get accustomed to. Others, such as the Air X are noisy, and these are the only ones we have experienced or been neighbours to in strong winds.

Bill tried coupling a small alternator to the propeller shaft of the boat by way of a 10:1 geared pulley system to get a charge when sailing with the gearbox in neutral. It never worked out well. Churning up the oil in the gearbox absorbed so much of the power that there was not enough to power the alternator. If we could have had a mechanical clutch to physically separate the gearbox from the shaft, it might have been different.

Solar panels seem to have stopped getting cheaper and also stopped getting more efficient. Microchips have fallen sharply in price, but the solar panel type of silicon chip has not. Why not? Our enquiries are met with shrugs. Given that they only give off peak power for a couple of hours per day and fall off to zero for about

A small solar panel makes a useful extra power source.

14 hours, at present prices they make a totally uneconomical proposition as one's principal source of charging power. However, a small panel to keep a starting battery topped up while you leave your boat unattended seems to be a good use, as does a panel for the battery of an outboard with electrical starting. This would keep the battery up when on passage, or when the dinghy has been on its davits for a long time.

HYDRAULICS

For boats over 40 feet, hydraulics systems are good for fittings like power windlasses or even for sheet winches. With the coming of power-driven headsail furling/reefing gears that do not cost more than the boat, a hydraulic motor is best, for the motor has to be fitted at the worst possible place for anything electric: the very stemhead itself. Perhaps the electric motor itself can be sealed, though such seals are never totally reliable. Remember that the wiring has to reach the motor and pass through the forepeak and then a deck-fitting and it is vulnerable to sea water.

It is also possible to have a hydraulic drive for the propeller shaft and these have improved in efficiency recently. They do allow the engine to be sited in a more convenient place. The problem is the hydraulic whine that comes from oil circulating at high speed in pipes. This is tolerable in a wooden or glass-fibre boat, but a steel boat seems to act like a guitar and amplifies the noise to such an extent that the boat becomes an environmental health hazard. With the right installation one does not need to have a second hydraulic pump to drive auxiliary fittings such as a windlass.

Hydraulic bow-thrusters are better than electric and do not need large batteries, and on that note we will move on to domestic matters.

10 • Victualling, and Other Domestic Considerations

'Many suppose anything is good enough to serve men at sea.'

THE GALLEY

Apart from the heads, nothing will get more use on your boat than the galley. If you wish life aboard to be the peaceful and enjoyable experience we all hope for, it repays much thought and planning. You will not get it completely right to start with, but your first cruise will show up any design faults and mistakes in emphasis. These should be rectified. Even small inconveniences can become very irritating if encountered several times a day, and are intolerable in bad weather.

'The Cooke roome where they dresse the victual may bee placed in diverse parts of the shippe'

Think of the following things:

- Does the galley work at an angle of (say) 40° on both tacks?
- Will the lockers or cupboards open without depositing their contents on the floor?
- Is everything strong enough for the cook to hang on to, or fall against?
- Are the things that you need in bad weather easily and conveniently stowed? (If the pan you need is at the bottom of a pile of seven, Murphy's Law makes it certain that the 45° roll will come just as you have them all out on the floor to reach the one you want.) Items in constant use should have prime space, closely followed by the mugs, bowls and stores needed in bad weather. Separate the pans (especially if they are non-stick) with cardboard picnic plates to prevent noise and scratches.

Drawers in the galley sometimes make more sense than cupboards or shelves, especially if they open fore and aft. All need strong catches of some sort: drawers can have a vertical retaining bar, a swing catch, or be the lift-and-pull-out kind.

Magnetic catches are not usually strong enough against the G-force of heavy groceries and a big wave, though having said that my magnetic knife rack hangs on to its cargo in all weathers, others have found this too.

If the crew is small, it is of great benefit to have plates and cutlery conveniently to hand. My ordinary single-decker washing-up plate rack is held in place on the drainer with two strong cup hooks; I have found this and its contents able to withstand even very violent motion, as does a deep cutlery drainer fixed to the wall, which holds enough knives and forks for two, and the most used kitchen tools.

• Cookers •

The kind of cooking stove you choose needs some thought. Bill mentioned the different fuel options in Chapter 6 Below Decks in some detail; I need not repeat them here. Top-of-the-stove cooking is fine for holidays, but for living aboard you will want to cook as you did on shore, and you will need to bake bread, which means that an oven and grill is desirable.

Mini all-purpose ovens are available these days, some with a hob on top. These are the smallest option, and cope quite adequately for a singlehander or small crew. At the other extreme are cookers for big charter yachts, rather like Agas. They are wonderful, I had a small version on *Fare Well*. It ran on diesel and had the added advantage that the stainless steel bolster that covered it was the right size to take a folded sheet. This meant that if I folded the washing carefully and placed it, still a little damp, on the warm bolster, I could walk away and let the ironing do itself. The stove was not gimballed, but was mounted athwartships, so pans slid sideways, not into your lap. (Its fiddles always prevented a serious loss of soup.) It heated the water too, and had a strong crash bar.

That model had become too expensive when we fitted out *Hosanna*, and for the same money we got an electric cooker, a mixed gas and electric hob, and (having the space) a microwave cooker, plus a generator to run all these appliances. I no longer regret the exchange, though the ironing no longer does itself quite so satisfactorily.

Gas stoves have the great advantage of instant heat and adjustability. Both the diesel cooker and the coal stoves still to be found in older boats are hot to use in the tropics; cold lunches become the order of the day. There are now good gas stoves that do not look as if they have been made from Meccano.

• Microwave ovens •

Many boats nowadays are thinking of installing microwave cookers. As always, the Americans are in the forefront. The advantages of microwaves are short cooking times, and therefore less power consumed; they do not heat up the galley in the tropics, and they fit into a small space. Though their output is measured as 600 watts, be aware that they will actually draw between 1000 and 1500 watts. They are now being made specially for yachts (ie expensive), with a built-in inverter so that they may be used with battery power, otherwise an AC generator is needed. See the chapter on Power for recent improvements in inverters (giving you the opportunity of buying a basic microwave from the High Street sales). A drop-down door model, such as I began with, is best on a boat, but they are hard to find, so you must allow space for the sweep of the door. In case you break the glass sheet or turntable (replacements are difficult to get and extremely expensive), take with you a suitable Pyrex dish as a spare. Since the best way of cooking in foul weather is in two-minute bursts below, then back up on deck for fresh air, you can see the handiness of a microwave oven (see photo page 180).

You can use it as a meatsafe in cool weather, and it's an excellent stowage for goodies either to set or defrost, or just sit, safely away from pets, children or flies.

The small all-purpose oven-grills with a hotplate on top, mentioned above, are sometimes combined with a microwave oven. These are very convenient where space is limited, but their power consumption is as much or more than a full-sized electric oven, and at nearly 3000 watts is more than small inexpensive generators can cope with. In my experience the combined microwave-grill works less efficiently than the two would as different items, and cooking for six on one of these I would find a headache, but this must be balanced against the saving of power and expense.

• *Other ways of cooking* •

Whatever you choose to cook on, have another method of cooking, just in case. An all-electric galley is no good if the power fails, and it is possible to run out of gas. In *Hosanna* I have a split hob, with three gas burners and one electric plate (these hobs are domestic and now easily obtainable, and we found screw-down fiddles to marinise them). The saloon is heated by a wood stove, on which we often cooked our lunch while converting *Hosanna* in the boatyard, using an upturned biscuit tin on a trivet as a Dutch oven – if it wasn't stew in a heavy casserole. A small charcoal barbecue is not only wonderful for sunny anchorages, but can be a useful cooking back-up in good weather; or that old standby the single-burner Primus (the self-pricking one) or even a small Camping Gaz stove in case of dire need.

Remember that your stove (and you) may have to cook at a sharp angle, or even crashing up and down (I had the dubious satisfaction of knowing that my diesel stove on *Fare Well* would function at a 60° angle: we were stranded in this position for a day or more, so it was quite important at the time). You will therefore need either a gimballed stove or well-designed, high fiddles to keep your pans in position in a seaway. I prefer a fixed stove with fiddles, as the gimbals take up extra space, but if you spend long days heeled over on one tack you might have a different view. In addition, check that water cascading down a hatch will not put out the stove and prevent its use in a storm, as has happened on some racing yachts. At a time when hot food is most needed, you will be glad that your stove is in a safe, dry spot, and that you can brace yourself to use it without a waterfall descending on your head.

• *The sink* •

The sink, as Bill has said, is best with natural drainage. This has been a help to us on some occasions of emergency, such as bailing out the engine-room. Since both were in the centre of the boat, it was a fairly easy matter, with two of us, to bail straight into the sink. When we were fighting an engine-room fire it was possible to get water to it with a good deal of control, for the same reason. As regards one sink or two, while some swear by a double sink, even if they are too small to wash large pans in (it does make an extra catchall while working), I prefer one bigger one: if only because it drained one bucket of bilge water before the next one arrived. Small sinks save water, but this is achieved at sea by placing a smaller plastic bowl in the larger sink, which has the added advantage of cushioning against breakages. I also get mad if the sink is too small to immerse a dinnerplate.

A board that fits over the sink for extra workspace is commonplace now, but was not when we built *Fare Well* over 30 years ago. We invented our own, wood on one side and Formica on the other. When not in use it slotted into a specially made groove alongside the stove. This board was for bread or pastry. A separate one, smaller but thicker, is carried as a chopping block, and a cleaver goes with it, as meat and fish often come in their original state in the places we go.

We prefer a decent-sized sink large enough to immerse a dinner plate; you can always save water by using a plastic bowl inside it, which also cushions against breakages.

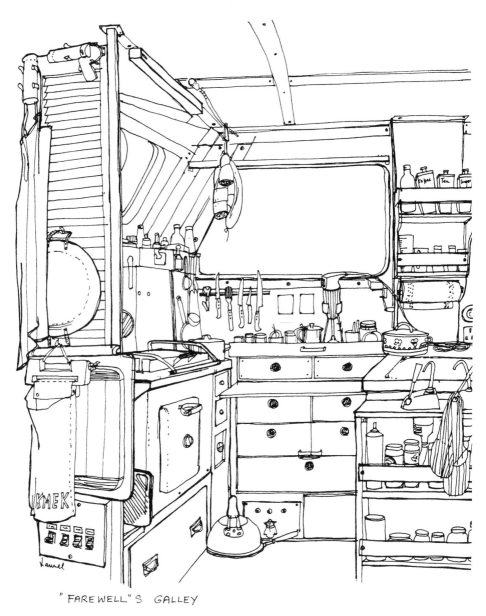

" FAREWELL"S GALLEY

• *Equipment and appliances* •

Avoid the temptation to clutter precious workspace with domestic appliances that will not work without shore power. Go back to the mechanical aids our grandmothers used, and if you want them handy, create storage space for them. I would prefer to take such things as hand mincers and coffee grinders (rather than a bulky electric mixer or food processor which are too big for most galleys, though again our sample of cruising boats lists several whose galley pride *is* a mixer). You will not, as on holiday, be either camping or eating out all the time, so be sure your equipment suits your style of cooking. If you are a dab hand at cakes, take cake tins. I use the non-stick loaf tins, which I keep cushioned from scratches with paper towels or picnic plates and are still rust-free after several years' use at sea. If you are good at patés or potted tongue, take the containers you know to be the right size, and the shaped piece of wood to press their contents. We use G-clamps for this. Take an elegant dish for your speciality: sometimes you may want to splash out, joining the neighbouring boat for a combined dinner; and a little style is a welcome change. Not that a salad for 20 people does not taste just as good from a plastic washbowl – take several stacking ones, they have many uses.

Spend time looking for your favourite tools in stainless steel. It took me years in the old days to find a pair of stainless tongs – without which I cannot even boil an egg – that fitted nicely to the hand. Nowadays good kitchen tools are readily available in stainless steel from specialist kitchen shops. Chromium plate soon loses its shine when subjected to the chafe and roll of a boat, and then rusts disgustingly. Strong plastic can be a good alternative: sieves, ladles, and potato mashers come to mind, but strong is the operative word.

As well as my tongs, the things I would not be without are:

- A pressure cooker.
- A well-engineered hand beater.
- A wall tin opener that will not rust in a few days, invaluable when fast sea stew is needed.
- A small spatula or butter spreader.
- A hamburger press (mine is plastic, very old, and still in good shape) in which you can quickly make chickenburgers, meat and/or veggieburgers, fish cakes, and so on.
- Bamix Magic Wand. Once my only electrical kitchen gadget, this is the neatest handheld mincer and beater I have ever come across. It consumes 100 watts on 240 volts AC or the inverter, and used with a tall jar or jug will purée soup, beat cakes or chop vegetables. It was designed for the blind and is very easy to clean. I have not seen it marketed recently, Braun do a similar one if not quite so elegant. I now have
- A mini chopper, since arthritis is stopping my chopping.

You will need something to measure with.

- A set of stainless steel measuring cups are useful: I found the plastic ones too breakable.
- A polythene jug marked in centilitres has lasted till it is all but illegible. Fortunately these are cheap and readily available.
- I once thought a miniature diet scale would be great for weighing, but it was too small, too fragile, apt to capsize and extremely unreliable. I go now

The Bamix 'Magic Wand'.

for a compact battery operated electronic scale these days. It takes no more space than a paperback, can be used with any container, and weighs in kilos and pounds, which when cruising is essential. Mark One lasted eight years and was still working thanks to some rather dodgy amateur soldering (ours) so to be on the safe side we are on to Mark Two. The batteries last more than a year.

- A timer, preferably the four-hour kind with not too loud a tick, can be invaluable not just for cooking but reminding you of watch changes, weather forecasts, the morning VHF net and the noon sight. Fasten it firmly to a dry bulkhead, as landing in the washing-up bowl is not good for it.

Other cruisers list among their essentials:

- A gas match.
- A magnetic knife sharpener.
- A corkscrew!

Consider your gadgets from this point of view:

- Do I use it a lot?
- If it is electric, is there a mechanical substitute?
- Is it robustly made, of a rust-free material? If not, can I be bothered to cosset it by building a special stowage?

- Is it reasonably resistant to going wrong, breaking or getting trodden on?
- Is there a simpler way of achieving the same result?
- Is it robustly made of rust-free material?

Having said that, I would be the last person to discourage you from taking any beloved device that you would be unhappy without. Be sure that it has a safe stowage, and try to protect it from the corrosive salt air.

Saucepans should be good quality, tall for their width and have well-fitting lids. They should not deform if dropped, and have well-insulated handles. I have never regretted the stainless steel pans I bought for *Fare Well*, pricey at the time, but after 30 years of constant misuse are still as good as new, bar one whose handle rivets have failed.

You will need a frying pan or two. If you take only one, have it large, light and strong, unless you are addicted to cast iron. (Seriously, Bill interjects, a small yacht and Le Creuset pans don't mix.) A lidded skillet is useful, and lidded casseroles (good-quality enamel seems to last well, but the cheap ones chip too quickly). Our cruiser survey shows the average number of pans in the galley to be 10, with the extremes at 4 (mingy) and 25 (OTT). Nesting stainless or aluminium dishes of various shapes and sizes are handy, as they have many uses either for cold food or in the oven.

• *Finding things that fit* •

This is tremendously important, and not just in the galley. Be sure to measure exactly the space available in your oven and get ovenware that fits well. It saves spills if the pans don't skid from side to side (most yacht ovens are too wide, imitating those on shore), and nothing is more irritating than finding that your two most used dishes don't quite fit side by side, or even one above the other. If you fit a drawer with a cutlery tray, make sure no space is wasted, even cutlery can be too large or too bulky. A 3in drawer will take such a tray.

Holders for this or that are not always standardised, though this is improving. We used to have to saw an inch off Greek kitchen rolls to fit UK holders but now we're in Europe and everything is metric. One of your drawers needs an internal measurement of 33cm by 8cm high if you want to take advantage of catering size rolls of foil and food-wrap. Even expensive state-of-the-art kitchens on shore rarely allow for this, except by wasting a lot of space.

• *Other ideas* •

I find the brown rustic ovenware that you can buy almost anywhere now can be used on calm days or in harbour. We have broken only one in 30 years. Mine are mostly oblong and the largest one fits the oven exactly and will do lasagne for ten or bake a huge fish.

We don't find it necessary to use plastic glasses. We buy sturdy French glass,

Arcoroc or Duralex, they seem to bounce happily off most things except steel plate, and we don't break any more than a household ashore would.

One very large aluminium pan can be carried in case of lobsters. We have one, but keep it in an inaccessible place with the large serving bowls that are required on such occasions inside it, since it is also useful for large quantities of rice and spaghetti. Lightweight moulded wooden bowls and trays from the Far East are worth the space, they are unbreakable and last for ever. Wickerwork baskets don't last long, but they are lightweight and cheap.

FARE WELL'S BASIC GALLEY EQUIPMENT

IN USE DAILY

2 stainless steel saucepans
2 non-stick frying pans
Asbestos mat with handle
1 wooden spoon, 1 wooden turner
Stainless steel tongs
Kitchen knives and cutting board
Stainless steel measuring cups
Small spice jar containing (5:1) salt and
    pepper mix

Potato masher, slotted spoon
Ladle (with hooked end so it does not
    slip into the pan)
Wooden garlic masher (also pushes food
    into the mincer)
Tin opener
Hand egg beater
Bamix Magic Wand
Non-stick loaf tins
Stainless steel colander

IN USE WEEKLY

Pressure cooker
Omelette pan
Large plastic bowl for mixing and rising
    bread
2 casseroles, enamel, lidded
Fireproof earthenware
Assorted wicker baskets

**IN USE LESS OFTEN BUT WORTH
THEIR SPACE**

Hamburger press
Large paella pan, also good for frying
    large fish
Huge pot for lobsters or rice/pasta for 20
    people
Hand mincer

Hosanna's galley is as big as the mini-kitchen in a London flat, but when we return to a smaller boat the above would still suit me well, though as I age I have had to add one or two (hand) devices to a strong wristed husband for peeling vegetables, levering ringpulls and unscrewing the tops of jars and bottles.

Oh yes, and sharp, strong scissors for getting into those hideously impossible blister packs.

Before we leave the galley, let me remind you to find space for the indispensable roll of paper towels, and for the teatowel and handtowel which otherwise are always on the floor among the spilt sugar, rice and onion skins. There should of course be a better place than the floor for such things, which brings us to:

• *Rubbish, garbage, trash and hygiene* •

As packaging gets more and more copious (and impossible to get into) our problems of rubbish increase. There is something to be said, I wrote in the last edition, for unwrapping all your goods at the supermarket exit, and leaving *them* with the problem of disposal of all the boxes, plastic, paper and card. Today I'm quite sure that the health and safety mob would slap my wrists for advising you to hump raw food back to the boat without hygienic wrapping on it.

Some larger galleys have a free-standing rubbish bin just as you might find ashore, but this roams about in bad weather, and in smaller spaces it is probably better to have the kind that is fastened behind a cupboard door. The most convenient bin I have ever had either ashore or at sea is my present one, an exact copy of the one we had in *Fare Well*. It is fixed behind the door under the draining board to my left, the door drops forward on a chain just long enough to allow the bin-lid to open, and it is in exactly the right place to scrape plates into as you place them in the sink. It is lined with recycled plastic bags, two of them, because one always has a hole in it. At sea you will use it only for plastic items, since when you are hundreds of miles from shore, decomposable rubbish has to be tossed overboard.

Paper and food waste will disappear very quickly, into the maws of fish. Tins, if punctured, will sink and rapidly disintegrate, two miles down. Bottles are filled with sea water and sunk. We try not to throw plastic overboard anywhere. In harbour or near beaches and seashore, keep your rubbish and land it when you can, putting it in the appropriate containers if available. (It may, alas, yet end up in the sea, we have seen it dumped over a cliff by the local authority.)

If you have ever been woken at dawn by the relentless clonk of floating bottles along your hull; maddeningly loud and arrhythmic to screaming point (you are waiting not just for the proverbial second shoe to drop, but for the next ten green bottles), you will not, after a party, drop your bottles over the side to perform their *musique concrète* through the anchorage, waking more people than a change of wind among a ten-yacht raft-up. Perhaps the only legitimate use for firearms on board is for potting these offending bottles and sinking them. (Some of these comments may offend certain eco-conscious readers, but those who propose the laws and requirements of environmentalism must be realistic. We find legislators do not take into account circumstances of which they have little knowledge, and being at sea for 20 days with modern packaging is one of them. In fact there is a general exception for ships offshore, in that they are not required to keep on board anything that might be a health hazard to the crew, including corpses. It makes sense. We all have to try not to take unreasonable advantage of it.)

The galley floor is best kept clear and clean, since your dinner will occasionally land on it:

Always clean your galley floors:
The portion dropped there may be yours.

You don't want to slip on a greasy floor, either, so choose your flooring with care to be both non-slip and nice looking. It's hard to know if a soup-coloured floor is clean.

We have a rule that engine room dirt is not to be washed off in the galley sink. Bill disobeys it constantly, so I have to provide a sludge-and-rust coloured towel which he carefully avoids using. So any diesel puddings are his fault.

While I am ordinarily rather a slob at washing up, tending to leave it till I feel like it, I get more diligent if there are flies or wasps about. If there is nothing to attract them in the way of sticky surfaces and leftover food, there is nothing for them to wipe their filthy feet on. Sometimes they even go away.

• *Keeping your cool: refrigerators, ice boxes and other coolers* •

Fewer and fewer long-distance yachts nowadays travel with no means at all of cooling food. A refrigerator is both a boon and a tyranny; it makes a lot of difference to one's life, but it eats power, and goes wrong oftenest among one's gadgets. (See Chapter 6 for comments on fuels.) Nevertheless 100% of the cruising yachts in our recent survey have a fridge aboard, and 42% had a freezer as well. What a change that is! Top-opening fridges make sense on a boat, but most of them have poky openings which make both access and cleaning difficult. Our fridge could be defrosted in about ten minutes as it drained into the engine-room sump. We had wire baskets made to fit it, four at the top and four at the bottom. If we cared to use the extra power, the bottom would take frozen food. Defrosting and cleaning was done as a combined operation, both of us working fast: remove the eight baskets, hose down with fresh water, dry off and replace baskets. If the bottom was not full of frozen food, we put in a half-gallon container of sea water, frozen if possible (friendly fish markets will sometimes do this for you), to act as an extra cool bank. This also helps in case of a power failure. In this dire event, do not open the cabinet. Try to increase the insulation by covering it with a sleeping bag or deck cushions while the failure lasts. After more than about 24 hours (given a tightly packed, well frozen and well insulated mass) you may have to decide if a big cook-up is going to be necessary to save the food.

Ice boxes of the type that take a large block from the fishhouse were found in many yachts, and the ice lasts a surprisingly long time: ten to twelve days in the tropics and three to four weeks in cooler waters. Keep the ice as dry as possible by draining off any standing water. You should have no trouble finding ice, either in the Mediterranean or the West Indies, but it is heavy. Anywhere there is a fish market, there will be ice. If you can get half-gallon (2 litre) containers of sea water frozen for you, as is sometimes possible in the specialist freezer shops in the Med and the States, you can pack your box with these and obtain a drier cold. In the Pacific, however, ice is harder to come by.

Ice cubes are worth a mention. The usual flat trays are of little use on a boat; they spill when you heel. For years I searched for a top-opening untippable ice cube maker. When the answer appeared it was, like all the best ideas, astonishingly simple, a compartmented disposable plastic bag, filled from the top and then tied off, which will fit good humouredly into odd corners of the freezer. This excellent idea is now available everywhere.

With no refrigerator or ice box we are back to Grandmother's meatsafe, a wooden box with fly screen panels placed somewhere dry and airy, and if possible cool. An insulated polythene cool box in a dry bilge can be effective. Other cooling methods you will have are the sea water, which is often no cooler than the air, and the evaporation principle, used by the earthenware butter and milk coolers. A cloth or muslin dipped in fresh water causes rapid cooling as the wind passes over it, as does the Osokool type of porous box with a well for cooling water. (This water should be fresh, as salt will clog the pores, but little is needed.)

MARKETING

Marketing should be a pleasant experience, spiked occasionally with culture shock, and cushioned with coffee and cold drinks.

Those of our American friends who are used to the ecofriendly brown paper bags that go straight from the supermarket into the boot (trunk) of their car, will

A floating fruit and vegetable stall is a welcome sight for the live-aboard folk at Aegina, Greece.

do well to acquire a capacious shopping bag, several in fact. The ubiquitous string or nylon net bag of Europe comes to mind, which is great for stowage on board but less good for bringing home the bacon, since sharp items protrude and bite the calves of the hapless marketer. The best sort of bag is something waterproof and rather shapeless, perhaps with a drawstring top, that will subside into the inevitable pool of water in the bottom of the dinghy without disintegrating or the contents taking harm. Such a bag can also be carried on the head, which is much better for your spine than hanging off-balance at the end of one arm. I often see yachties with rucksacks, another way to carry quite a heavy load safely. Europeans shopping in America, *per contra*, will soon realise that the paper bags supplied by Piggly Wiggly, while ecologically sound, will not survive a soggy dinghy ride, and will take their own shopping bags with them to America where they can be difficult to find.

Most cruisers find room on board for some sort of trolley for heavy items, where taxis are unobtainable and deliveries unknown.

• *The joy of shopping* •

Entering a 'supermarket' on a Greek island (the Panemporion, or Everything Shop), you will find a dim cave, smelling of wine, olives and sheep cheese. The shutters are closed to keep it cool. It is dark, the floor is uneven and the clutter is unbelievable. Only the owner knows where the lamp oil is, or what lies buried under the empty fruit crates, or how long he has had that dusty pile of rubber knickers for a previous generation of babies. (For today's babies he has a rather less dusty pile of Pampers.)

Be careful how you step back or you will be caught behind the knees by the gigantic weighing machine that stands on the floor, and end up sitting in an open sack of rice. The bolts of cloth on the shelf are brown, brown and black; there are innumerable battered boxes of coloured thread and large hanks of natural wool for weaving the local rugs. Wine is from the barrel, olives from the vat and lamp oil from a drum: bring your own bottles. As it is several days since the last ferry, the vegetables are not what they were and the last of the fruit went this morning, but then you should have bought your produce on the day of the ferry, as everyone else does. However, there is wine, feta cheese and olives, and the bread that comes fresh every day, hot and redolent of the wood oven it was baked in up the hill. (The baker's van will toot on arrival, and you join the village women for the morning chat round the van.) It makes shopping so easy when there is very little choice. Who needs 25 different kinds of bottled water?

Compared with this, the supermarket in the Virgin Islands really was a supermarket. The packets and tins were on self-service shelves and showed signs of having been wiped over fairly recently. There was a great deal of strip lighting though only a quarter of it was working. There were trolleys, some with a full complement of wheels, and there were a few baskets that did not snag your clothes with broken wires. Almost everything available in the States was available here – tins a little bent and packets a bit battered by the long journey, and rather expensive; but here were your hominy grits, your canned chicken-and-dumplings, your Hershey bars and Betty Crocker cake mixes. (Was that a beetle in the cornflakes? Probably.) Local produce was tucked away at the back in coarse grey paper bags: the dried beans, cornmeal, black-eyed peas and delicious transparent tubes of split pea soup mix, like a miniature barber's pole of orange, yellow and green. Here too were the bottles of Hot Pepper Sauce, and a cold box for the sows' ears, pig's tails and chicken gizzards. Were there beetles? Yes, some, but at least they would not be resistant to every known bug destroyer.

That supermarket in turn was luxury itself compared with one we found in ex-Communist Romania. The shelves were almost bare, with about six packets each of staples such as flour, sugar, powdered milk, and huge bricks of soap. After the previous night's rainstorm the pasta section (all two feet of it) was flooded, and tin baths were strategically placed to catch the drips still coming through the roof. A few tins of tuna, carp and luncheon meat, plus locally made jam and honey, comprised the gourmet section. UHT milk was unknown, and there was no salt. I find it all intensely interesting going from one extreme to the other. I love to know what people eat, and how they cook it, and where better to find out than the shady covered markets of Europe or the Western world, where a cool breeze wafts through with scents of fruit and spices, where the cries of the vendors are accompanied by the country tattle of chickens, goats and donkeys and good food is to be had at low prices.

I get my heavy shopping over early: it's cooler. (In Yugoslavia you may find everything sold by seven o'clock in the morning.) My 'donkey', who is only too anxious to leave, takes the heavy stuff back to the boat, or waits at the café, leaving me to the leisurely delights of tasting, chatting, balancing price with quality and discovering new things. No one in a supermarket has time to chat as the market ladies have. They will tell you how to prepare and cook unfamiliar things, that if you wait a week the peaches will be cheaper, that the market will be closed tomorrow for a Fiesta, that the broad beans are new and tiny enough to be eaten raw with cheese. They will tell you how to clean squid, and never to boil endives. I discover treasures in obscure corners, I observe how things are bought and by what name, and what is in the cupboards at the back of the stall. With a bit of luck I come home with something cheap and delicious for lunch, which is well deserved since everything has to be logged in and stowed somewhere first, a time-consuming chore.

Having done it, though, you can then go off and anchor in a quiet bay and not worry about shopping for a while; only about trying the new recipe one of the market ladies gave you. The language of cooks and those who are interested in cooking is surprisingly easy to follow: if you don't know the word a little mime helps. Before I learnt the Greek for eggs I had to act the hen admiring her product, which used to cause great merriment; perhaps life is less fun now that I know more words.

STOWAGE

'How the Ordnance should bee placed, and the goods stowed on a ship.'

Stowage is a fine art. There are three requirements:

1 Your goods should be safe from bending, breakage, beetles and bilge water.
2 They should be accessible.
3 You should be able to find what you want easily.

To take the last point first, I recall how Clement Freud, taken on to cook magnificent dishes for a long yacht race, prepared a splendid scheme of labelled lockers, a detailed inventory of every bit of food he had in them, and a delicious daily menu. Alas, the ship had to leave immediately the stuff was delivered on the quay. It was bundled in anywhere it would fit by the frantic crew and Freud lost all track of it, getting occasional nasty surprises during the trip.

Whether you keep an alphabetical 'where to find it' notebook, or a list of the contents of every locker and drawer taped just inside it, or have a phenomenal memory, it matters not as long as you can find what you want. A filing system by which everything beginning with, say, S goes in the same place sounds alluring, but has practical drawbacks. One is that you get incompatible substances oddly mixed together, like soup, sandals and seizing wire; and the other is that of nomenclature: B for butterscotch, or S for sweets? B for bandaid or P for plasters?

The Set Theory works well: stow like things together. It is logical, which helps other people to find things. Thus your paint locker is also the logical place for solvents, brushes and sandpaper; as the Bosun's locker is for all sorts of nautical bits and pieces which do not fit into the come-in-handy box, which all cruisers know and love if not by that name.

We start with the heavy things, which ought to go near the bottom of the boat. That means the dry part of the bilge.

Tins

You will read many an account, in books about world-girdling or Southern Ocean racing, of the tedious task of varnishing all the tins and painting on some sort of shorthand to indicate the contents. (This led to a friend of ours saving a tin of 'goose' for his birthday, only to find on opening it that it was gooseberries.) We do not do anything to our tins. We then put them in the bilge, group them by kind in different-coloured plastic bags. (A dry bilge should be the norm for cruising; if you have reason to believe that your labels will soak off, change to a drier boat.) The plastic bags are merely to help separate a batch of tinned soups from the sort of tinned meat that goes with salad. There is also a bag with party delicacies in it, for birthdays and such. (The portion of the bilge which contains the sump, bilge pump and/or strum box must be kept free of anything which could clog the pump if the worst should happen, so it is a good place to put hard objects with no extraneous bits to float off, such as drums of antifouling or gallon jars of detergent, well wedged in against chafe.)

The 'everything' shop. Meganisi

If you have room, large flower pots and square plastic buckets make good separators, and the latter are always handy: we find we lose overboard one plastic bucket per storm, on average. Beer crates are also good for stowing other things, but too large for many boats.

Bottles

The bulk of these can stow in the bilge, too. If you get your duty frees there may be quite a lot of them. We used to pack ours carefully with corrugated paper, but when we ran out of it we found that jamming them in head-to-tail was just as effective: breakages are almost unknown, though a beer bottle popped its crown cap due to excessive fizz.

Those bottles that you want handy can be stored in cradles, on their sides as in a cellar, or behind a retaining bar, in circles cut to fit or an arrangement of pegs. All these restraints need to be at least 3 inches tall if you want to prevent clinkage when rolling.

Glasses

These go with bottles. They can go in similar circles, or be slotted into a holder if they are stemmed, or be packed fairly tightly into a drawer. The cheap French glasses will stack, but sometimes jam together unless separated by a leather tag. It is also possible to fit a bracket rather like a toothmug holder for glasses, and it's very good policy to have one to hold the helmsman's glass or mug within reach. We find these holders very good for jars of pencils and have them everywhere, with a circle of rubber or foam plastic at the bottom to prevent rattles.

Plastic containers

These should be of flexible polythene rather than the hard transparent acrylic, which breaks too easily. The lids should fit well (Tupperware has been a boon to yachtsmen, but there are many brands as good or better these days) to keep out beetles and dampness. A determined mouse can chew through them and a rat will be through in two bites. (Keep a cat.) Nevertheless they are indispensable for dry stores such as flour, cereals, pasta, rice and all the things that cannot be left in their original paper or plastic bags. (The heavy polythene used for five-pound bags of rice seems to be beetle proof, provided you protect them from chafe, but no barrier to a determined rat; see section on Pests.)

Other storage solutions

I have seen very impressive galley drawers built to fit their containers, all top-labelled and awesomely neat. My herb drawer is less orderly, as the jars and bottles are all different sizes and shapes; I've never known a serious cook able to stick with one brand of herbs and spices, ranged neatly in racks to fit as in the glossy magazines: we are not to be regimented like that. At least mine are all top-labelled and easy to find.

A combination of square and round shapes also means that you can get a jar out when you want it. This was not the case with a drawer I once saw packed tightly with square containers of the same height: it looked wonderful but you could not get a finger between them to lift a container out. This was not what I meant when I said that everything must fit where it stows.

I find the pierced plastic storage baskets now on sale useful for things that are not used every day. All the curry and Chinese ingredients go in one, to be got out when needed, all cake and pudding things go in another, and so on. If you are very short of space, put your herbs and spices into the small self-sealing plastic envelopes that are sold for jewellery, labelling them carefully. They should then be kept in the dark, so a biscuit tin might be better for your collection than Tupperware in this instance. Buy whole seeds and pods, they keep much longer than ground ones.

A ready-use shelf near your stove should hold all the things that everyone needs constant access to, such as tea, coffee, cocoa, salt and sugar; it should also hold half a dozen tins of bad weather food (see Bad Weather Cooking).

In Spain, it is possible to buy strong polythene milk containers with a double-sealed screw-on lid. I found these ideal for large quantities of wholemeal flour and the like, the 3- and 5-litre sizes suited me best. Similar containers are obtainable in Greece for storing olives. The cylindrical ones stowed in the bilge and did not chafe as the squarish ones containing soft drinks or detergents did. We had supposed that the latter would stow beautifully in the bilge, and so they did, but after six months or so in close contact with their bedfellows they began to chafe and crack at the corners, and the resulting orange flavoured foam was astonishingly hard to mop up. We still use such containers, but are much more careful about protecting them from chafe.

• *Storage tips* •

Remember that foil packets of instant mashed potato and dried soups and vegetables are irresistible to weevils, which can eat through them with ease: put all your packets into a lidded box. Cardboard boxes and packets are also not beetle proof, put the contents into glass coffee jars, which though heavy seem very strong and we have not broken one yet. Take extra lids though: they do break. Cut out any instructions from the packet and tape them to the jar.

Oblong bins often sold for cleaning materials can be screwed in suitable places such as the engine room. A shelf or bracket for them to stand on prevents them breaking away from the screws if they are used for heavy items. Ingenious use can also be made of flowerpot holders and deep sink tidies: for the brushes and scourers by the sink and in the heads or shower for organising everyone's toilet gear. Stainless steel and plastic tool clips have many uses, from preventing the washing-up liquid falling in the sink to actually holding tools. We wish the stainless ones were to be found in a wider range of sizes.

Nets are good for fruit and vegetables, since they are airy, and if strung horizontally, help to minimise bruising. Net bags, hung from hooks so as to occupy those almost unusable spaces, can be used for a variety of awkward objects.

Cardboard boxes are not recommended. Some yachts will not even allow them on board long enough to unpack the groceries, but unload on the quay because they are believed to harbour cockroaches. While the cockroach, according to one of my authorities, is an innocent little creature and one of the few to whom no blame can be attached for carrying any disease, it breeds fast, is aesthetically unpleasing and crunchy underfoot. The Pests section in Chapter 7 will help you to deal with it.

Other almost unusable spaces, such as behind linings, I have seen used to make little shelves for cassettes, hidey-holes for insecticides and rat bait where the cat and the children can't get at them, or once where there was a rather larger space, holes were cut in the lining and various brushes stuck through them, with their heads poking through and the handles in the space behind.

Large shelves can be made more practical by the use of plastic baskets; you can even colour-code them. They are good for sewing materials, the bulkier items of first aid (bandages, rolls of adhesive tape) and personal gear.

SHORT-TERM VICTUALLING

In previous editions we detailed lists, country by country, of what to buy where, what is hard to find and what to store up with. It seems no longer necessary to go into so much detail, since shopping in Europe has evened out since the coming of the EU, and everyone is far more knowledgeable about exotic foods. What neighbourhood does not have its Thai or Serbian restaurant these days? You still won't get pork in Muslim countries (except in certain parts of Turkey), ground ginger in Greece, soda water and Bramley apples in France, and anything left alone in its natural state in the USA. We are, however, going to be more specific about the cost of living this cruising life, which is a great deal less than many suppose.

Some people prefer to do all the shopping at once, and hire a taxi, donkey, rickshaw or tuk-tuk to get it back to the ship. On the Intra-Coastal Waterway in the States you can often borrow a 'courtesy car' to do this. In Europe, stores will sometimes deliver to the quay; it's worth asking. If the heavy shopping is done a day or so early there is plenty of time to stow things properly and choose your fruit and vegetables with care. If you then get them back to the boat without bruising and stow gently, they should last well.

• *Storing bread* •

Most Mediterranean bread is meant to be eaten the same day. If the baker takes the trouble to bake every day, he reasons that you should pay his bread the respect it deserves by buying it daily. Wrapped bread, which keeps a week, is looked upon with scorn and is only available in the larger centres. You can give your daily loaf a longer life, after you have enjoyed its first crusty day, by keeping it in a clean polythene bag, and thereafter placing a hunk of it for immediate eating in a lidded casserole in a moderate oven for a while. This needs a certain amount of judgement as you want the result to be close to fresh bread, not a dried-up rusk. A damp tissue in the casserole helps. When this has all gone, you will need crispbread or crackers, or bake your own. The long-keeping 'half-baked' loaves available in England and America are beginning to appear in the yachtier centres of Europe. The equivalent of *pain de compagne* (country bread), in almost any European country, keeps three or four days.

• *Storing meat* •

Meat for a week is easy if you have a fridge. With the possible exception of France, Mediterranean butchers do not hang their meat and it benefits enormously from a sojourn in your fridge of at least four days, especially lamb or beef.

If you have no fridge or ice box and the weather is hot, take raw meat for one day (perhaps two if you have a cool spot for it), cooked meat for one more day, and cook up a double batch of meat in the pressure cooker which you put somewhere cool and do not open.) (The manufacturers frown on this idea because the cooker is not hermetically sealed, but we find the contents keep a day or so and are free of dust and flies.) Thereafter you will have to rely on tins, and dried and preserved forms such as hams and whole salami in its infinite variety; a boon to yachtsmen as they should hang in the air anyway.

• *Dairy products* •

Eggs and butter all keep well enough for a short cruise. Salt butter keeps better in normal conditions, but if you want to keep it in the freezer use unsalted butter. You will need a keeping kind of milk: condensed, powdered or UHT (Long Life); the same goes for cream if it is wanted. Enjoy good cheese, its life is short even under the best conditions (5° to 10° C and 85% humidity). Soft cheeses last a few days, semi-soft, such as Port Salut, St Nectaire and Provolone, will last a week or more, the harder cheeses like Cheddar, Edam, the Tommes of France and the Gruyères will keep up to three weeks.

Even for a week, put biscuits, crackers or cookies in an airtight container. There is something horribly demoralising about soggy biscuits.

LONG-DISTANCE VICTUALLING

'Gammons of bacon, dried neat's tongues, Beefe packed up in vinegar . . .'

Long-distance means long enough to cross an ocean, though the same consider-ations apply to a long cruise among the more isolated communities where supplies may be difficult to get; we were more benighted going down the Danube, especially in the ex-communist countries, than we ever were in remote Greek islands or the West Indies. A month to six weeks should encompass most ocean passages if one takes the more practical routes between ports.

Not enough attention is paid, I believe, to food for long passages. The lad who airily assured me in Barbados that he and his all-male crew had crossed the Atlantic on beer and cornflakes was pulling my leg (I hope), but there is more than a grain of truth in what he said. I've seen the least experienced youngster sent off at the last minute to victual the ship with a hastily compiled list in which liquor had clearly been discussed at length, but which was vague as to kinds and quantities of other items. I have sometimes been spotted as a yachtswoman and asked for advice right there in the market a couple of hours before departure. If you are starting from England, explain to the manager of your local Cash and Carry Store that you need bulk stores for a long voyage, and you will usually be allowed to shop there on a one-time only basis. Supermarkets in ports often give a discount to long-distance cruisers if they spend more than a certain sum. It's worth a try.

• *Planning* •

Where do you start? Where do you begin when planning food for a long voyage? Some swear by Frederick M Gardner (see below); I went by multiplying a head count *times* meals *times* portions. On our transatlantic crossing to the West Indies I was glad of the surplus remaining at the end of the voyage, as tinned and bottled stores were expensive and sometimes hard to find in the Windward Islands.

While we try to live on local produce where we can, to do so in the West Indies would have caused deprivation to the carnivorous males among the crew as steak dinners ashore were largely beyond our means. Luckily, the widely available chicken, frozen, fried or both, saves them from carnal famine.

• *How much do you need to take?* •

Carry food and water for twice the normal expected passage time, plus emergency provisions and water for a further ten days. You do not want to end up 'down to the last tin of corned beef and licking the dew off the deck', as one of our single-handed friends described his landfall. Mr Gardner's famous list, 'The care and feeding of a Yachtsman', lists items by weight and calls for 5½lb of food per man per day, of which 14½oz was meat. To that he added a gallon of liquid per head per day for drinking.

So he expects four people for 40 days to consume over a ton of food. It takes a bit of organising. I studied this list with great interest before our first long ocean passage and came to the conclusion that our crew of three men and two very tiny women would consume rather less than that. No way can I eat nearly a pound of meat a day. So I decided to think in terms of the number of meals per day and the portions required, and allow a bit extra each time in case of extreme hunger. My deliberations will be found further on and are easily modified for larger or smaller appetites.

Protein
After the first week, if you are a carnivore you will have to rely on tinned meat and fish, with eggs, cheese, vegetable and nut proteins if you are not.

Dried and preserved meats such as hams and whole salami in its infinite variety are a boon to yachtsmen as they should hang in the air anyway. How long will salami keep? In 1944 we returned to the house we had left in 1939. In the deserted larder we found, hanging lonely under a shelf, a forgotten salami, given to us by a grateful Czech refugee at the outbreak of war. In that drear time of rationing we seized it with glee. It was used, slice by precious slice, in all kinds of ways; the smallest dice giving an exotic flavour, a bit chewy after all those years but still delicious.

Take dried fruit, peanuts and peanut butter, powdered milk, wheatgerm and cheese to add a little more wham to your spam, and see the section on food-combining for further meatless protein.

• *Tinned goods* •

If you have no freezer you will need plenty of tins of meat. These should be solidly packed protein, not the kind that is full of gravy where you find only two walnut-sized lumps of gristle with difficulty by using a magnifying glass. Good tinned meat and fish is expensive, but is worth the money especially if you have no fridge. Good buys are corned beef, chopped pork, sausages, stewed steak, luncheon meat, ham and tongue, and for special occasions pheasant or grouse if you can run to it. Fray Bentos steak and kidney pie is good, and they make an excellent range of pie fillings: steak and onion, steak and mushroom, and steak and kidney, which were extremely popular with the crew, much better than the tinned steak and kidney puddings, where the duff was of doubtful consistency and the filling rather meagre.

Also popular was the stewing steak from Ireland, brand-named Casserole, and Libby's Beef Stew. Newforge's Irish Stew tasted good, but we had to add more meat to it. Meatballs which I thought would be great with spaghetti, turned out to be pasty and flavourless. I washed the gravy off them and replaced it with a good strong Italian ragu (spaghetti sauce) full of onion, tomato and basil, which made them a bit more interesting. If you get tired of tinned hamburgers you can make much better meatballs from them. French tins of cassoulet (gourmet pork and beans) are wonderfully ribsticking stuff, add some pork boiling sausage (vacuum packed, keeps well) to pep up the protein. I no longer give space to tins of spaghetti. The real thing is so much better, and almost as quick and easy, especially if you cheat and use ready-made sauces. The same goes for tinned soup (I make an exception for *soupe de poisson*); there is always something to make fresh soup from, even if it's potatoes, onions and milk, and a stock cube. There, too, is something worth its space: a variety of stock cubes of different flavours to add interest to soups, stews and risottos.

BODRUM MARKET

Tinned chicken is always a disappointment; it is too soft in texture and the flavour is changed. The best we found was the chicken and dumplings of the Southern USA. However I carry a few small tins of chicken in jelly to add variety and extra protein to bad-weather soups and risottos. Tinned patés are always a good idea, as are hams and tongues if you can afford them.

Vegetables that survive canning best are petit pois (tiny peas), haricot beans (get some of them au naturel rather than in tomato sauce, for a wider variety of uses), *garbanzos* (chick peas), spinach, sweetcorn, beetroot, celery (the texture is wrong but the flavour is good), tomatoes (very useful), lentils, green beans, broad beans and mushrooms (but dried mushrooms have better flavour and weigh less).

In Spain, tinned cauliflower and Brussels sprouts are available; we found them rather soft, but the cauliflower made quite good *Crème du Barry* soup, and the sprouts, fried with onions, made an occasional change. Carrots are useful for a touch of colour, but fresh ones kept so well that I hardly ever needed the tinned variety. We carried assorted tinned Chinese vegetables, but missed the crunchiness of the real thing.

Tinned fish are very handy in all varieties. Octopus and squid survive canning well; mussels taste tinny. Tinned kippers and salmon make good paté or kedgeree. Paella mixture (a small tin of mussels, squid and octopus available in Spain) can make a good fishermen's risotto as well. Pilchards can make a pie with potatoes. Sardines make a delicious *spaghetti con le sarde*, while anchovies make a good spaghetti sauce when mixed with garlic, chillies and olive oil. Tuna is useful. Crabmeat is dear, but put some in the 'treats bin', a tin will feed a good many people in a risotto or seafood quiche.

Take a little tinned fruit; your fresh fruit supplies ought to last well; but something like pineapple, raspberries or gooseberries can make a treat. Tinned fruit cake is worth taking, as it is time and fuel-consuming to make.

Other tinned goods that I found valuable were the small tins or jars of spaghetti sauce available in Italy in four flavours, or the less good and rather sweeter ones now available everywhere in Europe and the USA, to which more meat, fish or mushrooms could be added to make a very satisfying meal, especially with wholemeal spaghetti.

Many of these tins can, of course, be used for cold lunches, perhaps accompanied by a cup of hot soup if the weather is cool, or a salad if it is hot.

• *Dried food, cereals, grains, pulses and flour* •

These are particularly important to vegetarians. Grains, seeds, cereals, and dried pasta will keep for at least a year. Grains and legumes add texture and crunch to tinned food and have a fresher taste. They will keep a year at least and they add texture and crunch to tinned food and have a fresher taste. Dried haricot beans, split peas, lentils and chick peas are all good in spite of the jokes, and all add protein to the diet. Fresh water is necessary to reconstitute and cook them. Rice keeps indefinitely and is essential in my cooking: both white and brown, but the brown takes longer to cook (soak it for 24 hours first). Dried pasta of all kinds keeps splendidly as long as beetles are kept away – they love it too. Wholemeal pasta is available and makes a more wholesome food, but it does not taste the same. Burghul (bulgar or cracked wheat) makes interesting pilaf and is a change from rice.

Muesli and similar mixtures keep better (6 months: the nuts in it deteriorate first) than crisp breakfast cereals (like cornflakes, which sog very quickly and take up much more room). Note that nuts go off much quicker than dried fruit, so do not mix them in advance.

You will need bread flour: white and wholemeal, and ordinary flour, but take a tin of baking powder to make your own self-raising flour. Now here's a thing: can I find baking powder or cream of tartar in airtight tins these days? They are all in cardboard or plastic containers marked 'Keep in a cool dry place'.

White flour if kept dry and beetle-free keeps eight months to a year in damp-proof containers. Brown and wholemeal are supposed to last about 6–8 months because of the greater fat content, but in my experience are usable for much longer. All flour is best kept in the dark.

Wholemeal bread mix is worth its space. Cake mixes can be useful when time is short but keep less well than separate ingredients because the fat content spoils. Ready-mix packets, such as cake, pastry, scones and dumplings, have a shelf-life of about 6 months, but those with no fat, such as bread-mix and pan-cakes, keep about a year, and the bread-mix is usable for much longer if you add extra easy-blend yeast.

BREAD MAKING

YEAST

Life is now easier with easy-blend dried yeast (patent name Fermipan) such as Harvest Gold or McDougal's which keeps (they say) for 9 months, longer in my experience. Sprinkle it in with the other dry ingredients.

There are times when a loaf of really solid high-protein bread is worth a whole tray-ful of bridge rolls. Try this one:

HIGH PROTEIN BREAD

1 packet (10oz 280gms) wholemeal
   bread-mix (Grannie Smith, McDougal's,
   etc) or use 280gms of wholemeal flour
Add to the dry mix:
1/3 cup wheatgerm (a generous half oz)
   (This product does spoil rather
   quickly, unfortunately)

1/3 cup soya flour
1/3 cup instant powdered milk
1/2 teasp (or 1 sachet, 6gms) Fermipan
   (instant dried easy-blend yeast)

Into the 6 fluid ounces of handhot water you will use to mix the dough, stir a tablespoon of molasses, black treacle or dark honey; add to the dry ingredients, mix well and knead for five minutes. You won't need a bread tin if you then shape it into a bunloaf or cob. Put it on a greased baking tray; place it, tray and all, inside a large polythene roasting bag (take with you several of the turkey roasting size), secure the bag with a wire tie and leave in a warm place to rise for an hour. Bake 35 to 40 minutes in a hot oven, and eat with enormous pleasure.

You will notice in the list of ingredients on the bread-mix packet ascorbic acid: vitamin C. This is not to do you good, but to cut out one of the usual two rises. If you make your bread from scratch, you can do the same, by adding a crushed 50mg vitamin C tablet per 1.2kg of flour, or a pinch of vitamin C powder for the recipe above. Vitamin C powder can be bought at a pharmacy.

DIE-HARD BREAD

You have no oven? After kneading the above recipe, shape it into a round and put it in your pressure cooker, gently warmed and well oiled. Cover with a damp cloth. When the dough has doubled in size remove the cloth, put the cooker over high heat for three minutes, with the lid on but the pressure valve open. Then turn down the heat to as low as possible, using an asbestos mat or flame spreader if you have one, and cook, still with the pressure valve open, for 30 to 35 minutes. Turn the bread over and cook a further few minutes to brown the top. This really works, I've done it.

Collect and take with you recipes for quickly made top-of-the-stove breads such as griddle scones, soda bread, bannocks and scotch pancakes. I have about 40 such recipes; they can be a life saver when morale needs a boost.

• *Sell-by dates* •

On long voyages you will outsail many sell-by dates, don't panic; they are the manufacturer's get-out, and need not be regarded as written in stone. If it looks, smells and tastes all right, it probably is. The only thing past its date that has made me really ill is shelled walnuts – in England.

• *AFD (air freeze-dried) foods* •

These are made in quite a few varieties now. Apart from the well-known dried soups you can get beef, chicken and shrimp curries, farmhouse stew, savoury mince and beef stroganoff, and all kinds of rice dishes. They need fresh water to prepare and take time to cook. Their texture tends to be rather monotonous, but they have their place especially for bulking out leftovers. It's worth reminding you that the average shipboard beetle gnashes its way through foil packets with disturbing ease, so keep them in a metal or plastic box, and be conscientious about putting the lid back. In Italy you can get an excellent freeze-dried mixture of about ten diced vegetables, intended for minestrone. There's an English equivalent, too. A handful of this in any soup or stew is good: you can also use the whole packet with a little salt pork, bacon, or boiling sausage and pasta, for a dish you can stand the spoon up in.

Dried fish

This is always heavily salted. Throughout the Mediterranean and in parts of the West Indies you will see boxes of rough-looking sheets of cardboard, vaguely fish-shaped, light on one side and dark on the other. It is, in fact, fish – called bacalao, baccala, stockfish or salt cod. It keeps for ever without refrigeration and is very good when properly processed, but even if you get a preliminary amount of salt out by soaking it first in sea water and then fresh, it still needs rivers of fresh water washing over it for 24 hours before it is edible, so it doesn't work at sea.

Dried mushrooms

They are a splendid idea: they have much more flavour than tinned ones. The French, Italians and the Chinese have very good ones, soak in a little warm water for 20 minutes.

Dried egg

I have mixed feelings about this. It's probably all right in cakes; otherwise use it to eke out the breakfast scramble or omelette. To make scrambled eggs entirely with dried eggs brings back too many wartime memories, but today's kids might like it, knowing that there are plenty of other things to eat and bacon or Bacon Grill (tinned) to go with it. (Address in Appendix.)

Dried and salt meat

Whole salami has already been mentioned. If you have no fridge or ice box, a piece of smoked bacon will hang in an airy place, dusted with black pepper to keep the flies away. Hams are trickier, since the cut section dries a bit, but a leg of mountain ham we bought in Yugoslavia lasted all of a Mediterranean summer. It was heavily smoked and we hung it in a net inside greaseproof paper, changed regularly. Similar hams are to be had in Spain, Italy and France. Vacuum-packed smoked and salted meats keep from six weeks to two months and are worth their space for snacks: sliced ham, prosciutto (Parma ham), sliced salami, liver sausage, and that valuable standby: boiling sausage; the Dutch ones are excellent. Some vacuum packs of bacon will be useful for a few weeks, but a large piece of smoked streaky bacon (*poitrine fumée* in France) will keep much longer and taste better: keep it like the ham, in greaseproof paper.

• *Dairy produce for long voyages* •

Long Life milk (UHT) and cream keep for five months, and we think it is nearer to fresh milk than either powdered or condensed; it is a matter of opinion. (We were amused to find that it arrived in the States while we were there in 1982: hailed, of course, as 'new', when we'd had it in Europe for several years!) A little of the instant powdered milk can be useful in some recipes: ie bread. Get the powder in plastic containers for best keeping. Long Life cream tastes better on tinned fruit than tinned cream, and is fine for cooking. Nothing beats fresh milk for cereals or just drinking, but I have yet to meet a cruising boat with a cow on board.

Cheese

Sad to say, cheese is a problem. It is best kept in a cool humid place such as the vegetable drawer of the fridge (not the freezer, which is ruination to cheese). Any soft or semi-soft cheeses will not survive the first week, say goodbye to Camembert and Brie after seven days. See also above (Short-term victualling).

Semi-soft cheeses (St Paulin, Tommes, St Nectaire, Wensleydale) will delight you for a week or so if you wrap them tightly with foodwrap to exclude the air. Roquefort and other blues should be wrapped in a damp cloth and put in a plastic box, to keep a couple of weeks or more. The harder cheeses need careful selection and dedicated care for their well-being in order to last; Edam, Cheddar and Gruyère and similar are best in plastic bags with frequent attention to prevent sweating and pare off mould.

That said I have had some success with a cheese keeper made by Tefal (see Appendix) which humidifies the naked cheese it contains; they last at least twice as long, and the hard cheeses a great deal longer. Be warned, it is bulky, and needs to be kept in the fridge.

If you can find a whole 'stoved' Edam cheese (Edam *étuvée*, available in France and the Low Countries), you are in luck, it keeps indefinitely. So do the granite-like Parmesan (in the piece) and Sbrinz, its Swiss equivalent, which will happily break your teeth after a round the world voyage. Some of the industrial cheeses, vacuum packed or wrapped in foil, keep well until opened, such as Philadelphia and other cream cheeses: study the sell-by dates, and take boxes of small portions of wrapped processed cheese of various kinds for the night box. There are such things as tinned camembert and brie, made in Bavaria. If you keep them long enough you might have sufficiently forgotten what real cheese tastes like to find them amusing. Vacuum packs of grated cheese are useful, and keep several months.

The only way to have yoghurt after a couple of weeks at sea is to make your own from a good Bulgarian culture.

• *Eggs* •

Fresh eggs need no refrigeration: indeed EU regulations make the chilling of eggs illegal. Buy your eggs from a hen personally known to you, along with her assurance that they are new laid, ie this morning's or at a pinch yesterday's. Do *not* wash them. It is not an old wives' tale that eggs should not be washed: it

is illegal in the EU for eggs to be washed before packing. The reasons are: a new-laid egg is protected from bacteria by a film thoughtfully provided by the hen for the purpose; this film is removed by washing. Also, a dry egg is impermeable to bacteria but this impermeability breaks down if the shell becomes moist, and while the egg is wet, germs can pass through the shell and set up premature spoilage. (In the USA eggs are washed *and dried* at the packing stations under strictly monitored sanitary conditions.) In Europe, if you are fussy, you may gently brush off loose dirt and feathers, but leave any washing until just before you cook the egg.

It will now be clear to you why an egg that has been chilled should be avoided: on removal from the fridge condensation occurs, the shell becomes moist and bacteria can enter, shortening the life of the egg.

Keep your eggs carefully packed (we found fibre trays cut to fit square plastic buckets which we kept in the bilge were perfect) at a temperature of about 10°C/50°F; a cool dry bilge for example, and they will keep for a month with no further attention. On the average transatlantic crossing in either direction you should have no trouble.

How to deal with a bad egg

As this is now a rare event in Europe and the USA, I revive some forgotten tips. After three weeks, start to test your eggs in a glass of fresh water. If they sink they are fine. If they float with a bit of the shell above the water, have ready a clean yoghurt pot or other disposable container: avert the nose and break the egg into the pot. If it is bad, you will know at once. Do not pour it down the sink: unless you have a salt water pump at the sink you will waste too much water flushing away the smell. Just deep-six it over the side, pot and all. If you are doubtful, you did use a clean pot, so it will be OK for well-flavoured omelettes or ginger cakes. If your egg is undecided whether to sink or float it is probably not young enough to be a breakfast soft-boiled egg, and the whites may refuse to whip, but it will still be usable for most purposes. A flattened-out runny yolk or white means the egg is old, but not necessarily bad. Broken yolks also indicate a stale, but not necessarily bad, egg.

No, you cannot test them in salt water because they would all float.

A new-laid egg (up to three days old) is very hard to peel when hard-boiled, and takes longest to cook, but you won't have that problem for long. If your journey is going to last longer than a month or five weeks, some of your eggs will need to be preserved. This is done by sealing the shell, either by putting the eggs in water-glass (a solution of sodium silicate obtainable these days only from very old-fashioned chemists) or smearing them with petroleum jelly (Vaseline). Make sure you get the odourless kind: eggs absorb smells and tastes very easily. In waterglass, the new-laid eggs that my mother put down in wartime kept for a year. After six to nine months you could not count on unbroken yolks, but otherwise they were great.

• *Fats, and oils* •

Outside the fridge, salt butter keeps better than fresh sweet butter but it is harder to get in the Med and more expensive as it is usually imported. Keep all fats as cool as you can. Margarine keeps longer, melts less easily, and now seems to be less good for us than was once thought. Learn to cook with olive oil (that *is* good for you), it keeps a year or more, like other cooking oils. Lard keeps very well indeed, more than a year. Packets of suet do not melt, and keep about six months.

• *Boil-in-the-bag and foil dinners* •

Some are very good indeed, though they are expensive and the portions are small. They have an inestimable value for no-fridge voyagers, as they have a long shelf life. They make good celebration food. Stowed so they do not chafe through they last almost indefinitely. Chicken and duck in these packs are infinitely better than tinned.

In Italy a boiling sausage known as Cotechino or Zampone is put up in the same way. It keeps for years. It can be boiled in the bag, and is excellent hearty food sliced and eaten with lentils, mushy peas and mashed potatoes. All these sealed packs can be boiled in sea water. Other sausages such as garlic and liver sausage to be eaten cold are appearing in the UK in long-life foil packs too; no need to refrigerate any of these.

• *Variety of foods* •

Do not rely on just one kind of food, and one kind of cooking even on a short trip, not for the sake of variety, but actual survival. I heard recently of a racing crew almost succumbing to despair; they had been furnished *only* with boil-in-the-bag meals, but the alcohol cooker that should have heated them was ruined by salt water in a storm, and a single Sterno burner was all that remained to cook for ten people. Freeze-dried food is useless without the fresh water to mix it with, and something to heat it, and even tins need an opener (carry two or three). As a last resort in storms you could take a few of the self-heating cans now available. They are very expensive, but in dire need you might feel a hot meal was worth the money. If you ring the changes with freeze-dried foods, tinned, vacuum-packed, salted, and good old long-keeping standbys like rice and dried pasta, with fresh bread, onions and potatoes, lemons and oranges you probably won't even need vitamin tablets.

• *Other ways of preserving* •

Vacuum-packed bacon and cold meats keep very well in a fridge or ice box, as does paté. Even if you have no fridge there is a great deal of choice. Paté will keep for a month, potted in jars under a layer of butter to seal it. You can keep a brine crock (I use Tupperware with a well-fitting lid to prevent spills) and salt down pieces of pork, hocks, trotters, slabs of belly or tongues. If you leave them in the crock for three days they are mild enough to cook in the pressure cooker without previous soaking, and will then keep for up to two weeks in a cool dry spot, though my guess is that they will get eaten fairly rapidly. Not for nothing were the sailors of yore called 'salt horses': a little practice in the ancient art of salting and pickling may stand you in very good stead if you wish to cruise in the wilder parts of the globe, even in the Eastern Med and the north coast of Africa where the Muslim culture makes pork and charcuterie hard to find.

Bill and I became genuine salt horses on one Mediterranean cruise. I was looking for a tongue to salt before cruising eastwards, and in an Italian market allowed eagerness to overcome caution when I found one after a long search. I bore it back to the corner of the market where my 'donkey' was waiting with the heavy stuff. Beaming, I showed him my prize. He sighed, and pointed out the stall where I had bought it, where I could now plainly see the horse's head that adorned the sign. I had bought horse tongue. I pickled and cooked it just the same – it was excellent: we ate every bit with relish. In the south-west of France they pot down goose and duck in the autumn; the meat is cooked gently in goose or duck fat, potted and covered completely with the fat in stoneware jars. It keeps for a year in a cool larder. My food bug authority worries about this, so if you want to experiment make sure you get an authentic recipe and follow the instructions carefully. The dish is known as *confit d'oie* (goose) or *confit de canard* (duck). I made some to take with us when we left England: we ate it and survived. In French supermarkets this duck and goose confit are now available in vacuum packs which keep well. You'll also find it tinned.

Bottling
Bottling jars are quite robust. I take a few containing Bramley apples, and apple and blackberry, since they seem to be unavailable tinned. Supermarket apple sauce is woefully tasteless, and cooking apples are unknown even in Europe.

• *What to put in the freezer* •

If you are fortunate enough to have a freezer (42% of the cruising yachts in our survey have them), and still more fortunate to have one that works, pack it with the solidest meat available. It is a waste of space and energy to fill it with bone, gristle and other bulky inedibles. Choose cuts with a minimum of bone or none, and reduce chickens to legs (or thighs and drumsticks) and boned breasts. Put them into packs of the number of portions needed for a meal. Do the same with chunks of stewing beef or lamb: you will be very glad at sea that you took the trouble to remove all the fat and gristle and pack it in convenient meal-sized portions. Chops, whether pork or lamb, should be parcelled according to crew numbers, or in two's, enabling you to add small amounts of protein to rice or pasta dishes. Shrimps are good packed in hundred gram packages; small amounts to add to fish soup, paella or risotto are handy sometimes. Fillets of cod or haddock make a change if the fishing is not going well. Hamburgers can be made into meatballs, or cottage pie, get the best quality you can. The same goes for mince, get really good quality and put it up in meal-sized parcels which reflect the number in the crew. Keep a careful record of what is in the freezer, where it is approximately (baskets help, or different coloured bags), and cross it off the list as consumed.

I would grudge freezer space for prepared dishes, vegetables (except spinach and green beans), puddings and junk food such as pizza, but you might not agree. Morale is a funny thing – if you feel that frozen doughnuts or Black Forest cake might at some point do the trick, don't let me dissuade you! In the freezer, sweet butter will keep for 6 to 8 weeks, salt butter rather less. (The reverse is true outside the fridge.) Margarine or low-fat spread keeps longer than butter.

• *The care and treatment of sick vegetables* •

There is no reason why you cannot eat fresh vegetables from the Canaries to Barbados, or the West Indies back to Europe. Oddly enough, this will be more difficult coming east from the Americas or going across the Pacific, for it has little to do with the length of the journey.

It has everything to do with whether your fruit and vegetables have been wounded in the chill-room of the supermarket, or killed in the gas chambers of the commercial fruit merchants. If they have, then for keeping purposes they are not worth a damn, as you must have noticed. Regrettably, since we first wrote 12 years ago, things have deteriorated further, it is now very hard indeed in the western world to buy genuinely fresh vegetables that have not been chilled.

You have only to compare the potato clamp at the frosty field's edge, the onions drying from hooks in the barn, the apples laid neatly on the attic floor to keep all winter (and what a memorable smell that was for the children!), the pumpkins stacked on the outhouse roof in bright orange rows, and the pomegranates and persimmons left on the tree to burn like lanterns in the autumn night, as used to be common (and still is where life is simple), and then think of the expected life of the produce you bought this morning at the supermarket. If you don't put that cucumber in the fridge at once it will dissolve into a pint of greenish water by morning. The lettuce has suffered already in the car. The cabbage and oranges may last till the weekend. Not much else will.

Chilling kills fruit and vegetables. They die of hypothermia. Buy them straight off the tree, out of the ground or off the vine, from the farm or market (but never from the supermarket of the western world). Choose them with the care you would give to selecting your next child from the orphanage, carry them gently without bruising them, and cradle them like babies in a cool and airy spot. If you wash them at all (to rid them of slugs or beetle eggs) dry them with great care and thoroughness to prevent mould. Unlike babies, you go through the whole lot daily and throw any doubtful ones overboard. We kept our main stock of fruit and vegetables in the dinghy under a canvas cover raised over the oars to give a through-draught; it was easy to check them over.

Since almost any packet of fresh fruit and veg from a supermarket says: 'Keep refrigerated'; you'd need a refrigerator as big as a double-decker bus. Recently I have been using Stay-Fresh bags, intended to keep your vegetables and fruit fresh for much longer. You are supposed to keep them in the fridge, but I experimented with keeping them in the dinghy, as one does. The results are quite encouraging, and I now use them regularly for green and red peppers, carrots, celery and other vegetables.

• *Fruit and vegetables: How long do they keep?* •

East-to-west Atlantic crossings, November to March   You will be buying your stores in a Mediterranean climate, in the markets of Spain or Portugal, the Canaries or Madeira. Quality and variety are excellent and prices are reasonable.

- *Will last six months*: pumpkin (if you do not pierce the skin), potatoes, onions, kept loose or in nets, lemons wrapped in foil.
- *Will last a month or more*: carrots, Jerusalem artichokes and parsnips buried in earth or sand. (These last three I now put in a Stay-Fresh bag.) Citrus fruits, cooking and eating apples, are best kept on trays with hollows to separate them – you can get these from fruit farms or some supermarkets. Tomatoes, if you choose them hard and all shades of green and wrap them separately in paper towels or newspaper (but not foil because the acid in tomatoes eats through it), and put in a cool dark place. Check daily, eat the reddest and throw out any squashy ones.
- *Will last about three weeks if the skins are undamaged*: melons, cucumber, marrow (do not pierce it), avocado pears, hard white cabbage, kept loose.

- *Will last two weeks kept in Stay-Fresh bags*: whole green peppers, celery, leeks, Romaine and iceberg lettuce, fresh figs, courgettes. The latter benefit from wrapping as for tomatoes, and careful watching. If the flower has not dried off the end they are particularly subject to mould.
- *Will last ten days*: aubergine, globe artichokes, pineapple, cauliflower, green beans.
- *One week*: lettuces (check for slugs, etc): be sure they are dry and wrap firmly in Clingfilm. The big Romaine lettuces and the Iceberg keep especially well. Soft fruit, figs, grapes, green runner beans. Mushrooms seem to keep best if kept separated in eggboxes. They dry and shrink a little, but are edible for about a week.
- *Eat first and fast*: spinach and broccoli (a Stay-Fresh bag extends its life by a couple of days only), cabbage greens or spring greens, watercress, Dutch lettuce, and anything slightly bruised.

The above times are based on choosing undamaged fruit and vegetables checked for wild life, and picking them over daily for signs of decay. The Stay-Fresh bags need checking too, moisture in them should be blotted with kitchen paper before replacing the produce and sealing well. The bags may be washed and re-used several times. This all sounds like a lot of work, but fresh food on a long crossing is really worth some trouble, and if it's like most long voyages, you'll be glad of something to pass the time. For vegetarians, this advice is essential.

Despite all I've said about chilling produce, if you like chilled salad, and you have a fridge or ice box, it is of course permissible to chill all these things just before serving. After all, you have to kill a chicken before eating it.

West-to-east crossing, in May to August   You will be buying your produce in the West Indies, North America or Bermuda. For the US or Bermuda, the notes on European shopping apply, with some alterations for the change in season. You will have to 'think seasonal' to avoid chilled produce. Remember: get it out of the ground or off the tree (or from under the hen).

Bermuda is a special case; you will find it harder to follow the rule that a chilled vegetable is a dead vegetable, because a large proportion of green stuff and fruit is chilled and imported from the US for immediate consumption. At great expense, I might add. Never mind, it's only 18 days to the Azores. Actually, there are a few market gardens in Bermuda, but they require some hunting down.

FRUIT AND VEGETABLES ON THE OTHER SIDE

The West Indies have some unfamiliar edibles worth describing:
- The large variety of roots (yams, eddoes, tannia, dasheen) keep well for months in a dry place. Yams and sweet potatoes are big enough to have

doubtful pieces excised: use the mutilated ones first. Sweet cassava can be kept buried the same way as carrots and artichokes. (It is the bitter cassava from which the poisonous juice must be extracted; it is mostly used for laundry starch.)

- Christophene, in appearance like a pale green knobbly pear but a better keeper, cooks like a crisp marrow. Aubergine is often called melongene or eggplant, and keeps up to two weeks.
- Pawpaw should be bought green, when it can be used as a vegetable until it turns golden, then it is eaten as a fruit after a week to ten days.
- Coconuts have a long life: while they come to no harm from a bump or two, it is worth stowing them securely or they crash around the boat like cannonballs.
- Mangoes keep about a week.
- The huge bananas known as plantains are only for cooking; as they are very starchy you can treat them like potato.
- Breadfruit has the same function and keeps well. It grows on one of the most beautiful trees in the Caribbean.
- The bunch of bananas is the badge of all long-distance cruisers in the West Indies, hanging somewhere in the rigging. Even if you put a few 'hands' in the dark and cool to slow the ripening, you will still have to eat them fast when their time comes. You will need recipes for banana bread, banana curry, banana milkshake, banana cake, banana pudding, fried bananas and rum-buttered bananas, just for a start. Bananas will cost you about a penny each, if you shop right. Be sure you hang them the wrong way up, which is actually the right way up, the way they grow (ends suggestively uppermost, hands pointing to the sky).

HOW TO LIVE CHEAPLY ALMOST ANYWHERE

• *Before you go* •

In these days when quick and beguiling TV dinners have led many of us to forget how to cook basic cheap meals (if we ever knew) you will have to do a bit of home-work. Talk to your grandmother, or at least the older generation, about what they ate in the old days. Consult the library. Collect recipes, especially from countries outside the wealthy West. You must learn to cook inexpensive things unfamiliar to you. Try and find an old cookery book that tells you how to deal with unusual things (I swear by André Simon's *Guide to Good Food and Wine*, a small book published 1952, which tells me what to do with kangaroo, hippopotamus, laver (seaweed) or cassowary for example, not to mention how to mix a Manhattan cocktail, should I feel like one). More useful to cruisers than anything by the latest TV chef, however expert in rocket salad and balsamic vinegar he may be.

Learn about protein combinations (see below). Preparing food and cooking will take longer than is the habit these days, because you must leave pre-packed convenience food, where there is any, on the shelf of the supermarket. Look for the cheaper cuts of meat, and cook them long and slowly in the pressure cooker. The good news is that not only will you eat better than you ever did, and be healthier; you will thoroughly enjoy experimenting with savoury recipes that are a delight and a wonder at a third of the price of fish and chips.

The West Indies
One can live cheaply, but a bit primitively, on rice, breadfruit, eddoes, bananas, fish and rum.

The Far East
You can live for a week on a few pounds, but you must learn to shop locally, and eat what the inhabitants eat, ie the soup noodle buffet at 30 pence a bowlful, instead of the smart tourist joint at usual European prices.

The Mediterranean
Live on seasonable vegetables and fruit, and don't be tempted by the delicious but costly delicacies available from the *rosticcheria* or the *traiteur*. Fish can be dearer than meat, except for sardines and picarel, so if you can catch the fish yourself, so much the better. We live without stinting ourselves on £60 a week for food and drink for two people. We could halve this easily without suffering much, and often we do, for short spells. Eating and drinking out a couple of times a week comes to about £20, that's optional of course.

• *Combining protein-rich grains and cereals* •

Meat, fish, eggs and chicken are complete proteins.

On long voyages among remote islands, such as the Antipodes–Red Sea run or across the Pacific, you can find your diet short of meat and fish. The same can apply if you cannot afford large quantities of meat.

It is worth studying the following facts with care and in more detail than I have space to give here. (The Small Planet books listed in the Appendix will tell you more.) Certain grains and legumes, eaten together, increase those proteins usable by the body to more than the sum of their parts, which explains why the poorer nations thrive on combinations of:

- rice with lentils
- cornmeal and kidney beans
- bulgur and chick peas
- barley and beans

and why even baked beans on (wholemeal) toast is a complete protein.

Take with you: dried haricot beans, lentils (all colours), split peas, soya beans and soya flour, chick peas, butter beans, peanut butter, and powdered milk; and combine

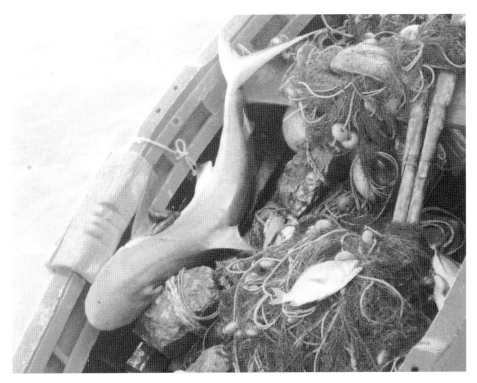

You can often buy fresh fish from the fishermen's boats in the Caribbean.

them with brown rice, bulgur, wholemeal grains and pasta, for nourishing pilafs and spaghetti dishes. Add cheese, or spoonfuls of powdered milk or wheatgerm, small pieces of meat or fish if you have them, and plenty of spice and flavour. These protein-rich mixtures get you out of trouble if the fresh food runs out, and are excellent dishes in their own right, extremely varied and tasty. Recipes will be found in Middle East and Indian cookbooks, so do not be lulled into substituting tins of baked beans in tomato sauce, which make everything taste of sweet ketchup. The pressure cooker will make short work of the dried vegetables, which can be cooked in stock or soup to add different flavours to suit whatever meaty morsels you have.

OTHER ITEMS YOU MIGHT NEED

The best way to remember every item you will need is to imagine your way through a day, from the moment you rise till the time you go to bed, and write down everything you eat or use. Thus you will not forget the toilet roll, can-openers, matches, washing-up brush, tartar sauce, marmalade or salt. Then do it again going through events that crop up only weekly or monthly. (Yes, ladies, don't forget those; or your Pills either.) As Captain John Smith reminds us, at sea '. . . there is neither Ale house, Taverne, nor Inne to burne a faggot in, neither Grocer, Poulterie, Apothecary nor Butcher's shop.'

TRANSATLANTIC FOOD

My thinking went thus:
Meat for five people for supper for five weeks, using up the frozen meat first.

SUPPER

First two weeks: Day 1, Hamburgers. Day 2, Chicken. Day 3, Tinned. Day 4, Pork chops. Day 5, Steaks. Day 6, Party night. Day 7, Rice or spaghetti.
Following three weeks: Day 1, Tins. Day 2, AFD Curry. Day 3, Tins. Day 4, Steak-and-kidney. Day 5, Rice or spaghetti. Day 6, Party night. Day 7, Tins.
To my great astonishment we caught a fish, so one night we ate that. Party night food had been thought of, and was tinned pheasant or frozen duck (Bill's birthday), or national dishes mostly Chinese or Italian.

LUNCH

These were bread (home-made when the bought bread gave up after the thirteenth day) and cold meats, galantines and pâtés, salami, etc with salad as long as it lasted (till the nineteenth day), cheese and fruit. If it was a cold day, we added hot soup.

BREAKFAST

Very important, after everyone had done at least one and maybe two night watches. We used combinations of eggs, bacon, porridge, sausage and beans, bacon grill, and kippers, plus toast and marmalade, and hot drinks. Cereal bars of fruit, nuts and honey make wonderful emergency breakfasts.

NIGHT WATCH FOOD

Sweet biscuits, chocolate bars, cheese portions, wholemeal crackers, nuts and raisins, dried figs, fruit cake.

WHAT WE CARRIED

For five people. We already had on board pickles, jams, sauces, salt and pepper, stock cubes and other staples bought in Italy, France, Spain and Gibraltar.

TINNED MEAT	SIZE	TINS	SIZE		TINS
Hot dogs/frankfurters	15 oz	6	Meatballs	15 oz	8
Stewing steak	15 oz	18	Irish stew	15 oz	12
Breast of chicken	3½ oz	6	Sausages	15 oz	6
Corned beef	7 oz	12	Roast beef	7 oz	7
Bacon grill	7 oz	4	Roast pork	7 oz	7
Bacon grill	12 oz	6	Roast lamb	7 oz	4
Tongue	1 lb	6	Pie fillings	(15 oz)	
Ham	1 lb	3	Steak-and-kidney		6
Steak-and-kidney pie	15 oz	2	Steak-and-mushroom		6
Steak-and-kidney pud	15 oz	6	Steak-and-onion		6
Steak-and-kidney pud	7 oz	12			

TINNED FISH

Kippers		9	Crab	7 oz	6
Prawns/shrimps	7 oz	15	Mussels	3½ oz	3
Pilchards	15 oz	15	Oysters	7 oz	2
Salmon	7 oz	7	Sardines		12
Squid	7 oz	3	Paella Mix	3½ oz	2
Tuna	7 oz	6	Anchovies		2
Chopped clams	15 oz	2	Herring Roes		2

OTHER TINS

Chopped pork	7 oz	6	Fabada (Spanish pork and beans)		1
Pork and beans	7 oz	6	Paella	15 oz	2
Sausage and beans	7 oz	6	Ravioli	30 oz	3
Pheasant	15 oz	1	Cassoulet	2 lb	1
Game pie filling	15 oz	1	Fruit cake	2 lb	1
Chinese goose	7 oz	2	Soups	15 oz	12
Liver pâté	3½ oz	2	Oatmeal	500 g	1
Pâté de campagne		3	Spaghetti sauce (Bolognese)		6
Sweet biscuits	3 lb	1	Spaghetti sauce (Matriciana)		6
Biscuits for cheese	3 lb	1	Spaghetti sauce (clams)		6
Spaghetti sauce (mushroom)		6			

TINNED VEGETABLES

Pelati (tomatoes)	15 oz	12	Brussel sprouts	15 oz	12
Pease pudding	7 oz	7	Ratatouille	20 oz	2
Mushrooms	7 oz	9		15 oz	3
Leeks	5 oz	2	Red peppers	7 oz	5
Cauliflower	15 oz	7	Garden peas	15 oz	8
Spinach	15 oz	7	Petit pois	12 oz	4
Celery	15 oz	4	Water chestnuts	7 oz	2
Beans, green	15 oz	5	Bamboo shoots	7 oz	2
Haricot beans (natural)	15 oz	12	Bean sprouts	7 oz	6
Macedoine (mixed veg)	15 oz	6	Curried beans	7 oz	4
Butter beans	15 oz	3	Heinz beans	15 oz	3
Beetroot	7 oz	2	Carrots	15 oz	5
Broad beans	5 oz	2	Sweet corn	10 oz	12
Chick peas	15 oz	3	Red cabbage	15 oz	2
New potatoes	15 oz	12	Lentils	15 oz	4

TINNED FRUIT

Pineapple	15 oz	3	Peaches, large		3
	7 oz	4	Raspberries	15 oz	4
Pears, large		3	Fruit salad, large		3

TRANSATLANTIC FOOD continued

TINNED PUDDINGS

Syrup sponge	8	Jam sponge	2
Chocolate sponge	2		

FROZEN

2 Large pizzas	5 Steaks
10 Loin of pork chops	1 lb Chicken pieces
2¼ lb Chicken breast	1 Duck
24 Beefburgers	

IN FOIL

Cotechino (sausage)	Chicken curry, 12 portions
Minestrone	

PERISHABLES

		2 kg Green tomatoes	2 kg Cucumbers
10 kg Potatoes	10 kg Onions	1 kg Green beans	1 kg Carrots
2 Cauliflowers	4 Cabbages	1 kg Lemons	
6 Aubergines	1 kg Green peppers	3 kg (10) Grapefruit	
1½ kg Courgettes	10 Avocadoes		
3 kg Sweet apples	3 kg Acid apples	6 Large white loaves	6 Large wrapped
4 kg Oranges	4 kg Green bananas	12 Bread rolls	wholemeal
3 Melons	1 kg Red tomatoes		loaves

FRESH GROCERIES

3 lb Streaky bacon	16 lb Butter 5 x 7oz
2 lb Vacuum packed bacon	3 lb Turkey galantine (whole)
3 lb 5oz Garlic sausage (whole)	2 lb Ham
1½ lb Liver sausage	1 Pork boiling ring
2½ lb Cheddar cheese	1½ lb Double Gloucester cheese
2 boxes Cheese portions	8 dozen Eggs
36 bars Bournville chocolate	36 bars Kit-Kat chocolate
2 pkts Crispbread	Nuts and raisins 24 small packets
Wholemeal crackers in packets of 4 x 24	

DRY GOODS

Plain flour	2 kg	Tea bags	250
Wholemeal flour	8 x 3.3 lb	Dumpling mix	½ lb
Rice	2 x 5 lb	Batter mix	6 pkts
Spaghetti	10 lb	Dried yeast	1 tin
Chinese noodles	4 pkts	Instant-blend dried yeast	3 pkts
Sugar	8 kg	Paper towels	6 x 2 rolls
Long-Life milk	36 litres	Toilet rolls	6 x 2 rolls
Long-Life cream	12 pkts	Nescafe	1½ lbs

DRINKS

Beer	144 cans	Orange squash	½ gal
Lemon and lime squash	½ gal	Wine	40 litres

WHAT WE ACTUALLY USED (23 DAYS)

All the beer! All the fresh vegetables, and the following in tins:

Ham	1	Pheasant	1	Lentils	1
Steak-and-kidney	2	Tongue	1	Brussels sprouts	2
Steak-and-onion	2	Roast beef	3	Bean sprouts	1
Steak-and-mushroom	2	Roast lamb	3	Pease pudding	3
Chicken breast	1	Crab	1	Mushrooms	3
Bacon grill	3	Salmon	2	Bamboo shoots	1
Meatballs	1	Kippers	3	Fabada (Bean stew)	1
Stewing steak	1	Prawns	1	Haricot beans	3
Sausages	2	Soups	6	Pelati (tomatoes)	2
Sausage-and-beans	4	Ravioli	2	Water chestnuts	1
Irish stew	5	Spaghetti sauce	6	Potatoes	1
Game pie filling	1	Cream	1	Heinz beans	1
Chopped pork	1	Jam sponge	1	Raspberries	2
Corned beef	2	Carrots	1	Pears	1
Chicken supreme	2	Peas	4		

We had 2 dozen eggs left, fresh fruit (oranges, lemons and grapefruit), and plenty of useful basic stores which stood us in good stead in the West Indies.

When we were within four days of Barbados the beer ration (jealously watched by the men) went up from one can a day to two, and then, to their great joy, to three.

DEEP-SEA COOKING

SONG OF A SEA COOK

I think what pleasant thoughts I can
While bending o'er the frying pan
But truth to tell, I'm ill at ease:
It's hard to cook in seas like these.
But break the eggs and stir the pot
And try to be what you are not:
A cook with stomach not upset
Who hasn't lost her breakfast yet.
Why do they always ask for more
When half the stew is on the floor?
How can they eat so heartily
When I can't even drink my tea?
But peel the spuds and cook some duff

(Three pounds of flour should be enough)
They'll eat like the proverbial horse
Even if served with Diesel sauce.

• Cooking in bad weather •

'*. . . give every messe a quarter can of beere and a basket of bread to stay their stomacks til the kettle be boyled . . .*'

If you are the sort of cook that most of us are, fine on deck but subject to sickness down below unless horizontal, you have to develop a method if you are not to starve yourself while feeding the crew.

One method is to bring all the ingredients up on deck, in one or more washing-up bowls, and do the preparation up in the fresh air. This is suitable for put-together meals like salad and sandwiches. Enlist help and it will be done fast, but half of it will be eaten prematurely.

A variation of this is the do-it-yourself buffet. Again washing-up bowls are used, to avoid everything landing on the floor of the cockpit. You cannot, of course, lay things out nicely on a plate, so recourse is made to smaller bowls and plastic boxes with lids. Larger ones can contain potato or tomato salad, smaller ones sliced meat and salami, or tuna transferred from the tin. This is where I would use paper plates on the wicker plate-holders available in the States, or wicker breadbaskets, which save washing up.

At some point in the day, however, you will have to serve something hot, since that is what is really popular in bad weather: a steaming pot of something rib-sticking such as soup, stew or risotto.

For this I have a second method based on one-minute dashes to the galley, interspersed with fresh air up on deck until it is time for the next dash. (An extractor fan in the galley also helps.) There is no need for gourmet cooking under these conditions. Your crew will be more than grateful for that simple dish known to all sailors under various names such as lobscouse, slumgullion, potmess: in fact, Sea Stew.

Force 8 Stew

Choose a moment when you are feeling particularly strong, and make your first dash. Bad-weather stores should be handy in the galley, so if you also have a wall

tin-opener it will take you no time at all to put in a large deep pan: one tin of meat, one tin of vegetables, one tin of soup and one tin of drained potatoes. (It does not seem to matter what kind any of these are, the result is invariably excellent, though some mixtures you may discover to be more favourite than others.) Light the stove and put the pan on, with lid. Turn the heat very low. A pressure cooker is deep and works well; put the lid on but don't bring up to pressure. This mixture is very thick, and at intervals further dashes will be required to prevent it burning and to turn the whole mass over with a wooden spoon. When the entire contents are gently bubbling, serve in large mugs to three people.

This is the most delicious food you ever had if you are cold, wet and hungry. Starch seems to be needed for queasy stomachs to work on, so risottos and spaghettis are also good, but they are a little more time-consuming to cook.

Force 6 Stew

This is made with fresh vegetables and potatoes instead of tinned ones, as the cook should be feeling stronger. Veg cleaning and preparation can be done on deck, using helpers, but watch your knives don't get chucked overboard with the peelings. Anyone who is too sick to eat Sea Stew should be encouraged to eat at least some wholemeal crackers, and if you boil a kettle for a hot drink, try them with bouillon or Bovril, which may go down better than tea or coffee. It is good to give the stomach something to work on: we find porridge and brown sugar very heartening too.

• Another bad-weather recipe •

We lay just inside the pierhead at Bastia in Corsica at the day's end in howling wind. We saw a tiny yacht with storm jib and close-reefed main sailing in, towing a 40-foot charter yacht. There seemed to be no one aboard the charter boat so Bill went to help. As they came alongside a tiny girl swung her huge tow round to us, released it, and allowed us to berth the charter yacht stern-to while she, the skipper, finished berthing herself. There were four seasick Germans in the charter boat who had done nothing to help her or themselves, but were quick to dash ashore and up to the restaurant. We invited the skipper and her student crew on board for a drink: Bill wanted to say 'well done' to Anne-Marie of the famous Breton sailing school at Glenan for a magnificent piece of seamanship. Let alone his penchant for five-foot girls.

Anne-Marie agreed with us that in such weather it was best to stay with our boats, and that we could happily eat together, having much in common. At that moment a great gust tore the Germans' inflated dinghy from its fixings on board and carried it across the bay. Anne-Marie sighed, and with immense aplomb went off in her dinghy to get it back. When she returned and had made it fast properly she cooked one of the best bad weather dishes we've ever had. What a girl!

ANNE-MARIE'S PATATES AU LARD – A BRETON SAILOR'S DISH

All you need is a pressure cooker, a Spanish onion per person, lots of potatoes, and a big hunk of poitrine fumé (smoked belly of pork). Onions and meat in the bottom, then the potatoes. No water is needed, the onions and pork bathe the potatoes in delicious juices and make the gravy. Pressure-cook it for ten to fifteen minutes. Food for the Gods – and Goddesses.

During Hurricane Alberto, in the Gulf Stream north of Bermuda, we had hot food the first day (eggs for breakfast with oatcakes and coffee, soup for lunch with fruit cake, and Sea Stew for supper). Then water got into the batteries and for the only time in ten years the stove would not light and we had cold food that day. The following day Bill got some of the batteries going again, and as the huge seas were beginning to subside we celebrated with an enormous lunch of T-bone steaks and tinned raspberries and cream. Gosh, it was good.

Once the alarms of the first day of the hurricane were over we drank a lot of coffee, some of it laced with brandy.

On the 'cold' day we had rum punch, which boosted morale without confusing the brain too much, and ate apples and chocolate and fruit cake, with the occasional ham sandwich.

It is noticeable that people who normally spurn puddings and cakes and sugary drinks, such as all three of us, turned in a time of worry and crisis to sweeter food and drinks. We were also immensely hungry, perhaps partly because it was hard to sleep through the noise and violent motion.

This brings us to:

OTHER USEFUL WAYS TO COPE WITH BAD WEATHER WHEN COOKING

- Use a damp sponge cloth or dish towel on the table or worktop to anchor plates and mugs.
- Pour drinks out fore and aft, not athwartships: who holds, also pours. Don't fill saucepans or mugs too full.
- Hand things up to the cockpit, in a wicker breadbasket for each person. This will take a mug of stew, bread, implements, and an apple or tomato.
- Mugs are better than bowls, which are better than plates.
- There should be somewhere where the helmsman can put a drink safely, without it ending up on the deck.
- The high-friction Dycem plastic, which we call 'Sticky blue', can be cut to fit any surface. It has been so successful that we have been able to dispense with fiddles except on the cooking stove. A similar product called Scotgard is also available. (Address in Appendix.)
- Used and empty utensils should be put straight into the sink ready to wash up, so they do not roll underfoot and get broken.

• *Night watch food (the night box)* •

Night watches consume a lot of energy and except in pilotage waters they can also be very boring. You can count on the night watch losing all sense of morality and burrowing like alley cats in a dustbin through the cook's precious stores. If you do not want your menus totally disarranged, and large desserts intended for tomorrow to disappear without trace, you must provide a tempting and adequate night box. A large Tupperware bread bin might just be big enough.

It should contain both sweet and savoury items, such as dried fruit and nuts, cheese (wrapped portions are handiest), wholemeal crackers, chocolate bars and boiled sweets, cereal bars or granola (a sort of solid muesli, available on the diet and health shelves of the supermarket. They keep a year and make excellent bad-weather breakfasts); fruit cake and biscuits. If you are on a long passage where fresh fruit is limited, make it crystal clear whether fruit is allowed as an extra or counts as part of the daily ration, since it is impossible to satisfy a three-apple-a-watch man with the stores carried on a small boat. Some yachts fill Thermoses with soup and coffee for the night watch, others (if the autopilot is working well) find that the watchman gets a welcome break by making his own hot drink.

• *Food for morale* •

'And after a storme, when poor men are all wet, few of those but wil tell you a little Sacke or Aqua Vitae is much better to keepe them in health than a little small beere or cold water, although it be sweet.'

When morale is low, break out some treat or delicacy: a tin of Dundee cake or shortbread, tins of *boeuf bourguignon, cassoulet* or smoked salmon paté. If the weather is fine and spirits need to be raised, pancakes, drop scones or new rolls with honey do wonders.

Find an excuse for a party: celebrate (or commiserate) something: the best day's run or the worst, 500 miles, 1000 miles, the day we saw the whale; and get everyone to help with the best dinner you can manage. Give a prize for the most inventive costume or headgear, or the best limerick. I always keep a bag of small presents on board. Whenever I see anything small and attractive ashore, I add it to the bag. Thus one can always cope with an unexpected birthday or find a suitable prize. You can also run a sweepstake on the noon-to-noon run.

WATER

Skip will not let me wash my hair
Nor yet my grubby underwear;
'The water's getting low,' he shrieks,
'We've just enough for ten more weeks.'

Water, the lack of it, and where to get it, occupies the mind of cruising people a

One of the pleasures of the cruising life is eating alfresco on deck. Here we are mid-Atlantic celebrating our first 25,000 miles of cruising.

great deal. The habit of being mean with it must become second nature. If you run to the luxury of hot water, you cannot allow the tap to run hot without saving the cold water that comes out first. On our boat this is done by having a jug of the right capacity kept in the galley: when the jug is full, the water will be hot and the jug of cold can (and must) be used elsewhere, in the kettle for instance.

Our bathroom is right forward, a long pipe-run from the cylinder. Bill has installed a diversion in the hot water pipe so that, by turning a tap on, one can divert the cold water run-off back into the tank. One must not forget to close the tap before having a hot bath.

'. . . a little pumpe made of a Cane, a little peece of hollow wood . . . to pumpe the Beere or water out of the Caske, for at sea wee use no taps'

Small toddlers love pumping water and turning on taps. So, unfortunately, do guests. Make sure that the water is not frittered away without your knowledge; a press-and-release tap would help, being harder for a toddler or guest to use than a Whale pump or a foot-button.

Have plenty of buckets. One cannot have too many, as one always seems to lose one (plus a doormat) in every storm. Then when it tips it down in the West Indies or the Pacific, you can fill your buckets and have a water frolic. Some people can plug their cockpit drains and turn it into a huge swimming bath.

If you are really short of water it is possible, indeed desirable, to use fresh water twice. First, where hygiene is essential, such as washing oneself or the dishes.

Having done that, the resulting water, according to its state, may then be used for the galley floor, or engine room overalls. Hair needs a lot of rinsing, but the water used is usually still clean enough, if a bit soapy, to wash clothes in. Judgement has to be used here. To shore-people who have water to wash cars with, this must seem rather revolting. (We did say that the life is not all paté and champagne.) I can assure you that Bill, coming up from the engine room with filthy hands, is quite glad of leftover washing-up water to get the worst off. All galleys should have a salt water tap, if only for firefighting!

A very refreshing gambit that takes a minimum amount of fresh water goes like this: heat a cupful of water to boiling and put it in the bottom of a warmed jug. Hold your face over the jug, under a towel as if you were inhaling balsam. Your face will be nicely steamed. Wipe off the grime and salt with a tissue and hand the jug to the next person in the queue, reheating the water as necessary.

Water that has been used to boil potatoes or pasta can be used for soups or freeze-dried food, but go easy on the salt. Water drained from tinned vegetables can be used for the same purposes or to boil potatoes.

Water was even more desperate in a submarine on 40-day patrol in Bill's time in the Navy. No washing was allowed at all except that there was a bucket of sea water and nearby one solitary bucket of fresh for 60 men for a week. One washed dirty hands in the sea water, then rinsed them in the fresh, which gradually turned into diesel soup. Long passages can lead to similar problems in a yacht without adequate water tanks and to an inevitably smelly crew. Larger-scale washing was 'bottom half Tuesday, top half Thursday, and on Saturday, all over lightly with an oily rag'. Submariners say one gets used to it because everyone smells the same. Submariners' wives say they can identify their husbands in the dark by the smell of diesel. As long as it is their own submariner climbing into bed, not someone else's.

• *Can you cook in sea water?* •

To illustrate an important point: once in Yugoslavia we went on a Club Mediterranée sailing barbecue, the first of the season, which was going to be done in style, huge amounts of meat with rice and spaghetti cooked on a remote beach. Everyone helped. Well, nearly everyone. Some of the men went off to taste the wine at the local tavern three kilometres away, and returned disgusted. 'One has drunk a wine of the most execrable,' said a tired Frenchman, 'and one has spat all the way home.' He began to wash his mouth out with wine from the huge jars we had brought with us. 'Which one is the water to cook the rice?' I asked, looking towards the jars. 'That's all wine,' said the organiser, 'we will use sea water.' 'Have you done this before?' I enquired with some doubt. He brushed my worries aside with superb confidence: what do the English know about cooking? So we duly cooked rice and pasta for 40 people in sea water. Both were so salty as to be totally inedible, and I have since found that the same thing happens with potatoes. You cannot cook vegetables in pure sea water. Not in the Mediterranean, anyway.

I have done some tests, and find that 5% of sea water makes it quite salty enough. That is 1 part in 20, or 1 fl oz of sea water to 1 Imperial pint of fresh. You would have to be pretty desperate for that to make any difference.

• *Laundry at sea* •

Proper washing machines are still not often carried by the long-distance cruiser, (20% in our survey) but their use is growing. There is a small plastic washing machine that I have seen on live-aboard yachts, which seems to please its owners, being light but solidly made. It is on the market in France for about £80. As they don't heat the water they don't use much power; but they do use a lot of water, which is probably why I have seen them in use only in marinas or close to a dock-side tap (see photo page 116).

A hand-operated one is sometimes available from UK mail order catalogues for about £30. Laundromats are rare in the Med. Smaller boats do the washing on the quayside.

When water is pretty short, as it always is on long-distance cruises, the time comes when the Skipper's shorts are sufficiently redolent to be capable of independent movement and will come when you whistle; with the embarrassing affection of an elderly and appallingly smelly dog. Now is the time to consider washing in salt water. Any strong liquid detergent will wash satisfactorily. If it is choppy, put the clothes in a tub and let them slop around with the motion of the boat doing much of the work for you. You must get the salt out by a rinse in fresh water; otherwise your clothes will be stiff, the salt will attract moisture so that they never fully dry, and you could end up (particularly with tight jeans) with a painful skin rash caused by chafe, or worse, 'gunnel bum' (salt water sores).

In places where it rains, such as an east-to-west Atlantic crossing, it pays to see a shower coming and get out the clothes and buckets to benefit by it. To get one-self and the clothes one is wearing thoroughly soaked in fresh water can be very refreshing, and is usually an occasion for much hilarity and splashing about. The west-to-east crossing is considerably colder and normally contra-indicates such skylarks, but it would depend on the degree of desperation.

Acquire an old-fashioned washboard and that useful article known as a dolly or

Washday ancient and modern: Greek washboard, a copper posher, a wooden 'milking stool' dolly, an all-plastic clothes peg.

posher. Washboards are still found anywhere there are no washing machines, such as the Greek Islands and the West Indies. The dolly is rarer, but it is not hard to make one of the milking stool variety illustrated. If you were used, on shore, to a washing machine and a tumble-dryer, you will be surprised and pleased at how much longer your clothes last when you wash by hand, provided of course you don't lose them overboard when you've pegged them out to dry.

Before I learnt the art of clothes-pegging I lost overboard two good towels, a pillowcase and a woollen jersey. All sank to the bottom with extraordinary rapidity before we could seize the net. Spring-clip pegs, I learnt, are not strong enough. Lead the washing line across the wind if possible, and use pegs that have no metal parts to rust, the old-fashioned Gypsy peg or all-plastic ones. Turn the clothes inside out (the strong sun will fade them quickly otherwise) and peg them firmly in such a way that they parachute across the wind. Lead the line through arms, legs or belt loops if you can. They will dry in no time. Bring them in while still a little damp, fold carefully and stack in a warm place. As they finish drying, they will 'iron' themselves with no further attention.

PRACTICAL HINTS FOR BOATWIVES AND SHIPS' HUSBANDS

• *The WC and shower compartment* •

Sea water used for flushing the loo causes scale to form. Putting some vinegar in the bowl from time to time, especially if you are leaving the boat for a few days, helps to minimise this, as does a daily sprinkle with washing up liquid. An occasional cautious catharsis with the delightfully named Greek product 'Drastico' (hydrochloric acid as far as I can make out) is abhorred by the manufacturers, but works absolute wonders.

The second most important habit to acquire at sea (the first being not to waste water) is to put nothing down the loo that could lead to a blockage. It helps everyone to remember this if there is a separate lidded bin for hairballs, cigarette ends, matchsticks, dental floss and even more unmentionable items. If your taste is for waggish notices on brass plates, now is your chance to let rip. Otherwise a simple green cross painted on the lid will indicate its use to most people. It will not stop children from poking about in there to see what it contains, but that all comes under the heading of a broad education. My children learnt a lot that way.

• *Thoughts about the accommodation* •

Which is what the yacht brokers call your living space. We find we need safe places for spectacles these days. Pockets for them – and indeed for anything that needs to be readily to hand, such as seasick pills, sunscreen cream, finger plasters, bottle openers and so on – can be made from felt, leather, fabric or any suitable material, and screwed or stuck to the linings or cockpit in strategic places. Doublesided sticky pads can be used to fix not only these but digital clocks, perpetual calendars, navigating gimmicks, and even pictures and photographs if they are not too heavy. Fewer screwholes keep up the resale value!

Magnetic racks

You might doubt that these would be of any use at sea, but we know many yachts who use them. We have one for kitchen knives and one for small tools. Only the big carving knife and the heavy ratchet screwdriver get jerked loose by a choppy sea: they are fine for smaller items. Don't site magnetic racks near a compass, it goes without saying.

Seaboots

Stow these upside-down on dowels of suitable length. This not only helps them to dry but prevents them from filling up with rubbish and dead wasps.

Plastic foam offcuts

Keep a bag of these to stifle any clinks and bumps that can disturb your sleep in choppy seas: cassettes, bottles and glasses are the worst offenders.

Vacuum cleaner

A cylinder type vacuum cleaner has many uses apart from the obvious one. Ours helped us to build the boat. It was second-hand even then and has swallowed everything from wood shavings through nails and screws to lumps of rubbery caulking compound, drilling swarf, rust chippings and grinding dust. Put together backwards it can be used as a heavy duty blow-dryer for newly painted areas, or even damp bilges if you should be so unlucky. We are thinking of coarse painting, naturally. (We would not blow dust and flies on the sort of paint and varnish where dogs must not sneeze and cats must not tread.) There are now some battery-driven vacuum cleaners that are worth their space for light duties: crumbs, fluff, loose dust, even dead insects if they are small ones.

Cottons and canvases

Few can stand up to sea water and hot sun, but lining your curtains with heavy cotton prolongs their lives. Cockpit and deck cushions are usually vinyl covered, which lasts well but sticks to hot bare skin. Most people make loose cotton covers and accept that they will need replacing frequently. It's worth it not to find your thighs securely stuck to the cushions in hot weather.

Sticky labels

A practical thought: you can buy sticky labels in the form of little coloured circles. Get several different colours, and use them to match plugs with sockets, so that a red spot plug fits a red spot socket. Or use them to highlight important electronic buttons that the designers try to hide from us by camouflage and incomprehensible icons: charcoal on charcoal seems to be flavour of the month.

DUTY FREES OR BONDED STORES

Not only have the rules changed considerably, but duty free stores are more difficult to get. We are not talking about the rip-off 'duty frees' on the cross-Channel ferries, no cheaper than Continental supermarkets, and recently ended. The real article out of bond is available if you are bound for a destination outside the EU, and will cut your booze costs considerably. The difficulty is to find a bonded warehouse at all, let alone one who will deign to supply a dozen cases to a yacht, instead of a truckload to a cruise liner. When we did find a willing supplier we found that procedures were now much simpler. No longer was our booze embarked under the eagle eye of the Revenue men and sealed with lead excise seals. The paperwork was done, and the goods came on board just before sailing, and we pushed off from Southampton bound for Istanbul. The further your destination and the larger your crew, the more you are allowed. No cheating, we did actually get to Istanbul. It just took us a year or so. Cheers!

AND FINALLY: THE PLEASURE OF IT ALL

Two occasions I shall miss dreadfully if I ever come ashore. One is the impromptu cruising barbecue, on a beach perhaps, with half a dozen dinghies hauled up on the shingle, and the yachts nodding at anchor a short swim away. The fire is already crackling under many and different grids and grills; bring your own meat or fish, something to drink, and 'a dish for the table' that everyone can share. The meal langours deliciously on into the warm afternoon with chat and laughter: memorable days.

The other is of wonderful meals for two on board after a good day at sea, not in themselves so Epicurian, were it not for the beauty of the day, the good temper of the sea, the satisfaction in our progress, and the sharpness of our hunger. With such a sauce, anything tastes good.

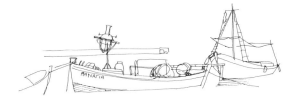

11 • Misadventures

*'. . . some accident that requires the help of all hands . . .
which in most voyages doth happen.'*

CRIME

There are two sorts of crime relevant to yachtsmen: those committed by yachts-men and those against yachtsmen, with the occasional merger of the two.

One of the features of long-cruising is its suitability as a way of life for the criminal whether retired, resting, or active. In recent years the professional criminal has become aware of this, which is sad because inevitably the processes of identifying, tracking and arresting them will impinge on the freedoms of the cruising yachtie. It must be achingly obvious to all engaged in cruising that our way of life is an ideal cover for terrorists. Not only that, but the illegal immigration trade has also started to imperil our freedoms.

When a minimum number of criminals were involved with small boats, the forces of international law and order did little, for attempts to track individuals would have been inordinately expensive. The occasional cigarette smuggler was arrested, but there was no great international co-operation, for one country was not over-concerned about another's smuggling problems. But the alarming increase worldwide of narcotic abuse has brought yachtsmen to the notice of authority.

• Drug and people-smuggling •

Drug smuggling is of two broad types: the highly professional operations of organised crime, and the more casual, small-scale activities of individuals. The 'casual' smuggler is of any nationality and can operate anywhere, though there is much activity close to the USA. The American authorities try hard, but their closeness to anarchistic small states poses a difficult problem.

Elsewhere, there seems to be no longer any co-ordinated campaign against limited abuse by the user, but the attitudes of countries vary and most will sling the book at any hop-head they happen to stumble across. We have no experience, but anecdote says that those who get caught usually do so because they have to be investigated for some other, totally unconnected matter, which might be quite innocent. It is not our remit to advise on what is non-nautical good behaviour.

Now that yachts are being increasingly used by professional criminals, it pays, therefore, not to get the wrong side of any Continental Customs or other para-military patrols under any circumstances.

Much the same applies to people-smuggling, with or without the hyphen. Do not leave your boat unattended in any unguarded mooring in North Africa. (Marinas are probably OK.) Yachts are stolen, loaded with immigrants and driven towards Sicily, Calabria, or southern Greece. Possibly Spain too. The crims decamp in a RIB when close offshore and then leave the yacht to drift onto the beach when the immigrants are entitled to be treated as shipwrecked mariners and given help and shelter. Understandably, coastal patrols get upset about this. At one time in the little yacht harbour at Rocella Ionica, we counted six fast patrol boats based there. There was an operational control, the senior officer of which was an old friend, with whom we discussed the problem. We were left in no doubt about the seriousness of what can only be described as a conflict.

These people-smugglers are often armed. A young Greek coastguard from Meganisi was shot by Albanians when trying to make an arrest. Beware of Albania.

Much of the unpleasant types of traffic in the Mediterranean (and the Caribbean, too) occurs under the Red Ensign and there is no doubt that the British flag is falling into disrepute, to the inevitable disadvantage of British yachtsmen in general. Ownership of these yachts is vested in companies set up in the Channel Islands, Gibraltar or some other idyllic colony; the shares are held in the names of nominees; by some vagary of the Merchant Shipping Act, the yachts can be registered not only in these places but also in any British port. Regard warily a Red Ensign yacht aboard which neither captain nor crew speak English.

Laundering the cash proceeds takes place in many ways, but one of them is by buying and selling yachts through certain brokers in the south of France, the transactions passing through parts of the world that tolerate financially dodgy banks, ie Switzerland, Liechtenstein, Luxembourg and the Channel Islands. Normally, we are against interference by governments in the private affairs of individuals, but in these circumstances the case for the abolition of banking secrecy is manifest. The crooks are exploiting the system.

• *Pilfering* •

That apart, most crime perpetrated by yachtsmen is petty, and typically against their fellows. French yachtsmen in the Caribbean have a poor reputation. This is hard on those pleasant, honest Frenchmen who wish to enjoy civilised cruising.

So far as crime against the yachtie is concerned, the wanderer is somewhat at the mercy of the petty pilferer. It is impossible to live in tropical heat and turn one's boat into a fortress: the open air is an essential ingredient to living. Fortunately there are few places where pilfering is a serious problem, for the more primitive the culture, the more likely the inhabitant will have strong conceptions of hospitality and a lack of covetousness. Most of us try to steer clear of big cities, where most of this nuisance occurs.

Theft in big cities

From the experiences of ourselves and friends, we think it unwise to leave a boat unwatched, even for short periods, in open harbours in big cities. By open harbours we mean those where there are no dock gates with police or Customs men controlling entry by the public. Typical among open harbours where care is needed are Barcelona, Cartagena, Baltimore (USA), Brindisi, Marseilles and Palermo. There are plenty of others. Most yacht marinas in or near a city are prime targets for thieves, and this particularly applies where the marinas are open to public access, such as Antibes, Athens, and many along the French and Italian Riviera. This leads to many boats in these marinas being fitted with intruder alarms, and given the intrinsic unreliability of marine electronics that means sleepless nights for all crews living aboard when these things go off semi-continuously. In fact, the intruder alarm fitted to small craft goes off in error so often that no one pays any attention.

In some countries, notably Italy where urban dishonesty is part of the culture, there is a very fierce desire to protect the property which a person has, even if he stole it from someone else in the first place. Marinas in Italy tend to have a more positive security system, sometimes leading to a sort of prison camp mentality. One, near Rome, was surrounded by a double chain-link fence, with vicious dogs running unleashed between them. There was only one gate, double locked, and a scrutiny before entry that stopped just short of body-searching. There was a conscientious night patrol, but in spite of all this, thieves arrived by water one night and stripped several boats of their electronics. This marina, unlike some, welcomed live-aboards as reliable watchmen who actually paid the marina, not vice versa, for the privilege of keeping watch. We wrote this paragraph some time ago and have left it in to give a flavour. We believe Italy is facing up to its intolerable lawlessness. Things are improving.

If you are frequently leaving your boat unwatched in any marina or large port, locking up is essential. Doors and hatches in seagoing craft are generally stoutly made and good locks can be fitted. But these are not necessarily the whole answer because thieves are often adept at undoing them. It is worthwhile devising a complex door or hatch opening system that is apparently contrary to logic. We know of one case where such an entrance to a boat was attacked and battered without the raiders gaining entry, even though it had not been locked.

For our own part, we had until recently lost very little to the pilferer, which indicates that too much worry probably attaches to the question. The total over the years was a teak-handled knife, a tape recorder that we left on deck while we were ashore, and two fenders which might have been badly made fast and, of all things, a steel derrick. Our total financial loss was probably less than the cost of a good lock. But note that we steer clear of cities.

However we have suffered at last. In 2000, when we returned to England for a major refit, vandals and thieves raided *Hosanna* three times in 60 days. On the second of two occasions when we were on board, Bill (who used to play wing-forward for a United Services XV) tackled one of two, a teenager wielding an oar, and was so angry he almost managed to wrestle the lout over the side into the tideway. Just as well he was unsuccessful for this was not long after the unfortunate Tony Martin murder case. Bill had no weapon except the oar wrested from the intruder, who ran away with his co-thug. The third time, though, while Laurel was in hospital, we were properly done over and thousands of pounds of wanton damage was done and goods stolen. The sad thing is that the police cared only that we were unreasonably upsetting their statistics by reporting three separate crimes. They tried to amalgamate the three break-ins as one crime, but we reasonably pointed out that since they had no idea who had done it they could not say the jobs were done by the same people. Screw their crime statistics. The English provinces, once so civilised, are now part of the anarchic jungle. We were, however, offered counselling. They seemed to think that more important than catching the criminals.

Unfortunately one can no longer rely on scrupulous honesty anywhere in Europe. We have even had something stolen in a Greek island, something unthinkable 20 years ago. But on the whole, Greek islanders are honest and one can leave cars unlocked with goods inside them and nothing is touched. We recently returned after visiting the Boat Show in England to find we had left the inner door to the 'verandah' open. Nothing was disturbed.

Illegal Albanian immigrants are another matter. It seems a shame to tar them all with the same brush but there are too many bad lots to do otherwise.

A British catamaran needed her marine windows replacing. The owner was a swallow (summer visitor) and made arrangements with a Greek professing to provide a service for yachts when their owners were absent. They gave him the job of fitting the windows during the winter. He in turn handed the job over to a gang of Albanians. Not only did they not do the work, but they lived on board until they had sold off the yachtsman's possessions and then decamped. The Greek police shrugged their collective shoulders. *Ti tha kanate?* (What can you do?) Equally bad, was that the Greek contractor refused to admit any liability for the workers he had hired and walked away from it saying, in effect, 'Sue me, you won't win.' In that he was probably correct. Do not involve yourself with the civil courts in any Mediterranean country. Criminal courts are a different matter. Not completely different, but. . .

One point to watch in regard to petty theft: in many places it does not pay to report it. Get local knowledge. Your chances of getting your property back in any case are virtually nil, but to report it is to involve oneself with officialdom, sometimes to have one's freedom of movement restrained and, final indignity, the local Customs may assess you, the loser, as having imported the item and charge you duty on it, effectively multiplying your loss. This last unfair and unreasonable insult is the clincher. Fortunately the EU has minimised the effect of this insult.

Inflatables and other tempting items
The most common stolen item is an inflatable dinghy, with or without outboard motor. There seems to be a worldwide market for these items, and I am surprised

In some places this flotilla of dinghies would be a tempting target for thieves, but here in rural Greece there is no problem.

the *Financial Times* does not list them under 'Commodities' with the day's range of buying and selling prices: 'The Zodiac market moved narrowly today with a fair supply from St Lucia which found ready buyers. Avons were in steady demand and gained £40. Metzeler lost ground in early trading with a large batch of nearly new from Palermo, but recovered later to close the day £20 lower.'

Normally, inflatables are cut adrift from the parent yacht during the night. Old West Indies hands hoist their dinghies in at night, or else reeve wire painters, but these are difficult to make really secure. The ease with which an inflatable can be stolen and then hidden for later disposal is a very important factor in your choice of which type of tender to carry. Customising your inflatable with logos and designs, however silly, is an excellent idea.

Liferafts are occasionally taken, for their cost is substantial, but as they are more easily traced they do not find such a ready market.

Running rigging and on-deck gear is sometimes stripped from a yacht. In Brindisi this can be done by real experts while the crew are sleeping peacefully below. Brindisi is a bad port both from the point of view of real theft and pilfering, the latter being done both by local urchins and by the swarms of hitch-hikers waiting to embark on the ferries for Greece. This may be improving (2005). The fact that Corfu suffers from thieves is due not so much to Greek dishonesty but almost entirely to young tourists. But it is in Italy that thieves used to have real *chutzpah*. At Palermo, thieves who had been locating the dinghy they wanted found to their dismay that the owners had chained it to the stern davits. So they stole the davits too.

There is also an active market in entire yachts, mostly confined to those produced in quantity, which are less easily distinguished one from another. The liability of having a particular type of yacht stolen is in direct proportion to its ready resale: so it does not necessarily pay to buy yachts with high resale values, which can anyway change. And recall our comments above about illegal immigration.

In Antibes the yacht over-wintering next to us, a German-owned Amel, was visited for several days by an overalled young man in a battered van, who did certain work aboard, arousing no suspicions. Nor was anyone alerted when the yacht sailed, ostensibly to the boatyard for slipping. It was by chance that a friend of the owner (who was at that time home in Germany) saw the yacht in Palma, Majorca, and went across to greet his chum. Finding a stranger on board he suspected something was wrong, phoned his friend and brought in the police. The thief was arrested, and it subsequently transpired that he had selected the yacht some time before and had negotiated a series of West Indian charters for her before actually committing the theft.

Other points about theft

Theft of all types is endemic in the French and Italian Riviera and in or near any large Italian or Spanish town. Be wary in Athens, Egypt, and to a lesser extent Tunisia and Morocco, and the touristy parts of Portugal.

Don't be too suspicious in tiny places like Bequia (WI) where one is visited by small boats containing native people, very friendly for the most part, some begging, some selling, some offering to do your washing, but fundamentally law-abiding.

PLACES WHERE THEFT IS VIRTUALLY UNKNOWN
- The rural areas of Greece and Turkey.
- The more isolated and rural areas of southern Italy (away from tourist centres).
- The Canary Islands (away from tourist centres).
- The Azores except for Punta Delgada.
- The out-islands in the Bahamas.
- The rural parts of Yugoslavia.

In all other areas, unless you have local knowledge to the contrary, assume that tourism has attracted those that prey on the tourists, and observe a little, ask a little, get to know the local feeling. It pays to take at least elementary precautions against petty theft.

WHAT PRECAUTIONS?

- Do not display ostentatious wealth ashore. Even modest possessions by North American or European standards are wealth beyond dreams for many people. To them, possessing a yacht of any kind means you are a millionaire, even if you built it from scrap with your bare hands.
- Do not leave dinghies in the water, or leave boarding ladders down, or ropes and fenders overside while at anchor overnight.
- Do not sleep on deck, if you are seriously worried about a place.
- Fasten hatches and large openings in a part-closed position that will allow ventilation but not admit a person, or a hooked implement.
- Put attractive items such as bicycles out of sight; don't leave them on the quay.
- Take reasonable care, but do not reduce yourself to a fortress mentality all the time.

• Piracy •

Many people contemplating long-term cruising are concerned about piracy, which is the taking of a vessel or the robbery of crew, cargo or equipment on the high seas, ie away from harbour. This crime has been much played up by the press, particularly in the USA with respect to piracy in the Caribbean, to the level of mild paranoia. In the chandlery at Bahia Mar, Fort Lauderdale, I waited to buy sandpaper while an American bought a rifle, a sub-machine gun, and two pistols for about $1200. While they were being gift-wrapped I enquired where he was bound with such an arsenal and was told the Virgin Islands. I could not help observing that he would be better off without them, which led to a frosty attitude on the part of the shop-keeper, who furnished, in season, many such armouries.

From which, you may gather, we ourselves are not armed. In my experience firearms are a positive liability; or to put it another way, gun-toting yachties have more problems from carrying weapons than the unarmed get by not so doing. Now, since our experience with intruders in Great Yarmouth, we wonder whether we are right after all. I suspect anger might have caused me to use a gun had I possessed one. Not a good idea. Clearly the firearms issue is something each of us has to work out for himself.

• To arm or not to arm? •

'To be a good gunner, you must learn it by practice.'

Consider the question of how to use these weapons. Guns are for killing people. It is no use having one unless you are prepared, instantly and without stopping to think, to point it at someone and fire to kill. The typical handgun is a very inaccurate weapon, and cannot be used to wound without seriously hurting. Apart from practised target shooters, it is only possible to pump bullets in the general direction of the target and hope one of them will do sufficient damage to stop an assailant (if it is in fact an assailant, see below). A rifle is not a close-quarters weapon (unless it has a bayonet: God help us) and is designed for comparatively accurate longer-range work. Anyone with any experience of naval gunnery will know of the great problems attached to sighting from a platform moving randomly in three dimensions. Skilled naval gunners with complex control gear hardly ever hit anything (they fire broadsides in the hope that one in ten shells might possibly hit the target): what chance has an excited amateur?

All these weapons must be kept clean, lightly oiled, and ready for instant use if they are to be effective. In many ports they must be declared, probably landed under police control and collected again before sailing. There are heavy penalties for transgressions of firearm laws, which differ from place to place so that one is never sure what they will be.

In real life one is also faced with the problem of identifying an assailant as such. Some time ago, an American yachtsman (it is almost always Americans who get into trouble with guns) panicked and shot dead one of the crew of a Spanish trawler near Alboran. The trawler was approaching to swap fish for foreign cigarettes, a common practice at that time. That trigger-happy yachtsman became a sadder jailbird.

So how do you tell if the boat approaching is friendly or vicious? Do you shoot anyway? Hardly. And do you think that if they are real pirates they will be unprepared for your rather limited self-defence? They'll be ready, and they'll blast the hell out of you at the first shot, or ram you. The only people you will discourage by arms will be friendly ones.

We once went into Aghios Andreas Bay at the southern end of Ithaca to find an American ketch the sole occupant. No doubt he was irritated at having his solitude spoiled, but the situation hardly called for his appearance on deck with a shotgun, telling us to get out of the bay as it was only big enough for one. It is the impulsive exploitation of the enhancement of power given by a weapon that is so dangerous in the hands of a person who is temporarily, or even partially, unstable. What did we do in Ithaca? We told him mildly to grow up, there was plenty of room. We had children on board, who took lines ashore as we anchored. He became quite friendly next day, and congratulated us on our seamanlike approach to anchoring. This story, which we have related from time to time, later came back to us as having happened to someone else. I hope there are not really two gun-toting nuts around the Ionian Sea.

I believe that the very ownership of a weapon fosters paranoia. If already a little unstable, it becomes more accentuated and even dangerous. I hope I get over my current feeling of paranoia, but it has to be faced that if the forces of law and order fail, the citizen is tempted to defend himself as best he can. Boathooks, even a dinghy oar, aren't a bad weapon. I just wish I'd hit him harder.

• *Murder and violence* •

This probably happens more often at sea among a dissident crew than in harbour by persons unknown.

What about attacks in harbour? Apart from our own direct experience, we mean. These do happen. Whereas we have no personal knowledge of any authentic example of piracy, we do know of other people who have suffered personal injury in harbour. It is necessary to consider whether these incidents would have been prevented with firearms. They all concerned intruders boarding a yacht. At least one of the yachts carried arms but had no chance of using them. Two of the three cases were murders, in St Vincent and in Port of Spain, Trinidad. That in Friendship Bay, Bequia, was almost murder. Two of the yachts were American, one was British. It is impossible to be sure, but I believe that the mere possession of firearms would not have altered the outcome of any of these cases, where the murderers had been able to get to close quarters before being observed. The St Vincent government did not appear to investigate the crime committed there with any energy whatsoever. Trinidad did at least produce and sentence a culprit.

Do not make too much of these terrible events. They are deplorable, but much less common than a mugging if you had stayed at home.

The whole thing is a question of prudence once again. Nothing will eliminate robbery and/or violence. But in places where it is known to occur, then some vigilance will reduce both its probability and its impact. Port of Spain is a big commercial port and not a noticeably congenial place for a yacht (though nowadays it seems to be getting better).

ACCIDENTS

'Master, let us breathe and refresh a little, and sling a man overboard
to stop the leakes.'

Not all damage to boat or person is caused by a criminal. Mishaps happen. In our experience most accidents between craft are trivial, most are clearly defined as to fault, and in most cases the defaulter makes amends instantly and without quibble. Three times we have suffered minor damage while made fast. Once in Boulogne from a member of the Royal Motor Yacht Club, who departed shouting 'Sorry, old man' and who did not answer our letter asking for the cost of a new starboard light. Twice by Italians, who volunteered compensation immediately and paid in full.

The problem is that chasing compensation in foreign countries, in foreign languages and via post, is a most unrewarding and frustrating pastime. Better to do a modest deal on the spot while the other fellow's conscience is still troubling him, than to hold out for full and complete indemnity. Most yachtsmen are decent types, thank God, and long may it last.

Major damage is a different matter. Here insurance is a very definite help, for even if the perpetrators cannot be traced or brought to book, underwriters can be expected to settle in the terms of the policy, or even a little more in some cases.

If you commit the damage yourself, to another vessel or a person, then you will probably appreciate being insured. This is a mischance all the more likely as yachting centres get more crowded and increasing numbers of novices take to the sea with certificates obtained at evening classes, fondly believing they are competent. (Don't talk to us about fast-track qualifications, that oxymoronic term. Any craftsmanship qualification needs an element of time and experience.) To sail without good third party cover is foolhardy and anti-social, especially as more and more people new to the sport bring a motor-car mentality to sea with them. One must also remember the fortune that many modern yachts represent in money terms, and the high cost of cosmetic repairs.

• *Personal accidents* •

Minor damage to the person is discussed in Chapter 15, which is about treatment that is totally within on-board resources. But one can have major accidents or mishaps that require surgery or hospital treatment, and though this cannot be considered a minor matter it will have to go in that chapter too, together with some comments on health insurance.

Not all accidents to the person happen on board, or even to your own crew. Everyman's mishap diminisheth me, to parody a good quotation. We once had a difficult time helping fellow British yachties coping with the problems involved when a singlehanded yachtsman was killed in a motor accident in Italy. The British Consul at Florence was not merely unhelpful, he was positively discourteous.

Laurel and I frequently travel about together in little excursions from our ship, and it is always a possibility that an accident to one would involve the other too. Such accidents do not have to be fatal to be bothersome to strangers. And the problems ensuing, if temporary neighbours whom you have only met the day before, or local officials, have to trace your relatives or whatever, are so great that some small precaution should be taken.

Every cruising yacht (short-handed or not) should have displayed close to the main hatch a small, semi-permanent notice saying, '*In case of urgency or difficulty, contact . . .*' One should also leave a will in a place of safety, and in the case of couples (because the likelihood of both dying at the same time is greater than for shore-dwellers) consult a lawyer about whether special clauses should cover this aspect. If so, draw up compatible wills.

On a less gloomy note, it is a good idea to have a square foot or so of surface, close to the main hatch, painted in blackboard paint. We leave messages on it in chalk, or at appropriate moments write up announcements of pure joy.

• *Accidents at sea: the legal position* •

I have mentioned already the obligation to go to the assistance of a vessel in distress. This is detailed in Section 6 of the [British] Maritime Conventions Act of 1911, the terms of which will have been enacted by all nations signatory to the Convention.

We are *obliged*, so far as we can without danger to our own vessel, to render assistance to every person (*even if such a person be a subject of a foreign state at war with Her Majesty*) who is found at sea in danger of being lost. Failure to do so is a misdemeanour. This is further amplified by the Merchant Shipping (Safety Convention) Act 1949, which should be read. (It is too long and detailed to include here: copies can be had from Her Majesty's Stationery Office.) The procedure for dealing with casualties on board is in Section 73 of the Merchant Shipping Act 1970. Casualties (and note that the ship herself can be a casualty) must be reported to the Department of Transport as soon as possible, and in any case not later than 24 hours after arrival at the next port. The report should contain a description of the incident, give details of injuries to personnel and damage to the ship, the name and official number of the ship, her position, next port of call and ETA, and should go to any DTp Marine Office, or the Maritime Coastguard Agency (MCA) at Southampton. (For web address see Appendix.) There is growing evidence that the MCA is catching the same disease as the Health and Safety Executive, of which the first symptom is an inability to leave well alone. As we write, new rules on reporting nautical accidents are being proposed. The first draft I saw verged on the lunatic in its possible application to small craft. I am told that the Chief of the MCA was with P & O earlier on in his career. That would not surprise me.

• *Births, deaths and marriages* •

Also coming under 'accidents' we have births, deaths and marriages at sea. The law covering deaths is given in the Merchant Shipping (Returns of Births and Deaths) Regulations 1979. A master is required to make a return of births in a ship, or of deaths in or from a ship. It should be made as soon as practicable (but within six months) to either a Marine Superintendent in the UK, a British Consular Office in foreign countries, or the equivalent of a Marine Superintendent in a Commonwealth country. There will also be local procedures if a body is landed at a port (the Regulations warn), but the UK regulations apply whether or not the body is landed, buried at sea, or recovered.

The official record of a birth or death is in the register entry made by the Registrar following the receipt of such a return from a Master. There is no legal obligation to recover a body sighted at sea, because of the dangers of capsizing, disease etc, but sightings should be reported to the nearest authorities. Do so by radio, if possible. If reporting by person, the report in a foreign country should be made to the British Consul in the hope of avoiding local problems. That is the official position; there must always be a strong incentive not to sight bodies at sea.

Marriages

Seems a shame to put this under misadventures, but marriages on board have a legal basis only when conducted by *an authorised person*, and when the ship is in the territory covered by that person's authority, and the official record would be held under the law of that territory. A British shipmaster is not, and never has been, an authorised person, and there is no UK machinery for recording marriages at sea. An entry in a log book is not, of itself, legal evidence of a marriage. As the old joke says, marriages solemnised by the Captain are valid for the duration of the voyage only.

• *Shipwrecked mariners* •

If wrecked, the yachtsman is normally *not entitled* to be treated as a shipwrecked mariner for the purpose of repatriation, and any in this unfortunate difficulty would be treated by a Consul as a normal distressed British subject. And God help them if my experience of British Consuls is anything to go by.

It is worth noting that while on the high seas a British registered ship is considered an extension of British Law, but once she enters the territorial waters of another state the situation is not so clear, particularly if citizens of that state or their property are affected.

LOSS OF SKIPPER

A particular disaster that worries a lot of wives, mates and less experienced members of a crew of two, is the loss of the skipper, whether he is the man overboard or temporarily inactive through injury or sickness while at sea. It is such a real worry to some that it justifies a word or two.

The crew must be able to handle the craft, even if only under power or with reduced sail. Even for a novice this is not as impossible as it might seem, especially when needs must. Some people are afraid to discuss this, particularly wives with their husbands, but it is worth making the effort because the conclusions will never be forgotten.

In any event there are a few simple precautions to be taken. In times past, in big ships it was normal for the wireless office to be given the ship's position every watch so that in emergency they had an approximate position always at hand. (This problem has eased considerably with DSC radio.) In a yacht I always plot the position at least once every four hours in the oceans, and at least every two hours in soundings, whether by fix or DR. I always have, in the ready-drawer, charts for diversionary ports to which I might have to go for some emergency, and my plan for the voyage lists some of them. Because Laurel is the Met Officer she is always aware of wind patterns and the weather. Now, with GPS, there is no excuse for not coping with the navigation. Like most yacht-wives, she uses the VHF from time to time so she is at home on the radio as most people are. (Examinations for VHF ought to be unnecessary. VHF is not nearly as complicated as a mobile phone.) She is not so hot on engineering but she can start, stop and use the engine.

• *Internal damage to the yacht* •

Even with good care and maintenance, things do go wrong in ways that are dangerous. I once had a shaft coupling disintegrate off Ushant. It had been badly machined by someone I was entitled to expect to do it well, and the chatter of the bad fit destroyed the metal by fatigue. The shaft dropped back leaving a 2-inch diameter hole. Fortunately one of my crew on that occasion was a professional cabinet maker: I have never seen a wooden plug made so fast, but it took a lot of getting in against the water pressure. It could not be put in the outer end. The lesson I drew from this was to have ready-made plugs for all the openings in the hull. This would now be considered normal. It wasn't then.

FIRE AT SEA

Perhaps the most frightening possibility is fire at sea. We had one and I was fortunate in having been trained in ship firefighting. The experience is instructive. I had fitted a ventilating fan above the batteries and the exhaust side had Tannoy brand ducting secured by clips supplied by the manufacturers. The ducting consisted of a wire spiral thinly covered by plastic. In the compartment there was a deckhead-mounted Noxfire automatic extinguisher.

At about 0330, somewhere northwest of Corsica (we always have a bad time round there), sailing in a very rough sea at the tail end of a gale, Laurel, who was on watch, called me to say there was a smell of burning. I opened the hatch to the engine room and found the whole space full of flame and smoke. I shut the hatch; the fire was clearly beyond the capacity of extinguishers and I naturally thought that the automatic one had gone off but had failed to cope. In fact, it never did go off.

After some time I managed to get the fire under control using a very fine spray of sea water. As the smoke cleared I saw the cause. The ducting had fallen out of the clips, which were clearly not adequate for the extra strains of violent motion in bad weather (a feature that is distressingly common in items designed by whizz-kids who have never had a wet shirt). The ducting had dropped on to the battery terminals, rolled about and soon worn away its thin plastic coating; the wire had shorted across the terminals, igniting everything nearby, helped by the contents of a plastic can of paraffin that I had been idiot enough to stow there.

LESSONS LEARNT

(Some of them I knew already, but needed a reminder.)
• Cheap and flimsy fastenings just will not cope with the violent movement of a small boat in heavy seas.
• Contrary to popular advice, it is a good precaution to cover batteries, but the covers must permit the passage of gases. A strong plastic mesh would be effective.

- Paraffin and any cans of any fuel, particularly in plastic containers, should be stowed on deck.
- Automatic extinguishers, even when in date, cannot be relied on and are therefore not worth the money.
- Butyl insulated wiring, specified by Lloyd's as being fire resistant, burns as merrily as other, less expensive, plastics but is more difficult to extinguish.
- Our thick-walled plastic diesel fuel lines did not ignite or melt, even though damaged. This may be because the engine was running and the tubing was cooled by the flow of oil in it.
- The sort of fire extinguishers that can be carried in a small craft, while adequate for a minor outbreak in the early stages, cannot cope with a serious blaze.
- Crew that cruise a lot need to have actual experience of putting out electrical (the most frequent cause) and fuel fires using only a water spray. Not a jet, but a spray of as fine droplets as one can get. It is cheap and effective, but it is a definite skill which the long-cruising yachtsman should acquire.
- Boiled batteries do not work.
- The mess from a fire is horrible, and hard to clean up.
- We were in more physical danger from the fumes of burning plastic battery cases, wiring insulation etc than we were from heat and flames.

BRIEF COMMENTS ON FIGHTING FIRES IN SMALL CRAFT

'Captain, we are fowle on each other and the shippe is on fire.'

• The nature of fire •

To start, a fire needs three essential elements: fuel, oxygen and a source of heat. I think that for our purpose we can ignore some of the more esoteric chemical fires which the full-time fireman may have to deal with, and consider the more simple ones. In a yacht there are fuels galore for a fire: diesel oil, plastic linings, foam upholstery, the resin in fibreglass, paints, wood, cooking fat and gas to name the more obvious ones.

Heat is necessary in two ways: the fuel has to be raised to its ignition temperature, below which it will not burn. This varies with the material, and for some is remarkably low. In addition, a source of heat has to be applied (even if momentarily) at a temperature known as the flash point and this triggers the flame. This also varies with the material and again can be quite a low temperature.

To extinguish a fire, break the triangle of fuel, oxygen and heat. One can:

- Remove the fuel
- Cut off the supply of oxygen
- Lower the temperature of whatever is burning

or preferably do a combination of these.

Port Gaios in Paxos

Even if the flames are put out, if the temperature of the fuel is not lowered below its ignition temperature the fire can re-start.

We remove the fuel by, for example, throwing it overboard. Very effective, but sometimes not practicable. We can remove the oxygen by smothering the fire, with a fire blanket or foam, for instance. We can cool the fuel with water or certain chemicals.

• *Fire extinguishers* •

These are essentially for first aid. They are useful and necessary to provide a very quick means of dealing with minor outbreaks which have been detected in the early stages. Of course they are also helpful even with major fires, for in these circumstances every little helps.

Given that their chief effectiveness is against small fires, one should choose extinguishers that do not themselves cause a great deal of damage, inconvenience or mess. In every case that I have seen a dry powder extinguisher used on a small fire, either afloat or ashore, it has caused more mess and damage than the fire. This experience cannot be extrapolated indefinitely because the fire, if unchecked, would obviously have gone on to cause a great deal of damage, but it does contain a lesson.

One should also get an extinguisher that is easy to use. Instructions to beat the

top on the floor, shake for a minute, then point away from the fire for five seconds are too complex to remember, and far too difficult to absorb if on the edge of panic.

Extinguishers with certain chemicals are dangerous to the user. Carbon tetra-chloride (Pyrene) is a close and poisonous relative of chloroform, and must not be inhaled for any length of time, especially if there is any alcohol in the body. There are extinguishers loaded with halon, an inert composite gas similar to the freon once used in refrigerators. We used it when careless welding in the engine room of *Hosanna* set alight some rags soaked in spilled diesel oil. It was extremely effective; only one squirt was required. It is, however, supposed to affect the ozone layer several miles up, and has been banned due to 'Green' pressure. The gas is much heavier than air; no one has yet explained how it gets up to the ozone layer since it does not rise! Yes, I know all about the Brownian diffusion of gases, but that does not apply in a centrifuge, and the earth's atmosphere is just that. Most professional firefighters are angry that halon has been banned, and none more so than those at sea, because the ban is not necessary. When used on a fire it undergoes an endothermic reaction, one which absorbs heat from outside itself, thus cooling the fuel as well as depriving it of oxygen. It becomes a completely harmless substance after this and does not affect the ozone layer. At sea we cannot use copious quantities of water. Halon is so far and away the best product that to deprive us of it for an unproven theory is criminal, and possibly lethal to ships' crews. It discredits the whole Green movement. The RYA should have stood out against this ban. What are they for?

In 2005, we have heard of a halon substitute. My expert informant tells me that it is not so effective, not having the endothermic reaction potential, but it is probably the best extinguishant legally available. (I understand halon is still in use aboard oil rigs, whose crews' lives are reckoned more valuable than ours.)

Apart from the halon substitute which is expensive at present, carbon dioxide is the best alternative for use in a boat. It is a heavy gas and does no damage. Because of weight it does not leak away from the boat, as it would do in a caravan, for example. It is effective against fat fires in the galley. It is possible to use some of the contents on a small fire and still have the remainder usable if you are unlucky enough to have another; a very important point at sea where replacements are unobtainable. Like halon, it works on all oil fires, but, unlike halon, it does not cool the fuel, so after putting out the flames that has to be done. The failure to cool means that CO_2 is not so good for dealing with fires in carbonaceous or solid materials, unless some other method of cooling is subsequently used. It replaces oxygen so you need to watch out that you can still go on breathing.

Foam extinguishers are really only for oil and petrol fires. They make a horrible mess and do not cool effectively. They need a certain skill to be fully effective and are probably not really suitable for small yachts.

Automatic extinguishers usually work by having a fusible plug which melts in heat, or by having an electronic actuator which senses smoke. I have known the former go off by accident, and also to fail to go off, but I have never heard of a case on a boat where they went off as promised. In my view they are a snare and a delusion and are best avoided, though surveyors, who must find something to grumble about in every yacht they survey, are keen to recommend them in insurance surveys. (So far, in more than a dozen insurance surveys I have seen, the number of idiot recommendations exceeds the sensible ones by a proportion of three to one.) I have no field experience of the other type in action, and prefer to put my faith in that unfailing sniffer device: my wife's nose.

So, what sort of extinguishers do we have? In defiance to authority I still have five halon extinguishers because I value my skin. I would only use them if I were to be in desperate need and I assure you that in those circumstances only a suicidal nincompoop would worry about the ozone layer. They are easy to check if up to pressure and ready to work. But I will conform to the law during our next refit.

One must be sure to renew extinguishers according to the makers' recommendations, and it is now difficult to replenish halon extinguishers. In my professional career I fought two serious fires at sea, and have spent much of my life since thinking about the problems which might have killed me. I am going to repeat that I disapprove strongly of the banning of halon as a result of 'Green' pressure. It should be permitted for use at sea. There are alternative firefighting techniques for use on shore which are not available to the ship-firefighter. Let's be Green, yes, but let us also be merciful to those in peril on the sea.

Any other firefighting materials? Yes, a fire blanket is worth keeping, both to smother a small fire or to use as a means of removing burning material. It's cheap and has nothing to go wrong. But remember a blanket does not cool the fuel: this must still be done, and very quickly.

Sprinkler systems, which ought really to be called spray systems, are worth installing in large yachts, especially in machinery spaces when it may not always be possible to get in to fight a fire. They give off a spray of very fine droplets of water, usually sea water. As their effect is not carefully aimed they do a fair amount of devastation, particularly to furnishings, so in my view are not recommended for automatic use, when they could be expected eventually to go off unasked. For an automatic system in the engine room I would prefer halon or carbon dioxide, but remember that engines cannot run on it. If the access is down a hatch, do not go leaping gaily down when the fire is out. There will be no oxygen for you to breathe, and maybe toxic smoke as well. Again the burning material will not be cooled, and could therefore reignite if the gas is dispersed.

• Big fires •

We define this as a fire beyond the capacity of your hand-held extinguishers. It may not be very large, but perhaps it is very intense and very soon could be large. In a yacht there is only one firefighting material available in sufficient quantities: water. You are surrounded by it, but to succeed you must use it skilfully. Water can be used against almost any type of fire if used well.

Fire brigades are occasionally called to deal with ship fires in port. Very soon there are dozens of 3-inch hoses snaking aboard, and before long, the weight of water in the vessel either sinks her or destroys her hydrostatic stability by creating free surface which capsizes her in her berth. The Bootle Fire Brigade hit the jackpot in 1953 with the *Empress of Canada*. It certainly puts the fire out, which enables the firemen to call it a success. It usually writes off the ship, puts a busy berth out of action, and may cause more financial damage than letting the fire burn itself out.

At sea, one is obsessed with preserving the ship, so make sure every bit of water let into her will be used to the maximum advantage. The jet of water, used so often and so dramatically on fires in buildings, has a point in enabling firemen to get water to the seat of a blaze they could not otherwise reach. It also blasts apart solid material and cools it. In its place, it is the right way of doing things. In a ship, and especially in a small ship, it is seldom the right way. Notice I do not say 'never' or 'always': there is no such conception in firefighting.

Water serves the important purpose of cooling. The most effective way of doing this is not by conducting heat away but by evaporating, which uses up a large amount of latent heat energy. In most circumstances, therefore, it pays to deliver the water in an ideal form for instant evaporation – a very fine spray.

A fine spray also acts as a sort of curtain. As the fire uses oxygen, it draws in more air and feeds itself. The spray curtain, though not a complete screen, reduces the flow of air to the fire. As the water droplets evaporate efficiently they turn almost instantly to steam which, because it has many times the volume of the water it came from, helps to create an effective barrier to air.

Jets of sea water conduct electricity well. A perfect spray of fine droplets, because the droplets are separate from each other, will not conduct. In practice, of course, a spray is never perfect, but at the ship firefighting school, I have taken part in experiments showing that a fine spray of sea water can reach to 75cm away from a high-voltage source without the nozzle giving more than a mild tingle to a person holding it with bare, wet hands. *This is not for repetition with backyard lash-ups*: it is potentially a very dangerous thing to do and the experiments were very carefully controlled, but it demonstrates that in the presence of low-powered electrics it is acceptable as a last-resort firefighting method.

The conclusion I draw from these last three paragraphs is that a fine spray can be used effectively against any likely fire aboard a yacht. Ideally the spray should be under some pressure: it can be pumped by hand using a galley pump. If enough pressure is obtainable the JetSpray hose 'gun' used aboard many boats for washing down decks and paintwork is adequate. If pressure is low, then a shower fitting is better than nothing. A rose from a watering can is good, but something of a rarity aboard a yacht. Rather than chuck buckets of water over a small fire (which can actually help it spread) I have found that dribbling water drops from a sponge can be more effective.

How do you use a spray? The spray's weakest effect is against solid materials. In this case use it to drench the burning items and to keep wet the adjacent area. Even when the flames are out, continue cooling until the surfaces stay wet. If in doubt remove charred matter with a knife or coarse rasp and cool again because it might still be very hot inside.

• Galley fires •

Of course halon, CO_2 or the fire blanket are best used first. One must also cut off the supply of fuel to the stove. A lot depends on the state of a fat fire. If it is entirely inside a saucepan (and one should endeavour always to use deep cooking utensils in a boat) put a lid on it and cool the pot down. Don't let any water get in the fat or it will spatter explosively. If the fat has spilled and spread, then we have an oil fire.

• Oil fires •

If the area of oil that is burning is large, use the fine spray curtain as if you are holding an umbrella against a strong wind, and slowly sweep the surface of the oil to try to reduce the burning area and to 'gather' the burning part into an ever-decreasing area. Do not leave any burning patches behind; go back and sweep again, slowly. You are both cooling it and reducing the oxygen supply. You will not succeed quickly. Try not to use more water than the fire is evaporating. If the oil is sloshing about in a moving boat this can be helpful because it is assisting cooling somewhat, but it does make containment with the spray more difficult. If there is a lot of oil (and water) in the bilge try to pump it out; ecology comes a poor second just now. The oil, even if hot, is unlikely to cause problems in the pump. It is important to cut the leak off as soon as possible so it may be necessary to concentrate on cooling the site where the isolating cocks are before tackling the main blaze, if more oil is actually leaking into it. I had this problem in one of the major fires I helped fight at sea. The engine room was on fire with hot oil fuel pouring from a burst 4-inch diameter feed pipe. The stop cock was adjacent to the seat of the fire. We had to empty the 200-ton oil tank into an empty fresh water tank. So even in 1952 we did our best to avoid pollution, long before the Greens got going. Seamen do try, but only seamen can possibly know the balance of the arguments at sea.

• *Electrical fires* •

There is not really any such thing: electricity provides the initiating heat and flash point and it is other matter that burns. The problem is usually that the electricity goes on supplying a source of great heat, which hinders attempts to extinguish the fire and also constitutes a hazard.

Usually the trigger of the fire is a short-circuit, which may or may not be arcing and therefore may not be easy to see. Try to identify the problem point and cut off the power to it. Smoke can prevent you from being able to see, so this is not always by any means easy. It is possible to use a spray curtain to contain the smoke to some extent, enabling you to see the seat of the fire. Apart from the regenerative potential of a continuing short-circuit, this type of fire usually turns into one of the others. A particular problem is that when plastic electrical insulation burns it gives off poisonous fumes.

• *Smoke* •

Many of the comforts of modern life produce toxic smoke when they burn, for example fabrics, upholstery, mattresses and plastic linings. Others produce carboniferous smoke which is not necessarily poisonous but which stops us breathing. Incomplete combustion can produce carbon monoxide which is poisonous. Sea water mixed with battery acid gives off chlorine, which is deadly.

Some of these toxic gases are lighter than air, and in fire conditions, when they are hot, most can be expected to rise. Under most conditions it pays to approach fires giving off a lot of smoke by keeping as near the deck as possible. Wet cloth over mouth and nostrils will filter particles, but will not stop most toxic gases. It hardly seems worth lumbering up a boat with breathing apparatus, but if necessary, it may be possible to improvise with a diving face mask and some tubing.

• *Understanding firefighting principles* •

All this is easy at a firefighting school. The important thing about actual fire-fighting, when every fire is different, is to be aware of the principles, to know the methods (and if possible to have exercised their use) and then to use your intelligence. The tradition of rushing to a fire is a very good one, but on arrival do not go mad and waste your resources. A few seconds to determine the nature of the fire and to plan the battle will be amply repaid.

The point at which you call for outside help depends on what help is available, what means you have to call it, and the relationship of the fire to your resources. If in doubt about your ability to cope and help is available, take a moment to call for it.

Most port authorities insist on a fire brigade being called, because they have an obligation to protect other vessels. They usually have power to tow away a burning ship to a safe berth and similar draconian rights. In these circumstances, ie in port, you must summon help, but unless the fire is beyond your control remember you are still in command of the ship.

Before you set sail (I refrain from saying before you burn your boats), if you can, find a fire brigade that has a specialised ship-firefighting team. There are not many of them, but Kent in the UK is one. I am sure that one of the Fire Officers would spare a moment to let you practise with extinguishers. Getting the feel of the equipment in advance is a powerful advantage.

IN CASE OF FIRE

- Call the whole crew.
- Get to the fire quickly, but calmly.
- Determine the generative centre of the fire.
- Assess the dangers of toxic gases and take precautions.
- Cut off any outside supply of fuel, or potential fuel.
- Select your firefighting apparatus.
- Attack the generative centre if it can be reached. If not, determine your route to it.
- Keep on until flames are out.
- Thoroughly cool the previously burning material.
- Check at frequent intervals afterwards that you have not overlooked any hot spots that are smouldering.

'The fire is out, God be thanked.'

DISMASTING

Other mishaps to the yacht involve the loss of mast, and canvas. We carry enough spare or alternate sails to get by, perhaps less efficiently but nevertheless practically, if some are blown out.

Here Bill is cutting free the rigging after Hosanna *lost her foremast.*

Loss of a mast is more serious, and is best dealt with by getting them strong enough at the start. The extra cost will probably be less than the excess on your insurance policy. Cruising boats should not go around with the bendy fishing rods sported by the racing folk. It helps to have a two-masted rig too, but only if there is no triatic stay. (I am not sure triatic stays contribute very much anyway.)

What to do if you lose a mast is very well covered in salty books on seamanship. Racing yachtsmen write about it frequently in magazines, but mostly they have large crews of gorillas to heft spars about. All the more reason for the cruising man to consider his double-strength masts and rigging, and then double again to be on the safe side.

Yes, I have been dismasted. Twice. Once while racing on the Harwich-Hook Race in the 1960s, and once recently in *Hosanna*, and both in almost exactly the same place off the Kentish Knock Light Vessel. Racing, we were grossly over-canvased and deserved it. *Hosanna*'s solid wood foremast had rotted round a knot under the paint, and the vibrations of motoring (yes!) into a short, steep sea brought it all down. At 0400 of course. The two of us managed to get all 400 kilos of it back inboard, and we continued south to Ramsgate. We have a galvanised steel mast now. No mucking about.

LOSING A RUDDER

Problems occur rarely in mid-Atlantic. The recent report of a modern, expensive yacht whose spade rudder broke off in mid-Atlantic in perfectly normal Atlantic weather is unusual. Unable to effect a repair, they had to scuttle their yacht. Unsupported spade rudders hung right aft are not advisable for use offshore. The stresses on a rudder when running before a biggish sea are very great; one only has to watch gybing racing yachts broaching madly in a high wind, their transoms in the air like hens with their backs to the wind. Add to this the forces when the stern is atop a breaking wave with tons of sea water sloshing first one way and then the other in seconds and you begin to wish there was some re-inforcing pintle lower down. Not a pansy little skeg stuck on apparently with sellotape, but a beefy great extension aft of a proper keel.

I'm not saying the yacht in question was flawed in design or build. Perhaps, as the builders pointed out, there could have been an unknown previous unfair strain on the rudder that had weakened it. But that leads on to the next reason to avoid spade rudders. The rudder itself is part of the lateral resistance (and therefore of the balance) of a yacht. To compensate, the fin keel is further forward than would be the case with a long-keeled yacht. When and if this large area right aft is removed, the yacht becomes severely unbalanced. In the case under discussion, the crew reported that they could not steer the yacht at all. This astounded me. I have never come across a yacht that cannot be steered without a rudder, it was one of the first things we learnt in the old sailing days, but I have to believe what they say. The implications are shattering. On this evidence alone, I would avoid spade rudders.

• *So, how to steer without a rudder?* •

When loss of rudder happened to me in an ex-German Navy yacht (a very old wooden one whose rudder stock had been consumed by gribble inside the tube) we did not try to rig a jury rudder, but steered downhill by rigging the boom squared off one side and the spinnaker pole squared off the other. From the ends of each we streamed a coil of rope, each coil at the end of a four-part tackle. By shortening in or paying out one side or the other we could keep the yacht (a 30 square metre racing yacht) on course in 10 foot waves. (See drawing opposite.)

Before the ARC started, yachts having trouble on the transatlantic were few in number. It was rare. Probably because everybody knew they would be alone and took great care. It seems to me that accidents on the transatlantic voyage have increased. I have no figures; it is an impression. Perhaps the news gets round faster these days. One can hardly blame the organisers of the ARC. They lay down minimum standards and inspect the boats. Weather and sea conditions should be good and are so most of the time. I wonder, though, if people are now induced to make the passage in yachts that are too light for the infrequent bad moment. They are production yachts that sell in their hundreds and have made many

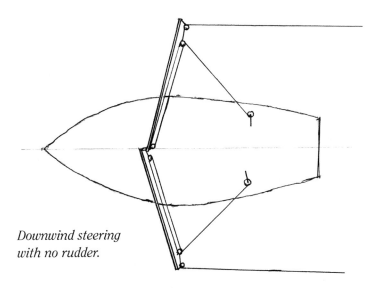

*Downwind steering
with no rudder.*

passages in safety. The query is about their reserve of seakindliness that is needed for those rare nasty shocks that most yachts seldom experience. No evidence, no data to speak of. Just a gut feeling. I worry about people making a passage in a boat that I would not, myself, have complete faith in.

LIGHTNING STRIKE

During the various talks we have given we have been surprised at the interest shown in lightning at sea. *Fare Well* was struck once, and Bill was struck once before in a small warship; it is one of those very rare sea-going experiences which seems to fascinate everyone.

Quite a long while ago *Yachting Monthly* had a correspondence on what policy to adopt when entering a violent thunderstorm, and one writer advocated donning rubber gloves and boots. Bill, being rather a rude sort of sailor, wrote in, suggesting that someone had forgotten to include a condom. The then Editor, Des Sleightholme, doyen of yachting wits, wrote back gleefully that he felt the comment a little ripe for publishing in those days, but finished with the following:

> *The lightning flashed, the thunder crashed,*
> *The mate of the watch turned pale,*
> *For St Elmo's fire struck his rubber attire*
> *The moment he touched the rail.*

It is St Elmo's fire that one is more likely to encounter, especially in a steel boat. In a GRP boat or a wooden one, there is a lot to be said for having a bond between the sea water and the top of the mast. Of course the standing rigging does this if the mast is not metal, the only link required being between the chain plates and the water. The reason for such a bond is to keep the electric current flow on the outside of the boat.

Thunderstorms in the tropics, and also in the Med, can be much more violent than we in temperate zones are used to. We once counted 42 lightning flashes within one random minute. In these circumstances it is obvious that there is a huge potential difference between the atmosphere and the sea.

It is only when this difference is unable to disperse peacefully that it runs riot and strikes. During a night thunderstorm one will often see St Elmo's fire (a brilliant display from the masthead looking like a 'sparkler' type of firework). This discharge is helping to prevent the violently damaging strike.

I was on deck both times when struck, and it was difficult to assess exactly what was happening. Both times there was an enormous display, several metres across, of St Elmo's fire at the masthead, and it went on for some time. In *Fare Well* (then in the Gulf Stream) the sparking increased rapidly in intensity as I watched. I felt the sensation usually described as one's 'hair standing on end', even though I was wearing a cap. It was an extraordinarily strong sensation. It developed into a feeling of being lifted off the ground a few inches, of stopping breathing, of being held by the back of the neck like a rabbit, of being absolutely unable to move at all. Those below felt nothing.

It is well to remember that even in the Med, severe storms can strike. We were lucky not to suffer damage when we experienced force 10 in Bodrum harbour.

During this time I was aware that the sparking at the masthead had turned into a brilliant ball of light about 7 metres in diameter, and that the rigging was glowing white.

Suddenly, as if by throwing a switch, it all turned off. I fell to the deck in a state of shock, and all the fire and sparks at the masthead disappeared. Notice that I have given no time-scale for these events. I was not aware of any sensation of time passing. It is possible the whole sequence took place in a second, it might have taken 10 or 20; I have no idea.

What was the damage to a steel boat?

To me personally, nothing that a good breakfast could not put right. There are few things that do not yield to a good breakfast.

The problem was: no hot breakfast yet. The only interior part of the boat affected was the wiring, which suggests to me that the current flowed in the skin of the boat (the Faraday box effect) and set up a strong magnetic field that induced current into some, but not all, of the wiring. It must have done so at great speed, for in some cases the wire had melted before the fuse had blown. Generally wires melted or insulation blew open at sharp corners, and the damage took the form of a directional blast along the wire. It was as if the current had a linear momentum and could not negotiate the tight bend, mounted the banking and left the track like a racing car.

Some physicists I have discussed this with deny that such an effect is possible, but I have seen it, and I have found one scientist who says there is some evidence that very violent flashes of current have what he called a 'plasma effect'. Well now.

Question: Was that a lightning strike or a very bad attack of St Elmo? Answer: Who knows? Next question: What can one do about it? Answer: nothing more than I said above.

If it was just bad St Elmo, then in the thunderstorm going on at that time, it suggests to me that a good electrical path up to the top of the mast, together with a good area of conductor in the water (we had recently had a spectacular grounding in coral which had taken a lot of paint off our keel), inhibits a strike by organising a very effective discharge. If it was a proper strike, then compared with the devastated condition of both wooden and GRP boats that have been struck (all I have seen have taken fire), I cannot help feeling that a boat built of a good conducting material has advantages for the tropics.

What else was damaged? All the electronic fittings on the mainmast were blown apart, but to my amazement I found that some of the instruments themselves (those which had been switched off) survived the blow. All the electronics on the mizzen mast, including the Decca radar, survived. Our radio sets all survived (they were switched off, and their aerial plugs removed: my practice in storms). Several electric motors did not. The stator coils in the generator had to be re-energised.

As for the standing rigging, it appeared to be undamaged, possibly because the current was flowing over the surface rather than inside the wire, and of course the wire was soaking wet in the heavy rain, which may have cooled it. Anyway it survived several more years of use and abuse.

There was one other important effect which does not go under the heading of damage: compass error. The whole ship became highly magnetised and the compass was wildly out. Fortunately we had logged the direction of the swell a couple of hours before the storm, so we had an angular reference. Without that, in completely overcast conditions and 400 miles from land, we would have had absolutely no idea of which way to go.

It turned out that the compass deviation was about 90° to start with, but within an hour this had fallen to 35°. A week later it was about 15°, but it took three months to fall below 5°. It never did return to its former state; after about six months we adjusted the magnets to remove the last couple of degrees of deviation.

It wasn't much fun clearing up the mess, but it was a fascinating intellectual exercise trying to sort it all out.

All in all I feel there is not enough objective evidence in existence to justify any heavy expenditure on this problem. One can, however, take the simple precautions I outlined at the start. At least they won't do any harm. And the compass problem shows how it pays to keep the log up to date.

EMERGENCIES OUTSIDE THE BOAT

These are emergencies which can lead to the abandonment of the enterprise, its interruption or a temporary trip home for one of the crew: illness of a close relative, for example. It really is impossible to give advice to cover so many different problems in so many possible places, and at widely varying times. We have only had to make two out-of-routine or emergency trips home in 29 years, one from a Greek island, and one, half-expected, from southern France.

I used to counsel maintaining a contingency fund of cash on board to cover both fares and additional costs that will be entailed in such an event, if there is any chance of it occurring, but with the coming of ATMs and easy availability of cash, that is less important. It is possible that a real family emergency while cruising the South Pacific could be ruinous.

• *Back up and outside help* •

There are those who worry about disasters, that they might be unable to cope. I think most of us have worries of this nature to some extent. It is natural. And if it induces an atmosphere of prudence and care it is a productive worry. To set sail with a literally careless abandon is dangerous and childish, and it is not macho because real men *care*.

The sea is a dangerous place, though there are times when the dangers are hidden. A live-aboard needs a different approach to that of the Solent week-ender. The live-aboard must adopt and maintain a quasi-professional attitude. This is vital because the sea becomes most dangerous when you forget that it is dangerous.

Some get over their nervousness about dangers by a decision to make their first ocean crossing in company with an organisation like the Atlantic Rally for Cruisers (ARC) or on a round-the-world jolly such as the Blue-Water Rally. It's a free world and there are those for whom the sociability and jollity, combined with inevitable outbreaks of competitive spirit, are welcome enough to attract them, even though the fees for participation are, in our opinion, unjustifiably high. But I would not say that organisations such as the ARC enhance security at sea. They might even give a false sense of security and induce lack of care. One cannot be dogmatic about this.

In the first place, the Atlantic crossing itself from the Canaries to the Windward Islands is unlikely to be other than a comparatively safe voyage. The voyage *to* the Canaries before you start your crossing is far more difficult and dangerous: thus more appropriate for a passage in convoy.

In spite of all the aids to communication, all the chatty radio nets, boats inevitably disperse on a long voyage and end up miles apart. Finding another yacht in distress is not easy; one's sea horizon at deck level is only about 4 miles and yachts are not equipped with direction finding equipment. Even with the ARC, you cannot rely on outside help coming quickly, though recent events show that it can be done. For ocean cruising you must have an attitude of independence, of self-reliance, of self-confidence. The ARC may be ideal for those 'doing the triangle' (Europe – Caribbean – Bermuda – Europe, all in one year starting in October), but if you have longer distances in your sights, we think, and it is only an opinion after all, that you should start as independently as you will have to go on. More on the ARC in the chapter on Social Life, of all places.

MAN OVERBOARD

With all this goes the problem of falling overboard. I fell overboard in calm weather in 1949 from the deck of an ocean-racing yacht in the Channel near the Nab Tower. It was during the dark, just before dawn. I had no life-jacket on, and without a motor to help them, my colleagues had to abandon the search for me. I was recovered unconscious by the Royal Engineers Rowing Club out for an early morning row off Southsea.

Yachts then had no guardrails; we had no safety harnesses, and life-jackets were the enormously bulky kapok-stuffed kind that prevented all movement, so when racing we didn't wear them. Things have changed now, with well-designed lightweight life-jackets and clip-on harnesses readily available. USE THEM when on deck alone, especially at night. There is no longer any need to take chances, believe me. Falling overboard at sea from a cruising yacht should be all but impossible. Make it so.

I subsequently spent three weeks in Haslar hospital with pneumonia and other chest complications, some of which still affect me. Not recommended.

There's another man overboard lesson for all of us here. When I was rescued, I was barely conscious and was taken by the REs to the Royal Naval MO of the Guard who sent me straight to hospital. Because nobody knew from whence I had come, nobody cancelled the full-scale search that was going on until several hours later. Lesson: if you are involved in a rescue, or survive by your own efforts, then inform the authorities ASAP. The rescue personnel often risk their lives. They must not do so unnecessarily.

• Recovery •

One of the useful things to have on deck in the event of a man overboard is a moderate length (50 metres, say) of light floating rope about 8mm diameter. The rope should have a metre-long loop at the end, and being floating, will not get in the screw. Given the two circumstances: that manoeuvring is difficult and the victim is conscious, it is possible to come close enough and turn so that the rope is brought across the victim. If the yacht can then be stopped, it is possible to haul him alongside, but he should not normally be towed. Better to let the rope go from on board and pick it up again if you have too much way on. There are now commercial kits which perform the above function: they are not expensive and have the right sort of fittings.

I believe in the use of the engine in recovery. My experience is that even when running under spinnaker, the engine at full astern will not destroy steerage way and will save valuable yards while the sail is being furled: a point of importance for short-handed crews. Beware of trailing cordage when furling.

Loss of anyone aboard is a terrible disaster. Its effect and the awful fear of it can be mitigated by a discussion and decisions of what to do if the disaster happens. That is probably enough to make sure it never does.

It is different in harbour. You relax, have fun, go to the taverna and come back giggling and full of bonhomie. Who wears a life-jacket on an evening like that? Yet this is when the unthinkable happens. In our last three years at Levkas, eight yachtspeople have fallen into the water, incurring some nasty cuts and bruises but mercifully without fatality. One would certainly have drowned had his dog not given the alarm. Two were from a dinghy, but all the other six fell in while trying to board or leave a yacht which was moored bows-to a low pontoon. This often involves trying to scramble over or round the anchor, or over a pulpit rail down a rickety ladder in sometimes stormy conditions (a generalisation, but not a completely unfair one). It is easier to come into a Med berth bows-to, but our conclusion is that it poses serious risks for those on board unless proper steps (literally as well as metaphorically) are taken to make clambering over the stem and anchor safe and easy in the dark, in pouring rain and high wind, wearing oilskins. We recently lost a valued friend who fell in at Levington Marina and drowned for cause unknown.

Why not lower the anchor into the water for a start? Not only would it be out of the way, but its chain cable hanging down would provide a good hand-hold.

And one useful thing the Health and Safety Executive might do productively is to require marinas to have more emergency ladders on their pontoons.

See also under 'falls' in Health and Welfare at Sea, Chapter 15.

THE PANIC BAG

Having advised that a good rigid dinghy is in many respects better than an inflatable liferaft, I have to remind you that the latter does have a survival pack of sorts on board. Therefore, if you use a rigid dinghy as a lifeboat, you should have a pack to help you survive. We call ours the panic bag. Some people object to the use of the word panic in this context, saying that it is the last thing one should be aware of in this circumstance, but I disagree. Actually using the word reminds one of the danger of panic, and inhibits its formation.

Ours actually consists of two bags: the First Panic Bag, which is kept in the dinghy on passage, and the Second, which is kept reasonably handy for grabbing if there is time. For those with an inflatable liferaft, it might be worth comparing my lists with the contents of the survival kit provided therein, and making up a bag to contain the difference. (You cannot check the raft's pre-packed supplies: they are quite often not as promised.)

Our lists are based on consultation with a survivor friend, and also my own 600 miles in the Indian Ocean in an open boat.

THE FIRST PANIC BAG (for 2 people)

4 x 8 pint water in opaque plastic bottles	Tweezers	2 'space blankets'
2 strong drinking cups (Melaware)	Small compass, mirror	300ft codline
4 red flares, 4 orange smoke day markers	Needles and thread	Fishing line, spoons, hooks
	Cotton wool	Greek style foul-hooks for fishing
Torch, spare bulb, spare batteries	Small bottle TCP antiseptic	Greek 7-pronged harpoon head (a barbed minia-
200 multivitamin pills in plastic jar	Tube of antibiotic cream 100 tablets broad spec- trum antibiotic	ture Poseidon's fork)
100 Horlicks tablets	Tube of sun screen oint- ment	Gaff for fishing Set of small chartlets in a plastic bag
1lb boiled sweets	Seasickness pills	Survival type solar still
Swiss army knife, dinner knife, spoon	Sponge (bailer is already in dinghy) 2 small hand towels	(RAF surplus type)

THE SECOND PANIC BAG (for 2 people)

2 inflatable cushions	Candles, matches in	Cereal bars in waterproof
2 single blankets	screw-top jar	container
2 wool sweaters	Araldite (epoxy glue)	Can-opener
3sq yds 4oz canvas	More boiled sweets	2 pairs sunglasses
Some fresh lemons in foil	4 more pints water	Bucket
2 parachute flares	More sunscreen ointment	2 sunhats
Small funnel	8 assorted tins of food	

Items that date and deteriorate must be replaced when time-expired. And let's hope that, like us, you get 30 years of cruising and never have to reach for the panic bag.

LIFERAFTS

It appears that the MCA have made the carriage of a liferaft compulsory for British yachts going more than 20 miles off the coast. In my view this measure is quite wrong. There is nothing to stop those who have 100% faith in liferafts from carrying them. We have lost three friends who placed reliance on inflatable liferafts. They are designed as a short-term safety device and they do not stand up to a prolonged use or, put another way, there are instances where they have not done so, and a failure rate in such a device, however small, is not acceptable to us. They require frequent, very expensive maintenance in circumstances where one cannot be certain that the maintenance has been conscientiously performed. They may be better than nothing, but that is not good enough when survival depends on them.

I prefer a well-designed rigid dinghy with built-in buoyancy, and a good spray hood, preferably a sailing dinghy, sensibly fitted out as a potential life-saving device according to my own actual experiences of what is involved.

POSTSCRIPT

How did I survive hours in the Channel without a buoyancy aid? Actually, I can only surmise: there was a naval enquiry into the event, if only because my shipmates abandoned the search, for which they were rebuked. (Unjustly, I felt. They had decided to head for shore and get help. They had no radio.)

First fact: it was a calm sea. I was wearing a completely new and experimental plastic smock. Up to 1948, naval oilskins were just that, oiled canvas coats, black and stiff as boards, miserably uncomfortable. Somebody had designed a new outfit: trousers and smock of heavy black plastic. Much better! It had a wide neck so you could wear a towel inside, and a drawstring round it. I had been given one of these for trial and had kept my thieving hands on it ('rabbited' in naval slang) when the trial was completed. I was wearing it, well towelled and drawstring tight at the neck. The Royal Engineers (motto: *Ubique*) reported that it had ballooned with air and had kept me head-up and afloat. They gave me a hot shower (Wrong! We now know) and fed me tea until I vomited, bless them, and because I seemed to be OK, they took me back to my mess. (Also a mistake as I ended up hospitalised with pneumonia, but we did not know about hypothermia in those days.) And 56 years later I still have (and occasionally wear) the original plastic oilskins that saved my life. Beat that, Henri Lloyd! Only joking.

12 • Navigation

'If you don't know where you are going you will probably end up somewhere else.' – PETER AND HULL, The Peter Principle

Cruising books of 20 years ago had to have a chapter (at least) on this subject, and in the early cruising symposia we attended it was clear many inexperienced yachtsmen were nervous about it. (Unjustifiably, in my view.) Now the situation has changed completely. They are not nervous enough, GPS has made it seem too easy.

This is at first sight tough on me (Bill) for this is my professional speciality and it seems that my Fellowship of the Royal Institute doesn't carry much weight these days. But if you thought that would get you out of a homily on the subject – think again! You get full value in this book. Navigation has changed, but it's still there. And there is still need to avoid complacency.

For a long time now, the navigator has been obsessed with knowing the ship's position. It was not always so. My fishermen father, grandfather and other ancestors didn't work like that. They plotted backwards from where they wanted to go and sailed (literally in their case – we are talking of sailing smacks) so as to maximise their chances of getting there with no instruments but with a lot of knowledge. They knew not where they were; their position would have badly affected by trawling up and down the North Sea for several days, probably under overcast skies in winter. Many boats were lost, and the memorial at Lowestoft is crowded with names of the drowned, including not a few Coopers. Position was all a mystery.

Their method was the one used by the unfortunate Sir Cloudesley Shovell who wrecked the British fleet off the Scillies in 1707. Some say that the wreck was caused by his inability to discover his longitude, and an American woman has written a best-selling book passing on this misapprehension. For misapprehension it is. It was not ignorance of the longitude that wrecked the fleet. They did not know their *latitude*. Because many of you may be faced with a similar voyage under sail, from Spain to the English Channel, let's look into it.

The technique then was to think of the destination: the Channel. Note that it resembles a sleeve. (So it is called in French: *La Manche*.) The 'cuffs' of this sleeve are dangerous, but they are 35 leagues apart; an important distance immortalised in the sea shanty *Spanish Ladies*. Once inside the cuffs, you can head eastward, with nothing south, into a gradually narrowing channel until you see somewhere you recognise. Old charts abounded in sketches of the coastline for this purpose.

When well offshore, you did not know your position. You chose a course that would take you in the general direction of your destination with the minimal chance of danger. You hoped something visible would turn up in time. Old navigators were optimists. They had to be. Gloomy navigators are a modern phenomenon.

Any sailor at that time could work out his latitude using either the sun by day or Pole Star by night, if they were visible. So the method was to head due north from Spain until one was at or near the mid-latitude between Ushant and Scillies, then turn east and keep a good look out. It's still a prudent method if you sail without electronics.

Unfortunately for Sir Cloudesley, the weather stayed rotten and they saw neither sun nor stars. He *estimated* his latitude to be about right and turned to the eastward. He had underestimated both current and leeway in the bad weather, and had overshot the required latitude. His fleet ploughed into the Bishop and Clerks Rocks at the sleeve's northerly cuff in a westerly gale. Even had he known his longitude, he would have been in trouble for he was heading for a lee shore with limited manoeuvrability. He could not have turned the fleet round. In the context of the time, it was not incompetence, but ill-fortune. We could all do without that.

We all like to think this couldn't happen nowadays. But it could, and it does. Why? Because paradoxically, the art of position fixing which came after Sir Cloudesley has now been advanced to such a fine art, with such exactitude, that we have come to pay too little attention to where we are going. We tend to think statically, glorying in the latest perfect fix. We now have GPS and waypoint navigation. Our boat is exactly *there*, with absolute three-metre certainty. And it's a doddle, isn't it? It can be. It can also be dangerous for we have not yet got

Island of Ustica in the Tyrrhenian Sea

ourselves into the habit of thinking dynamically. Marine accident reports are still full of accounts of those who let the ship run on a mile too far while brewing the cocoa (so to speak).

ELECTRONIC NAVIGATION

Each science terms of art hath wherewithal
To express themselves, call'd technologicall.

Our recent survey has shown that 84% of cruising boats now carry a computer or laptop, some both. Twenty-odd years ago we met our first cruiser (American of course) with a computer on board; a thing of great wonder, and some chortling; what on earth would you *do* with such a toy? Now we know.

Nowadays, we can connect together our GPS, our compass, our echo-sounder, our computer (with its electronic charts), our log (if we have one) and the radar. Unfortunately we can also connect the CD and DVD player, but that's another story. We can call up the chart on screen, click where we want the destination waypoint to be. The track will appear on the 'chart' and we can select the largest scale to check that nowhere does it cross a shoal. We can use various windows to display other views and other instruments.

We should check the nearest dangers to the track-line and make sure there is a good margin of error. Some programmes highlight dangers according to pre-entered characteristics of the ship and do everything for you. By engaging the autopilot, we will follow that line, sails or motor permitting, wind and currents also. From that time on we are *not navigating by position mode*, we are dynamic. All we have to do is to let our gizmos follow that line. (But not, please, while watching the DVD.)

There are two cautions:

- If, for various reasons, we wander off track *the process must re-start* on a new track, and we must closely examine the new track for dangers. This is often overlooked, especially when caution drops in bad weather. Remember, do it right and never, ever completely trust the little b****r.
- Be careful about selecting waypoints from a book. Firstly there are few books printed without a basket of misprints. Secondly, others will also select the same waypoint from the same book because it's easier. Such is the accuracy of GPS that in poor visibility, you could all arrive at the way-point at exactly the same moment. Wham bam, damn-damn-damn!

IT HAS HAPPENED. It used to happen, too, with Decca. It is known as an EAC, Electronically Assisted Collision. Never take the charted position of a buoy, for example, as a waypoint. You might end up hitting it. According to a yachting magazine, four Solent yachtmasters in a fast motor yacht have just done that.

• *Hitches and glitches* •

There is a story circulating of the airliner that on take-off greeted the passengers over the loudspeaker, but instead of 'This is your Captain speaking . . .' they heard: 'You are on an experimental flight. The aircraft is being flown by computer and there is no pilot on board. There is no need to worry. The system has been carefully checked and nothing can go wrong. HIC. go wrong. HIC. go wrong. HIC. go wrong . . .'

Twice in my cruising experience, I have noticed that GPS has been officially switched off during defence crises for several hours. We are told it won't happen again. Ho ho ho!

Another time I knocked against the power connection. The set appeared to be working correctly, and it was 20 minutes before I noticed that it was showing the last known position by internal battery-operated memory. It had no satellites. I only noticed because the ship was no longer on the expected course.

It has also been known for the waypoint to be entered incorrectly owing to the buttons on the damned thing being smaller and closer together than the end of a finger. The Big Finger Syndrome. The GPS is dumb. It needs looking after. Do not trust the little b****r. It can bite.

After years of resistance, I wouldn't now be without it. But I have a second one with an independent power source. I quite expect the two of them to discover each other one day and gang up on me. 'This set has detected another GPS on board. You have performed an illegal operation and we will both shut down immediately' will flash on the screen. And the second one will answer 'So there!'

Here is another word of caution. The Royal Institute of Navigation has produced a document written by its Vice President (the president is an air navigator), Bill Sandford. There can be few better authorities. I quote:

'It is now widely accepted that to use a system like GPS as sole means (of navigation) is unsafe.' He goes on: 'Satellite signals are so weak at the point of reception [that] they are vulnerable to interference.' In addition, 'Signals are simple to jam . . .' and jamming can be accidental as well as malicious.

The sort of people who throw rocks from motorway bridges can jam GPS with very simple equipment (my comment).

Now, extra satellites are being provided and when Galileo kicks in during 2009 we will have 50 satellites. But nobody can give any guarantees at all that satellite navigation will be a continuous service. Nations are pressing the IMO to establish e-Loran as an alternative system that is not satellite based. Britain is building a transmitter at Rugby, hoping it will be operative in 2005.

A Dutch professor has designed a small receiver that will filter all signals from e-Loran and satellites and automatically select the most reliable. It will do this in conjunction with an ordinary PC. It is in limited production (Jan 2005) but is still too expensive for the average yachtie. Just hang on a bit. When we have something like that, then we can go totally electronic. Not before.

With the plethora of electronic gadgetry that yachts carry nowadays, a sturdy gantry is a better option than cluttering up the mast and it supports the gangway effectively.

You think that GPS will no longer go down? Well, in the last couple of months, GPS was suspended for a short period without warning, for reasons unknown, and it caused a large tanker in the Dover Strait to alter course 30° before the watch officer noticed. Fortunately without mishap.

Ignoring the question of what such a big ship was doing on autopilot in the Dover Strait, we have to accept that the 'gather time' before the watch officer observed the error, decided what to do, and then got around to doing it, is dangerously significant.

Of course, I don't want to worry you, but . . .er, well, don't throw away those paper charts and don't sell your sextant to the antique shop just yet. GPS should be checked with another method and be subject to eye-ball supervision.

• *Navigation first aid kit* •

Let's examine what to do if you experience an electronic crisis. Let us assume that being an imprudent sailor (of course you're not), you have nothing on board to navigate with. Rats ate your charts, you have no power, not even your electronic compass. No radar. No VHF.

Now I know that if you have taken the trouble to buy this book, and read this far, you are not a complete idiot. You will have considered such an improbable possibility or, at least, you are likely to do so from now on. Especially out of sight of land, there are elementary precautions that you really must take just in case the above scenario occurs.

Every half hour note down by the old steam method (a non-indelible pencil and paper):

- Your current position (lat and long from the GPS).
- The direction the waves are moving in, or coming from.
- The wind direction.
- Your approximate speed over the ground (speed made good on the GPS).
- Distance to go to destination waypoint.
- Bearing of destination waypoint.
- ETA at destination waypoint.

You must then relate your desired course to the wave direction. Wave direction is slower to change than wind, which can be capricious.

Now, even if you do not have a paper back-up chart, we presume you have a pilot book (some say they take up too much room, but they are worth their space in emergencies) and are not navigating, as one motor yachtsman we met, on an AA road map. A *good pilot book* is part of your first aid kit, and there will be enough information in it to draw your own rough chart. Yes, there will be, and I have done it several times, the most notable occasion being off Great Yarmouth at 0400 on a stormy night. (Don't ask why I had to do it. Suffice to say that all the warnings I give are based on bitter experience.) The Admiralty Pilots are best. Most yachting 'pilots' are pretty poor for navigation first aid purposes and even in these days of GPS, do not give latitudes and longitudes of salient landmarks. They call themselves 'pilots', but in truth they are guide books for nautical tourists going from one marina to the next, and I am going to suggest to Imray that they make a point of improving on this point in future editions. The RCC Pilotage Foundation who is behind many published pilots, should also see to it where necessary. Now that everyone uses GPS it is essential that pilot books can be used as back-up in case of trouble.

If you fail to make the notes suggested above, have only a yachting guide aboard and your system goes down, then you are in much the same state as navigators in the 13th century. The Pope's advice to them at the time was to pray to the Virgin Mary for guidance. There are no statistics on the reliability of this procedure.

• *Charts* •

Paper charts in Britain have become ridiculously expensive. Even in the USA, where the government subsidises them, they do not exactly come cheap. Electronic charts are the answer, but they have to be used with care. Several sources are available and you must get the one that suits you best. None are perfect. The programme that enables you to have access to them doesn't cost much, but the individual charts do when you add them up.

The charts can be up-dated by a download, which is also expensive. I expect prices to fall one day.

The disadvantage of the electronic charts system is that it is much more difficult to absorb the whole picture on a small screen than on a spread-out sheet of paper. Voyage and cruise planning is easier, and a lot more enjoyable with a paper chart.

Is the electronic system dependable? I would say that it is reliable to over 99%, but that operator error is probably several times as likely. The charts, individually, are accurate; it is system failure you worry about, and that means computer crash. And they do crash and they get harder use in a small boat than in the comfort of your own home. So, what to do? Paper charts as well? Or a second computer?

We still have Bill's enormous collection of paper charts, some of them now aging, having been given to him by a grateful and generous Queen when he left the Royal Navy, but all of them useful in their time. This collection, added to over the years, now amounts to about 600 charts. At present prices these would cost new about £10,000.

A world folio of electronic charts would cost in the region of £4000, but you are unlikely to want a world folio. Unfortunately, most standard folios are designed for big ships and contain charts of little use to a yacht. The areas seem to be designed to make the yachtsman pay as much as possible to cover popular sailing grounds. Cherry-picking the charts you want is expensive; the unit cost is high. Shop around.

There are various illegal copies of standard electronic chart systems available, most originating in Russia. We are ourselves interested in protecting copyrights, and have to disapprove, but I have checked over one of these on a neighbouring yacht and it seems to be OK, though it contains certain gaps and cannot be up-dated. And no, we cannot and will not offer you a source in the Appendix. It could be difficult to find a source while in the UK, for pirating is heavily frowned on there, but in some countries electronic pirating is commonplace. The problem for the law-abiding is that the legitimate publishers of electronic charts cannot get a fair return on their investment, if half (say) of the market are getting the product free so, inevitably we have higher prices all round. Homily over.

• *Navigation systems* •

Electronic charts should be used with a system. Though there are comparatively few publishers of charts, there are several makers of navigational systems. Some systems offer you a choice of chart suppliers. However, if you are going down the electronic road (and by the time this is published, I think you should), unless you have already got a large investment in paper, you should purchase the package so that everything is compatible. Cherry-picking can lead to problems. Some systems will only work well if everything, compass, radar, echo-sounder, autopilot, etc is their own make. I left the Raymarine stand at the Boat Show with that impression, though I found their system impressive. Everything from the one maker? Is that good or bad? I'll have to leave that to you.

Unfortunately, the sales pitches of the various suppliers are strong and, though they will be straight on facts, they can be a little over-enthusiastic on performance, particularly in ease of use. The salesman will flip happily about the system and make it look easy, but unless and until you become equally at home with it, expect a fair amount of frustration. Most systems are about as simple as Windows is itself. One system we have tried is almost impossible to switch off.

ANCHORING

What, is the anchor away?

The other subject I want to cover in this chapter is anchoring. Why in this chapter? Well, the choice of anchoring position, the state of the bottom, the amount of cable, the anchor bearings and setting an anchor watch in bad weather are the responsibility of the Navigating Officer. That's big ship practice. In yachts it's all up to the skipper. I was raised in both yachts and big ships. I think you will be able to tell.

There are many misconceptions about anchoring, and while cruising abroad, you will probably anchor far more than the typical UK-based sailor. We once went

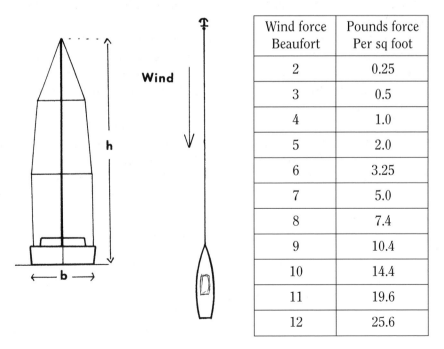

Wind force Beaufort	Pounds force Per sq foot
2	0.25
3	0.5
4	1.0
5	2.0
6	3.25
7	5.0
8	7.4
9	10.4
10	14.4
11	19.6
12	25.6

*Table giving the force on a yacht exerted by a steady wind from right ahead (based on Martin's formula). First calculate the frontal area by multiplying **b** and **h** (in feet) as shown on the diagram to the left. Then use the square footage in the table.*

410 consecutive nights in a variety of places, with an anchor down in one way or another.

Manufacturers and magazines grade anchors by their 'rated break-out pull'. This is obtained by subjecting the set anchor to an increasing steady strain which is measured on a spring balance. Eventually the anchor will break out, and that is the RBP. Obviously, the higher the figure the better. But that is not the whole story.

While in the River Danube estuary, *Hosanna* lay to single bower anchor in a 7-knot current (measured on log). She was docile, neither sheering about nor

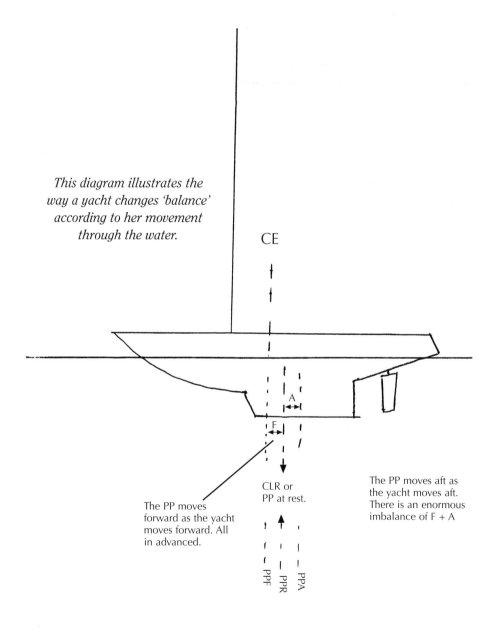

This diagram illustrates the way a yacht changes 'balance' according to her movement through the water.

CE

A

F

CLR or
PP at rest.

The PP moves forward as the yacht moves forward. All in advanced.

The PP moves aft as the yacht moves aft. There is an enormous imbalance of F + A

PPF

PPR

PPA

snatching; a completely steady strain. Obviously the anchor was doing the work of an engine driving the ship in smooth water at 7 knots. That, I know, takes 180hp. The equivalent wind that would have to blow on the ship's frontal area to develop that power would be on the borders of Beaufort scales 11 and 12. With such a wind blowing, she'd surely drag. Why didn't she? What is the difference?

The RBP is not the vital factor. Of course it helps, and when lying stern to the quay with an anchor out, Med-mooring fashion, then the anchor has a steady pull and the RBP is relevant. But not when at single anchor. Why not? And what is significant?

Let us digress and consider the way a yacht pivots. If at rest, she will pivot about the point referred to by yacht designers as the geometric *centre of lateral resistance* (CLR). Yacht designers contrive the combined centre of effort (CE) of the wind blowing on her sails, hull and rigging to be a noticeable distance ahead of the CLR. You might expect the yacht then to be unbalanced while on a reach, say, and her head to pay off (lee helm). And it does not, or should not. This is because the designer knows that when the yacht is moving forward through the water, the CLR, which navigators call the *Point of Pivot* (PP), moves forward and it is a matter of the designer's judgement and skill how far forward he assumes it will move. The faster the yacht moves, the further forward moves the PP and we see the weather helm increasing as hull speed is neared. In fast planing boats, the PP moves so far forward that it is actually ahead of the boat's stem and we have the phenomenon of the boat apparently skidding sideways as she tries to round a sharp corner.

Following all that (you still with me? Keep trying, it gets better). you find that if the yacht is going backwards (making a sternboard) the PP moves aft. You will notice this effect as you try to go astern with a cross wind. The bows will pay off embarrassingly and some yachts are so badly designed that they will not steer at all in this way.

Now, back to the yacht at single bower anchor in a strong wind. Her sails are furled but she still has a CLR from her hull, masts and rigging. This is probably before (ahead of) the CLR with sails set because the mast, which is usually forward, has a strong effect. Unlike river currents, the wind is never constant in either speed or direction, especially close to land which is where we tend to anchor. She may be lying docile, head to a wind which we will define as the *mean wind line* (MWL), when there comes a gust from, say, 30° on the starboard bow. This new force can be resolved into a force blowing along the line of the ship and another blowing across her beam. The force blowing her backwards (at this moment the stronger of the two resolved forces) will tauten the cable and move her astern so that her PP, already abaft her CLE when at rest by a distance F, will move even further aft by a further distance A (see diagram). The lateral resolved wind force will have an enhanced turning effect on her bows owing to an imbalance of A + F, and she will pay off sharply and sheer off in a direction about 60° to the mean wind line under the constraint of her cable.

Even if the wind now returns to the MWL, the yacht will still experience sufficient turning force in a strong wind to prevent her responding to the pull of her
anchor cable until she sheers off sufficiently to pull it straight. She will 'fore-
reach', dragging the loose cable with her. Sometimes one can get into a sort of
pendulum rhythm like this as the yacht sheers off one side of her anchor and then
the other.

The effect is not confined to yachts. HMS *Implacable*, an aircraft carrier, while
riding out a force 10 in Invergordon, fore-reached either side of her anchor until
she was actually to windward of it (the anchor was marked by a danbuoy).

You can see that if the cable is being pulled hard sideways, then the RBP is

irrelevant. At some point, the anchor will be jerked sideways and be made to turn which means one fluke will break out on one 'tack' and the second fluke on the other side. The anchor drags, and usually starts to move too fast to dig in again. If at this moment the wind is on the ship's beam, then you stand no chance. She will gain way downhill.

How to avoid all this? For this is what we are on about here.

The ability of the anchor to turn without breaking out is important. Ships' anchors with their two big flukes cope quite well with one fluke usually holding on while the other digs in. Nevertheless, the anchor has a tendency to walk back.

Most yacht anchors are designed for the steady pull. The Bruce anchor is excellent for this and was developed to hold oil rigs which lie in a spider's web of cables in which anchors and cable loads are static. The Danforth type is a bit like a big-ship anchor and tends to hold quite well but walk back. The CQR was designed for flying boats of the old Imperial Airways and these did not lie at all quietly under anchor. The CQR was given a hinge which helps it cope while being swung about. It is not as good as the others with a steady pull. (See also Anchors page 91.)

Is there nothing that can be done to mitigate against this phenomenon? Yes, and I remember the *Implacable* incident for the rebuke I got for not taking action earlier. It was a gentle rebuke for I was only 20 years old at the time. Quite young to be left in charge of a 40,000 ton ship with 2000 men on board.

The first measure is to let go as much cable as you can in the searoom you have available, it is doing no good in the cable locker. But you do not veer all of it straight away. When there are 4 'shackles' still to go, let go the second anchor and veer 4 more shackles on both of them while the ship is head to the mean wind. The short cable reduces the sheer to one side and brings her head round more quickly.

Big ship shackles are 12½ fathoms or 75 feet (15 fathoms in merchant ships). That measure is unrealistic in a yacht. We, in *Hosanna*, as we did in *Fare Well*, think in terms of a shackle of 5 fathoms, or 30 feet, and we measure and mark our cable like that. I think that figure makes sense (NB 10ft = 3 metres).

How much scope do we use? It is related to the depth of water and to the nature of the bottom. Both should be taken into account. The scope is not a direct proportion of the depth. We never sleep with less than 3 shackles (90 feet) of chain cable out, no matter how shallow the water. Above 15 feet, I use 4 times the depth, and above 20 feet, five times. Then above 40 feet the ratio moves the other way so that in depths over 60 feet, I use 3 times the depth once more, or in deeper water still, all the cable I have got, tailing it with nylon in extreme cases. In the Boxing Day tsunami, some yachts at anchor off Phuket with plenty of cable out came to no harm.

• *Second anchors* •

The greatest is the sheat anchor, and never used but in great necessity.

So far as possible, I try to avoid having to lay out a sheet or second anchor because ours is not self-stowing. It is hard work handling anchors weighing 200kg on one's own. All right in calm conditions, but the elements are not always kind. As it swings about while hung on the derrick, I get a good insight into how a matador feels.

Incidentally, did you all notice that *Mirabella*, the big yacht that dragged aground off Cap Ferrat, reportedly lay to a Bruce anchor of 600kg? (Report in *Yachting World*, among other sources.) She is 8 times the length of *Hosanna*, and ours is 200kg. Warships of her size would carry bigger anchors, but she is lighter

Here Fare Well *enjoys a peaceful mooring at Man 'O War Cay, Abaco, Bahamas.*

weight. There is more to this loss than I am aware and I would like to know more because I find the whole story puzzling.

The *Implacable* story brings up another lesson, as most things that happen at sea do. The reason I had not taken any action at that time was that, if I had veered more cable, I noticed that the ship's swinging circle could possibly have covered a shoal if the wind were to have backed 120°. Exposing the ship to that risk required command approval. As the youngest and most junior officer, I hesitated to disturb the beribboned hordes of Midian who, once called from their slumber, would have prowled and prowled around and though they would not have criticised me directly, would undoubtedly have decided that I was over-cautious, lacked moral fibre etc, and had disturbed them needlessly. It was a no-win situation. As you grow more experienced, you learn to take pleasure in calling your seniors out to get as wet and cold as you are.

The real lesson is that if it is a matter of ship-safety, then do not hesitate: call the skipper and the watch below. They shouldn't complain. Better be safe than wrecked.

If you want a way of reducing the yacht's tendency to sheer about at anchor, try the riding sail illustrated below. This specially made sail is far better than setting a reefed mizzen which will slat about and damage itself. This one stays mostly full of wind and its V setting makes it act sooner.

One small thing: on those rare occasions when the wind blows across the swell and rolling becomes a nuisance (it happened to us in Mustique in the West Indies, and also at Pargos in Greece), it is possible to spring the cable to point ship across a moderate wind (see illustration on page 283).

Lastly, and we include this because the Boxing Day tsunami of 2004 must be still fresh in most people's minds (at the moment of writing all of us are still in shock), a word on tsunamis.

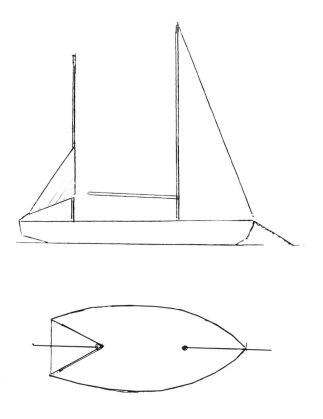

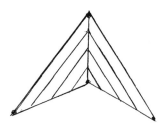

This riding sail, set as shown, will keep the yacht docile and head to wind. Set it round the mizzen mast and sheeted to both quarters as shown. Left is a diagram of the sail opened out in plan. Note all edges should be taped and the cringles strongly worked.

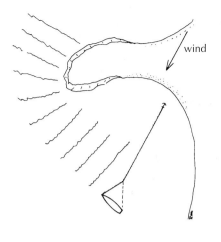

*Springing the
anchor cable.*

TSUNAMIS

You may think the chance is pretty remote. Many off-chances happen at sea and some background deeply bedded knowledge might well save your life. Tsunamis can be caused by an underwater earthquake, and the worst of them occur when one tectonic plate slips and drops, perhaps sliding under another. This causes a deep depression in the sea level immediately above the drop, followed by resonance. On the surface the waves fan out, achieving a speed of $\sqrt{gh}$ knots, where g is 32 and h is the depth of water in feet. In deep water they cause vessels no problems at all, the height of the wave would probably not exceed 5 feet, and the wavelength might be a matter of miles, but the waves, up to about five or six together and often preceded by a trough, could achieve speeds of 400 knots.

No problem in deep sea then, but waves have their own depth well below the level of the trough, and when this reaches shallow water, the under part slows down, the crest continues to rush on, piles up much higher, until it falls flat on its face, creating the breakers we are used to on the sea shore. At Miyako Bay in Japan (1896), it was about 10 feet high at the bay entrance but reached a height of 93 feet at the head of the bay. In general though, if you are anchored in deeper water, you would be OK. One yacht we have just heard from was anchored off Phuket, unusually in 17 fathoms. They survived. Many yachts anchored further inshore did not. So, if you get a tsunami warning, go directly to sea and do not pass go on the way. That was the advice of the Royal Naval Navigation School in 1949. I see no reason to doubt it in 2005.

Do we think it couldn't happen close to home? It is not unknown in the Med, though there hasn't been a big one for a long time. In British waters, we would be badly affected by a tsunami if there was a repeat (and it is quite likely one day) of the great Lisbon 'quake of 1755, the worst in recorded memory. It happened just onshore so there was only a minor tsunami, but if the next one were to occur a few miles away out at sea, we'd know all about it in Britain.

One last point I would like to make. In 1949, when there was a mild tsunami in the Indian Ocean, the Royal Navy had an East Indies Squadron based at

Trincomalee in what was then Ceylon. The ships were sent out at once to all the colonies, including those such as India which were recently independent (and there were many colonies at that time). They were sent out also, as my ship was, to the scene of other natural disasters such as cholera or plague epidemics, floods and famines, earthquakes, attacks by pirates and Arab slave runners. The British Empire was not as bad as it is sometimes painted. I was there and am proud of what my country used to do.

There is no East Indies Squadron now. And no body, government or otherwise, has taken its place as conscientious and efficient suppliers of immediate aid.

13 • Communications

'What cheere mates, is all well?'

That I, at my age, should try to teach anyone about communications! My six-year-old grand-daughter would be more useful. She can cope with G3 mobile phones, entirely without any help.

I recall being Second Navigator in an aircraft carrier and on watch as Fighter Direction Officer. After a visit by a flight of US Naval aircraft, the cousins ranged on the flight deck and prepared to fly off. Over the radio we heard:

'This is Triple Nickel Natch, gimme de woid and I'll make like a boid.' Our senior officers needed smelling salts. Fortunately, I had been on exchange to the US Naval Academy at Annapolis and knew the language. I decided to reply in British idiom:

'5557, OK to piss off. Out.' I was rebuked for inattention to procedure. That happened quite often in my early naval career. The word is Communication, after all. If it succeeds, does it matter what form it takes?

Occasionally, yes, when there is a danger of misunderstanding. Even so, when our young are now sending each other text messages of startling incomprehensibility (only to those who do not know the language), authority needs to relax a bit its habitual caution.

VHF RADIO

Which leads me to wonder why it needs a whole day for RYA approved 'schools' to teach people how to use the DSC version of VHF when six-year-olds, entirely untaught, can cope with infinitely more complex communications, send text messages and take your digital photo? The only possible answer is that by making it a completely unnecessary all-day course, they can charge higher prices.

I was at sea when marine VHF started in the Royal Navy. We called it TBS, standing for Talk Between Ships. Even in wartime with all the dangers attaching to misuse of a completely new device, nobody had to have instruction in its use. We just got on with it, as kids do now with the mobile phone. I do not think it led to the loss of any ships except for U-boats and that was the idea.

When the technology was released for civilian use, the shock-horror in Britain at the time would lead one to imagine that the end of the world was nigh.

International Agreements. Regulations. Examinations. Certificates. And all this was worse in Britain than anywhere else because British politicians and Civil Servants have always believed that private use of radio waves destroys Britons' sperm counts.

In the West Indies, where marine VHF is generally unregulated, it was used before mobile phones by anybody, for such purposes as booking a restaurant table, ordering a taxi, or even making a hairdressing appointment. (Call sign: Teeny-weeny-sweeny.) In Greece where there are hundreds of yachts on bare-boat charter, there is no effective control over the use of marine VHF. It is used all the time. Flotillas have their own operating channels, and nobody will convince me that the typical flotilla client is an experienced, let alone certificated, mariner. Various groups of private yachties operate a 'net' at fixed hours of each day to exchange information. It is used by children, and I've even heard it used by dogs. We could listen to chatter all day long if we wanted to. *It does no harm.*

And procedures? One can cope far better without formal procedures on a phone than one can on VHF with all its stilted rubbish (which, however, I admit is of help when speaking to foreigners). New thinking is needed in this area. But what about emergencies?

Right, I agree that this is important. When the new DSC etc is compulsory for all craft (and I have no objection to that) distress calls will be automated. There remains the periphery of distress and also port control and VTS use. The latter concern mainly professionals, but yachtsmen are occasionally involved. Techniques and procedures are simple. Qualification for this could be included in the Yachtmaster® syllabus and exam, and also in Helmsman's Certificates. Apart from that, there is need of a small number of designated 'yachtsmen's channels' for yachtie and marina chatter and for the use of which no licence would be required. See how many civil servants that would lay off. Keep it simple.

• *HF (Ham) Radio* •

Bill originally thought (in the 1970s) that it might be as well to get his HF Radio Amateur's Licence (for Ham radio) because its use would be cheaper than marine HF. He got it, but he found that most nets were dominated by an 'in group' who had little or no time for anyone coming in from outside, however much the group claimed otherwise. Most of the people on the air were Americans and the chatter was close to anarchy, far worse than marine VHF and largely irrelevant to a seaman. Bill packed it in; sold the set. We have no HF transmitting capability, even when on ocean passage, and feel better without it.

If you are already a committed aficionado, and it's one of your hobbies, your views and perspective will be quite different. In the old days Ham radio buffs did much useful work in many difficult areas, but that was before the arrival of the mobile phone and the internet. Your coastal SOS, these days, is as likely to be sent by mobile phone, and nobody regulates that.

MOBILE PHONES

When we were dismasted off the Kentish Knock (which, for the benefit of Solent sailors, is just outside the Thames Estuary) and it looked like being a few hours before we got control again, we thought we had better tell the Coastguard that while we needed no assistance, we were temporarily not under command with no steaming light and nowhere to display 'not under command' lights. We were completely unable to get any response on VHF, but we got through first time with a 999 call to the Coastguard on our mobile phone which was inside a steel wheelhouse at deck level. Since then we know of numerous other instances where mobile phones have been more use than VHF in an emergency. The authorities really must acknowledge this, but try getting the MCA to face the facts of modern nautical life . . .

In our last edition we published a table of relative costs of communication by various methods. Such tables appear helpful but in fact they are out-of-date by the time of publication even in magazines, let alone books. There are so many variations now that we have decided not to repeat the process. This is a topic that is more suited to yachtimags.

I have done vast research into this and am not a lot wiser. I am going to proffer a précis of what I think I have learned, and I am particularly indebted to a magazine called *PC Pro* who published an almost incomprehensible (to me) article on this very subject. Nerd, I am not, nor geek, whatever that is. I have delved fearlessly into it and done some mining. I hope they do not mind. Here goes. (We are talking about mobile phones.)

It is no use publishing tables of usages and rates (they say so too). There are too many variables and everything is changing at the speed of light. As we state below, get it all clear before leaving the UK.

Be wary of pay-as-you-go services and make sure they support data. Some do not. If Compuserve or AOL is not to your taste go to www.gric.com and there you will find hundreds of companies covering 150 countries and offering over 15,000 dialling locations available at local rates. Check before leaving the UK that the service you select really works. And check with your own ISP how much extra the GRIC service costs.

Don't invest heavily in the latest pocketsized thingummy. Choose tried and trusty hardware, and as a general rule buy it in the UK or USA, where you speak the language and can ask questions. If possible get the seller to set up the service for you. It isn't that easy, so make him sweat.

Almost everything electronic costs more outside the UK, except for the USA who have a different mobile phone system. (You don't think they'd have the same as everyone else, do you? Come onnnnn!) Generally speaking (as most people are these days) your mobile phone should be T3. Nowadays most are, but check before you buy.

Souzouki Shop, Chios.

E-MAIL ETC

Another method to contact the folk back home is e-mail. Come in six-year-old grand-daughter again.

E-mail is easy, BUT. The problem is doing it as cheaply and reliably as possible. I do not propose to advise anyone on how to run a business from a yacht. People do, now that they can. Somehow, I get the impression that this was easier a couple of years ago. Now that business users in the UK and USA use broadband, they have become much more profligate with the amount of material they push out. Yachties are constrained to use comparatively slow baud-rates, and downloading masses of irrelevant pictorial decoration is irritating and expensive. Not many countries in our comfort zone have broadband at all, let alone in those outposts where we yachties go.

While on the move one has to use a mobile phone for e-mail by one means or another or else use an internet café or marine HF. The internet café is not necessarily cheap, usually a minimum charge of anything from one Euro to seven or more and printing out at so much a sheet can run up a big bill. We have seldom found a baud-rate above 18,000, which is horse and cart stuff in advanced countries. And most Continental internet cafés have a nicotine-laden atmosphere that could peel the skin off a lemon. Marine HF comment later.

While under way from place to place we use Compuserve as our ISP. We wish there was a better one available. Compuserve seems to make no realistic attempt to control unsolicited messages (spam) which end up costing us a small fortune, but at least it works. We either dial the UK access number, which is outrageously expensive, or get a connection via the nearest country which is merely expensive. This requires a little trouble getting sorted out as one needs different script files for every country. If using Compuserve or AOL, which are world-wide organisations, get it done while in the UK. You will be lucky to find anyone on their advice line who knows about all this, but persevere. You will spend hours on the phone listening to 'don't get confrontational' music, but at least it will be done. One gets there in the end. And even then, they didn't tell us that Greek land lines work on a different system called *equant*. We had to discover this for ourselves and find which insignificant little box to tick while Laurel murmured soothing words to calm me down. There, now you know. Check up on that.

Mobile access is improving. There are several ideas which I have not tested. Vodafone have a G3 datacard that promises promises, but at a hefty price. I was quoted as a small user, £200 for the card that you plug into the PCMCIA slot on a laptop + £11.75 per month for up to 5mb. That's a lot. I'll wait for the price to fall.

While in Levkas we have found a friendly local business which will let us take in our laptop, plug it into their land-phone line and send and receive e-mail via a local number. Greeks, for all their faults, are a generous, friendly race.

Others use pocket-phone, which depends on mobile phone facilities, and others use GPRS. Unfortunately the latter requires a contract and, in spite of EU membership, Greece will not permit foreigners to sign contracts unless they have a Greek tax reference. This is best avoided.

The RCC Journal gives details of what sounds like an economical system if you have a lot of traffic. It is called SAILMAIL. For more info see Appendix: www.sailmail.com.

In Levkas marina, there is a WLAN set up by a German company and we originally got quite excited about this as it promised a fast baud-rate. Firstly, it turned out to be wickedly expensive even before one had sent or received a byte. Secondly, one was not given a trial transmission and it turned out that the baud-rate was not that marvellous and varied considerably. And thirdly, the signal is badly interrupted by all the aluminium masts in the marina so that reception is patchy. At a berth right next to the antenna, the service is excellent. Not, in my opinion, a suitable service for a marina unless you happen to berth alongside the antenna.

• *Laptops* •

One thing to think about is that aboard the average cruising boat there is no necessity to miniaturise everything. Generally you do not have to carry things about with you when using mobile phone data transmission, so a standard laptop will do, or even a proper PC in a larger boat. Getting a mini-thing with a match-box size screen will impose eye-straining limitations and miniature keyboards are not usable for adults with BFS (Big Finger Syndrome).

You cannot afford a substantial folio of paper charts at present day prices. Carrying a full-size laptop or PC aboard is going to be the norm in future; in our recent survey of cruising yachts we mustered 83% with computers and/or laptops. (See chapter on Navigation.)

Make sure your laptop has a screen that is readable in bright light. Some cheaper ones fail in this respect, and it's annoying to have to look at them under a blanket like a Victorian photographer. These are those made with the old TN screens that have been around since the 1970s and which have 'fudged dither' as a disadvantage. Whatever that is. Better ones are MVA which don't dither at all, and finally there is IPS which is fragile. Ah well! Let's wait for Super IPS, when we can afford it.

There is a good market in used, reconditioned and cleaned conventional laptops which are available very cheaply, especially those with a US keyboard. Try the UK magazine *Micromart*. We don't understand the articles but the ads are useful.

• *Satellite phones* •

Satellite phones such as Iridium, Globalstar, Thuraya and Thane are expensive. You will pay about $5000 for widespread (but far from world-wide) coverage, plus call charges. Slightly cheaper ones will work up to about 200 miles offshore. The company to consult for this and other schemes is G Comm at www.g-comm.co.uk – helpful people.

• *Snail mail etc* •

This gradually deteriorates and we must expect the service to go on doing so. The once ultra-reliable GPO (or whatever it calls itself this year) has joined the Continentals in running a haphazard business. Without knowing with whom and where the fault lies, we reckon we get about 85% of letters sent to us, but only about 75% of packets or small parcels. Larger parcels are better except for those sent by couriers such as DHL to Greece. These seem to get to Athens as quickly as promised, but then go on a long holiday. We have had several items sent this way at great expense, but *not one* has actually been delivered. It is somewhat the same in provincial France, where the 24-hour delivery promised often turns out to be 4 days. And no prospect of compensation either. One has to face the fact that much vaunted and advertised services only apply to capital cities.

• *The man with a cleft stick* •

Undoubtedly the oldest, and most reliable, method of communication, its yachting avatar, is the chum coming out to join you for a few weeks. Anyone doing this can expect to bear a heavy burden. Easyjet has been known to cower at the prospect of a plane load of people *Hosanna*-bound, with spare parts in their luggage.

14 • Inland Waters

'We say a calme sea or becalmed, when it is so smooth the ship move very little, and the men leap over boord to swim.'

We did not include this as a subject in previous editions because we decided against diluting the image that we felt was behind most people's longing. Since then we have paddled in the ditches of Europe and found that sometimes the skills required have been greater than at sea and even more hair-raising. Let's stop being patronising. There are many who use the French canals as the first stage of their transatlantic, or voyage to the Med, and like it so much they decide to stay there. An increasing number take the inland option right off as the increasing membership of the Dutch Barge Association (DBA)

The French waterways have a lot to offer in terms of scenery and tranquil settings; here Hosanna *is moored at Abbeville on the River Somme.*

shows. We have often been asked to go more into the pros and cons, if only because changing one's mind can result in trying to live aboard an unsuitable boat.

The verb to sail, as in *Sell Up and Sail* – what does it mean? The Royal Navy has long been held as an authority on nautical terms, and they use the word to describe a ship under way from one place to another no matter her means of propulsion. So I can use the word sail to mean navigation on inland waters.

One would not normally seek to live aboard a sea-going boat on inland waters. One reason is that seaworthiness makes demands on the boat's design and equipment. One could not get the same accommodation length for length, ton for ton, or pound for pound as in a boat specially designed for inland waters. Inland craft can be fitted out to a much lower specification, do not need the safety equipment and will have a lower insurance premium. One can get a much bigger boat for the money.

Another reason for the inland option is that one avoids seasickness and some people are badly affected in this way, even with modern drugs. That is undeniable. The notion, often quoted, that it is safer to sail inland waterways than the ocean, is up for debate. Counting our three most hair-raising experiences in nearly 100,000 miles of live-aboard cruising, I would put Hurricane Alberto at the top, but number two would be the River Danube in flood, and the next would be the River Rhine in flood. Even on the canals, we have experienced some anxiety. Friends of ours shudder when they recall their experience in their own boat when a lock-gate collapsed, causing fatalities in a big cargo barge.

But these are rare events and one can be less or more adventurous as you will, and as experience grows.

There are plenty of specialist books on inland cruising and some are better than others. We have written four anecdotal books to give a flavour, and there are always the brilliant Roger Pilkington books. To our mind, the books which ought to give the nuts and bolts all lack something vital. Marian Martin's formal exposition of the rules and conventional signs, *The European Waterways* (Adlard Coles Nautical), is a must, but it has the flavour of a school text-book. On the whole we think that Marian's book combined with either our books or those of Roger Pilkington would be a reliable source of information. Well, we would say that, wouldn't we? For factual details on individual French waterways, David Edwards-May's revised and up-to-date edition of *Benest*, an old classic, is undoubtedly the best. For maps go for the *Cartes-Guides de Navigation Fluviale*. All are available from Stanfords map shop in Long Acre or from Kelvin Hughes, or should be. We give these in detail because they would be of interest also to sea sailors bound the inland way to the Med.

Outside France there are many different sources, too numerous to mention here. If seriously interested, subscribe to the *Blue Flag* (the journal of the DBA), the best magazine covering all inland waters from a navigational point of view. They will always help with practicalities. Maps and guides for the Danube are not so easy to select or get. I am trying to get the Danube Commission to release their data and so produce some charts. It's an uphill struggle. In the meantime, Germany, Austria and Hungary are well served, but further on there are problems. See also the section on books in the Appendix.

What about the inland waters of the UK? We know nothing about them, except the Broads. The Broads are governed by the Broads Authority, which is dominated by extreme Greens for whom all boats seem to be anathema. Even though there are now only a quarter as many hire boats plying the Broads, the number of floating inspectors prodnosing about has increased enormously. The River Thames is much the same as the Norfolk Broads, over-run by *gauleiters*.

People do live on the British canals. Let's give some credit. The restoration and revitalisation of the British canal system is mainly due to amateur enthusiasts, and they have achieved wonders. But the fact remains that to us, most of these canals are miniature. A narrow boat resembles a floating exclamation mark. No advice from us on this question then, but there are many magazines covering this system and we note that the enthusiasts are a nice lot of people.

There is one feature of living aboard on the inland waters. Wintering is, in our opinion, not so pleasant. Whenever sea-going yachties get together over a winter they always have an active but informal social life. In our inland winters, with one exception, we have found this is largely lacking. For a start, the weather inland is much colder and people pull the duvets over their heads and tend to hibernate. They don't come out much. The other reason is that usually there are fewer boats gathered together in one place, and even fewer live-aboards. Winter on your tod can be lonely.

15 • Health and Welfare
at Sea

*'The Chirurgeon is to be exempted from all duty but to attend the sicke and
cure the wounded; and good care would be had he have a certificate from the
Barber-Chirurgeon's Halls of his sufficiency . . . for which neglect hath beene
the losse of many a man's life.'*

Nowhere is it more obvious than on a long-distance cruise that sickness is
more a state of mind than of body. Most cruising people find that as the
pace of life slows to 5 knots on average and the world shrinks to the size
of their boat, many bodily ills dwindle and disappear. We get colds only when we
go back to the UK. On the other hand, you have a better chance of doing yourself
an injury on a boat of cruising size than might be the case if you had stuck to golf
and lawnmowers. Well, Bill thinks not; he used to do the mowing, and he once
played golf. He loves the safety of our boat. He is an escapee from gardens.

FIRST AID COURSES

But injuries happen and while you need no longer exempt your Chirurgeon from
all other duty, it would be well, as Capt John Smith points out above, that he have
a certificate. But where from? It has to be said that the Red Cross and St John's
courses are neither heroic nor practical enough for the long-distance cruiser.
Even if we have access to advice by radio, we are likely to need practical skills such
as giving injections, administering a drip, stitching wounds, and the control of
pain and infection. When we first wrote about this, many doctors in the British
Isles still had a deep-seated mistrust of allowing any Tom, Dick or Harriet to
acquire such paramedical skills or even read about them, though in the USA there
was a crash course (the Intensive Survey of Medical Emergency Care), designed
by a doctor/sailor. So in the first edition we wrote that there were no medical
courses in the UK for long-distance yachtsmen.

However, since we persuaded *Yachting Monthly* that our idea for a Long
Distance Cruising Symposium would be feasible and popular the programme
daringly included First Aid at Sea, the scene has greatly changed, though we
think there is still a need for more and better. That very first cruising seminar in
1987 was a runaway success, and the herald of many look-alikes; they are now
commonplace. Even the RYA now runs them, complete with a talk on First Aid at

Sea. With luck you can catch Professor Noel Dilly's talk on the subject, riveting, useful and hilarious.

Many years ago, when there were no such courses, the only one Laurel could find was the Ship Captain's Medical Course, which was obviously intended for professional seamen. The Lowestoft Nautical College, with some astonishment, admitted her, a woman among the assembled ships' captains and mates, and she found the course wonderfully reassuring. She reported:

The Medical course is based on the *Ship Captain's Medical Guide* (known

SYMI — Aegean Sea

as The Book) which all British merchant ships are required to carry on board, as we did ourselves. We always carried a copy for long cruises in *Fare Well* and latterly in *Hosanna*, and found it very useful in emergencies. Embarking on our travels, I felt I wanted some practical knowledge to add to the drugs and equipment which we carry. It was all very well having the stuff on board, but did I know how to use it all? No, I did not. Many people ask how we cope with sickness or accidents at sea. The only response that we can make is: 'As best we can, it doesn't happen often.' One knows that help is not within reach, and that the High Street surgery is 4,000 miles away. When the crunch comes, you are your own barefoot doctor – you, with the worried look and the shaking hands. I ought, I felt, to be able to give an injection, and take a stitch-in-time with a suturing needle.

I began badly. The bridge was up, I was ten minutes late, and already I'd missed the whole of Preparing a Cabin for a Patient and half of Vital Signs. Yes, the course was dense and intense. We went at the pace of a motorcycle scramble. We learned how to take blood pressure, record temperature, pulse and breathing, how to test urine and why. ('Nurses in the old days used to taste it to find what was in it', said Rosie SRN, our Mentor; thank God we now use Labstix.)

From Observation and Care of Bed Patients, we learned to face the enema, and to give rectal infusions (to fight the Demon Dehydration, the killer in many and varied diseases and conditions). We learned how to cope with Malaria, we saw a slide cassette on Heat Exhaustion and Heat Stroke.

Fortified by lunch, I then discovered more than I care to know about Sexually Transmitted Diseases, a lecture beautifully sung by a Welsh doctor. He began *pianissimo* with the diseases we'd all heard of, went into a fugue of oddities that were new to some of us (the males usually), and ended up with a threnody on AIDS, then a new disease.

Next day we pelted through Poisons, including gases relevant to the cargoes of Shipmasters, but not very likely on a yacht.

We roared past Resuscitation, hurtled through Haemorrhage, and halted for a while for Hypothermia (something that anyone who goes boating on the lake ought to know about, let alone long-distance cruisers).

We galloped past Gallstones, shot through Surgical Emergencies, were mesmerised by Mental Illness and Myocardial Infarction (which up to then we had called heart attack).

We ended with Bodies (disposal of) and Burial at Sea.

And all the time I would ask: 'But suppose you haven't got room on your boat for all that apparatus/equipment/vast array of drugs?'

Improvisation can save your bacon, as I well know, and Rosie often assured us with examples. Here's some of mine:

> We were leaving Port Mahon (on a Friday of course) when Bill was freeing the anchor from a heavy rope encrusted with barnacles, when a huge fish-hook caught deep in the pad of his middle finger. My first action had to be taking the strain off the rope, and therefore the finger. The second was to check that the boat was still safely anchored. The third was to sit down and think a bit.
>
> 'Push the hook through the skin (if no vital organ is endangered), nip off the barb, and withdraw', said the First Aid book. But they hadn't seen stainless steel Spanish fish-hooks; they're more like something you find at the butcher's, with a whole ox hanging from it. Which was not far from the truth, as I pointed out to the Skipper at the time: he was not amused.

A brief effort to obey the First Aid book with the aid of bolt cutters threatened to amputate the finger and was quickly abandoned for a Stanley knife, 'sterilised' with brandy.

Both patient and 'doctor' then drank some of the brandy (not recommended in The Book) and, shaking like leaves, cut out the hook, which was baited with something slithery that looked very evil. I wish I knew what, as the wound healed clean and with great rapidity, and we might have made a fortune selling it to a drug company. Observe that it never occurred to us to row ashore and find a doctor. One loses the habit.

I also recalled putting the Skipper's neck in traction with a handy billy and a seven-kilo gas bottle over a pulley, and under 'Burns' in the appropriate chapter you will find an ingenious use for the raingauge.

Back to the course. In two and a half crammed days we learned to stitch gaping wounds in surprisingly resistant foam rubber ('very like the real thing', said Rosie) and not to put our unsterilised finger on the knot. Knowledge of stitching I could have used on a couple of occasions for small wounds.

We learned to inject oranges. We learned to approach the plastic model of Resusci-Annie with confidence, despite her lying on the floor with her lungs exposed and a feral grin on her face. Her bared rubber teeth looked as if they could bite you if she didn't care for your technique, or your aftershave. I added the Brooke Airway to our First Aid list.

When it came to exam time on the third afternoon, we all regurgitated sufficient material (some of it only half-digested) to pass; Caroline of *Heartsease* and I were the first women to do so at Lowestoft who were not Shipmasters or mates.

What did all that make me? Certainly not the Doc. But next time something happened, I had a modicum of confidence to add to common sense. I hoped to reassure my victim that my panicky search through The Book would bring help and relief. Raising morale is my strong point. Even without the brandy. And I was more determined than ever to harp (to the point of boring my readers) on *prevention* of accidents and illness at sea. Stop it happening, and you don't have to treat it.

SURVIVAL AT SEA

There was no such course for yachtsmen when we began sailing. We have survived 60 years of sailing despite that. Now there are, we urge you to include one in your programme. The RNSA runs one in conjunction with the RYA.

FINDING HELP WHERE YOU NEED IT

It is to be hoped that you will have gone to sea in a state of good health, as far as can be ascertained by check-ups and dental work before you go. Cherish this happy state of affairs by thinking 'prevention' rather than 'cure'. Catch it before it happens. Eliminate the chances of sickness and bodily damage to your uttermost. Since this attitude goes hand in hand with the watchfulness that every good seaman cultivates, the quicker it becomes second nature to you the sooner, paradoxically, you can relax and enjoy your cruise. By 'looking for trouble' you are avoiding it!

At sea you are dependent on who may be within call. Advice may be available by radio: a call of Pan Pan Medico should produce results if any doctor is monitoring, or any merchant ship or shore station picks up your call.

If you are within reach of land, English-speaking doctors who have been properly trained may be found world-wide by joining IAMAT, the International Association for Medical Assistance to Travellers, a non-profit making organisation. Otherwise MASTA (Medical Advisory Services for Travellers Abroad) is a world-wide advisory health service for travellers. Approved by (and next door to) the London School of Hygiene and Tropical Medicine, they will tailor a Health Brief to your individual requirements (from £9 to £30 according to the number of countries you will visit), with details of all inoculations required, information and a list of medical items to take with you, and up-to-date 'health newsflashes' from all over the world, via their computer bank. Long-distance yachtsmen would need the more comprehensive service which could be very good value. They also run a health insurance scheme. Forms are available at branches of Boots, chemists, or direct from MASTA. Addresses and websites for all these will be found in the Appendix, together with other extremely useful sites with detailed (free) medical advice for travellers, including updates on what plague is endemic where and what inoculations to get. The doctor's surgery by cyber-café has arrived; you can describe your symptoms and receive reassurance and advice.

HEALTH INSURANCE

Be sure to take with you form E111, included in the excellent booklet Health Advice for Travellers, or the card that will shortly replace it, if you wish to benefit from reciprocal health agreements in Europe. It is available at Post Offices, and see the website in the Appendix.

Though health insurance is a luxury if cruising the waters of EU member states (generally, the health service of anywhere in the EU is better than in Britain, and we can say that from experience) it is another matter in the rest of the world where all medicine may be private. When we first wrote it was impossible to get world-wide continuous cover. It is still not easy. It is necessary to shop around to get quotes. Big companies are not interested because their underwriting is geared to mass processing. Smaller ones have insufficiently large books to be able to spread the risk, and the remainder blow hot or cold depending on the way their risks are spread. Quotes can even vary from month to month.

All medical insurance is expensive, and usually excludes the very disease you are most likely to get. We made the decision long ago to do without it. In over 30 years of full-time cruising, we have paid for the usual small accidents, visits to the surgery and dentists, and two major operations. We are still ahead of the game after two private hip operations, and healthy for our age.

In the EU, if your form E111 is in order and you do the paperwork, you will pay for attention but get the money back, as you will for prescriptions and surgical procedures, though sometimes only a proportion of it.

In the USA they will take your credit cards before allowing your suffering body into the hospital; this is where you may need insurance.

Three points:

- Get a policy with a watertight repatriation clause.
- Insurance for the USA will be expensive, though cheaper if taken out in the USA.
- For EU countries, don't forget form E111 (or the card that replaces it). The omniscient smart-card complete with iris recognition, fingerprinting and your DNA, along with your bank balance (for the USA), is another matter. You'll probably cope with that better than I will.

WHEN YOU GO

Take with you 'The Book', and/or *The First Aid Manual* published by the Red Cross and St John's Ambulance Association. If you have room, consider taking the following books:

1 A copy of the *BNF* (British National Formulary) or *MIMMS*, which give comprehensive information about drugs, very useful abroad. A polite request to the prescription counter of any large pharmacy usually produces an old copy, as it is a biannual publication.
2 *Where there is No Dentist* and *Where there is No Doctor* (specify whether you want the International or African edition) from TALC, address in Appendix. What was the difference between the International and the African edition, I asked the young man who answered the phone, thinking they dealt with different bugs and diseases. 'The pictures,' he said. Of course.

There follows, in alphabetical order, not the First Aid advice you will get from the above books and websites, and other helplines specially conceived for yachtsmen, but a useful list of preventive measures, which is less often come across.

PREVENTIVE MEASURES

AIDS and STDs
It used to be sailors who spread Sexually Transmitted Diseases (STDs). Now that everyone travels, it is the tourists and the businessmen who spread the plague. That doesn't stop sailors catching it, though.

- Take the obvious precautions, and a long hard look at new and sexy friends.
- Carry condoms with you at all times, you never know whom you might meet. We gave a lift to a young man in Corfu, desperate to catch the next plane out. Matter of serious illness in the family. 'A close relative?' we asked sympathetically. 'It's me,' he said, 'I've got the clap.'
- Remember that condoms have a limited shelf life, and are hard to find in remote places. Buy them where you can be sure of the quality – we are sure the tale of rubber workers in Catholic countries pricking every tenth condom with a pin to re-establish God's little lottery is not true, but you get the drift. Give them a balloon or water test if you are uncertain. Fun and educational for all the family. If bought loose and wholesale, it helps to shake a little talcum among them, to preserve the *preservatifs*.
- Consider asking your doctor for an AIDS kit if you intend going to certain parts of the world where AIDS is especially rife. Thus if you had to go ashore for any kind of treatment you would take with you your own syringes, needles, blood-giving set, sterile swabs and plasma. (MASTA, see Appendix, has information on this.)
- Avoid accidents needing blood transfusions, and don't go in for tattooing or piercing in dodgy places, both geographical and anatomical.
- Carry a Brooke airway and surgical gloves for giving First Aid.

Appendicitis

This is the great bugaboo that once frightened everyone. Many transatlantic yachtsmen used to have an 'elective appendectomy' in order to avoid any possibility of trouble. This would need to be discussed with your doctor. We feel that nowadays hospitals take away the disease you came in with and give you several new ones in exchange: this is even acknowledged by the medical profession in a fearsome Greek-derived term: *Nokosogenic* (meaning arising in the hospital) disease. Stay out of hospital and stay healthy, we say. However, it is a worry. We know of no one who has died of peritonitis at sea since the 1960s: it seems that modern antibiotics can hold the situation until help is at hand.

Births

(For prevention see under AIDS, above)

It is *very* difficult to get any kind of contraceptives in large areas of the world. To be safe, take a good supply with you, and have several different methods in case you run out.

Lady, if you are seasick to the point of vomiting, or have even a short attack of diarrhoea, or vomiting, or both, the effectiveness of your Pill could be endangered. Talk to your doctor before you go about the possible effect of seasickness on your sort of Pill: it might be necessary to use a supplementary method for the rest of that cycle.

Bites

For mosquitoes see *Malaria* and Chapter 7 on pests.

Fleas Repellants such as Deet should work for all biting insects. The drill for fleas is to undress in the bath, shaking every item of clothing so that the little beast lands in the water (it will be obvious that a shower stall doesn't work quite as well). I miss the Keatings powder that one shook among the sheets in the good old pre-war days when one picked up fleas on the bus, at Saturday cinema, and in Woolworth's. It even smelt nice, though it felt a bit sandy. I suspect some veterinary flea powders are similar. Ask.

Ticks These can give you or your pets nasty diseases; the one good use for a lit cigarette is to encourage them to drop off. Otherwise ether works, but see Chapter 7 on pets and pests.

Animal bites see *Rabies*.

Bodily damage

A yacht is made of hard and unyielding substances, which in bad weather get up and hit you, causing bruises, cuts, and concussion, cracked ribs or broken bones. The old Salts used to say: One hand for yourself, and one for the King.

A yacht big enough to go cruising in is under the sway of enormous forces. If something breaks or casts loose it can cause serious damage to people or boat. Part of seamanship, therefore, is learning how to approach and tame your tiger whether it be a flogging sail or twin boom with the minimum of danger.

Below decks
- Learn the motion of your boat: when she may jerk or spin, as in a gybe all-standing or the wash of a big ship, or a sudden squall.
- Make sure that handholds are numerous, in the right place, and that these and anything that can be used as such are *strong enough*. We have seen (for instance) tables on production boats that collapsed into matchwood when crashed into by a 7-stone weakling.
- Expect the Captain to warn you, if at all possible, that a big wave or jerk may be coming.
- Climbing the mast at sea should be attempted only in dire necessity.

On deck
The deck of a yacht is never smooth. It is dotted with cleats, rings, bitts, upstands, screwplates and deadeyes, all waiting to bite your feet. So:
- Wear good deck shoes to protect your feet from damage, as well as for traction. Bare feet are fine in harbour or at anchor, but GET YOUR SHOES ON for manoeuvres. Shipboard work often cannot wait while you hop around holding your toe and yelling.
- Use preventers and guys to limit the swing of spars, and prevent gybing. Again prevention is better than cure, so:

- Check halyards for weaknesses, ropes for chafe, wire for kinks and broken strands (the latter are a constant source of lacerated fingers).
- Replace bent shackle pins, and tape up protruding split-pins or enclose them neatly in plastic tube.
- If the weather threatens, shorten sail early to lessen the forces you have to control. Even a handkerchief of canvas in a force 8 can bat around like a tin roof in a hurricane, and a rope can assume the murderous quality of an iron bar wielded by a maniac.

Listen to the Flotilla. They believe that nothing can hurt them; after all, what could possibly happen on two weeks' holiday in such lovely sunshine?

'I'm coming in a bit fast: stick your foot out and hold us off that big motor boat, will you, Harry?' The luckless Harry tries to stop 5 tons of fast-moving boat in zero seconds: oh dear, he's hurt his foot. But as the boat recoils, Dad is very busy at the tiller end:

'Maude, can you let a bit more anchor line out? What? No more? Well tie another rope to it then – be quick, I can't quite reach the quay. HOLD ON, MAUDE! What did you let go for? Stop crying, it's only a rope burn. Fred, take a line ashore, will you. No, I can't seem to get any nearer, we've run out of anchor line: surely you can jump that?'

Fred, challenged, jumps at the precise moment when the cleated anchor line brings the boat up short. He is lucky if he is precipitated into the water rather than onto the rough concrete quay, which will result in numerous cuts and abrasions if not worse.

The same abrupt halt has probably thrown Mum against the cockpit coaming, a frequent cause of cracked ribs. All it needs now is for Sandra to stub her bare toe against a cleat, and on leaving, for Susan to jam her fingers in the anchor cable roller and Dad to get a hernia heaving up the anchor, unaware in all the excitement that the ferry has come in and laid several hundredweight of chain across it. We have watched all these accidents happen, and a lot more, but not all to one boat, at one time, mercifully.

A few more anti-injury hints:

Bill looks remarkably cheerful after suffering an attack by the wind generator.

- Don't fill a bucket of water from the sea if you are sailing fast. Even at 5 knots the jerk can almost dislocate your shoulder.
- So can an unexpected gybe if you are holding the mainsheet in your hand. 'Never cleat the mainsheet' goes back to our dinghy days; it is not valid for bigger boats.
- Anchor chain can crush fingers or hands; I have a healthy respect for ours. On *Fare Well* it was very heavy. I kept my hands well away from it by looping a short length of codline through the links when I needed to move it: this could be let go instantly if the cable began to run out unexpectedly, or even cleated up to stop it if you were quick.
- Release with care those dinky little elastic sail gaskets with a plastic knob at each end or they will snap back and knock your teeth out and probably break your glasses as well.
- Finally, wearing a lifejacket can save you a few bruises, as will a padded jacket with integral buoyancy.

Body odour

This delicate matter must be mentioned, since the chronic water shortage on board often prevents normal bathing and showering.

- Be aware that your clothing affects your smell. Man-made fibres all engender smells in the smalls after a couple of hours. Cotton, wool and linen may be worn for much longer before they need washing. You may decide that the easy-care qualities of polyester/cotton mixtures are worthwhile, but you will have to wash them more often, thus using more water.
- Canvas shoes and trainers need washing whenever you have access to a shoreside hose, otherwise the smell can become intense enough to glow in the dark; leather deck shoes are more expensive, but kinder to your feet and mates.
- Personal hygiene can be assisted by moistened wipes. Do not use those saved from restaurants in the interests of economy on anything except your hands: I shudder to think of the effect of the lemon-flavoured variety on tender portions of the anatomy. There are specially made ones for this purpose such as Bidette and Femfresh. In the UK we now have moist toilet tissue, but it has not reached the Eastern Med yet. A huge box of baby wipes is worth a great many baths. For women, throwaway Brief Savers are a godsend (if only there was a male equivalent: a sort of paper jockstrap).

My greatest contribution to clean cruising is probably the discovery that the Debutante brand plastic bowl (withstands boiling water and is graduated in pints and litres) fits exactly into the Lavac bowl to form a bidet. I was so excited by this discovery that I bought a second plastic bowl, but the first one has lasted ten years without breaking.

Bill is under the delusion that underarm deodorants are effective. Overuse of anti-perspirants (not the same thing) is thought to cause dermatitis.

Breaking fingernails

You need strong short nails at sea. There are preparations to paint on and strengthen them, but you can also 'eat' them strong by including plenty of gelatine in the diet: eat straight jelly (Jello) cubes if you like, or dishes in aspic such as oeufs en gelée, brawn or pig's trotters, oxtail. Wearing gloves can spare you damage: not the delicate little pair from the Yotte Shoppe which exposes your finger ends, in our experience one of the most vulnerable and easily damaged parts of the body, but a strong leather or plastic-palmed pair. The yellow ones sold for bargees in European waterways prevent injury either when dealing with wire rope, or that popular French mooring system called the *pendille*, where you pick up a fixed rope between the quay and a mooring buoy, and slide it through your hands to bring it to the forward anchor winch to make fast. As the rope spends a lot of time in the water, it is covered with coral and small, sharp crustacea. Those on shore can be heard tittering as you lacerate your hands and bleed into the scuppers. A pack of false nails take little room for those who fancy a little silent boasting among well-groomed people ashore.

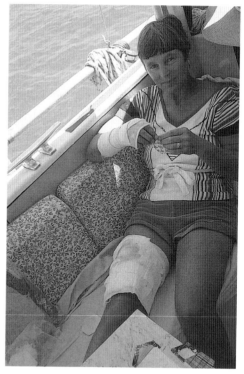

Burns and scalds

Every cook must evolve his or her own way of coping with hot pans in a choppy sea. Some advocate seats and straps in the galley, but I prefer to be free to leap aside. With good fiddles it is not the pans that move, it is their contents, so it makes a lot of sense to have deep, tall pans, with well-fitting lids, and not to fill them too full. Pressure cookers are excellent because the lid stays on. A wide-based kettle with a whistle closing the spout keeps boiling water in the right place. You need a safe place to put a hot pan down where it will not slide, and insulated pan and pot handles. A large cover-all apron of tough plastic helps to protect you from splashes.

Should you be unlucky enough to sustain a burn or scald, help to prevent blisters by rapid cooling, in cold

Some knowledge of first aid is essential when cruising as you often have to deal with your injuries without professional help, as in this case when Laurel was barbecued by Bill.

tap water if it's available, or with an eyewash pod. (See First Aid kit page 323.)

It is also important, with a bad burn or scald, to prevent dehydration. When Bill accidentally barbecued me four hours away from civilisation, we were acutely conscious of this. Following instructions in the *Ship Captain's Medical Guide*, he fed me lemon squash with a little salt in it, half a pint every half hour, and measured my output in the rain gauge, driving the boat at maximum speed all the time, I should point out. He also radioed ahead for assistance. On arrival (at an Eastern Mediterranean port with a hospital) we had waiting for us on the quay willing hands to help Bill berth, a French doctor, an English doctor, an English nursing sister, and an American nurse (all live-aboards or on holiday in yachts). All of them advised us not to go near the hospital, and were delighted with Bill's lemonade, now satisfactorily coming through me every five minutes, and tickled by the rain gauge idea. With such good care, the burns on thighs, arms and hands healed in no time; I convalesced in the cockpit on a clean sheet.

Crew members can get burnt if you have an on-board barbecue (usually the kind that gimbals on a stern rail). At anchor smoke and sparks blow harmlessly away aft, but moored to the quay it pays to study the wind direction. We know of two cases of burns caused by thoughtless use of methylated spirit: firelighters are much safer. We keep a fire extinguisher and a fire blanket near the cooking stove in case of galley fires. (Firefighting in yachts is covered in Chapter 11.)

Ciguatera poisoning

This is caused by eating fish from certain coral reefs in tropical waters. It manifests not only with the usual food poisoning symptoms: nausea, vomiting and diarrhoea; but can also produce tingling and numbness in the fingers, toes, lips and tongue; joint and muscle pains, weakness and cramps; fatigue, fainting and headaches; and itching made worse by alcohol. To confuse the issue even more, any or all of these symptoms may be present, and they may be so slight as to be barely noticed, or severe enough to include breathing difficulties. Some sources say the death rate (mostly from breathing difficulties) is 2–3%, others 1%; further sources say that it could be less as the milder cases are not reported.

In by far the majority of cases, unpleasant as these symptoms are, they will go away in time, though muscular weakness may persist for quite a while.

Ciguatoxin is found in a small organism that attaches to the algae on certain coral reefs, where it is eaten by small fish. These are then eaten by larger fish, and as the food chain gets longer, the toxin is concentrated until in the larger predatory fish it becomes a danger to those who eat it.

Distribution This is the hard part, as the distribution of the affected reefs is sporadic and capricious: it is not yet understood what factors make some reefs harbour the organism, and others (though quite close by) not. So while one can say with truth that ciguatera is present in reefs in the Pacific, Japan, Queensland, the Great Barrier Reef and the Caribbean, that is not the whole story. North of Antigua in the Caribbean, ciguatera is present in some reefs. To the south, the

Windward Islands and the Grenadines are free of it. French Polynesia is widely affected, Raratonga is not.

What is certain, in all the myth and rumour which abounds on this subject, is that the local fishermen, be they Polynesian, Caribbean or Floridans, know with fair exactitude which reef and which fish species to avoid. They will also volunteer much folklore on testing fish for poison, ranging from cooking it with a silver coin (which turns black if the fish is toxic) to trying it out on the Mother-in-law. No reliance can be placed on these methods, as only very sophisticated laboratory tests can detect whether the fish is affected. Neither heating nor canning destroys the effects of the toxin. So what to do?

Local knowledge from a reliable source is vital. If in any doubt, do not eat the larger predatory fish: grouper, barracuda, emperor, sailfish etc. (One source describes over 10 kilos as large.) Do not eat moray eel. Do not eat the roe, liver or other offal especially from large fish.

Research is going on in Queensland, Tahiti, Japan and Hawaii, among other places, to establish accurate tests for ciguatera in fish.

Test for ciguatera One such is now available. It's not cheap, and has a limited shelf life, but if you catch big fish in affected areas you might find it useful. See Appendix.

Colds
Just go to sea. The virus disappears after a week to ten days, and you will catch no more colds until the next supermarket.

Cystitis
This is a urinary tract infection. If you are subject to it, make sure you drink a lot of water, wear cotton next to the skin, and take your favourite remedy with you.

Dental problems
Some old Salt Horses, chiefly from the New World, used to suggest having all your teeth out before a long cruise. This seems to us a draconian solution, especially as our teeth seem to last much better nowadays. It should suffice to ensure that you are 'dentally fit' before you leave. Tell your dentist your plans, and he will be careful to miss nothing.

Thereafter, look after your teeth. I will not insult your intelligence by telling you how, since we are all over-exposed to dental hygiene. Here are some thoughts that might not occur to you, however:

- If you wear dentures, take them out if you feel seasick, they are too easily chundered overboard. Of course you will take a spare set in case of accidents.
- Take a dental first aid kit (see Appendix), which should contain a temporary filling mixture, and cement to repair bridgework, or even broken

teeth. The designer of such a kit recounts the dreadful story of a woman who tried to replace her front crowns with super-glue, all that was obtainable in the remote island where she found herself. The glue engendered heat as it set, causing unimaginable pain and damage.

- Lost fillings may be temporarily replaced by granny's remedy: equal parts of oil of cloves and powdered zinc oxide. Mix this well, and work it into the well-dried cavity. It will set in about a quarter of an hour, and last until you can get it seen to.
- Oil of cloves on cottonwool is a harmless local painkiller.

Departure stress

Leaving home and friends can be grievous. Husbands and lovers could help a lot by trying to understand how serious a bereavement this is; the male has no roots, it seems; certainly not the ones who go to sea, and feels less pain on upheaval. The tumbleweed male should allow plenty of time for his partner to adjust to transplantation (in the gardening sense). Unlike plants, this will be worst *before* the actual uprooting; on sailing day the relief will be balm to everyone's pain but the weeks or even months before you go will be hard.

Bereavement is a sense of loss, of people and things that are loved and respected. It is not necessary for the people to actually die, or the things to be destroyed for you to feel bereft; bereavement is also caused by leaving treasures behind, whether human, animal, abstractions or objects. Bereavement is something to be reckoned with. It is a very germane consideration. Men come up against it with a jolt when they unexpectedly lose their jobs. Some people suffer severely from bereavement when they retire, and grieve for their lost jobs and status. If they have no absorbing hobby they can die of despair. In the same way women will grieve for family, friends and the house they leave behind.

Happy are they who are encouraged and comforted while they work their way through this painful stage. Grief is extremely hard work, and very time-consuming for the person undergoing it; and the support group will need great patience. He will need to check the urge to say: 'Aren't you making rather a meal of this?' or 'Dear oh dear, you are going on a bit.' Of course she is. That is how she will work through it.

Diseases, avoidable

'They fall sicke of one disease or another . . .'

Unless there are positive medical objections, it makes sense to acquire vaccination, immunisation, and inoculation against smallpox, tetanus and typhoid (TAB).

Some parts of the world will not allow entry without an International Certificate of Vaccination, against smallpox and/or yellow fever.

It may also be advisable, according to where you intend to travel, to have shots against cholera and polio, and gamma globulin shots against hepatitis and some other viral infections. Babies should have the triple vaccine (diphtheria, whooping cough and tetanus) unless your doctor advises otherwise. It is not considered advisable for babies under nine months to have yellow fever shots, but you may insist, in writing. Children should have the triple vaccine, plus immunisation against polio.

Discuss with your doctor the advisability or otherwise of all these precautions, and whether to include shots against tuberculosis and German measles for your children (tuberculosis is making a disturbing comeback), and whether you should do something about malaria, the increase of which is causing concern.

Detailed lists are available in a leaflet from your local Department of Health and Social Security, and the DoH website. The Scottish NHS site is especially good. Try also the Hospital for Tropical Diseases and MASTA (Medical Advisory Services for Travellers) whose addresses will be found in the Appendix.

Ear itch

Many people get this infuriating complaint when swimming. Ear plugs or a good bathing cap are the obvious answer. Otosporin (on prescription) seems to work.

Eye damage

Whether you wear spectacles or not, have your eyes tested before departure. You will need good sight by night as well as day, and if glasses help, wear them. Tell the optician your plans and discuss with him whether the lightness and toughness of plastic lenses outweighs their tendency to scratches. Take spare pairs (and your prescription) with you. Keep them on with chain, elastic or string: whatever suits you. Do not keep them in a breast pocket: I have seen many a pair of specs go to the bottom of the sea as their owner bent over a rail; otherwise they fall down a hatchway and get broken. Fix a steel tag to them and you might get them back with a Sea Searcher magnet: we have rescued not only spectacles but keys, fountain pens, bolts and wing nuts, fish traps and bicycles.

If you still use the sextant for sunsights be extra careful not to glimpse the sun directly through the telescope. This is easy to do on days when the sun is fitful. It can burn the retina, causing irreversible damage which may not be noticed at the time. Professional seamen seldom wear sunglasses, preferring to train their eyebrows to jut like yardbrooms and to observe the world through slitted eyes. We feel that Polaroids (polarising glasses) can be helpful if you are looking up-sun. They are also essential in tropical waters, to enable the look-out to pick out coral heads underwater. If bright reflections give you headaches, add a broadbrimmed hat or an eyeshade.

There's nothing that drives you out of your senses
Like constantly losing your contact lenses.

Talk to your optician about the advisability or otherwise of using these at sea, and ask him to check for colour blindness, which would preclude unsupervised night watchkeeping. Eyes are priceless: guard them well.

Falls

Much of what was said under Bodily damage is equally valid for falls. Apart from damage to fingers from tools, we observe falling to be the major cause of damage to yachtsmen, resulting in a wide variety of lesions, from bruises and scrapes to the very common cracked ribs, through broken bones of all kinds up to skull and vertebral fractures.

Good handholds and the right shoes go a long way to avoid these injuries. In weather when the ship's motion is very jerky, clip on and hold on, and only move when necessary.

Bill and I hold opposite views about cockpit cushions. I like plenty of them to cushion me when I get thrown off balance; Bill thinks there are too many, as he falls over them if they get dislodged.

A padded coat or lifejacket can save bruises to the upper part of the body. I sometimes inflate my pilot jacket a little to enable me to bounce off hard edges.

Your steering or helmsman's seat should be difficult to fall out of, as well as comfortable to sit in.

> *Mop, ah, mop those spills away,*
> *Before you crack your vertebrae.*

Flip-flops are for wearing ashore only. They are highly dangerous. We knew a paraplegic who acquired his injury by catching the rung of a ladder between his toes and the sole of his flip-flops. He fell 30 feet. Finally:

Never pee over the side of the boat even in calm seas. It is an excellent way to fall overboard, however alluring it might be not to have to go below. The Search and Rescue Organisation of Sweden found that 75% of male bodies discovered floating in harbour had their flies undone. There is evidence to show that attacks of faintness (known as vaso-vagal inhibition chaps) can occur if you get out of your bunk suddenly and stand up on deck to 'pump ship'. How about constructing a 'pig's ear' as the Navy calls it? Make a funnel from the top of a plastic bottle: an opaque one for aesthetic preference; attach it firmly to a length of hose which will reach over the side, then hang the business end within reach of the cockpit. A little ingenuity with the design of the funnel even allows us disadvantaged females to use it, instead of getting our bottoms splashed by the rollicking seas in the toilet bowl.

Finger damage

You don't want to lose them. Rings are sometimes responsible for nasty injuries, including that unpleasant one known as skinning, when the ring catches on something and is pulled off your finger. That said I have worn three rings for 30 years at sea without problems, all of them almost as flat as a wedding ring. Keep your dress rings for going ashore. Minor damage to fingers is frequent from whatever cause; have plenty of adhesive plasters on board. Warming them helps them to stick.

Heat exhaustion

This is nothing to do with sunstroke; it is caused by working in hot humid conditions. The danger arises with temperatures of over 27°C, 80°F, combined with high relative humidity. Increasing bad temper and bolshiness on the part of a normally co-operative crew is an indicator. A sufferer will:

- Be cool, sweaty, and pale.
- Have a weak and rapid pulse.
- Have weak and rapid breathing.

If profuse sweating leads to dehydration with nausea and weakness, system failure can ensue and lead to heatstroke, see below.

Prevention Allow the cook a heavier hand with the salt, include in the diet salt fish such as anchovies, highly seasoned salami, and a great deal of water to drink. Keep cool and stay in the shade if possible. Stokers in the Navy used to be given pints of salty lemonade to prevent heat exhaustion.

Heatstroke, sunstroke

This is more catastrophic, but less common than heat exhaustion. The sufferer will not be sweating, and will become very hot.

Prevention Acclimatise yourself gently to hot weather and strong sun. Wear light clothing and a hat. Stay in the shade and keep decks and crew cool with buckets of sea water. Drink plenty of fresh water and don't be mean with the salt.

To avoid sunstroke or sunburn, make sure that your boat is well equipped with a suitable awning to provide plenty of shade.

Heart attack

If you have a good healthy heart, rejoice and keep it that way.

- Take exercise.
- Avoid being overweight.
- Eat less fat and convenience food, more fruit and vegetables.
- Avoid stress.
- Avoid cigarettes.
- Drink a couple of glasses of red wine a day, rather than two bottles only at the weekend.

If you have had a heart attack, your doctor will have told you what you should be doing as well as the above. So sail away and do it.

Herpes (cold sores)

Avoid sun on the lips, as it excites the herpes virus into action. So does wind, dryness, and a raised body temperature. Wear a shady hat, and use a sunscreen. Lipsalves are not recommended, they may dry the skin more than they help, but Vaseline is safe and effective. If you feel the tingle that precedes a cold sore, we find Zovirax works.

Hypothermia

'Not so much as a cloth to shift him, shaking with cold.'

In our young days, something vaguely termed 'suffering from exposure' attacked mountaineers, fell walkers, and shipwreck survivors. Old people and babies died, too, in their homes. After years of study and research, it is now called hypothermia and is recognised as a killer. Not only in cold climates, take note. It is now suggested that yachtsmen at risk, whether in the water or in a liferaft, actually succumb to hypothermia oftener than drowning. If they are in the water, it is hypothermia which probably causes them to drown.

Since this is at present the most likely cause of death at sea, know the enemy. Hypothermia is a serious loss of heat from the deep areas of the body. If the inner body temperature falls below 32°C (87°F) the prospects are not good. Your clinical thermometer is no use for these deep body temperatures, which are caused by heat being leached away from the body without being replaced. This can happen when immersed in cold or even cool water, when exposed to wind without proper clothing, or, as in the case of the very old and the very young, through non-functioning of the body's heat regulators.

The time it takes to get into this condition is idiosyncratic; if you are strong and physically fit – even dare one say, fat – you will last longer than someone of smaller build who is equally fit. Well-covered people have an initial advantage as they store more heat, but lose their edge when they tire more rapidly and become exhausted. Children cool faster than adults. Cold water leaches the heat away faster than cold dry air, but wind chills you very fast.

Prevention Your sailing clothes are important. They should protect you from wet and wind, and have some insulating (air-retentive) properties. The former is provided by waterproof foul weather gear, and the latter by wearing under it anything that will trap air, such as a knitted garment, or a foam lining. Underwear should be of the kind that wicks moisture away from the skin. Those furry garments sometimes called Polar suits trap the air in the pile, and are comfortable. However as they are of man-made fibres, a woollen jersey over them is a good idea, as wet wool is a better insulator than wet nylon and actually generates a little heat.

Even on a warm night, a sudden strong wind can chill you rapidly. It is as well to have a windproof jacket and a woolly hat handy. Preventing loss of heat from head (20% heat loss is through the scalp), hands and toes becomes important in colder climates, and there is no substitute for wool. Wet nylon socks will not keep you warm, but having said that, once you get to survival level anything is better than nothing.

SIGNS TO WATCH FOR

- The person may not realise that he is dangerously cold.
- He may be shivering. (This is beneficial, as it generates heat.)
- He may be awkward and clumsy, and his movements and speech may be very slow.
- His mind may feel like porridge, and a state of lethargy can set in, preventing self-help.
- If you suspect hypothermia, *prevent further heat loss*.
- Remove the person from the water or wind.
- Get him below. If possible replace wet clothes with dry ones, otherwise wrap him in a foil space blanket.
- Cover the head with a woolly hat, and mouth and nose with a closely wound scarf, to prevent heat loss from the lungs.
- *Do not leave him alone*, as he is capable of irrational behaviour, including removing all his clothes.
- Keep him horizontal, even after he thinks he's OK. (See after-drop, below.) If he is conscious, give warm (not hot), sweet, drinks but *NO ALCOHOL*, which causes central heat loss and a dangerous fall in the blood sugar.

It is much more important to *prevent further heat loss* than to try artificial warming by means of hot water bottles or baths, as this can bring the heat to the body surface at the expense of the deep organs. If the sufferer can get into a warm bath without help, it is safe for him to have one, but watch him even if he says he's OK now, thank you, as a lengthy period of care is needed to prevent the after-drop which occurs after rescue and some warming, and can lead to complications:

in Bill's case collapse, double pneumonia and three weeks in the Naval Hospital (see Chapter 11 Misadventures).

Survival in the water

Stay with the boat or wreckage. Float, don't swim. Swimming dissipates heat. If you are not alone cluster with the others, and try to roll into a ball, to reduce the heat loss from your body.

Infantile diarrhoea

This is probably the most dangerous thing that could happen to your baby or toddler, apart from severe sunburn. The baby becomes progressively dehydrated until he is seriously ill. To combat dehydration in children (and adults as well if need be) you can obtain a double-ended plastic spoon which has been developed for Third World mothers. Salt goes in one end of the spoon, and sugar in the other, and both are stirred into boiled water until dissolved. This cheap and simple device has saved more lives than kidney machines. The address to send for the spoon is in the Appendix, but if you encounter any difficulties here are the quantities:

Life-Saving Fluid) ½ teaspoon salt, 2 level tablespoons sugar or honey, dissolved in a litre of boiled water. (Dissolving is important because your body cannot use the salt otherwise.) One glass for a child (and two for adults), to be taken after every attack of diarrhoea. (Up to a litre a day for children.)

Alternatively ask your Chemist for Dioralyte sachets, a ready-made mixture of sodium chloride (salt), potassium chloride, soda bicarbonate and glucose, for mixing with 200cc (7oz) water. They will be more expensive than the salt and sugar mixture, but can be used even for tiny babies.

Legionnaire's disease

This risk is present if the boat is left for a few months, when plastic water tanks and pipes encourage the growth of the Legionella bacteria, which are then spread in a fine droplet spray from the shower. After a spell of disuse, clean empty water tanks and pipes, with chlorine, then flush through thoroughly with plenty of fresh water before refilling.

Low morale

'For when a man is ill or at the point of death, I would know whether a dish of buttered rice with a little Cynamon, ginger and sugar . . . bee not better . . . than salt fishe . . .'

Sooner or later the time comes when nothing goes well, and everyone feels low and grouchy. I have said earlier that food and drink are important: now is the time to break out something special for the next meal. In the meantime, splice the mainbrace or have a coffee with some rum in it, or eat a whole candy bar.

The aftermath of bad experiences takes its toll of all the crew, not always in the same way. Some talk a lot, some do not talk at all. Some sleep at once, some cannot sleep. Some are elated because it is over; others worry in case it happens again. All need comfort and reassurance. What we sailors have known about for years and dealt with by simple humanity has now a fancy name: post-traumatic stress, and become the province ashore of professional counsellors. These do nothing that tact, understanding, and mutual support from your mates cannot do as well or better. Talk it all through, as often as is needed. A recognition that it takes different people different ways, is at the heart of everyone's recovery.

If you find it hard to sleep after an exhausting (even frightening) experience, a tablet of Serene or Kwells is an effective calmer, without fogging your head in the morning, as stronger tranquillisers are apt to do. Usually, however, our best practice after such events was to talk the shock away for an hour or two over a stiff brandy or gin, to cut the adrenaline. When we felt sufficiently unwound, we went to bed and usually slept like logs.

Morale on board is a delicate flower. It has to be nurtured and tended with care. We have met yachts where it seems to have broken down completely: everyone moving well away from each other in a heavy silence, speaking to us and other strangers without looking at us, in tones that are too loud. Someone is often crying down below; and you can bet she will be the first to recover.

I have said something already about mutual support between skipper and crew. This must extend, gentlemen, to allowing your ladies a good cry, after an exhausting or terrifying experience. Most women are immensely strong mentally and can also call on more physical strength than might be thought, if need be. They will do whatever is necessary, beyond what you could have hoped for. They will fight fires, pump valiantly, bail like demons, staunch the blood, and hang on to the uttermost.

They will cope, beyond the point of pain and exhaustion, like the human beings they are. When there is no more to be done, they are likely to burst into tears. Men react indignantly to this. They feel it as a reflection on their actions; but crying is no more a criticism of him than his heartfelt swearing at a sulky generator is a reflection on her. What is more, tears are as beneficial as a cold beer on a sweltering day. Better, since there is evidence to show that a natural anaesthetic is released into the brain when someone cries. No wonder it is such a relief. Try crying a bit more, chaps: it's good for you.

> *After the storm is over*
> *Indulge in a real good cry,*
> *Swallow a whisky and water*
> *And dinner with lots of pie.*
> *Comforting words should be spoken*
> *Helping you sleep till morn,*
> *Harmony need not be broken*
> *After the storm.*

Malaria

This dreadful disease is caused by the bite of certain mosquitoes, in certain areas of the world. It is on the increase and must be taken seriously. We are collecting more and more evidence that shows that taking tablets of Brewer's Yeast alters the taste of your blood to the point where mosquitoes cease to bite you, where the bite is merely irritating.

In areas where malaria is rife, where the bite can be lethal, you *must* take proper precautions *well in advance.*

There are pills to prevent malaria. You must start them early, and continue after you leave the area known to be infested. IAMAT, previously mentioned, and MASTA, and the Department of Health, have very good information. Unfortunately malaria is becoming resistant to the present range of remedies. See also Chapter 7 on pests, but the following preventative measures should also be taken:

- Avoid mosquito bites, either by burning pastilles or coils, using sprays, or creams, preferably containing Deet, when awake and active.
- When asleep use a mosquito net.
- In the evenings wear long sleeved shirts and trousers tucked into socks.
- Proof your portholes with gauze.
- Take your preventative pills rigorously, starting well before, and continuing well after, following instructions implicitly.

Dengue fever

This is also caused by a mosquito bite, but a different mozzie. As there is *no vaccine* for this, *avoid bites* as above but by day as well as night.

Malnutrition and deficiency diseases

Most ocean passages last less than a month, so it is very unlikely that you are going to stagger ashore with beriberi or pellagra at the end of your voyage, especially if you paid attention to the chapter on victualling. However, multivitamin pills take up no space at all and might be useful. One of the really long sea passages is that made by cruisers from Australia and New Zealand, who come across the Indian Ocean and up the Red Sea to the Mediterranean. The time for this is the dry Northeast Monsoon, which means that fresh water is critically short and hard to replace. We have seen these folk arrive in the Mediterranean in poor shape, skinny (easily remedied) but with salt-water boils and ulcers that are hard to heal. The protein-rich cereal mixtures in Chapter 10 (Victualling) could help to prevent these. For the boils (gunnel bum) see skin problems, below.

Noxious diseases of all kinds

Your life will be changing completely. Would it be so hard to use this opportunity to stop smoking? Apart from the good effect it will have on your health and finances (and you will not find low-tar and filter tips in the remoter areas) smoking in the confined space below decks of a small yacht is literally nauseating and conducive to seasickness. Think about it.

Rabies

Get your ship's cat or dog vaccinated (see Chapter 7), and in areas where rabies is endemic, warn the children not to pet animals they may find ashore. Animal bites must be treated seriously in any country where rabies is a possibility. Try and educate your children out of the pretty pussy mindset, to treat all animals, wild or domesticated, warily and with great respect, *look, but don't touch*. Mangy animals can cause ringworm in humans. If bitten, even if you have been vaccinated against rabies, seek medical help. In the meantime clean the wound as best you can with cetrimide or alcohol; gin or vodka will do.

Seasickness

This above all can spoil your enjoyment of (anyway) the first two days of your voyage. There is much that can be done to minimise its likelihood and shorten its duration. You could be one of those who are never ill at all, or one of the unfortunates who are very sick indeed for a long time.

It is a comfort to know that on a long voyage the large majority of people are over the worst on the second day. Thereafter a sensible regime will prevent its recurrence, even in rough seas, unless prolonged galley or engineroom work are attempted.

To cut seasickness down to a minimum:

- Don't go to sea with a hangover.
- Go into a rough sea with the stomach warm and comfortably full of something fairly stodgy: stew with lots of potatoes, or pilaf, or pasta or porridge, not curry or spicy food.
- Have an extra jersey handy; it is important not to get chilled and you might not want to go below for it. Best start off too warm: you can always discard.
- Try not to get too tired. Do whatever is necessary, and rest between tasks, up on deck if you can.
- Spell the helmsman, drive a bit. Drivers are seldom sick.

Preventatives The most effective drug, statistically, is hyoscine hydrobromide. The stronger pills need a prescription, milder ones are available over the counter as Kwells (tablets) or Scopoderm TTS (skin patches) which are better if you are likely to vomit. Avomine (promethazine theoclate) and Dramamine (dimenhydrinate) are almost as good; it is a question of finding out what suits you and taking it at least half an hour before it is likely to be needed. Sea Legs (meclozine) may be taken the night before sailing. Stugeron, Marzine (both cinnarizine) and Valoid (cyclizine) are less likely to make you drowsy, and are therefore less useful as mild sedatives. None of these drugs should be accompanied by alcohol, which is anyway not a good idea in bad weather.

When storms begin
Lay off the gin.

Some people find pressure wristbands, working on the acupuncture theory, to be very effective.

If you can, keep eating and drinking. If you cannot face real food, nibble dry crackers or crispbread, and have an occasional sweet fizzy drink: a swallow or two of beer is surprisingly good, ginger ale not far behind; it's the fizz that counts.

As a last resort, lie down, for'd if running before the wind or aft if going to windward. (This takes one set of the semi-circular canals in your ear out of action, and so you feel less giddy.)

> *Take in time your seasick pill*
> *Otherwise you will be ill.*
> *Tummy warm and full of food*
> *Helps to keep you feeling good.*
> *Too much booze the night before*
> *Makes you toss your cookies more.*
> *Cold your body, head and toes,*
> *Overboard your breakfast goes.*
> *Nibble, nibble all the day*
> *To hold your queasy tum at bay;*
> *A gill of beer or ginger ale*
> *Will stay your stomach through the gale.*
> *Should you feel that death is near,*
> *Lying down you'll feel less queer.*

Skin trouble

Ulcers and boils (gunnel bum, in the racing world) are caused by constant contact with salt water, such as occurs on the long run from Australia up to the Red Sea. With water so desperately short, none can be spared for washing to remove the salt from the skin.

It would be well worth taking a large quantity of wet wipes: even one a day would get some of the salt off. Paper pants make a lot of sense, too. Cocoa butter is soothing, and speeds healing. Vaseline (petroleum jelly) is good too. Note that what chemists call a 'cream' is often not as good for the skin as 'ointments', as the latter are based on oil. However some swear by nappy rash cream. Multivitamin pills also help skin healing; a good diet is even better, see Chapter 10 on Victualling.

Stomach upsets

> *'. . . And then if their Victuals be putrified it indangers all'*

Assuming that you have had your TAB shots, get further immunity by eating and drinking locally. Take the normal precautions of peeling fruit and vegetables just before you eat them, or washing them in fresh water. If you feel stronger measures are needed, wash in:

- Tincture of iodine, 8–10 drops in a litre of water.
- Bleach: 1 teaspoon to 2 litres of water.
- Permanganate of potash crystals, enough to turn the water a light pink.

Boiling the water we have not found necessary anywhere, but with a small baby you may feel it essential, or if you yourself are susceptible and worried about the water source. Purifying tablets are available, both for large and small quantities of water. Most are based on chlorine. Small water filters are available on the market for travellers.

Since a chronic water shortage leads to skimping the washing up, it is sensible to have two separate chopping boards. Keep one strictly for raw meat, fish or chicken, and stow its appropriate knife with it. The other is for cooked meat, bread and cleaned raw vegetables for salads. It too has its own knife.

Stomach disorders are usually caused by one of the Fs: food, flies or faeces, so keep the first clean and cool, murder the second mercilessly (see Chapter 7) and don't skimp the personal hygiene and hand washing: use medicated wipes if water is really a problem. Keep some in the heads, with a bin for used ones.

We ran into trouble with stomach disorders on our return from America, when we visited Tangier. In the two years we had spent in the ultra-sanitised States we had obviously lost our resistance and Tangier is not a good place to be sensitive in. We suffered somewhat, but our Mediterranean immunity soon re-established itself.

Remember that alcohol is a great bug killer ashore. *'Take a little wine, for thy stomach's sake, and thine often infirmities,'* as St Paul advised St Timothy. Our eminent authority states that 'a little wine' can be reckoned as up to half a litre (red wine) a day!

Stress

You have gone to a great deal of trouble to leave stress behind. Make sure that you also leave behind such lingering habits of the old life as hurrying to get somewhere, working from morning till night, or putting the engine on merely because it is faster. There will be quite enough to challenge you in the months ahead without looking for extra work. Use the lazy windless days to store well being and energy, as well as learning how to cope when the weather turns foul, things go wrong and everyone is needed to the utmost. This is certain to happen, even if you neither girdle the Earth nor round Cape Horn. If you do decide that you want to do these heroic things, beware that a sense of compulsion does not creep in, and with it a loss of that carefree feeling that you are doing what you want and not what you must. That is not the way of laid-back cruising. Nor is the driving urge to 'get your ticket punched', as we have heard circumnavigation and crossing the

Atlantic described: trying to do this in a limited time probably causes as much pointless hassle as staying in the cut-throat world of business or fighting for your job ashore.

Cruising without stress is to leave behind the TV, the computer, the newspapers, and the punishing daily onslaught of the world outside. Shrink to your own little world of the boat, the sea, and the sky. Take no count of hours, only days and nights, have no time limit and girdle the world almost by accident, strolling from island to island and continent to continent.

> *Blue sky and green water pour into your mind;*
> *The balm of the world, landsman's daughter,*
> *You sought so long to find.*

Sunburn

Millions of words of warning are printed every year, yet one sees the boiled-lobster effect wherever there is a bit of sun and wind. Patience and a good sunscreen lotion are all that is required; you cannot get a deep-water suntan in three days, you will merely have your skin crispy-broiled. Take a total sunblock cream: apart from prevention it can alleviate even a nasty sunburn. Protect noses, lips, bald pates and the tops of your feet. If you stayed in the shade for a fortnight in hot sunny weather, you would still achieve a pleasant tan and no burns. Conversely you can burn out of doors even on a cloudy day.

Sun is not always beneficial. Even with a good protective tan you can get skin cancer, which is sharply on the increase.

Thrush (vaginal candidiasis)

This distressing complaint can be discouraged by wearing loose-fitting cotton (never man-made fibres) next to the skin. The Pill can predispose you to thrush. Take with you something to cope with it, like Canesten.

Water contamination

To prevent:

- Do not let the water hose fall in the dock.
- Keep the hose clean and protected. (It will last much longer if you don't leave it in strong sunlight, though this can give you a wonderful hot shower.)
- Before you top up, direct a jet at the tap or standpipe to clean it: shore people can be very careless where they walk their dogs.
- 30 grains of stabilised chloride of lime to 100 gallons of water will destroy all organisms in it, but so will a little alcohol in your drinking glass and it tastes better.

Worms

See also Chapter 7. If you are interested in (herbal remedies) try 3–6 grains (≏ ¼ gm) of (fresh garlic) bulb, or ½ teasp of the juice. Or, to eliminate round and thread-worms, and paralyse tapeworms: steep shredded pomegranate bark in a tightly closed container, reduce by half, and take 4oz followed by a purgative. Better to use modern remedies such as Pripsen, which do not require purgatives afterwards.

THE MEDICINE CHEST

'. . . *Also that his chest be well furnished bothe for Physicke and Chirurgery and so near as may be proper for the clime you go for.*'

Here follows a list of what we took (after much discussion with our doctor and other authorities); what we used it for; and whether we used it at all. In the 30 years since our first departure many improvements and discoveries have been made, so I also give an update and a list of additions that we found necessary. (POM) means a prescription was necessary. Ampoules are for injections.

WHAT WE TOOK AND USED:

(POM) Ampicillin: Broad-spectrum antibiotic. *Update: (POM) Amoxil.*

Aspirin tablets, soluble: Headache and colds, minor aches.

Cream of magnesia: Indigestion. *Update: Aludrox.*

Burrow's Solution: Still available as Aluminium Acetate lotion, for fungus infections. *Update: Canesten cream.*

Chloramine tablets: For water purifying. *Update: Sterotabs, Katadyn Micropur.*

(POM) Diazepam 5mg capsules: Nowadays strongly discouraged, as addictive.

(POM) hyoscine hydrobromide (Scopolamine): For seasickness.

Kaolin and Morphine mixture: BNF: 'Concrete mixture', for diarrhoea.

Kwells tablets: Useful as a mild sedative.

Multivitamin tablets: To prevent deficiency diseases.

Paracetamol capsules: For headache, toothache, colds, etc.

(POM)Tetracycline tablets: Broad-spectrum antibiotic.

LATER WE ALSO ADDED:

(POM) Distalgesic tablets: For moderate to severe pain. *Update: (POM) Dihydrocodeine*

Nurofen: For flu, rheumatic aches, toothache.

Scopoderm TTS: hyoscine hydrobromide skin patches. For seasickness.

Stugeron (Cinnarizine): For seasickness.

(POM) Tetanus vaccine.

(POM) Xylocaine cream: Local anaesthetic.

WHAT WE TOOK BUT NEVER USED:

(POM) Adrenaline ampoules: 1:10,000: Shock or severe drug reaction.

(POM) Atropine: Narcotic, relaxes gastro-intestinal tract. *Update: (POM) ProBanthine.*

(POM) Benzedrine, 4 tablets: For emergencies requiring short-term prolongation of alertness.

(POM) Benadryl Antiallergic. For allergic reactions. *Update: (POM) Benadryl Semprex.*

Codeine: Now withdrawn from sale. See Paracetamol above.

(POM) Decadron: Severe allergies, shock and venom. *Update: Piriton.*

(POM) Diazepam ampoules: Potent tranquilliser. Discouraged nowadays.

Dioralyte powder: Against dehydration after diarrhoea.

(POM) Gelusil tablets: Antacid. *Update: Aludrox tablets.*

(POM) Lasix: Diuretic, for use after near drowning in salt water.

(POM) Lomotil: For severe diarrhoea.

(POM) Naprosyn tablets: Muscular and skeletal pain (eg discs).

(POM) Nitrazepam, 5mg capsules: Sleeping tablets, for short term use only.

(POM) Penicillin V.K. tablets: Antibiotic. *Update: (POM) Magnapen.*

(POM) Pethidine ampoules: Narcotic for pain relief.

(POM) Septrin tablets: For those allergic to Penicillin. *Update: Methoprim.*

Senokot tablets: for Constipation. A rare condition, we found.

(POM) Xylocaine ampoules: Local anaesthetic.

As you see, about one-third of this list was never used in 30 years of travel from America to Turkey, from Calais to the Ukraine. The more heroic measures were there if they were needed, kept in a locked drawer. We were told later that we would have been justified in using one of the narcotic painkilling ampoules on one occasion; but it was run-of-the-mill remedies we mostly needed: antibiotics, paracetamol, kaolin mixture and mild painkillers. As it should be.

• *Before you go* •

Thorough discussion with a qualified person will be necessary, not only because you will need prescriptions (and not necessarily on the NHS (National Health Service) either) but also for an explanation of how and when to use these things.

THE FIRST AID KIT

These are now available tailored to yachtsmen's needs, and can be bought as add-on Modules according to how far offshore you are going. (See Appendix.) Be prepared to spend £35 on a kit to allow for a three-hour wait for help, about £200 on Module 1, to £1000 for a full Marine medical kit (all four Modules).

Whatever container you keep this in, it ought to be fairly near the cockpit (which tends to become the casualty centre) and easily accessible. A *list of the whereabouts* of more bulky items (large dressings, bandages, and the applicators for the larger sizes of tubegauze, for example) should be stuck into the lid or otherwise firmly attached.

List One is what we took when we started, List Two contains later additions due either to increasing age or experience. (POM) means we needed a prescription.

LIST ONE

WHAT WE TOOK AND USED:

Acriflavin ointment: For burns

Adhesive dressing strip and Elastoplast (finger plasters): We use hundreds of these. The waterproof ones don't seem to stick as well as the fabric ones.

Anti-sting cream: Mosquito bites, wasp and jellyfish stings.

(POM) Aureomycin ointment: Antibacterial, for cuts and abrasions.

Calamine cream: Minor skin itch, and sunburn.

Clinical thermometer (see Fever Tester in List 2).

Cotton wool

Crepe bandages: Can be washed and reused.

Butterfly sutures: Never successful, as the victim was always sweating and no matter how much we swabbed they would not stick.

Eye bath: For washing out foreign bodies with saline solution.

Fisherman's Friend: Rubbing ointment (no, not the pastilles!) for sprains, wrenches and muscle pain.

(POM) Furacin ointment: Antibacterial, for burns or wounds.

Golden Eye ointment. (withdrawn, see Neobacrin).

Mercurochrome stick: Used like Iodine, stays on better in sea water.

(POM) Neobacrin: Eye ointment.

(POM) Nystan ointment: Thrush and athlete's foot. *Update: Canesten cream.*

Roll of adhesive plaster (tape): The Bandaid type from America came unstuck within ten minutes: we were glad to get back to Elastoplast.

Safety pins.

Scissors and tweezers: NEVER TO BE TAKEN AWAY AND USED ELSEWHERE!

Sterile packs of wound dressings in several sizes.

TCP antiseptic liquid: For disinfecting minor cuts.

Tubegauze bandages and applicators, in 4 sizes from toes to torsos: We used only the two smaller sizes. A particularly neat form of bandage.

We took a gross of disposable hypodermic syringes, with needles. We have never used them, and today's suspicious world being what it is, we recently took them to a pharmacy for safe disposal.

LIST TWO

ITEMS WE ADDED LATER AND WERE USEFUL:

Aerosol burn spray: Now kept near the stove.

Cicatrin: Antibiotic powder for wounds. Less painful to apply than ointments.

Fever Tester: A temperature-sensitive plastic film applied to the forehead; takes up no room, is unbreakable, but cannot be used rectally. There are several kinds of plastic thermometers nowadays.

Ice Pak: A once-only shake-and-apply ice pack for bad bruises. No need to store in the fridge. We got ours in the USA, but now obtainable in the UK (see Appendix). We also now use a freezing spray which can be reused many times (Urgofroid, made in France). If you have a freezer there is nothing better than a pack of frozen peas for bruises and sprains.

Low voltage electric blanket: For aches, flu, and general misery.

Nobecutane spray: Forms a sterile plastic coating over wounds or burns.

Oil of cloves and zinc oxide powder: For temporary tooth filling.

Sterile burn dressings: Sofra tulle, Opsite etc.

Nowadays I add P20 sunblock to this list.

ITEMS ADDED BUT NEVER USED:

A Brooke Airway: For resuscitation.

Disposable mini enemas (Microlax).

Disposable scalpels: After the fishhook episode.

Fluorescein stain: For finding damage to cornea.

Labstix: For testing urine

Prepacked sutures, already attached to needle. For closing wounds.

Rectal thermometer (Blue bulb): For measuring hypothermia.

I would now add Crewmedic's eyewash pod for sterile flushing of eyes, wounds or burns, since running tap water is not available at sea.

Murphy's Law being what it is, since we got the scalpels and sutures we have not required them again.

May you also never need what you have prudently taken with you.

16 • Cruising Grounds

'One to the top to look out for lande.'

In discussing the type of yacht and her gear there has inevitably been some emphasis on voyaging and bad conditions. Your typical boat dweller is not out to score miles or win trophies, or even to get unnecessarily wet and tired; it is simply sensible to consider the worst, so that in the vast majority of cases, the cruiser is well within tolerable limits of safety and comfort. In looking at cruising grounds, the emphasis must be on the pleasant side of life afloat, although everywhere has its share of trouble which I will have to mention. Once again, there is a lot of subjectivity. Forgive me. How could it be otherwise?

Ocean crossing for the likes of us is not a case of long-lasting heroics. (They may happen, but are not part of the plan.) We prefer the more congenial places which can be reached without taking dubious risks, or by extreme physical effort. Thus our own ocean experiences have been confined to the nicer parts of the Atlantic and Indian Oceans. I have also sailed professionally in most of the really nasty parts of the world because my monarch told me to and I assure you that no yachtsman should go there seeking pleasure. Don't even think about it. Well, think about it if you like, but think well.

Things have changed somewhat over the years. There are nowadays many more people living in yachts than there were and there is no doubt that some traditional cruising grounds have become more crowded. Very often we, long-distance live-aboard cruisers, 'discover' a wonderful cruising ground that is well detached from commerce, only to find that, eventually, an airstrip is built, the charter yacht industry moves in: flying dozens of crews out for short holidays in locally based yachts. You can't fight this. It's difficult even to grumble, though we have a go at it now and then. But the two forms of yachting are not wholly compatible.

The short-term charter sailor seeks to cram into his fortnight as much activity as he can. He is in holiday spending mode and he spends in a concentrated manner. The long-term cruiser is less frenetic, more careful with his money and his rate of expenditure has to last all year instead of just a special fortnight. The charter parties raise prices, their operators often negotiate special concessions for berthing and so on, and inevitably the yachtie moves on to discover somewhere else to which the vandals of industrial yachting will inevitably follow him.

And with more and more live-aboards, too, we are getting significant numbers of the more adventurous. One has only to read such publications as *Roving Commissions* (the annual journal of the Royal Cruising Club) to see the extraordinary places some yachties go. Would you believe one couple spending two years in the Antarctic Circle? Someone else seeking out the North West passage round Canada? A voyage from Britain to the Arctic Circle and then from the White Sea to the Black Sea through the Russian Rivers? A voyage across the northern Russian coast from Norway to the Bering Strait? But these are a special sort of yachtie.

Cruising grounds, did we say? The world can be the live-aboard's cruising ground.

THE WEST INDIES

Traditionally, most people contemplating this life have had a palm tree in the vision somewhere. This is changing, but I have to start somewhere and it is perhaps best to start with the West Indies. Most of this archipelago has a mixed colonial history, and the main population is of African descent from slaves, or in some cases of Spanish origin. There are many Indians in Trinidad. Some islands are very poor with unstable or uncertain economies, others have become more prosperous by exploiting tourism. It is a sad reflection that the islands in worst shape are very often those that were British possessions.

To nautical tourists such as ourselves, there is an inevitable pull towards the Windward Islands (the Grenadines, St Vincent, St Lucia, Martinique, etc) and afterwards to the more diffuse Leewards: Dominica round to the Virgins. The parts farther west: Puerto Rico to Cuba, once less attractive for political reasons, are beginning to offer scope for visits, and even the Central American isthmus, once best avoided except for the brave, is being cruised again. There are also the islands off the coast of South America from Trinidad to Curacao, the smaller of which are becoming more popular; though being downwind of the main group they are not so convenient to cruise.

The fly in the ointment for the private cruising yacht in this whole area is the large fleet of bareboat charter yachts. Some are essentially private craft let out on the occasional charter and these are no problem; the difficulties arise from what I call industrial chartering. The boats are almost always badly equipped, badly maintained and often badly sailed. The usual customers are Americans. Now, the USA probably has more private cruising yachts than the rest of the world put together, and probably more competent yachtsmen to sail them. In the same proportions she has also more boorish idiots, and it seems that many of these holiday in a bareboat in the Caribbean.

Search and rescue facilities in this area are scant (there are exceptions, notably Barbados), and these charterers, used at home to nannying by the very efficient US Coast Guard, put out a scandalous number of distress calls, many for trivial reasons and others for want of elementary prudence. British (and other nationalities) registered vessels are bound by law to answer distress calls. Sadly, the

professional, crewed charter yachts, many of which are British flag even if only of a debased kind, have been driven to ignore these calls or they'd never get their work done.

In addition, the bare-boat fleets have established bases which reserve for their exclusive use facilities which were once available to all. Either that or they charge discriminatory rates for private boats that are not acceptable to live-aboards. People on a three-week holiday from a very prosperous country can outbid longer term visitors for the scarce resources, and cause high prices, the main benefits of which go to external investors and do not reach the local people. Local politicians should remember that the local tourism that keeps their islands solvent was pioneered by private yachtsmen, and it is ungrateful to squeeze them out.

The pleasures of the area outweigh the minor irritations. There are wonderful anchorages and beaches, and the sailing between is excellent. We found, almost without exception, the local people friendly, extrovert and cheerful, the officials good humoured and courteous. Generally the poorer the community the nicer the people and officials, and it was in the more prosperous Virgin Islands that we found the only examples of rudeness, and even those were not too bad.

Formalities are generally not irksome. Almost every island is a separate sover-eign state, so that a lot of clearing and entering has to be done and a lot of expensive courtesy ensigns carried. Most islands make a moderate entry charge, and some yachtsmen resent this because harbours tend to be open anchorages with few port facilities; but considering that the islands are poor, such a charge is hard to find unreasonable.

The cost of living in the islands is based on the US dollar (apart from the French islands, which are heavily subsidised by France). Much of the foodstuff is imported from the USA, often by air, so that these items are expensive except the ubiquitous frozen chicken. Stocking up in Martinique with its Gallic attitude to the importance of food is a pleasure after months in the non-French islands, as apart from the wealthier, more developed islands, up-market foods are hard to find. Yacht chandlery supplies have improved except in the less developed islands, but are not cheap. Repairs can be undertaken at Antigua and Grenada, where there are boatyards with reasonable craftsmen, slipways, and berths with electricity for a self-refit.

So we wrote in the last edition. In 2004, Hurricane Ivan devastated Grenada (for a good report see *Yachting World*, November 2004) which was supposed to be impossible as Grenada was thought to be below the hurricane belt. Even underwriters thought so and they are a suspicious lot. Well, it isn't so any more. A book like this can never be up to the minute. For the latest news the magazines are the only source.

From the pictures in *Yachting World* of the devastation, one must question the wisdom of laying up yachts with their masts stepped, no matter where in the world. Laying-up seasons always have the worst weather. Elsewhere, we post a picture of yachts blown over in the Med. When not actually sailing, the mast is a sore thumb sticking up and is a nuisance.

Mail from Britain or the USA to the Caribbean Islands is generally quite good. Air communications are very good and air freight is recommended for parcels. European flights go regularly to Antigua, Barbados, Grenada, Trinidad and the French islands; and the smaller inter-island air services are busy and efficient, if sometimes a little hair-raising. Landing on Union Island or St Bart's is not for the faint-hearted. It is as well to have medical insurance with a repatriation clause in the West Indies because facilities in the islands are limited.

Diesel fuel is conveniently obtained in only a few places, but as the wind is so reliable, pleasant and free, diesel does not loom large in most people's minds. The most convenient points that we found were at Grenada (St George's), Martinique, English Harbour and St Thomas. If a really large amount of fuel is needed, go to Venezuela, where it is extremely cheap.

The weather is pleasant during the European winter. The temperatures are moderated by the tradewind, which is usually about force 4 but does rise occasionally especially in certain channels. The most we recorded in one winter was force 6 off Kick 'em Jenny, near Grenada, where the seas were also unusually disturbed. It rains every few days, usually a sharp shower which should be used for topping-up tanks, for fresh water is not easy to get in quantity. During this season hurricanes hardly hever happen.

In summer the weather is not so pleasant, but to compensate there are fewer tourists. The weather is hotter, wetter, a bit more capricious, and hurricanes do happen though they are not by any means an everyday event. The old rhyme tells you when they start:

> *'June too soon,*
> *July by and by,*
> *August you must,*
> *September remember,*
> *October it's over.'*

Not scientifically reliable but a rule of thumb. The global warming industry tells us that it will become more and more unreliable. Already, on 18 June, 1982, we were damaged in Hurricane Alberto farther north, off Bermuda. If you are in the Caribbean there is a wealth of local knowledge, of hurricane holes in which to get secure, and what precautions to take. These matters are out of the scope of this book; my hurricane experiences (two) have both been well offshore; the best place to be, we think, in a good boat. It is quite another thing close to land.

One thing I would offer on the subject of lying to anchors in a hurricane hole. Though I have never ridden a hurricane out while at anchor, I have ridden out some pretty violent storms, and this is where having your mast(s) in tabernacles is a real advantage. The windage of a stepped mast is enormous (wind power increases quite sharply with height) and tends to be well forward causing sheering about at anchor. If the mast(s) can be lowered in good time, and made fast securely, the yacht will have probably less than half the frontal windage and will be better balanced. She'll stand a much better chance, and you won't need the sails for the time being: believe me, you ain't a-going to sail anywhere during the blow.

Well out to sea, the winds are steadier, the seas tend to be longer, lower (except in the dangerous semi-circle) and more predictable, one does not notice the rise in sea level caused by the extraordinarily low atmospheric pressure, a rise that builds up as it approaches shallower water and causes the celebrated tidal wave (which is not tidal at all), and one has plenty of searoom.

In these waters, charts and navigational publications are hard to get. For electronic or technical repairs, I found English Harbour a good centre. Most services can be contacted on VHF. In fact, in the West Indies, almost everyone can be contacted on VHF: Sam Taxi, the scuba shops, the restaurants, and even hairdressers. Some restaurants make a general call on channel 16 to inform all stations that their menu for tonight is on channel 68, and bookings can also be taken thus. The radio is seldom silent, but on the whole the system functions very well: it is because everyone uses the radio that one finds it useful in a way not possible in over-regulated Europe (especially in Britain) or the USA. The radio discipline is better than on Long Island Sound or in the Solent at the weekend.

As one goes farther west the cruising gets less congenial. Big money dominates the Virgin Islands scene, and prices rise. By the time you reach St Thomas you are in an American city and the supermarkets are well stocked, but the people lack the good manners of the poorer islands, and crime rates are higher. The welcome is often still good, but there is something missing.

The US Navy makes a nuisance of itself (quite unnecessarily) exercising north of Puerto Rico. Cuba used to be off-limits for British insurers, but I expect this is changing. I have not been to Jamaica recently, but have heard reports that it is not currently advisable.

One reads a lot of alarmist articles in magazines about piracy, violence and robbery, and we discussed our views on this in Chapter 11.

If you are required to leave a boat, say for an emergency visit home, the marina in St George's, Grenada has good security; alternatively there are facilities in English Harbour. Up-market marinas, at up-market prices, exist in Antigua, Tortola, and St Thomas and St Lucia.

CHRISTMAS IN THE WINDWARD ISLANDS

We lay at anchor in the big sheltered bay of a small island. An occasional sharp blow from the wrong direction needed prudence to watch neighbouring yachts keenly in case their crew were ashore when we all changed places like the crossover sequence in a barn dance. Mostly, however, the weather was warm and lazy, we rowed ashore daily for brown loaves freshly baked in a wood shingled cabin. A covey of boys would 'watch your dinghy, man,' for a copper or two if instead of hauling it up the beach at the Frangipani, you hitched it to the wooden staithe that led on to the open space where, if anything was for sale, it would be sold. Had someone killed a pig, landed some bonefish, or brought in some vegetables?

Apart from this when-it-happens-man market there were round this space a small, simple grocery store not much bigger than a garage, an everything shop mainly for tourists, and a tiny Barclays' Bank. The Frangipani was a restaurant-bar kept by the Prime Minister with a few rooms to stay in and a sandy dance floor by the beach. It was also the yachtie's mail drop, which gave us an excellent excuse, 'just going for the mail . . .' and there was a complex of chalets for tourists further round the bay. That was about it.

If you wanted serious Christmas shopping you took the schooner to the big island, a wet and windy passage lasting an hour and a half. You went early, and were back by 13.30, offloaded all the packages, boxes and parcels for the grocery store and the bar. Frozen chicken took its chance in the hold with everything else, and was slightly defrosted when it arrived, to be refrozen as quickly as possible in the store's minute freezer. Nobody suffered from eating it.

Dark came at six. After a carol procession in dinghies round the fleet, singing in about six languages, the lamplight gold against the velvet blue star-sprinkled sky we rowed ashore in shorts on Christmas Eve for rum punch, barbecued New York strip steak, and a jump-up to the island's steel band.

• *Westbound across the Atlantic – the easy way* •

Go south till the butter melts then turn right, there is not much more to it. If leaving Gibraltar, it is better to wait for a *levanter* (east wind) but that often brings poor weather generally. If you are coming from the north, it usually pays to keep well out, and you can sometimes carry the Portuguese trades almost down to the Canary Islands.

Most yachts call at the Canaries, a good place to store ship before crossing, and there can be quite a social scene there in November. The tradewind belt moves north in winter, and it is better to wait for it to establish itself up to 15° N or so, which usually happens in November, but you should never timetable these things if you want to have fun. The wind then increases, and by January is much stronger. If going to the Caribbean for a long stay, it might be worth spending a couple of months in the Canaries, or making a diversion to the Cape Verde Islands.

Only freak weather should disturb the easy tedium of the transatlantic passage. The occasional squall enables everyone to strip off and have a free shower, but make sure there is enough rain to wash the soap off before putting it on.

For the nervous, competitive, or extremely sociable, there is the ARC (Atlantic Rally for Cruisers).

• *The Bahamas* •

Moving northwestwards from the Caribbean Islands, you come to the Bahamas, another independent ex-British colony. It was peopled largely by loyalists from the revolting American colonies about 1778 and these white people with their black slaves were the forebears of many of the present inhabitants. In the north, the Abacos, much of the populace are so firmly Nonconformist that you might imagine you were in Scotland. You might, but it would be difficult, for the weather and scenery are very different. The Bahamas are flat, palm-clad, sandy islands set on a series of broad shallow banks penetrated by the odd deep-water tongue of ocean. The local industries are tourism and drug-dealing, but the latter is a closed shop and the participation of amateurs from outside is much resented and dangerous. It can still be dangerous so if you innocently see something you shouldn't, be tactful, and rather short-sighted.

The southern islands are more remote and less densely populated, with scope for some very quiet cruising, though provisions take some looking for. The northern islands are close to Florida and have large numbers of shorter term visitors. There is a bay called No Name Bay south of Miami which we selected as a good dawn jumping-off place for a day sail to the Bahamas: so did half a hundred others. The Florida Channel between that state and the Bahamas is one of the busiest waterways in the world, with some very long commercial multi-barge tows using it, and it merits some care when crossing, especially at night.

The Bahamas are islands where souvenirs are few and an artist/craftsman could earn a bit, but the cost of living, being so dependent on nearby Florida, is high.

The Islands ought to be prosperous. The currency is at par with the US dollar, but there are local notes in circulation, as well as American ones. The officials are pleasant, courteous, but not noticeably industrious or efficient. Communications are good with Florida, and then from Miami are excellent. Mail and telephone services seemed to be good. The banking system, where it is of British or Canadian origin, is above average.

The other sort of banks, the coral ones, require care. Paradoxically, the old British charts are the best. One of these, No. 1496, was engraved in 1844 with the last new edition in 1907 and its detail is first class. I occupied myself for some time with checking several of the areas of the banks, and though there were some differences I would say that if used with a little prudence and common sense, this chart is infinitely preferably to the US chart of recent publication. But any chart cannot cope unaided. The latest supplement to the British Admiralty Pilots should be carried, but even better are some of the recently published yachtsmen's guides. The *Chart Kits* published in Needham, Massachusetts by the Better Boating Association are a good investment and based on US government charts. They are cheap, too.

Care should be taken when using GPS in conjunction with older charts. We don't have to emphasise this, do we?

There are several places to leave a yacht in the Bahamas, but none of them are ideal and many are over-expensive. Unless one's departure is very urgent (in which case Marsh Harbour suggests itself), it would be better to head for Florida, a short trip away. There one finds every possible facility.

• *Northbound from the Caribbean* •

If bound for Florida it is better to go south of the Bahamas Islands. There are some doubts about the surveys east of the Bahamas; ever since a flag officer of the Royal Cruising Club was wrecked there the charts have been assumed to be wrong.

Seriously, though, there have been quite a few yachts lost in those parts; one should think carefully before closing the low-lying banks. Whether the charts are wrong, or there are unrecorded strong currents, I do not know; nor, I suspect, does anyone else yet. It is not one of the most important bits of ocean.

If bound for the Bermudas, it is as well to start from east of Puerto Rico to be reasonably expectant of a reach. There are no problems. The Bermudas are well lit and clear of off-lying dangers to the south.

Heading to the USA from the Bermudas ought not to be difficult, though we once took 12 days for the 630 miles. I know from bitter experience that this is a passage where one should take a lot of care about the weather. Excellent forecasts are broadcast from Portsmouth, Virginia by voice on SSB, and some of them are in English. The others are in what my American friend called 'Dixie'.

One of the important features of these forecasts is the relaying of the positions of the edges of the Gulf Stream. This ocean-going river flows at up to 3 knots in this part of the world and makes a lot of difference to a yacht's course made good. The edges are well defined: the northern edge particularly can be recognised with some exactitude by observing the sea-water temperature, which will fall several degrees in a few hours when bound northwards out of the stream. Because of the current flow, very nasty seas can build up when the wind is opposite this current. Gales from the northeast quadrant can be particularly dangerous.

Watch out for fog in the colder waters approaching the New England coast. As soon as possible get the local weather forecasts from the special coastal VHF stations. Also beware of shipping bound to or from New York. There are off-lying dangers near the New England coast so do your homework first and carefully. Take note that by some administrative lunacy, the offshore buoys off Nantucket, that would be so useful for a position check in bad weather, all have the same light characteristic: flashing white, every 4 seconds.

If having left Bermuda you are tempted to return for any reason, then consider very carefully before doing so. The off-lying reefs to the northwest of the islands are dangerous; and very dangerous in bad weather, being poorly lit and comparatively steep-to.

THE EAST COAST OF THE USA

There are many people who spend their lives cruising the Intra-Coastal Waterway between Chesapeake Bay and the Florida Keys. The Chesapeake is a bay of great size, which can get very rough on occasions but has many delightful places to visit: Washington, which has been largely rebuilt by the industrious natives since my ancestors burnt it; Annapolis, the home of the US Naval Academy; Jamestown, St Michael's, Oxford and Cambridge. Some of these places are as delightful as their prototypical English towns.

The Florida Keys are a string of islands connected by a causeway, extending round into the Gulf of Mexico. Very low-lying, and dangerous in severe storms.

The Intra-Coastal does extend north of the Chesapeake, as far as New York (where we moored in the middle of Manhattan for less than the price of a hotel room), but the depths are not sufficient for most sea-going sailing craft.

It is superfluous to say much about the USA. The natives are friendly: however terrifying they may be as tourists, on their home ground they are charming, hospitable hosts, generous and efficient, with a vast and constant appetite for apparently tasteless food. But the country changes. The west shore of the Chesapeake, close to Washington, is rich, sophisticated and comparatively crowded. Progressing southward through the backwoods (literally) of South Carolina or Georgia, one finds people of less material wealth, and many of those at the supermarket checkouts are on welfare.

The Waterway country is evocative of the Norfolk Broads on a vast scale, with trees, reeds, herons, bitterns, flat country, estuaries and a similar state of mind

*The Intra-Coastal Waterway between Chesapeake Bay and the Florida Keys
provides delightful cruising: indeed some live-aboards love it so much that they
never leave. It is also used by some giant barges.*

among the local people. It is sometimes a long way between settlements; there are
remote anchorages, quiet and beautiful, oysters for the gathering, strong tides
and many bridges which open very efficiently; the fixed ones have a minimum
high water clearance of 65 feet (except for one at Miami, which can be avoided by
a short hop at sea).

There is only one lock: at Great Bridge in Virginia. The water in the Waterway
is spread very wide, but it is shallow. A draught of 2 metres (6ft 6in) is pushing
the limit, and one must expect to touch bottom occasionally, especially near the
southernmost inlets.

Provisioning is often difficult as in most US communities all the stores are now
in out-of-town shopping malls, approachable only on wheels. For this reason
some isolated marinas have a (sometimes rather battered) 'courtesy car' which
one may borrow free for local use.

The bigger yachting centres are crowded and made hideous by speeding water-
hogs in fast power boats; which makes the southern part of Florida's waters less
attractive. But there are plenty of good marinas where one can leave a boat to do
some touring, and good facilities everywhere for hauling out and refitting.

American marinas are different from those we have become accustomed to in
Europe. The mega-marina does exist, of course, and is very much better run than
its European counterpart, but the typical US marina is a comparatively small
family affair, often with only 30 to 50 berths, sometimes a little scruffy but almost
always with a real, friendly welcome.

The climate is surprising. In winter, southern Florida is pleasant, but from St Augustine northward expect some cold spells. It can be bitterly cold in North Carolina. In summer, the whole area is hot and humid and has the world's biggest and hungriest mosquitoes. Spring and autumn are delightful.

US officials vary. We found Customs officers everywhere to be courteous, helpful and on the ball. The Immigration people were appallingly aggressive. Check for visa requirements. Sometimes needed, often not, the US administration are volatile and apparently given to occasional bouts of xenophobic panic. Live-aboard yachties do not rate that highly on the scale of visitor desirability. We are familiar with this feeling world-wide: persons of *no fixed abode*, such as us, whose boats may well be far more valuable than a house, are vagrants, gypsies, chicken-stealers, with no credit rating, and only a short way off being responsible for all the looting, pillage and rape reported to the local police. But let's not get carried away on that hobby-horse.

Do not fall into the trap of regarding US Customs or the US Coast Guard as merely benevolent nannies to the large number of incompetent skippers who crash from mishap to ineptitude on the coast. There is massive drug smuggling through the creeks and inlets of the Intra-Coastal, and the Waterway is well patrolled. The Coast Guard, though apparently staffed entirely by teenagers, is very much on the alert. They run the rescue service, maintain navigation marks, and keep watch on channel 16 and also on 22A, which foreign vessels do not have. The US Coast Guard seemed to be permanently confused about our failure to reply on this channel. Note that several VHF channels have different user designations in the USA.

Older European mobile phones do not work, but we are told that T3 and better phones will.

Buoyage is different, adhering to IALA System B. Well, it would be, wouldn't it? Whoever imagined Uncle Sam would accept what the rest of the world think reasonable. It's a wonder they accept the Collision Regulations. Come to think of it, some of their motor-boaters clearly do not.

The electricity supplied from shore in most marinas is another oddity. Voltage is 110V, alternating current of 60 cycles instead of 50.

The regulations against pollution are strict, and in the case of yacht heads and holding tanks are so draconian as to be unenforceable. There being no pump-out stations, ordinary marine heads may be used at sea. I understand the whole situation is under review, when some of the ecological over-enthusiasm may be tempered with realism. On the Great Lakes, and in the canals and lakes north of New York where there is little outlet of water to the sea, the situation is different and the laws are enforced with vigour. There, marine heads may not be discharged overboard.

A brief word about the north, though these waters are not really our province as the sailing season is so short. Cruising the New England coast is delightful, though it does require alertness and good navigation because of the strong tidal streams, especially farther north, and the frequency of fog. Navigation marks are good and facilities are excellent. In fact the whole of the US coast is good cruising, and the people badly need to meet a few foreigners.

SUMMER IN RHODE ISLAND

We arrived in the dead of night, battered from the hurricane we had been through a week before, just north of Bermuda. We felt our way towards America in thick fog. The Coast Guard plane that had been sent out to find us had flown north/south at our request, to give us a compass check. That was after we'd told him we needed no assistance, but which way was America, please, as our compass had been shot in the lightning strike which unkindly followed the hurricane, and the sky had been too overcast to take sights. The fog hid the light of the harbour of refuge at Point Judith till we were only a mile or two away. We crept in and with utmost thankfulness dropped anchor at two in the morning.

When we woke we found ourselves surrounded by lobster pots, and had some difficulty getting out, now we knew they were there. Newport was dressed overall, bands playing and crowded with people, all waving. 'Nice welcome,' we said. Then we found ourselves in the middle of the start of the America's Cup, so it wasn't for us after all.

There could be no doubt about the welcome that we got at Avondale when we brought our crew Nora home next day. We would be there for months repairing our wounded boat, and were never wanting for company, loan of a car or a television, entertainment, or a hot dish supper.

• *Eastbound over the Atlantic* •

The most common route is via the Bermudas and the Azores. The passage to Bermuda poses few difficulties that we have not already discussed in the reverse direction. From Bermuda head northeast until the latitude of 40°N is reached, then steer along the parallel until a couple of days or so west of the Azores. The popular time for this voyage is May/June and then the weather will not be hot: often it is jersey weather all the way, and the winds can be variable and sometimes irritatingly light. There is always a chance of some strong winds, but most of the severe depressions should pass well to the north. (I do not guarantee that.)

Shipping is mostly light, especially compared with the yacht traffic in May or June when something like 150 yachts arrive in the Azores each month from the west. The Azores are an easy landfall, and a very impressive one after some 18 days at sea. Nevertheless they have been missed completely; I do not know how, but they have. The welcome is good and the living is cheap. From the Azores to Gibraltar, Portugal or the English Channel presents no special problems in the summer months.

THE MEDITERRANEAN SEA

We have referred to the changes that have taken place in the live-aboard world. The principal one is that proportionally fewer new-comers to the way of life are setting out for the tropics and very large numbers are heading for the Med. Not all are contemplating permanent peripatetic residence in a boat. Many want to spend only the summer on board (the swallows, we call them), and others are planning to live on board and cruise only until they find the ideal villa. Some have no intention of cruising at all. The boat becomes a houseboat aboard which they live while taking advantage of the liberal labour regulations in the EU.

The numbers coming in these several categories have multiplied many-fold in the past five years and this has reflected in the increased sales of previous editions of *Sell Up and Sail*. It is almost exclusively the British who are responsible for this rapid expansion. Other nationalities have always lived on board too, but their total numbers haven't changed that much, except for the Swedes. And, would you believe it, Sweden is the only European country to have published a translation of *Sell Up and Sail*. Well!

The Americans have mostly disappeared; only the hardy and level-headed remain, knowing that their exposure to the terrorism their President promises is less likely to take place in the yacht cruising grounds of Europe than in an American city.

What has come over the British? Laurel has done a survey of a substantial number of live-aboards we have met over the past three years and she will discuss this later.

Because of the phenomenal increase in new-comers to the Med, we will go more deeply into it, especially as the whole northern shore, with the exception of former Yugoslavia, is in the EU, and Turkey wants to join. So do both Croatia and Serbia but they have to turn over their war criminals first and, as they regard them as heroes, that will take time. Even North Africa has become more friendly. This leaves only the palpable hatred surrounding Israel and maybe things will improve there soon. A few Israeli yachts are seen cruising, but they dare not fly their country's flag.

In the EU, we were supposed to have freedom of movement, but that does not seem to apply to yachts. Or only in theory. In practice, various nations which depend to a large extent on the income from tourists, find all sorts of nasty little ways to irritate visitors.

We have long pointed out that in a car we may cross frontiers without even stopping. By contrast, in a boat at some frontiers *wholly within the EU*, one can sometimes spend two hours of bureaucratic meddling by heavy-handed jobs-worths. Bill recently spent three days at Brussels pleading for all this to change. We do not expect to live long enough. He says he has never encountered a more blinkered and self-satisfied bunch of idle bums. They make the British Civil Service seem positively entrepreneurial. On the way home Bill threatened to join the UKIP. He won't. He hasn't voted since the 1960s.

Mediterranean countries seem occasionally to go mad and throw all sorts of oppressive measures at visiting yachtsmen. They seem to take it in turns, which keeps us all on the move. Greece is always on the edge of administrative chaos alternating with bouts of xenophobia. But the last countries to throw their weight about were Portugal and Spain. Mostly the problems are based on whether one is or is not a resident; the taxman demands a pound of flesh if he decides one is. As the rules of residence are not standardised (why not: practically everything else is?) the whole subject is dogged by capricious officials. Never mind, the joys of the area outweigh the irritations.

The Med is a wholly different cruising ground to those we have discussed. History and scenic beauty rather than the quality of the sailing are the chief attractions. Generally navigation in small craft is not congenial to most people in December to March, and should be indulged with caution also in November and April. It is around the equinoxes that conditions become especially capricious, and quite like British weather. Depressions that come in from the Atlantic are deflected at the last minute, and forecasts become unreliable. In high summer the weather is usually dry and stable. Winds over much of the Med are characteristically moderate then, though there are places where usable winds are good.

We have often cruised the Med in winter, and we have not been alone. There are always a number of antipodean boats coming up through Suez, and some of these are on a limited time world cruise, so that they do not want to lay up for long. They form the nucleus of winter cruisers, and we have had some good social times out of season, sharing off-beat moorings with some very congenial fellow wanderers. This is what it is all about.

The Strait of Bonifacio, and the Sicilian Channel particularly close to Cape Bon, have predominantly west winds and east-going currents. In the Aegean, the

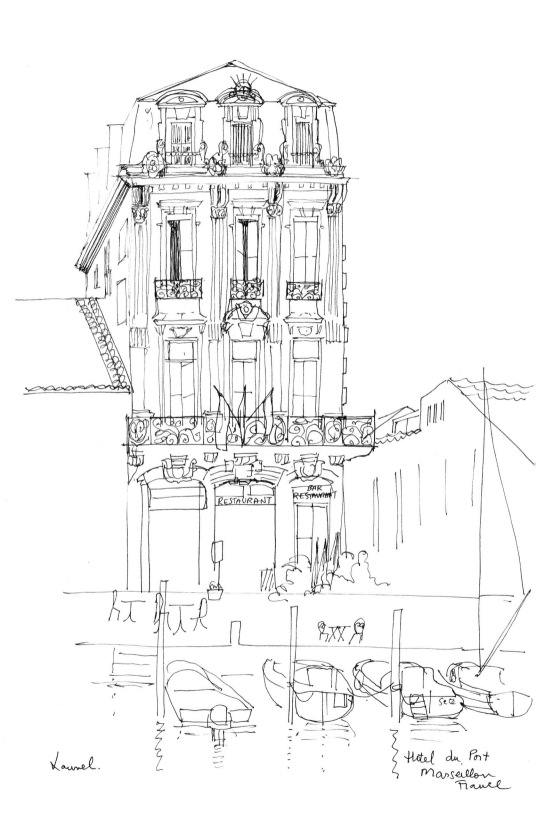

Laurel.

Hotel du Port
Marseillon
France

Greece rates highly on our list of good cruising grounds. Here we have anchored
Hosanna *at Sounion and climbed up to the temple to admire the view.*

summer (Etesian) wind, often called by its Turkish name *meltemi*, can blow for
three or four months from between northwest and northeast, sometimes reach-
ing gale force, when ferry and even air services are interrupted. A particularly
troublesome bit of sea, winter or summer, is the Gulf of Lions. (In 1958, HMS
Cumberland of 12,000 tons suffered almost a million pounds worth of damage
there in one god-awful night.) It is not so much the wind strength that causes
problems to the small-craft navigator in the Med; there is often a very short and
steep sea going with it, and it is this which does the damage and causes acute discomfort. Even to ships with a 23 feet freeboard.

We do not think we need to go into all the Mediterranean countries in detail
because, since writing the original edition, there are now many adequate guides
(I hesitate, as a one-time professional, to call some of them 'pilots', but that is letting my prejudices hang out), so we will confine our comments to generalisations
that are relevant to live-aboards. In addition, because we have spent the last two
years in Greek waters, we will go into that in more detail later on as a sort of
sample.

The welcome for live-aboards has changed somewhat over the past few years, but the increase in the numbers of live-aboards is not the reason for the cooler welcome. Very often live-aboards or long-term cruisers have pioneered yachting tourism in less frequented parts of the Med, and others have followed us. Easily accessible cruising grounds, such as the Riviera, have long been well-known, over-crowded and expensive.

For many years the difficulties of private yachting for short periods, such as are available to the ordinary family who have to work for a living, were such as to limit the number of yachts. This started to change with the flotillas which frankly saturated the more congenial places such as the smaller Ionian Islands. These holiday-makers, who were not always well-behaved, changed the local culture during the summer. Tavernas changed their style, their menu, their service, and their prices. People on a short-term holiday have, comparatively, money to burn. But it was the sheer numbers that tried to crowd into tiny little ports with no regard for local feelings that caused the problems. A few local people have profited, but many have seen their home villages spoiled for no personal gain. And so the yachtsman as a class has become unwelcome in some places, or at least not as welcome as was once the case.

SPRING IN THE IONIAN

In the little harbour of Vathi in Meganisi one Easter weekend, the local people prepared to enjoy their celebrations, which are as important to them as Christmas is to Nordic communities. There were two live-aboard yachts there, a German boat, and ourselves, both of us long known to local families. We had been invited into the church, where Laurel helped to polish the brasses soon to emerge from the black shrouds of Lent, and Bill watched a young lad being coaxed to pass on hands and knees beneath the *epitaphios* that stood in the midst of the church, to bring him good fortune for the coming year. The *epitaphios*, a symbolic bier decorated with flowers symbolising the crucifixion, is processed around the harbour on Good Friday. This is the solemn climax to a long and bitter fast, during the 42 days of which many will eat only pulses, seeds and bread, no meat, fish, cheese, eggs, not even olive oil. The butcher goes on holiday.

In the midst of the procession, two separate flotillas arrived unexpectedly. The local population of about a hundred, marking the last days of a rigorous and austere Lent, was overwhelmed by a noisy invasion of about the same number, their shouts drowning the plainsong and their skimpy holiday clothes looking crude and tasteless beside the decorous black of the worshippers. The flotilla leaders were outrageously unsympathetic, encouraging their punters to push their way in to photograph the procession.

After dark, Judas is burnt in effigy, spouting fireworks. Of course, this is like Guy Fawkes, fun for everybody, and the flotillas were welcome to join in. The taverna owners and staff however were unable to do so; they had not yet opened for the season, they had had no advance warning and were frantically rushing around organising a scratch meal for an unwelcome and demanding group.

The hordes left for elsewhere next morning, and the island enjoyed Easter in peace. At midnight, the cry of 'Christos anesti!' went up in complete darkness. A match flared in the church, the altar lamp was lit, and from it candle after candle lit and twinkled, one person to another, becoming a rivulet of light spreading round the harbour and up the hill, as folk reached home and the windows lit up. If you can get your candle home alight, and mark a cross in smoke on your door, your year will be good. As the church was on the quay, we didn't have far to go.

Next morning we were invited to share kokkoretsi and scarlet eggs for Easter breakfast, and help spit-roast the lamb for later in the day. As we turned the spit, the villagers told us that they might ask the harbour to be closed to flotillas for Easter the next year.

While it is true that certain centres pose comparative overcrowding problems for those of us who were lucky enough to enjoy the Med in its uncrowded days, when it was much cheaper to live there than now, it is noticeable that the new-comer is still as enchanted by the life as we have been. So the harbours of the Balearics are overcrowded but, apart from the very high season, there is still pleasure to be had. Likewise in Greece.

We know of certain places in high season where the charterers do not get to. They are not necessarily as beautiful or convenient as the better-known spots, but they are often cheaper. No, we will not publish a list of our own secret places, but if you take to this life, and go to the Med for a long stay, you will get to know them. During the winters, when the yachties foregather, the word gets round. We are quite a strong, but friendly, union.

The cost of living has risen in the popular cruising grounds. Mainly this is due to the Common Market, the EEC or the EU.

> *It escapes no blame*
> *by changing its name.*

Things have not necessarily been all for the better as Brussels has come to the poorer parts of the Med. There has been, it is true, massive hand-outs to backward communities, but in the best Med tradition, these have often created a few millionaires, rather than benefiting the whole population. With Brussels has come more imports: marvellous! You can now buy packets of Krokkiweet on the tiniest island, but with it has come better packaging of everything, therefore much more rubbish, and higher prices.

Whereas prices in Greece and Turkey were once much the same, since Greece has been in the EU, her prices have risen to a much higher level. Nowadays the cheaper places are the less sophisticated non-EU countries, such as Turkey and

We meet . . . raft up and have a party before sailing on.

North Africa. In the latter case it is as well not to visit Algeria owing to their tendency to kill foreigners to teach them a lesson. Egypt is also not wholly secure, but Tunisia and Morocco will give you a good welcome, though the climate is desperately hot in summer.

The Dalmatian coast of Yugoslavia, as was, is getting back to normal; the boats returning are for the most part German or Austrian. Alone of the northern yachting countries, Germany and Austria (is there any real difference?) are close enough to ex-Yugoslavia for people to pour over the Brenner pass for a long weekend provided the boat is in Croatia. There are good marinas in Croatia and in 2003 they were cheaper than in Greece. Opinions differ, but there are often reports of surly officials, and this matters because they are not full members of the EU. We recall also, that Croatia was largely responsible for the break-up of Yugoslavia with its concomitant genocide.

As examples, we give comparative marina costs (in euros) for typical marinas in Croatia, Greece, and Turkey. Assume a yacht of 12 metres LOA.

Marina	All year	Winter only
Croatia	2000 to 4500	approx 2400
Greece	3080	1440
Turkey	2304	1257

NB. In all cases, the price includes electricity (up to 15 amps) and water. The prices are not for any particular marina, but they are our own attempt to get a comparison. Note too that in the eastern Med, one can usually do a deal in an under-used marina.

Military matters cannot be ignored further east. Insurers prefer yachts to keep west of longitude 33° East unless an extra premium is paid. This puts a strain on visiting Israel and Syria. All is not exactly rosy west of this meridian, Greece and Turkey are making real efforts to bury the hatchets (2004). Each country sent teams to help in each other's earthquakes recently. The Cyprus situation looks as far as ever from resolution, but membership of the EU, with access to the obscenely large hand-outs to Mediterranean countries, seems to have concentrated minds. It is likely that Cyprus and Turkey will soon reach agreement. One lesson the Greeks have been slow to learn is that they cannot push Turkey around, because if they do: Wham! Perhaps an end to this squabbling is one of the major benefits of the EU. Dammit, there must be some.

• *Wintering* •

The Med climate is cold on winter nights, even if sunny at lunchtime. Greatcoat weather in places like Malta during the *gregale* (NE gale). Most people like to find a good, cheap, safe berth to endure winter. Many try to find work, and this is possible within the EU countries for EU citizens. Most have maintenance to do, perhaps a short trip back to the homeland to see how Mum is, or the grandchildren are getting on. An extension of a previously mentioned problem is that many of the best winter berths are nowadays filled with laid-up bare-boats, most of which finish their season early enough to occupy the more congenial and safer parts of the harbour, doing nothing for the local economy for months on end. Further secure berths are pre-empted by those yachties who have given up all pretence to cruise any more and who have taken a job ashore and use their boats only as fixed houseboats (this last is a noticeable product of the relaxation of restrictive labour laws within the EU).

WINTER IN THE ARGOLIS PENINSULA

We are in a huge sheltered bay; on one side is a long quay, partly occupied by fishing boats and the tourist *caiques* laid up until next season. In the middle of the bay, dozens of yachts are anchored, most of them stripped for the winter and laid up until spring. There's room at the quay for eight or ten yachts which have crews on board. Some of these earn a little by working for the local boatyard on the boats laid up. We see each other daily, often in the local store, or at the post office (a portakabin on the quay), sometimes aboard each other's boats, casually for the day temperature is pleasantly warm and there is work going on. The tourist shops have closed till spring, and so have many of the bars and restaurants, but Manoli's one-storey taverna under galvanised roofing never closes. On Sundays that's where we meet at lunchtime. We sit outside if it is sunny, Manoli clucks and tsks because he thinks it's too cold, and we have to bring the chairs out ourselves. Tough, us northerners. We are English, Scots, German, and Dutch. We swap stories and info. Some of the local ex-pats join in – the boatier sort. We drink Amstel beer or Manoli's homemade wine (the taste is something else, and has to be acquired). Invitations for the coming week are given and exchanged, a midday barbecue is feasible, a run to the local county town, or even to Athens, in someone's car. We eat *patatas tiganitas* (fries, the best in the country, Manoli says) and plates of *marithaki* (large whitebait). Our lunch, most of it liquid, costs us about 80p a head ($1.20), pretty affordable, that. Home, then for the more energetic, a walk round the bay with a dog, perhaps. For us, back on board for a feet-up until dusk when we might need to light a driftwood fire as the sun goes down. There are no newspapers in winter; we entertain ourselves with a book of crosswords, a paperback from the last swap session, and music from Greek Radio 3.

More and more general harbours are using EU subsidies to turn themselves into up-market (comparatively speaking) mini-marinas which, in Greece at any rate, charge local boats a preferential rate at the expense of the foreign tourist, for the attraction of whom the EU money was originally intended.

But one gets by. The chosen wintering ports change. And it has to be admitted that there is a type of live-aboard who does tend to foul the communal nest. Most of us tend to overlap onto the quay a bit, even if only temporarily while repairing something, for all live-aboard boats are encumbered. Some turn the quay into a junkyard. Others fall ill and cannot readily move on, or run out of funds and owe money, leading to their boat going rapidly downhill; as a class we have our share of personal disasters, and there is no welfare system to come and help.

In 1995/6, for example, many boats left Greek waters for Tunisia and Turkey, where they were made welcome. Greece had introduced an exorbitant scale of charges which led to open harassment by their Port Police (I have already referred to the incident of painting the guardrails), and though the worst effects were ameliorated, many found that a winter in Tunisia was a lot cheaper, the weather as well as the welcome was warmer.

• *Documents and nautical qualifications* •

We were taken to task by some readers of the first edition who had not yet set off deep cruising, for saying little about this subject, and several people at the early cruising symposiums, which we initiated, were clearly troubled by it. (Bill has never considered taking the Yachtmaster® Certificate, as a Master mariner with a lifelong experience in sail. Laurel has no certificates at all, bar the Ship Captain's Medical Training Certificate, and Coastal Navigation (Theory) from the National Sailing School.)

There is a simple reason why we said nothing about it. Apart from the ex-communist bloc countries, documentation has never given us any real bother and we didn't think the subject merited space. Now (2005) we can say that it merits less space than ever, especially in the Med, where EU citizens can cruise about EU countries' waters with few formalities, rather in the same way that Americans can cruise from state to state in the USA. Except when some local bureaucratic idiot temporarily upsets the applecart.

Even elsewhere, there is no point in going minutely into it country by country because the detailed rules are constantly changing. Please let us reassure readers who are planning their voyages: be sensible, but don't worry.

The requirements are different in virtually every country, and often in different ports within the same country. Ensure that the boat is properly registered in your own name, because boats registered in the name of companies in Panama, Guernsey, Gibraltar, etc can get into difficulties; this is often a signal of someone up to no good. Remember that Part One Registrations have to be renewed every five years at a cost of £50. If you do not do so, you will have to go through the ridiculous expense of taking out a new registration. Bureaucracy rules, OK. Keep the registrar informed of your contact address. He will issue a reminder.

If the boat is in your name, the formalities pertaining to the craft will give no trouble. They may take a long time, but time is not of the essence.

You can save time if you make out copies (several) of your crew list. These lists should not only have the names in full of everyone on board but also passport numbers, dates and places of birth, maiden names (and once we were asked for names, dates and places of birth of our parents too). Do not worry. Stay calm.

We know of a Frenchman who cruised his yacht with an old British registration certificate of a yacht that had been scrapped. (The administration of the Small Ship Register encourages this, but the RYA dismiss this glitch as unimportant.) He had renamed his boat to match. He never had any trouble. You, being honest and essentially law-abiding, are not going to have any either.

No one has, so far, *ever* checked the number carved on our main beam, to see if it matches the ship's papers.

I assume you have proper passports that are in date. I assume you have taken the precaution of getting a visa for those countries who are scared to let you in without one, or who wish to extract the maximum cash from your visit. I assume you have found out if any vaccinations or inoculations are required, both for yourselves and any pets, and that you have the appropriate certificates. It's all tedious on occasions, but really quite simple. Do not worry.

If planning to go to both Israel and Arab countries, or if you wish to go to Northern (Turkish occupied) Cyprus and also want to go to Southern Cyprus or Greece afterwards, then you can get a second passport in advance if you tell the passport office what you want to do. Greece cannot refuse entry under EU law to an EU citizen but they can be difficult. Don't mix the passports up, keep one for the sheep and the other for the goats.

Hosanna *leaves the massive lock at Gabçikovo on the Danube in Slovakia.*
Photo: Captain Brinkmann.

Be careful about giving passage to persons of countries that are regarded as 'difficult' in the country you are heading for. Even this is not as bad as it sounds.

• *Stories* •

During the days when apartheid was at its worst, we arrived in Antigua with two South Africans on board in the days when the redoubtable Sergeant King was in charge of immigration there. Our friends wished to disembark and fly home. Within a short time, thanks to a friendly approach, our friends went ashore with the scourge of the Caribbean smiling happily and helping them with their baggage. People, even officials, are fundamentally approachable if you are tactful.

Some years ago, friends of ours embarked the young Greek boy-friend of their daughter for a short cruise and headed for Turkey without thinking. Their guest, when he discovered which harbour they were entering, was petrified. He expected to be decapitated or worse. The Turkish immigration officer told the quaking youngster he was very naughty to have come without a visa, then threw his arms round the boy's neck, kissed him and said 'Welcome to Turkey'. Well, he was a good-looking young lad.

Turkey now demands visas for Britons in retaliation for something they imagine Mrs Thatcher did to one of their diplomats' children. Visas can be obtained at the Port of Entry without any difficulty, and are more of an irritant than a penalty. Do not worry.

Most countries are beginning to demand evidence of third-party insurance cover. We rather approve of this. We advise getting a certificate in the local country's language from your insurers; ours (GJW) provide this automatically.

In all our cruising (except for ex-Iron Curtain countries) we have never been asked for documents issued by the port we have left, nor for de-ratting certificates, though once we were asked to produce evidence of good health. Any evidence. We wrote out our own certificate and stamped it with the ship's own 'official' stamp, which we put over the top of some left-over British postage stamps. It did the trick. Do not worry.

Check:

- Passports in date and visas.
- Boat registration.
- Boat insurance if applicable.
- Vaccinations and inoculations (including pets').
- Yachtmaster® Certificates or equivalent or better evidence of personal competence.
- If European, make sure you have VAT evidence.

Remember that people do arrive in the most awkward countries improperly documented and still have a good time, provided they are not aggressive or tactless. So do not worry.

We have made certain exempting clauses with respect to ex-Iron Curtain coun-

Eel setts in the Camargue, France.

tries. It is likely these will be visited more and more in the future, and as they have not yet adapted their systems to the notion of freedom of passage, especially in yachts, you may find some difficulties. These are often soluble by the gift of a bottle of wine: costing (in Romania, for example) 80 pence, and well worth it.

One meets more and more yachties coming from these countries. One, Andreu, from Moldova, told us hair-raising stories of the problems he had had getting permission to sail away from Odessa in the Ukraine in the boat he had built himself from government surplus items he had salvaged from the scrap-heap of an armament factory. (You do meet some interesting people in this mode of life.)

We have described in another book our experience of a recent impromptu visit to the port of Ismail in the Ukraine. They wouldn't let us enter the country, as we had no visas and could not go to Kiev to get them, but they were perfectly polite about it, and we could have obtained provisions and shelter if we had needed them. All we suffered was inconvenience. (They allowed our cats ashore without a visa.)

In Romania, on the other hand, the bureaucracy was labyrinthine and byzantine: crooked in both senses of the word. The moral is that if visiting a country whose border forces are subject to political paranoia, you will need to have both patience and papers in apple-pie order, and probably have to drop dollar notes into various palms as well. This last is more difficult. We cruise with a small wad of one dollar bills for use in these sorts of emergency. They are often of more use than a passport.

But *do not worry*.

Now, routeing (as opposed to routing, a different process altogether).

ROUTES

In previous editions we have included comments on various ocean routes that yachts use for getting from one area to another. There are nowadays many books going into this subject in more detail than we have space for. We think it better to leave the subject to them because, if you are serious to the point of going, you will want the detailed information.

Nonetheless, if you are doing your fireside planning long before setting out, it is as well to be aware of your first hurdle: that is getting away from Great Britain in the direction of warm waters with or without palm trees. Your choice at this stage will affect your yacht's dimensions and characteristics, or vice versa.

You will have the choice of an inland route via the European waterways, or the Bay of Biscay. Let's look at the latter choice first.

For a European, the first problem to be faced is getting away. If I say that a voyage direct to North America or the West Indies is contrary to the spirit of the casual wanderer, I think most readers will by now know what I mean. So, we rule out 30 days of beating westward into the winds of a series of depressions. This means that the first leg of a transatlantic voyage is south, not necessarily to Gibraltar, but in that direction.

This is also the open sea route to the Mediterranean. There are other ways of getting there, and they were mentioned in the chapter on inland waters. For the moment then let us look at a passage to Gibraltar or its vicinity.

• *The Bay of Biscay* •

Your first challenge (if you choose to accept it).

It is a sad fact of geography that the first ocean crossing which northern Europeans make on setting out is the Bay of Biscay, a difficult stretch of water for southbound sailing vessels. A sad fact also that if you, a cruiser climbing a learning curve, are plucked out of trouble by helicopter, your 15 minutes of fame will be attended by castigation, condemnation, little respect, and a week later total oblivion. Whereas a racing yachtsman (an expert who should know better), whose Southern Ocean rescue involves expenditure in megamillions, is treated as a hero and there will be a book and a film. It seems hard.

The reputation of the Bay of Biscay stems from the depressions that are characteristic of its weather patterns, causing strong westerly winds which blow craft into the bay. With a long gale, or a series of short ones in quick succession, the average yacht has difficulty not only in getting out of the Bay, but also in surviving the gale itself, for room to manoeuvre gets steadily less and less the more one is embayed. Further into the bay it shallows, making the seas steeper and more dangerous, and the last part of a typical gale has the wind from the north-west: the worst possible sector.

Sailing captains of old, leaving the English Channel in weather other than a set-fair anti-cyclone, would steer west until longitude 8° west, when they would turn south. It took longer, but that way they stood a fair chance of not becoming a statistic. It seems to us that cruising yachts manned by small inexperienced crews should think of doing something like that. Top quality yachts with huge crews of experienced gorillas do as they please, but families, especially with children, should play safe at the beginning of their world cruise.

An alternative is to coast to Cork in Ireland, getting gradually accustomed to the life and having shelter to run to if there is a bad forecast, and then start from there. They're lovely people in Cork, and it's well worth a visit.

In any event, keep well outside the Ushant traffic separation scheme and special tanker channel; it is better to double Ushant out of range of the Ushant light. You should do so even if the separation scheme were not in operation, because if bad weather comes, the wind is more likely to be west than any other, and it will almost certainly be accompanied by a current pushing a vessel into the Bay. Only experienced yachtsmen should attempt to pass inside Ushant.

The western coast of Spain is not a comfort zone in bad weather. I would pass down the Portuguese coast well out to sea, out of sight of land, and only close the coast near Cape St Vincent. This headland has a traffic separation scheme round it, which is of doubtful necessity and a hazard of itself. Sailing vessels should round this cape very close-to with an easterly wind, in which case they are obliged to foul the badly planned northbound lane, though there is seldom very much traffic. With a north-westerly wind, which is the most likely, it is well to stay off-shore out of the way of the northbound traffic; keep a good offing if bound for Gibraltar in order to avoid the Banks, for though there is depth for a yacht, the seas can be very unpleasant there.

The distance from Falmouth to Gibraltar is 1080 miles, and from Cork it is 1098 miles. Most cruising boats average between 100 and 130 miles per day. I had my best day's run ever in *Fare Well* southbound some 30 miles off the Portuguese coast, logging 190 miles with only 37 square metres of canvas set. But we still took 12 days for the passage because we were hove-to for 48 hours in a Bay of Biscay storm.

• *Bordeaux and the Canal du Midi to the Med* •

There remains the case of those who fancy sailing down to Bordeaux and then passing through the Canal du Midi to the Med. Unless you are experienced, with an experienced crew in a well tried boat, wait until the weather is set fair. The coast round the Gironde estuary is low-lying with offshore sandbanks. Of course you can coast hop, but it's not that easy.

• *Freighting your boat* •

Finally, a word about sending boats as freight. Transporting boats about Europe by truck is well-known, but one can also send boats, quite big ones, aboard ship. There are special ships running regular services.

Cost For example: a 12 × 4.50 metre boat, shipped transatlantic, would cost $19,000 each way with a 20% discount if paid up 5 months in advance. Under certain circumstances it is possible to travel with your boat. Consult Complete Freight at www.completefreight.net.

CRUISING IN COMPANY

It had (truly) never occurred to me, Bill, that anyone would be seriously nervous about an Atlantic crossing in the trade wind belt. It first came up when we invited a relative to come over with us in *Fare Well* in 1982. He brought his wife, a lovely lady, an experienced small-boat sailor, and a valuable member of the crew.

Halfway over, she appeared on deck with a face of thunder, and her shame-faced spouse was clearly in for some rough handling. It transpired that the only way he had been able to get her across the Atlantic was to tell her that we were making a short trip round the Canaries, as she thought an Atlantic crossing would be stormy. She had been shanghaied! Fortunately, it was a calm voyage; the only really rough bit had been between Gibraltar and Tenerife, running before a wild Levanter (east wind), which the lady hardly noticed.

Given that sort of feeling, we should have expected that someone would propose a transatlantic voyage in company. Jimmy Cornell, an experienced ocean sailor, started the series of Atlantic Rallies for Cruisers (the ARC) which, backed by *Yachting World*, have been a great success, and have pleased many people. We mentioned this briefly in the chapter on safety matters, but it is important enough for other aspects of it to crop up again.

We do not propose to carp at the ARC. We like to be on our own at sea, so it would not suit us. We like to pick our own ports of departure and arrival and, most important, take our own time. The fee for the ARC is substantial. Their brochure quotes £530 (2005) for a 12-metre yacht (plus £100 surcharge for multihulls) plus £50 per adult on board. The requirements for the gear to be carried are somewhat eccentric in places (a requirement to carry dressing lines of international code flags, for example, which do not come cheap). One must have Inmarsat or equivalent, which is very expensive. We also do not feel personally happy with a sort of military drill book impression that the brochure gives, though this may be more a matter of the organisers' lawyers covering their legal liabilities in this litigious age. A competitive atmosphere with prizes has grown more and more apparent over the years, though we understand that a decision has been taken to downplay this in future. Those caveats are our own personal views, and the fact that so many have enjoyed the experience indicates that there are many yachtsmen who welcome Jimmy's initiative. He has given pleasure to many. If you feel you would like that way of cruising, try www.worldcruising.com. The ARC is no longer run by Jimmy Cornell; it is now a commercial enterprise.

Another, eastbound, transatlantic rally is the ARC Europe, also run by the World Cruising Club. It is a similar set-up and we have similar feelings. Still . . . same website as above.

We comment on the safety/security aspect of the ARC in the chapter on Misadventures.

There have been other rallies on a 'round the world' basis, making several stops en route. One is called the Blue Water Rally. A rally of this scope has to be expensive and I have heard quoted £8500 + £500 per person. The circumnavigation takes just under two years, which seems to us to be a bit hectic. We feel that a slower boat might find it a bit of a strain. We would. There is specifically no racing and of that we approve. We have been unable to discuss this rally with the organisers. We have spoken to fellow yachties who have taken part but not to enough of them to be in a position to comment. Consult their website if it appeals to you.

Bill, who knows the Suez Canal very well (he once was a Suez pilot), thinks there could be advantages in making the transit of the canal as a group, whether a formal one or just an ad hoc arrangement. Probably the same applies to the Panama, too.

We have to face the fact that yachting in all its forms has expanded greatly over the past 50 years. Growth appears to be exponential. Many coastal yacht clubs and marinas are full; almost the only yachting still with growth potential is the long-haul cruising world. It is all going to get more and more crowded as more and more countries take up yachting. And perhaps the rallies have their place for the inexperienced to get their feet wet. People vote with their feet. Or boats, as the case may be.

But there is another feature of all rallies that worries us, and it is not a criticism of the organisers in any way. This is that they are a potential vehicle or example for future official interference with our freedoms. We can envisage (just) the day when yachts will be forbidden ocean passage except in such a convoy. They will be expected to have their gear approved and pay a contingency fee against the possibility of needing assistance. Oh dear!

17 • Social Life, Entertainment, and Etiquette

'... then all the rest may do what they will til midnight.'

Entertainment might seem an odd subject for those to whom sailing itself is an entertainment, but when the navigation of a vessel from one place to another is the prime motive, some forms of diversion are needed.

READING

This is the most obvious pastime. People used to books cannot easily manage without them. There are no libraries available to the wanderer, so one has to have reference volumes to taste. Most yachts carry a paperback library comprising those loved books which are read over and over again, and also those less loved books that are enjoyable once and are then swapped with other yachts for similar works.

Swapping paperbacks is a continuing process. It is sad that British and American paperback publishers use a form of unsewn binding that falls apart. (It is called 'perfect binding', not because it is any use whatsoever for the purpose (and it isn't), nor because it is perfect for generating profits for publishers but because it was invented by a Mr Perfect who should clearly roast in hell.) Most books bound this way can be read or consulted about three times only before the spine breaks. To bind reference books in this way is little short of fraud, and they are certainly unfit for the purpose for which they are sold. Purchasers should try returning them by the dozen to the bookshops under the Sale of Goods Act – that might stop the practice. Many yachting centres have secondhand bookshops, where your nearly new paperbacks may be swapped.

Nowadays there are internet bookstores which will deliver world-wide. The trouble is that you still have to wait for them to arrive by post and so you can only take advantage where you are immobile and have a good postal 'drop'; Poste Restante is not usually reliable enough, though most marinas understand the requirement for a good postal service for their clients. Beware of giving a UK address for reference. These companies sell on their client list and you will be bombarded by e-mail spam.

More and more reference books are becoming available on CD for use in computers. This saves on space and weight in a boat library.

GAMES

Apart from reading, games are played rather more by the typical yachtie than by his land-dwelling friends. Some, including me, indulge themselves with a chess computer programme, but it is not the same thing as playing with real live people. Draughts (or checkers) and backgammon (or tavla) are played a lot.

A very popular game is Scrabble. There are certain difficulties playing it with our American friends owing to their inability to spell. We solved the problem by using the Shorter Oxford Dictionary when aboard our boat, and Webster's when in theirs, but they had the worst of it because Webster's is kind enough to have both American and English spellings.

Bridge and Scrabble can be played against a computer. Personally I find computer Scrabble unsatisfactory owing to their use of Chambers Dictionary, which seems to me to be about another language entirely.

Of course ex-naval people can play uckers, a complete mystery to the uninitiated.

MUSIC

The simplicity of cruising life encourages you to make your own entertainment, here Sue of Tala *treats us to an impromptu concert on her backpackers guitar.*

The Royal Cruising Club has a song book, and at a suitable time aboard their boats the skipper may hand them round like hymn books so that the anchorage resounds with song. The accompanying instrument for sailors' songs has traditionally been portable and easily stowed: a pipe, concertina or harmonica. Later the fiddle came in. Then, of all things, the yacht piano, which solved the ballast problem I suppose. Now we have electronic keyboards (where will it end?) and guitars. The traditional Spanish guitar, of thin wood put together with non-waterproof glue, has minimal aptitude for life in a yacht, but innumerable boats consider it is worth its valuable space. The Backpacker's guitar is handier. We have the obligatory guitar. Someone should invent one, the inside of which can be used as a locker. Not content with the guitar, Laurel bought a dulcimer kit in the USA and amused herself building it while sailing back over the Atlantic. I hold my breath every time we see a double bass.

We have just come across a yacht with a full-scale karaoke kit on board.

HOBBIES

Sailors of old did not have a lot of spare time, but they had various diversions including decorative knotting (macramé), knitting, scrimshaw and some wood-carving. These are all enjoyable pastimes today, though real whales' teeth are getting as scarce as hens'. These pastimes all have the virtue of taking up little space, and when well done the products can be sold.

The first problem is that more and more of the old seafaring hobbies are condemned as environmentally unfriendly (to whose environment is not clear), and are therefore banned by landlubber legislators. The next problem is that many well-practised shoreside hobbies do not translate to the sea-going life. Collecting is difficult because of space and the importance of protecting vulnerable and valuable items from sea damage. Postage stamps and books, for example. I have not heard of anyone actually having a model railway in a yacht, but I expect one exists somewhere. I sometimes wish I had an old-fashioned Meccano set.

Almost any art or craft except possibly stained glass, fresco painting, mosaic and monumental masonry can be practised, and cloth crafts are particularly appropriate. Laurel once did a lot of patchwork; she says it is an occupation which can be done in any corner at any time and is easy to put down or take up. Let your imagination run along those lines and do as you will. Take any special tools with you, and spares too for they are sometimes unavailable or hard to trace.

One of the chief entertainments while cruising is the social life, meeting and getting to know other yachties or passers-by. One sometimes does not have a lot in common with the people on the quay. Nor even with those in the next boat, except the sea and common experiences, but one can learn a lot from others. We'll discuss wintering later.

RADIO

When on board on our own the radio is invaluable. It is wise to keep some track of world events; you do not want to arrive somewhere in the middle of a coup d'état, or after a natural disaster. The BBC World Service news broadcasts keep you in touch, though political in nature and unwontedly occupied with Africa. Its entertainment is not so hot, but this is not its prime function.

The broadcast frequencies for any area vary during the day, and also from month to month as they have trouble from sunspots or human interference. Check frequencies in use via the internet.

Local national and provincial radio is heavily dependent on taste. In the West Indies you get reggae morning, noon and night. In Europe all countries have an approximate equivalent to the BBC Home Services, and most countries have a programme with cultural leanings. France Musique is excellent, and has the great asset that its announcers have almost perfect diction which is a great help in learning the language. (How foreigners get on trying to learn English from the multi-dialect broadcasters we have in the UK I cannot imagine.)

Turkey and Greece both have classical Third Programmes. The Greek one is not bad. The Turkish programme was airing trad jazz when I last heard it.

In the USA, we found Public Radio to be good in quality and not only because they sometimes use BBC material.

The best domestic radios are those with digital tuning and 'scan' and 'save' buttons. There are several on the market.

Digital radios are available that latch on to satellites for perfect listening. We are told that there are fewer and fewer free-to-air programmes (as is the case with satellite TV), so you may have to pay for a contract of some kind. This area is in a state of flux.

TELEVISION

Television is an effective language teacher. By watching children's programmes, one gets talk in a simple vocabulary with simple grammar, usually spoken slowly and clearly. (The Teletubbies are an exception.) Advertisements can be in simple language, and repeat phrases over and over again, with pictures.

Entertainment from terrestrial television abroad is patchy. One finds an occasional piece of excellence that is relevant to us, the foreigners, but not often. In larger countries where audience figures justify the expense, films are dubbed in the local language. In smaller countries, such as Greece, they are broadcast in English with local sub-titles. This is the case in Greek cinemas too. Incidentally, those who studied Greek in school will find it of little use. It's rather as if a knowledge of Chaucer's English would be of any use in 'ackney.

Now there is satellite TV. The more commercially centred programmes cannot be obtained legally as the companies insist on a telephone connection and tell us they will not license their special receiving decoders for use in ships and boats. However it is possible to get pirate decoders through various shady gentlemen who advertise in papers like *Exchange and Mart*, or *Loot*. One can, in many cases, buy a suitable receiving box locally, but these are always more expensive than in the UK. Check the internet carefully. You need to be sure that your cruising ground is within the satellite footprint. The BBC, for example, have carefully chosen a footprint that makes it difficult to receive throughout the Med. It is possible, but with an inconveniently large dish antenna. The two best satellite dishes for yachtie use are Astra 2 and Hotbird.

There are still some free-to-air broadcasts by satellite, mostly news or shopping. The gear can be obtained from any retailer. You can install it yourself, though retailers dissuade you and offer to do so for a large fee. The problem in a yacht is pointing the antenna in the right direction and keeping it there. The boats near us as I write have mounted their winter antennae on poles fixed to the

Satellite dishes are becoming a common sight on cruising yachts.

piling. It is nice in winter to wake to the soothing voice of Charlotte Green impeccably reading the news.

Last week, our omni-directional terrestrial TV antenna blew off the foremast-head in a gale and fell over the side. I recovered it, decanted the sea water from it and from its co-ax connectors, and propped it on a boathook secured to the guardrails. It worked better than ever, thus destroying some of my more secure beliefs in electronic technology and UHF propagation.

In the Med, video tapes are becoming a bit passé among yachties, though in the more populous centres, where there are land-lubberly ex-pats, there are usually places to buy English language videos. One should be careful about video recording and playing, recorders/players must be compatible with the TV set you have on board and the local system. Multi-system videos are available but at a hell of a price.

Multi-standard terrestrial television sets are available. We have a 14in Grundig which will work on 230 volt AC or on 12 volt DC and receive everywhere, including France, but not for America. For the USA, we found that a British TV set would receive the picture but not the sound. As a temporary expedient we bought and placed next to the TV, a little radio set costing $5 tuned to the TV frequencies, intended for those who cannot bear to miss the latest soap. Even when out walking.

With the coming of flat screens and multi-media, the carrying of a good TV set will become much easier. Eventually it will be your music and photo album, will work off your computer or laptop, display your video, e-mails, play your DVDs and cook you a steak and kidney pudding. We will have to wait until they come down in price.

We tried to get more info on this at the boat show, but it seemed everyone wanted to sell satellite equipment of the most expensive, gyro-stabilised kind. Perhaps this is the way things will go. We found a complete blank stare at the mention of French terrestrial TV, some of which is excellent. 'But you can get British programmes on satellite . . .' or 'there are French programmes on satellite too . . .' Sorry mate, there are better solutions somewhere without having to pay the dirty digger a fat subscription. This will sort itself out in time.

WINTER IN A GREEK ISLAND MARINA

Some 30 yachts have crews on board, and during the winter days we can be sociable or not, as the fancy takes us. A lively morning VHF net lasting about ten minutes keeps us informed as to arrivals and departures, weather, wants and difficulties, and social events. Several times a week we meet in the evening at the clubroom which the marina management has provided free. Sometimes there is a quiz. Once a week the extremely popular pot-luck supper is held, often on a theme such as Chinese New Year or Australia day, when we stagger to the clubroom with steaming dishes covered in foil, when we drink draught wine (at a price that the British can only dream about) and chat, swapping tips and hints and anecdotes, and invitations are exchanged. There are Greek lessons, keep fit classes, and a music group. (Up to six guitars, a banjo, and Laurel's transatlantic dulcimer.) We can revise our first aid, learn Dutch cooking, or new handicrafts. We visit yachties in hospital. (One of them has had both his knees done) and those of us with cars give lifts to those without.

We keep busy, but all of us are longing for the spring barbecue, and good sailing weather again.

YACHT CLUBS

Talk of social life leads us to consider clubs and associations of interest to the long-cruising yachtsman. There is a tendency not to belong to clubs. We are thus exceptions, though we question just what benefit we get from some. Loyalty dies hard.

We have to consider this mainly from a British point of view, as we know less about other countries' clubs than citizens of those countries. It is likely that the generalities we make about British clubs will apply to all.

Clubs (other than local ones) which set out to, or actually do, help the cruising yachtie are:

- *The Royal Cruising Club* is the senior of them all in terms of date of founding (there is no other measure of seniority in this context). Its membership is limited in number and very mutually supportive, but not at all snobbish. Its members really do get about the world, and tend to be well-informed, excellent seafarers. Their foreign port information (available only to members) is top in its class. As well as that they have a Pilotage Foundation, founded with a legacy from an old member, which edits, publishes and subsidises cruising guides that are valuable to yachtsmen cruising in less frequented places, and which would not be a commercially viable work.

- *The Cruising Association* is very active. It has an excellent clubhouse in London with charts and information for consultation by those planning a voyage. We meet many members, and admire their creditable levels of skill. The subscription is modest and their newsletter is first class. They also operate an efficient crewing service, a sort of yachtie marriage bureau (hope that does not cause offence). Skippers must be members, but the service is open to non-members as crew on payment of a fee.

- *The Little Ship Club* has been kissed by Prince Charming and is now wide awake. It has excellent courses for those wishing to improve their skills. It is a little expensive for those living near London as its excellent clubhouse (in the City) caters for the stockbroker lunching community.

- *The Royal Naval Sailing Association* is a very active club (it started all the round the world racing, for example: the first three round-the-world solo voyagers were all members), and has a fantastic spread of Hon Local Officers world-wide, almost all of whom are superior in every respect to those attached to imitating clubs. Supposedly for serving or retired Royal Navy, Reserves, and those associated with the Navy, their membership is falling as the Royal Navy declines and we old salts die off, and their interpretation of their original entry qualifications is nowadays less rigorous. They have over 6000 members so can afford a good service at a moderate subscription. Worth joining if you are eligible, in spite of a mild remnant of old service pomposity.

- *The Ocean Cruising Club* is a classless international club for those cruising the oceans. (There are American, Antipodean and Belgian members, but the Germans decided to have their own outfit.) Qualification is a port-to-port voyage exceeding 1000 miles in a small yacht (<70 ft) though in our experience it is far more difficult in a large yacht with a small crew than in a small fully-manned yacht. It is run by people more interested in sailing than administration. It disseminates valuable information through its well-edited magazine *Flying Fish*, and constitutes the second largest batch of members that we meet in harbour and on the high seas. It ought to offer apprentice membership for aspirants.

• *The Seven Seas Cruising Association* is run from the USA and is specifically for live-aboards. All members are Commodores and we find the sensation that all are chiefs with no Indians rather eccentric. One drops to Associate membership if one moves ashore, even for short periods, and that is a good idea. The membership qualification is loose, so that one finds a high proportion of live-aboards are house-boat dwellers on the US east coast waterways. A very friendly lot – full of extrovert American enthusiasms and informality.

We were once in favour of a club for European live-aboards, but were nervous of initiating anything that would either fail because all the membership were so busy sailing that there would be no administration, or alternatively it would, like so many clubs, end up by administering itself into the position of taking in its own expensive washing, thus achieving nothing at great expense. On the whole, I think that view is correct. We do not need it.

All these clubs we mention publish a mixture of journals, newsletters and information sheets. All, except for the Ocean Cruising Club, publish in A4 format. I do wish the others would realise that, whatever advantages A4 has ashore, it is too big and clumsy for a small boat's bookshelf. Hats off to the OCC. A5 is the convenient size on board, and that should be the criterion. It is also easier to send through the post and does not cause nearly so many problems in marina letter-racks.

• *Royal Yachting Association (RYA)* •

I have had a stormy association with the RYA. I first joined in 1948, when it was called the Yacht Racing Association (YRA). Many of us think it should never have changed its name. I occasionally resign on principle, and then re-join because it is an essential force in the modern world where our nautical freedoms are threatened. It doesn't always take action I approve, in fact it generally does not, but that's life. Now, in 2005, those freedoms are being even more heavily assailed and the RYA and the EBA (the European Boating Association, which the RYA initiated) are the only protection we have against the hordes of bureaucrats, both Brussels and local, that cast continually about to see whom they may regulate more closely.

We have recently spent three days in Brussels, having been invited to a meeting to discuss harmonisation of regulations for inland waters throughout Europe. The main pre-occupation of most delegates was not about those rules, but discussing where and when to have the next meeting so as to maximise their enjoyment of the event. Nothing was achieved. It was our first such venture and likely to be our last. But the point is that the RYA had a man there who was much respected and, unlike most delegates, he was competent, succinct and intelligent, and he seemed to be able to listen to rubbish all day without losing his temper. (Bill distinguished himself by telling one Assistant Commissioner, an Austrian, that he had the outlook of a Nazi. They won't invite Bill again.)

There are some new regulations from our own MCA which are quite over the top. And to my horror I find these were accepted by the RYA without serious protest. But protest there will be, there *must* be, because the regulations, obviously directed towards the inexperienced and ignorant, are inappropriate and dangerously restrictive when applied to the competent.

So now, unlike in previous editions, I urge yachties to fork out for membership, and shout rather loudly. I like President Johnson's saying about a protesting aide: 'Better if he's inside the tent pissing out, than outside pissing in.' So get inside the tent and . . . well, this is where the metaphor breaks down.

When we started serious yachting as boat-owners (58 years ago) there were no regulations inhibiting us except international law and the collision regulations. There was precedent and etiquette which we respected. Nowadays, it seems that new restrictive orders are published every year by one body or another.

Bill recalls being the navigating officer of the duty destroyer based at Portland in 1956. They were called out in mid-winter to assist a yacht in trouble. She was being sailed by a single-hander with absolutely no experience. He had left a Solent port (Little Yarmouth, he thinks) against the advice of the Harbour Master in order to sail round the world. Against the opinions of his fellow officers, Bill defended the yachtsman's right to do that, though it was at that moment an unpopular view. He believes, though, that people who sail inadvisedly in appalling conditions cannot expect the rescue services, not excluding the Royal Navy, to spend millions on getting them out of trouble. Yachtsmen should expect to cope on their own, and should advance their learning and expertise before trying something dramatic or potentially dangerous. The sea is always dangerous but has a nasty habit of beguiling you into thinking it is not.

Nevertheless, recall the telegram on the subject of letting children on their own over-night in a small boat in Arthur Ransome's *Swallows and Amazons*. 'If not duffers wont drown. If duffers better drowned.'

FLAGS AND THINGS

We fly the blue ensign. Three times last year I overheard remarks from summer sailors containing the word 'snobbery'. I rather resented that. Let's spare a moment to consider British ensigns.

Historically, ships carried flags or banners of their owners, who were once the great feudal lords. When the Monarch wanted a fleet he commanded the lords to provide their ships which assembled into a fleet, but each ship still flew the flag of its own lord. As fleets got bigger the potential for disaster increased and we find the first examples of casualties due to friendly fire. To avoid this, the King decreed that all ships should fly his flag.

As Britain dominated the seas, the fleet got bigger and the large number of sailing ships became difficult to control. It was divided into three squadrons, the red, the white and the blue, each with its own admiral. To distinguish them, they flew a flag of the appropriate colour with the king's emblem (the Union Flag) in the upper canton. Note that the red was the superior squadron (and hence the senior flag) while the white came next and blue was the tail-end Charlie. So much for the superiority of the blue ensign!

The three squadrons disappeared in about 1850 when the navy turned to steam and it became easier to manoeuvre an entire fleet as one unit. During the next 40 years, fighting ships flew the white with a red cross superimposed, merchant ships, which were still liable to be summoned on the Queen's behalf, flew the red. There was chaos among yachts. For example, my own club, the Royal Norfolk and Suffolk, founded in 1851, flew a white ensign without the red cross and continued to do so until the 1890s when after an acrimonious correspondence with the Admiralty and the Prince of Wales, they were obliged to give it up under the threat that the Lords Lieutenants of the two counties would be imprisoned for treason. They were offered the right to fly the blue ensign, but declined as it was considered lower class. There's snobbery for you! They ended up with a red ensign defaced with the Prince of Wales' own personal badge.

So you see, it is the superior *red* ensign which is the symbol of snobbery.

Personally, I believe this system of ensigns has had its day. The white clearly belongs to the fighting navy, the red should be reserved for commercial shipping and the Merchant Navy who earned it during World War II (by God, they did!), and all yachts should fly the blue, defaced if desired by their club emblem. Don't talk to me about whether a ship flies, wears, shows, displays or flutters its blasted ensign. You know what I mean.

Actually, I like flags. Gay things, in the true meaning of that adjective. But one can get over-obsessed with what used to be called flag etiquette. Etiquette is defined as the 'generally accepted code of behaviour', so that if one belongs to a club or association which expects its members to conform to a certain practice, that is a reason for conforming. It is, in any event, economical to lower the ensign at night when nobody can see it, because they cost quite a lot, and soon wear out if left flying all the time.

Legally, a British ship has only to show an ensign on entering or leaving a foreign port (Merchant Shipping Act 1894 et seq). The ensign she may use is also laid down, and the Royal Navy is supposed to, but no longer does, police this. In addition, a lot of countries expect to have their ensign displayed by visiting vessels, and in some cases, Turkey is one, the courtesy ensign is a legal requirement.

Some naval officers are confused about flags and come to believe that naval practice and regulations apply to all classes of ships. They do not. And as the Visual Signalling branch of the Royal Navy has been swallowed up by the sparkers, there are not many naval personnel who have any knowledge of the rules.

Courtesy ensigns by tradition were flown at the foremasthead. In yachts this was usually kept for the club burgee, but nowadays few cruising yachts belong to clubs, and if they do, they usually fly the burgee at the port crosstrees. The starboard crosstrees are then for the courtesy ensign. This is because mastheads are now often cluttered with electronic decorations. There are some clubs that insist their burgee *must* be flown only at the masthead, and it is interesting that for those that wish to, the masthead can be so arranged as to permit this. I think it looks better.

Many smaller yachts have their ensign tied to the standing backstay, where it stays until it rots. This is almost the current etiquette, so if you do the same no one is likely to notice. But it does add to the cost of living, and it seems to me desirable to have some sort of halyard so that when one remembers one can haul the flag down to prolong its active life. Beware of buying your red ensign from a foreign source; they are always incorrect as to design and even proportion and they show you up. The red ensign, for example, should have a length twice its breadth. Foreign made flags conform to the European norm where the proportion is usually 3:2 instead of our 2:1. In so many ways we differ from Europe.

International Code Flags are a waste of money, unless you wish to dress ship for a celebration or take part in the ARC. You will need flag Q on arrival in some countries, though no longer within the European countries, unless coming from outside the Union. Apart from that, most flags carried will be courtesy ensigns, which have become a bit of a nuisance since so many former colonies have become jealous little republics.

The best way of dealing with the problem of multiple courtesy ensigns, since they are so expensive, is to follow our previously given advice and carry a sewing machine and a couple of yards of material of each of the primary colours, plus some different coloured fabric marking crayons to do the intricate bits without which no modern flag seems to be complete. If possible, arrive in a country with its courtesy ensign hoisted. Try not to be mean with size; flags are generally hoisted high and can look very tiny, which hardly seems a courtesy. In some places yachtsmen have been fined for having a tatty courtesy ensign.

Recently the whole question of flag etiquette has come under debate in the journal of the RNSA. The fact that old-and-bold naval officers are at last questioning outmoded practices should augur well for a change in the position. But the Royal Navy which occasionally has the ability to move fast is slow to change its traditions. Unlike the USN. Bill recalls seeing a notice on the bulletin board at US Naval Academy, Annapolis, saying: 'the following will be a tradition as of now . . .'

• *Dressing ship* •

It is a present day nautical convention to hoist strings of decorative flags between mastheads and down to stem and stern in order to celebrate various occasions. Not many observe it, except a few British and Dutch with the odd American or German. We do it because I like flags and think it looks good, but we do not do it for those rather formal occasions laid down by the Admiralty. (The Admiralty now calls itself the Ministry of Defence (Navy): not by me, it ain't.) We did it at Meganisi in Greece where we were staying at the time of the Feast of Saint Bissarion, the local patron. It is an island of merchant navy men, and several called by to thank us for the courtesy. It all helps to make the yachtie more welcome.

Fare Well *looking smart with gleaming topsides and dressed overall.*

We once did it on Trafalgar Day while in France, and a French Naval Captain observed 'This is a good day for the France.' '*Comment?*' we replied, a little surprised. 'Well, we shot Nelson that day.' A different side to the coin. Everyone enjoys a sense of humour; we made another friend.

The usual form for dressing lines is to alternate the flags of the code with the pennants and substitutes. The order does not really matter – just make a colourful show.

Our dressing occasions are: the birthdays of crew, Trafalgar Day, St George's Day, Christmas Day, New Year's Day (when we also hoist a full string of courtesy ensigns for the past year, known as one's brag-line), plus any special dates for the country or port we are visiting.

HOW TO BE A POPULAR YACHTIE

The considerations that apply to flag etiquette apply also to yacht etiquette – the arbiters are no longer those elderly blimps from Cowes or the New York Yacht Club who have for so long arrogantly imposed their values on Anglo-American yachting. The arbiters now are the people who actually sail, and they comprise many nationalities. The form nowadays can be summed up:

1 Cause the minimum inconvenience to other yachts' crews.
2 Help another yacht berthing close by you.
3 Give assistance willingly, and without legal haggling, to anyone in difficulties.

These three tenets are obvious to most people who want to sail. In more detail, certain usages have grown up around them, and I will give those I have noticed. If I have missed any, then I apologise to whomever I have offended.

Diesel generators Their use is growing, and it has to be faced that many yachts have them and need them. In general, most confine generating to the forenoon. There is a growing tendency for a second run in the dog watches, between about 1600 and 1800, which is not so nice, but tolerable. In port, you should not run generators before 0830, between 1230 and 1600, or after 1900 unless you want to incur the justifiable wrath of your neighbours. Incidentally, the petrol driven, so-called silent, air-cooled mini-generators are not noticeably more quiet than the latest generation of diesel generators.

In 2005 the use of generators at all hours has become more common. Charter yachts are likely to run their air-conditioning 24 hours a day, and even among the smaller yachts the practice is on the increase. There is a law in Greece forbidding the running of noisy machinery anywhere between 1400 and 1700, the better to further the *ipnos*, or afternoon sleep, but it is rarely observed nowadays. We suggest it should be observed in boats, extended to include the late evening and night-time. At anchor, when yachts are some distance apart, the convention can be relaxed, particularly if it is windy, but in close anchorages such as Bequia or Union Island it ought to be observed.

Dinghies In Europe, dinghies left ashore are inviolable. You should make yours fast on a long painter so that it can be shoved to one side to allow others to get alongside to land. In areas where Americans abound, and particularly where their racing circuses congregate, the unsolicited borrowing of dinghies is not uncommon. Americans seem to tolerate this noxious practice, which is generally anathema to our older civilisation. Either take precautions or be surprised.

Anchors (what again?) Be particularly careful when berthing bows- or stern-to a quay not to lay your anchor cable(s) across others. In many places it cannot be avoided, however. The first to arrive at Navpaktos, in the Gulf of Corinth, is obliged to be the last to leave; the centre of this tiny circular harbour resembles a diagram for a multi-part Matthew Walker knot, tied in cable. A great deal of tolerance is needed. It is difficult when big yachts and little ones intermingle for they have different manoeuvring characteristics, and therefore different berthing techniques, something that newcomers find difficult to appreciate. It comes with experience.

Untangling foul anchors is an example of the willingness of yachties to help each other. Usually anyone with a dinghy down will paddle out to do his stuff. Greek yachtsmen are particularly good about this. If you are moored stern- or bows-to with the usual taut cable, and someone fouls it when weighing, you have an obligation to respond to reasonable requests from the fouler, who is probably in the best position to know how he is foul. He will probably ask you to give him some slack, for a yacht without a power windlass is unlikely to be able to haul a tight chain to the surface so that he can unhook his anchor. Even if he has power, if he hauls up a tight cable he is likely to haul up your anchor with it, so some slack is usually desirable. If wind conditions are troublesome run your engine at modest revs to hold your stem off the quay. If you are the fouler, and haul out the anchor of a berthed boat, try to re-lay it as close to its original position as possible.

One does *not* buoy anchors in a busy port; the chaos if all did so can be imagined. If you are worried about foul anchors use a non-floating trip line taken back to your bow. In an open anchorage an anchor buoy can be of help to another yacht in avoiding anchoring too close because sometimes one's cable lies in a curve on the bottom. In a crowded anchorage it is a help to a newcomer shaping up near you to tell him how much cable you are lying to. It is the responsibility of the late-comer to keep clear of those already anchored, and this continues unless the first-comer changes the state by veering or shortening cable, or by letting go another anchor.

> *The last to haul or the last to veer,*
> *He's the one who must keep clear.*

• *Berthing* •

It is usual to help with the ropes of a yacht berthing next to you. In the Med, where harbours are often crowded, it can be anti-social to berth alongside the quay. There are exceptions, such as Poros in the Aegean, or Khalkis, but for special reasons. Anyone berthing in this way has to be prepared for others to berth alongside them without any ceremony. In the Azores, Bermuda, Baltic and some Canaries harbours, yachts sometimes lie alongside six or more abreast. Outside yachts (other than tiddlers) must have breastropes to the quay, and springs to their neighbours. Utmost co-operation is needed, and is usually forthcoming to a measure that breeds friendships.

The old convention of always crossing over the foredeck of a neighbour is gone: many voyagers now have a proper sleeping cabin in the fore part of the yacht, and in warm climates often a wide-open hatch. It is proper to enquire (by day) how you should cross, and the responder should also pass on the information he has already got from yachts inside him.

• *Footwear* •

The real seaman wears deck shoes because he knows that stubbed toes can be debilitating, and also that quaysides are often fouled by disease-ridden dogs. Dilettante yachtsmen who spend more time polishing their yachts than sailing them have an elaborate ritual of donning or doffing shoes like a crowd of Japanese at a temple. But you cannot expect an outside crew to take off their boots just because you bagged the inside berth. Face the fact that if the deck of your yacht will not stand up to deck shoes it is not fit for its purpose. They are *deck* shoes for heaven's sake. On the other hand the shoe wearer has an obligation to see that his shoes are clean. And his feet too, of course.

• *Smoking* •

Do as you like in your own boat, but in harbour do not throw cigarette ends overboard. Many yachts put their dinghies down in harbour, and it's too easy to start a fire in one and it might be a petrol fire.

• *Garbage* •

The French and Italians tend to leave plastic bags of garbage on the quay, thereby encouraging rats, stray dogs and cats, and incurring the wrath and disrespect of others who mostly look for the garbage skip. This is often full, when there is nothing to be done except to leave the garbage alongside it. In the Caribbean and elsewhere, pay no heed to little boys who paddle out to your anchorage and offer to dispose of your garbage for a fee. They will rummage through it for anything of interest, and then leave the rest on that pretty little beach where you wanted to swim.

• *Quiet* •

Quiet times vary from place to place. Some are still heaving at 0300. A few miles away, at another port, the inhabitants will all be asleep by 2230. Local people may welcome the income from tourism, but do not want to pay too high a price for it. Ascertain and respect the local convention. A Greek law forbids the use of machinery between 1400 and 1700.

• *Helping out* •

There is a tradition of helping others with navigation information. Where they are otherwise unobtainable, charts etc are loaned for photocopying, which is of course illegal in the case of most countries' charts, but not for Uncle Sam's. Linguists pass on the weather reports, and any yacht who has been in the port more than a few days should pass on the whereabouts of sources of essentials (water, or gas bottles) or even non-essentials that are particularly interesting.

Usually anyone who owns or hires a car will offer a supermarket service to the others in the port. This could get onerous, but people are mostly sensible and do not take unreasonable advantage.

Lastly, let us put the European Union in perspective because we have been hypercritical earlier on. It has another side. It has given us many cruising bene- fits, not the least being the Customs Union. It has not yet standardised port bureaucracy, but it is working on it. One can travel from country to country with little trouble, though illegal immigration prevention causes problems in places. The impecunious can take on some work and avoid being stranded. We won't vote for Britain quitting the Union so long as it does not become a United States of Europe, and we wish we might live long enough for the various pains in the bum to be sorted out.

May you all have fair winds and fine weather, wherever you sail.

Appendix 1 • Books

• *Seamanship, maintenance and repair* •

Rigging Handbook, Brion Toss, Adlard Coles Nautical
Metal Corrosion in Boats, Nigel Warren, Adlard Coles Nautical and Sheridan House
Heavy Weather Sailing, Peter Bruce, Adlard Coles Nautical
Navigation for Yachtsmen, Mary Blewitt, Adlard Coles Nautical
Celestial Navigation for Yachtsmen, Mary Blewitt, Adlard Coles Nautical
VHF Radiotelephony for Yachtsmen (GMDSS edition), RYA
VHF Radio Operator Examinations (GMDSS edition), RYA
Cruising French Waterways, Hugh McKnight, Adlard Coles Nautical and Sheridan House
Inland Waterways of France, David Edwards-May, Imray
The European Waterways, Marian Martin, Adlard Coles Nautical and Sheridan House
The Yachtsman's 10-language Dictionary, B Webb, Adlard Coles Nautical and Sheridan House
Reeds Skipper's Handbook, Malcolm Pearson, Adlard Coles Nautical

• *Health and victualling* •

The Ship Captain's Medical Guide, HMSO
Where there is No Doctor and *Where there is No Dentist*, TALC (Teaching Aids at Low Cost), PO Box 49, St Albans, Herts AL1 4AX   Tel 01727 853869
North Atlantic Seafood, Alan Davidson, Penguin Books
Mediterranean Seafood, Alan Davidson, Penguin Books
Charcuterie and French Pork Cookery, Jane Grigson, Penguin Books
Diet for a Small Planet, Francis Moore Lappe, Ballantyne Books
Recipes for a Small Planet, Ellen Buchman Ewald, Ballantyne Books
The Great Cruising Cookbook, John Payne, Sheridan House

• *Potentially useful websites for books* •

www.sheridanhouse.com (Nautical publishers)
www.adlardcoles.com (Nautical publishers)
www.bookfinder.com (Worldwide secondhand hard-to-find books)
www.bookharbour.com (Kelvin Hughes, books and charts)
www.nauticalbooks.co.uk (New and secondhand nautical books)

Appendix 2 • Useful Websites and Addresses

• *General* •

www.ybw.com (IPC magazines: Yachting and Boating World Forums)

The Foreign Office   Tel 020 7238 4503/4504 (Information about political risks abroad)

Sailboat Buyers' Guide: The Complete Guide to Boats and Gear, SAIL magazine (source for all marine products) www.sailbuyersguide.com and www.boatus.com.

• *Health* •

www.cigua.com (Ciguatera poisoning)

www.healthatoz.com (health A to Z, USA)

www.fitfortravel.scot.nhs.uk (NHS Scotland)

www.doh.gov.uk/traveladvice (Department of Health, UK)   Tel 020 7210 4850

www.surgerydoor.co.uk/trl (Clinic by Internet)

www.masta.org (Medical Advice Service for Travellers Abroad)   Tel 0891 224100

www.sentex.net/~iamat (International Association of Medical Assistance for Travellers)

www.crewmedic.com (Modal First Aid Kits, eye-wash pod)

www.dentanurse.com   Tel 01981 500135 (Dental repair and first aid kit)

TALC (Teaching Aids at Low Cost) PO Box 49, St Albans, Herts AL1 4AX   Tel 01727 853869 (Spoon for babies)

• *Weather* •

www.met-office.gov.uk/datafiles/offshore.html (British Met Office)

www.meteo.fr (Meteo France)

www.nws.noaa.gov/om/marine (USA Weather Service)

www.nhc.noaa.gov (National Hurricane Centre)

www.wetterzentrale.de (German source giving a nine-day forecast)

www.franksingleton.clara.net

www.gric.com

• *Navigation* •

www.nms.ukho.gov.uk (Notices to Mariners for UK charts)
www.imo.org/imo/library/piracy/623rev1.pdf (Information on piracy)
www.rin.org.uk (Royal Institute of Navigation)
www.pcmaritime.co.uk (Nav and met programs)
minories@kelvinhughes.co.uk (Charts)

• *Communications* •

www.bbc.co.uk/worldservice (BBC World Service)
www.shiptoshore.co.uk (Organises mail forwarding etc)
www.ipass.com (How to access your ISP when abroad via a local number)
www.stargate3.co.uk (Pocketmail)
www.marinecomputing.com (Installation and advice on Inmarsat Mini-M and C)
www.inmarsat.org (Inmarsat organisation)
www.kvh.com (Makers of Tracphone for Mini-M)
www.tt.dk (Thrane and Thrane phone-makers for Mini-M and C)
www.rme.com (Inmarsat C compression software)
www.pinoak.com (Pinoak)
www.globewireless.com (Globe Wireless)
www.sailmail.com (Sailmail)
www.pentacomstat.com.au (Seamail)
www.xaxero.com (Software for Seamail)
www.airmail2000.com (Info on e-mail by ham radio)
www.win-net.org (Radio ham e-mail shorestations)
www.shortwave.co.uk (Shortwave shop for HF radio gear)
www.gmdss.com.au (For comprehensive info on GMDSS and DSC)
www.icselectronics.co.uk (Ditto, but this is a slow downloader)
www.radio.gov.uk (Radio authority for British Government)
www.g-comm.co.uk (Satellite telephones)

• *UK Domestic* •

Hozelock Ltd Haddenham Aylesbury Bucks HP17 8JD (Plastic clothes pegs)
Lee Sanitation   Tel 0044 1295 770000, Fax 0044 1295 770022
www.aqua-marine.co.uk (Domestic gear including refrigerators)
www.tek-tanks.com (Makers of fridge cabinets and tanks in plastics)
www.penguineng.com (Refrigerators, etc)
www.spectrawatermakers.com (Watermakers)
www.lakelandlimited.com (Stainless kitchen tools, Bamix, Stayfresh bags,
   Tefal cheese-keeper)
www.yachtpeople.com (Scootguard non-slip sheeting)

• *Chandlery* •

info@bluewatersupplies (VAT-free equipment)
www.aquafax.co.uk (Wholesalers, but very helpful people)
www.mailspeedmarine.com

• *Education* •

Calvert School 105 Tuscany Rd Baltimore MD USA. e-mail:
   inquiry@calvertschool.org
www.bbc.co.uk/education
www.atschool.co.uk (To keystage 2)
www.oceantraining.com (Navigation, meteorology, VHF radio etc)

• *Insurance* •

insure@gjwltd.co.uk
www.bishopskinner.com (Third Party Insurance)

• *Freight* •

www.completefreight.net

• *Cruise in Company Rallies* •

www.worldcruising.com (ARC, ARC Europe)
www.yachtrallies.co.uk (Bluewater Rally)

• *Yachting clubs and organisations* •

www.rya.org.uk (Royal Yachting Association)
www.cruising.org.uk (The Cruising Association, London)
www.ssca.org (Seven Seas Cruising Association, Fort Lauderdale, US)
e-mail office@ssca.org (Seven Seas Cruising Association)
www.oceancruisingclub.org (Ocean Cruising Club)

Index

First published 1989
This compilation © 1989 by Bloomsbury Publishing Ltd
The copyright of the individual contributions
remains with the respective authors © 1989.
The extract from the screenplay – *Tender is the Night* © 1950
by Malcolm Lowry, reprinted by permission of the
Estate of Malcolm Lowry and Sterling Lord Literistic, Inc.

Bloomsbury Publishing Ltd, 2 Soho Square, London W1V 5DE

A CIP catalogue record for this book
is available from the British Library

ISBN: 0 7475 0506 3

10 9 8 7 6 5 4 3 2 1

Jacket illustration by Jeff Fisher
Photoset in Linotron 202 Sabon by
Rowland Phototypesetting Ltd
Bury St Edmunds, Suffolk
Printed in Great Britain by
Butler and Tanner Ltd, Frome, Somerset

CONTENTS

Illustrations

'We Shall Find Out'

GAVIN EWART

On sticks, on walking frames, upright or falling,
the old ones in the block are silently calling;
with mute appeals for cleaning, cooking, shopping,
they trespass on our time – and Time's not stopping,
inexorable, like water boiling eggs.
They're all, as we jollily say, *on their last legs.*

Of helping, what they need's a double helping,
as at their heels those hounds of time are yelping.
Home Helps and Meals On Wheels. When life is ending,
it isn't loving, it's more like befriending
they want from us, the not-yet-too-far-gone,
who still can hear and see and pull clothes on!

Father, James Gray, on the beach at Hayling Island, England, about 1948

Mother, Barbara Gray, Hayling Island, England, about 1948

Simon and Nigel, Quebec, 1941

Still Trying

SIMON GRAY

I was born on 21 October 1936, in a mock-Tudor house on Hayling Island, off the coast of the county of Hampshire in England. I don't believe I was forewarned of the event, and have no idea of how I took it. I don't know whether my parents worked for me devotedly or whether I was a happy or unhappy accident. My mother's tendency to recrimination leads me to suspect that if I hadn't been wanted she'd have told me so, and blamed me for turning up. My father was always reticent about both major and minor matters, so I've no idea which he viewed me as. My brother, sixteen months older, exhibited a very positive response by gazing at me in angry disbelief, then climbing on to my mother's bed and assaulting her. Or so my mother was subsequently to claim.

My memory of my first three years is very feeble. We had a nanny, though my father was at the time only beginning as a general practitioner of medicine, and wasn't well off. But then *everybody*, as my mother said years later, had a nanny. My mother's family, by the way, was always presented to us by our mother as straight-down-the-road London middle class. Her father, dead just before my birth, had been a doctor. Her mother, dead just after my birth, was a teacher. It was only after my mother's death that I discovered the usual family horrors – a touch of madness here, alcoholism there. My father's family was Scots, of humble origin. His parents had emigrated to Canada when my father was eight, and my grandfather had become a fairly successful employee in a large corporation in Montreal. My father was therefore brought up a Canadian, coming to England only after he'd qualified at McGill University. His accent, during the years I knew him properly, was Anglo-Canadian. In the weeks of his dying this accent slipped away, like a first skin, until for a brief period he spoke with a pronounced Canadian accent. In his last days that too slipped away, and he spoke in a strong Scots accent, the accent of his childhood, with which he hadn't spoken for some sixty years. In our beginnings are our ends, I suppose.

My only clear memory of my first four years in Hayling Island is, in fact, to do with my father. He perpetrated what I considered a serious injustice on myself in favour of my older brother. I sought him out, and informed him in a voice shaking with rage and fear that he was 'a big silly'. I then ran. He ran after me,

9

caught me and did something in the parental style of those days that I can't recall, though I've often tried. I have an impression, too, that when younger and confined to a pram, I discovered the principles of locomotion. By rocking my pram violently I was able to roll myself along the garden path. This evidently was a deeply satisfying experience. I continued to rock myself into sleep and then through it, emitting strange singing noises, until well into my late thirties, when the freight of life, probably, in the form of alcohol and cigarettes, dragged me down into an inert, snoring slumber. Now I set myself to it I recall the sea – its smell and sounds, and sitting on the vast sanddunes in the sun in the company of my brother and a Great Dane on whose back we used to ride. But no friends (perhaps we didn't have any). No family meals (perhaps we didn't have those, either). And very little of my mother, which suggests that the nanny performed her duties satisfactorily. But then I don't remember the nanny, either. There may have been more than one, now I come to think of it.

When the war began in earnest, my brother and I (five and a bit and four respectively) were evacuated to Montreal to live with our grandparents, while my mother drove vehicles (I'm uncertain as to their type) for the air force base on which my father was a medical officer. I think they had what used to be called 'a good war', i.e., made friends, went to lots of parties, grieved regularly. My brother and I also had a 'good war', I suppose, in that we were fed copiously, and the only dangers we ran we invented for ourselves. There were initial problems. Some of these were settled easily. We were moppety like English children with lispy voices, who had to make rapid adjustments if we were to survive at the ferocious state schools to which our grandparents sent us. A visit to the barber eliminated the moppet by eliminating most of our hair while bringing our ears into dramatic prominence. It didn't take long to change our accents either – I would say that the lisp was battered out of us during recreation periods over two weeks. One of our evident advantages – we'd never experienced it before – was our freedom: not comparative, virtually absolute. Our grandparents were too old and too out of the habit of children to know how to look after us. Their sense of responsibility ended with our being fed. Besides, my grandmother, I realised retrospectively, was an alcoholic. She spent many hours self-confined with bottles of sherry in a dark bedroom at the back of a large dark house. My grandfather worked in Toronto, returning only for the weekends. He was short, Scots, chain-smoking, and uncommunicating. The only other member of the family was their daughter, a spinster so out of tune with children, at least of this rapidly metamorphosing kind, that she spent most of the day being somewhere else, doing something else. We never knew where or what, as she didn't have a job. I once found her in the kitchen crying over a photograph, I don't know of whom.

Our lives were therefore spent on the street. Within a short time we'd become members of a local gang, the leader of which was, as I still think, the most beautiful girl the world has ever known. She organised all kinds of forays, mainly in search of cigarettes. (I was up to ten a day before I was seven.) Or money to buy cigarettes. And candy. And comic books. But this was business. Her primary preoccupation was the realisation, or more accurately half-realisation, of her own intense fantasies. She was now the leader of an outlaw group; now a pirate princess; now a gun-toting nurse; now a nun consigned to martyrdom. She wrote down all these scenes and cast them impeccably – at least from my point of view, as I was her faithful lieutenant/mascot and accompanied her right to the end, which was invariably her death. She was shot, hanged, tortured to extinction, or burnt at the stake, I crouching beside her in her last moments, the rest of the gang grouped around her or spread at her feet. (I think it was this experience that alerted me to what Richard Harris must have felt when playing the last scene of *Mutiny on the Bounty* – Marlon Brando dying interminably and the wretched Harris thrusting his face into the camera line, in the hope that he too would make it to the final cut – as his nose and chin just about did, to terrific comic effect for connoisseurs of that sort of thing.) On one occasion I did get to cradle her head on my lap, and it was into my eyes she smiled as she sighed her last. When I went back to Montreal some fifteen years later, when an undergraduate at Cambridge, I enquired after her of my grandparents and my aunt. My aunt told me that she had died at eighteen, of leukaemia. I don't know what depressed me most. The brute fact, or that I hadn't been there in my customary role, seeing her through it.

My addiction to cigarettes increased to the extent that to keep up with my demand I was compelled to increase my supply. And therefore my income. My solution was to write an imaginary address for my parents on an envelope, and stand outside the post office, sobbing. When asked what the matter was – about one in five adults took the trouble – I would explain that I'd lost the money for the postage stamp, and piteously hold out the envelope, adding that it was to Mum and Dad at home in England. A reasonable number, about one in three of those who stopped in the first place, obliged. Generally the only trouble came from old ladies who wanted to extend their charity, and take me home for a good meal. This operation, which throws a poor light on me but a favourable one, I believe, on human nature, came to an end when a burly man I'd solicited introduced himself to me as a policeman, and said that, if he hadn't been on his way home, he'd have put me under arrest. He added that from now on he'd be watching me. It's my belief, forty years later, that he still is.

At the end of the war our parents, who I've no doubt expected – memory and imagination being what they are – their rural moppets back, were alarmed to find themselves in possession of two streetwise, jug-eared, crew-cut thugs. My mother particularly loathed our accents – my father had one rather like it buried deep within himself, don't forget. She set about working on it, and as a backup, sent us to the local private school. We were the only two boys as it was a girls' school, and in no time we were saying 'water' and 'tomato' as if we'd never been away. But of course we had, and probably in some respects never quite came back. I'm fairly sure that the experience of being an alien twice in four years explains whatever needs explaining in my novels and plays. This simple diagnosis is complicated by the fact that almost ten years later I was back in Canada, along with my older brother, a younger brother (born when I was nearly ten), and my parents. My father, who had qualified as a pathologist in the immediate post-war years, had re-emigrated, though he hadn't returned completely, preferring to settle in Halifax, Nova Scotia, rather than in Montreal, where his parents and sister still lived. (My grandparents were in their eighties when they died. My aunt died of cancer in her early fifties. They went within weeks of each other, of unrelated illnesses but no doubt according to some psychic domino system.)

My own years between returning from Canada and returning to it were spent going through a conventional middle-class education, though by an unconventional route and in a distinctly unconventional manner. After the girls' school, my brother and I did two years at Portsmouth Grammar School as boarders, about which I have a general memory of perpetual cold, and a particular one of a small brute of a dentist who went at one of my front teeth as if he were an irritable and incompetent carpenter wrestling with a recalcitrant nail. I screamed so much that at one point he cuffed me, and when he finally sent me out of his surgery, blood still streaming down my jaw, informed me that he hoped never to have to see me again. A reasonable hope, as I fell over several times on the way back to the boarding house, once almost directly in front of a bus, the driver of which probably thought I was the first of the juvenile drunks. I do recall two teachers: Miss Foster because she was pretty and kind; Mr Watson because he read Dickens with a passion and wit I have never heard equalled, even by professional actors, and who therefore introduced me to literature and, now I come to think of it, to the theatre as well.

After we'd been at Portsmouth for two years, my father moved to London, where my brother and I were sent to the kind of preparatory school since made famous in English fiction, to which this perfectly corresponded. The headmaster was a mild-mannered classicist with an ageing mother. He was also a black marketeer, as a number of us discovered one afternoon when we strayed into his cellar, and found sides of beef and legs of lamb hanging there. It was a time of severe rationing, and what we were looking at was clearly the quota for a week for over a hundred boys. But as it was a day school, and our lunches were taken at a restaurant down the road, it was obvious, even to us, that the headmaster was making the kind of claim on national resources that could have landed him in jail. Under the circumstances his general air of bewildered benevolence was a tribute both to his criminal capacities and to his natural temperament. I can easily recall two of the other teachers – indeed, will never forget them. One was a long streak, about six foot six, I should imagine, of sadism. He beat us ritualistically, though savagely, with a gym shoe for offences too obscure for his victims ever to be clear about. He was finally sacked. The other was a short, pudgy, and very clever pederast. He was extremely fond of me and would cuddle and fondle me for hours, beat me when the fancy took him, and generally, with soft smiles and roaming hands, kept me in a state of excited subjection until one day my mother met him. I was taken away immediately, sent to a cramming school for a few months – after so much dalliance I'd slipped behind somewhat in my studies – took my public school exam, and scraped into Westminster. My brother, who'd left a term before me, scraped into St Paul's.

Westminster School is attached to the Abbey, and within walking distance of the West End. Cloistered and cosmopolitan, it attracted (at least in my day) teachers who were relaxed, tolerant, and urbane. Several of the older ones had found the atmosphere of the school so congenial that, having arrived as pupils at twelve, they stayed on for the rest of their lives, with only a necessary intermission at Oxford or Cambridge to pick up qualifications for their return. Most of the younger ones were just back from the war. They'd had enough experience of discipline to know that it is only valuable when it makes sense. There were still vestiges of traditional public school authoritarianism, of course – fagging systems with prefects having the power to administer beatings – but the prevalent atmosphere worked against them, insidiously corroding them, so that by the time I left they hadn't so much been abolished as allowed to wither, almost unnoticed, of neglect. Even in my first year the few senior boys who took their power seriously were regarded as aliens really, not only by members of the staff, but by their juniors and victims. They would have been happier, was the

13

feeling, at another school. At indeed almost any other school in the country.

I can't say that my years at Westminster were so much happy in themselves as a source of subsequent happiness, happiness remembered. At the time I was too much in it and of it, and anxiously apart from it, given my perplexing background and the sense, which never wholly died, that all the other boys belonged there by linear right – the right pre-prep school, followed by the right prep school, followed by Westminster – as their fathers had, before them. Those that didn't belonged by a finer right, being scholarship boys, intellectual aristocrats whose status was confirmed by the gowns they wore at all times until lights out. They were boarders, and lived together in one house. I was a day-boy – day-boys were an undistinguished because reasonably large minority – and resented it, particularly the feeling that the life of the school went on after I left it each evening. It was home that seemed to me the prison. Not of my family's making, but my own, out of my sense of exclusion.

But my abiding uneasiness came from the conviction that I was a fraud. My education was pitifully deficient, as I'd come to Latin late and to Greek not at all. My admired fluency as a writer of essays also seemed to me fraudulent, something I'd picked up as I'd picked up the proper accent and manners, acquired by observation and imitation, and without proper content. If the boys and the masters couldn't see the Montreal gangster lurking behind the façade, I knew he was there all right, waiting to expose himself in a gesture or an expression. As it happened, he didn't expose himself at all. He was quite simply caught. By the police.

What happened was this. I'd been given a Georgian penny for my birthday by a great-aunt on my mother's side. A spectacularly useless present, I thought, even by the standards of great-aunts, until one day, returning home with a couple of friends (outsiders like myself, one being short and squat with a permanent smirk that was an accident of feature but taken as deliberate commentary; the other unnaturally tall with a contemptuous manner – the consequence, I imagine, of his having to deal with a drunken father who turned up inexplicably at the school from time to time), I noticed at the underground station a ticket machine that delivered sixpenny-halfpenny tickets and one shilling and sixpence change if one put in a two shilling piece. On impulse I put in the Georgian penny, and a halfpenny, and duly received the ticket, and three sixpences. The rest, once I'd discovered that you could buy Georgian pennies for twopence, was elementary. The three of us bought as many as we could afford, and raided ticket machines all over London. We went at it for months, on the way to school, on the way back, until our income vastly exceeded our capacity to spend it. Eventually two policemen, who had spent hours, if not days, crouching behind the machine we hit most regularly, rose from behind it one morning when I'd dropped in my Georgian penny and my halfpenny, and arrested us. Two of us, me and the small, squat smirker. The third member of the gang had risen too late to join us, and had had to go straight to school.

We were escorted to the police station. Our statements were taken. Our parents were summoned to remove us. A week later, after spiritual preparation by my mother ('You fool, you!' and, 'You've brought disgrace on the family!' and, 'That a son of mine . . . !') I duly appeared with the smirker before a juvenile court. The smirker's father was a barrister, and he'd persuaded a colleague to come and speak in our defence. It was a memorable speech: moving, sagacious and once or twice funny (although I didn't laugh), and nearly tipped the case against us. The magistrate turned irritably towards us when the barrister had finished, clearly recognising that anything he'd looked forward to saying in our favour had already been said, leaving only what was to be said against us, which he said. He let us off, however, with a suspended sentence, on class grounds, I suppose. At least I can't believe that two state school boys would have been treated so lightly. My father reimbursed the underground to the tune of fifteen pounds. As I had twenty pounds concealed under my bedroom floorboards, which I handed over to him, he made a clear profit of five pounds. I doubt whether it was a consolation.

I went back to school terrified that news of my criminal career would have leaked into it, and that I'd be expelled. But nothing was mentioned until years after I'd left, when my housemaster, who was an exceptional teacher of English, let slip that he and the headmaster had known all about it before the court hearing.

I would like to report that this episode marked the end of my tendency to deception, and it's certainly true that after it I became compulsively, not to say preposterously honest in financial matters, to this day lingering on a bus past my stop to give the conductor the fare, for instance. But the profounder deception, the intellectual one, continued. My essays became more and more skilful exercises in avoiding the issues raised in their titles. My contributions in class were offered only for their epigrammatic effect, my characteristic demeanour a posturing arrogance assumed to distract attention from the fact that I still knew virtually nothing. Not that I didn't read. I read all the time. But always and only novels. Tolstoy, Dostoevsky, Dickens, George Eliot. Also the works of Hank Janson, an English writer of American crime fantasies, whose forte was sex, particularly bondage. His works went under the floorboards, in the cavity in which I'd hidden my bags of stolen sixpences. I don't believe now, after twenty years of university lecturing in English, that this was a poor reading list for a sixteen year old, even the Hank Jansons, but there was no English side at Westminster then, and what I should have been reading was history books – histories of Europe to be precise, with special concern for the Middle Ages. It was on this subject, or rather around and around this subject, that my essays were written, deftly, fluently, and emptily. And the style I evolved, courteously aloof from the facts, as if I didn't want to insult the reader (the master of the History Sixth; followed by the master of the History Seventh) by asserting what I assumed he knew, contained here and there touches of real passion quite unrelated to the subject – sweat, so to speak, breaking out on the face of the liar.

But I was believed. Genuinely courteous back, both the History Sixth and History Seventh masters assumed I knew the facts that I assumed they knew and nominated me as a candidate for an Oxford scholarship. I was saved from this exposure by Fate, in the form of my father's sudden discovery that he could no longer afford my school fees. Further, that having had to pay them, and my brother's, had so drained him financially that he was forced back to Canada. Hence, Halifax, Nova Scotia, at the age of seventeen. This meant, by the way, that I escaped yet another (as I was sure it would be) humiliation – my National Service. I had had three fears there: One, that I wouldn't care for it. Two, that it wouldn't care for me. Three, which really contained both one and two – that I wasn't officer material. When reproached by friends for 'getting out of it', I explained that several years in Canada equalled about two years in the Army, as if this were a piece of moral accounting.

Of course, nobody who came across me during my four years in Halifax would have believed that for me this was in a sense a return visit. In those days (I haven't been back for over twenty years) it was a late-Victorian coastal town, clean of air, with vast beaches and a pervasively moral atmosphere. Along the main street there were almost as many churches as there were banks. In honour of my refined educational background, I allowed my hair to hang to the nape of my neck – in my first week a policeman stopped the traffic to exclaim at its length – and my Westminster drawl contrasted pleasingly, to my ears anyway, with the nasal Scotian twang. The irony of a chap destined for the quads of Oxford (if they'd let him in) actually finding himself on the campus of Dalhousie University was one that I further enjoyed by bringing it to the attention of the natives. I sauntered about the college (which now contains one of the largest collections of Rudyard Kipling in the world) with T. S. Eliot's poems in one pocket and a pencil and a pad of my own verses in the other. I saw myself as an intellectual sophisticate fallen among provincials. It was only years after I left that I discovered I'd been seen by almost everybody else as the campus pansy.

My career as a student was a succession of triumphs. I was treated by Anglophile professors and associate professors and assistant professors of English with something close to awe. Quite a few of them were New Zealanders; others were underqualified (i.e., had been to London rather than Oxford or Cambridge) Englishmen. Some were mere Canadians even. Anyway, whatever they were, they seemed more apprehensive of my seeing through them than I was of their seeing through me. My essays were passed about the department, and sometimes on into other departments. Once a professor (or assistant, or associate) of economics searched me out in the library, where I held court by isolating myself in a far corner and working on my verses, to congratulate me on a slimy pastiche I'd produced of the later Henry James, borrowed from an equally slimy but far more skilful pastiche by Max Beerbohm. In seminars I could force abdications with a phrase. Fellow students scribbled my rehearsed throwaways into their notebooks. Those teachers in whose eyes I glimpsed any hint of the sardonic I simply boycotted. This helped guarantee my reputation while satisfactorily undermining theirs.

I also made two close friends. One was the son of a rabbi from Poland who'd invented (or so I understood it) an incisive new circumcision technique. The other was the son of the principal of a Baptist theological college, in whose library I once came across a sort of illustrated treatise on the administration of corporal punishment to young females. I was tempted to steal it. (Which reminds me that last year I was shown around the library of the Harvard Club in New York. The only book I opened – an art history – had concealed in it a [male] homosexual magazine. I wasn't tempted to steal that. But these two incidents are obviously packed with unexplored information – about Baptist ministers; the Harvard Club; and possibly my instinct for books.) Anyway, in the company of these two friends, Louis and Graeme, I read Shakespeare, Plato, Aristotle, Kant, Heidegger, Sartre, Camus, etc. With them I went to Western and gangster films, discussed life and sex (we took them to be synonymous) and to them I showed my poems and my various novels. We founded together a literary magazine called *Ground*, and had numerous editorial meetings which were mainly devoted to excluding from the board a fellow student who we suspected might be more talented than us. We sold annual subscriptions to the mayor, all the professors (associates and assistants), to the prominent doctors, to the lawyers, etc.; and finally produced one issue, after which the three of us left

Halifax. Not together, as a matter of fact, but to pursue our different careers. That solitary issue I now like to think is a collector's item, as it consisted almost entirely of major works by me, published under my own name; and minor works by me, published anonymously, as fillers.

I also had one or two experiences with girls – those who were of an intellectual bent themselves, and therefore thought there was some cachet to be gained from cuddling the campus pansy (who also, by the way, had a weight problem, owing to an uncontrollable addiction to candy bars, hamburgers and Coca-Cola). But on the whole I kept sex down to those conversations with Louis and Graeme about life, or firmly back in the head from which I expressed it into socks and handkerchiefs, in the usual manner of adolescents, which I no longer was. The campus pansy/intellectual was in one or two respects, perhaps, a mite retarded, though in his desires heterosexual enough for two. I suppose this was the inevitable penalty for remaining an English public school boy – which, come to think of it, I'd never properly been. But there were other factors besides the self to frustrate one's yearning for sexual experience in Nova Scotia. For one thing, as my mother reminded me, there was the shortest possible distance between the first kiss and the altar. And then the shortest possible distance between the altar and the first set of nappies. It was, in this respect, quite Mediterranean, although the morality was the consequence of a chilly Puritan, rather than a hot-blooded Catholic moral climate. I don't believe, in all the time I was there, I heard of one broken engagement, though I know for a fact there must have been. A friend of mine, a native who knew the rules but was the victim of an undisciplined nature, had the happy experience of hearing his engagement to one girl announced over the radio while having lunch with the family of another girl to whom he had also just become engaged. The trouble is that I can't remember the outcome, although it's obvious that he couldn't allow both engagements to stand. He later, by the way, embarked on a political career. But it was an added problem in Halifax that, small-town in every respect, it had a magnificent public communications system. Nothing private happened without it being announced on the radio – except the utterly unannounceable things, which were subsequently announced as engagements. There must have been adulteries and divorces even, but I never worked out the radio codes for those.

As soon as I'd taken my Dalhousie degree (a most distinguished one romantically marred by a couple of low marks in a couple of compulsory science courses, which demanded both application and a show of real knowledge) I departed for Clermont-Ferrand in France, to teach as an 'assistant' at the Collège Technique. I left behind my parents, my older brother, who was studying law at Dalhousie, and my younger brother who, a decade later, was to assume my role on the campus although in a less clear-cut fashion, as his generation was more liberated than mine. Nevertheless he did pretty well. A straight-down-the-line heterosexual, he was suspected of all my pansy tendencies.

It had long been my ambition to get to France – really since reading Sartre, Camus, and Cocteau, and being much taken by the early death of Raymond Radiguet, the author of *Le Diable au Corps*. I wanted his experience, without the actual death, if you follow. Or possibly I wanted the death, followed by a speedy resurrection as a young, famous and doomed novelist. But it turned out that it was quite difficult to be a 'Frog' in France, if you weren't born to it. By the end of my first week in Clermont-Ferrand, as I sat in a café puffing Gauloises and sipping 'marcs' with five or six other young English and American personages who were there on roughly the same terms as myself, I felt I was on the right lines. But in fact by the end of the year I still hadn't acquired an older French mistress to initiate me into the mysteries of the heart, etc. I hadn't acquired a younger one either, though I'd have willingly tried to initiate her into the mysteries, as far as I understood them. What I had acquired was a girlfriend, English like myself, and further like myself in that she'd spent the last few years in Halifax, Nova Scotia. She was teaching in a town in the south and sometimes I went down to see her, or she came up to see me. Our sessions together were a torment for both of us, as I was (a) hopelessly in love with her and/or (b) wild with lust for her while she was (a) probably in love with the son of one of the town's gendarmes and (b) not really sure she enjoyed my company, as it was emotionally intense and could turn physically hectic whenever I misinterpreted a signal – a companionable smile, for instance. The conversations that followed my yearning lunges and her methodical parries constituted, for her, the meat and wine of our relationship. When we weren't together, which was usually, I wrote her long letters, or simply lay on my bed in my small, rented room *en famille*, wretched. So when it comes down to it, life, in its usual perverse way, had provided me with exactly what I thought I wanted – someone to initiate me into the mysteries of the heart, etc. At least I doubt if any French mistress, of whatever age, could have taught me more about unhappiness. After I left Clermont I didn't see her again for years – not until I bumped into her at a party in London when we were both in our late thirties – literally bumped into her, as I had to step briskly sideways to avoid somebody's stumble, and found myself making contact with a short but ample mound of flesh, off which I then sort of ricocheted. It wasn't simply that she'd become very fat, but that she'd also become almost circular. If she'd been togged out in bombazine she'd have been a perfect reincarnation of Queen Victoria – apart from the slightly unsteady way in which she was holding a glass that turned out to be full to the brim with brandy. Her conversation was affable though slurred. Nothing, as far as I could make out, had happened in her life at all, apart from this steady rounding process. She lived by herself in a town on the south coast, and taught English to foreign students in a language school. Still, my wife enjoyed meeting her at last – my 'Scandinavian sprite' whose ghost I'd summoned up in the early days of our courting to haunt her.

Gray and wife Beryl with daughter Lucy and son Ben, 1973

Two Poems

PETER DALE

SOUVENIR

The very earth on which they stood
   is gone: three fists of withes,
poor pollards tilted at the wood's edge,
   reeds like scythes up-ended, crossed.

Beneath clouds slabbed with storm,
   their image skimmed with light . . .
Far friend, I hope with you a faded torment –
   Hindsight seems the last betrayal.

CRANE'S BILL

Delicate misty bloom
   huddled away like your words,
a crane's bill of powdery blue,
   mute for all its worth;

not to be gathered or pressed
   where it may grow again.
Let it grow here for the present
   we never took nor gave.

Sweet Ladies, Good Night, Good Night

SCOTT BRADFIELD

'Women only seem like nature when nature's not around. But women are more deliberate than that. A woman's love is completely artificial, just like her cosmetics. Woman's love has design and strategy in it, unlike man's. I think men have been getting bad press for a few thousand years now, or ever since some woman elicited poetry.' Arnold Bromley was picking at his right ear with a twisted paper match and sitting at the counter in Coco's on MacArthur Boulevard. Empty saucers and a single coffee cup sat before him on the counter. One saucer was tracked with chocolate cake topping, the other with coffee and cream.

'Did you want more coffee?' the waitress asked. Her name was Michelle. Michelle was an undergraduate in pre-med at the University.

Arnold looked at her a minute. She was thin, pretty, and immensely un-interested. 'I guess I'll just have the cheque,' he said.

Then Arnold drove to Estelle's place and found Estelle in bed with a man whose name, he learned later, was Bob Reilley. Estelle, as it turned out, had met Bob Reilley at a neighbourhood Safeway approximately two days before.

'There's something I've been meaning to tell you,' Estelle said. Bob Reilley had pulled a towel over himself and, out of courtesy, was putting out his recently ignited cigarette. 'I don't think I've been entirely fair with you lately, Arnold,' she said. 'Frankly, I think you can find a woman who'll treat you a lot better than I do.' Bob Reilley yawned distantly, gazing at his extinguished cigarette in the glass ashtray beside the bed.

Arnold let himself out the front door and pushed Estelle's keys through the mailbox grate. He got in his still-warm car and drove around for a few hours. This time, he stopped for coffee at Denny's.

He looked at the menu just long enough to give himself time to unwind. He already knew the menu by heart.

'Chocolate cake and coffee,' he said after a while.

The tiny plastic nametag on the waitress's blouse said Mary-Anne.

*

'Sex is only more acute than love. But that doesn't mean love is any less real,' Arnold said.

Her name was Jilly, and she worked at I. Magnin. She wore sheer skirts and nylons and bright, almost fluorescent make-up. She had beautiful legs.

'Love's the way we learn the world's immediacy, and so we need it more. Love holds things in context. Love's the melody, and sex just the individual chords in a song. That's why love's so much more important to us when we're alone. Sometimes I think I'd give up my entire life for love. Sometimes I think I already have. Would you like to stop here? Would you like an ice-cream?' They were standing outside Hagen-Daz in the enormous shopping mall. The mall was filled with couples, families, and running children. The windows displayed elegant clothes, furniture, table settings and expensive toys. The air reverberated with golden light. Plastic stools and benches down the centres of each aisle were crowded with dazed, expressionless shoppers and their baggage. The shoppers seemed to be contemplating nothing. They seemed very enervated, and annoyed with themselves for feeling so tired.

'How about a chocolate chocolate-chip ice-cream?' Arnold said. 'Does that sound good? Did I tell you, Jilly? Did I tell you you have beautiful legs?'

Jilly had a boyfriend named Bob. 'But you're a lot more interesting than Bob,' Jilly said. 'You're always saying interesting things. It's not easy for a person to feel very intelligent about themselves when Bob's around. All Bob ever talks about is his car. This is what he's going to do to his car. This is what he's bought for his car. It's like living with Instant Replay. It's like living with Bob's car. Sometimes it's like not living with anybody at all.'

Jilly broke up with Bob, and Arnold knew he was on warning. From that day forward Arnold tried to be as interesting as possible. He took Jilly to movies, museums, sporting events, RV and boat shows, carnivals and circuses. He told her about politics, language, culture, literature, theatre, war, domestic surveillance, wok cooking, the history of unions, home-made salad dressings and just about anything else he could make up. But then one night at her apartment he just wanted to watch television. He couldn't think of anything interesting to say and, for that one night, he didn't really feel like saying anything interesting, either.

Jilly broke up with Arnold the following weekend and went back to Bob. 'I'm a one-man woman, Arnold,' she said. 'And I'm afraid Bob's that man. It's not that I don't still care about you a lot. It's just I think you'll be better off finding the sort of woman that's right for you, and I'm afraid that woman's just not me. Now here, I've packed all your things in this bag, so if you could take just a quick look around. I'm expecting Bob here any minute. If you see his truck, try to step on it, will you? You'll know it's Bob's truck if it says "Bob Reilley's Plumbing Supplies" on the side.'

Arnold purchased new shirts and after-shave. He purchased new shoes. He restyled his hair and purchased a blow dryer. He even purchased a new futon with a straw mat base, hand-painted sheets and matching pillowcases. When he got home and looked at himself in the mirror, he liked what he saw. He looked different and he smelt different. He looked like a man who knew what he wanted from life, and was prepared to go out and get it. He smelt like a man who wouldn't take no for an answer.

'I guess I've always been an other-directed sort of person,' Lydia Sanchez said, eating mushroom *linguini* at Marie Calendar's in El Toro. 'A lot of people are self-oriented sorts of persons, because they've never progressed beyond the nipple-stage. That doesn't mean I'll let other people take advantage of me. And *that* doesn't mean I'm just thinking about myself because I won't let other people take advantage of me. When you let other people take advantage of you, you're doing them a severe disservice. You're not letting them learn what it's like to live in a real world where people don't let you take advantage of them all the time. I received an EST summer scholarship when I was eighteen years old. I was audited by scientologists and believe it was the most profound, unforgettable experience of my entire life. Now I like to think of myself as a sort of Rosicrucian Buddhist, and I'm presently attending night classes at Valley College to receive my BA in cultural anthropology. During the week I'm a receptionist for Dr Brady, Credit Dentist. You know Dr Brady, don't you? He has those awful commercials on TV. In reality, though, Dr Brady happens to be a really nice man.'

Arnold looked over both shoulders, trying to locate the waitress who had virtually disappeared with his order of gin and tonic. Marie Calendar's was filled with young, attractive and well-groomed couples, all very much like Arnold and Lydia, who shamelessly flirted not only with one another, but with members of the many other attractive couples seated at tables around them.

As if in afterthought, Lydia said, 'I really love eating at Marie Calendar's.'

Arnold loved Lydia because she did to him in bed everything he could possibly hope for and didn't even wait for him to ask. They had many wonderful times together for almost ten days. Then, like rain, it happened. One night Arnold brought the makings for sandwiches over to Lydia's apartment and they watched television together. 'You know, this is all anyone ever needs,' Arnold told her, gesturing with his pastrami salad on French roll. 'I mean, we've got decent food, we're in love, and there's a good movie on TV. It's not like we need those things other people need to be happy. You know, like fancy restaurants, or going to big stage shows. You know, like *Cats* or something. It just goes to show you don't need a lot of money or anything just to be happy.'

That night, after Arnold had gone home alone, he felt it break in the dark air. It wasn't a sound so much as a beat, like a sudden shift in temperature, or some seismic tremor deep underground. Arnold sat up in bed suddenly. He looked around his dark room at the lopsided bureau, the paperbacks on their shelves, and the tiny Casio electronic alarm clock on the orange crate beside his bed. There was something reproachful about it. The time was 3.45 a.m.

Lydia stopped returning his calls. 'Is your machine working all right?' Arnold asked her answering machine. 'Or are you just not getting my messages?' Finally, early the following month, Arnold went to Hamburger Hamlet and had three quick gin and tonics on an empty stomach. The gin filled him with resolve, fortitude and self-confidence. 'Call it arrogance if you want,' Arnold told himself, getting back into his car. 'That's fine by me. You've just got to be a little arrogant in this life if you're ever going to amount to anything.' He parked outside Lydia's office on Van Nuys Boulevard and waited for her to come out.

'I want you back in my life,' Arnold said when she appeared. She was accompanied by two young women who wore dental assistant uniforms. They both smiled at each other over Lydia's shoulder, as if they had been anticipating Arnold's sudden courage all along. 'I want us to spend the rest of our lives together,' Arnold said.

Lydia removed the bolus of pink gum from her mouth and placed it delicately on the back of a wooden bus bench. Her eyes were deep, black and remorseless. 'No,' Lydia said. 'No, Arnold. I'm afraid I don't think that would be a very good idea at all.'

His name was Bob, she told Arnold finally in a letter. Bob Reilley. She and Bob were very much in love. But that didn't mean she wasn't still concerned for Arnold's own happiness and peace of mind. She sincerely hoped that, someday, after they had both, as she put it, 'straightened out their lives emotionally and had gotten to know themselves deep inside', they could be friends again. Perhaps, at some elaborate reconciliatory dinner, he could meet Bob face to face, and she could meet his new girlfriend, and they would all feel very, very happy things had turned out so very well for everyone after all.

*

Arnold began putting on weight. He drank Budweiser by the case, and spent all his free time in front of his cable television, dialling the remote control and watching baseball games. He began checking books out of the library concerning low blood sugar and dietary disorders. Then, suddenly one morning, he noticed his hairline was receding. For the first time in his life he developed faint rashes of acne around his jaw and neck, particularly after he shaved. He felt generally tired and listless. His apartment seemed to be growing tinier and more unkempt. The new hand-painted sheets on his futon even began to unravel. Every few weeks or so he went to the supermarket filled with predictable resolve. He purchased fresh vegetables, low-carbohydrate oils and salad dressings. When he returned home, however, he already lacked sufficient energy for mixing them together. Over succeeding days the carrots and celery shrivelled and diminished in the refrigerator. They began to resemble shrunken heads and genitalia, or the archipelagos of fantasy kingdoms in garish paperback books. Sometimes they mildewed and he threw them in the trash.

'Love's an illusion we can't always afford,' he said at Sambo's. The half-eaten chocolate cake was turning stale on his plate. The waitress, whose name was Polly, brought him more decaf. 'Sometimes love isn't love at all. Sometimes it's just the past. Sometimes it's just some moment we never really knew.' Arnold grew silent for long periods of time, watching the steam unravel from his coffee. There always seemed to be something important he meant to say, but he couldn't recall exactly what that something might be.

'I live right down the street,' Polly said when he brought his bill to the register. Polly had bright, flat white teeth. Polly was in the University drama department. 'Why don't you give me a call sometime?' Polly said.

He took long walks now rather than drove. At work, many of the female employees began showing him obvious and elaborate concern.

'Something wrong? Something wrong at home, Arnold? Bad financial investments? Vitamin deficiency? Have you ever heard of Epstein-barr virus syndrome? Do you know a lot of young men are diagnosed with Epstein-barr virus syndrome these days? It's mainly dietary, Arnold. It means there's something seriously wrong with your diet.' Sometimes one of the women's long, brightly-lacquered hands would flash and lightly brush Arnold's warm forehead. When they came up close to him he could smell their moist perfume. A silk sleeve might brush his bare arm. He might catch a glimpse of cleavage.

'You need someone who'll take care of you,' they said. 'You need someone who loves you. Why don't you lie down for a minute, Arnold? Why don't you come over tonight and I'll fix you a nice, hot dinner?'

SWEET LADIES, GOOD NIGHT, GOOD NIGHT

Arnold, suddenly out of breath, would walk quickly from the office and into the men's room. There, among the harsh fluorescents (which felt to his skin more like texture than light) he would gaze at his florid, spotty face in the bright mirror, and feel the heart pounding in his chest like something mechanical and estranged. His stomach and colon fluttered. That spring he began to develop a bleeding duodenal ulcer. Whenever he returned home, the message light on his answering machine was flashing.

'Hi, Arnold? This is Vicky. Do you remember me? Do you remember San Diego? I was just thinking about you. I mean, if you wanted to give me a call or anything, I'll be at home. OK, Arnold? And if you don't want to give me a call, well, that's all right, too . . . '

Bob Reilley's plumbing supplies franchise was located in Tustin, and one smoggy, humid day in April Arnold drove out to his office carrying in his right-hand jacket pocket a Smith Model 686 .357 Magnum which he had purchased earlier that month at Grant's for Guns in Costa Mesa. The gun felt very heavy in his pocket. It was a clean, comfortable sort of weight, however. There was a lot of security in the weight of a .357 Magnum, Arnold Bromley thought.

'It's not like I haven't been through all this before,' Bob Reilley said. 'It's not like I don't understand exactly how you feel, or why you've aimed all your misdirected frustration at me.' Bob Reilley was leaning back in his padded leather swivel-chair. His feet were propped up on the desk, and his hands folded behind his head. Bob Reilley had changed a lot since that evening more than two years ago when Arnold had discovered him in Estelle Constantine's bed. Bob Reilley had developed a very significant belly, flaky red hands and face, and a large bald patch across which he had combed elaborate swirls of greasy, dyed-black hair. 'I do sympathise with you, Arnold. I really do.' Arnold thought that Bob Reilley was just about the most nondescript-looking man he had ever seen in his entire life.

Arnold took a seat on the unsprung sofa facing Bob Reilley's desk. The sofa was inadequately covered by a thinning ozier bedcover. Arnold had let himself in through the unlatched back door of the abandoned plumbing supplies office, where the long aisles were filled with dismantled shelves, refuse, and long intricate ropes of dust. Only one, semi-charred fluorescent bulb flickered overhead. The door marked 'Manager' had already been open when Arnold had walked in and found Bob Reilley asleep at his desk.

Without removing his feet from the desk, Bob Reilley reached behind himself for one of two half-empty bottles of Jim Beam and a glass from the bookshelf.

'It always hurts to know we're not the only one. It always hurts to learn love isn't something that's been waiting for us, but just something that happened to be around when we got there. Look, if it's any compensation, I've been through it myself, you know. I mean – excuse me. Would you like a drink?'

Arnold looked thoughtfully at the proffered Jim Beam. He held the gun in both hands, the handle leaning against his crossed right knee. 'No, thank you,' he said.

'Well, don't want to let it go to waste.' Bob Reilley finished his glass and poured another, taller one. 'As I was saying – I've been through it myself, Arnold. It's not like I'm some heartbreaker or something. It's not like I just run around Southern California trying to make time with other men's women.' Arnold wiped his nose with the back of his hand. Then, thoughtfully, he wiped the back of his hand against the thigh of his grey slacks. 'Look, we're both single guys, right? Every woman we meet's just *bound* to belong to *some* damn guy or another, right? Women aren't like us, Arnie. They don't sit around brooding very long when things are over with some guy. They move on. So what are guys like you and me supposed to do? Keep our eyes on the obits or something, like apartment hunters in New York? The race goes to the swift, Arnie. The quick and fleet of foot. Don't tell me you've never done it. Don't you start playing holier than thou with that stupid gun.'

'This isn't personal,' Arnold Bromley said, indicating his heavy gun with a breezy gesture. 'This one's for abstractions. This one's for love.'

'Oh, my. Sorry, Arnie.' Bob Reilley had spluttered Jim Beam all over the back of his arm. 'Love. I get you. We're talking love now, are we?'

Bob Reilley wedged his glass between his thighs and poured it full again, splashing some into his lap. The abandoned offices echoed with the buzz and flutter of the broken fluorescent. Bob Reilley's voice seemed to increase suddenly in both volume and confidence. 'That's what women are for, are they, Arnie? Love. Love and beauty, right? You tell me about it, Arnie. You see those fucking empty shelves out there? What do you think those empty shelves used to contain? Well, I'll tell you what they used to contain. They used to contain the most complete hardware maintenance equipment selection in the tri-county area. That's what love does to a guy. It takes a big successful business and turns it into nothing. There was one girl, Arnie, she broke up with me, right? For six months she phoned me ten or twelve times every night and called me a bastard for letting her break up with me. She showed up on my porch with a hand-axe. I took it away and the police arrested me for assault. Women send their boyfriends after me all the time. They want to teach me lessons because I didn't love them enough. They want to teach me lessons because I loved them too much. I've had my telephone number changed about a hundred times. Do you want to know how many women are out there, Arnie? How many women in the world there are who hate my guts? I haven't any idea, Arnie. I really don't. Women aren't action, Arnie. They're judgement. And I think judgement's a lot worse than action just about any day.'

Bob Reilley took another long drink and wiped his mouth. 'So what are you going to do with that gun, Arnie? Shoot me? Put a bullet in my head? I'm really scared. I go to bankruptcy court on Friday. I've been sued, assaulted, defamed, perjured, disavowed and once, I was once almost even impaled. How do you think things'll turn out in bankruptcy court this Friday, Arnie? The judge's a woman. So's my lawyer. Women are everywhere, Arnie. It's not like the good old days. Today there are women in government and banking. There are women in distributorships, construction, and even controlling the entertainment industry. My broker was a woman. We went out two weeks or so. I lost $73,000 after that one was over, Arnie – $73,000. Then, in February, one of them burned down my house. It was a nice house. The insurance policy had lapsed. No, my insurance agent wasn't a woman. But my insurance agent's wife was. My insurance agent's wife was probably the biggest mistake of them all, Arnie. Two nights in a Best Western in La Jolla. If I could go back in my life and change just one thing, it would probably be those two nights with my insurance agent's wife in La Jolla.'

'You're right,' Arnold said, holding the gun just as firmly. 'Women aren't nature. Women are judgement. Women are language.'

'It's like there's nothing we can do, Arnie. We're damned if we do and damned if we don't. It's like no matter what we do or how we behave, they'll still be able to say anything they want about why we did it. What's our behaviour matter if they can just remake behaviour's rules any time they want?'

'It's a losing battle.'

'It's like time.'

'It's like we're always being betrayed by our own bodies.'

'It's women, Arnie. It's not us. It's not you and I, pal.' Bob Reilley got up from his desk. 'We got to stand up for one another, right, Arnie? We got to stick together.' He was walking slowly, confidently across the room. His right hand reached out for Arnold Bromley's gun. 'It's ridiculous for *us* to be arguing, isn't it? It's language again. It's like we're playing right into their hands.'

Arnold Bromley stood up too. 'No, Bob. This isn't language. This is reality. And now, if you don't mind, I think I'll get back to language again.' At that point, Arnold shot Bob Reilley six times in the back of the head as he made his break for the door.

In the storage aisle, the fluorescent extinguished with a sudden, audible pop. Everything went completely black.

'Good night, sweetheart,' Arnold said. 'Good night, Bob.'

Two Poems

PETER PORTER

DESKTOP CONFESSION

It is the brain which publishes our lives.
The fingers fight on any keyboard to
Invent the self, the total which survives,
The secret fundamentalist who
    Loves me but hasn't heard of you.

The screen lights up, the processor reveals
Its hoard of words, its everything that is;
The little brain is shocked, so it appeals
To death and summary, and 'hers' and 'his'
    Are timed and ticked, with *sic* and *viz*.

Consider the girl whose head's between her legs,
Think of the minutes stalled in days and hours,
Making novels fly, grading rhymes like eggs –
The evanescent words, the paper flowers,
    The shining Freudian lakes and towers,

These are confession's public instruments,
The only way a private voice can win.
Great houses send their several compliments,
This time you really get beneath the skin,
    You lift the lid and peer within.

Alas, there's nothing there to see; we come
From an unprinted blackness, one by one
Into the light; our books applaud, and some
Live in our minds longer than things we've done,
    Old desktops warping in the sun.

WITTGENSTEIN'S DREAM

I had taken my boat out on the fiord,
I get so dreadfully morose at five,
I went in and put Nature on my hatstand
And considered the sinking of the Evening Lands
And laughed at what translation may contrive
And worked at mathematics and was bored.

There was fire above, the sun in its descent,
There were letters there whose words seemed
    scarcely cooked,
There was speech and decency and utter terror,
In twice four hundred pages just one error
In everything I've ever said – I looked
In meaning for whatever wasn't meant.

Some amateur was killing Schubert dead,
Some of the pains the English force on me,
Somewhere with cow bells Austria exists,
But then I saw the gods pin up their lists
But was not on them – we live stupidly
But are redeemed by what cannot be said.

Perhaps a language has been made which works,
Perhaps it's tension in the cinema,
Perhaps 'perhaps' is an inventive word,
A sort of self-intending thing, a bird,
A problem for an architect, a star,
A plan to save Vienna from the Turks.

After dinner I read myself asleep,
After which I dreamt the Eastern Front
After an exchange of howitzers,
The Angel of Death was taking what was hers,
The finger missed me but the guns still grunt
The syntax of the real, the rules they keep.

PETER PORTER

And then I woke in my own corner bed
And turned away and cried into the wall
And cursed the world which Mozart had to leave.
I heard a voice which told me not to grieve,
I heard myself. 'Tell them,' I said to all,
'I've had a wonderful life. I'm dead.'

Emergency Landing

MARTIN AMIS

When it comes to flying, I am a nervous passenger but a confident drinker and Valium-swallower. And although I wasn't exactly goosing the stewardesses or singing 'Viva España' (this was a BA flight to Malaga), I was certainly in holiday mood. In fact I had just called for my second pre-lunch cocktail – having enjoyed, oh, I don't know, a good three or four on the ground – when I began to sense that something was up.

Suddenly withdrawing the half-dozen meal-trays she had just laid out, the flustered blonde stewardess told me that the bar-service had been suspended. In answer to my very anxious enquiries, she told me that the bar-service would soon resume. I was still grumbling to myself about this when the Captain's voice came on the public-address system. 'As you have probably noticed,' he began (I hadn't), 'we have turned full circle and are heading back to Gatwick. For technical reasons.'

Now I saw that the sun had indeed changed places, and that we were flying north over France towards the Channel. Unworriedly I resigned myself to the usual frustrations: the six-hour wait, the free orangeade, the bun-voucher. Now I saw also that the stewardesses were systematically searching the overhead compartments. So. A bomb scare. But this bomb didn't scare *me*.

The Captain came on again. In a bored voice he levelled with us about the 'alert'; then, more urgently, he added that, in view of the time factor, it was now thought necessary to make an emergency landing, at Dinard. At this point, still feeling no more than mildly devil-may-care, I took the second half of my Valium 5, helping it down with a swig of duty-free whisky. I offered the bottle to the girl in the window seat, whose clear distress I began, rather grandly, to pooh-pooh. The bottle was then taken from my hand by the stewardess and fondly restored to its yellow bag. We speared down on Dinard, not in the cruising, wallowing style that aeroplanes usually adopt for landing, but with steep and speedy purpose.

Seats upright. Place your forehead on the back of the seat in front of you. There will be more than one bump. Don't be alarmed by the reverse thrust. Leave all your hand-baggage. Move as quickly as you can to the exits and slide down the escape-chutes. When you are on the ground – run.

EMERGENCY LANDING

I glanced, for the first time in my life, at the benign cartoons of the safety-procedure card. Then I hunkered down for the final seconds. I thought of my wife and eight-month-old son, whom I was flying out to join. I had escorted them to Gatwick ten days previously, on the same morning that the Air India jumbo had been blown to pieces (or so we then thought) over the seas of south-west Ireland. My apprehension at Departures that day had been far more intense than anything I was feeling now. What I was feeling now was, mainly, relief that my wife and child weren't with me. Had they been, everything would now be different. For a start, I wouldn't be drunk. I placed my wallet on my lap (I had no jacket), and waited.

The 737 landed like a skimmed stone, like a bomb itself, like a dam-buster. The reverse-thrust came on with such preternatural power that the tail seemed to lift, as though the whole aircraft were about to start toppling end over end. In this weird squall of gravity and inertia, my wallet shot off my lap and slithered along the floor, four or five rows away. Now the plane was quenched of its speed; seatbelts clicked, and immediately a pressing queue had formed in the aisle.

My paramount concern at this point was, of course, to find my wallet. Coolly lingering in a vacant three-pack, I was well placed to watch the passengers flee past me to the end of the aeroplane. As they awaited the stewardess's order (the doors had to open, the chutes had to inflate), the passengers pressed forward, four or five women – perhaps those with children – in the forefront. Physically they showed no more agitation than, say, people in fairly desperate need of a bathroom. But their voices contained an edge of panic. In those few seconds I remember only one word being spoken, and often repeated. 'Please . . . Oh please.' Soon the stewardesses were urgently shooing them down the aisle. I waited. Then, grumbling and swearing, I crawled around in search of my wallet and scattered credit cards, which had themselves been torn loose by the G's.

At last I strolled to the door. 'Sit and jump,' said the stewardess. Those elongated dinghies are a lot less stable than they look, but down I went – wheee! – and jogged away from the aircraft, which, I saw, had reached the very brink of its runway and had jarred to a halt midway through a ninety-degree turn. Five yards from its nose lay the edge of a lumpy brown field.

Around me was being enacted the formless drama that perhaps invariably succeeds every incident of mass crisis or jeopardy. I can only describe it as a scene of peculiar raggedness, with sights and sounds somehow failing to coordinate. A man keeled over in the grass, clutching his heart and moaning loudly. A girl with a sprained ankle was being helped away three-legged to safety. Busily the stewardesses gave comfort where they could. I myself – with, no doubt, egregious nonchalance – attempted to console a weeping woman. There was a good deal of crying in the air, brittle, exultant. Soon the French security guards were shepherding us tenderly across the field to the terminal.

After a shock (I later learned), the body needs a lot of sweet tea. But the drinks were on BA, and most people drank a lot of brandy, which (I later learned) is the very thing the body needs least. I compromised by drinking a lot of whisky, and remained in capital fettle throughout the five-hour wait. The evening soon became an exercise in maximum *esprit de corps*, with the passengers informally dividing into two camps: those who were saying, 'I've never been so scared in my life,' and those who were saying, 'You think this was bad? This was nothing. Let me tell you about the time I . . . ' My position was, I suppose, unusual. I had not felt fear; but I knew that fear would have been an appropriate feeling.

Now, all writers secretly maintain a vampiric attitude to disaster; and, having survived it, I was unreservedly grateful for the experience. Here I sat, not in Gatwick but in Dinard, enjoying a good free dinner and pleasant camaraderie. And when I flopped into bed at five the next morning – replacement aircraft (the original was later searched, fruitlessly), baggage identification on the dark tarmac, the incident-free completion of the journey – I felt like a returning hero, a man who had come through a testing time, without a scratch, without a wince.

And I was wrong. For the next few days, although outwardly cheerful enough, I was pretty sure I was dying – and of natural causes, too. My body was subject to strange tinglings. Throughout my tragic siestas I lay there trembling and boiling, as if a tram station or a foundry had established itself beneath the bed. I watched the world through veils of helplessness. This was no hangover. This was old age.

My wife suggested that I was suffering from delayed shock – which, I admit, gave me quite a turn. Although I had privately diagnosed a brain tumour, I was still reluctant to identify the malaise as an after-effect of something that had bothered me so little. My body, however, continued to insist on the truth. Hoaxers and other operatives in the terror business will be relieved to learn that, when it comes to fear, there's no such thing as a free lunch, or a free dinner.

So much, then, for my valour on the fields of Dinard. I emerge from the incident with another new experience, and no credit whatever. I was as brave as a lord, as brave as a newt. Chemically numbed at the time, my fear – of which there had clearly been plenty – had just burrowed deep and waited. I had sneaked out of the restaurant without settling the bill. The body's accountants had redressed the ledger, with interest. And for nearly a week I was wearily picking up that tab.

Two Poems

JAMES LASDUN

SELF

Sometimes I almost have you then I don't,
Always one frame ahead of me you move
Into a room, talk, scrawl a line, make love;
I copy every gesture but I can't
Quite catch you up. As accidental others
Reeled into family ciné films, your soul
Must have been turned round idly like a jewel
In the minds' eyes of extras – schoolfriends' mothers,
Shopkeepers, waitresses – what did they see?
How did they misconceive you, or did one
Happen to catch the stone's full fissured dazzle?
I know you less than even so glancingly,
I, who should be closer to you than son
Or lover; I'm not even on your trail.

AZTEC HOTEL

Staying on; the imagined future of a coast
Opened like Tenochtitlan to the white men,
Who never came: a Bauhaus/barracks ruin,
Terrace and private bath for every ghost.
The sun drifts like a coin in oil. A swarm
Of winged priests, each its own obsidian knife,
Murders the feathered serpent into life;
Their bodies swell and redden on my arm . . .
Verdigris'd whitewash, crimson bougainvillea
Spurting from concrete pillars like a wrist's
First leap of blood . . . A set of six chrome rungs
Drops to a hot blue void. Despair,
A dry pool where a bald hen roosts,
Quetzalcoatl cackling on stone tongues.

Pigaunt

MARY SULLIVAN

When my father spoke on the telephone with a certain mixture of belligerence and fear, we knew he was talking to his sister Alice in Bath, Somerset. We hung round listening, trying to make him laugh and laughing unkindly ourselves. On Alice's rare visits, he and she had only to be in the same room to quarrel. In later life I was amused by their identical expressions of teak obstinacy, until others told me how often I wear that same expression myself; and I am jolted by something of her I see in the mirror from time to time.

I first remember Alice in her forties. She was built like a telephone box, and used her height and bulk to intimidate. She had a loud, nasal voice; fat pouches encroached on her fine eyes. I see her endlessly chomping the sweets and chocolates given to her, in spite of wartime rationing, by her various protégés.

Some of these people were Catholic refugees met through her church work; she called them 'my lame ducks'. Some were the young men and women she took up with at the office where she held a clerical post: these she hoped to convert to Catholicism. In such relationships she was genial and generous; several of those she befriended were still writing to her fondly many years later.

Alice's missions began in the early twenties, when she was about twenty-five and living in Battersea with her widowed mother, Bridget Shiel, her younger brother, Jack, and an orphaned cousin named Kathleen. In Alice's adolescence, an epileptic sister, Ellen, had been her special care. When the child died at ten or eleven, Alice threw herself into the religion which for the rest of the family was not much more than a tribal custom, diligently observed but seldom thought about or discussed. She attended mass daily, and made her confession as often as she was allowed by the parish priest, Father Lynch, who was brisk with her scruples and discouraging about the possibility of her vocation.

Alice removed to a neighbouring parish to worship, and soon became a nuisance to the priest there, who mentioned the matter to his friend, Father Lynch. One evening the Shiels were visited by Father Lynch, asking to speak with Alice and her parents.

Young Jack, sitting quietly on the dark stairs, heard Father Lynch talking pleasantly to Alice, cajoling, reminding her that there was plenty of time for God to show her what she should do. He heard his parents embarrassedly echoing the priest's words; then Alice crying, shouting, hiccuping; he heard his own name.

Soon after that, Alice left school and went out to work. The cousin, Kathleen, then a small child, came to live with the Shiels in rooms they rented from an engine-driver. In their shared bedroom, Kathleen was required to kneel before a picture of the Sacred Heart to recite her night prayers, ending with a hymn led by Alice in her developing contralto. When Alice came to bed, she lifted the blankets off the little girl. If the child's hands were between her legs or near her crotch, Alice awoke her and in silence arranged Kathleen's arms in the shape of a cross on her breast.

Jack won a scholarship to Battersea Grammar School, putting his foot on the ladder that would take him quite away from railwaymen's rented cottages. His parents beamed and boasted. Alice lettered a text in red and black, and stuck it to the mirror in Jack's room: 'What shall it profit a man if he gain the whole world, and suffer the loss of his soul?'

When she was about twenty-two, Alice tired of the minor religious leagues and sodalities which had absorbed her great energies. Now she joined the Catholic Truth Society, whose speakers competed with the politicians, fundamentalists, anarchists and flat-earthers at Speakers' Corner, Hyde Park. Nervous but determined, she learned to stand up to the heckling, whistling, and ironic clapping and cheering with which her random audiences greeted her witness. Those who knew her then have told me that she dealt rather wittily with her opponents. I imagine it was such an exchange, and the black-haired large handsomeness of her youth, that caught the attention of Gerald Poole.

The Shiels never knew exactly how Gerald made his living. He called on them to be formally introduced not long after he took Alice to tea at Lyons' Corner House for the first time; soon he was often to be found holding court in their kitchen. His cheerful cockiness, curly brown hair and natty clothes charmed Alice's mother. Kathleen, whom he tickled and teased, fell in love with him immediately. Jack was less delighted; sometimes, when Gerald accepted a third cup of tea, Jack pointedly gathered up his books and slammed off to study in his cold little bedroom.

Alice's father, observing the strength of her feelings for Gerald, made an effort to discover something about Gerald's background and prospects. All he learned was that Gerald claimed to be thirty-four, though John Shiel put him a little older; that Gerald had come to London from Suffolk, where he had no family left; and that he was something to do with a firm of estate agents, though which one, and where, he never precisely said.

Gerald told Alice he lodged with an aunt in Finchley, rather out of the way for their Sunday trips, and besides, the old lady was not very well, and easily put out by visitors. Every weekday evening Gerald wrote to Alice. Sometimes he put on the back a little comic sketch of himself leaning on the counter in the all-night post office at the end of the Charing Cross Road. The daily arrival of his blue envelope became a joke among the Shiels, though Alice never laughed as she snatched up her letters to read in private. When her mother pressed to know if Gerald meant to marry Alice, she blushed and muttered that there was such a thing as spiritual friendship. Jack picked up this phrase; when they heard Gerald's jaunty rap on Sundays, he said, 'Ah, the spiritual friend,' and put his hands together as if to pray.

Gerald went once or twice more to hear Alice at Speakers' Corner. Then he said he would learn more quickly about God and the church if Alice were to concentrate on him; so they went on Sundays to Epping Forest, along the banks of the Thames, and to the London Zoo.

One day an oblong white letter, postmarked Finchley, arrived instead of the square blue one. Gerald's wife wrote to say that if Gerald had promised marriage, he was not free; and that he was not free anyway, and wouldn't Alice agree once she knew about the gambling and the debts?

Alice had to agree. Weeping, she burned his letters. She cried in her room in the evenings, and for some weeks went to confession at a different church every few days. She was so wretched that even Jack was sorry and gave up mocking for a time.

The sudden death of John Shiel from meningitis appeared to drown Alice's first grief in this new sorrow that overwhelmed them all. She had felt that her father was on her side in her battles with life, even though his overt pride was in his clever son. This loss propelled her back into all kinds of church activities, and, as she slowly recovered, she began to collect people at work and anywhere else she could, with their conversion in view.

Jack had recently finished at university and was now a civil servant. At home he took his father's place, in that his mother deferred to him, waited on him, and was slightly nervous of him; all of which Alice watched sourly.

Cousin Kathleen, now eighteen and earning her living, was engaged to a merry young man called Arthur Bentley. Lingering on the front steps one night, they heard Alice rattling the chain on the other side of the door, and issuing meaningful coughs.

'Good evening, Alice!' Arthur shouted through the letterbox. 'Fine weather for the time of year!' Arthur's unshakeable good humour wore down Alice's defences, and in time she dropped her most outrageous attitudes with them. Alice and Jack kept up their nursery scrapping and sniping into old age, but a lasting kindness grew up between her and the Bentleys.

Kathleen's account of Alice's life before I was born was necessarily not as full as the one I had from my father, but it contained details of a kind he preferred not to remember. Alice's mother, my grandmother, was a watery sort of person, dominated by both her children, but with one sure weapon against her daughter: Alice's unmarried state. Kathleen has often told me how this fact, trailing all its associations, was demurely slipped into my grandmother's remarks whenever she and Alice disagreed: how Alice could be made to droop and crumble.

It was Alice who found Jack his wife. Rosie Gaynor, intelligent, uninstructed, flighty, came as a junior to the office where Alice was supervisor. Alice singled her out for the missionary treatment right away. The offered friendship, and the novelty to her of religious ideas, beguiled Rosie for a while; but at that time in her life she was too lazy and too hilarious to pursue any such thing very far, and was anyway sceptical by nature. Alice tried hard with her pamphlets and little talks, but eventually she had to give up.

When first introduced to the Shiels, Rosie had been in awe of Jack and his books, and the high hopes people had of him. Jack had dismissed her, as he dismissed all Alice's acquaintance. Rosie continued to visit in Battersea; by and by it seemed not to matter which of Alice or Jack received her; at last it was understood that her friendship was with Jack alone.

There followed a passage of several years when they were sometimes a couple, sometimes friends among a changing group of friends. Each threatened to marry elsewhere but did not. In the spring of 1935, they were on holiday in Brighton. It happened that, at the aquarium there, Rosie saw Jack lift some little boy on to his shoulders to look at the fish over the heads of the crowd. In that moment it struck her that if they went on as they were, she would find herself dancing at his wedding, and not as his wife. She told him this; he told her other things; six weeks later they married, with Alice in a tremendous hat, first among their guests.

When I was born, two years after my brother Patrick, my parents moved to an outer London suburb. When the war began, my father's work exempted him from conscription, while Alice was assigned to a civilian post in the offices of the Admiralty. An exploding shell destroyed the house in Battersea where she and my grandmother still lived; they came to us as a temporary arrangement which stretched to several months.

Alice and my father had each become accustomed to ruling a household: now they shared one, with all their old antipathies intact. My mother kept the peace as well as she could, but had her own difficulties with her sister-in-law. Alice had an alarming habit of suddenly smacking our faces when Patrick or I displeased her. My mother, intervening, said that it was affronting to us and was wrong, no matter what we had done. Alice said that we were hopelessly out of hand, especially Patrick, who needed much firmer treatment.

He had been something of a favourite with her at first, a handsome, bright little boy of nearly six. She played with him boisterously; she had my mother dress him in his sailor suit, and took him off with her to church, and on visits to friends in her old parish. Alice sometimes teased Patrick about his sticking-out ears, something both our parents had at different times asked her not to do. When Alice and Patrick returned from an outing one Sunday, he let fall that Alice had remarked on his jug-ears to her friends, and had smacked him when he objected.

Everyone had something to say except my grandmother, who hid in the kitchen. Patrick cried; my mother defended him and reproached Alice, who, guiltily overbearing, declared that Patrick was already spoilt, and should be punished when he was pert with adults. My father told Alice to lower her voice, and, when she continued to boom, asked her to come and speak to him in his study. This made my mother laugh; they all turned to her in surprise; somehow the moment passed, the quarrel evaporated, and the household lurched back to its usual condition of rumbling unease.

A few weeks later, Alice and my parents were sitting at the table after a meal. They were listening to the radio news, which in those wartime days often induced an atmosphere of excitement and fear, uncomprehendingly absorbed by Patrick and by me. Patrick had broken the spring of his clockwork train. He brought it to the table, but finding that my father would not attend to him, began to run it backwards and forwards among the crumbs on the tablecloth. He balanced a piece of bread on the funnel of his toy; when it fell off, he picked up the morsel and ate it.

Alice leaned across the table. 'Patrick,' she said, 'I don't like eating with a pig.'

'Alice!' my mother began sharply, but my father cursed and bent closer to the radio. What he heard made him hold up his hand for silence. They listened with frightened faces, and Patrick with his train disappeared under the table.

PIGAUNT

Soon after this, Alice was transferred to the Admiralty department which had moved to the relative safety of Bath in Somerset. It was decided that my grandmother would follow when Alice had found them somewhere to live.

The night before Alice left, my mother made a rabbit pie for our last meal all together. My father brought home some cider, and after a glass or two he began to sing uproariously, 'Run, rabbit, run, rabbit, run, run, run!' We thought it was wonderful.

Patrick stood on his chair and waved his fork; he gazed round delighted; his eye fell on Alice, absently picking out and eating the crumbs of pastry in the piedish. He pushed his face towards her. 'I don't like eating with a pig, Aunty,' he said in a low, serious voice.

Alice reached out to slap him, but feeling the eyes upon her, dropped her hand. 'You're going to have to do something about this child,' she said furiously to my father.

'Oh, you asked for that, Esmerelda,' he replied, laughing.

Alice rushed from the room. Patrick began to jump up and down on the chair, screaming, 'Pigaunt, Pigaunty, Pigaunt, Pigaunty!'

'Stop it, that's enough, get down!' my mother said, cuffing him, but she was laughing too.

Alice moved into a flat in Bath, at the top of a Victorian villa in Henrietta Street. My grandmother joined her there, and our household settled back into its own courses.

Patrick found that he could make either of our parents laugh on quite unsuitable occasions, by murmuring primly, 'Pigaunt,' while I, without really understanding the joke, could be wound up to hysteria if he only framed the letter 'p' at the right moment.

More than a year passed. I started at Patrick's school, to which my father took us on his way to the railway station. We did not connect a tumbled public building, or a gap newly smashed in a familiar row of houses, with what news the radio urgently put out several times a day. We were often hurried in the night to a dank, underground shelter, where we lay on metal bunks, listening to the near, loud, deathly sounds of war; but what interested us were the snails crawling up the wet walls, and the shrapnel, currency at school, we would pick up on the roads in the morning.

On a Friday in March, 1943, my mother met us from school and took us to see *The Wizard of Oz* at the Regent Cinema. There was a solemn thrill in the occasion, for we had only ever seen one other film. At the moment in the story when the black-and-white screen is suddenly filled with the bright acid colours of the land of Oz, a needle of excitement pierced me; I seized my mother's arm and turned to her in joy; but she put her hand on mine most soberly.

It was dark when we came out. Patrick and I cantered about rowdily on the way home, full up with what we had seen. As we turned into our own street, my mother said, 'This time next week you'll be in Bath.'

'In Bath? In the bath? All wet?' Patrick shouted.

'No, daft, in Bath, in Somerset, where Nana and Aunt Alice live.'

'What? Pigaunt? Really?'

'I think you'll have to stop saying that,' my mother told him.

'Not to *live* there?' I asked.

'For a while,' she answered. 'You won't have to be in a shelter there, it'll be safe.'

'Will we go to a new school? Will Pigaunt take us?' said Patrick.

'Alice will. Aunty Alice. Or Nana,' said my mother.

I stood still. 'Why can't you take us?'

'I will take you, darling, I'll take you to Bath.'

'No, to school, you can take us to school.'

My father came up behind us. He was carrying a bag of oranges, a great rarity then; he held them up for us to jump at. He knuckled our heads with his signet ring, and we all went indoors together.

Each day my mother described some new detail of the life we were going to, as she prepared our clothes and gathered our possessions. 'Nana's going to look after you. She knows what you like to eat, doesn't she? And she'll tell you your story when you go to sleep.'

'Yes, only when you're not there,' I said, looking at her calmly.

'I'm going to be here, darling, or who would look after Daddy? It's for you to be safe, you see.'

'Supposing Pigaunt slaps us?' said Patrick.

'I don't think she will, Pat,' said my mother. 'We've specially asked her not to do that any more. And you must remember not to say that word from now on.'

I was surprised that Patrick worried about the Pigaunt. It was obvious to me that my mother would protect us, though it was indeed a puzzle to know how my father would get on by himself in London, which was, it seemed, suddenly so dangerous.

Rathwick Villas stood separately from the beautiful sweep of Georgian houses in Henrietta Street, though built of the same stone, and like them smoke-blackened and rain-worn. On the top floor of Number 2, an attic room was used for eating, with a tiny kitchen made out of a cupboard across the landing. The high-ceilinged sitting-room below was sparsely furnished, not much having been rescued from the ruined Battersea house; but the wind-up gramophone had survived, with some old records of music hall songs; the Millais picture *Bubbles* was there, and a set of wedding china in the glass-fronted case.

Alice and Nana shared a large, bleak bedroom; Patrick was given a small room, down a flight of stairs lit ruby-red by a stained-glass stripe in the window. For me a mattress was laid on a pile of trunks and boxes in a corner of the big bedroom, under a mournful picture of the Sacred Heart, and partly concealed by the flank of a dark wardrobe. My mother slept there with me the night we arrived. Although we were cramped and uncomfortable, I was completely satisfied with this evidence of her protection.

I went out with Patrick in the morning to explore the park opposite. The low, overgrown entrance led down a slope and out upon a wide, bowl-shaped lawn, ringed with shrubberies and studded with closely-set trees. We tried the rustic seats in a piss-smelling log cabin, and we knelt to poke sticks into the goldfish pond in a bare winter rose garden. We were soon cold, and came back to the flat, looking for my mother. She was sitting with her coat on, drinking tea with Nana, her small suitcase at her feet.

'Where are you going? I'll come with you,' I said.

She put her arms round me. 'I'll see you soon.' She kissed Patrick. 'Be a good boy.'

Nana took me on her lap. 'Say goodbye to Mummy, now.'

Patrick and my mother went downstairs together, and we heard the front door bang. I said firmly and cheerfully, 'She'll come back soon.'

'Not for the time being,' said Nana. 'Look, let's empty the cases and put everything away, shall we?' And after a while, 'There we are, Margaret. What are you going to do now?'

The Convent of the Holy Redeemer stood on a corner, in a wide avenue lined with large, square villas. It was a mean, mustard-coloured copy of some French château, but the lovely surrounding lawns and walks and arbours softened its grim aspect even in the leafless cold.

Alice held me by the hand at the yellow oak front door; Patrick stood behind us.

A young, fat-cheeked nun appeared, wearing a sacking apron over her grey habit. 'Oh, good afternoon, Miss Shiel! And Patrick and Margaret, is it? Reverend Mother's waiting for you in the parlour – this way,' she said.

We followed her along a dim tiled corridor, where brown radiators were cold to my passing touch.

Reverend Mother looked very old to me, papery, with a soft, hissing voice. 'Miss Shiel. And these are your brother's dear children. Sit down here; Sister Gabriel will bring us some tea, won't you, Sister?'

I moved to the wooden bench she had indicated, but Patrick stood with his hands in his pockets, watching Sister Gabriel go out. Reverend Mother turned to him, moving shoulders and neck in one, in order to see round the angle of her starched coif. 'Sit down, young man,' she said. 'I hear you're quite a handful. Well, well. You're going to be in Sister Paul's class, I expect your aunt told you? No hands in pockets there, you'll find.' Patrick put his hands behind him, his ears turning red.

'He is rather wild,' said Alice. 'No proper discipline at home, of course, and I believe their London school was dreadfully rough. I'm surprised at my brother really.'

'Now, Patrick, you've begun Latin, I suppose, but perhaps not French?' said Reverend Mother.

'What are those?' said Patrick.

'I see. And where have you got to in Maths?' she asked smoothly. 'Arithmetic, I expect you call it?'

'Oh, I can do sums,' said Patrick.

'Good. And will you read this to me?' said Reverend Mother, handing him a book which Patrick was surprised to find was about Robin Hood. He read aloud with amusing liveliness, but, when he looked up for approval, saw that Reverend Mother had turned her attention to me. 'You'll be in Miss Grundle's class,' she said. 'And if you manage well, you can move up in the autumn term. That's after the summer holidays, you know.'

'I won't be here then,' I replied. 'My mother's coming soon to take me home.'

'Oh, but what will your aunty do without you? And your granny?' said Reverend Mother, smiling and catching Alice's eye.

Sister Gabriel returned with a tray of tea. Seeing that Patrick and I left most of ours, she asked permission to show us over the school. Once alone with us she took our hands and, stepping outside, suddenly ran with us across the empty playground. There were lights and voices in the school, and in the dingy hall which Sister Gabriel said was the common room, we found four or five tall girls, with a much younger one seated at a piano. They surrounded Sister Gabriel.

'What's for supper? What's for pudding? Have you got a stamp I can have?'

'Why are they at school on Sunday?' said Patrick.

'Boarders,' said the tallest girl. 'We live here all the time. There are some others that go home at weekends, like now, and everyone else comes just in the daytime. Are you starting this term?'

'Yes,' said Patrick.

'No,' I said. 'Well, we are, but we're going home soon; our mother will come and fetch us.'

'Oh, shut up,' said Patrick.

'I've been here three years,' said a red-haired girl. 'I wish my mother would fetch *me*.'

'Cecily,' said Sister Gabriel to the small girl who had been playing the piano, 'take Margaret to see Miss Grundle's room, would you? I think Patrick would like to look at the gym.'

'Will I have to do gym with girls?' said Patrick.

'No, just with the day-boys,' said Sister Gabriel. 'We'll come back and wait for you here, Cecily and Margaret.'

'I was in this class four years ago,' said Cecily, idly banging desk lids in Miss Grundle's room. 'She's stricter than the nuns, and she hits you if she hears you call her Grumble.' Cecily, with her experience, and her tidy plaits with little crinkled curls on her forehead, seemed more than a child: somehow an intermediary between me and the powers that kept the red-haired girl in this place for three years without her mother.

'My brother calls my aunt something,' I said.

'What? What, then?' said Cecily.

'Something rude.'

'What?'

'P . . .'

'*What?*'

'Pigaunt!' I said loudly.

'Oh, Pigaunt, how funny! Has she heard him?'

'She did once. He just says "p" now.'

Cecily lost interest. 'Let's go back. Sister Gabriel might let us make toast.'

We started school at the convent the next day. Nana took us to and fro at first; then she came to meet us on Pulteney Bridge, halfway home, and in a few weeks we came and went alone.

In Sister Paul's class, Patrick, whose dangerous reputation had gone ahead, sat at an inky desk with Kennedy's *Shorter Latin Primer*, while in Miss Grundle's always strangely quiet room, I entered upon similarly hopeless relations with

long division, and the subject and object of a sentence. As time went on, Patrick's failures were recorded and punished, while mine were merely deplored. No efforts of ours, and no abilities of other kinds counted in our favour. We were unsuitable for this superior education, and we remained out of our depths, in glassy boredom tinged with fright, as long as we were at the convent school.

Now and then I saw Cecily with her friends, in the playground or the big meadow, passing on the main stairs or at a nearby table in the dining-hall. She spoke to me only briefly; custom was against it, as I quickly came to understand. I had chosen her nevertheless. I told her my mother was coming tomorrow, next week, next month, and made the claim again as fast as time disproved it. Cecily was only nine or ten herself, and completely limited by the convent, as I was not, but for a long time she was patient with my tedious confidences.

Sister Gabriel, who worked in the kitchen and in the vegetable garden, was pleasant with the children, especially the younger ones. She would bring back a ball that landed among her cabbages, and join the game for a while, shouting orders and giggling. She spoke cheerfully to Patrick when she met him alone in a corridor, evicted from a lesson because of his invincible ignorance of the dative case; once, a toffee appeared by his shoe after she had gone clumping by.

At playtime Patrick flew about like a bullet. He fought boys at random, tearing their clothes and his own; he threw stones at Sister Gabriel's chickens; he climbed to the top of the walnut tree in the meadow and stayed there until Reverend Mother was fetched and ordered him down.

Alice passed on to our parents the convent's complaints. After my father's death forty years later, I found her letters in a box with the ones Patrick and I wrote home every Sunday. She described marching Patrick to apologise to the nuns for this or that misdeed, and she was blunt enough about his poor school record and mine; but there was some humour in what she wrote, and a misleading air of being almost on Patrick's side.

I saw that in my own letters I had never referred to my mother's return, though for months I believed in it as I believed the next day would break. Patrick's letters ended with a little cartoon, accurate and charming: Sister Gabriel chalking out an ink blot on her white coif; or Nana absentmindedly wearing her carpet slippers in the street.

Our parents could not have divined from any of the letters from Bath the dreariness of Patrick's perpetual disgrace, or the pure quality of my obsession. They knew what an unlikely guardian Alice was; but at that time thousands of London children were sent to live with strangers, and those that remained were in constant danger. Our safe-keeping with people to whom we belonged must have been something to hold on to in their own turmoils, and not to be unsettled by faint reports of our childish difficulties.

My grandmother ran their home in Rathwick Villas for her daughter as if Alice were the man of the house. Patrick and I were kept out of the way when Alice came home from work in the middle of the evening. Alice took us to mass on Sundays, and occasionally on some expedition, but all the practical details of our care were given to Nana. She showed Alice the domestic accounts on Friday nights; hastened to clear the rooms of our mess when Alice was expected; and in the kitchen hid her bottle of stout behind the flour bin, for fear of Alice's disapproval.

In the cold, stuffy room I shared with them, I was often awoken late at night, Alice's bulk looming over my corner box-bed, the covers turned back, and my arms arranged for me in a cross on my chest.

Once I whispered, 'I'll tell my mother.'

Alice heard me. 'It isn't your mother who is hurt by sin, it is Almighty God.'

Alice sometimes brought home from her office a shy young man or a polite girl, who for a while came to mass with us on Sundays, and to lunch afterwards. We glimpsed another Alice then, the good-natured, generous aspect of her that earned the affection of those she befriended, and of which my parents later spoke as flickering out unaccountably, even in the midst of some shocking and absurd piece of behaviour.

Alice, who was always busy with parish affairs, served on a committee to do with Catholic refugees. The members met at the flat, where my grandmother waited on them in her usual stolid way; but when a Pole named Karol Horoch was present, I more than once heard Nana muttering to herself as she came away from the sitting-room. Karol, having been assisted by the committee, now attended its meetings, and had taken to calling at odd times, alone. He brought flowers and sweets to Alice and my grandmother; he kissed their hands; he sprang to move chairs for them or to adjust the angle of a lamp.

Karol had not heard of his wife and children in Poland for several years. He spoke of them to Alice by the hour; sometimes he cried. He tried to talk to my grandmother if he called when Alice was out, but Nana was impatient with his muddled English, and embarrassed by the loneliness and need which even Patrick and I could discern.

My grandmother complained openly about Karol; she said he came for what he could get, and that he gave her the creeps. Alice was reproachful; Nana made some scoffing reply, from which the bitterly spoken words '*any* man!' became separated and lie in my memory, two stones.

When Father Lane came to stay early in the summer, Nana kept her thoughts to herself. Thomas Lane was the present chaplain to the London convent Alice had attended. He wrote asking her to find him a couple of nights' lodging in Bath.

Alice was flustered and delighted. 'Father Tom can have Patrick's room, Mother: Patrick can come in with us, and Margaret – Margaret, now.'

Listening as I put on my shoes to go to school, I thought what an interesting bed the sitting-room sofa would make, and how jealous Patrick would be.

'Why not give Father Lane the sofa? It's only a night, or two,' said Nana.

'No, no, a *priest*, Mother! I'll have a word at the convent this evening,' said Alice.

It was arranged that I should spend Thursday and Friday nights of the following week at the convent. Plainly the idea was impossible, and ten days' time was to me a remote and meaningless distance. I simply withdrew my imagination from the matter. The days passed; I appeared biddable enough; suddenly it was too late: I found myself at tea with the boarders after school on Thursday, and night coming.

'They can't put you in our dormitory,' said Cecily, 'it's full up during the week. Where do you think this kid'll sleep, Ros?' she asked the red-haired girl, who was eating bread and jam and reading.

'In that little room, sick-room, sort of, next to Sister Paul, I should think,' said Ros, looking at me. 'What's the matter with you?'

'Nothing,' I said. 'I wondered, I mean – '

'What's up?' said Ros. 'I expect you're homesick; is that it?'

I stared from one to the other.

'But you don't *like* your aunty!' said Cecily. 'You call her – ' She stopped.

'Let's go down to the meadow,' said Ros, 'see if they've mended the swing. Come on, Margaret, it'll be all right.'

Sister Gabriel sent me in long before the others, but when Cecily came to say good night, I was still dressed and sitting on my bed.

'You'd better be quick, Margaret,' she said. 'Sister Paul will be up for prayers in a minute. You're supposed to be asleep.'

'I've got to go home,' I said.

'You can't, it's dark. What for?'

'My mother might come,' I said. And then in a rush, 'Supposing she comes and I'm not there? Supposing she goes away again?'

'Oh, I see,' said Cecily, and sighed. 'She hasn't come all this time, has she? You always say she's coming, but she never does.' Cecily spoke kindly, but her reasonable tone stifled hope. I began to cry. 'Look, your brother, what's his name? Patrick, he'll be there, won't he? So she'll know you must be somewhere. And your aunty would tell her,' Cecily said. We heard Sister Paul on the stairs. 'Oh crumbs, get into bed, quick,' said Cecily, and was out of the door before I could speak.

I lay in bed in all my clothes. I kept still. I heard from along the passage Sister Paul leading the prayers and the girls' responses; footsteps, other voices, a door closing. After a while I heard Sister Paul getting into bed in the room next door. I slept, and woke to complete darkness. I felt horror of the strange place. I got up and went out into the corridor. In the blackness I fell over the fire-bucket kept at Sister Paul's door. Light came from her room and she appeared, wearing a cotton hood instead of her coif, and without her round spectacles. 'What's this noise? Margaret! Margaret Shiel! What are you doing?' Then, seeing that I was fully dressed, Sister Paul said furiously, 'Have you been out? Where have you been?'

'No, Sister,' I mumbled. 'I thought – I tried – I wanted – '

Sister Paul pushed me back into the little room. 'Get undressed at once, now. Get into bed. Patrick Shiel's sister! A great girl like you! Your aunt will be pained by this, very pained indeed!'

I lay in the dark again. I thought of my mother looking for me in the empty streets and, when a rasping bell awoke the convent in the morning, I did not know whether I had thought or dreamt of her all night.

Sister Gabriel came to look for me when lessons ended on Friday afternoon. 'I hear you don't like it with us,' she said. 'Is it my cooking?'

I looked down. Sister Gabriel turned my face to hers. 'You're to go home with Patrick,' she told me. 'But you must both wait for your grandmother, she'll come to the front drive.'

'What about the priest? Is she angry? What will my aunty say?'

'It's all right, you'll see. Go and get your things,' said Sister Gabriel.

'What did you have for breakfast?' Patrick asked me as we stood together in the drive. 'Anything interesting? Sausages? I hope that old twerp's got out of my room; isn't it horrible sleeping in your bed? They both snore, don't they, and Aunty whistles as well. And grunts.' He laughed. 'Puh. Puh. Pig! Pigaunt!'

I did not want to laugh, but laughter tore out of me. I sat on the gravel, bent over, choking.

'Am I going to stay at home tonight?' I asked Nana, as we walked through the town. 'Where will Father Lane sleep?'

'He's found himself another bed for tonight, for a very special reason,' said my grandmother. 'Look.' She pointed along the Grand Parade. 'I think you know that lady and gentleman.'

Our mother and father stood at the corner of Bridge Street. They saw us and held out their arms. Patrick reached them first. He put his head inside my father's coat.

'Were you looking for me, then?' I said to my mother.

'Oh yes, darling,' she said, laughing painfully, and holding me while I laid my wet cheek on her sleeve.

Alice returned from work that evening to find Father Lane had politely withdrawn, my parents booked into the guesthouse a few doors away, and that I had persuaded my mother to allow me to sleep with them there. 'Father Tom could have stayed, if Margaret's going to be with you,' said Alice angrily. 'What a way to arrive!'

'Your turn tomorrow night,' my mother said to Patrick.

But I slept in the guesthouse each night on a folding bed beside my parents. Sometimes I woke and got up to look at them. Sometimes I heard their voices cloudily through my sleep. I was consoled and triumphant.

Patrick and I were slippery when questioned about our progress at school. Discovering that our parents did not realise how well we could read, we dazzled them with that, and became vague when Latin or long division were mentioned. None of it seemed to matter. We went to the seaside at Weston-super-Mare. Patrick learned to swim in an afternoon, chucking himself blithely off a shelf of sand. We had a picnic beside the goldfish pond in Henrietta Park, watched from a distance by a child I sometimes played with in the evenings there. I made my mother call her over and give her a slice of our cake, so that the girl would know I had a mother too.

At school Cecily had heard that my parents had arrived. 'Will they meet you today?' she asked sharply.

'They brought us this morning; didn't you see them? And they'll come this afternoon,' I said.

Cecily, looking down from the playground wall after school, saw us go off with my mother alone. We went to a café near the Abbey.

'Daddy had to go back this morning,' my mother said. 'They sent a telegram.

He left you a present, look, and he's going to send you some books, both of you.' He had given us each a ten-shilling note. We examined them incredulously. I saw my mother look at her watch.

'*You're* not going, though,' I told her.

'I have to go this evening; there's a train at six.'

'Can I come to the station?' Patrick demanded. 'I know the way home. Can I?'

'You could live here,' I said to her fiercely. 'There's room in my bed; Nana would let you.'

'We'll come back at Christmas,' my mother said. 'We'll all be together again then.'

'I'll come on the platform with you,' said Patrick.

'Well, you're not going,' I said to her, folding my arms.

I did not speak as we walked home, and I kept out of the way while she collected her things. There was angry-sounding conversation on the top floor, then Alice flounced down to her armchair in the sitting-room. Nana stayed upstairs while my mother came to find us, to say goodbye.

When I heard the front door close, I went in to where Alice sat knitting forcefully, like someone signifying 'knitting' in a game of charades. I moved as if carelessly to the window and, looking down on Henrietta Street, I watched my mother as she went away.

Later that evening I followed Patrick to the park. He looked for his friends, but there was only the keeper picking up bits of paper with his bayonet-stick. We sat in the log-cabin.

'*Will* she come back?' I asked Patrick.

'Look, *shut up* about them, will you? She *said* they're coming at Christmas, didn't she? You heard. Don't go on about it.' I was silent. Patrick said abruptly, 'I'm not going to school on Thursday. Don't tell anybody.'

'Why not? Where will you go?'

'Oh, for a reason. Just somewhere. Don't tell anyone.' He punched my arm with each of the last words. I left him and went to look at the goldfish that lurked under the sheets of waterlilies. We could just hear my grandmother at the upper window, calling us in.

Cecily came up to me in the meadow the next day. 'Was that your mother? Why didn't your father come too?'

I said, 'They had to go.' And then before she could ask any more, I said quickly, 'Shall I tell you a secret?'

'You and your secrets.'

'Patrick's not coming to school on Thursday.'

'So what?'

'He's going home,' I said at random, 'right home, to London, I mean, he knows the way to the station.'

'Don't be daft,' said Cecily. 'He can't do that, he hasn't got enough money. You're making it up.'

On Thursday morning Patrick turned back when we were halfway to the convent. '*You tell anyone!*' I went on without him. Nothing was said at school and, as I walked home in the afternoon, Patrick came out from a big clump of rhododendrons in the park. He had been there most of the day, and had twice seen our grandmother go by, carrying shopping and humming. He was wet and hungry and bored. As we waited for Nana to come down and let us in, he said more savagely than before, 'You tell anyone and I'll smash you.'

'Patrick Shiel! Margaret! Come here!' Sister Paul was waiting as we came into school. 'Where were you yesterday, Patrick Shiel?'

'I was at home,' said Patrick. 'I was, um, I was ill.'

'Not at the station, then?' said Sister Paul heavily. 'Not on the train to London, I take it?'

'London? No, I was in the park.'

'Ah, were you? Very ill in the park? Then why does Cecily Talbot think you'd gone on the train?' Sister Paul showed a crumpled piece of paper. 'This is about you, Patrick; Cecily wrote this silly note. And what is this word? What is this dreadful word, Margaret?'

'Is it Pigaunt?' I said at last.

'You know it is. How could you speak like that about your aunt? What would be happening to you without her? She is a wonderful woman, every-one loves her here, and so should you. The things she does for the parish! Go into the chapel now, and tell Almighty God you're sorry. Reverend Mother is away this week; I shall write to your aunt myself, and she must speak to your parents.'

Patrick had to carry the letter home. Alice was still out when we went to bed; Nana left it on the sitting-room mantelpiece.

I woke while they were undressing, and as usual pretended sleep. I heard Alice at the mirror, slapping the sides of her jaws. There were creaks, rustlings, murmurs. The light went out. My grandmother began to snore. I heard weeping.

We expected immediate punishment, but none came. Alice never referred to Patrick's truancy and, if she sent Sister Paul's letter to our parents, we never heard of it. Gradually our apprehension faded; the affair moved off within a clot of silence, and sped into the past. I said no more to anyone about my mother's return.

We were back in our same classes and still more or less bemused by what went on there, when the autumn term began. Away from school we had acquired some freedom. We were allowed out in the city, and we went about with our friends from the park. My father sent us the books he had promised, and for the first time we had tickets to the public library, a kind of liberation in itself.

We were less completely subject to Alice and Nana. Alice's working hours became more erratic, and she was increasingly preoccupied at weekends. She still regulated our affairs through Nana, and oppressed us in details herself, but her peculiar, almost physical power over us, which was like a spell, had begun to dissolve.

Our parents were expected on Christmas Eve, but my father was recalled at the last moment, and they did not come until two days later. Patrick and I spent the time twanging with excitement and disappointment, racing up and down the flights of stairs, fighting, and hanging out of the sitting-room window to see along the street.

On Boxing Day we flew to answer the doorbell. The Pole, Karol Horoch, stood smiling, his arms full of flowers and parcels. 'For you, this one. For Patrick, this. And is your dear aunty here?'

'You have timed it well, Karol,' Alice called down. 'Jack and Rosie haven't turned up yet; there's plenty of lunch for you!'

Patrick's glance slid over mine.

'Oh, dear lady!' Karol bent over her hand. 'I could not come before.'

'Aunty's very giggly today, isn't she?' said Patrick to my grandmother as we were drying the dishes.

'Yes, well, no fool like an old fool,' Nana said.

'What does that mean?' asked Patrick with special airiness.

'It means that you and Margaret must take these cups down, and mind your own business,' she said.

The afternoon darkened over the park. Nana was in her bedroom. Patrick and I sat with Karol on the sofa. We were drowsy in the heat from the gas fire; Alice slept in her chair.

'There was a crow,' said Karol. 'This crow wanted to drink water, but could not reach it in the jug with its nose.'

'I know that story; I've got it in a book,' said Patrick.

'I want to hear it,' I said.

'It found a little stone, very small stone, and dropped it in the jug,' said Karol.

'Yes, and then lots more to make the water rise, I know,' said Patrick.

I reached across to hit him, and Karol lifted me and sat me on his lap. 'You tell us then, Patrick,' he said.

'I'll get my book,' said Patrick.

I was tall to be on Karol's lap; I felt foolish; I wriggled and met a hard yet yielding lump where I sat. Karol bent to me and laid his lips on mine. His tongue licked over my teeth and down into the floor of my mouth. A serious pleasure brightened and died in my body. I drew back from him and looked round to find Alice watching us with an expression I could not read. Patrick came back with his book. He and I sat on the floor; Patrick leaned against Karol's legs and began to read the fable aloud.

During his visit, my father looked at our school reports and went to call on Reverend Mother. He asked us if we would like to leave the convent and go to the local primary school, which would, he said, be like our London one. Alice banged the table and said she would not be guardian to Catholic children not at a Catholic school. My father said he might have to take us home, but on the last day of the year, he and my mother set off without us.

Patrick had been fired by those words, and he believed from day to day that we were about to go home. I was no longer a believer, and I turned away when he said, 'What's the first thing you'll do when we get there?' or claimed to know the day and hour we would arrive.

We went home at Easter. At our old rough London school, nobody was interested in our stories about the convent. By the next year, when the war ended, the time in Bath had become a far-off, seldom-mentioned episode, of which our separate recollections had begun to diverge.

Family visits were exchanged until my grandmother died; there was always a row about something. Alice continued to speak *ex cathedra* on matters of faith and morals, writing long, disapproving letters at each stage of our education, deploring our respective choices of career, and finally ex-communicating us when we made non-Catholic marriages. My mother handled the troubled relationship gracefully, but after her death my father paid Alice only a wincing annual visit, during which Patrick and I were not mentioned.

Alice knew something of us nevertheless. She had remained friendly with her cousins, the Bentleys, to whom I was much attached and saw often. When my daughter was born, Alice wrote me a pleasant, ordinary letter, a tremor, now, in the ornate hand. I had a second daughter. A parcel arrived from Alice containing a little dark-blue coat edged with red, which she had knitted for the baby.

I took it from its wrappings. I thought of Alice, now grown old, making this in the sitting-room at Rathwick Villas. I thought of Karol, and Father Lane. I thought of Gerald Poole, and the lost sister, Ellen, and clever little Jack.

Alice had been knitting when I stood at the window and watched my mother go away a second time. My mother went down the steps, across the road, past the tangled entrance to the park, along the curve of Henrietta Street, and out of sight. As she went, I thought: If I bear this now, I shall always be able to bear anything; but I was wrong about that.

Two Poems

CATHY BOWMAN

THE FOOT PEOPLE

In the middle of the Christmas table
the stuffed turkey glows, a declining empire
waiting to be divided, gutted,
and devoured by the ferocious appetites
of the Foot People. They repose on cushioned chairs,
twelve continents with flasks of hard
liquor and all of history next to their hearts.
Tonight they dine on a chorus of sweetheart
peas and huckleberries on canopied beds
of mint, bone-bone beans, bow-tied chives, fluted
eggs, sweet potato embers doused in drippings,
celery trumpets, and drums of platinum blond beer.
They wait for this meal all year. The fourteen-
year-old girl stares at her blow-dried wings
in the china plate. Cornbread rises
and dangles like the Tower of Babel.
All around her the Foot People quake.
Wrinkled cranberries twinkle half mad.
Her head feels like a captured moon tugging
at her stick bird body, bound in its new bra,
matching panties, and starched holiday dress.
Her moon head pulls like a long lick,
while the stick body pushes her into the nervous
hands of the chair. A voice corrects
from the right. She hates her knees. She hates her
lips. She toys and picks at the dark
meat she cannot eat. All around
her the Foot People yawl and yawl. When she tries
to speak blood slaps at her ribs. They yawl
and yawl. Blood slaps her face! Words flop on her

tongue like foamy waves. Her head buoys, her body sinks.
It's her mother's kiss she craves to cool her neck.
She looks down at her chest and thinks about
her nipples. They remind her of her feet.
No man would want to kiss them. She has her father's
feet. She calls her father's side the Foot People.
Now in the kitchen, six foot-aunts and the grandmother
tell her – *undo your dress.* They look below
her belly, above at her new breasts.
Then she gets the five rules for life,
one for each fat toe of the right foot. *The eyes*
of Texas are upon you all the live long
day, they sing well past midnight and no one
sees when her head begins to lift
the stick body higher, higher. Below
the table stretches like the great
rivers of the world, the Euphrates,
the Colorado, the Congo, while tobacco
smoke smears in a boozy tornado.
Bluesy candles snake dance in a line.
The oriental poppies glitter to infinity.
She opens the window, floats outside.
It smells like the ocean at night.
The trembling poplars wave to her like sisters.
She gets into her father's blue Buick and drives.

KING ARTHUR

Uncle Mitch, Mitch Mitchell, had a belt
so long and powerful it could go to work
for him when he was tired. That belt could
wrastle down an angel. You know, the one
on page fifty-six of *The Children's Living
Bible*. Even though their house was small
I think it had a closet all its own.
It was that strong. Brilliant, too. It had eyes
too. Eyes that could, when called upon, tell just
who had lied, cheated, arsoned, greed or thieved.
Exactly who had sniffed whose and put a finger where.
Just who in fact would be written in the Book of Life
or Death. It could, it was a fact, send us all straight
to hell with a smell of bacon fat and sulphur vapour.
You can bet your bottom dollar it was a thrashing
from King Arthur that burned little Mitchie's
hair such a violent shade of red. That poor soul
had about a million sinful freckles. *Pecas*
is the word in Spanish. But how we loved
his evil ways. He swore he saw King Arthur slide
into the moonlight and crawl across the border
into Juarez. Listen to that screech.
The belt is coming home now and he's looking
for someone to lick. From the branches
of the only fruit tree on the block the King
with court of giant June bugs kept the watch.
We couldn't get those peaches that we craved.
But that was all before the day Uncle Mitch,
Mitch Mitchell, got laid off from his shift
at Standard Oil. That night, my Aunt Yvonne,
sweetest one, hit the stereo. She cracked
open a fifth of 150 proof, sun of a gun
we're gonna have big fun down on the patio.
The moon fell in the sky like a cultured pearl
in a curvy bottle of Prell. Somewhere in the house
King Arthur recoils on the shelf.

The Bridge

STEPHEN WALL

On the evening of the day his wife finally left him Richard celebrated by making love to another woman. That was not, of course, quite how he put it to himself. Nevertheless, he felt a strong urge to mark the day of his release from a situation which had long been deteriorating, and a declaration of sexual independence seemed the appropriate way to do it. He had resisted temptation so far and much good it had done him. What was there for him to be loyal to now?

Julia had announced her departure at breakfast, a time of day when she was normally full of business-like energy and when Richard was not at his best – one of their many small incompatibilities.

'I think I should tell you, Richard, that I'm leaving today. I don't want to leave a note, or anything like that.'

'What do you mean, leaving? When will you be back?'

'Well, I'll be back soon to collect some more of my stuff, and we can talk about which things you want and which I'd like to have. There's no hurry. I'll give you a ring.'

'You mean you're *not* coming back?'

'Richard, I do wish you weren't so slow in the mornings. Why you try to read the paper at this time of day I can't think – you never take any of it in. I'm leaving today because I'm moving in with Peter.'

Although he had long anticipated what was happening, Richard didn't say anything because, now that it was real, he felt too ill to do so. Julia, with the intuitive perception of the married, realised this, and was touched.

'You'll be all right, darling. It's for the best, really it is.'

He saw that her eyes had that shine they always had when she was close to tears. She rose from the table, kissed the top of his head as she passed, and said, as she went out of the room, 'You know we don't love each other any more, not as we should, not as we did.'

Richard turned round and was about to say, How can you possibly think that, but by then she was already upstairs, collecting her bits and pieces. He didn't move from the kitchen. Shortly afterwards the front door opened and then shut again.

*

Fortunately his day at the office wasn't too strenuous. One of the firm's more demanding authors had to be given a less expensive lunch than he felt was his due, but Richard's amiability in such situations was so practised that by the end of the meal his guest had become quite docile. During the afternoon Richard tried to make some headway with a manuscript on which a decision was needed, but after a couple of hours at it he found he had little idea of its contents, let alone its merits. Best to leave it to the weekend, perhaps, and take it home. At least it would be quiet there now.

About tea-time one of the newer editors rang to ask if she could see him on a matter trivial enough for it to be obvious that it was a pretext. When she came in they smiled at each other uncertainly. After a pause, Richard said, 'Sue, I've been meaning to thank you for coming to Brighton with me, for that presentation. I'm afraid I talked too much afterwards, though I can't remember what about. Sorry about that.'

'That's all right. It wasn't the first time a man has told me the story of his life in a bar. Perhaps some of it was true. I enjoyed it anyway.'

'I'm not sure what the truth is any more. By the way, are you staying for drinks tonight? It won't last too long. We might go on somewhere afterwards, if you'd like to.'

She looked straight at him for a moment.

'All right,' she said.

The office party wasn't the conventional Christmas Saturnalia – it was the wrong season anyway – but a decorous send-off for a retiring director. As a recently elected member of the Board Richard had to be there, but he steered Sue away as soon as he decently could. During dinner they mostly gossiped about professional matters, and it was not until they'd reached the sorbet that Richard said, after looking round the restaurant as if to be sure there was no one there he knew, 'I'm sorry if I seem a bit subdued. The fact is my wife walked out this morning – not dramatically, you understand – we'd both been expecting it for some time.'

Sue put her hand over his, on the table-cloth.

After his confession Richard felt increasingly relaxed. It was a great relief to be with a woman who as far as he was concerned had no history, but who appeared to find him agreeable.

As they walked away she took his arm and said with light irony, 'I think this is the point at which one of us is supposed to say, My place or yours?'

Richard thought of his empty house, the breakfast things still on the table, the unmade bed. 'Oh yours, I think,' he said, equally lightly, 'don't you?'

Her flat was some distance away, not far from the river. In the taxi they kissed each other speculatively. Inside, her room was unexpectedly warm. 'I can't bear coming back to a cold place,' she said, 'especially when one lives alone – at least, most of the time,' she added, with a certain archness. Richard let the implication drift past. He liked being with Sue and was beginning to desire her, but he could not pretend an interest in her private life, not at this stage.

They sat on the sofa together while they had some more coffee, and began to kiss again.

'I must leave you for a moment,' she said.

When she returned she stood just inside the room holding the door-handle, naked to the waist. He stood as she came up to him so that he could touch first one breast and then the other with his fingertips. Their breathing quickened; she took off the rest of her clothes and began to undress him; they fell to the carpet. Richard knew that his need for the imminent release was uncontainable, and that it would not bring him what he wanted. He cried out, and then continued to sob, before quietening gradually. 'Was it so wonderful for you?' she asked. He buried his face more deeply in her neck. 'I'm glad it was,' she said. 'Don't move. I love your weight on me.' After a bit he turned his head the other way. At floor-level he could see some fluffy slippers pushed under a chair. Looking up, he realised that a portable television set on a small table had been casting its pale eye over the proceedings.

He disengaged himself with the usual slight embarrassment while also attempting the tenderness he felt was the least he could show. 'It's very late. You must get some sleep.'

'You can stay here, if you like.'

'That's sweet of you, but I have to go home for some things I'll need in the morning.'

'Well, it's nice to know that I'll see you in the morning – at the office,' she added, seeing that he looked blank for the moment.

'Yes, of course. At the office,' he said, and kissed her lightly on the cheek before he went.

The night air felt raw, as it does in London. Richard walked away from the flat, not thinking much about his direction, and soon found himself at the Embankment. Not many people about now, but vehicles, released in batches by the lights, still slid along the wide road beside the river. He crossed it, and leaned on the stone parapet. He suddenly felt so tired he could hardly move, and let himself slump over it. A car drew up and two uniformed men got out.

'Are you all right, sir?' said one of them with the studied politeness of a man expecting, but scrupulously not wanting to anticipate, a drunken reply.

'I'm fine, officer, thank you,' said Richard, trying to appear urbane. 'Just a little faint, that's all.'

'Live near here, do you, sir?'

'Not far,' said Richard, moving off, 'not far.'

The police returned reluctantly to their car – slightly piqued, Richard felt, at his apparent sobriety – and drove away.

He walked slowly, and then more slowly, along the pavement, from one street lamp to the next, until he came to the iron bridge. His feet began to hurt, but, although it was dry, he could hardly take his shoes off. He began to cross the bridge and looked down at the river, black as the tarmac in parallel with it. Which way was the tide going? Hard to tell. What had happened that evening seemed further away now than his breakfast conversation with his wife. He tried to recall what it was like when he first made love to her, but it was a blank, as if the recent scene had automatically erased all its predecessors. But when he was halfway across and had begun to think about what to do in the morning, his memory cleared. It came back to him completely – the place, the time, all the little details he thought he'd lost for ever.

'Don't go,' he shouted, as if to someone on the opposite bank. 'Don't go,' he cried again, gripping the bridge's iron railing as if his life depended on it.

a.

b.

It's Raining...

... It's Pouring

october 1988

Presque un Chef d'Oeuvre · Nearly a Masterpiece
November 1988

Paul Klee et son violon.   Jan. 1989.

V'là l'bon Vent

November 1988

31

Hotels

CHRISTOPHER REID

In the first hotel
I opened my wardrobe
to an ambush from childhood:
a sweet, tugging fragrance
I couldn't name.
Shuttered windows
gave on to a blind drop
and the portamenti
of amorous cats.

*

In the second hotel
I noted that the wallpaper,
although of a strictly
geometrical pattern,
was upside-down.
A hornet arrived
the following morning,
loose-jointed, like a gunslinger.
Then it flew away.

*

In the third hotel
none of the corridors
ran into each other
quite where expected.
My Gideon's Bible
was marked at *Lamentations*
by an envelope addressed
to Mrs Minnie Fireberg,
Utica, NY.

*

CHRISTOPHER REID

In the fourth hotel
I fell asleep
about nine o'clock.
Woke five hours later.
A woman in the street
was practising her giggling.
A bottle smashed.
Dawn crawled slowly
with its traffic chorus.

*

In the fifth hotel
the complimentary stationery
carried the most
vainglorious letterhead
I have ever seen.
Why didn't I steal some?
The plumbing shuddered
in every limb
at the twist of a single tap.

*

In the sixth hotel
the phone was pink
and its weight felt wrong
as I lifted the receiver.
It was no one I knew.
Advice and prohibitions
in several languages
were posted by the lightswitch
in a passepartout frame.

Stumps of Time

ANGUS CALDER

Kate and I went to the first meeting of the Scottish Constitutional Convention in Edinburgh at the end of March, 1989, thinking that history might just be made before our eyes, that a mechanism might be in the making which could deliver Scottish Home Rule. A good day for it, spring sunshine, but no sense of crowds converging in excitement. Outside the Church of Scotland Assembly Hall, shouting Unionist insults at the delegates as they entered, was a small mob of young people, evidently led by a certain Edinburgh councillor. These could immediately be classified: Rangers supporters. A piper playing 'The Sash' completed a cameo of irredentist (as it were) Protestant Unionism, embattled against Scottish National sentiment.

Inside the great grim hall itself, in the seating reserved for the general public, we fell in with Douglas Dunn. He'd come, he told us, in the hope that the occasion might provide a poem. His verses could surely not be heroic. The occasion was 'historic', so speakers kept assuring us, but it didn't feel 'historic'. It was nearly boring – though not really boring – to hear politicos making their predictable pronouncements; beaky Donald Dewar for Labour, scoutmasterly Malcolm Bruce for the Democrats, MPs on their best behaviour. Everything well sorted out in advance, no danger of undue excitement. One warmed to the Green Party spokesman as he complained about the paucity of women among the delegates, cooled off again as he tried to summarise, in his allotted seven minutes, his party's entire policy, and ran well over the limit.

At this point, I adjourned, with Douglas, for a jar in Deacon Brodie's. Douglas reckoned it was high time that Labour politicians employed speech writers: even Dewar, a lawyer, couldn't get nouns and verbs into proper relationship with each other. I said that what had been missing was armed men in the streets outside, gunfire, menace in the air. And that the Welsh would have done it better. There'd have been singing. A throaty old man from the valleys would have evoked the shade of Nye Bevan. I was thinking of my recent trip to Cardiff.

2.

Every two years, Edinburgh is invaded by many thousands of Welshmen with red and white scarves. They start arriving days before the rugby international and occupy accommodation which they booked last time. They pack out every pub in town, singing. Some women, I know, find their friendliness unwelcome (taking, as it can do, the form of unsubtle propositions). But most people say they 'love the Welsh'. The Welsh are always dubious about their team's chances beforehand. If it wins, they are generous with praise of the defeated Scots. If it loses, their grief stirs the deepest pity, but one doesn't hear of them turning nasty and smashing up bars.

For some years, I have provided modest pre-match entertainment, on behalf of the Open University in Scotland, for Welshmen associated with our Cardiff office. This year, I laid on a spot of curling at the ice rink near the Murrayfield rugby stadium. Enthusiasm for this sport is guaranteed by the fact that few beginners fail to get at least one good stone up the ice at first outing. In 1991, I have promised to organise a grand international tourney, Wales versus Scotland (or, rather, my pals versus them).

Hence my welcome in the Cardiff office where I went to conduct a little OU business and watch Wales play England was even warmer than on previous occasions, when I've arrived to cheer Scotland at the Arms Park. And it was a great pleasure for me to be wholly, for once, on the Welsh side. Every Scot or Irishman I know who follows rugby agrees that the beating of the English, by any one of the other teams in the Five Nations Championship, is a cause for joy almost as great as a win for one's own country. In 1989 Wales had lost their previous three games, badly. The like of such an inept Welsh team (the product, all concurred, of bizarre selection policy) could not easily be remembered. The English, by contrast, looked extremely powerful, and stood to take the Championship if they beat Wales. But I was sure they wouldn't. I knew the Arms Park.

It must be the most exciting sporting arena on earth. It's in the centre of the city. Crowds flocking to it create the impression of a whole people on the move. It is impossible to believe that anyone in the principality can be indifferent as to the outcome. The general will of the Welsh expresses itself in the famous singing of 'Land of our Fathers', rolling with sweet menace round the ground. The Arms Park is compact. The stands are steep. Even sitting where I was near the top of one of them, one feels very close to the drama on the pitch. There were, I guess, plenty of English supporters there. But what could they do against the fervour of thousands massed behind every Welsh scrum, the yearning for Welsh victory which seemed to clutch the legs of the English backs and freeze all their brilliant speed? 9–6 to Wales. Not a great game, but a victory. And that, certainly, did feel like an historic occasion.

3.

Seriousness and sport are often seen as incompatible. I sometimes encounter (though not in Scotland or Wales) fellow 'intellectuals' who find it impossible to understand why I get fretful around four forty-five on a winter Saturday if I'm not within reach of TV or radio to hear the Scottish Premier results, why, given the choice, a Murrayfield International would take precedence for me over an expenses-paid weekend in Italy, and why I get bad-tempered if vital engagements force me to pull out of even the least consequential curling match. Yet sport is manifestly much more than useful exercise, or relaxation. For *aficionados* it provides moments of glory, personal or national – and also, of course, of trauma – as intense as our brief lives can sustain. It interacts with the real, as opposed to the 'serious', History of Our Times. It usurps ground which zealots believe should be sacred to religion or politics.

I remember, back in the mid-seventies, when Welsh rugby was at a zenith (remember King John? Phil? Gareth? JPR?) a prominent member of Plaid Cymru complaining to me that all this sporting success was bad for his party. So long as the Welsh could beat England at rugby, he believed, they wouldn't be bothered about mere political independence. Recent research has suggested that the suicide rate in Scotland rises after Tories win general elections, falls after Scotland's appearances in World Cup football finals. Perhaps the inept displays put on by Scottish teams after heroic efforts have taken them into four successive finals are consolatory for depressives: 'At least there are other poor buggers more useless than me.' Or perhaps the phenomenon has to do with enhanced sociability, sense of communality, when everyone in Scotland seems ready to talk about the one thing which matters, anywhere, to whatever person.

We needed a Trinidadian Marxist, C. L. R. James, to persuade us that sport is 'culture' and crucial to national identity. It was he who concluded that in the West Indies cricket has been an art form as central to society as drama was in Ancient Athens. With 'seriousness' he could write (in 1969) of the great all-rounder Garfield Sobers: 'All geniuses are merely men who carry to an extreme definitive the characteristics of the unit of civilisation to which they belong and the special act or function which they express or practise.' Sobers' 'command of the rising ball in the drive, his close fielding and his hurling himself into his fast bowling' were 'a living embodiment of centuries of tortured history'.

I think James for once went over the top in that essay. I can see how the fury of great West Indian fast bowlers can be related to centuries of black servitude, but can recall nothing 'tortured' about Sobers' supremely graceful batting. (I swear I once saw him drive – not pull – a good-length ball past square leg, behind which I was sitting.) However, James's general point is taken. The unpredictable genius of Andy Irvine, long Scotland's rugby full-back, did indeed seem to express a history seen by fellow Scots as one of daredevil valour, mighty improvisations – and hideous defeats and failures. He could muff a simple tackle, drop a high ball as the enemy bore down on him, pass fecklessly in front of his own posts under pressure.

I quote from Norman Mair's report in *The Scotsman*, 19 February 1980, of a match against France which Scotland won 22–14: 'Having been roundly booed by his own home crowd as he attempted to kick a goal with six previous failures behind him, including a short-range penalty from almost in front of the posts which would have squared the half-time score at 7–7, Irvine was lionised as he left the field. He had contributed two tries, a touch-line conversion and two penalty goals to the most extraordinary return from the dead you will find outside the pages of the Bible.' I was there, in the stand, behind Scotland's posts, as gathering darkness began to obscure the play at Murrayfield, with twelve minutes to go and France, with a 14–4 lead, still applying pressure. Twice one saw Scottish backs begin movements deep within their own half which culminated in someone (one learnt only afterwards that it was Irvine) pouncing over the French line for a try. Unfortunately, for some time thereafter, the Scottish team played as if there was no need to amass points early – such a Highland Charge in the dying minutes would see it through. This rarely worked out.

I notice in the same yellowing newspaper that Hibs had placed George Best on the transfer list; he'd played only five matches for the club, and had just failed to turn up for a cup tie. I'd feel it tasteless to speculate as to how the decline and fall of that peerless footballing talent related to the crisis in his native Ulster which began soon after he first displayed himself to terraces ready to dote on his every movement. I was lucky enough to see him, sleek and new, play for Manchester United against Arsenal at Highbury in a 'forward line' (what an old-fashioned concept that seems now) which included also Bobby Charlton and Denis Law. They provided a spectacle of thrilling attack to match the Welsh Rugby backs of the seventies at their greatest.

What is it that makes us call a games player a 'genius'? It isn't just the capacity to make spectacular scores, remarkable shots. It is what is called 'class', a nasty locution which I try not to use, though 'timing', my preferred substitute, is rather tame. It is the capacity to handle easily and gracefully basic sporting tasks which others strain at or turn into drudgery. It is what one spotted when one first saw a very young Paul McStay in the Celtic midfield: he seemed to have an extra half-second at his disposal in which to pass the ball, to create a time of his own amid the typical frenzy of Scottish Premier Division football. I remember once in a Lords Test Match (I cannot recall whom England were playing, and apparently lost my scorecard) Cowdrey and Barrington coming together at some point when the match was off the boil. For half an hour or so, before rain stopped play, they patted and nudged and pushed the ball here and there, comfortable singles, leisurely twos, as if batting was easier than mowing the grass. When Robert Jones, the Welsh scrum half, kept punting the ball behind the English pack and driving them back at the Arms Park in 1989, the formidable English flank forwards appeared sluggish: he had 'all the time in the world'.

And I suspect what exhilarates second-raters and coarse sportsmen such as myself, who feel an emotion like passionate love as sporting 'genius' displays itself, is this: in dreams, if not in reality, we have performed just so. Out of time, weightless, we have, however briefly, achieved the difficult, feeling it was easy. That double take-out I curled in last night, for instance . . . I fear I may now be boringly personal.

4.

I am playing my first game as left wing three-quarter for the school second fifteen. A centre called Bayliss, brilliantly blond in the autumn sunlight, passes out to me just inside our own half. I race successfully for the opposition line, and touch down. When Scotland score at Murrayfield it is that memory which sweeps, as it were, through me: not thoughts of another moment, a few weeks later, when speeding to score I was tackled, admirably, by a saturnine youth playing for Reigate Grammar, and broke my left collarbone in the fall. Soon after that prudence decided me to give up a sport to which, being averse to violence, I was not well fitted.

I kept up my cricket, however. And in this case, the example of sporting idols was decisive. I have what is called a 'reasonably good eye', though I have worn spectacles since I was four; the phrase refers to reflexes, really, rather than vision. However, my physical co-ordination is poor. My batting never displayed a hint of 'class'. I have had a few amusing moments bowling very slow, high off-spinners which – if they were allowed to pitch – would turn at forty-five degrees, but few skippers have considered the likely cost in runs (say 10 an over) worth the remote chance that a wicket might fall. Nevertheless, I played cricket for years in teams above my station, not coarse at all, including good, even excellent players. How? This could sound like a homily: I worked very hard at my fielding, before I converted myself into a wicketkeeper, a stopper not a true stumper, but reasonably brisk with it. My 'out-cricket' (odd phrase), I think, persuaded selection committees to persevere with me.

An example, from my early thirties, when I was already wondering sometimes if I was too old for the game. I have been dropped from the second eleven of Carlton, that famous Edinburgh club. It is Saturday morning. I have a hangover. The phone rings. 'John Jamieson's just called off. Can you be at Jock's Lodge for two o'clock?' Marginal players can't afford to turn down such requests. Head splitting, I trauchle up to the Royal High FP ground, and find that I am due to impersonate the said Jamieson at number 3. JJ was Carlton Seconds' unanswerable riposte to claims that Boycott or Tavare was the most boring batsman of the epoch. He batted as if scoring strokes could only be acts of incredible folly. He pushed forward again and again, pad close to bat, as if no other movement were possible . . .

I remember a good, flat pitch. I remember thinking: I must keep my head down, eye on the ball, concentrate. After some five overs from which I gathered no runs, I was back in the pavilion. I suspect, though I do not remember, that the dreaded straight ball on a good length had been enough to topple my castle.

Others scored runs. (It was indeed a good wicket.) And when Royal High batted, our captain, a tall man bowling spinners with a high, angular action, caused them a bit of bother. For a time we clustered round the batsmen expecting catches. But their skipper arrived and drove us away. Runless, catchless, I found myself patrolling the square leg boundary as Royal High batsmen began to take charge. I felt seedy and glum, till I stepped out of time, weightless.

Their skipper, a powerful man, pulls. The ball is soaring for 6. I run twenty yards to intercept it, leap, pluck it out of the air. The game is drawn but back at the Carlton clubhouse, team mates tell the Firsts about that astonishing catch.

There'd been other such moments. Once, playing for my school seconds, I'd picked up a full-blooded leg drive centimetres off the turf while fielding at forward short leg, and then scooped up a hook as it rushed fiercely to ground at square leg. One of the other side joked – and this thrilled me exquisitely, 'Who's this you've got playing for you? Tony Lock?'

5.

Not long ago, I learned from Allan Massie, the novelist (also an excellent sports columnist, at one time, for the *Glasgow Herald*), that he too was at the Oval that day in 1956 when Lock took the catch I best remember, and he too remembered it.

'Typhoon' Frank Tyson had made his return to the England team for the final test of 'Laker's Series' against Australia. He was not the fearsome fast bowler he had been Down Under a couple of winters before. His first ball sailed full pitch over the batsman's head innocuously, like that of some novice warming up in a public park game. That chunky, accomplished Australian opener Colin Macdonald was unruffled by three more uninspired deliveries. Tyson's fifth ball came down towards his legs, just the ball to clip backward of square. Macdonald executed the shot, keeping the ball down. Lock, a big man with scant fair hair who looked from the seating bald and even aged, swooped, plucked up one-handed the certain boundary, threw it casually skywards. Macdonald ct Lock b Tyson 3. As *Wisden* records: 'Australia's troubles began with a sizzling right-handed leg slip catch by Lock when Macdonald seemed to have achieved a perfect glide.'

It has saddened me to see some of the shine taken off the memory of the wonderful Surrey team of the fifties for which Lock played, by the ineptitude, as successive Chairmen of Test Selectors, of two of its key figures, Bedser and May. I will return to this topic later. Here my concern is with what the Oval and its heroes meant to me as a boy growing up in what used to be 'Surrey'.

I first went there, when I was thirteen, to see the 1955 South Africans, for whom Roy McLean scored 150 in 210 minutes. It must have been a delightful innings, but being a bigoted Surrey partisan, I resented it. What I loved was the ground itself, that paradisal vista of brilliant green turf aborded by gasometers. There was a smell in the air which during early visits I supposed to derive from my own Marmite sandwiches: it took me a long time to realise that a local brewery provided it. From the stands beside the pavilion, one looked towards the centre of London, a city still blitz-scarred, but still mostly human in scale and Dickensian in associations. The cars, the roads built or converted for them, and the property developers, had not yet eaten its heart away. I could cycle a dozen miles from Sutton to the Oval without fear, along the tatty, cheerful high streets, escaping from the ghastliness of 'outer suburbia'.

And I could watch the most successful county combination of all time, which took seven successive championships between 1952 and 1958. The records of the 1957 season represent its dominance at peak. May topped the national batting averages by a clear ten runs. There were three other Surrey players in the top twenty. The bowling figures make astonishing reading. Four Surrey bowlers figure among the top six. Lock, with 212 wickets at 12 runs apiece was in effect as far ahead of the field as May. Laker, Eric Bedser and Loader all averaged under 16 for large hauls, and Alec Bedser (only twelfth in the rankings) took 131 wickets for 16.56. This was a perfectly balanced attack. Loader, who scooped up a Test hat trick against the West Indies that year, had 'genuine pace' – in other words, he was fast enough to hustle sound openers out on good wickets. This complemented the medium-fast skills of Alec Bedser, still a fine opening bowler in his late thirties. His gentle-seeming approach to the wicket, followed by the immaculate arc of his arm, was a supreme example of 'timing' which created the illusion of almost placid ease, whereupon his leg cutter spat viciously off the turf. Laker was always a joy to watch: his relaxed-looking off spin, I gradually noticed, would tease out top-of-the-order batsmen when they appeared to have settled down. After which Lock, bustling diagonally up to the wicket, faster than most left-hand spinners, would scythe rapidly through the tail. And Eric Bedser's little-sung off spin won matches on its day.

However, it is the fielding statistics for 1957 which are the most extraordinary of all. In those days a fit cricketer would play maybe thirty first-class matches in an English season. A very good wicketkeeper, like John Murray of Middlesex that year, might just claim over 100 victims, some 80 of them caught. Surrey's admirable Arthur McIntyre caught 51 and stumped 9. For Surrey, though, Micky Stewart (normally forward short leg) took 77 catches, a record 7 of them in one game. Barrington (slip) got 64, the legendary Lock took 63, and May (slip) claimed 29 – more than such an excellent close fielder as Ikin of Lancashire, who played in every one of his county's 28 fixtures.

Obviously, the might of the bowling attack meant that many more catching chances were offered than fielders for other teams would see. But the opposite also held true. The daring and brilliance of Surrey's close fielding, six or seven men near to the batsman, Stewart close enough to pick his pocket, Lock breathing audibly 'round the corner', gave the bowlers many wickets. Stuart Surridge had shown the way. An unpretentious reserve fast-medium bowler and entertaining tail-end batsman (his cover drives hit on the up for 6 towards the gasometers were of his own patent) Surridge led Surrey to the first five of its seven successive championships. He was clearly a shrewd leader, but, more important, in close fielding he led by example. The threesome of Stewart, Surridge and Lock forming a 'leg trap' for Laker's off spin had been, as they say, 'awesome'.

I could not emulate the peerless elegance of May's batting – his cover drive, lofted leg drive and late cut were all unequalled in easy grace. I was never going to be able to walk back staring thoughtfully skywards like Laker, turn, take a few steps, and squeeze another good length off break devilishly off the pitch into the batsman. But I could stand where Micky Stewart did and take catches. I began to realise in my late thirties that only the coarse game stretched ahead of me when I was playing for West Lothian Seconds. I had been ousted as wicketkeeper in favour of a lad aged fourteen who has gone on since to represent Scotland. I could no longer move in quickly and dangerously from cover point as Bernie Constable had done for Surrey, nor fly round the outfield like the young Barrington. And now I found my close fielding was going. I still stood close, but with faltering reflexes I was putting myself in danger.

Nevertheless, at least the lesson in 'out-cricket' learnt from my Surrey heroes had kept me in respectable cricketing company, up to the point where I cheerfully joined Marchmont, founded as an Edinburgh 'public parks' club by a Goanese Communist and chiefly recruiting from Asians, Irishmen and members of the Labour Party.

6.

I have a pal, Syd Harrex, an Australian poet, who told me when I last bumped into him that he was compiling a collection of pieces about *non-English* cricket. Fiji or Holland, yes. England, no. Poms out. I took his subversive point. 'Cricket writing' has tended to imply 'fancy Pom prose'. Cricket is seen (even by C. L. R. James) as something quintessentially 'English'. That is one reason why men grumble in Scottish bars when the landlord lets the Test Match appear on TV. Rugby is occasionally tolerated, since Scotland quite often beat England at it (and in the Borders it is the 'people's game'). But cricketers are often regarded as apostates from the true Scottish faith, which is football.

However, Scottish cricket, like Fijian, has its national characteristics. When Freuchie (Fife), played into Lords by bagpipers, won the UK Village Cricket Championship a few years back, their attack was labelled 'the mean machine'. Its grudgingness was as typically Calvinist as Irvine's fitful heroics were Jacobite. The main Scottish leagues, even at second-eleven level, involve 100-over games on pitches which are usually slow. Sides have been known to bat 80 overs, for under 200 runs, merely to deny a rival advantage under a complex points system. Because the slow pitches are unpredictable, often bad, anyone who can bowl straight 'little medium pacers' just short of a length, over after over, will take many wickets and concede few runs.

My old Carlton and Marchmont comrade, Doug Jones, who like most sensible people drinks in the Auld Toll Bar, recalled for me just now that Brian Hardie, of Essex but formerly of Stenhousemuir, once held the record as the slowest-ever scorer in County cricket – 4 runs in 142 minutes. He came back to play as a guest for his old club when Doug was in action for Carlton Firsts against it. He pushed forward, bat behind pad, remorselessly. When a Carlton spinner tempted him with drivable balls outside the off stump he indeed drove each in turn, but along the ground straight to a fielder. Doug, in the covers, soon felt his hands stinging. Hardie, who never looked like getting out, totally in command, progressed to a half century in some 50 overs. Even that, I riposted to Doug, must have been electrifying compared to an overcast afternoon at West Lothian's ground (aptly named Boghall) when I, unselected, had volunteered to umpire. For no obvious reason, Holy Cross Accies' openers batted out some 11 overs, against bowling of no special merit, before one, perhaps by some accident, scored a run. He was extremely bitter when I gave him out l.b.w. on the front foot soon after. The ball was straight, not rising or cutting – and besides his play had goaded me to fury.

A favourite 'coarse cricket' anecdote bears on this national thriftiness. The Australians are playing at Perth against Scotland. Dennis Lillee – perhaps the finest fast bowler 'of all time' – is with the party but not engaged in the match. He strolls into a public park in the environs of the city, and finds a cricket match about to begin. One of the teams is short. Lillee agrees to make up numbers and at once finds himself opening the bowling. His first ball pitches, rears, and sails past batsman and wicket keeper for 4 byes. Same with the next . . . After one over he's taken off. Too expensive. I don't believe this story, for all the circumstantial detail supplied by the friend who told it to me; Lillee was a very great bowler largely because he adapted himself so well to varied conditions. But *si non è vero* . . .

West Lothian plays at Linlithgow. A very ordinary housing estate is adjacent. The clubhouse has been a centre in summer for young lads whom it has 'kept off the streets'. Hence, like one or two other clubs in Lowland Scotland (Stenhousemuir, Aberdeenshire spring to mind), West Lothian were able to develop a 'youth policy' based on wide acceptance of the game amongst the junior soccer-playing classes. Young Davy Fleming, who supplanted me as second-eleven wicketkeeper, was not, I gathered, a success in the classroom. But his 'timing' in his early teens was as exceptional as Cowdrey's: he could make the stock forward defensive prod look attractive. As happens in other sports and in other countries, Scottish cricket gave him a chance of prestige and respect which his other capacities could hardly have provided. I once took an American friend, very left wing, who was stridently convinced that cricket was a snob's sport, to the West Lothian Clubhouse on Saturday. She was disarmed by the proletarian ambience – the chugging fruit machines, the sharp demotic humour.

So there is a 'Scottish Cricket', not likely to produce a world-beating side, but quite widely played and wholly different in atmosphere to the game as conducted in the Home Counties. And also from the Asian-dominated sport on matting wickets which I entered with huge enjoyment, during three years' teaching in Nairobi.

The University put two teams into competition in the 'Commercial League'. There was no way I, or any other white lecturer, would get into the A Team. Not only was it a crack side, its selection policy was controlled by intricate negotiation between different Asian groups. A substantial portion of the immense variety of the Indian sub-continent was represented amongst East Africa's Asian population, on the whole united by middle-class aspirations, but divided by religion, caste and region or country of origin. Come to think of it, I wonder if I got to keep wicket for the B team because my chief rival was a Eurasian without a strong group behind him?

I hope I don't give an impression of exclusiveness or bitter hatreds. I think a Ugandan African student made the A team, and the skipper of the B team was a business studies lecturer from Derbyshire. The Commercial League rules permitted each entrant to include one 'outsider' from the crack Nairobi clubs. In the season which I am recalling, Mohammed Senior was our choice, a steady fastish bowler, grafting sound batsman, a good 'bits and pieces man'.

But our star turned out to be Manohar Singh, a University employee. He had represented Kenya as a fast bowler, but taking him behind the stumps was easy. Despite a good action, fair pace, and respectable line and length, there was no devil left in his attack. His batting, however, made our season, in which we got through to the semi-finals (whence, if successful, we would have gone on to meet University A in the final), compiled our highest total so far – and lost by 10 wickets.

We were not supposed, merely 'B' as we were, to give Education much of a game. This side had its pick from Nairobi's Asian schoolteachers. Nor were we doing too well chasing a high target till turbaned Manohar went in to bat. Early on, he got hit in the face – sweeping, I think. Dramatically, he fought on, blood from a nosebleed streaming down his visage. He thrashed the Education bowling every which way, embodiment of the Sikh fighting spirit. The shell-shocked Education captain could think of no better ploy than to keep on bowling himself, his own spinners. These, as I found when I got out to the wicket, came pleasantly on to the bat of a person temperamentally inclined to slog. At one point Mohammed Senior, serious and avuncular, who was umpiring, advanced down the wicket to me and said, 'Do you realise you just took 10 off that over?' I hadn't. 'Keep cool,' he said. 'We're getting there.' And so, thanks to Manohar, we did.

I played in my early twenties for a West London side which usually included three or four West Indians and can confirm that their game was something special; a devout faith in sound technique (they'd admire Barrington, for all his slow play) was coupled with a relish for heroics and dramatics. It was a ferociously scarred Jamaican army man, briefly a guest member of that side, who taught me, in the course of an unbeaten, match-winning fifty partnership for the last wicket to which I contributed maybe four, that it is easy to run a bye if the keeper, standing back, fumbles the ball. (At least, if you have the respectable speed off the mark which I then possessed.)

7.

So where do all these anecdotes and cogitations leave the C. L. R. James thesis that cricket expresses culture and history? It stands up quite well, I believe. Consider English cricket, that object of Syd Harrex's Pom-phobia.

Most people (above all, C. L. R. James) believe that English cricket in the Edwardian era, when its first-class batsmanship was still dominated by ex-public school amateurs, experienced a Golden Age. Be that as it may (I have my doubts about how purely amateur men like Fry and Ranji were, and note that Australians, even South Africans, often did damn well against the high-born English heroes) there is a consensus that English cricket was badly hit by the First World War, that torment for patriotic consciousness, in which 'Englishness' was crucified in Flanders. However, by the late twenties, when Chapman's great side triumphed in Australia, it had made, like the economy, some resurgence.

How does one weigh the undoubted individual 'genius' of Bradman against all the other factors which might have contributed to the Australian counter-attack over the period 1930 to 1948? His run-making feats are astonishing, and will almost certainly never be equalled. But can the sublime self-confidence, the transcendental omnicompetence, of that boy from the outback not be related to the currents which, during his career, swept Australia decisively from 'colonial' to 'independent' status? Certainly, the atmosphere in 1932–3 when that (mean) Scots captain Douglas Jardine launched 'bodyline' fast bowling with the express intention, partly successful, of checking Bradman, was one in which self-righteous Aussies felt free to complain about cheating Poms.

That Surrey team of the fifties lent its best men to English sides which were the last to enjoy clear supremacy over all other cricket-playing nations. If the shock West Indies triumph in England in 1950 relates to the dwindling of Britain's Imperial power, England's successes under Hutton and May may provide some insight into the British culture of the following decade.

Hutton's generation had served in an exhausting but successful war. May's were 'toughened' by National Service. Ironies sprout around these facts. It was in tune with the spirit of the People's War and Attlee's Britain that Hutton should become the first professional to captain England. However, since National Service meant that young men went later to university, this was the last era in which Oxford and Cambridge could put up a serious show against the counties. And the latter for the most part (even Hutton's Yorkshire) continued to prefer amateur, ex-Oxbridge, captains. Surridge and May used a different dressing-room from the nine other men in their victorious Surrey side. There were contradictions in cricket corresponding to those involved in Macmillan's patrician leadership of a Tory Party dedicated to full employment and welfarism. That Surrey side could be seen as projecting a hierarchy not unlike that of the Army still swollen with National Servicemen, still the basis of claims to Great Power status. Surridge was the popular CO, May the smart young commissioned officer, Alec Bedser the perfect sergeant major, with Corporal Barrington preparing to succeed him. Admirable pros, such as Constable, Fletcher, Clark, provided enough batting to keep the show going, never presuming above their station as privates. The specialist arm was a likely source of disturbance. Of the 'three Ls', Loader and Lock emigrated to Australia, Laker quarrelled with Surrey and ended his career with Essex.

Thirty years later, the seeming equipoise of the late fifties in which old-fashioned institutions such as Oxbridge, the House of Lords, the Monarchy – and county cricket – had flourished in an atmosphere of national complacency looks as remote as any version of the Edwardian Golden Age. Empire vanished in the sixties, political consensus in the seventies. The quasi-tragic pathos involved in the spectacle of Bedser, then May, sending out team after team of undifferentiated (and now highly paid) professionals to be destroyed by the West Indies, humiliated by New Zealand, shamed even by Sri Lanka, derives from the status of these men as giants of a bygone era, in which cricketers could not play for one county this year, another the next, fine professionals earned craftsmen's wages, and public school chaps still received the deference thought due to breeding rather than the less rooted respect given to money. The counties themselves have been re-organised on or out of the map. 'Middlesex' has disappeared, even 'Yorkshire' is cruelly divided.

The impression which England cricketers so often give now, that they are spoilt, peevish, overgrown children with plenty of yuppie greed but little 'bottle', would have caused general horror in the late fifties. I quote *Wisden* on Surrey's 1957 eleven: 'They played, acted, thought and looked like the magnificent champions they were.' Whatever resentments may have simmered in the pros' dressing-room, the tabloid press got little or nothing to chew on and spit out.

At the Oval in the fifties, the members of Surrey CCC in their special section, and the mostly working-class crowds around the ground, were part of a unified-seeming culture in which the policemen were still thought of as unfailingly decent and social classes, acting corporately, could combine to maintain the dignity of a 'Great' Britain. 'Unified-seeming' – the other face of class was seen in industrial disputes and general election results. More than any other 'advanced' country Britain was obsessed with 'class', divided by 'class'. To say that the wonderfully graceful professional Graveney was a 'class' batsman was virtually to coopt him to the gentry.

I return to Scotland, 1989, to that comic-horrific scene on the Mound. It should be notorious now, even furth of the country, that about three-quarters of the Scottish population not only voted against Thatcher in the 1987 General Election, but went on opposing, according to polls, in the same three to one ratio, every policy her 'Quisling' ministers thrust upon them. I write in the past tense, lest implicit extrapolation from these facts should suggest generalisations which in a few years' time might look very silly.

If football is to Scotland what cricket is to West Indians, then Rangers cannot be dismissed as a quaint Proddy anachronism or unimportant exception. They are the richest club in Scotland, with the biggest support, which has accepted a policy of buying outside Scotland, taken so far that seven or eight Englishmen may be on the Ibrox pitch sustaining the psyches of the faithful. There is no natural correspondence between Thatcherism and sectarianism, but there is between Thatcherism and wealth. Rangers' management using the club's enormous resources can set up private old people's homes, install luxurious private facilities of all kinds at Ibrox, buy their way into control of TV companies . . . newspapers . . . anything. And the club's tradition is militantly Unionist. Union Jacks blossom on the packed terraces as Rangers score against Celtic, a club with Irish Nationalist associations.

The politenesses of inter-party compromise inside the Assembly Hall – 'The Sash' repeated on the pipes outside – as a good C. L. R. Jamesite I am not sure that impolite youths in red, white and blue scarves can be ignored. I fortify myself against possible future disappointments (how can older Labour supporters than I, with personal memories of 1945, square how they felt then with the realities of our *fin de siècle*?) by reminding myself that whatever has happened since, I did see the 'three Ls' rampant below the gasometers. Whatever stupidities have disfigured my life, I did help Manohar Singh defeat Education. Whatever becomes of Scotland before or after I die, I have heard great generations of poets read to enthusiastic packed halls, I have willed the team of our small country to struggle into four successive World Cup finals – and I was there when Irvine scored 16 points in twelve minutes to beat the French.

I turned to the talkative French couple beside me, now fallen silent, and muttered, insincerely, '*Dommage.*'

Serfs

DYAN SHELDON

Everyone is drunk. They are all talking and laughing a little too loudly – Sara, Richard, Melanie, Claudia, James, Alex, Doug, Bob, Liz, Zeena, Charley, Tel, that guy, what's-his-name, from the legal department, Folkstone's secretary, Princess Grace, and that lovely blonde from computers, the one whose boyfriend, looking like something from the night of the living dead, sometimes comes to pick her up after work on his Harley Davidson, what a waste, a girl with a face and a bum like that, she's going to have to get rid of him, him with his ponytail and his dangling ear-rings and his skull and crossbones tattoo, if she wants to get ahead – all of them pissed as newts. Though, if you think about it, and Mike is thinking about it, it doesn't make any sense to say pissed as newts. Newts barely move let alone consume bottle after bottle of the house white and red. It would make a lot more sense to say pissed as corporate workers at eleven o'clock on a Friday night. Pissed as managers and accountants and salesmen and secretaries out for the night when they have some reason to be out, when they don't have to go to work the next day. Pissed as people.

Drunkest of all, of course, is Frank. He sits at the centre of the table, or, to be more accurate, and at this point in the evening Mike would like to be accurate, at the centre of the several tables that have been pushed together for them, his food untouched, his jacket off, his hair uncombed, his lips stained red with wine. At the moment, he is concentrating on wrapping his tie around Folkstone's secretary's head like a bandana. But she won't sit still. Some old pop song is playing in the background, something sweet and bouncy about daydreaming, and Princess Grace is moving in her seat to it, waving her hands and shaking her tits and bobbing her head so that the tie keeps slipping and Frank keeps falling against her.

Mike catches the waiters exchanging a smirk. The waiter on the right, a man who clearly doesn't want as much as a one-second delay when they finally call for the bill, looks fed-up and wary and bored. But the one on the left is still trying to look patient and agreeable, still trying to look as though it didn't take thirty minutes to get all the orders and that it then hadn't turned out that Melanie forgot to ask for a starter and Doug changed his mind about the chicken and

Bob was only enquiring about the Camembert in a general way, what he really wanted was the *ratatouille*. The waiter on the left is still trying to look as though he doesn't know exactly how the evening will end – with someone being sick outside the loo and someone else breaking a glass, with a fight over the bill and at least one person missing a coat or a purse or a briefcase, screaming so that the other diners can ignore them no longer. Of course I'm not accusing you, my good man; all I'm saying is that that is where I left it and it's bloody well not there now, is it? – but the one on the right isn't hiding the fact that he has seen it all before, and would be happy never to see it again. Mike straightens his own tie, hoping that no one thinks he's as drunk as everybody else.

'Hey, y'know what, Mike?' Frank shouts down the table to him. 'Y'know what I just thought?'

Mike pours some bottled water into his glass, impressing himself with the steadiness of his hand. 'No, Wookey, what'd you just think?'

Frank grins, a jack-o'-lantern smile, his eyes focusing on something behind Mike's head. 'I just thought, you know, that this is an office party and I don't even have a fuckin' office any more.'

Several people laugh, Hah hah, that's pretty good, Frank, an office party without an office.

'What do you think of that, Mike? An office party and I don't have a fuckin' office.' He sweeps up his glass and knocks his bread plate off the table.

Folkstone's secretary, getting up to go to the ladies, slips and lands in Doug's lap. 'Whoops,' she says.

Doug wraps his arms around her and kisses the back of her head. 'Boy,' he smiles, too far gone to pretend that he's kidding, 'I'm sure glad my wife's not here.'

Mike, who is also glad that his wife's not here, signals to the waiter for the bill.

Frank returns from the floor, several napkins clutched in one hand and a wholewheat roll in the other. 'Hey, you know what, Mike?' he calls, struggling back into his seat. 'You know what? You could call this the last supper, couldn't you, Mike?' He looks first down one side of the table and then the other at his disciples, the women who have typed his letters and taken his messages and made sure he got copies of the right minutes and memos, the men he has made decisions and plans and jokes with, sitting all together in their blue and brown and grey suits around the boardroom table, talking seriously, even solemnly, about the South Africans or the Americans or the Japanese.

Frank Wookey's last supper. He picks up someone else's glass. 'To Frank Wookey's last bloody supper,' he shouts, and the others raise their glasses to the toast, stomping their feet and cheering, Yeah, yeah, you tell 'em, Frank, that's the way. Frank stands up, swaying only slightly, and throws out his chest. 'And just wait till you see me rise from the dead,' he shouts. ''Cos I will, you know. This isn't an end. It's a beginning. Frank Wookey's going to rise from the dead. Just you wait and see.'

The tramp, dark in the dark, tucked into a doorway with bags of garbage piled up around him like a soldier in a trench, and smelling, Mike decides, like the cesspool at the end of the universe, is talking to himself. Frank is talking to himself, too. Frank wants Mike to give the tramp some money. In all the years they have known each other, Mike has no memory of Frank ever wanting to give money to a bum before, except once, at Christmas, when they'd been drinking champagne and Folkstone's secretary was with them, wrapped around Frank, but tonight he does. Tonight Frank is concerned about his fellow human beings. Frank says they'll never know what brought this poor bastard to this doorway, will they? Maybe some awful tragedy. Maybe his child was killed and he started drinking and his wife left him and he lost his job and his home and . . . Mike pulls him away. 'Don't be stupid, Frank,' he says. 'Things don't happen like that.'

This is not the first time Mike has had to take a drunk Frank Wookey home. He has helped Frank home from office Christmas parties, department dos, retirement celebrations, company picnics, and the awards dinner the year Frank won the Most Valuable Employee pin, gold with a diamond chip. This is not the first time a drunk Frank Wookey has told him how he's his best friend in the world, staggering beside him, draped over one shoulder like a scarf, repeating, in long, sour mouthfuls, 'You're my best friend, Mike, you know that? You know that, don't you, Mike? My best friend in the world.'

Nor is this the first time that Mike has answered, 'Yeah, Frank, I know. You're my best friend, too. Wookey and Hammond, the team to beat.' And they have been best friends. Wookey and Hammond. Working together, drinking together, going to matches together, taking their wives out together, visiting each other's homes, taking their families on holiday to France together last year and to Cornwall the year before that. Wookey and Hammond.

Frank lunges to the left and takes them both into the side of a Rover. 'Whoa,' says Frank. Mike, his weight against the car, straightens them out. His only friend as well. 'Whew, Mike,' says Frank, holding on to the roof and making a sound somewhere between a laugh and a retch, 'I've really tied one on this time, haven't I?'

He wonders if he'll have to carry him. 'Yeah, Frank,' Mike says, stuffing the tie back into his pocket and trying to smooth down his jacket a bit, 'you really have.'

'I don't think I've been this drunk since Stevie was born. Remember that, Mike? Remember how drunk I got when Stevie was born?'

He wraps him over his shoulders again and they begin to two-step past the rows of cars, two steps to the left and two steps to the right and two steps forward. 'Vaguely.'

'Still,' says Frank, his voice enormous in the mausoleum-like silence of the parking lot, 'this is a special occasion, too, isn't it, Mike? After all, it's not every day a man gets to start his life over, is it? Not every bloody day.'

'No,' says Mike, 'not every day.'

Frank starts to cry when they're about halfway home. Frank's crying is not one or two quiet, manly tears, a small crack in the voice, a just-noticeable thickening of the consonants, but great, half-swallowed sobs that shake his whole body. Mike grips the wheel. For some reason, Frank falling apart when they're on their own is more embarrassing than it happening with the others. At least then there would have been someone to exchange looks with, someone else to talk to while Frank got it all off his chest. One of the women would have sat beside him, holding his hand, saying, It's all right, Frank. Everything's going to be fine. Mike's eyes move between the road and the rear-view mirror. 'Pull yourself together, Frank,' he urges. 'You're almost home.'

All this past week, with the reshuffling announced on Monday and the redundancies announced on Wednesday and being told to have his desk emptied by today, Frank barely flinched. 'I've been wanting a change,' he said on Wednesday. 'A man gets stale. It's no good living your whole life in a rut, is it?' And everyone had agreed that a change of direction was a good thing, like a second chance at life, you had to think of it as a golden opportunity. 'Hey, I'm good,' Frank said on Thursday. 'What do I have to worry about? Nothing, that's what. Not a thing. When I think of all the offers I've had over the years . . . they'll be beating my door down by the end of the week.' And everyone had agreed that a man of his experience and reputation wasn't going to have any trouble getting another job, not on your life.

But this is Friday night and now Frank sits slouched against the door, his face into the night, all his things from work in a cardboard box in the boot, including the asparagus fern that used to sit on his windowsill and the pictures of Kate and the kids that used to sit on his desk. 'What if I don't get offered something else?' he asks in a choked voice. 'Huh, Mike? What if I don't get something? I'm forty, you know, not thirty. Not one of these whizz-kids, managing director by the time they're twenty-nine. What'll I do if I don't get another job?'

Mike concentrates on the road ahead, on not going too fast or being seen to weave, on not being pulled over and breathalysed by some cop who's barely out of his teens. He wishes that Frank would either pass out or just shut up. As far as Mike's concerned, being best friends means that it's all right for Frank to vomit out the car window or even all over the upholstery, but it doesn't mean this. They're not schoolgirls, for Chrissake. Mike slows down for a changing light that, were he really sober, he would have run. The car stops.

When you come right down to it, he and Frank don't usually talk about anything. Sure, they complain about things – their wives, their neighbours, their kids, the interest rates – they argue about things – the government, the environment, Arsenal as compared to Real Madrid – and until last Monday they used to moan a lot about the job – how much they hated it, how it drained you and bored you and left you with little energy for anything else, how much they loathed office politics, all that shit, how they had both sort of fallen into their jobs without planning to, how Mike had always wanted to run his own business, and how Frank had always wanted to write, always started things (a novel, a play, a story about his children's pet chicken) but never had the time to finish them – but they don't really talk. Mike looks up at the sky, surprised that the stars are almost visible. They never talk about what they're afraid of. The tape that's been playing ends, the light goes green. Does anyone? The car jumps forward. Not fucking likely. He looks over at his best friend, crumpled in the corner like an empty bag. He thinks of his wife, tucked up in bed at home, dreaming of whatever it is she dreams of. Who would you talk to? He flips the cassette over.

'You'll be all right, Frank, don't worry,' he says. 'A man doesn't put all those years into something to wind up with nothing, does he? A man doesn't work to have the best life he can only to lose it all overnight.'

Frank rummages in his pocket for a tissue and comes up with his tie. He uses it to dry his eyes. 'But what if I don't? What'll I do if I don't come up with something?'

'But you will.'

'What if I get demoted? What if I'm only offered something junior, something with a smaller salary? What am I going to do then, Mike? How am I going to pay the mortgage? Do you know what my mortgage is? And the credit cards. And the kids' schools. And the loan payments – '

'Don't worry, Frank, don't worry. Something will come along.'

'Don't you remember Larimer, Mike? Remember he was head of export? You know what happened to him, Mike? He sells for a greeting card company, Mike, that's what he does. Head of export. And what about that guy, Jesus, what was his name, you know, that good-looking Irish guy everybody thought was such hot shit and then he got the push. He killed himself, Mike. He threw himself in front of a train.'

'Don't be ridiculous. He was drinking a lot, everybody knew that. It was an accident.' They pull into Frank's driveway. Frank's driveway is oval, as though it belongs to a great house and not a four-bedroom mock-Tudor with a patio out the back. In the bend of the drive is a bit of grass and a silvery-blue ball on a concrete stand. 'You'll see, Frank. It'll all be for the best. Maybe you'll even have a chance to start that novel now.'

The porch light comes on and Frank again begins to cry.

Sober as a newt by now, Mike drives home with the top down and the stereo up and ten years of Frank's life in a box that used to hold dogfood in the back of his car. He should have known when Frank told him not to say anything to Claire that he wouldn't have told Kate what had happened. 'How could I tell her?' Frank wanted to know. 'You know what she's like. I'll tell her when and if I have to.'

The two of them sat in the car while Frank pulled himself together, waving at Kate, wrapped in a blue robe and scowling in the doorway. 'Frank?' she called, her voice the only sound disturbing the dreamy suburban night. 'Frank? What are you doing? Where have you been?'

Frank stuffed his tie back in his pocket. 'Would you have told Claire?' Mike said that of course he would have told Claire, she's his wife, isn't she, how could he keep her in the dark, but now he wonders if that's true. Not that she's his wife, of course she's his wife – he has one friend, Frank, and one wife, Claire – but that he would have told her. What good would telling her do?

She is his wife, Claire, the woman who washes his clothes and keeps his house clean and looks after his kids and fixes his meals, the woman who sleeps in his bed and sees that the bills are paid on time, the woman he yells at or fucks when he's had a bad day, the woman he fucks or takes out to dinner when he's had a good one. Claire, tone deaf, efficient, methodical, earnest, serious, humourless. Claire of the cold feet and bony hips, famous in certain circles for her cherry soufflé and her model children. What good would telling her do? She'd say to him exactly what he said to Frank, Don't worry, it'll be all right, you'll get another job, a better job, in no time at all, everything's going to work out fine.

And then, when he didn't get a better job, another job, if he didn't, she'd start to worry, she'd look at him with her old eyes but she'd be seeing something new. We can't afford this, she'd say. We can't afford that. What about the house? she'd want to know. What about our holiday? What are we supposed to do without the company car? she'd cry. But your career, what about your career? I thought that you were being groomed, I thought that you were headed for the top; what was all that work for? All those meetings? All those late nights at the office? All those missed meals and birthdays and school plays, those cancelled holidays and theatre tickets and dinners with friends? She'd turn her back to him whenever they were together – in the kitchen, in the living-room, in the garden, in bed – What did you do? her silence would ask him. What did you do wrong?

Eventually, of course, they had to get out of the car. Kate wasn't going back inside, and she wasn't going to let them sit out there all night while she shivered on the doorstep.

'You're drunk,' she said to Frank as they staggered up the flagstone path. And then to Mike, 'He's drunk. Why do you let him get so drunk?'

'We tried to call, Kate, really,' he said, concerned, sincere, smiling into her angry eyes. 'There was a little celebration in the office, you know, and then we decided to go for – '

'I was worried sick,' she snapped, her arms folded against her chest. 'I thought there'd been an accident.'

Frank pitched up the steps and hurled himself through the open door.

'No,' said Mike, 'no accident.' He handed her Frank's jacket. 'Everything's fine.'

The Hammond home is dark and, except for the sound of his key in the lock and the door opening and his footsteps slowly creeping down the hall and into the kitchen, silent. It is a beautiful home, large and spacious, two full bathrooms and a downstairs loo, its lawn landscaped and its interior decorated, its kitchen fitted, its windows double-glazed, a dream house if ever there was one. He turns on the light and stands there for a few seconds, Frank's box in his arms, looking around, wondering whether to have another drink or not.

Claire never waits up for him. She never leaves a note for him propped up against the sugar bowl: Damian needs some help with his maths, Elena's upset because the cat hasn't come home, I said you'd take her out to look for him first thing in the morning, Did you remember the sun-dried tomatoes? Your dinner's in the fridge, just bung it into the microwave, love C. On the wall beside him is the oversized calendar that contains the history of their weeks. Monday, dentist, piano, man to prune trees. Tuesday, swimming, Brownies. Wednesday, tennis, new strings, Elena supper Chloe. Thursday, hairdresser, new shoes. Friday, movie, pizza, call about rug. She no longer even bothers to pencil him in. He decided in favour of the drink.

The tune from the restaurant is stuck in his head. *What a night for a nightcap*, he sings to himself as he takes out the gin and a glass and the juice and a trace of ice cubes, *What a night for a nightcapping boy, I've been having this sweet drink, Fills me up with this feeling of joy . . .*

Friday night, he thinks, Friday night. When he was a kid Friday nights were special. Friday night, the beginning of the weekend. It was always Sundays that he hated. Sunday, the day before everything went back to normal. Sunday, when all the fun came to an end. Even when he wasn't a child any more he felt like that. He'd wake up on Sunday and think: Shit, back to work tomorrow, back to the grind – but on Friday morning he'd wake up thinking: Thank God, I can make it through today, it doesn't count, it's Friday, and then there's this whole long weekend ahead. He wasn't hungry at supper, but he's suddenly hungry now. He hunkers down in front of the refrigerator. Everything inside, carefully wrapped in Clingfilm or packed away in plastic containers, looks cold and dead, specimens – a bowl of boiled potatoes, a chicken leg, a slice of pizza, a block of cheese, leftover baked beans, spaghetti sauce. Not any more, though. Now he wakes up on Friday morning and thinks: Oh hell, Friday, two more days and it'll be Sunday and the week will start again. Just as he woke up this morning. Oh hell, Friday, the weekend's almost over. He slams the refrigerator door closed. It's as good as Monday right now.

He sits down at the table with his drink and a packet of something that tastes like pickled onions and is shaped like monsters' feet. It's like eating nothing. No, it is eating nothing, pickled onion flavour nothing. He looks through Frank's box as he bites off tiny, crunchy toes. Some photographs, a calendar, a print of a sailboat gliding across a sunset, a magnetic paperclip holder, a clutch of pencils and ballpoint pens, a corkscrew, a gold fountain pen, a tie, a diary, a half-dead plant, a box of painkillers, a bottle of after-shave, an electric razor, a bright red mug – Frank's life.

He sips his gin. *What a night for a nightcap, What a night for a nightcapping boy, dumdedumdedumdodedodedodo.* The real song has some line about time in it. He tries to remember, closing his eyes and picturing them back in Triolo's Ristorante, somebody, maybe Frank, saying, 'Hey, you remember this song?' Some line about time not being on your side, something something not really on your side, and falling on your face on somebody's lawn, something about falling on your face on somebody's new-mown lawn. He reaches into Frank's box and comes up with the chrome cylinder Frank used to keep his pens in. I could certainly manage that, he thinks, flat on my face in the grass.

He bites a foot in half, dunks the other half in his drink. And this is his life.

This is his life – their life – and if he suggested to Claire that now might be a good time to change his life, their life, while they were still young and possible, jumping instead of being pushed, a good time to sell up and go somewhere new, maybe start his own business, do something different, something that made getting up in the morning an event to be looked forward to and not something you do because of the mortgage payments and the overdraft, then she'd tell him he was crazy. Crazy, she'd say. Give all this up? What for? Crazy, she'd say. Do something else? Like what? she'd ask. Well, I don't know, he'd say – as though he had never given it any thought, had never lain awake listening to his own heart beating and watching the room materialise in the morning light, making up a new life for himself. He gets up and goes to stand by the sliding glass doors that lead from the kitchen to the sunroom. Claire calls it the conservatory. I think I'll go sit in the conservatory, she'd say. I think I'll serve tea in the conservatory. But it isn't a conservatory, it's a small glass box at the back of the house, just like the small glass box at the back of the house next door. Well I don't know, he'd say, I always thought I'd like to set up a little shop somewhere, you know, imports, crafts and jewellery and stuff like that, from South America maybe or Asia. Places like that can do very well, Claire; nowadays there's quite a demand. A shop? She'd look at him as though she'd never seen him before. You want to give up a prestigious job to become a shopkeeper? You want to risk everything, our security, everything, so you can sell cheap rugs and woven baskets? She wouldn't laugh, Claire's not a laugher, she would sneer. I thought it might be nice to do the buying, he'd say, you know, travel a bit, meet different people, learn something new. She'd manage a laugh at that. You sound like you're about fifteen, she'd say, mimicking him, *travel a bit, meet different people, learn something new*; for God's sake, Mike, what's come over you? And she'd laugh so hard she could hardly breathe. What about me? she'd rightly demand when she was back in control. What about me and the kids and our lives? We're happy as we are. We love this house. We love this community. We have friends here. We belong. Damian has his piano and his football. Elena has her violin and her swimming. Their schools. My clubs, my charity work, my Brownie troop, my tennis lessons. What about us?

He stares through the glass of the doors and the glass of the sunroom and out into the night of the back garden, but he can see no lawn, mown or otherwise, can see nothing but himself staring back, a tired-looking man, no longer really young, maybe, but young enough, prosperous, well fed, well cared for, successful, a man in a good suit, with a good haircut, a glint of gold on his wrist – a man who looks nothing like the man he once wanted to be.

Claire stirs as he slides into bed beside her. 'You're late,' she says sleepily, turning over so that her front is against his back, her breath warm on his neck. 'Anything special?'

'No,' he whispers, not really wanting to wake her. 'You know, the usual.'

'Frank get home all right?'

'Yeah, Frank's all right.'

Claire says, 'Ummm.' She tucks her legs behind his, puts an arm around him. 'So you had a good day?' she asks, though it is hardly a question.

He closes his eyes. 'Umhum,' he says. 'Terrific.'

'That's good,' says Claire. 'We did too.'

What a night for a nightcap, he sings in his head, collapsing into sleep, *dumdododedumdodo . . . and fall on your face on somebody's new-mown lawn.*

Two Poems

FLEUR ADCOCK

THE RUSSIAN WAR

Great-great-great-uncle Francis Eggington
came back from the Russian War
(it was the kind of war you came back from,
if you were lucky: bad, but over).
He didn't come to the front door –
the lice and filth were falling off him –
he slipped along the alley to the yard.
'Who's that out at the pump?' they said
– 'a tall tramp stripping his rags off!'
The soap was where it usually was.
He scrubbed and splashed and scrubbed,
and combed his beard over the hole in his throat.
'Give me some clothes,' he said. 'I'm back.'
'God save us, Frank, it's you!' they said.
'What happened? Were you at Scutari?
And what's that hole inside your beard?'
'Tea first,' he said. 'I'll tell you later.
And Willie's children will tell their grandchildren:
I'll be a thing called oral history.'

WHERE THEY LIVED

That's where they lived in the eighteen-nineties.
They don't know that we know,
or that we're standing here, in possession
of some really quite intimate information
about the causes of their deaths,
photographing each other in a brisk wind
outside their terrace house, both smiling
(not callously, we could assure them),
our hair streaming across our faces
and the green plastic Marks & Spencer bag
in which I wrapped my camera against showers
ballooning out like a wind-sock
from my wrist, showing the direction
of something that's blowing down our century.

Berlin

IAN McEWAN

FIRST NIGHT

There was another man sitting in the front passenger seat of the Beetle when Leonard went down on to the street with Bob Glass. His name was Russell, and he must have been watching their approach in the rear-view mirror, for he sprang out of the car as they approached it from behind and gave Leonard's hand a manly shake. He worked as an announcer for RIAS, he said, the American radio service. He wore a gold-buttoned blazer of a shameless Post Office red, and cream-coloured trousers with sharp creases, and shoes with tassels and no laces. After the introductions, Russell pulled a lever on his seat and gestured Leonard into the back. Like Glass, Russell wore his shirt open to reveal a high-necked white vest underneath. As they pulled away, Leonard fingered his tie knot in the darkness. He decided against removing the tie in case the two Americans had already noticed him wearing it.

Russell seemed to think it was his responsibility to impart as much information as possible to Leonard. His voice was professionally relaxed, and he spoke without fumbling a syllable or repeating himself or pausing between sentences. He was on the job, naming the streets as they passed down them, pointing out the extent of the bomb damage, or a new office block going up. 'We're crossing the Tiergarten now. You'll need to come by here in daylight. There's hardly a tree to be seen. What the bombs didn't destroy, the Berliners burnt to keep warm in the Airlift. Hitler used to call this the East-West Axis. Now it's Street of June Seventeen, named for the Uprising the year before last. Up ahead is the memorial to the Russian soldiers who took the city, and I'm sure you know the name of this famous edifice . . . '

The car slowed down as they passed West Berlin Police and Customs. Beyond them were half a dozen Vopos. One of them shone a torch at the licence plate and waved the car into the Russian sector. They drove through the Brandenburg Gate. Now it was much darker. There was no other traffic. It was difficult to feel excitement, however, because Russell's travelogue continued without modulation, even when the car crashed through a pot-hole.

BERLIN

'This deserted stretch was once the nerve centre of the city, one of the most famous thoroughfares in Europe. Unter den Linden . . . Over there, the real headquarters of the German Democratic Republic, the Soviet Embassy. It stands on the site of the old Hotel Bristol, once one of the most fashionable . . . '

Glass had been silent all this while. Now he interrupted politely. 'Excuse me, Russell. Leonard, we're starting you in the East so you can enjoy the contrasts later. We're going to the Neva Hotel . . . '

Russell was reactivated. 'It used to be the Hotel Nordland, a second-class establishment. Now it has declined further, but it is still the best hotel in East Berlin.'

'Russell,' Glass said, 'you badly need a drink.'

It was so dark they could see light from the Neva lobby slanting across the pavement from the far end of the street. When they got out the car they saw there was in fact another light, the blue neon sign of a co-operative restaurant opposite the hotel, the H.O. Gastronom. The condensation on the windows was its only outward sign of life. In the lobby a man in a brown uniform silently handed them towards a lift just big enough for three. It was a slow descent, and their faces were too close together under a single dim bulb for conversation.

There were thirty or forty people in the bar, silent over their drinks. On a dais in one corner a clarinettist and an accordion player were sorting through sheets of music. The bar was hung with studded, tasselled quilt of well-fingered pink which was also built into the counter. There were grand chandeliers, all unlit, and chipped gilt-framed mirrors. Leonard was heading for the bar, intending to buy the first round, but Glass guided him towards a table on the edge of a tiny parquet dance floor.

His whisper sounded loud. 'Don't let them see your money in here. East marks only.'

At last a waiter came and Glass ordered a bottle of Russian champagne. As they raised their glasses, the musicians began to play 'Red Sails in the Sunset'. No one was tempted on to the parquet. Russell was scanning the darker corners, and then he was on his feet and making his way between the tables. He returned with a thin woman in a white dress made for someone larger. They watched him move her through an efficient foxtrot.

Glass was shaking his head. 'He mistook her in the bad light. She won't do,' he predicted, and correctly, for at the end Russell made a courtly bow, and, offering the woman his arm, saw her back to her table.

When he joined them he shrugged. 'It's the diet here.' And relapsing for a moment into his wireless propaganda voice, gave them details of average calorie consumption in East and West Berlin. Then he broke off, saying, 'What the hell,' and ordered another bottle.

The champagne was as sweet as lemonade and too gassy. It hardly seemed a serious drink at all. Glass and Russell were talking about the German question. How long would the refugees flock through Berlin to the West before the Democratic Republic suffered total economic collapse through a shortage of manpower?

Russell was ready with the figures, the hundreds of thousands each year. 'And these are their best people, three-quarters of them are under forty-five. I'll give it another three years. After that the East German State won't be able to function.'

Glass said, 'There'll be a state as long as there's a government, and there'll be a government as long as the Soviets want it. It'll be pretty damn miserable here, but the Party will get by. You see.'

Leonard nodded and hummed his agreement, but he did not attempt an opinion. When he raised his hand he was agreeably surprised that the waiter came over for him just as he had for the others. He ordered another bottle. He had never felt happier. They were deep in the Communist camp, they were drinking Communist champagne, they were men with responsibilities talking over affairs of state. The conversation had moved on to West Germany, the Federal Republic, which was about to be accepted as a full member of NATO.

Russell thought it was all a mistake. 'That's one crappy phoenix rising out of the ashes.'

Glass said, 'You want a free Germany, then you got to have a strong one.'

'The French aren't going to buy it,' Russell said, and turned to Leonard for support. At that moment the champagne arrived.

'I'll take care of it,' Glass said, and when the waiter had gone he said to Leonard, 'You owe me seven West marks.'

Leonard filled the glasses and the thin woman and her girlfriend walked past their table, and the conversation took another turn. Russell said that Berlin girls were the liveliest and most strong-minded in all the world.

Leonard, remembering what the decorators had said, tried out the opinion that as long as you weren't Russian you couldn't go wrong. 'They all remember when the Russians came in '45,' he said with quiet authority. 'They've all got older sisters, or mothers, even grannies, who were raped and kicked around.'

The two Americans did not agree, but they took him seriously. They even laughed on 'grannies'. Leonard took a long, triumphant drink as he listened to Russell.

'The Russians are with their units, out in the country. The ones in town, the officers, the commissars, they do well enough with the girls.'

Glass agreed. 'There's always some dumb chick who'll fuck a Russian.'

The band was playing 'How You Gonna Keep Them Down on the Farm?'. The sweetness of the champagne was cloying. It was a relief when the waiter set down three fresh glasses and a refrigerated bottle of vodka.

They were talking about the Russians again. Russell's wireless announcer's voice had gone. His face was sweaty and bright, reflecting the glow of his blazer. Ten years ago, Russell said, he had been a twenty-two-year-old lieutenant accompanying Colonel Frank Howley's advance party which had set off for Berlin in May 1945 to begin the occupation of the American sector. 'We thought the Russians were regular guys. They'd suffered losses in the millions. They were heroic, they were big, cheerful, vodka-swilling guys. And we'd been sending them mountains of equipment all through the war. So they just had to be our allies. That was before we met up with them. They came out and blocked our road sixty miles west of Berlin. We got out of the trucks to greet them with open arms. We had gifts ready, we were high on the idea of the meeting.' Russell gripped Leonard's arm. 'But they were cold! Cold, Leonard! We had champagne ready, French champagne, but they wouldn't touch it. It was all we could do to make them shake us by the hand. They wouldn't let our party through unless we reduced it to fifty vehicles. They made us bivouac ten miles out of town. The next morning they let us in under close escort. They didn't trust us, they didn't like us. From day one they had us fingered for the enemy. They tried to stop us setting up our sector.

'And that's how it went on. They never smiled. They never wanted to make things work. They lied, they obstructed, they were cruel. Their language was always too strong, even when they were insisting on a technicality in some agreement. All the time we were saying, What the hell, they've had a crappy war, and they do things differently anyhow. We gave way, we were the innocents. We were talking about the United Nations and a new world order while they were kidnapping and beating up non-Communist politicians all over town. It took us almost a year to get wise to them. And you know what? Every time we met them, these Russian officers, they looked so fucking unhappy. It was like they expected to be shot in the back at any moment. They didn't even enjoy behaving like assholes. That's why I could never really hate them. This was policy. This crap was coming from the top.'

Glass poured more vodka. He said, 'I hate them. It's not a passion with me, I don't go crazy with it like some guys. You could say it's their system you got to hate. But there's no system without people to run it.' When he set his glass down he spilled a little drink. He pushed his forefinger into the puddle. 'What the Commies are selling is miserable, miserable, and inefficient. Now they're exporting it by force. I was in Budapest and Warsaw last year. Boy, have they found a way of minimising happiness. They know it, but they don't stop. I mean, look at this place! Leonard, we brought you to the classiest joint in their sector. Look at it. Look at the people here. Look at them!' Glass was close to shouting.

Russell put out his hand. 'Take it easy, Bob.'

Glass was smiling. 'It's OK. I'm not going to misbehave.'

Leonard looked around. Through the gloom he could see the heads of the customers bowed over their drinks. The barman and the waiter who were standing together at the bar had turned to face the other way. The two musicians were playing a chirpy marching song. This was his last clear impression. The following day he was to have no memory of leaving the Neva.

They must have made their way between the tables, ascended in the cramped lift, walked past the man in the brown uniform. By the car was the dark window of a shopping co-operative, and inside a tower of tinned pilchards, and above it a portrait of Stalin framed in red crêpe paper with a caption in big white letters which Glass and Russell translated in messy unison: *The unshakeable friendship of the Soviet and German peoples is a guarantee of peace and freedom.*

Then they were at the sector crossing. Glass had switched the engine off, torches were shone into the car while their papers were being examined, there were sounds of steel-tipped boots coming and going in the darkness. Then they were driving past a sign which said in four languages: '*You are leaving the Democratic Sector of Berlin*' towards another which announced in the same languages: '*You are now entering the British Sector*'.

'Now we're in Wittenbergplatz,' Russell called from the front seat.

They drifted by a Red Cross nurse seated at the foot of a gigantic model of a candle with a real flame on top.

Russell was attempting to revive his travelogue. 'Collecting for the *Spät-heimkehrers*, the late homecomers, the hundreds of thousands of German soldiers still held by the Russians . . . '

Glass said, 'Ten years! Forget it. They ain't coming back now.'

And the next thing was a table set among scores of others in a vast and clamorous space, and a band up on the stage almost drowning the voices with a jazzed-up version of 'Over There', and a pamphlet, this time in only German and English with clumsy print that swayed and danced:

BERLIN

Welcome to the Ballhouse of technical wonders, the place of all places of entertainments. One hundred thousand contacts are guaranteeing . . . (the word was an echo he could not place) *. . . are guaranteeing you the proper functioning of the Modern Tablephone System consisting of two hundred and fifty Tablephone sets. The Pneumatic Table-mail Service is posting every night thousands of letters or little presents from one visitor to the other – it is unique and amusing for everyone. The famous RESI Water Shows are magnificent in their beauty. It is amazing to think that in a minute eight thousand litres of water are pressed through about nine thousand jets. For the play of these changing light effects there are necessary one hundred thousand coloured lamps.*

Glass had his fingers in his beard and was smiling hugely. He said something, and had to repeat it at a shout. 'This is better!'

But it was too noisy to begin a conversation about the advantages of the Western sector. Coloured water spouted up in front of the band, and rose and fell and lurched from side to side. Leonard avoided looking at it. They were being sensible by drinking beer. As soon as the waiter had gone a girl appeared with a basket of roses. Russell bought one and presented it to Leonard who snapped off the stem and lodged the flower behind his ear. At the next table something came rattling through the pneumatic tube and two Germans in Bavarian jackets leaned forward to examine the contents of a canister. A woman in a sequined mermaid suit was kissing the bandleader. There were wolf whistles and cheers. The band started up, the woman was handed a microphone. She took off her glasses and began to sing 'It's Too Darn Hot' with a heavy accent. The Germans were looking disappointed. They stared in the direction of a table some fifty feet away where two giggling girls were collapsing in one another's arms. Beyond them was the packed dance floor. The woman sang 'Night and Day', 'Anything Goes', 'Just One of Those Things', and finally 'Miss Otis Regrets'. Then everyone stood to cheer and stamp their feet and shout *encore*.

The band took a break and Leonard bought another round of beers. Russell took a good look round and said he was too drunk to pick up girls. They talked about Cole Porter and named their favourite songs. Russell said he knew someone whose father had been working at the hospital when they brought Porter in from his riding accident in '37. For some reason the doctors and nurses had been asked not to talk to the press. This led to a conversation about secrecy.

Russell said there was far too much of it in the world. He was laughing. He must have known something about Glass's work.

Glass was serious in a punchy way. His head lolled back and he sighted Russell along his beard. 'You know what the best course I ever took at college was? Biology. We studied evolution. And I learned something important.' Now he included Leonard in his gaze. 'It helped me choose my career. For thousands, no, millions of years we had these huge brains, the neo-cortex, right? But we didn't speak to each other, and we lived like fucking pigs. There was nothing. No language, no culture, nothing. And then, suddenly, wham! It was there. Suddenly it was something we had to have, and there was no turning back. So why did it suddenly happen?

Russell shrugged. 'Hand of God?'

'Hand of God my ass. I'll tell you why. Back then we all used to hang out together all day long doing the same thing. We lived in packs. So there was no need for language. If there was a leopard coming, there was no point saying, Hey man, what's coming down the track? A leopard! Everyone could see it, everyone was jumping up and down and screaming, trying to scare it off. But what happens when someone goes off on his own for a moment's privacy? When he sees a leopard coming, he knows something the others don't. And he knows they don't know. He has something they don't, he has a *secret*, and this is the beginning of his individuality, of his consciousness. If he wants to share his secret and run down the track to warn the other guys, then he's going to need to invent language. From there grows the possibility of culture. Or he can hang back and hope the leopard will take out the leadership that's been giving him a hard time. A secret plan, that means more individuation, more consciousness.'

The band was starting to play a fast, loud number. Glass had to shout his conclusion, 'Secrecy made us possible,' and Russell raised his beer to salute the theory.

A waiter mistook the gesture and was at his elbow, so a fresh round was ordered, and as the mermaid shimmered to the front of the band and the cheers rang out there was a harsh rattling at their table as a canister shot down the tube and smacked against the brass fixture and lodged there. They stared at it and no one moved.

Then Glass picked it up and unscrewed the top. He took out a folded piece of paper and spread it out on the table. 'My God,' he shouted. 'Leonard, it's for you.'

For one confused moment he thought it might be from his mother. He was

owed a letter from England. And it was late, he thought; he hadn't told her where he was going to be.

The three of them were leaning over the note. Their heads were blocking out the light. Russell read it aloud: '*An den jungen Mann mit der Blume im Haar. Mein Schöner*, I have been watching you from my table. I would like it when you come and ask me to dance. But if you can't do this, I am so happy when you would turn and smile in my direction. I am sorry to interfere, yours, table number 89.'

The Americans were on their feet casting around for the table, while Leonard remained seated with the paper in his hands. He read the German words over. The message was hardly a surprise. Now it was before him, it was more a matter of recognition for him, of accepting the inevitable; it had always been certain to start like this. If he was honest with himself, he had to concede that he had always known it really, at some level.

He was being pulled to his feet. They turned him about and faced across the ballroom. 'Look, she's over there.' Across the heads, through the dense, rising cigarette smoke back-lit by stage lights, he could make out a woman sitting alone. Glass and Russell were pantomiming a fuss over his appearance, dusting down his jacket, straightening his tie, fixing the flower more securely behind his ear. Then they pushed him away, like a boat from a jetty. 'Go on!' they said. 'Atta boy!'

He was drifting towards her, and she was watching his approach. She had her elbow on the table, and she was supporting her chin with her hand. The mermaid was singing, 'Don't sit under zuh apple tree viz anyone else but me, anyone else but me.' He thought, correctly as it turned out, that his life was about to change.

When he was ten feet away she smiled. He arrived just as the band finished the song. He stood swaying slightly, with his hand on the back of a chair, waiting for the applause to die, and when it did Maria Eckdorf said in sweetly inflected English, 'Are we going to dance?' Leonard touched his stomach lightly, apologetically, with his fingertips. Three entirely different liquids were sitting in there.

He said, 'Actually, would you mind if I sat down?' And so he did, and they immediately held hands, and many minutes passed before he was able to speak another word.

SIGNAL ACTIVATION

She was emptying a teapot into the small kitchen sink where two saucepans balanced on top of a stack of dirty plates. He was watching the thick material of her skirt, how it moved in delayed motion, how the warm cashmere just covered the tops of the pleats and how she wore football socks inside carpet slippers. All this winter wool was reassuring to Leonard who felt easily threatened by a provocatively dressed woman. Wool suggested undemanding intimacy, and body warmth, and a body hiding cosily, demurely in the folds. She was making tea in the English style. She had a Coronation caddy, and she was scalding the pot. This too put Leonard at his ease.

In response to his question, she was telling him that when she first started work at Twelve Armoured Workshops, R E M E, it was her job to make tea three times a day for the C O and the 2 I C. She set down on the table two Army issue white mugs, exactly the same as the ones he had in his apartment. He had been entertained to tea a number of times by young women, but he had never met one who did not trouble to decant the milk into a jug.

They warmed their hands around the big mugs. He knew from experience that unless he made a formidable effort, a pattern was waiting to impose itself: a polite enquiry would elicit a polite response and another question. Have you lived here long? Do you travel far to your work? Is it your afternoon off? The catechism would have begun. Only silences would interrupt the relentless tread of question and answer. They would be calling to each other over immense distances, from adjacent mountain peaks. Finally he would be desperate for the relief of heading away with his own thoughts, after the awkward goodbyes. Even now, they had already retreated from the intensity of their greeting. He had asked her about tea making. One more like that, and there would be nothing he could do.

She had set down her mug and had put her hands deep in the pockets of her skirt. She was tapping her slippered feet on the rug. Her head was cocked, with expectation perhaps, or was she marking time to the tune in her head? Was it still 'Take back that mink, those old worn out poils, What made you think . . . ?' He had never known a woman tap her feet, but he knew he must not panic.

It was an assumption, lodged deep, beyond examination or even awareness, that the responsibility for the event was entirely his. If he could not find the easy words to bring them closer, the defeat would be his alone. What could he say that was neither trivial nor intrusive? She had taken up her mug again and was looking at him now with a half-smile which did not quite part her lips. Aren't you lonely living here by yourself? sounded too wheedlingly suggestive. She might think he was offering to move in.

Rather than tolerate more silence, he settled after all for small talk and began to ask, 'Have you lived here long?'

But all in a rush she spoke over him, saying, 'How do you look without your glasses? Show me, please.' This last word she elongated beyond what any native speaker would have considered reasonable, unfurling a delicate, papery thrill through Leonard's stomach. He snatched the glasses from his face and blinked at her. He could see quite well up to three feet, and her features had only partially dissolved. 'And so,' she said quietly. 'It is how I thought. Your eyes are beautiful and all the time they are hidden. Has no one told you how beautiful they are?'

Leonard's mother used to say something of the sort when he was fifteen and he had his first pair, but that was hardly relevant. He had the sensation of rising gently through the room.

She took the glasses and folded down the sides and put them by the cactus.

His voice sounded strangled in his ears. 'No, no one has said that.'

'Not other girls?'

He shook his head.

'Then I am the first to discover you?' There was humour, but no mockery in her look.

It made him feel foolish, immature, to be grinning so openly at her compliment, but he could do nothing about it.

She said, 'And your smile.'

She smoothed away a wisp of hair from her eyes. Her forehead, so high and oval, reminded him of how Shakespeare was supposed to look. He was not certain how to put this to her. Instead he took her hand as it completed its movement and they sat in silence for a minute or two, as they had at their first meeting. She interlocked her fingers with his, and it was at this moment, rather than later in the bedroom, or later still when they talked of themselves with greater freedom, that Leonard felt irrevocably bound to her. Their hands fitted well, the grip was intricate, unbreakable, there were so many points of contact. In this poor light, and without his glasses, he could not see which fingers were his own. Sitting in the darkening, chilly room in his raincoat, holding on to her hand, he felt he was throwing away his life. The abandonment was delicious. Something was pouring out of him, through his palm and into hers, something was spreading back up his arm, across his chest, constricting his throat. His only thought was a repetition: So this is it, it's like this, so this is it . . .

Finally she pulled her hand away and folded her arms and looked at him expectantly. For no good reason other than the seriousness of her look he began to explain himself. 'I should have come sooner,' he said, 'but I've been working all hours of the day and night. And actually, I didn't know if you'd want to see me, or if you'd even recognise me.'

'Do you have another friend in Berlin?'

'Oh no, nothing like that.' He did not question her right to ask this question. 'And did you have many girlfriends in England?'

'Not many, no.'

'How many?'

He hesitated before making a lunge at the truth. 'Well, actually, none.'

'You've never had one?'

'No.'

Maria leaned forwards. 'You mean, you've never . . . '

He could not bear to hear whatever term she was about to use. 'No, I never have.'

She put her hand to her mouth to stifle a yelp of laughter. It was not so extraordinary a thing in 1955 for a man of Leonard's background and temperament to have had no sexual experience by the end of his twenty-fifth year. But it was a remarkable thing for a man to confess. He regretted it immediately. She had the laughter under control, but now she was blushing. It was the interlocking fingers that had made him think he could get away with speaking without pretence. In this bare little room with its pile of assorted shoes belonging to a woman who lived alone and did not fuss with milk jugs or doilies on tea trays, it should have been possible to deal in unadorned truths.

And in fact, it was. Maria's blushes were brought on by shame at the laughter she knew Leonard would misunderstand. For hers was the laughter of nervous relief. She had been suddenly absolved from the pressures and rituals of seduction. She would not have to adopt a conventional role and be judged in it, and she was not about to be measured against other women. Her fear of being physically abused had receded. She would not be obliged to do anything she did not want. She was free, they both were free, to invent their own terms; they could be partners in invention. And she really had discovered for herself this shy Englishman with the steady gaze and the long lashes; she had him first, she would have him all to herself. These thoughts she formulated later in solitude. At the time they erupted in the single hoot of relief and hilarity which she had suppressed to a yelp.

Leonard took a long pull of his tea, set down the mug and said, 'Ah,' in a hearty, unconvincing way. He put his glasses on and stood up. After the handclasp, nothing seemed bleaker than setting off, back down Adalbertstrasse and descending the U-Bahn, and arriving at his apartment in the early evening darkness to find the breakfast coffee cup and the drafts of his foolish letter all over the floor. He saw it all before him as he adjusted the belt of his gaberdine, but he knew that with his confession he had made a humiliating tactical error and he had to go. That Maria should blush for him made her all the sweeter, and hinted at the scale of his blunder.

She had stood too and was blocking his path to the door.

'I really ought to be getting back now,' Leonard explained, 'what with work and everything.' The worse he felt, the lighter his tone became. He was stepping round her as he said, 'You make a terrific cup of tea.'

Maria said, 'I want you to stay longer.'

It was all he wanted to hear, but by now he was too low to enact a change of heart, too drawn to his own defeat. He was on his way to the door. 'I have to meet someone at six.' The lie was a hopeless commitment to his anguish. Even as it was happening, he was amazed by himself. He wanted to stay, she wanted him to stay, and here he was, insisting on leaving. It was the behaviour of a stranger and he could do nothing, he could not steer himself in the direction of his own interests. Self-pity had obliterated his habitual and meticulous good sense; he was in a tunnel whose only end was his own fascinating annihilation.

He was fumbling with the unfamiliar lock and Maria was right at his back. Though it still surprised her, she was to some extent familiar with the delicacy of masculine pride. Despite a surface assurance, men were easily offended. Their moods could swing wildly. Caught in the turbulence of unacknowledged emotions, they tended to mask their uncertainty with aggression. She was thirty, her experience was not vast, and she was thinking mostly of her husband and one or two violent soldiers she had known. The man scrabbling to leave by her front door was less like the men she had known and more like herself. She knew just how it was. When you felt sorry for yourself, you wanted to make things worse. She was touching his back lightly, but he was not aware of it through his coat. He thought he had made his plausible excuses and was free to depart with his misery. To Maria, who had the liberation of Berlin and her marriage to Otto Eckdorf behind her, a display of vulnerability of any kind in a man suggested an approachable personality.

He opened the door at last and turned to say his goodbyes. Did he really believe that she was fooled by his politeness and the invented appointment, or that his desperation was invisible? She could have kissed him and enticed him back that way. But, as she explained later, she wanted to save those, she wanted their first kisses to be leisurely and free of calculation. He was telling her he was sorry he had to dash off, and expressing gratitude for the tea again, and offering his hand – a handshake! – when she reached up and lifted his glasses clear of his face and strode back into her sitting-room with them. Before he had even started to follow her, she had slipped them under a chair cushion.

'Look here,' he said, and, letting the door close behind him, took one step then another into the apartment. And that was it, he was back in. He had wanted to stay; now he had to. 'I really do have to be going.' He stood in the centre of the tiny room, irresolute, still attempting to fake his hesitant English form of outrage.

She stood close so he could see her clearly. How wonderful it was, not to be frightened of a man. It gave her a chance to like him, to have desires which were not simply reactions to his. She took his hands in hers. 'But I haven't finished looking at your eyes.' Then, with the Berlin girl's forthrightness Russell had praised, she added, '*Du Dummer! Es macht mir sehr glücklich wenn dies für dich das Erste Mal ist.* If this is your first time I'm a very lucky girl!'

It was her 'this' which held Leonard. He was back with 'this'. What they were doing here was all part of 'this', his first time. He looked down at her face, that disc, tipped way back to accommodate the seven-inch difference in their heights. From the top third of the neat oval, the baby hair fell back in loose curls and straggles. She was not the first young lady he had kissed, but she was the first who seemed to like it. Encouraged, he pushed his tongue into her mouth, the way, he had gathered, one was supposed to.

She drew her face back an inch or so. She said, '*Langsam.* Plenty of time.' So they kissed with a teasing lightness. The very tips of their tongues just touched and it was indeed a greater pleasure. Then Maria stepped round him and pulled out from among the heap of shoes an electric fire. 'There is time,' she repeated. 'We can pass a week with our arms just so.' She embraced herself to show him.

'That's right,' he said. 'We could do that.' His voice sounded high-pitched. He followed her into the bedroom.

It was larger than the room they had left. There was a double mattress on the floor, another novelty. One wall was taken up with a gloomy wardrobe of polished wood. By the window was a painted chest of drawers and a linen box. He sat on the linen box and watched her plug in the fire.

'It is too cold to get undressed. We'll go in like this.' It was true, you could see the vapour on your breath. She kicked off her slippers, he untied his laces and took off his coat. They got under the eiderdown and lay with their arms round each other in the way she had prescribed, and kissed again.

It was not a week but several hours, just after midnight, before Leonard was able to define himself in strictest terms as an initiate, a truly mature adult at last. However, the line that divided innocence from knowledge was vague, and rapturously so. As the bed, and to a far lesser extent, the room, warmed up, they set about helping each other undress. As the pile on the floor grew – sweaters, thick shirts, woollen underwear and football socks – so the bed, and time itself grew more spacious. Maria, luxuriating in the possibility of shaping the event to her needs, said this was just the right moment for her to be kissed and licked all over, from the toes upwards. This was how Leonard, halfway through a characteristically meticulous job, came to enter her first with his tongue. That surely was the dividing line in his life. But so too was the moment half an hour later when she took him into her mouth and licked and sucked and did something with her teeth. In terms of mere physical sensation, this was the high point of the six hours, and perhaps of his life.

Before that was complete, there was a long interlude when they lay still, and in answer to her questions he told her about his school, his parents and his lonely three years at Birmingham University. She talked more reticently about her work, the cycling club and the amorous treasurer, and her ex-husband Otto who had been a sergeant in the army and was now a drunk. Two months before he had appeared after a year's absence and had hit her round the head twice with an open hand and demanded money.

This story temporarily erased desire. Very gallantly, Leonard got dressed and went down to Oranienstrasse to buy a bottle of wine. People and traffic circulated, oblivious to the great changes. When he returned she was standing at the stove in a man's dressing-gown and her football socks cooking a potato and mushroom omelette. They ate it in bed with black bread. The Mosel was sugary and rough. They drank it in the tea mugs and insisted it was good. Whenever he put a piece of bread in his mouth, he smelt her on his fingers. She had brought in the candle in the bottle and now she lit it. The cosy squalor of clothes and greasy plates receded into the shadows. The sulphur smell of the match hung in the air and mixed with the smell on his fingers. He tried to recall and recount in an amusing way a sermon he had once heard at school about the devil and temptation and a woman's body. But Maria misunderstood, or saw no reason why he should be telling her this or finding it funny, and she became cross and silent. They lay propped on their elbows in the gloom, sipping from their mugs. After a while he touched the back of her hand and said, 'Sorry. A stupid story.' She forgave him by turning her hand and squeezing his fingers.

She curled up on his arm and slept for half an hour. During that time he lay back feeling proud. He studied her face – how scant her eyebrows were, how wonderfully her lower lip swelled in sleep – and he thought what it would be to have a child, a daughter who might sleep on him like this. When she awoke she was all fresh. She wanted him to lie on her. He cuddled up and sucked her nipples. When they kissed, it was right this time to be free with his tongue. They poured out the rest of the wine and she chinked his mug.

Of what followed he remembered only two things. The first was that it was rather like going to see a film that everybody else had been talking about; difficult to imagine in advance, but, once there, installed, partly recognition, partly surprises: the encompassing slippery smoothness, for example, was much as he had hoped, even better, in fact, while nothing in his extensive reading had prepared him for the crinkly sensation of having another's pubic hair pressed against his own. The second was awkward: he had read all about premature ejaculation and wondered if he would suffer, and now it seemed he might. It was not movement that threatened to bring him on. It was when he looked at her face. She was lying on her back, for they were what she had taught him to call *auf Altdeutsch*. Sweat had restyled her hair into snaky coils and her arms were thrown up behind her head, with the palms spread, like a comic book representation of surrender. At the same time she was looking up at him in a knowing, kindly way. It was just this combination of abandonment and loving attention that was too good to be looked at, too perfect for him, and he had to avert his eyes, or close them, and think of . . . of, yes, a circuit diagram, a particularly intricate and lovely one he had committed to memory during the fitting of signal activation units to the Ampex machines.

Night Train

CRAIG RAINE

Moths go over and over the glass,
puffs of French chalk,
like someone checking for fingerprints.

Between two barbed wire fences,
on the verge of the underworld,
the train is arrested. Irrevocable

as a declaration of love,
this silent, stolen masterpiece,
this aching gallery of gilded light

and now we would like it to leave.

Extracts from The Good Doctor –
A Comedy

NIGEL WILLIAMS

ACT ONE.

The urology clinic of a hospital somewhere in England. On stage are JOHN, *a registrar just on the right side of forty and* STEPHEN, *a consultant on the wrong side of the same age.*

JOHN: I want to feel. I want to help. I want to care.
    But I'm a doctor; I am so aware
    That charity, like courage, has its bounds,
    And GPs, surgeons, housemen on their rounds
    Have moments when they could not give a toss
    About some clown's contracting cancer, possibly
    There are those who would say
    They feel for every patient, every day.
    I don't believe them. I'll lay even money
    Comedians don't eat, sleep, or dream funny,
    And stockbrokers at play on the golf course
    Don't think about the movements of the Bourse.
    Why –
STEPHEN: The only patient I find pleases
    Is one who's got the interesting diseases.
    It's my career. How can I best advance it?
    Can I write this one up in this month's *Lancet*?
    Tenderness, humanity, respect, I've kissed 'em
    All goodbye – the urinary system
    Is now my love and speciality.
    Not people's hearts or brains, but how they pee.
    That's all I see of people. Toms, Dicks, Harrys, Billys
    Are not themselves, but kidneys plumbed to willies.
    Relax, dear boy –

JOHN: I can't. I wish I could. All that is real
 Is that I cannot care. I cannot feel
 For patients as I should. And yet one face
 Is everything to me –
STEPHEN: She's from this place?
JOHN: She is.
STEPHEN: Oh John, you are in love.
JOHN: It's worse
 Than that.
STEPHEN: Don't tell me –
JOHN: What?
STEPHEN: That she's a nurse.
 Say she's a stranger, say she's some stray face
 Glimpsed in a theatre, a bar, a place
 A million miles away from our work here.
 Love doesn't go with medicine, I fear.
JOHN: Love's not the word, Stephen, you cynic.
 It's worse than love, and closer to the clinic
 Than anyone could fear. It's passion, Steve,
 Passion far stronger than you would believe.
 I don't know when it started. Years ago
 Maybe, and don't they say that when it's slow
 Love is more real. I've worked with her for years,
 And, though to strangers Angela appears –
STEPHEN: Angela, you said –
JOHN: I did.
STEPHEN: Oh John, it's far
 Worse than I thought. She is my registrar.
JOHN: As I am.
STEPHEN: John, she's –
JOHN: What?
STEPHEN: Well, she's from Leeds
 For starters.
JOHN: So what?
STEPHEN: And her big heart bleeds
 For every patient who walks through that door,
 No matter what the bugger's in here for.
 She'll hug and kiss and pet and hold the hand

Of minor infections of the prostate gland.
A urine specimen that isn't right
Is sure to lose her beauty sleep that night,
And her compassion has a wider radius
Than a cystitis or a hypospadias.
The politics of medicine, that's her thing!
She's not only softhearted, she's left wing!
Mere mention of the letters NHS
Is guaranteed to bring on quite acute distress.
She weeps at articles in magazines,
On funding for dialysis machines,
And sobs, screams, yells and pulls out hair
At lack of staff for geriatric care.
There's no way I, a fat-cat rich consultant,
Can tell this girl I'm not a beast, exultant
When someone from the working class expires.
She thinks that all successful men are liars.
JOHN: Well, maybe truth, which is what I live for,
Is only to be found among the poor.
I don't want a position and a suit,
But to be a good doctor. Yes, there's beauty
And passion in being a physician,
I feel.
STEPHEN: Look. You're in love? Or on some mission
To change yourself and others?
JOHN: Both. I feel
My love is part of my desire to heal.
As for her politics, well, our profession
Has lost, I think, its most crucial possession,
The feeling for humanity. I love
Because she loves, and love for others starts
The highest form of duty in our hearts,
Which once again is love, if she loves me
(I don't know yet if she does) it will be
Because I share her passionate concern
That people should mean more than what they earn
Since –
STEPHEN: Listen, John, will you do me a favour?

THE GOOD DOCTOR

The feeling for humanity's the flavour
Of the month, this month, with her, but in a week
She'll find that Jesus got it wrong, the meek
Do not inherit any of the earth.
And people get exactly what they're worth.
It's just a phase with her. I know the type.
She gets off on the pleasures of the gripe,
But solidarity with Nicaragua
Won't match some dude's new XJ6 Jaguar.
And you're not being honest either, succour
The poor and needy if you must, then fuck her.
Don't try to combine principles with wooing.
Heal as a doctor. When in love try screwing.

JOHN: It's all OK for you, you have your life
    Perfectly organised, a perfect wife,
    Who, when you play around, swallows the story.
    And your life fits your principles, Tories
    Are always hopelessly corrupt –

STEPHEN: I beg your pardon –

JOHN: Please don't interrupt.
    You start your patients on the NHS
    And then say, 'If you would like private –'

STEPHEN: Yes.

JOHN: See? He admits it. Such hypocrisy!
    The doctor using nationalised facilities
    To train and foster surgical abilities.
    And then, when he's acquired what it takes
    He prostitutes his skills to Arab sheikhs.
    Your attitude to sex is just as bad,
    Like every Tory you're a closet cad.
    Family life, sacred to Margaret Thatcher,
    Adding on cubits to her moral stature?
    I'll tell you what she means by family life –
    Do what you like, but don't divorce your wife.
    Family life? Do me a favour, please.
    Try that on Parkinson and Sarah Keays.

STEPHEN: What is all this in aid of, John?

JOHN: I want
　　Your help.
STEPHEN: Well, you put all your charm up front,
　　Don't you? You have a funny style of charm.
　　'Can you assist me while I break your arm?'
　　A curious way of asking. D'you impress
　　Your girls this way? You want help do you?
JOHN: Yes.
STEPHEN: Well, why start up political debate
　　When what you want advice on is a date?
　　In spite of what you may read in Kate Millet,
　　Add politics to sex and you will kill it.
　　The General Synod's views about gay vicars
　　Will not get you into our Angie's knickers.
JOHN: Look, I acknowledge what is wrong with me
　　Whatever people say – I disagree.
　　I didn't study medicine at university,
　　But got my first-class honours in perversity.
　　I even find a lot to criticise
　　In things I say when I soliloquise.
　　If Angela was here I'd say, I bet,
　　'In my view Kinnock is a hopeless wet.
　　And any person who is socialist
　　Will not appear on my kosher list.'
　　That's how I am. And if I twist your arm
　　It is because you are the one with charm.
　　Perhaps if I get you to plead my case,
　　I'll see my future written in her face.
STEPHEN: Well, isn't this how Africa was won?
　　Ask someone you despise to get things done.
　　The man who's thought to be completely naff here
　　Is thought OK at dealing with the kaffir.
　　Be warned! I may not be in love like you.
　　I may be Tory – I have feelings too.
JOHN: I thought about that.
STEPHEN: Angela is not –
JOHN: Your type. Precisely. What she hasn't got

Is what you want most. Angela is clumsy,
Strict, fierce, girlish . . .
STEPHEN: And I like them Mumsy.
What do I have to say, John?
JOHN: Just convince
Her of my worth. From frog to prince,
Is the short journey that I plan to make
Through your sweet talking, Stephen, if you take
Ten days and twenty lunches to persuade
Her, I don't care. I want to get it made.
That's all. And need some bastard with good looks
To talk myself in Angela's good books.

Pause. STEPHEN *looks deeply serious. Then –*

STEPHEN: I'll do it.
JOHN: Honestly?
STEPHEN: Of course I will.
Like every roué who's over the hill,
Seduction in the abstract is my sole
Delight these days. *How to Get Hole*
By Steve Maclune MD. Learn from its pages
How to get laid in seven easy stages.
As for the Real Thing, I've had sufficiency.
Others can get Acquired Immune Deficiency . . .

ANGELA: I never know how serious you are.
STEPHEN: I'm getting serious.
ANGELA: Me too. What's far –
STEPHEN: More crucial is that I'm married. Yes.
I won't deny it and I must confess
That my wife understands me very well.
Exclusive marriages are made in hell.
We both of us agree that love is blind,
And, bearing that important fact in mind,
When she shows extra marital affection,
I'm pointing in the opposite direction.
I think the fact that Ellen has affairs

Shows in a curious way she really cares.
When she says, 'You're the best of all in bed,'
I know something important's being said,
Since she has had so many different men,
She knows whereof she speaks. Though, now and then
I feel a twinge of something like regret,
I think it is the best arrangement yet
For civilised and caring, modern blokes,
Who would not stoop to furtive, shameful pokes
At girls they would not dream of calling lovers.
The guilt! The pain! What if the Wife discovers?
No, I am open with her, and we have no shame,
No guilt, no lying and no endless blame.
She has affairs with Scandinavian men,
Mainly from Gothenburg, though now and then,
She gets her rocks off with a Greek or Turk,
She likes the northern punters. They're hard work,
But, when you get them going, she maintains,
They shag like rodents going into drains.
The other reason she prefers it Norse
Is – she can't speak the language, though of course
She knows a few of the more basic words.
ANGELA: Half of me says: What he says is absurd.
    The other half says –
STEPHEN: Do what you really feel,
    For politics and Reason cannot heal
    The hurt that I can see in you, my dear.
ANGELA: I always thought one should be very clear
    And rational and now –
STEPHEN: What?
ANGELA: Now I feel.
    And feeling is the only thing that's real.
    Feel this floor, see that light, feel this white blouse.
    Oh what is it, d'you think, that so can rouse
    A sleeping spirit? Here, feel my hand.
STEPHEN: Your pulse feels normal.
ANGELA: Now, please understand.

This lady won't be pleased if you have mocked her.
Treat me as Angela, not as a doctor!
STEPHEN: You are a doctor, aren't you?
ANGELA: Stephen, please
Don't wind me up. Don't play with me. Don't tease.
Something is happening like spring or rain –
STEPHEN: (Oh Jesus, here she goes a-fucking-gain!)
ANGELA: Something is shining and the stars above –
STEPHEN: (I want a screw and she talks about love!)
ANGELA: Shine. Something is happening to my heart. Land –
STEPHEN: (All randy women sound like Barbara Cartland!)
ANGELA: Is more land. And sea, sea. Fire, fire –
STEPHEN: (Call the ambulance. Why is it that desire –)
ANGELA: I can see every grain of sand upon the beach. Hey –
STEPHEN: (Prompts boys to vulgarity and girls to cliche?)
ANGELA: The elements of life, for once shine clear!
STEPHEN: (I feel a sudden urge to disappear.)
ANGELA: I'm in love, Stephen!
STEPHEN: (Jesus!)
ANGELA: Oh, your face!
There's something magical about this place!
Don't laugh!
STEPHEN: I wouldn't dream of it. I take
Love very seriously. Make a mistake
And suddenly you're ruining your life!
I made this observation to my wife,
When she became tied up with one named Sven,
Not the most sensitive of Swedish men.
I reasoned with her, told her to keep calm, though
She did spend a weekend with him in Malmö.
It turned out he was having an affair
With somebody called Olaf, an au pair
Hired by the relatives of friends of ours.
Love is a dangerous thing. Its hidden powers
Make fools of all of us. It's very quick!
I thought you thought I was a right-wing prick.
ANGELA: Love is not rational. It doesn't come

To order. If you hear a different drum
You must march to its rhythm!
STEPHEN: What a bore, oh –
ANGELA: Who was it said that?
STEPHEN: I think it was Thoreau.
    Look, Angela, I can't think how we've said
    These things to one another, how they've led
    Us off from politics and into sex.
    It's all going too fast for me. What's next?
    Do I divorce my wife, become a Trot
    And throw away most everything I've got?
    Don't move too quickly, Angela. I'm me.
    Staid, cynical and tired. Forty-three.
ANGELA: Stephen, I'm making no demands on you.
    I really don't know what I'm going to do.
    I might sprout wings and head off for the ceiling,
    I'm talking, Stephen darling, about feeling.
STEPHEN: And magic, don't tell me, astrology.
    I'm sorry but my field is urology!
ANGELA: Everything's changed. That curtain over there,
    The white paint on the wall, the door, the chair,
    The distant hum of business in the wards,
    White-coated figures, who come on towards
    You while the lifts wink and descend,
    On down the passageways that never end.
    Nurses as trim as little ships sail out,
    All starch and purpose. Cleaners glide about
    In green drone's costumes through the corridors,
    Looping their mops on endlessly clean floors,
    While, in the concourse, all the visitors
    Stand like bit players, waiting for applause
    That never comes. Their eyes cannot meet yours.
    And in their hands are chocolates and flowers,
    A doll, a Teddy Bear, books for the hours
    Of waiting. Oh such weak gifts to appease
    The years of suffering, death and disease!
    And out beyond the hospital, the streets,

Black with November rain, houses repeating
Gables to the sullen, bleak, skyline –
STEPHEN: What paper do you work for? What's your byline?
ANGELA: Stephen, you silly man!
STEPHEN: I'm sorry, dear . . .
ANGELA: I see it, can't you understand? I see it clear.
Love, is the miracle of certainty.
When I walked in just now I couldn't see.
Now something's made me see and understand.
STEPHEN: Most likely your pituitary gland.
ANGELA: Don't tease me, Stephen, life is all before us!
STEPHEN: Women on heat don't see us, they ignore us.
ANGELA: Stephen, time has us all within its tow.
We roll and swim in on the tide, go slow
And easy, and we think the pace is ours.
It isn't. We are victims of the hours.
Life is a prison, swept clean by a clock's
Hands. Circle on circle. Ticks and ticks and tocks
And tocks, gone into nothing every minute.
That circle is our cage, and we are in it.

She touches him on the arm.

This is our only time. We are its measure.
Look to your left, behind you, there's pleasure
Slipping away. We're on a moving train,
Watching our lives from windows. Once in Spain,
We rode from Barcelona, all one night,
Southwards to somewhere, I forget where quite.
All I remember is the towns that came
Up out of darkness, and were gone once more.
We stood like sentries in the corridor,
Watching the streets, the lights, the brilliant bars,
All empty so it seemed, the shrouded cars,
Asleep in suburbs. Families flashed past
At supper. Housemaids pulled the blinds up, faster
And faster on we rolled, and, as I stared
Out at these lives, so briefly being shared
With us, I started to feel –

STEPHEN: What?

ANGELA: Well, scared.

STEPHEN: And what was there of which to be afeared?

ANGELA: Scenes, faces, gestures came and disappeared
    So quickly! Here was a sodium glow
    Above a motorway. Then, lights would go
    Suddenly neon, in a fairground park.
    But, in the end, always, there was the dark.
    The dark went on for ever, so it seemed,
    Those human touches, something we had dreamed
    Or painted on the violet night
    To charm away impermanence, our sight
    Betrayed by what we hoped that we would feel.
    Nothing was permanent, and nothing real,
    Except that darkness that went on and on
    To some plain where no light had ever shone.
    And then we stopped somewhere, in some small town,
    High on a bridge, and, as we all looked down
    Into a bedroom window's lighted square,
    We saw a young man and a woman there,
    Poor people, from their clothes, not prosperous,
    But looking at the darkness, just like us,
    Lovers perhaps, although they stood apart,
    Looking towards the train. And then my heart
    Said: You can keep your mountain greenery.
    Humans are my idea of brilliant scenery.
    People. The way they walk or talk or eat.
    People. Their noses, ears and lips and feet.
    People. Their passions and their petty lies.
    People. Their necks, their hair, their chins, their eyes.
    And, as I watched them, all those vanished scenes
    Were gathered up together, and it seemed
    As if our journey's past and future, places
    Seen and unseen, were waiting in their faces.
    And though things seemed to pass, in fact they stayed.
    I saw it and I could not be afraid.
    And love's like that, whether for wife or brother,
    Mother or husband. It's seeing the other.

I'm sorry, Stephen. That is what I feel.
Sorry it's sudden. But it can be –
STEPHEN: Real
Love is hard to find.
ANGELA: All the more reason
To grasp it if you think it is in season.
STEPHEN: You're hard to argue with.
ANGELA: I start abrasive,
But when got going can be quite persuasive.
STEPHEN: I'm not at all good, honest, strong or true.
ANGELA: You could be, Stephen.
STEPHEN: So it seems to you.
How do you know I want to be those things?
Beggars don't always fancy being kings.
ANGELA: I sense –
STEPHEN: What?
ANGELA: You've ambitions to be good.
STEPHEN: (I don't think Angela has understood
Quite where it is that my ambitions lie.
I think she'll go. The trouble is that I
Don't want to get involved in something big,
Where I end up being called Male Chauvinist Pig.
Too old for all of that. What is the use
Of any more soured, feminist abuse?)
I'm not entirely sure I've got enough
Of what you want. This sounds quite serious stuff.
ANGELA: Stephen, don't be so terrified of it.
I won't take much from you. Well, just a bit . . .
Fragment by fragment, piece by frightened piece,
And then, if you find you want to release
A little more, I'll say, Thank you, kind sir.
Whatever it is you would most prefer.
STEPHEN: It sounds OK to me.
ANGELA: Of course it is.
STEPHEN: Jesus, when she gets going, she's the biz!

ANGELA *is, indeed, very very close to him.*

ANGELA: Stephen –
STEPHEN: I know –
ANGELA: I feel –
STEPHEN: Indeed –
ANGELA: I do . . .
STEPHEN: (If this is talking what's she like to screw?)
ANGELA: Stephen –
STEPHEN: Yes, dear?
ANGELA: I feel –
STEPHEN: I know.
ANGELA: It's this –
STEPHEN: (Now time it carefully. Here goes. First kiss.)
> *He makes a pass at her, but she moves away. It's not so obvious as to be noticed, though. An experienced campaigner, he is quite unfazed.*
ANGELA: You see –
STEPHEN: Of course –
ANGELA: I feel . . .
STEPHEN: Indeed!
ANGELA: I ache!
STEPHEN: (I think she might be difficult to make.)
ANGELA: I want –
STEPHEN: I know!
ANGELA: I think –
STEPHEN: Oh yes!
ANGELA: I'm freezing!
STEPHEN: (Is this for real? Or is she just cock teasing?)
ANGELA: I hope –
STEPHEN: I know.
ANGELA: Yes?
STEPHEN: Yes.
ANGELA: Oh yes. I knew it.
STEPHEN: Fuck all the hanging round. Go on. Let's do it!
> *And he moves in for the clinch. He has not mistimed it. They kiss. For quite a long time. Very passionate. No words now.* STEPHEN *moves her towards the desk and the kiss continues there. Becoming steamier by the minute. At its high point,* JOHN, *looking very shaken, comes in through the door.*

JOHN: There's only one nurse left –

He stops. Sees them. Horror.
  What are you doing?
  It's gone beyond what you'd describe as queuing
  Out there. Jesus! What are we coming to?
  I wouldn't dare describe it as a queue,
  This . . . thing that stretches round the entrance hall.
  They're on the stairs, outside, they're wall to wall.
  Some have newspapers that they try to read,
  Others, alone with misery and need,
  Just sit and wait and stare and stare and stare.
  Surely, their faces say, there's someone there!
  This is like Bangladesh, Delhi, Calcutta!
  I think that I heard one old lady mutter
  She'd been waiting two weeks to see someone.
STEPHEN: Are there no nurses out there?
JOHN: Just the one.
  In the whole hospital, all I could see
  Was one sweet pupil nurse, who smiled at me,
  'I don't know where the others are, you see!'
  She said, and then, still trying this sad smile
  She told a patient, 'We don't have your file,
  But we are looking,' and the victim, grinning,
  Starts his life story. From the beginning.
  Address, name, rank and serial number,
  All meaningless, just one more piece of lumber
  To drift into th'administrative slough.
  The thing we feared would happen's happening now!
ANGELA: That's why these files are scattered on the floor!
JOHN: I can't think why it hasn't come before,
  Make no mistake about it. I would guess
  It's Armageddon for the NHS.
STEPHEN: It's probably some unplanned, wildcat, loopy
  Idea dreamed up by our friends from NUPE.
JOHN: I think it's just the entire system's choked.
  'Which doctor are you with? Have you booked

An appointment?' And the groans and curses
Are largely targeted at absent nurses.
Choose any explanation that you like.
There's just a shortage. They have gone on strike.
Someone has called a National Day of Action,
And not told us. Or the Red Army Faction
Have bribed as many nurses as they can
To stay off work. Maybe a ten-ton van
Of TNT was, by a kamikaze gnome,
Driven through Reception in the Nurses' Home.
I don't know why. But while you two have fun,
It's finished. Entropy has finally won.
I don't know who they are or what they've got.
They could be hernias or piles, foot rot,
Or large consignments of severe anaemia.
Strokes, hepatitis, Crohn's disease, leukaemia,
Heart transplants, TB, and severe nephritis,
Scabies and epilepsy and arthritis,
Queuing for hours. And when they reach the wards,
From what I saw – they'd do as well at Lourdes.
Because the doctors haven't got a clue
Who any of them are or what to do
With Mr So and So's impressive file
That just happens to be top of the pile,
When they're in front of them. 'My name is Sidney.'
'Right. You're the one with problems of the kidney!'
'Don't think so, Doctor. Last time that I come,
You said I had a crisis up my bum.
My kidneys aren't a problem. You checked 'em.
But there is something frightful up my rectum.'
Not that I can see many doctors left,
Apart from us. The whole place is bereft.

STEPHEN: **Look, may I ask you what it is you're saying?**
We have one nurse on duty?

JOHN: They are baying
For our blood out there, Stephen.

STEPHEN: Sit down, John.
Doctors and nurses . . . they can't all have gone!

JOHN: Why must they always be there? Why assume
    That they're like English strawberries in June.
    Nurses are a bit like books, have their shelf life.
    One went to be a typist, one a wife.
    One simply disappeared, faded away,
    Thinned out to nothing on a nurse's pay.
    One took herself and all her paraphernalia
    Off to a new life in Australia!
    And as for doctors, you would understand
    Them heading off for money in the hand,
    Rather than hanging round the NHS.
    The door's there, you'll be joining them, I guess.
STEPHEN: Look –
JOHN: Why or how a ministering angel goes,
    Or when a doctor's had enough, who knows?
    But why or how, the crisis has begun.
    In this part of the hospital, we're down to one.

He looks out of the door.

    Correction. Things are far worse than I feared.
    The one who was there, seems t'have disappeared,
    And as for doctors, well as I said, who
    Knows where they're coming from or going to.
    Off to their private clinics, aren't they, Steve?
STEPHEN: I'm staying here.
JOHN: I wonder why.
STEPHEN: Believe
    Me, John. I really tried on your behalf.
    But she was just all over me. Don't laugh!
JOHN: You've told her all about your little deals?
STEPHEN: It's difficult, John, Angie . . . well . . . she feels –
JOHN: I'll tell her.
STEPHEN: Do. She won't believe you, son.
    She says she thinks she loves me.
JOHN: WHAT?
STEPHEN: No fun
    For me I do assure you. It'll be
    OK, I promise you. She's not for me.

JOHN: Oh no?

STEPHEN: There is a crisis on, dear boy,
  No matter how much Stephen may annoy
  You, I'm afraid the two of us must start
  On something more than matters of the heart.

Their conversation becomes less private.

A Field Guide to Disposable Drink Containers

Monaghan Day

JOHN McGAHERN

On the last Monaghan Day that McQuaid came to the house Moran was on edge as he waited for him as he had been on edge every Monaghan Day, the only day in the year that McQuaid came to Great Meadow. Since morning he had been in and out of the kitchen where Maggie and Mona were cleaning and tidying and preparing for the big meal. Though Maggie was eighteen, tall and attractive, she was still as much in awe of Moran as when she had been a child. Mona, two years younger, was the more likely to clash with him, but this day she agreed to be ruled by Maggie's acquiescence. Sheila, a year younger still, was too self-centred and bright to ever challenge authority on poor ground and she pretended to be sick in order to escape the tension of the day. Alone, the two girls were playful as they went about their tasks, mischievous at times, even carefully boisterous; but as soon as their father came in they would sink into a beseeching drabness, change into sackcloth, cower as close to being invisible as they could.

'How do the lamb chops look?' he demanded again. 'Are these the best lamb chops you could get? Haven't I told you time in and time out never – never – to get lamb chops anywhere but from Kavanagh's. Has everything to be drummed in a hundred times? God, why is nothing ever made clear in this house? Everything has to be dragged out of everybody.'

'Kavanagh said the steak wasn't great but that the lamb was good,' Maggie added, but Moran was already on his way out again, muttering that not even simple things were made clear in this house and if simple things couldn't be made clear how was a person ever to get from one day to the next in this world.

The two girls were quiet for a long time after the door closed; then suddenly, unaccountably, they started to push one another, boisterously mimicking Moran, falling into chairs, laughing. 'God, oh God, what did I do to deserve such a crowd? Gawd, oh Gawd, not even the simple things are made clear.'

A loud imperious knocking came on the tongued boards of the ceiling in the middle of the rowdy relief. They stopped to listen and as they did the knocking stopped.

'She's no more sick than my big toe. Whenever there's a whiff of trouble she takes to her bed with the asthma. She has books and sweets hidden up there,' Mona said. They waited in silence until the knocking resumed, insistent and angry.

'Boohoo!' they responded. 'Boohoo! Boohoo! Boohoo!' The knocking made the boards of the ceiling tremble. She was using a boot or shoe. 'Boohoo!' they echoed. 'Boohoo! Boohoo . . . !'

The stairs creaked. In a moment Sheila stood angrily framed in the doorway. 'I've been knocking for ages and all ye do is laugh up at me.'

'We never heard. We'd laugh up at nobody.'

'Ye heard only too well. I'm going to tell Daddy on the pair of ye.'

'Boohoo!' they repeated.

'You think I'm joking. You'll pay for this before it's over.'

'What do you want?'

'I'm sick and you won't even bring up a drink.'

They gave her a jug of barley water and a clean glass.

'You know what day it is and McQuaid is coming from the mart. He's in and out like a devil. You can't expect us to dance attendance up the stairs as well. If he comes in and sees you like that in the door he'll have something to say,' Maggie said, but Sheila slipped back upstairs before she finished.

They draped the starched white table-cloth over the big deal table. The room was wonderfully warm, the hotplate of the stove glowing a faint orange. They began to set the table, growing relaxed and easy, enjoying the formality of the room, when Moran came in again from the fields.

This time he stood in the centre of the room, plainly unsure as to what had brought him in, his eye searching around for something to fasten on like someone in midspeech forgetting what they had to say. 'Is everything all right?'

'Everything is all right, Daddy.'

'Be sure the chops are well done,' he said, and went out again. No sooner had the door closed than Mona, released from the tension of his presence, let slip a plate from her hands. They stood watching dumbly in horrible fascination after it shattered. Quickly they swept up the pieces and hid them away, wondering how they would replace the plate without being found out.

'Don't worry,' Maggie comforted Mona who was still pale with shock. 'We'll find some way round it.' They were too sick at heart to mimic or mock this mood away. Anything broken had to be hidden until it could be replaced or forgotten.

Outside it was cold but there was no rain. It was always cold on Monaghan Day, the traditional day poor farmers sold their winter stock and the rich farmers bought them for fattening. Moran was neither rich nor poor but his hatred and fear of poverty was as fierce as his fear of illness which meant that he would never be poor but that he and all around him would live as if they were paupers. Moran had no work in the fields but still he stayed outside in the cold, looking at hedges, examining walls, counting cattle. He was too excited to be able to stay indoors. As the light began to fail he retreated into the shelter of the fir plantation to watch the road for McQuaid's car. If McQuaid had a big order to fill he mightn't come till after dark.

The light was almost gone when the white Mercedes came slowly along the road and turned into the open gate under the yew tree. Moran did not move even after the car stopped. In fact, he instinctively stepped backwards into the plantation as the car door was thrown open. Without moving he watched McQuaid struggle from the car and then stand leaning on the open door as if waiting for someone to appear. He could have called out from where he stood but he did not. McQuaid slammed the car door and walked towards the house. Not until McQuaid was several minutes within the house did Moran leave the plantation. He came slowly and deliberately across the fields to the back door. Though he had lived for weeks for this hour he now felt a wild surge of resentment towards McQuaid as he came into his own house.

McQuaid was seated in the armchair by the fire. His powerful trunk and huge belly filled the chair and the yellow cattleman's boots were laced halfway up the stout legs. He did not rise from the chair or acknowledge Moran's entrance in any way except to direct the flirting banter he was having with the girls to Moran. 'These girls are blooming. You better have your orchards well fenced or you'll be out of apples by October.'

The words were said with such good humour and aggressive sureness that it would have been impossible to take offence. Moran hardly heard; all resentment left him as quickly as it had come: McQuaid was here and it was Monaghan Day.

'Michael.' McQuaid reached out of the chair and took Moran's hand in a firm grip.

'Jimmy.' Moran responded with the same simplicity. 'Have you been here long?'

'Not long. I had a fine talk with these girls. They are great girls.'

Moran walked across to the curtained press where he kept medicines and took out a glass and a full bottle of Redbreast. He poured out a large measure of the whisky and brought it to McQuaid. Maggie placed a jug of spring water on the table. 'Say when.' Moran poured the water into the glass. McQuaid held out the glass until it was three-quarters full. 'You'll need it after the mart,' Moran said.

'I don't need it but I'll do much better than that. I'll enjoy it. Good luck, everybody.'

'How did it go?' Moran asked with a heartiness that didn't suit him.

'The same as every other Monaghan Day,' McQuaid said.

'Was it good or bad?' Moran continued.

'It was neither good nor bad. It was money. All the farmers think their cattle are special but all I ever see is money. If a beast is around or below a certain sum of money I buy. If it goes over that I'm out.'

'I've often watched you in the past and wondered how you know exactly the right time to enter the bidding, the right time to leave,' Moran praised. His fascination with McQuaid's mastery of his own world was boyish. He had never been able to deal with the outside. All his dealings had been with himself and that larger self of family which had been thrown together by marriage or accident: he had never been able to go out from his shell of self.

'I don't know how I know that,' McQuaid said. 'All I know is that it cost me a lot of money to learn.'

The girls had the freshly-cut bread, butter and milk on the table. The lamb chops sizzled as they were dropped into the big pan. The sausages, black pudding, bacon, halves of tomatoes were added soon after to the sides of the pan. The eggs were fried in a smaller pan. Mona scalded the large teapot and set it to brew. The two girls were silent as they cooked and when they had to speak to one another spoke in quick, urgent whispers.

'This looks like a meal fit for a king. It makes me want to roll up my sleeves,' McQuaid said in praise and plain enjoyment at the prospect of it as the plates were put on the table. He finished his glass of whisky with a flourish before rising from the chair.

The two men ate in silence, with relish, waited on by the two girls. As soon as McQuaid pushed his empty plate contentedly aside he said, 'These are great girls but where are the missing soldiers?'

'Sheila is upstairs with a cold.' Maggie pointed to the ceiling. 'And Michael is gone to our aunt in the mountains for a week.'

'Where's Luke, then?'

The girls looked from McQuaid to Moran and back to McQuaid again but they did not speak.

'We don't know where he is,' Moran said reluctantly. He particularly disliked parting with information about the house. 'You couldn't open your mouth in this house before he left but he'd be down your throat.'

'If I know you I'd warrant he was given his money's worth.' McQuaid laughed gently and when Moran didn't answer he added, 'The young will have their way, Michael. Anyhow, I always liked Luke. He is very straight and manly.'

'I respect all my children equally,' Moran said. 'How are your lads?'

'You know they're all married now. I don't see much of them unless they want something and they don't see much of me. They're good lads, though. They work long hours.'

'And the good lady?'

'Oh, the old dozy's all right. She needs plenty of shouting at or she'd go to sleep on her feet.'

They had married young and their three sons married young as well. They lived alone now in the big cattledealer's house with the white railing in the middle of fields. He was seldom in the house except to eat or sleep, and when he was all he ever did was yell. 'Get the tea. Polish the boots. Kick out that bloody cat. Get me a stud. Where's the fucking collar?'

'In a minute, Jimmy. Coming. On the way. It's here in my very hand,' his wife would race and flurry and call.

Then he would be gone for days. She would spoil her cats, read library books and tend her garden and the riotous rockery of flowers along the south wall of the house that he encouraged the cattle to eat. After days of peace the door would crash open. 'There's six men here with lorries. Put on the kettle. Set the table. Get hopping. Put wheels under yourself. We're fucking starving!' There was never a hint of a blow. So persistent was the language that it had become no more remarkable than just another wayward manner of speaking, and their sons paid so little attention to it that it might well have been one of the many private languages of love.

The dishes had been washed and put away. Mona went to join Sheila upstairs. Maggie was going visiting. Another night Moran would have questioned her, but not tonight.

Years ago Moran loaned McQuaid money when he had started in the cattle business but now McQuaid was the richer and more powerful man and they saw little of one another. They came together once a year to slip back into what McQuaid said were the days of their glory. Moran was too complicated to let anybody know what he thought of anything. Moran had commanded a column in the war. McQuaid had been his lieutenant. From year to year they used the

155

same handrails to go down into the past: lifting the cartwheel at the crossroads, the drilling sessions by the river, the first ambush, marching at night between the safe houses, the different characters in the houses, the food, the girls . . . The interrogation of William Taylor the spy and his execution by the light of a paraffin lantern among his own cattle in the byre. The Tans had swarmed over the countryside looking for them after the execution. They had lived for a while in holes cut in the turfbanks. The place was watched night and day. Once, the British soldiers came on Mary Duignan when she was bringing them tea and sandwiches. The Duignans were so naturally pale-faced that Mary showed no sign that anything was other than normal, and she continued to bring tea and sandwiches to men working on a further turfbank. Seeing the British soldiers, the startled men sat and ate though they had just risen from a complete meal.

'Mary was a topper,' McQuaid said with emotion. 'Only for Mary that day our goose was cooked. She was a bloody genius to think of giving the food to the men on the bank. She's married to a carpenter in Dublin now. She has several children.'

Moran poured more whisky into the empty glass.

'Are you sure you won't chance a drop?' McQuaid raised his glass. 'It's no fun drinking on your own.'

'I couldn't handle it,' Moran said. 'You know that. I had to give it up. Now I couldn't look at it.'

'I shouldn't have asked you then.'

'I don't mind. I don't mind at all.'

The reminiscing continued – the death of friends, one man marching alone throughout the night, the terrible hard labour it was for some men to die, night marches from one safe house to another, the rain, the wet, the damp, the cold of waiting for an ambush in one place for hours.

'We had them on the run by then. They were afraid to venture out except in convoys.'

'People who would have spat in our faces three years before were now clapping our backs. They were falling over one another to get on the winning side.'

'Many of them who had pensions and medals and jobs later couldn't tell one end of a gun from the other. Many of the men who had actually fought got nothing. An early grave or the immigrant ship. Sometimes I get sick when I see what I fought for,' Moran said.

'It makes no sense your not taking the IRA pension. You earned it. You could still have it in the morning,' McQuaid said.

'I'd throw it in their teeth.' Moran clenched and unclenched his hands as he spoke.

'I never question the colour of any man's money. If I'm offered it I take it.' But Moran was too consumed to respond and McQuaid went on. 'Then it began to get easier. We hadn't to hide any longer. One hot day I remember leaving guns and clothes along the river bank and swimming without a stitch on. Another Sunday we went trolling, dragging an otter behind the boat. Then they tried to bring in the General.'

'He wasn't a general. He was a trumped-up colonel.'

'Whatever he was we settled his hash,' McQuaid gloated. 'You had a great head on you the way you thought the plan through from beginning to end. You've been wasted ever since.'

'Without you it would never have worked. You were as cool as if you were out for a stroll,' Moran said.

'You could plan. You worked it out from beginning to end. None of the rest of us had that kind of head.'

'We had spies. We had men in the town for weeks. They were bringing the big fellow in on the three o'clock train. They were going to put on the big show. They had a band and a guard of honour outside the station, their backs to a row of railwaymen's cottages. They never checked the cottages.'

'They wouldn't have found us, anyhow.'

'Nibs McGovern met that train every day with his trolley to pick up the papers and the Boland loaves that the shops got for special customers. He was such a fixture that no one noticed him any more. It fell into our hands.'

'Looking back on it the plan couldn't have been simpler but we must have rehearsed it forty times. We all slipped into town after dark. Only Tommy Flood, the solicitor's clerk, gave any trouble.'

'Then we nabbed Nibs.' McQuaid laughed. 'Just as he was getting ready to go out on the town. We were lucky there as well. Nibs didn't go to any one pub in particular. Nibs was no trouble. He could think quick enough when he had to. We gave him whisky and hadn't to tie him up till the morning and that was only for his own good.'

'Then there was the waiting,' Moran said violently.

'I'll never forget it. Dressed up in Nibs's gear,' McQuaid said. 'The clothes were fit to stand up on their own, they were that stiff with dust and grease. The waiting was terrible. It's like getting old. Nothing happens and then the whole bloody thing is on top of you before you know it. The Tommies marching to the station. The band. Sound of the train getting closer and before I knew it I was out on that street pushing the trolley. The wheels were so loose I was afraid they'd fall off. The one thing we never thought of was to check the wheels. The overcoat was buttoned over the gun and the grenade. Even in the middle of summer Nibs wore that overcoat.'

'I had the stopwatch on you from behind one of the windows. I followed every step. I was afraid you'd get to the slope too soon. I was afraid you could run into our fire if you got too far up on the slope.'

'The gates were closed. The train came puffing in. The fucking band struck up "God Save the King". There were three fir trees beside the platform. They said they never grew right because of the smoke and steam. The Sergeant Major was shouting. They were all standing to attention. The Colonel or General or whatever he was came down the platform. There was another officer with him holding a sword upright. I kept pushing the trolley, praying to Jesus the bloody wheels wouldn't come loose. No one even looked at me or the trolley. The pair came along inspecting the troops. The one holding the sword was young. The Colonel was a big stoutish man with red eyebrows. All I remember thinking as I pushed the trolley and looked at the red face and eyebrows was: My friend, you are about to take the longest journey a man ever takes in this life. He took the full blast. The other man was still holding the sword upright as he went down. I pulled the pin out of the grenade. The line of soldiers was still half-standing to attention when I went through them. I hadn't to use the revolver. As soon as I got to the other side of the bank I threw myself down and started to roll.'

'That's all I was watching for. As soon as I saw you go down I gave the order to fire,' Moran said. 'Some of them were still standing to attention as they fell. They hadn't a clue where the fire was coming from. Then a few soldiers up at the goods store fired into their own men.'

'By the time I rolled to the bottom of the slope I could see the steady fire coming from the windows. I waited to get my breath before cutting across the road. I don't think I was fired on once. The first thing I did when I got behind the houses was to get out of Nibs's clothes.'

'They were beginning to fire back from behind the station. Michael Sweeney was hit in the shoulder. I gave the order to file out. Myles Reilly and McDermott stayed at the windows. They were our two best riflemen. When we got to Donoghue's Cross the road was cut and trees knocked down. We waited for Reilly and McDermott at the cross. Then we split up, half of us for the safe houses round the lakes and the rest of us headed into the mountains. We mightn't have bothered.'

'They were afraid to put their heads out and when they did they came in a whole convoy, shooting at women and children.'

'They were never the same again,' Moran said. 'News of it spread throughout the whole country.'

'You had a great head on you, Michael.'

'Only, for you it couldn't have come to anything.'

'I remember clearer than yesterday his eyebrows. Not often you see an Englishman with red eyebrows. I had so much time to look at him I can hardly believe it still, pushing the trolley, standing up in Nibs's clothes. I had already loosened the overcoat and was thinking as I looked at him: This very minute you are going on the longest journey a man ever takes and you haven't a frigging clue. Then I fired.'

'I was watching you with the stopwatch.'

'We didn't have to split up that day. They were afraid of their shite to come out of the towns. The country was ours again. Next we had the Treaty. Then we fought one another.'

'Look where it brought us. Look at the country now. Run by a crowd of small-minded gangsters out for their own good. It was better if it never had happened.'

'I couldn't agree with that,' McQuaid said. 'The country is ours now, anyhow. Maybe the next crowd will be better than this mixture of druids and crooks that we're stuck with.'

'Leave the priests out of it,' Moran said sharply.

'I'll leave nobody out of it. They all got on our backs.'

Moran did not answer. An angry brooding silence filled the room. McQuaid felt for the authority he had slowly made his own over the years, an authority that had outgrown Moran's. He would not move. Moran rose and went outside. McQuaid did not respond to him in any way when he came in again.

When Maggie returned she found them locked in the strained silence. Beforehand she had combed her hair by the light of the flashlamp, smoothed and rearranged her clothes, but even if she hadn't Moran would not have noticed this evening. At once, in the silence, she began to make tea and sandwiches. Mona came down and after whispering with Maggie disappeared again upstairs with a small jug of milk and some sandwiches. At last, out of the silence, Moran noticed McQuaid's glass was empty and attempted to pour him more whisky.

'Cap it,' McQuaid said and covered his glass with his hand.

'There were years when you were able for most of the bottle.'

'Those years are gone. We'll have the tea Maggie is making.'

Reluctantly Moran screwed the cap back on the bottle and returned it behind the curtains of the medicine press. The tone in which McQuaid had said, '*Cap it*,' smarted like a cut.

'Do you remember Eddie McIniff in Maguire's garden on night watch?' McQuaid asked. 'He could see all the roads from Maguire's garden. We were watching in case the Tans would try to infiltrate the lakes at night. Eddie used to shoot a lot of duck and could stand like a stone. One of the Maguire girls — Ellie or Molly, I think it was Molly, they were all fine-looking, tall women — came out to do her morning business and hunkered down under an apple tree a few feet away from Eddie. All Eddie did was to wait a bit and then leave over without a sound and lay the gun barrel across her back cheeks. I'd love to have seen her face when she jumped.' McQuaid laughed out loud. 'There must be nothing colder on a bare arse than a gun barrel that was out all night.'

Moran did not laugh. He looked helpless with the weight of his own disapproval. His two thumbs rotated about one another as they always did when he was agitated and looking for a way to strike.

'McIniff was blackguard enough to do that, but you'd think that at least he'd be ashamed to tell it.'

'What was it but fun?' McQuaid brushed the criticism aside. 'Didn't you have something to do with one of those Maguire girls? The rest of us had to scrape and scrounge for the girls, Michael, but whatever you had they always fell into your hands like ripe plums.'

'That was all talk,' Moran said, angry as ever at any baring of the inviolate secrecy he instinctively kept around himself.

'Your father was a hard man for the women in his day,' McQuaid said, addressing the two girls.

'I think Mr McQuaid does himself less than credit with that talk,' Moran said with quiet dignity.

'There's even rumours that you're courting again. Are you thinking of taking the plunge, Michael?'

Moran held a pointed silence. The girls brought tea and sandwiches.

'Ah, these girls will make some man happy,' McQuaid said. 'But you're a brave man, Michael. If anything were to happen to my old dozy, I'm afraid I'd live out my days in peace.'

The girls were able to laugh openly at last without any risk. The idea of the fat old cattledealer emerging as a romantic possibility was so preposterous that even Moran smiled.

'I'd take that pension, Michael. You earned it. Take what they'll give you. Never question the colour of money.' The talk turned to easier waters as they drank tea.

'I've got on without it long enough. Why should I take it from them now?' It was plain from the blustering way he spoke that he wasn't so sure.

'It never did me no harm. There were times when I was starting in at the cattle that it stood between me and the road. It doesn't make much difference now but a hell of a sight of worse things come through the letterbox at the end of every month.'

'I was thinking of taking it,' Moran admitted.

'Wouldn't it buy something for the girls here or put someone through school, even if you didn't want to take it for yourself? You should have taken it years ago. In this world you don't exist without money. And there might never be another world.' McQuaid could not resist this hit at Moran's religiosity.

'Man proposes . . . ' Moran said darkly.

'And God stays out of it.' McQuaid twisted round the old saw.

The girls had washed and put away the cups and plates, covered the few squares of sandwiches that remained with a damp cloth. 'Mr McQuaid's room is ready,' Maggie said as they prepared to take their leave for the night. 'The bed is aired.'

'Oh, I forgot,' McQuaid said hastily. 'I have to be hitting the road any minute now. I should have told you earlier but it must have slipped the old mind.'

Moran did not protest. Covertly, leaning far back in his chair, he watched McQuaid from under hooded eyelids: in all the years they had been coming together on Monaghan Day, McQuaid had always spent the night in the house.

'I told my old lady I'd be home,' McQuaid lied as he rose. 'Otherwise she'd have gone over to one of the boys. She gets afraid on her own in the house at night.'

Having waited long enough to see if they were needed, the two girls went up to Moran and kissed him on the lips as they did every night.

'Good night, Mr McQuaid.' They offered their hand.

'That was a great meal. Ye are a great pair of girls. If you ever get up our way, call in to see my old lassie.' He took and held their hands.

'Good night, Mr McQuaid,' they repeated awkwardly before leaving the two men alone.

McQuaid sat down but almost immediately rose again. As on all the other Monaghan Days stretching far back he had come intending to stay the night. Tonight a growing irritation at Moran's compulsion to dominate, to have everything on his own terms or not at all, had hardened into a sudden decision to overturn the years and quit the house at once. As soon as Moran saw McQuaid on his feet again he knew the evening, all the evenings, were about to be broken up, and he withdrew back into himself. He would neither plead with him to stay nor help him with his leaving.

As soon as McQuaid met Moran's domination of the evening with this sudden violence he was anxious to be conciliatory. 'Well, thanks for the meal and evening, Michael. It was a great evening.'

For a time it seemed that Moran might choose to remain seated and force McQuaid to make his own way out of the house. When he did rise in the chair it was slowly and grudgingly, and he followed McQuaid out into the stone hallway as if he were finding it difficult to walk or move. He held his hand on the door's edge in the darkness of the hallway.

'Good luck, Michael,' the old cattledealer said a last time, but Moran made no answer in the darkness.

A brief moon between clouds outside sharpened the lines of boxwood that led to the wooden gate. McQuaid walked heavily and firmly to the gate. He did not bother to shut it, letting it swing open behind him. After opening the door of the Mercedes he leaned on its edge to clear his throat and spit on the yellow path.

'Some people just cannot bear to come in second,' he said loudly enough to be heard before getting into the car, reversing it round and driving away. Moran stood holding the edge of the door until the headlights disappeared, and he closed the door without shutting the iron gate at the road or the small wooden gate leaning against the boxwood.

In a cold fury he stood and sat about for a long time within, twice changing from chair to chair. After years he had lost his oldest and best friend, but in a way he had always despised friendship: families were what mattered, more particularly that larger version of himself – *his* family; and while seated in the same scheming fury he saw each individual member gradually slipping away out of his reach. Yes, they would eventually all go. He would be alone. That he could not stand.

He saw with bitter lucidity that he would marry Rose Brady now. As with so many things, no sooner had he taken the idea to himself than he began to resent it passionately.

On a Recent Indiscretion in Upper Egypt by a Certain Fulbright Fellow

JAMES FENTON

He fell among the fellahin.
He felt a fellow feeling.
They went in an alfalfa field
Where they began unpeeling.

The muezzin he caught sight of them
From the far minaret
And what he saw made him as mad
As a holy man can get.

He foamed and fumed and frothed at them
And pelted them with quince.
That Fulbright Fellow has not faced
His fellow Fellows since.

A fast felucca ferried him
Past the Nile's fair fronded fringes
But when he reached his consulate
His mind was off its hinges.

Farewell to the falafel farm.
Farewell the *foul mesdames.*
Farewell the fez, the Fatimids,
Farouk in thy pyjamas.

'Far from these fair fringe benefits
My feeble prospects beckon
For I shall fray my future away
In frigging Llanfairfechan.'

JAMES FENTON

The fellah in this episode
Who hailed from Wadi Halfa
Has found that Fulbright Fellowship
Where it lay in the alfalfa.

And fiendishly invested it
In French securities
To furnish his fond flock with funds
For foreseeable dynasties.

And the moral of this episode
May be set forth forthrightly –
Don't go fellating fellahin:
You're a Fulbright Fellow!
It's – unsightly.

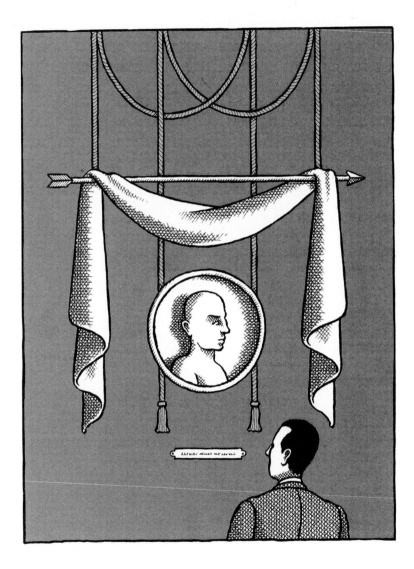

In November, 1948

PAUL BAILEY

I came home that November afternoon to find my father, in a restless fever, in the bed my mother shared with my sister. I did not sleep with him that night, or ever again.

I was eleven years old, and had been his bedfellow since the changes in first, my sister's body, and then mine had necessitated a separation of the sexes. We had only two small bedrooms in our little part of the house.

He sounded angry with the world, in his delirium. I was intrigued, rather than frightened. I wanted to make sense of what he was saying, but the words came out in sudden bursts, a few at a time, and I could not follow their course.

He shouted, often. He cursed his mother-in-law, whom he hated, whom he hated so much when he was well that he never mentioned her name. He said it now – to her face, it seemed. But she was a hundred miles away, in Hampshire, in the house he always refused to enter.

There were other names, unrecognisable to me, and – perhaps – to his wife of twenty years. They belonged, I think, to his comrades in the trenches, many long dead. He'd hinted once, on one of our Sunday walks together, that 'over there' had meant hell for him. 'I hope,' he said, 'you'll never get to fight abroad.'

More names, more ghosts. I listened to the roll-call, and was moved by a tone in his voice that was unexpectedly tender. Here was affection rising up, and the expression of it gave his features a brief serenity. I can't remember who the distant recipients of that tenderness were. How could I? It was the calm on him then that struck me.

His rage returned, and with it a name I found strange – exotic, even. It was Esther he berated, Esther he scorned, Esther he hit out at.

'Who's Esther?'

My mother answered by telling me not to ask silly questions, and to go and do my homework.

(Esther, I learnt in 1985, some months after my mother's death, was my father's first wife. She had gone to live with another man while he was in Flanders. I owe my existence to her unfaithfulness.)

*

IN NOVEMBER, 1948

The doctor, who had diagnosed my father as having a severe chill, acknowledged that pneumonia had set in. An ambulance came, and my father was taken to the local hospital, of which it was said that if you went in with a sore finger you left without a hand.

This happened during the night, while I slept alone, fitfully. In the morning, the other bed was empty. It had been made, with my mother's usual fastidiousness.

I did not need to be told what my brother told me, with much hesitation and embarrassment, on the afternoon of 28 November, when I came home from school. My sister's tears were evidence enough, but I had already gained my knowledge from the ghosts and, especially, the mysterious Esther. I had not been able to concentrate on my studies all that week because of them. They had signified something terrible, and when I learnt that it was death I was not surprised.

The children of Arthur and Esther attended their father's funeral. They had been born before the First World War, and were now middle aged. Laurence, my half-brother, had a wife with an even more exotic name than Esther. She was called Esmé. 'To think we have an Esmé in the family,' said my mother.

Molly, my half-sister, was a civil servant, and obviously brainy. I was told throughout my childhood that, if there was anyone I took after, it was Molly. She had offered to adopt me, I heard later, to relieve my parents' ever-present financial burden. The offer was declined. What a different life I might have led, in her spacious house, with her brainy husband, among her brainy friends. The Professor, as I was called, who had 'more brains than were good for him', regretted for a time that Molly hadn't whisked him away from the house near the gas works.

The following year, Laurence wrote to my mother to say that Esmé had given birth to a son, whom they had named after me. There were no further letters, and we lost touch with Molly.

The two of us were waiting in line for our Christmas meat in the crowded butcher's when my mother, whose reserve in matters of the heart was fiercely maintained, all of a sudden opened her mouth and howled. What a rare luxury grief afforded her that day: the expression – and in public, too – of her deepest, darkest feelings. The rawness of her misery stunned everyone in the shop to silence.

The howling stopped, and my mother dabbed at her eyes with a handkerchief. 'What a fool I've made of myself,' she said. 'I can't think what came over me.'

Munich

CAROL RUMENS

Utopia – nowhere
I could ever place
Until that morning.
We had left the sleeper
Blackly streaming
South like an *Anschluss*,
A riderless nightmare.
I was still wishing
Vienna, Vienna,
As her breath touched me.
She was pure city
And her brightening forth
In the moment between
Waking and blinking
The heavy gold-dust
Out of my surmise,
Was familiar as only
A constant hope is.
We called her 'München',
Tender with surprise.

A sixties child
In a fire-touched brocade,
She curtseyed across
The Marian sky.
If she had willed
Her forgetfulness,
We couldn't blame her.
We too were wide-eyed,
We too, faintly poisoned.
As the day withdrew,
She possessed us differently.

CAROL RUMENS

Her shadow found you
And the catch in her voice
Was the buried gracenote
Of the Slav.
She turned and turned
Her Russian face
And I heard her whisper
– Extinguishing, enchanting –
Of divorce and marriage
It is divorce
Cuts the deeper heartline:
There can be no future
That is not his past.

Bound to this course,
One night we sat
In futurist Odeonplatz.
Islanded, water-dazzled
Lorelei,
We softly murdered
A *song of the people.*
Our thin strophes
Were the circles where
A mail-coach butterflied
With its snow-faced driver.
As the storm encrystalled
His upturned room
And kneeling horses
To the arched, brilliant silence
Of a polar tomb,
He dreamed a letter home
And his blood-sugar, sinking
Slowly to zero,
Saw him through
To the death-drowsy, solemn,
Last 'I kiss you'.

MUNICH

Perhaps the blur, stinging
Our eyes, was him.
Beyond us too
Lay distances
Blanked by longing,
And, beyond these,
Expectantly
Fading towards us,
The radiance of footprints
We had each called 'family',
And betrayed.
And then I thought
Of a place too small
Even to spell,
A broken star
Where the map creased.
It blazed in the glare
Of an island's crime
Against her continent.
But we went on singing
Until history fell
In easy shadows
At the city's feet
And *peace in our time*,
Our breath said, peace
In our time.

On the Strip

D. J. TAYLOR

Sunset Strip, Hollywood Boulevard, is a clotted heatscape of a place, a serpentine coil of stores and diners split in two by a wide thread of tarmac, hazy with sun and exhaust fumes. Even at noon it has a silent, alien quality. The cars, fat Cadillacs with white-wall tyres, sleek roadsters with wound-down sunroofs, chug by in midlane or idle near the sidewalks, checking out building numbers or parking spaces. Apart from the odd driver manhandling a TV from shop doorway to the back of pick-up truck, and the prowling traffic cops, the street is deserted. The locals sit snugly behind the windows of bars and arcades. If you want to travel, you get a cab. If you want lunch you ring up and get it sent round. This, after all, as every newspaper will tell you, is the place where, not long ago, a tourist got arrested for *walking*.

The local newspapers, the *LA Reporter* and the *Hollywood Bee*, had a good laugh over that one. Nobody walks on the Strip. The traffic cop who lumbers past you (Los Angeles traffic cops look as if they live on nothing but ribs and beer) on the corner of Santa Monica can't decide whether cheery incredulity or cautious disdain is the best response. He settles for cheery incredulity. 'You're English, right? Sure I checked out your accent when you stopped for a paper back there.'

The traffic cop is almost certainly called Ralph or Hank. You can imagine him and the rest of the guys back at the station chortling themselves senseless over your naivety. ('Ho, boy! I come across this fruit taking a stroll down the sidewalk. You ever hear anything like it?')

'Seriously, though. I could see you were English the moment you walked up the street. We get a lot of English people here, kids mostly. Think they can hang out with the stars. Chicks who reckon on marrying Sylvester Stallone, that sort of thing.'

Twenty yards up the street a very old black man is trying to sell a brown paper package to a bored-looking Hispanic in a white suit. It is an uphill struggle. ('You wanna buy this stash? If you don't wanna buy this stash why you fuckin' talking to me? Fuck off.') Eventually the Hispanic catches sight of the traffic cop, gives a resigned Oh-God-you-trying-to-spoil-my-fun-as-*well*? grimace and lopes back to his car.

Ralph or Hank meanwhile is checking out a jeep-like vehicle which has stopped at the traffic lights alongside us, peering at the windscreen and finally going over to poke his nose into the aperture provided by six inches of wound-down window. Half a minute later and a pen is poked cautiously into the jeep.

He comes back slapping a fat notebook jubilantly against his thigh. 'Waddya know? Peter Coyote. He was in *Poltergeist*, the Spielberg movie. Whenever I see one of those guys I get them to sign my citation book.' He flourishes the notebook again. 'Danny Devito. Chevy Chase. Pacino. They're all down here. Take a look.'

Peter Coyote's signature is scrawled and anonymous. It suggests that Peter Coyote has a certain amount of difficulty in writing.

Ralph or Hank goes on. 'Sure, I once missed Robert Redford. The guy was sitting over there, across the street in a Mercedes. Would you believe it? Neither of us had a fucking pen.'

'Film is king' says part of a three-line graffito sprayed on the window of a tuxedo rental business a few hundred yards further down (the other two lines are: 'Television is furniture' and 'Rock and roll is life'). Here the movies are not what you go to on a Saturday night, but a constant topic of conversation, what you read about, what you tell your friends. Every newspaper has its celebrity page with an up-to-the-moment account of the latest studio deals. There are half a dozen Hollywood trade papers with headlines like 'Columbia Union Scam Rocks Network', even a porn magazine called *Smash Cuts* which purports to show stills from the low-budget steamers the stars made early on in their careers when $100 stopped the apartment being repossessed. Here on the Strip 'celebrity' doesn't mean politician, or chat show host, or writer or rock star. It means *movie star*.

Not that you meet many *movie actors* (the words are pronounced in slow, reverential tones) on the Strip. The stars live elsewhere, deep in the Hollywood hills, in condos by the beach down at Malibu, only hitting town to see their agents or attend one of the studio promo parties. Nevertheless, in the bars and the tacky breakfast diners the talk is of the $3 million that Dustin is getting for the remake of *On the Waterfront*, or what will happen to De Niro's career if he gets busted. They know these people. The Boulevard hangers-on, the hustlers who collect round the pool table in Schwab's to put nervous $20 bets on horses, the sad women who arrive at Di Magg's for the happy hour $1.69 double vodka and tonics could have been these people had fate been a little kinder. Hollywood is full of failed actors, unable to shake off their addiction. The old man who sweeps the streets down on Sunset probably had a supporting role in *Stagecoach*. The waitress who takes your order in the Ribshack is quite likely to have had a walk-on in *Easy Rider*, or been a subsidiary hostess on *The Dick Van Dyke Show* in 1968.

Mary-Beth takes orders behind the counter at Schwab's, a tacky but modish snackbar-cum-pharmacist at the South End. It is the sort of place where you might see a film star having breakfast. In fact, on this particular morning you can see a film star having breakfast – Dan Aykroyd, star of *Ghostbusters* and *Trading Places* (Mary-Beth calls him 'Danny' and doesn't charge him for the coffee refills).

'Sure, I came out this way after high school. 1969. 1970. Around that time. From Chicago. There isn't a lot you can do in Chicago if you want a career in show business. That was the time you could actually make it in movies, I mean you didn't have to have been at stage school, your pa didn't have to play golf with the head of East Coast Production at Universal, which is what happens now. Those days you'd meet a producer at a party, or in a bar – a lodda them used to hang round the bars – and he'd sign you up. You know, you'd be standing around in the beach party shots or walking the dog when Jon Voigt's limo pulled up. You remember the restaurant scene in *Five Easy Pieces*, the one where Jack Nicholson throws the plates on the floor? Yeah, well, I was sitting at the next table: the girl who's wearing the mackintosh and looks away when Nicholson starts talking dirty . . . I did a lot of films like that. I once got to screw Rod Steiger in a motel bedroom, I forget the name of the picture. The highpoint of my career. Screwing Rod Steiger in a motel bedroom. Can you imagine that?'

Mary-Beth is around thirty-five (in California 'around thirty-five' can mean forty and then some) and has the sort of complexion you don't see outside the front cover of *Vogue*: a tan skin, gleaming canines. She wouldn't look out of place as the sexy corporation boss in *Dynasty* or *The Colbys* or any one of the American sex and sin TV sagas which are looked on disapprovingly here as 'second-rate cinema'.

'Trouble is that sort of thing don't last. You know, the tits and ass roles. Your skin starts to go – I've seen it happen to twenty-five year olds: ten years surfing and they start to look like crocodile skin handbags. Your tits start to sag. And before you know it there's some eighteen year old out there on the set steada you. That's the way it goes, I suppose. Sure, I hung around the studios for a while – I worked in publicity at Columbia for a couple of years – but it wasn't the same. This was '77, '78. I nearly got a part in *Saturday Night Fever*, you know, the older woman the guy fools around with. After that fell through I just thought: Fuck it, I quit.'

A sidelight on life at the fringes of Hollywood. Even the beggars are film stars *manqués.*

'Hey. You lend me ten dollars?'

'How much?'

'Ten dollars. I got to get to an audition.'

This particular beggar is young, sharply dressed and looks as if he carries an Amex card. He has the resentful air of a stockbroker stymied by a timid client. Seeing that he isn't going to get the money he starts off on a guilt-inducing monologue. 'You're making a big mistake, man, you know that? You just screwed my chances of making it in movies. Straight up! They're auditioning for walk-ons in the new Bette Midler film, out on the Paramount lot, and I don't even have the price of a cab. Ten dollars, man. That's all it would take.'

'Five dollars?'

'You fucking limeys,' he says contemptuously. 'You slay me.' A little later, from the other side of the street, I watch him stop and light a cigar.

Hollywood is the most publicity-conscious place on earth, a town where even the ice-cream floats have their own public relations consultancies and the stack of press releases hitting the local newspaper offices each morning can be three inches thick. The radio stations play wall-to-wall advertising: law firms, shrinks, orthodontists. The hoardings rear up thirty feet into the sky: 'JOE'S BURGERS', 'STEP OUT IN SAFFERY'S SNEAKERS', 'SCUZZ PIZZA'. But, in the battle for column inches, for hoarding space and radio and TV chat, film, inevitably, conquers.

Promo week for *Who's That Girl?* and Madonna is in town. Well, not exactly in town but within a radius of a hundred miles and maybe attending a couple of parties. Actually the razzmatazz is fairly minimal, for despite the $16 million invested in *Who's That Girl?* these are tense times for Madonna the screen actress. *Shanghai Surprise*, the last film, was a conspicuous failure, pulled off the screens within weeks of release, and the rumours are that Hollywood investors are getting ready to shut off the money supply.

The Alhambra bar and diner's contribution to the spectacle is a Madonna lookalike competition, a preview copy of the film and a videotape of Madonna's innumerable hit singles. In the restaurant area I settle for a Madonna salad, pretty much the same as an ordinary salad except for an access of black pepper, but decline a Shanghai Surprise cocktail, a terrifying concoction made of curaçao and *crème de banane*. The lookalikes are arrayed on a small stage at the front: sullen, flat-chested women, none of whom bears any resemblance to Madonna, miming very badly to the out-take of *Like a Virgin*. There are even a few men, drag queens mostly, in gold lamé and cowboy boots, one of whom produces a surprisingly accurate rendition of 'Papa, Don't Preach'.

One very curious fact soon becomes apparent. Nobody *likes* Madonna.

'If you ask me she's got no business being in movies. She's a singer. Singers can't act. Look at Elvis.'

'Just another NIP (New York Italian princess). I give her two years. So what if she sold fifty million records? Sure, I went to see *Shanghai*. I walked out after half an hour, it was so bad.'

'I could take it when she looked like some greaseball off the street, you know, the type of girl you could see yourself balling. And the *Like a Virgin* stuff. I could get off on that. But now this Monroe thing. I reckon that's kinda offensive. I mean, who wants peroxide?'

There is a great deal more grumbling over the Jack Danielses and Bourbons which are being downed in preference to the Shanghai Surprise cocktail. Eventually the lookalike contest is won by a man, Steve from San Francisco, who takes the microphone to a chorus of shouts and wolf whistles. ('Ho boy! Hot! *Faggot!*')

Steve actually looks quite like his idol, apart from a very hairy upper lip. He decides to thank his mother and father ('for their support in my career') and announces that copies of his own personal video are on sale at the bar. Nobody seems very interested in the personal video. I find myself talking to a small, soberly dressed man in his mid-thirties whose name is Dwight. Dwight has receding, bouffant hair and turns out to be Steve's manager, quietly pleased with the night's work.

'Steve's one of my best clients, one of my very best. He could go professional any day. I want him to. It would give him the extra confidence, style. It's the one thing he needs.'

'What does he do for a job?'

'Steve? He works in the county assessor's office, valuing real estate. But he's one of the best. We took him to the impersonators' convention at Fresno last month and he caught third. And that was against, you know, the chat show people and the studio doubles. Ask Grace here. She'll tell you all about it.'

Grace is Steve's girlfriend, a skinny brunette who reminds you of an illustration by Kate Greenaway. Her eyes are misted over with tears. 'I'm so proud of him,' she says. What do Steve's parents think? 'Oh, they've been very supportive. They even came to see him at Fresno. That really knocked him out.' Later, while Steve is at the bar shaking hands and Dwight is eyeing up the Madonna salad, she says shyly, 'Do you have an English cigarette?'

Here in California they still make snuff movies. Snuff movies? Imagine the following sequence of events flicking away up there on the screen in front of you. The film is black and white, grainy, with smudges on the tape. The camera moves in on a wide, featureless room, without windows. Sitting on a chair, dead centre, knees pulled up to her chin, is a cheerful-looking girl, blonde-haired, who without further ado begins to take off her clothes, garment after garment, folding them neatly on the chair and then sitting down beside them. The tape crackles. A silent, expressionless muscle man approaches, also naked. What follows is standard hardcore – something you could see any hour of the day in one of the Strip's porno cinemas, tedious and unremitting, except that, at the height of this passionless frenzy, the muscle man brings out a knife from behind his back and starts to saw away at the girl's throat. The last thing you see before the screen goes blank is that rictus of glaring agony.

Snuff movies constitute the final entry on a roll-call of Californian horror which takes in Charlie Manson, the Family and the various psycho killers of the last twenty years. Either what you have just witnessed on the screen is ingenious simulation, the most brilliant play-acting imaginable, or homicide. Snuff movies make the average video-nasty look like *Bambi*. Nobody knows who makes them, how they get distributed, who watches them. They might not exist at all, were it not for the fact that people talk about them. You hear rumours of showings to select audiences of jaded Hollywood roués, of disappearing teenagers. Most people subscribe to the most brilliant play-acting imaginable theory.

Not long ago the police found the body of a seventeen-year-old girl dumped near an isolated bungalow deep in the Valley. The place had been uninhabited for years. Cause of death was given as strangulation. There was enough circumstantial evidence (two popped bulbs, shreds of masking tape) to suggest that somebody had recorded it on an eight-reel.

For some people the lure of celluloid can be, literally, a fatal addiction.

At On the Rox a bottle of champagne will cost you $120. A round of Alabama Slammers (Southern Comfort, sloe gin, orange juice, *crème de banane*) will set you back the price of a plane ticket out. For what is supposed to be Hollywood's chicest niterie, On the Rox is surprisingly downmarket, not much more than a single lounge with bar and pool-table tacked on as an afterthought. The clientele, pale-faced androgynes in seersucker suits, come here on the Dorian Gray principle: having had rather a lot of the good wine, they'd like to find out what the bad stuff tastes like.

The atmosphere is unexpectedly raucous and almost exclusively male. There are a lot of 'Hey Ned's and 'Howya doing, Marty's accompanied by palm-slapping, bear-hugs and two-minute handshakes. The only women are a scattering of 'meathook' girls, pink-skinned twenty year olds with impossible hairstyles and cantilevered busts, property of the Neds and Martys, who get to sit on the sofa drinking Coke. Ned and Marty and Zak and all the others work in the movies or rock and roll. They are the people who discuss distribution deals with Steven (Spielberg), or fix royal agreements with Jack (Nicholson) or tinker around with the tour dates for Bruce (Springsteen). They are the people who when the latest high-budget splatter movie bombs or the latest lavishly produced album fails to shift shrug resignedly and go back to their seafood platters. The stars come and go. These people stay around for ever.

The girls, when not tethered to sofas or Coke straws or Marty and Ned, are avid for conversation. This particular one is called Jaylene: blonde hair in lacquered cascades, flawless complexion. Jaylene turns out to be one of those girls who are *very interested in England.*

'Sure, I went there a couple of months back. A vacation? No, I was checking it out. Marty was doing some TV deal, so I just wandered around. Oxford Street. Soho. Isn't that right?'

It is. But tell me about yourself, Jaylene. What do you do?

'Uh huh. A little modelling here and there. I coulda had a chance of being a Playmate, but Marty figured it didn't go with his image, you know, balling a girl who gets on the centrefold and having people come up and look at you at parties. Besides, he didn't trust Hefner, if you see what I mean. So basically I do autos – you know, sitting on top of some heap of iron at the promo – a little TV. I was a hostess a while back on *The Dick Cavett Show*, only Marty reckoned it clashed with his schedules.' Later, Jaylene, in one of those breathless confidences-to-a-total-stranger, says earnestly, 'You know, I really *love* Marty, I really do.' I express a hope that Marty, a wizened little hamster with dark glasses, feels good about this.

Back at the bar a perennial Hollywood topic is being broached: the guys who didn't make it. Hollywood small talk tends to focus on the guys who didn't make it, the speed-freaks who bombed out after a couple of films, the addicts who overdosed three albums into a promising career, the actors who couldn't memorise their lines without cocaine. For the survivors, talking about dead comrades is a pat on the back, a there-but-for-the-grace-of-God exhalation that makes everyone feel a great deal better. Appropriately, On the Rox has its very own dead celluloid hero: John Belushi.

A crazed, sixteen-stone, paranoid maniac, Belushi – star of *Animal House*, *The Blues Brothers* and *Neighbours* – was found dead in a bedroom at the Château Marmont in March 1982. He was thirty-three. A post-mortem estimated the amount of cocaine in a hundred-centilitre sample of his urine at 55.72mg and later settled for a verdict of acute toxification. His brain simply ceased to tell his body to function. Subsequently the investigative journalist Bob Woodward wrote a book which depicted Belushi as a drug-crazed animal; the last week of his life an orgy of heroin abuse and destruction to which Hollywood turned a blind eye.

Wired, now a hotly resisted feature film, didn't make Woodward any friends. Jim Belushi, the deceased's brother, said that if he could somehow press a button and send a soul to hell it would be Woodward, no question. A similar sentiment seems to inflame the bar-proppers at On the Rox:

'That guy. How could he say those things about John?'

'I mean, we all knew Belushi had a drug problem. He was financing the deals out of the daily payments the studios gave him. It was just drug money. I've seen him do a thousand dollars' worth of coke in an hour; you never saw anything like it.'

'It was his friends that killed John.'

'And the studios.'

'And the fans. That was what killed him.'

The tide of anecdote ebbs and flows. The time Belushi trashed the jacuzzi. The time Belushi stole Hugh Hefner's popcorn at a party at the *Playboy* mansion. The time Belushi had a fight with Jack Nicholson. Back on the sofa Jaylene has fallen asleep, a formal, satisfied smile distinguishing her splendid features.

All of a sudden the party's over and there are lots of 'See you, Ned's and 'So long, Marty's, back-slappings, arm-wrestlings and hand-wavings. Jaylene wakes up and rises to her feet in a single, immaculate moment, lofts her hand under Marty's collar and scratches affectionately. More 'Nice to see ya's, 'Awright's and 'Move on up's.

Outside it is nearly dawn and haggard, grey light is spilling across the roof-tops. To the left, back down the Boulevard, a single green Cadillac is lurching perilously from one side of the street to the other. Far away there are firefly beacons winking in the dun sky. Marty wonders about going on to a breakfast party that somebody is having at a house in the Valley, shakes the Pontiac into action. As we move off, the first stream of cars can be seen away in the distance – evil metal rectangles cruising ceaselessly down the empty streets.

Two Poems

HAROLD PINTER

JOSEPH BREARLEY 1909–1977
(Teacher of English)

Dear Joe, I'd like to walk with you
From Clapton Pond to Stamford Hill
And on,
Through Manor House to Finsbury Park,
And back,
On the dead 653 trolleybus,
To Clapton Pond,
And walk across the shadows on to Hackney Downs,
And stop by the old bandstand,
You tall in moonlight,
And the quickness in which it all happened,
And the quick shadow in which it persists.

You're gone. I'm at your side,
Walking with you from Clapton Pond to Finsbury Park,
And on, and on.

POEM

I saw Len Hutton in his prime

Another time

   another time

Sweetie Rationing

CANDIA McWILLIAM

'In the main a discriminating man, Davey, would you not say? Not the sort to get in with . . . leave alone engaged to . . . ' Mrs McLellan's voice fell and joined those of her companions, good women in woolly tams.

With its freight of sugar ('freight' pronounced 'fright' to rhyme with bite and night in those days when the Clyde was still an ocean-going river), the cake-stand flowered high among the women. At each of the six tables in the tearoom there was such an efflorescence, encircled by blunt knives for spreading the margarine, and white votive cups. The celebrants sat in small groups. They had all been born in another century.

'Old ladies, that's the business. There's always more of them. The men don't hold on the same way. Then there was that war, too.' Erna's mother had told her right when she nagged her to take over the tearoom, even though it meant a move into the city. Erna's mother was known as a widow. Erna had not met her father. He was gone long before he was dead.

'What are you, Mother, if you're no' an old lady?' asked Erna.

'An old woman.'

Erna wondered about the difference. Her mother wore a scarf munitions-factory style and had brass polish round her fingernails from cleaning the number on the front door. Out by the lochan they'd had no number, but good neighbours. Now, in Argyle Street, the old woman went to kirk to get her dose of grudge at whatever new daft thing God had let happen. She had a top half which she kept low down in her apron-bib till the Sabbath, when it went flat under a sateen frock with white bits under the arms in summer and a serviceable coat over that in winter. Erna had always had shoes.

Well, now they had the tearoom, and Erna's mother had silver polish round her fingernails, from all the paraphernalia ladies use to take their tea in style. Cleaning the cake-stands was a long job because of the ornamental bits, curly at the top and four feet like the devil's at the bottom. Without the silver plates for the cakes, three of them getting smaller towards the top, the things were just tall skeletons. The plates were all right to clean. Wire wool made them shine up softly, like metal that has been at sea. Erna's father was said to have been in the

Merchant Navy. Erna did not know whether she herself was destined to become an old woman or an old lady. Marriage would tell. It would be soon, she guessed, from the way he was on at her.

At Mrs McLellan's table, the cakes on the bottom level of the cake-stand were almost finished. Not that it would be right to progress upwards until every crumb had gone.

'Discriminating?' Mrs Dalgleish, as though her hand were just a not totally reliable pet she had given shelter among her tweeds, took the penultimate iced fancy. 'You might say that, Mrs McLellan, but I might not.' The last cake, pink like nothing on earth, was reflected in the silver dish which bore it. Its yellow fellow was in the throat of Mrs Dalgleish, and then even more intimately part of her. When she had truly swallowed and licked all possible sugar from her lips and extracted all sweetness from the shimmery silence she had brewed among her friends, she went on.

Miss Dreever, who was excitable, never having been married, could not stop herself; she took the pink cake. She forgot in her access of pleasure to use the silver slice, but impaled it on her cake fork with its one snaggle tooth.

A doubly delicious moment: the ladies were free to progress up the shaft of sugar and to slip deeper into the story. Mrs Macaulay eased off one of her shoes at the heel. The ladies wore lace-ups perforated all over as though for the leather's own good. They were good shoes and kept up to the mark by shoe trees and Cherry Blossom; the good things in life do not grow on trees. Mrs Dalgleish had at home a shoe-horn, which she sometimes showed the lodgers; the late Mr Dalgleish had given it her, she explained, before he died. Only one lodger had ever dared to respond, 'Not after, Mrs Dalgleish, then?' The shoehorn was to save her bending. 'Though a widow has to do worse things than bend,' Mrs Dalgleish would say. She was not having a joke.

Nor was she today. 'Davey is no more discriminating than any of them when it comes to . . . women. And he's been cooped up in engine rooms for half his natural life. All that oil and steam. Not to mention foreign parts.' Mr Dalgleish too had been to foreign parts, but without the fatal admixture of oil and steam. Davey was an engineer, the sort with prospects. After the war, he'd done university.

'But the girl's not foreign, is she? Is her mother not from Kilmahog? Didn't you say that? And the wean brought up on Loch Lomondside?' Miss Dreever had a grouse-claw brooch which she touched with her own thin hand as she spoke. Since the war, she'd not got about so much, with her mother and the breakdown, but she did pride herself on her penetration beyond the

Highland Line. So many people lived in a country and didn't know the half of it.

'Yes, but a father from where, that's what I'm asking myself.' Mrs Dalgleish looked down at her wedding ring. 'Maybe I'll just try one of those coconut kisses.'

She gave a hostess's inclusive smile. 'Will you none of yous join me?'

In stern order of precedence, Miss Dreever last, the lowest in order below the sugar, the ladies took the cakes. The coconut was friable and soapy as Lux flakes, which the ladies hoarded to care for their good woollens. Today, Mrs Macaulay was in a lovat pullover, Mrs Dalgleish in ancient red, and Mrs McLellan (who had always been a redhead) had a heather twinset which had lasted well. Miss Dreever did not dress to please. She had the proper pride not to be eyecatching.

'Would the girl's father be an islander, then, Janice?' Only Mrs McLellan was allowed to call Mrs Dalgleish Janice. Sometimes they took tea in each other's houses. Mrs McLellan had a tiger skin on brown felt backing, which had seen better days not long ago.

Although the second rung of cakes had been reached, Mrs Dalgleish was not sure that the perfect moment for familiarity had arrived.

'Not an islander *or* a Highlander, Ishbel. And now we've all had quite enough of nephew Davey. What of your family, Miss Dreever?'

It was a bony, unappetising topic, though it had to be tackled at some point during these teas. Miss Dreever was an only child. Her fiancé (had he existed? the other ladies wondered) had been killed. No meat there, of the sort at any rate which you could really chew. Certainly no fat.

Miss Dreever's mother could not be discussed in safety because she intermittently went mad which upset Miss Dreever who had been raised in a tenement and bettered herself through reading. What a true relief for her to get out and about like this then, the once a week.

'You know me,' said Miss Dreever, 'always busy. There's Mother and the teaching and there is a chance I'll be the one to take the form outing this year. We're hoping the petrol will stretch to a beauty spot.'

Magnanimous, placated – how dull could be the lives of others – Mrs Dalgleish turned to Miss Dreever and looked at her. She was a poor skinny thing and probably had nothing in the evening but her books. Mrs Dalgleish had any number of activities. She never wasted a thing, not a tin, not a thread; there was all that putting away, all that folding, saving, sorting, to be done. She often had to stay in to do it, specially.

SWEETIE RATIONING

'Miss Dreever, dear, take that cream horn.' Mrs Dalgleish referred to a sweetmeat on the topmost rung of the cake-stand. The horn was of cardboard pastry and the cream was the kind whipped up from marge and hope and dairy memory, but it was a lavish token. The horn stood for plenty. The sugar on it was hardly dusty. In reverse order of precedence, the ladies took their cakes. Mrs Dalgleish was grace itself as she hung back.

Erna took away the teapot and freshened it in the kitchen at the back. She had torn the sole of her shoe jumping on old cans to flatten them for the dustbin man. She was glad she could get away with just drawing a brown line down the back of her leg to look like the seam of a nylon. All those old ladies had gams like white puds, and then there'd be the darning. With her shade skin anyhow she'd no need for stockings. He said so. She'd let him draw the line once, with her eyebrow pencil, but it got dangerous. Then it was her had to draw the line.

'Seemingly,' Mrs Dalgleish said as she distributed the tea, 'seemingly – though it could be talk, to do with which I will as you know have nothing – Davey's girl's father wasn't all he might have been. In the colour department.'

Miss Dreever wondered, in the instant before she understood, whether this future relative by marriage of Mrs Dalgleish could have worked in a paint shop. Then, clear as in a child's primer, came the bright image of a pot of tar, and the soft, dark, touching tarbrush. She bit the sweet horn.

Judgement

ANDREW MOTION

I was raking leaves in the front bed
when a helicopter wittered overhead

and I thought of a fish in a lake
the moment a waterbug paddles the far light.

My happiness disappeared. I had thought of death
and of everything that sails above the earth

brought low; I had watched the blood of my children
spill, and the solid stones at my feet crack open;

I had slithered so far into the underlying mud
I even flung out a hand for the hand of God.

*

Other times
I am underground:
in the small hours
when green minutes
drip from the clock
and wear me down
to the sort of bone
a scavenger dog
picks out of muck
and buries for later
but clean forgets,
so the years pass,
and the earth shifts,
and the bone turns
into nothing at all
like bone, or me,
or a single thing
waiting for light

JUDGEMENT

and what it shows
of someone else
who lies awake
all night beside me
and never speaks.

      *

For the first time in years
I am on my knees

in the sweet savour
of incense and soap.

The hand of God
is a burst of sunlight

torn through the head
of a window-saint;

the voice of God
is a fly in a web.

They are nothing to me.
I clench my eyes

and imagine a bed
overlooking a garden:

knee-high grass
and hysterical roses.

The day's almost done
and there's mist coming on.

A chestnut tree
by the farthest hedge

has the look of my wife
when her back is turned

and her head in her hands.
The best thing on earth

is to call her and ask
for a drink of water.

I call and call:
the kitchen tap;

a drink of water;
a drink of water

to taste and be sure
I am dying at home.

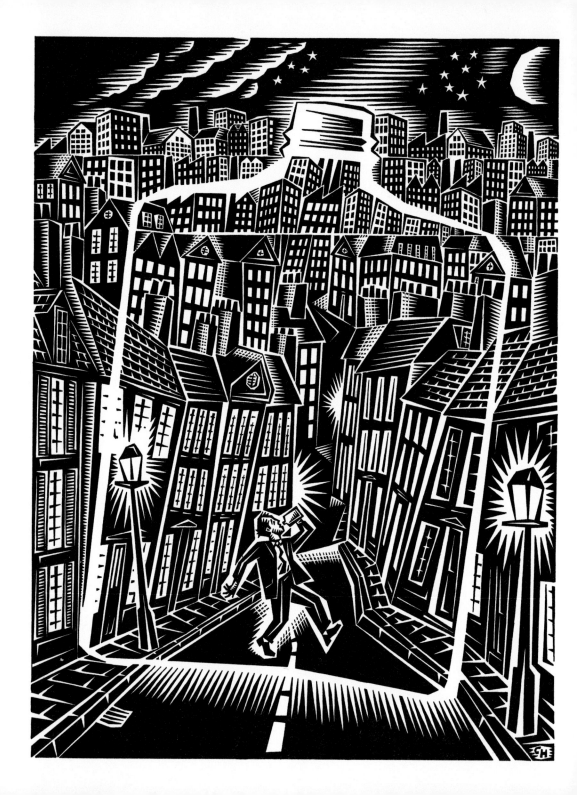

A Right Old Seeing-to

DAVID HOLDEN

It is there first thing in the morning, a bloodstained banner of conquest flapping from his mother's clothesline. I see it from the Lucknow kitchen and think: So much blood. Did he see-to Michelle or kill her? In this neighbourhood neither is ever out of the question. Especially after a night down the pub.

I turn to tell the guvnor Kevin. He sits at the kitchen table ploughing through a bowl of overmilked cornflakes, eyes nailed to the *News of the World*.

'Gazza's gone and done the dirty deed. Just like he said he would last night. Given her a right old seeing-to.'

'Aye, I couldn't help but see it. It's right outside my fuckin' window.' He grins through a mouthful of sogginess. 'His mother'll kill him when she sees. Fuckin' kill him, she will.'

'No doubt.'

'Just as long as we don't have to clean up the mess, eh, Jim?' He gets up, sighs, scratches his belly, puts the bowl in the sink. I nod. He pulls aside the grimy net curtains and peers out. 'I'm tellin' you, Jim, these people are no better than animals. *We're* supposed to be the animals, they're supposed to be the fuckin' Empire.' He lets the curtain drop.

He says that to their faces often, especially after they've had a few and are pounding on the bar for more. But even then Gaz and his crew consider Kevin an all-right bloke, because sometimes he deigns to buy a round. And when he does it's like a condensed Guy Fawkes party – laughing, shouting, displays and, most of all, singing. They all join hands around the guvnor, stare wearily into his fiery eyes, and give him a good Oirish song – 'Danny Boy', the only one they know. Because he's an all-right bloke, and because he can hear the tilltrilling like a frantic xylophone, Kevin lets them carry on for a good hour past closing. Then it's all business. 'Oh, Kevvie boy, the pipes're callin',' the last one wails as he's steered firmly beyond the pale. The guvnor slides the bolt home with a crack like a rifle loading. 'Fuckin' animals.'

At eleven o'clock I am behind the bar and at exactly eleven-fifteen, same as every day, Gaz is on the other side. He places his usual order in his usual tone, my personal swaggering Westminster chimes, 'Pint of lager-top, mate.' While I get it for him he drums on the counter top and looks out the front door, the one facing the tower blocks of Dickens Estate. He is waiting for one of his mates to arrive so he may commence the saga of the seeing-to. I push his pint across the bar. 'One pound thirty-five.' He pays without taking his eyes off the door. His fingers drum frantically. He is bursting to tell someone.

He won't tell me though. Because I don't exist. I am not a human being; I am an extension of the bar counter, a dispensing machine. In the rigidly defined Dickens Estate caste system bums and bartenders (particularly foreign ones) are at the bottom. I am an Untouchable, a victim of both my New Jersey upbringing and my ignorance of day-to-day Dickens Estate affairs. However, today I could improve my lot. I have seen the evidence.

Today is a good day – we both hear the door-handle jiggle not long after Gaz is served. Some days Gaz has to wait fifteen, twenty minutes before one of his crew arrives; I've watched him wait, beer untouched, for half an hour before the handle jiggles. Whereupon, it's, 'While you're at it, get Terry a drink,' as though he's just arrived himself, on his way to something much more important. I always cover for him wordlessly; as an Untouchable I enjoy a certain omniscience – accepted by my betters as long as it's mute.

Today it is not Terry but his younger brother Davey. At twenty Davey is five years less a man of the world than Gaz. But he is eager to learn, which is why he is usually the second person in the pub. He is a barrow boy and works for Gaz's father selling fruit and vegetables by the touristy tube stations near Dickens Estate – Covent Garden, Russell Square and Holborn. So far, his eagerness has stood him in good stead; recently he was given his own pitch around the side of Holborn.

It was the promotion Gaz would have received had he stuck to the business. But then Gaz always had other ideas. A fighter first – he'd already done some training. Then an actor. Or maybe even a singer. Something easy and painless to keep the money and birds ticking over until he really hit the big time. He tolerates Davey's greenhornness, his usurpation of Gaz's barrow boy birthright because Davey listens to him. Unlike most of his crew, Davey admires Gaz for being his own man, for breaking away. And for grudgingly including him in his Lucknow chalk talks.

Davey is full of the fight on last night's television. 'Did you see McCrory? He took that spic apart piece by piece. Did him good and proper.'

'Nah,' says Gaz, taking a long sip. 'I was busy.'

Davey's attention crystallises to a diamond point.

Busy is a great buzzword with Gaz's crew. Busy is a form of business and business is the only business. Done right (though not necessarily by the book) it pays out, like a bent fruit machine, a regular stream of money and girls. Gaz hasn't offered to buy Davey's drink so Davey knows he hasn't been money-busy; that only leaves sex.

'Yeah, so what you been up to – or *who?*'

Gaz says nothing, just looks intently and importantly out the front door. Calculating.

'You had it off with Queenie, didn't you?'

Gaz splutters into his glass. Queenie is a neighbourhood dosser whose hair is the consistency of congealed spaghetti. At opening every night she settles at the largest table, knowing that as it fills up somebody will feel sorry for her and buy her a drink. (I slip her the odd whisky now and again. We Untouchables look after our own.)

Davey's put a good one over on Gaz and milks it. 'It was Queenie, wunnit, Gazza? Old toothless Queenie.' And he starts to laugh.

'Aw, leave it out, Davey. Fuckin' hell, no need to wet yourself.' Nobody else has entered the pub and Gaz is getting angry. He's got to tell somebody and Davey's just blown his chance, braying there like an ass. What Gaz really needs are mates more his own age – geezers a bit more mature, a bit more sophisticated. Geezers who will appreciate the intricacies and raptures of the chase and capture. He drains his glass, goes to the door. Not a soul in sight. Jack Jones again.

Davey's still giggling. 'You want another drink, Gaz?' He dumps a wad of notes on to the counter. Gaz looks hard at the money then at Davey. It's mostly twenties with the odd fifty poking through.

'Good day on the stall yesterday,' Davey smiles. 'Busy.' His heavy gold bracelet, bought last night in the Boswell's Head, glints.

For a second Gaz is defeated, utterly lost. Then just as utterly he has a brainstorm.

'Pint of lager-top, mate.'

I am brought to a halt by his next conversation – not by the content but the recipient.

Me.

The bar extension. The dregs.

'Who d'you think's the best-looking bird comes in here?'

'Ah – '

'Come on, you're the bartender. You serve 'em all. You're not blind. You gotta have an idea.'

I recover gradually and fish for a half-knowing smile. 'I – um – take the Fifth.'

'Which fifth?' puzzles Davey, scanning the back bar. This is a new game and he doesn't know the rules.

Gaz slips me a wink. I find myself winking back. Complicity makes for strange caste systems.

'*The* Fifth,' he explains pedantically. 'One of them American legal terms. Like on *The Streets of San Francisco*. Means he ain't sayin'.'

'Oh.' The tables have been turned on a dime; Gaz presses on.

'So who'd you think?'

I know the correct answer and lay it before him, hyping it with just the right touch of awe. 'Michelle.'

'And who was in here last night, all night?'

'Michelle.'

'Was she in here alone?'

'Why, no, I don't believe she was.' (I fight down a tendency to ham my responses.) Davey's eyes are glued to Gaz, whose tone shifts from brisk QC to casual man of the world, posing a question whose answer is a foregone conclusion. 'Who did she leave with?'

'Why, you, of course, Gazza.'

My reply touches off two divergent repercussions: Davey looks like he's been cracked over the head with a pint jug and Gaz, who's never heard his name on my lips let alone in its familiar form, gives me a warning glare. Witness is excused. I turn my attention to Davey's pint, which he's knocked over.

In a world where men age bloatedly and women overnight Michelle was fresh and free as falling water. A glow of youth shone all through her – her beauty swept like a beacon over Dickens Estate, occasionally exposing a balding beergut knocking off a rouged-over wrinkle, and passing on. Her own mother was such a wrinkle, a middle-aged housewife dawdling on the dole; her father an Italian seaman, current whereabouts unknown, presumed knocking someone off back in Italy.

Michelle – named French by her mother to spite her father – came into the Lucknow often, always in the protection of a gaggle of girls who sat in one corner sipping Malibu and pineapple and eyed their out-of-pub boyfriends, who sat in the other and took no notice. Why Michelle came along I have no idea, except perhaps she was checking the fit of off-the-peg Dickens Estate existence prior to moving up to *haute couture*. She possessed no out-of-pub boyfriend – had endless aspirants both sides of the Lucknow door but never took them up – and on the night of the seeing-to the rumour was that the very next day she'd be lost for ever, swallowed up by the incomprehensibly northern world of Leeds University.

To Gaz's crew she was the ultimate pull. When her round came up all other activity would halt and a churchlike silence descend as she passed among them. Once at the bar though, it was every man for himself: offer her a smoke or a match or a line of chat or, if they'd been busy, buy her a round. She always declined, smiling. They never pushed it, the way they did with other girls. She would sashay back to her table with an armload of Malibu and pineapple, silence descending once again, broken here and there by half-spoken mutterings as each man invoked curse or blessing on her soul. That the only person on Dickens Estate earmarked for transcending it was both a girl and a darkie was something they could never come to terms with. Gaz especially because in his mind that earmark was meant for him.

I've finished mopping up Davey's drink and having performed my interlocutor's duties now stand with my back to the bar, drying glasses and surreptitiously consulting the back bar mirror. Gaz is winding up his account of last night's events. It differs from my memory only in the heroic quality Gaz attributed to himself – the epic myth is alive and well and being sung not by bards but barrow boys. Davey is enraptured, although his face clouds over when Gaz skips through the post-pub agenda with Michelle with almost no regard for detail. Did she get a right old seeing-to or not? Gaz seems to think so. Davey lets it go because the rest of the story is so good. Gaz finishes with the image of himself rampant against the rosy-fingered dawn, virgin-voided bed-sheet of victory snapping behind him. Davey is agog with the glory of manhood.

'Fuckin' hell, Gazza,' he whispers, 'fuckin' fuckin' hell.'

The next day at precisely eleven-fifteen I set a lager-top fizzing on the bar. By eleven-thirty it has gone flat. Davey's brother Terry comes in at twenty to twelve, Davey a few seconds later. Both make straight for the lager-top. Both look agitated. Terry waves off my query of a drink. He points to the pint.

'He been in yet?'

I shake my head.

'Bastard.'

'What you want him for?' says Davey.

'Connaughton,' snaps his brother. 'Manor House middleweight. Gaz was supposed to go a few rounds with him last night.'

'I didn't hear nothin' about that.'

'Yeah, well, you're a kid, i'n't ya?' Davey looks hurt. Terry acquiesces. 'We had to keep it quiet. There was a couple of quid involved. Didn't want the Old Bill fishing round in our pockets.'

Davey nods seriously. 'So what happened?'

'Gaz didn't show's what happened. Lost his bottle. I thought maybe he was with that Michelle bird – ' A possible leer of admiration traces Terry's mouth. 'You know, that Itie bint everyone's saying he – '

Now it's Davey's turn to be in the know. 'Bollocks!' he explodes. 'She's in fuckin' Leeds. Besides, he never knocked her off anyway. *She* knocked *him* off.' He snorts derisively. 'More like blew him off.'

'What?' says Terry. This is news. I creep a little closer myself.

'I was talking to her sister on the stall and she says it was *Michelle* done *Gaz*. Gave him a right old seeing-to. Said Michelle had some fuckin' crazy idea – she wanted to – you know – sort of have it away like, proper, before she went to university. Or some such women's libber shit like that.'

'Michelle? A *libber*?' Practically a dyke.

'Yeah – makes you wonder, dunnit? But listen – her sister says she picks Gaz, right, because he's harmless. You know, sort of stupid. So she let him chat her up that night, right, and buy a load of drinks, just so's she could get a bit of libber's wham-bam-thank you-Gaz.'

Terry is speechless.

'So they gets back to his place, he locks his mum out an' they start going at it like the clappers. On the settee.' Davey sniggers. 'Only fuckin' Gaz can't get it up.'

'No,' gasps his brother.

'Yes. Like a limp salami's our Gazza. Brewer's droop. Or worse. Half the night Michelle's trying to get him up. And when she does, her sister says he don't know what to do with it.'

'Christ,' moans Terry.

'Where to put it, how to use it – he might've stuffed it up his arse, for all the good it was doin' him. So she gave up. Left him there at half mast and walked out. Laughing like a drain she was, according to her sister. Bumped into his mum in the corridor, which only made her worse. Sister said the sound of her laughing woke her up three flights down.'

Suddenly there is bitterness in his voice. 'The cunt. The stupid cunt.'

After a profound silence Terry chortles, an older brother chortle. He sets Davey straight. 'Just like Gaz. Never could do nothin' right. All mouth and no trousers, that's Gazza. Now, if it'd been me locked in there with Michelle – ' He is stopped by the door slamming. Gaz's mother Peg, nose, ears and eyebrows struggling out of a wallow of wrinkle cream, careers into the pub.

'Where is he?' she spits.

'Don't know – ' sputters Davey, taken aback by the wildness in her eyes.

'His things are gone. I comes into his room this morning to wake him up so's he can cash his Giro and his wardrobe's empty. An' he's gone.'

Gaz has left without his dole money. This is unheard of. His mother looks from Terry to Davey. Terry shrugs; Davey straightens up on his stool. Peg leans heavily on the bar. She sighs loudly. 'You just can't control them these days. Oi, barman – what's yer name?'

'Jim.'

'Jim. Give me a large gin and tonic. And half a Guinness.'

For a second all three are lost in thought. I take away the lager-top, which jolts them back. 'In a lady's glass,' snaps Peg. 'And another thing – ' She stares at me preparing it. 'What's that little dago tart doin' sneakin' round my hallway last night?' She takes the drink from me before I can set it down. 'And why is one of my good sheets out on the line, covered in blood? He been fighting again?' She gets no answer from her gin and tonic, and by the time she's into the Guinness her son doesn't exist.

'So that whole story he told me yesterday ain't even true,' mutters Davey. 'Stupid cunt.' He motions for a bitter shandy.

'One thing's for sure,' says Terry. 'He ain't gonna show his fuckin' face round here for a long time. Pint of lager, mate.' I jump to comply.

And I think: If I wanted I could move up a second caste in as many days. For I possess the enlightenment these three boozing Brahmins so tirelessly seek.

I saw Gaz this morning.

It was at King's Cross station. I was coming out of the tube on my way to work. He was in a queue at one of the platforms. The sign said Leeds. His dress was studiedly casual but his demeanour blew his cover. His Sergio Francini bag drooped from his slumping shoulders. He was swilling from a can of supermarket lager he brought to his stubbly mouth in a frequent cigarette-like attack. He looked bottomed-out. He looked seen-to.

As he tilted his head back to capture the dregs his bag slipped off his shoulder, taking most of his fashionably baggy Georgio Avanti shirt with it. Along his collarbone a long snakelike gash of plaster emerged. He regarded it almost wistfully, then shrugged his shirt back on.

He remained in the queue until he reached the barrier, at which point there was some kind of problem. The ticket-taker pointed repeatedly to the ticket booth on the concourse, finally turning Gaz around and giving him a gruff push in its direction. He faltered after a few steps, paused, took in everything around him slowly, like a closing shot in a film, before finally shuffling out among the bums on Pentonville Road, his empty can cleaved to his bosom like a lost love.

So his secret's safe with me. I make his mother another gin and tonic. The whole world could be searching for Gaz and I wouldn't let on – not for all the tea in China. Not for all the chilli dogs in New Jersey. Not for all the *bhajis* in Bombay.

It's caste loyalty really. We Untouchables look after our own.

When I Was Young

DAVID MAMET

When I was young, the corner restaurant made a thing called a 'francheezie', which is the best thing that I ever ate. It was a hot dog sliced down the middle, filled with cheese, wrapped in bacon, and then sizzled on an open grill until it snapped.

And at the pharmacy they made a drink called a Green River, made with green syrup; or made with root beer, or any kind of soda that you wanted.

My father always had a Chocolate Phosphate, which is a thing we had in Chicago. It was made with chocolate, carbonated water, and a secret ingredient.

It was so cool and seemed dark in the drugstore, and smelt of vanilla and chocolate, and like nothing else in the world.

Even the water there was special. It was served in a white cone upside down on a cool silver base. And in the summertime, how cool that marble counter was when we had been out playing.

We played Kick the Canon summer evenings. Or we'd play ball in the streets, where the first manhole was a single, the second a double, so on down the street. And someone always watched out and yelled 'car'.

There was a row of garages back on our alley, tied together under a flat roof that ran the whole block, and sometimes we'd climb up and play football on top of the garage.

The policeman was named Tex, and he wore two stag-handled guns on his belt.

Times in the street, infrequently, there'd be a horse-drawn rag truck. The ragpicker either yelled 'rags, old iron' or that's something I remember from the stories my mother used to tell me of her old neighbourhood.

I remember that we had an organ grinder and his monkey who would come around. And I remember gypsies, though I don't remember how the gypsies looked or what they did.

At school we'd line up, boys on one side of the building, the girls on the other. When the whistle blew we would march in.

In eighth grade, I was a patrol boy. I wore a white belt and helped the crossing guard. There was a special way you learnt to fold the patrol belt, and wore it clipped to your pants belt during the day. When it dropped below ten degrees in winter, they gave the patrol boys hot cocoa.

WHEN I WAS YOUNG

And I remember in the schoolyard every spring, the coming of the Duncan YoYo man, dressed in his Duncan YoYo costume, who would demonstrate the latest models and the latest moves, and was an artist of such skill we were not envious, but awed.

We had a school store on the corner. Joe sold candles, pens and pencils and three-ring paper. Once he took a shoplifter, and cursed at him, and moved his huge bulk out from where he sat behind the counter and he caught the shoplifter and shook him on the sidewalk until the candy fell out of his shirt and on the street.

On Saturdays I walked two blocks to the theatre, and, for a quarter, saw fifty cartoons and a movie, which was usually a western, and I came back after dark.

Once they raffled off a bicycle and I think that I almost won.

I lay on my lawn in the springtime, on my back, and watched the winds blow high clean clouds over the lake.

My first friend told me that his father rode in a jeep in the war, and would have lost a foot when the jeep which they rode blew up.

Down the street a new family moved in. The man came by and borrowed money from all of the people on the block and never paid it back.

I learned to ride a bike. They say you never forget how; and I remember how it felt to learn. How it felt to be pedalling alone that first time, and I knew that it was going to hurt when I fell, and I didn't give a damn.

And we had the park and the beach and the museum, and I don't remember why I wasn't killed when we would spend the day climbing around the caryatids thirty feet above the ground.

We lived near the railroad tracks on the South Suburban Line.

When we went downtown, we bought tickets from the old woman in the old wooden booth up on the platform.

The waiting room smelt of steam and piss and in the winter it was the warmest place on earth.

They had black steam engines then, and when we waved at the engineers, they always waved back.

And now I'm older than my parents were when I was young.

The best thing since then, I think, is just being here with you.

A THANK YOU NOTE

I was recently riding on a London bus. Someone was smoking. The association of the rocking of the bus and the smell of good, non-filtered cigarettes took me back twenty-five years.

In my mind, I was, again, riding various Chicago buses to various jobs, schools, or assignations. And as I rode those beautiful buses, which felt so much like home, I smoked my Luckies and I devoured the world's literature.

I loved those bus rides and I loved those books. I was surprised, and, I suppose, charmed, to see that I still associate the rocking, the diesel smell, the toasted smell of someone else's cigarettes, with those vast, long novels – especially those of the Midwesterners: Dreiser, Sherwood Anderson, Willa Cather, Sinclair Lewis. Those big, long books about the prairies that never end, about an emptiness in the stomach, about a certain feeling, almost a love, of pain.

The old librarian at my high school once found me reading a paperback copy of *Lady Chatterley's Lover*, and chided me for my errant taste.

He felt he was expressing his regard for me by showing me his disappointment. He pursed his lips and said, 'Why do you read that stuff?' and even at the time I felt sad for him, and rather pitied him, both as a fool, for missing the pleasures of literature, and as a weakling incapable of constructing a better sexual advance. What effrontery. But he had seen a lot of me. I spent all of my afterschool time in the man's library, reading anything that had not been assigned.

In high school class I did read the assigned *A Tale of Two Cities*, which, apart from *A Christmas Carol*, is the only thing of Dickens I have ever been able to abide.

Call me a philistine, but I prefer the boredom and repetition of Sinclair Lewis, and the painful sincerity of Dreiser to butchers named 'Mr Cuttymeat' and so on; and I say, further, what of Thackeray, or even Wilkie Collins, either of whom Dickens, in my estimation, was not fit to fetch tea for. But then I seem to always get it wrong, as the librarian said. I think that Dostoevsky is not fit to be mentioned in the same breath with Tolstoy, nor Henry James with Edith Wharton. I do not like the tortured, and I prefer the truth in straightforward honesty to the 'art' revealed by whatever it is that we call talent.

Well, there, I've said it. And as long as I'm *coming out*, I might as well add that I think that Mozart couldn't adjust Bach's shoe buckles – an opinion which can be of interest to *no* one, and which I include solely because I have been trying to work it into cocktail conversation for many years and I have recently stopped drinking.

A THANK YOU NOTE

And I stopped smoking cigarettes long enough ago that they, when smoked by someone else, smell awfully good to me. They take me back to the days of my youth, and the beginning of my Love of Literature.

I have great gratitude to George Eliot, to Willa Cather, to the men and women beyond genius, to the simple writers to whom the only meaning of 'technique' was clarity. These people have been my great friends, my teachers, my advisers, for twenty-five years, from the time I thought Anna and Vronsky were romantic older people, to my last reading, when I was shocked to find that they were unfortunate young people.

To those writers – *how* can I feel they are dead –

Thank you for the insight that the only purpose of literature is to delight us. Thank you for your example. I am sorry that you were in pain. Thank you for your constancy.

Two Poems

JULIE O'CALLAGHAN

LOOK NO FURTHER

You can do anything in this room.
If you sit at this beech table
surveying the pine ceiling
with a plum in your mouth,
you could be royalty.
Up above the skylight
pine cones and wood pigeons are
sheltering me from the world.
A woven African basket
is stuffed like the horn of plenty.
A sink dispenses the source of life.
Cabinets with supplies
will treat your slightest stomach rumble.
A room of dreams:
What do you want to do?
Watch TV? Knit a sweater?
Listen to the radio? Eat an ice-cube?
Cook a dinner? Read the paper?
It's all here – look no further.

BANANA PEEL

A cockney man stands in my kitchen
holding with two fingers
an upside-down empty banana skin.
The tops of his beige PJs
are neatly tucked
into the elasticated waistband
of the bottoms.
His imitation-leather slippers
co-ordinate with the dark-brown piping
around the collar,
which further complements
his horn-rim glasses.
The banana skin flaps as he looks frantically
in all directions for the
regulation Marks & Spencer pedal-bin.

Extract from the Screenplay – Tender is the Night

MALCOLM LOWRY

Cut directly to the Isotta drawing up beside the statue of Diderot, DICK *driving,* NICOLE *beside him, the children together in the back; then a lovely shot of the huge statue of Diderot seated thoughtfully on his pedestal, with the spire of St Germain des Prés, and Les Deux Magots behind. It is a beautiful day and Paris at its best.*

DICK: Say goodbye to Monsieur Diderot, children.

LANIER and TOPSY (*in chorus*): Au'voir M'sieu Diderot.

NICOLE (*as the car drives away*): Au'voir, Paris . . . Au'voir, Café des Deux Magots . . . Au'voir, Montparnasse . . .

We see that NICOLE *is, on the surface, bearing up and trying to be gay, pretending it's a holiday, but an occasional sourceless smile betrays her great strain.*

LANIER: Au'voir, Tour Eiffel.

We see the Eiffel Tower in the background.

Daddy, will you help me build the Tour Eiffel when I get my Number Six Meccano?

DICK (*chuckling*): Sure will. But what gave you the idea I was an engineer?

LANIER: You helped me build the bridge . . . You need forty angle brackets, I don't know how many pulleys – and 500 nuts and bolts. And you make the elevator too.

Loses interest as they are passing a zoo – perhaps the Jardin des Plantes. Au'voir, éléphant.

TOPSY (*thinks this is silly or funny and laughs*): Lanier said Au'voir éléphant – he said –

They scuffle in the back seat.

We see, in passing, have been seeing, fragmentarily, a few of the advertisements we are now familiar with: 'Maurice Chevalier en Paris en Fleures', 'Les 10 Frattelinis', 'Grand Guignol', 'La Fosse aux Filles de Alexandre Kuprin'; while 'ZURICH SUISSE' appears sinisterly, as a sign in a travel agent's window. They pass a cinema with the electric bell already ringing. Instantly they are driving through one of the numerous lovely avenues of Paris, an avenue of trees, with a blowing fountain, where the road is fairly clear for a moment and DICK *puts one arm around* NICOLE's *shoulder tenderly.* NICOLE *rests her head on his shoulder gladly, as if almost wistfully hoping for she knows not what.*

TOPSY: Look – a blackbird –
We see a blackbird.

TOPSY *and* LANIER (*sing in chorus, to the tune of 'Au Claire de la Lune'*):
When you see one blackbird
Then they come in flocks
When –

DICK: Hey, stop being anagogical, you two back there.

LANIER: What's anagogical, Daddy?

DICK (*as we see a flock of blackbirds*): Metaphysically speaking, a darn nuisance. That's too near the knuckle, after Marie *and* Rainford . . . And since when have I lost my status as Dick?

LANIER (*scornfully*): All right – *Dick* then – but I call it bloody silly myself.

NICOLE *and* DICK *look at each other, laughing;* NICOLE – *showing strain – laughs rather cruelly,* DICK *is possibly preparing to reprove* LANIER. *(What hurts him is not the phrase* LANIER *has picked up, but the implied reflection upon the advanced 'psychological' method of bringing up the children, while the tone of* NICOLE's *laughter might be contemptuous of psychology itself, and hence his* amour propre.*)*

Suddenly the screen becomes a flashing moving wall of advertisements, pertinent and otherwise, almost instantaneously gone, but among which we glimpse: 'Théâtre des Arts, Le Dilemme du Médecin (The Doctor's Dilemma) de *Bernard Shaw;* 'Vieux Colombier'; 'S.S. Tenacité'; 'Théâtre des Arts, Oedipe le Roi, de *Sophocle';* 'Opéra, Elektra de *Richard Strauss';* 'Casino de Paris, Paris en Fleures'; 'Rex' (*an old, peeling advertisement);* 'Rosemary Hoyt en Fillette de Papa (Daddy's Girl)'; 'Vincennes, Emil Jannings *en Le Dernière Rire'.*

Cut to the Divers driving swiftly through the outskirts of Paris, past factory chimneys, glass factories, débris, whole vacant lots of rubbish, gasworks, millions of box-like structures precisely the same and everywhere ugly, ugly, ugly – a desolation beyond desolation.

NICOLE (*suddenly*): It seemed too bad to leave Rosemary like that – do you suppose she'll be all right?

DICK: Of course. Rosemary could take care of herself anywhere.

NICOLE: She's very attractive.

DICK: She's not as intelligent as I thought . . . She's an infant.

NICOLE: She's exactly the same age I was when we were married.

Suddenly referring to their surroundings which are getting worse.

Nom de Dieu! this is ugly . . . Do you suppose there's anything beautiful in life that isn't spoiled like this around the edges?

On an isolated blank building a toothpaste advertisement appears: a grinning Negro. NICOLE *groans abruptly.*

Oh!

DICK: Oh what?

We see the Negro again; DICK *glances back anxiously over his shoulder lest anything be said before the children, then even more anxiously at* NICOLE.

Better not think of it, darling.

NICOLE: Do you think we did right?

DICK (*slowly shaking his head, almost in a murmur, and keeping his eyes on the road*): From the standpoint of our responsibility to Rosemary –

NICOLE (*cynically*): Our responsibility to Rosemary!

Cut to the Divers driving through the country; it is exquisite countryside, trees, rolling fields with flowers, wheatfields with poppies, the long, beautiful, empty road ahead; milestones pass; a signpost: 'Paris – Bar-sur-Aube'. They are on the Troyes–Bar-sur-Aube road, heading for Belfort and the Swiss border at Basle or Vallorbe. Behind them the children are quiet, half-asleep. Through the fields the diminished Seine dreamily wanders after them.

NICOLE (*remotely but savagely, self-withdrawn*): How much we pass by, how much we lose.

DICK *looks at her anxiously.*

Perhaps for ever . . .

Cut to a long shot of the road ahead from the car: dissolve to the road under a starry night sky with a waning moon.

DICK: Lanier – are you awake back there?

LANIER *does not reply –* TOPSY *is asleep, but* LANIER *isn't.*

We all know it's long past your bedtime, but I asked were you awake?

LANIER: No, I'm in one of my difficult moods.

DICK: When I was about your age, Lanier, my old man liked to teach me the stars . . .

Cut to the car climbing a hill into the starry sky.

Cut back to a close-up of DICK. LANIER *is kneeling on the floor of the car behind him, his head close to* DICK's *and listening intently now.*

DICK (*pointing*): All right, you've got Andromeda. Now there, to the north, see those stars that look like an arrow? That's Perseus – see, Lanier?

LANIER: – mmn – well, sort of. Who was Perseus, Dick?

DICK: According to the ancient legend, he saved Andromeda from a monster of the sea . . . well, this business is rather complicated . . .

Cut to a close-up of NICOLE, *her head thrown back, resting against the seat; she is not listening to* DICK *and* LANIER, *she is staring up into the night sky with a remote, strange, secret smile.*

DICK'S VOICE (*during the close-up of Nicole*): But first he had to slay the Medusa . .

Cut from NICOLE'*s face to another long shot of the road and the sky. Lap dissolve to the car speeding along another road in morning sunlight. It is a glorious summer morning, and the little family, now by themselves without nurse or chauffeur, seem almost truly gay; for an instant we can almost forget the tragic goal they are approaching. In the back seat the children are singing and as we dissolve all of them, even* NICOLE, *take their parts in the beautiful, gay, ancient canon:*

> Frère Jacques
> Frère Jacques
> Dormez-vous?
> Dormez-vous?
> Sonnez les matines
> Sonnez les matines
> Ding dang dong
> Ding dang dong –

DICK *blows his horn in time with the last: Bam! Bam! Bam!*

But while they are singing we see that the country is wilder, and the road that stretches on ahead leads straight into the distant mountains, appearing now on the horizon. And looking closer at the little family as they sing, we can see that although the children, of course, have a wonderful feeling of holiday, NICOLE *and* DICK *are actually making a gallant effort.*

Dissolve to the car speeding along the same road, later in the day, towards these mountains, closer now, and more ominous as we approach the French Alps and the Swiss border. Cut to a close shot, in the car. DICK *and* NICOLE *are silent, the children are giggling, scuffling and half-arguing in the back seat, trying to sing 'Sur le Pont d'Avignon'. We see signs pointing back the way they have come: 'Bar-sur-Aube', 'Paris'. Signs pointing straight ahead: 'Strasbourg', 'Belfort', 'Basle'. DICK looks at NICOLE anxiously for she is gazing straight ahead at the mountains with a set drawn face.*

DICK: Pipe down, you kids, give that a rest.

The children start in again on 'Frère Jacques', and DICK tries to put a stop to this by blowing a long note on his horn.

NICOLE suddenly puts her hands over her ears, flinging a look almost of hatred at DICK and the children.

DICK (*to the children, glancing at NICOLE with anxious love*): Better give that one a rest too.

The children stop, subdued for the moment by DICK's tone of voice. NICOLE is staring ahead at the mountains rearing up their walls and cliffs ahead. It is not merely that we feel from her expression that she can no longer keep up the deception of a 'holiday', nor that as Switzerland and the mountains get nearer and nearer she becomes more despairing; we sense now an active hatred of the children, of their normality, their ability to be normal and gay, of their unity with DICK, and his with them, partly pretence though she knows that to be.

DICK (*sensing this mood in NICOLE and attempting to divert the children*): How about this one?

He begins to sing in the middle of 'The Kerry Dancers', the Irish song we heard Abe sing, a song so joyous one always forgets it ends by being heartbreaking.

When the clans began to gather

In the glen of a summer's night

And the Kerry piper's tuning

Filled our hearts with a wild delight –

As DICK is singing we see they are approaching a crossroads – the right signpost points towards Besançon and Dijon, the left towards Strasbourg; Dick slows, his song becomes diminuendo.

Oh, to think of it, Oh, to dream of it

Fills the heart with tears –

Oh, the thought of the Kerry dancers

Oh, the ring of the piper's tune –

We observe again, from NICOLE's standpoint, the sign pointing straight ahead: 'Belfort, Basle, Zug – ZURICH '–

Oh, the sound of the Kerry music

Gone, alas, like our youth, too soon –

NICOLE (*abruptly – we know from the way she speaks it is a ruse, yet it is also sincere, nor shall we ever know if it would have saved them*): Dick, why don't we turn off right and go back to Antibes? We could be in Besançon tonight, spend tomorrow night at Grenoble, and be home day after tomorrow. *All at once a mountain mist swoops down upon them, obscuring the road before us and the signposts, and as* DICK, *intent on driving, peers forward through the mist, suddenly right across the screen appears a huge sign in three languages: 'STOP! PAY TOLL!'*

The centre part of this between the two injunctions forms the roofed entrance to a toll bridge above which the vertical clearance is indicated. Beneath the 'Stop!' and the 'Pay Toll!' are ticket offices. There are other signs also of 'Achtung!' 'Notice!' 'Avis!' but the impact of the main sign has quickly devolved into English as it came towards us. (A materialised officer has raised his hand to stop the Divers' car: the next moment we see DICK *paying their money into the* guichet *through the car window – the border is actually perhaps a little further on, but there is a technicality of at least showing their passports here.) Cut to* DICK *groping his way in their car across the bridge in the mist.*

Cut to the Divers' car approaching the town of Zug – in the near distance we see a Ferris wheel, other appurtenances of a fair, what looks like a menagerie, etc. The mist has lifted, the sky is clear, and we see a signpost: 'Zug ½km, Zurich 5km'.

DICK: Well, we seem to have a fair.

LANIER: Oh, *do* let's stop, Daddy.

TOPSY (*almost jumping up and down*): Hee, bonjour éléphant, que vous me semblez beau. Bonjour, éléphant! Bonjour éléphant!

NICOLE: Oh yes, Dick, *do* let's stop and see the fair.

This too we suspect may be a ruse.

DICK (*smiling*): All right.

Cut to the Divers approaching the fair, through the menace of a shot of mammoth steam rollers that make way for them, upon each the legend 'Ich Dien'.

NICOLE (*suddenly and with vicous rancour*): She's quite smart.

DICK (*driving, and paying most of his attention to the car*): Who? Topsy? Sure she's smart.

NICOLE: Rosemary. Your ickle durl.

DICK: Oh, her . . . not very – there's a persistent aroma of the nursery.

NICOLE (*in a voice that might mean danger*): She's very *very* pretty. I can see how she'd be very attractive to men.

Cut to the Divers in the car approaching the edge of the fair.

NICOLE (*looking to one side, and showing she is losing contact*): See the little house – it looks like a painting that hasn't dried.

Instantly the house we are passing blurs, as through NICOLE*'s eyes; it looks something like the blurs we have seen in the psychological moments of* NICOLE*'s 'absence' in the flashback. (This gives us a knowledge of* NICOLE*'s state that exceeds* DICK*'s, preoccupied as he is to some extent with the car and the children, and we feel a mounting tension about, and with,* NICOLE*, and a growing apprehension quite on our own behalf as to what this may precipitate.)*

Cut to DICK *parking the Isotta.* NICOLE *gets swiftly out of the car immediately it stops without waiting for* DICK *to help her, on her face a secret strange smile which we see but which* DICK*, busy lifting the children out, does not. Meantime we hear the music of the fair and see the fairground – what we notice at first being not its kaleidoscopic quality, but simply its poetic beauty (escape). The camera follows the family walking through the outriders of the fair. On* NICOLE*'s face the smile flickers, derisive and remote. It becomes more remote, more derisive, as we realise that somewhere the mechanical steam music of the fair is churning out raucously the, by now, old tune 'Smiles'. Beneath this we can hear the whining and tinkling of a hootchy kootchy show. Cut to a sidewise near close-up of a screeching Punch and Judy show, with the word 'Guignol' above it. Slantwise the four appear, each half-turned to us on the screen,* TOPSY*, nearest, then* DICK*, who has both children by the hand, then* LANIER*, then* NICOLE*, furthest away.*

LANIER (*to* NICOLE): Look! A Punch and Judy!

As through LANIER*'s and* TOPSY*'s eyes, we see it first as possessing some of the magic of our first Punch and Judy shows.*

NICOLE: Yes, a Punch and Judy show –

NICOLE *seems to be orienting herself by anchoring to it, and the held sidewise shot of the Punch and Judy show wavers between magic and blurs. Not blurred, however, is the face of a small dark girl of about fifteen, who, happening to bump into them, smiles politely up at* DICK*. The churning tune 'Smiles' becomes suddenly louder and more awful.*

Cut into an almost head-on rowdy shot of the Punch and Judy show so that we are looking into it ourselves over their shoulders, with the family in the same order, though it is slightly angled and tilted. Cut into a shot of the whole fair, seen as a blur through NICOLE'*s mind, ghostly merry-go-rounds, ghostly steam rollers, in the distance a ghostly Ferris wheel, the ghostly Punch and Judy show now comes back into its rowdy aspect, as through* DICK'*s mind, to which we have temporarily transferred, so that it appears simply hideous. While these transformations have been going on we have scarcely had time to notice that* NICOLE *is no longer by* TOPSY'*s side.*

TOPSY: Daddy, is this the same Punch we saw last year in Cannes?

DICK (*as Punch starts belabouring Judy*): Couldn't be quite the same one if he is a year older.

TOPSY: He *could*, Daddy! He could, he's the very same one, I'm sure of it — isn't he, Lanier?

Judy now belabours Punch, squealing and scolding.

Lanier wouldn't know, but *I do* —

DICK (*as the camera holds the word 'Guignol' above the show a moment we feel he might be thinking it should be* Grand Guignol — *then returns to* Punch): No — I think he's got a few more grey hairs, this fellow — he's a sadder, if not wiser, man altogether.

While DICK *and the children are still watching the show, the squealing of Punch and Judy, the tinkling of the hootchy kootchy, the steam music churning out 'Smiles', seem to reach a climax together.*

Cut to NICOLE, *twisting swiftly and secretly, running through the crowd. Cut to* DICK, *at the Punch and Judy show. He realises she has gone, sees her, and runs after her. Suddenly, as he remembers he has forgotten the children, he wheels and runs back to them, drawing them this way and that way by the arms, as his eyes jump from booth to booth looking for* NICOLE. *Cut to a lottery wheel spinning seen at such an angle that we are sure what it is, then to the young woman in the booth behind it.*

DICK: Madame. Est-ce que je peux laisser ces petits avec vous deux minutes? C'est très urgent — je vous donnerai dix francs.

THE WOMAN: Mais oui.

Cut to DICK *leading the children hastily into the booth.*

DICK (*to the children, quickly*): Alors — restez avec cette gentille dame.

DICK *darts off again, but he has lost her. Cut to a circling merry-go-round — the source of 'Smiles' — blasting its steam music through its whorled pipes, with* DICK *keeping up with it till he seems to realise he is running beside it, and always staring at the same horse.*

Cut to a terrifying shot of an absolutely deserted flying machine, whose gondolas, while travelling at enormous speed, execute slow rolls, whizzing round empty – but with one cylindrical gondola broken and spinning crazily at a frightening rhythm different to the others, and making a dreadful broken grating sound.

Cut to a buvette, with DICK *elbowing through the crowd, then, while in the background, we see a suggestion of a sledge-hammer, plunging, circular motion of the loop-the-loop machine, to the apparition, ahead of him, of the words over a fortune teller's tent:* 'Votre Destin, Astrologie', *even, ironically,* 'Psychologie, Clairvoyant, Palmiste'; *cut to the fortune teller at the opening of the tent.*

THE FORTUNE TELLER: La septième fille d'une septième fille née sur les rives du Nil – entrez, Monsieur –

DICK *snatches up the flap, peers in. Inside we see a round horoscope, even as in a fragment of a nightmare, something about* Les Gémeaux célèbres Astrologiques, *Robert Edwin Peary, Sigmund Freud, née le 6 Mai 1856. Close-up of the horoscope. The horoscope begins to spin, instantly becoming a Ferris wheel, but seen in the distance beyond the crazily spinning empty flying machine with the broken, grating gondola; below this machine gazing up, its owner is now hopelessly standing.* DICK *begins to run past the flying machine towards the Ferris wheel. The Ferris wheel fills the screen an instant, then we see it slowly revolving against the sky, beyond it, the lake.*

Cut to a shot of the Ferris wheel motionless for a moment: in the gondola at the top we distinguish NICOLE. *The camera bears up upon her, and we see she is laughing hysterically, and then we hear her. The Ferris wheel begins to descend, and we are in the gondola with* NICOLE, *seeing the mountains, the lake, blurred, and the fairground, with* DICK *approaching now below, revolve, but in the peculiar fashion that is produced by the unique motion – jerk, swing, straighten out – of the Ferris wheel itself. As the wheel revolves* NICOLE's *laughter grows louder. Cut to a shot of the crowd taken from below looking up, among which we see* DICK *who, on observing the spectacle* NICOLE *is making of herself, has slunk back into it a little, a movement which exactly coincides with our reaction to* NICOLE's *behaviour in so far as we too are with* DICK *and still standing outside it.*

FIRST SPECTATOR: Regardez-moi, ça!

SECOND SPECTATOR: Regarde donc cette Anglaise!

The two points of view now begin to alternate rapidly. At one moment we are with NICOLE *in the Ferris wheel steadily increasing speed past the revolving blurred mountains, while her laughter becomes ever more and more diabolical: the next we are in the crowd with* DICK, *watching the wheel. Finally we are in the wheel with* NICOLE *as her gondola, slowing, approaches the ground and she catches sight of* DICK, *at which moment her laughter dies. Quickly she gets out and as* DICK *comes towards her she makes a gesture of slipping away. He catches her arm as she does and holds it as they walk away. They walk swiftly enough but the rapidity is accentuated by the now kaleidoscopic and nightmare vision of the various revolving mechanisms in the fairground. The confused dissonance of steam music still dominantly playing 'Smiles' also adds to the speed, but, beneath this, though we cannot notice it, a slower music in the score is acting as a kind of emergency brake upon both our emotions and the tempo, stating and restating a theme, at a much slower yet steadily mounting tempo, for, in spite of the drama here, the climax is not yet.*

DICK: Why did you lose control of yourself?

Cut to the same terrifying shot, though from the opposite side, of the unpopular empty flying machine with the revolving horizontal gondolas still whizzing round by itself with the owner standing there as if hopelessly smoking a cigarette below, and recurringly the one gondola gone crazy and gratingly spinning and spinning at a disproportionate speed to the others.

NICOLE: You know very well why.

DICK: No, I don't.

NICOLE: That's just preposterous – let me loose – that's an insult to my intelligence. Don't you think I saw that girl look at you – that little dark girl – oh this is farcical – a child – not more than fifteen –

DICK: Stop here a minute and quiet down.

NICOLE (*they have reached the buvette; she sits down, her hand moving across her line of sight as though it were obstructed*): I want a drink – I want a brandy.

DICK: You can't have a brandy – you can have a bock if you want it.

To the woman in the buvette.

Puis-avoir un bock, s'il vous plaît.

NICOLE: Why can't I have a brandy?

DICK: We won't go into that. Listen to me – this business about a girl is a delusion, do you understand that word?

The reiterated theme in the score now begins to act slightly as an accelerator rather than a brake on the tempo, the effect it has is as if it were part of the fair version of 'Smiles', which, actually recorded from fair music, it is trying to catch up.

Simultaneously the woman brings back the bock – she brings two but DICK

waves his aside, declining it, takes the other and hands it to NICOLE. DICK
lights a cigarette.
Cut to NICOLE: *almost finishing the bock.*

NICOLE: It's always a delusion when I see what you don't want me to see.
She drinks.

Cut back to the Punch and Judy show again, as through DICK'S *eyes, and
from the same angle, with the girl smiling up at* DICK: *cut to* DICK *at the
buvette: his eyes waver from* NICOLE'S; *instantly cut back to the Punch and
Judy show and we share* DICK'S *indirect guilt as we see* NICOLE'S *delusion
imply a psychological truth, for this time the girl smiling turns swiftly
first into* NICOLE *as we have seen her in the sanitorium, then into Rosemary, all this happening so fast that it too seems slightly to accelerate the
action.*

Cut back to DICK *and* NICOLE *in the buvette, beyond them we see
the words over the astrologer's tent:* 'Clairvoyant, Astrologie, Psychologie,
Palmiste' *etc.; and above that,* 'Votre Destin', *and the old woman standing
there.*

NICOLE (*finishes the bock*): Who do you think you are, Svengali?

DICK (*standing up*): Come on – we're going home. I mean we're going to
Zurich.

NICOLE (*roaring in a voice so abandoned that its louder tones waver and crack*):
Home. So home is the sanitorium, eh? And sit and think that we're all rotting
and the children's ashes are rotting in every box I open. That filth!

Dissolve, as 'Smiles' *begins again endlessly to repeat itself once more, to*
NICOLE *and* DICK *standing under the words* 'Votre Destin'. *Her words
have seemed to sterilise her and we see a sort of relief in* DICK'S *face, a
withdrawal of anger which is a withdrawal into pity on our part as* DICK'S
*face softens, the effect being that it has immediately softened after her
dreadful words.*

NICOLE: Help me, help me, Dick . . . You *can* help me!

While DICK *seems to waver, as if through his mind – though the image is
in fact objective – we see a muddy swirling onrushing flood, half-submerged
trees, then a dam: one sandbag is thrown against the dam; the water begins
to leak through, first on one side, then the other.*

NICOLE: You've helped me before – you can help me now.

DICK: I can only help you in the same old way.

NICOLE: Someone can help me.

Another sandbag is thrown against the dam.

DICK: Maybe so. You can help yourself most. Let's find the children. I left them with a gypsy woman in a booth.

The water leaks through past the second sandbag, both sandbags are swept away, they sink, though the dam still stands.

Cut to the lottery wheel spinning, sloping away from the screen, vaguely we notice LANIER *and* TOPSY *beyond it with several women and children, then* DICK *and* NICOLE *advancing swiftly through the revolving and plunging machines to see the children in the booth surrounded by women, examining them with delight like fine goods, and by peasant children staring at them. Cut to* DICK *giving the young lottery woman her ten francs; simultaneously the camera passes from the faces of the children who, deprived of their fun, look very unhappy and probably by now sense something of what has happened, to* NICOLE, *standing apart, evil-eyed, as if resenting the children, both as a real responsibility of the real world she would deny, and also as the cause of* DICK's *turning from her, and telling her to help herself.*

THE WOMAN (*to Dick*): Merci, Monsieur – Madame. Au'voir, mes petits.

The camera travels past the seemingly eternal screaming Punch and Judy show again to the car with the steam rollers beyond, returns to the children's faces, grave with disappointment as they trudge back and get into the car, DICK *and* NICOLE *silent beside them – they had been a little family, now each is weighted with mutual, yet terribly separate, apprehensions and anguish.*

Cut to an objective shot of the car as it moves off, threading its way through the steam rollers again; then we see DICK's *face at the wheel, tense and unsmiling, the children's faces, disappointed and half-fearful, and* NICOLE's *face, hard and distant, though she seems to be trying to control herself. But as we see a signpost: 'Zurich 4 km' her face becomes hard again. We now immediately shift our standpoint to a feeling of ourselves being in the car, which is climbing a hill through the mountainous country. We are with* NICOLE, *but we share her consciousness with that of the camera, and that of the film itself. Cut to a sign: 'Zurich 3½ km'.* NICOLE's *face gives way to the sourceless smile that already frightens us.*

DICK *cannot be, and is not, driving swiftly, but nonetheless we have the same or a similar sense of tension that we had first upon witnessing* Daddy's Girl; *then in Baby's configured account of the accident, but so far it is the tension alone that is similar. As we drive up the hill the sounds of the fair, the sound of the mechanical 'Smiles', now begin to drop away and the*

217

continually reiterated theme we had been scarcely conscious of in the score begins to disengage itself from these, becoming ever more and more rapid, and acting here something like a literal accelerator, instead of a brake. Still in the car we come now to a straightaway run parallel to the hillside and we actually do accelerate to gather speed for the circling hill beyond. Since there is no fence to the road, signs appear in French and German reminding us of 'Danger', of 'Dangerous Corner Ahead', a cross too appears by the side of the road, but this in no way suggests that DICK *is driving dangerously: the danger, on the contrary, is in the situation, ahead in the film, and to ourselves. The camera remains fixed on the ever unwinding road, and this accelerated run is just long enough for us to experience three combined sensations, that of increasing exhilaration we had when watching* Daddy's Girl, *combined with the feeling of certain but retrospective fatalistic disaster we possessed when watching the accident in the clinic sequence, to which is now added the unbearably horrendous anticipation of something imminently disastrous that is at the moment threatening, but exacerbated by the element of free will not present before, which leads us to hope against hope that accident may be prevented. Simultaneously the theme with its ever accelerating music disengages itself entirely from the fair sounds and music and mounts by itself: the effect is of incredible rapidity, and time becomes simply filmic. Cut to a flash of a signpost: 'Zurich 3¼ km'. Cut in again the flood – and we see the dam once more. The flood beats against the dam, leaking through it at every point and rising behind it. Cut from this to the similar scene of the car in* Daddy's Girl. *Cut into this a brief flash of the scene of* NICOLE *driving with her father just before the accident. Cut into this a huge close-up of Abe's face, drunk, succeeded the next instant by Peterson's face, the blood dripping. Cut into this a close-up of the bloodstained sheets, those first of Peterson, then those used to wrap* NICOLE'*s father, from this to the actual car we are in proceeding along the straightaway run: on one side of the road the cliffs rise like walls, on the other an immediate declivity falls away into an almost perpendicular drop into an abyss, with a few trees and underbrush clinging to its sides. Cut in a flash of a signpost: 'Zurich 3 km'. Cut back to the dam. It crumbles and is washed downstream in sinking fragments by the overpowering onrush of the flood and of a rising turbulent racing river that sweeps all before it. At the next moment, cut into the point in* Daddy's Girl *where Rosemary puts her hand on the wheel. There was a moon in that scene, which had been at night: it reappears here, for a split second as an isolated symbol of madness. Cut to a flash of a signpost: 'Zurich 2½ km' and*

back into our car going down the straightaway and at the same moment to
NICOLE *leaning over and screaming as she clutches the steering wheel from*
DICK, DICK's *hand trying to crush her mad hand down; then we are with*
the car for a final instant, as it swerves, rights itself, swerves once more, and
plunges off the road, tearing through low underbrush, but, as it falls and tips
twice, in rhythm with this, and as quickly as it takes to play five emphatic
chords on a piano, we have a close-up of Peterson's face, a close-up of
Rosemary, a close-up of the sheets at the Roi George, a close-up of the crash
of the Warren accident, and finally, emerging from a shot of the flood in
headlong and complete possession, the car settling slowly at an angle of
ninety degrees against a tree, as the children scream and NICOLE *screams*
and curses and tries to tear at DICK's *face.*

Close-up of DICK: *he seems to be thinking first of the list of the car; he*
pushes NICOLE's *hand away, climbs over the side and lifts out the children;*
then he ascertains the car is in a stable position. Now, looking at NICOLE,
he stands there shaking and panting while NICOLE *is laughing hilariously,*
unashamed, unafraid, unconcerned, as after some mild escapade of
childhood, so that no one coming on the scene would imagine she had
caused it.

We see a swift shot looking straight up the hill, showing the tearing destructive
path the car has made through the trees and underbrush as it plunged
downwards, another swift shot of the abyss below, where they might have
gone.

NICOLE *jumps out of the car, falling to her knees; she picks herself up and*
turns on DICK.

NICOLE: Ha!

Accusing and grinning, her face a grinning mask.

You were scared, weren't you? You wanted to live!

They confront each other, over the wreckage of their lives and the silent
terrified children, as DICK's *expression turns from shock to comprehension,*
to horror at her attempt on the children's lives, to anger, then to speechless
anguished fury (in which we can see his sense of his own guilt in being even
partly responsible for having brought her to this) yet finally, absolute fury.

DICK: You – !

Cut – slash – instantly and savagely to a shot of blazing windows facing each
other across a court, these windows confronting each other so violently that
they seem flaming, almost quivering with a fire within, so that it is both an
extension and a symbolisation of that blazing anger and hatred. As, on one

window, we see bars begin to form and become real bars, we realise that they are the windows of a court in the Sanitorium Zurichsee, whose name we see the next moment over the door: cut to the name 'Dr Frederick Dohmler' upon his door, then we go into his office.

Two Poems

DAN JACOBSON

A CORRESPONDENCE

(in the Chinese manner)

1

The moon rises as it has to, enlarged, enflamed, engorged
    with the day's heat.
Windows are open, doors too. Barefoot weather.
Outside, black leaves that lift their heads and hiss;
    then fall silent.
And in my heart – you, you, you.

Why you? I go to town; the train is full of women.
I walk in the street; they pass on every side.
It is clear to me, then, that randomness reigns.
Yet here I sit, still wishing you were with me now;
Or that we had never met;
Or that you had not been born for me to love.

Nothing else.

Never anything else.

2

Your letter was brought to me by a man in a peaked cap.
He had a sallow skin; it shone in the heat.
I offered him a drink of water but he refused it.
He said he had many other letters to deliver.

RECOLLECTION

It isn't her eyes or hands I recall
but the smell at the roots of her hair,
and the swerve of each strand as it starts from her skull,
    and the whiteness there.

The Babysitter

MAUREEN FREELY

It was 11 p.m. your time when I tried to reach you from St Louis. You *still* weren't home. This time a man answered. A man who only spoke Spanish. '*¿Bueno?*' he drawled. '*¿Bueno?*' I was sure I had dialled the wrong number, so I hung up and dialled again. The same man answered. 'Ricardo, *¿eres tú?*' he asked. I could hear salsa music in the background.

When I finally staggered through the front door of 2238 Hyde at four o'clock the following afternoon (and again, I'll spare you the details of my fiasco-ridden passage from coast to coast, suffice it to say that I was bumped off more flights in one day than most people are in a lifetime) . . . when I finally dragged myself and our nineteen thousand bags into the downstairs lobby, I could hear the same music floating down the stairwell.

I could not quite bring myself to accept that it was coming from our apartment. But the closer the elevator drew to the seventh floor, the more audible it became.

It was audible because – as I now discovered – the apartment door was open. Nobody noticed me walk in. I could have been anyone. A rapist, a kidnapper, anyone. And as far as I knew, the man on the couch could have been any of those things. It goes without saying that I had never seen him before in my life.

Let me describe him for you. He was young, black-haired, and wearing earphones. And boxer shorts. And nothing else. He was lying on his back with his feet propped on the far armrest and one arm distended above an overflowing ashtray. He did not notice my arrival. 'Hey, you!' I yelled. I got no reaction so I tried again. '¡*Hola, usted*!' He did not appear to hear me this time either. I was about to yank him to his feet when I caught sight of Maria.

Maria was on the balcony.

That's right. On the balcony. She was not simply 'on' the balcony either. She was on a chair on the balcony. And the chair had been pushed right up to the edge of the railing. At the moment I caught sight of her, she was not actually standing on the chair. She was kneeling on it. So her life was not in immediate danger. In other words, she was not teetering seven storeys above an asphalt driveway. She did, however, have one half of a plastic Easter egg in her mouth.

THE BABYSITTER

I know you'll be relieved to hear I didn't lose my cool. I moved swiftly but silently – locked my arms around her but pretended everything was normal.

She was glad to see me. Until I took the plastic Easter egg out of her mouth.

Her screaming stunned me. I staggered inside, still holding her close. I knew, however, that something else was wrong, something else was missing. At first all I could focus on was the safety gate. Where was it? It took me a few seconds to remember Jesse.

Where was he? Where was my son?

Clutching Maria close to my chest, even though she was trying to bite me, I raced through the apartment, calling Jesse's name. But he was not in the kitchen or the spare bathroom, or the children's bedroom.

The door to our bedroom was closed. I pushed it open with my foot. Peering through the billowing smoke, I caught my first glimpse of Eluisa.

During the three days I had been communicating, or rather, failing to communicate with this woman on the phone, I had developed a nightmare vision of her face. But let me tell you, her actual face was ten thousand times worse.

She had her hair in curlers and a hairnet wrapped tightly around them. There was an incongruous pink bow on top of the hairnet that made you even more aware of the tautness with which her yellow skin was stretched across her skull. She was wearing a quilted aquamarine dressing-gown whose stitching had begun to unravel. She had her feet in that footbath thing my mother gave you for Christmas. She was – it goes without saying, doesn't it? – smoking a cigarette.

Correction. Cigarillo. Another overflowing ashtray was precariously balanced on the cushion next to her. And I don't need to tell you about that sofa being made of the same highly inflammable material as the furniture in that hotel in Las Vegas. You know which one I mean. That one that burned to the ground, remember? In which most of the deaths were attributed not to the fire but to the poisonous fumes from burning furniture?

And that was not the worst of it. The worst of it was she was watching a video. A horror video. Yes, you guessed it. That's the one.

I myself didn't put two and two together. All I could think of was Jesse. All I noticed in passing was that the video was something horrible, sadistic, sick and grotesque.

Of course you couldn't hear the sound effects. Not with Joe Cubano and his Hundred and One Lowriders crooning away in the background. Anyway, our friend Eluisa was mesmerised. She had her eyes fixed on the set while she puffed away at her cigarillo and stuffed her mouth with peanuts.

Yes, peanuts. She had had a bowlful of them on the armrest. She had knocked it over a few times already, because there were peanuts all over the carpet. I don't need to tell you that just one of those peanuts lodged in Maria's throat could have killed her.

It may sound as if I just stood there gaping, unable to believe the scene before my eyes, but actually I didn't waste a moment. I went straight to the TV and turned it off. Eluisa looked at me and screamed.

I myself kept my cool.

'*¡Estoy el señor en la casa!*' I informed her. This piece of news made her scream even louder. So I said it again. Or rather, I shouted it. '*¡ESTOY EL SEÑOR EN LA CASA!*'

She lifted her hand to her mouth and then froze. 'Ahhh!' or rather, 'Aggghhhh!'

'*¿Dónde muchacho?*' I demanded. Suddenly Eluisa had jumped to her feet. Babbling and gesticulating, she went careering towards the bathroom. I followed her. She pointed at the bath. It was filled to the brim with water. And bubbles. And toys. But not Jesse.

'Hesse! Hesse!' she called. No answer.

She tossed her cigarillo into the toilet bowl and began to dredge the bath with her arm.

'JESUS CHRIST!' I yelled. I practically threw Maria on the floor. I plunged both my arms into the water. I can still remember how cold the water was, and my horrible relief when my arms did not brush against Jesse's corpse.

I turned to Eluisa. '*No está,*' I informed her.

She scurried out of the bathroom and opened up the walk-in closet. 'Hesse!' she shrieked. 'Hesse!' Her hairnet was coming off now, her curlers were askew. She gesticulated at a large pile of plastic dry-cleaning bags.

'JESUS CHRIST!' I yelled. For the second time in thirty seconds I nearly had a heart attack.

But Jesse wasn't lying suffocated in a plastic dry-cleaning bag. Nor was he spreadeagled on the asphalt driveway seven storeys below our balcony. He was playing Dr Who, in the service elevator.

That's right. The service elevator. The service elevator that is, as far as we can make out, the same make as the service elevator on Beacon Hill. You know, the one that the toddler walked into a year ago? Only to find it wasn't there? Remember? It was on the news? The parents were both lawyers? They had a Spanish-speaking babysitter? The child died?

I'm sorry if I'm upsetting you. But there's nothing I can do about it. I'm upset myself. I still cringe when I look at the service elevator door. I still recall my sinking stomach as I listened to the service elevator ascend the shaft, going click click click as it passed each floor, bringing Jesse's voice closer to us, bringing him within hearing range first of Eluisa's cackle and then my beseeching whisper. As it passed us again on its way down, giving me only the briefest glimpse of my son in his helmet. In his cape. In a fantasy world so impenetrable that he hardly seemed to register I was back when, after what seemed like hours of desperate tapping at the elevator window every time he passed, he came to a stop at our floor, and I opened the door, and the 'safety' gates, and tried to take him in my arms. Only to have him prod me with his laser sword and shout, 'Halt, intruder!'

'¡*Gracias a Dios!*' was Eluisa's reaction. '¡*Gracias a Dios!*'

As far as I was concerned, that did it.

I eighty-sixed her.

But if I thought I could erase her from our lives as easily as that, I was mistaken. Because the witch had left her poison behind.

I am referring, of course, to the soup.

I did not notice it right away. As I darted breathless and frantic around the apartment, emptying baths, picking up peanuts, restoring safety gates to their rightful positions, throwing away the disgusting aquamarine footbath my mother had given you because I knew I would never be able to look at it again without becoming nauseous, as I tried to erase all trace of her, I could smell something acrid, something halfway between smoke and steam fill the upper reaches of each room, but again, I did not put two and two together.

I thought I was imagining it. Because if you had to come up with a smell that could convey the full extent of my horror every time I opened up a drawer, or looked under a bed, it was that one.

Here are some of the things I discovered that the children said belonged to Eluisa:

Six pairs of silver lamé ballet shoes. Filthy.
One pair filthy stiletto gold lamé sandals.
Five false eyelashes.
One jock strap.
A plastic bag full of half-used candles.
Another plastic bag full of cat food and condensed milk.
Sixty-four prayer cards, all but one in Spanish.
A make-up bag filled with old lipsticks and eleven pairs of nail scissors.

A pile of magazines that had almost all the people's faces cut out of it. This was the woman you later told me was an Evangelist????

I don't know. I didn't know then either. Neither did Jesse.

'What do you think?' Jesse asked me at one point. 'Was she from outer space?'

I didn't know what to tell him. And I didn't know what to make of his sunny California smile. He had the same smile for everything. 'Halt, intruder, I'm pretending to be Dr Who. That's why I'm smiling.

'Oh, hi, Dad. It's you.' Same smile.

Same smile again for Eluisa as Dad hounds her and Joe Bolivia out the door. 'Gosh. That was quick! I thought she was going to be a babysitter for a long time. Well, guess I was wrong! Too bad. She gave us lots of treats. And she was teaching us the numbers in Spanish. Oh well. Maybe one day I'll see her on *Sesame Street*.' Same smile.

'So, Dad,' he says to me as he follows me, smiling, around the apartment, 'how did you like it on that planet? What did you say? Who told me you were on another planet? Mom, of course. Mom said that's why you weren't coming back for a long time. You know, you should have sent us a postcard.' Same smile.

Still smiling. 'Won't you ever give us peanuts, Dad? Not even a teeny weeny one if I stop eating with my mouth open? Not even after I'm six? Look, Dad, you missed one. No, three more peanuts over there. Look. *Uno, dos, tres.* Can you count to three in Spanish?' Still smiling. 'Why not? Didn't your mother teach you how to say *manzana* and *plátano*?' Same smile. 'She didn't? That's amazing.

'That's awesome.

'It's so easy, though. Look, Dad, here. I'm closing the door. That's *cerrada*. Repeat after me. *Cerrada*. Now I'm opening it up again. That's *abierta*. That's good, Dad. Now you know four words you can share with Eluisa. Oh yes, you do. You know *plátano, manzana, abierta* and *cerrada*. You don't think she's coming back? It doesn't matter. You can say it to the new one. All babysitters speak Spanish.'

Same smile. 'Do you still have all that money inside your head? Mom said all that money went to your head. I *didn't*?? You *don't*? Oh good.' Same smile.

Fathers came and went. Mothers metamorphosed and went up in smoke. Spanish-speaking babysitters came, ate peanuts, ran unattended baths, and split so fast they didn't even bother to change out of their disgusting bathrobes. Sisters howled. About everything. It was all in a day's work. I kept looking at Jesse, at his bright white California smile and his large phosphorescent-blue videoscreen eyes and thought: Where is the infant I held in the delivery room? Where is the little face that looked up to me with such sadness and wisdom? What had we done to our perfect child?

Nothing fazed him. Nothing was real. 'Oh, I know that cry,' he said when Maria bit my arm and screamed. 'She wants her bottle.' Bottle? I thought. I thought we had gotten rid of bottles years ago.

'Oh, I know that cry. She is probably angry because you threw away those God cards. She liked to play with them. Eluisa used to read them to her, even though she didn't understand. But you didn't mind, did you, Maria?

'Oh, I know that cry. She's hungry, the poor little thing. She wants to eat.'

'I don't want to go out until your mother comes home,' I told him.

'Oh, we don't have to go out,' Jesse said. 'We can have some of Eluisa's *caldo*.' He looked at me and smiled. 'Can't you smell it?'

This is not the worst part of the story. But it *is* the second worst. I advise you not to read it if you are feeling at all insecure.

The soup was in our biggest Le Creuset pot. You know, the one you never saw again after that day, because I threw it away.

It was bubbling away on the back burner.

It was grotesque.

It had whole, unscraped carrots sticking up out of it like icebergs, and the fat bubbling on the surface was two inches thick. It had a greenish tint to it. Not from parsley but from mould. But that was not the worst of it. The worst of it was that it was full of bones. Jagged chicken bones that looked like strands of meat until they stabbed you in the throat.

This was what our children had been 'living' on? It was all I could do to keep the scream out of my voice. I looked at my son. He was still smiling. 'I'm sorry,' I said to him with all the calm I could muster. 'But I cannot let you or any other human being eat that poison.'

'Eluisa made us *poison* for *caldo*?'

'Yes,' I said.

He looked impressed. 'Pick me up so I can see.'

I did.

'Wow,' he said. 'You're right.'

Maria screamed again. 'We have to eat something, though,' Jesse said. 'My sister's hungry.'

'We'll wait until your mother comes home and then we'll go out somewhere.'

'But she's not going to be back for ages.'

Oh yeah? I wanted to shout. Is that so? Where the fuck is she, anyway? But instead I said, 'Let's look in the fridge and see if we can find something else.'

We were looking through the stinking nightmare of the refrigerator when Jesse remembered something else. 'Something better,' he informed me. 'Something delicious. Something so delicious when you see it you'll start liking Eluisa and be happy she's one of the people in your neighbourhood when she comes back.

'The nice thing about Eluisa,' he continued, 'is that she brings us special treats to make us happy.' He went into the foyer and came back with a carrier bag that I had somehow missed. He reached in and brought out a mason jar stuffed with chocolate éclairs.

Yes, you heard me right. I said chocolate éclairs. After all your ranting and raving about nutrition and health foods, you had left your children in the care of someone who fed them chocolate éclairs. And they weren't even fresh, for God's sake. They had been sitting in the carrier bag all day, maybe all week. The cream wasn't even white any more. It was yellow. Naturally I couldn't let the children eat them. Naturally the children were upset. Especially Maria. When I took the jar away from her, she screamed as if I had chopped her arm off. I tried to pick her up, but she launched into a fully-fledged tantrum.

It was Jesse who thought of a way to calm her down. 'I think I have an idea,' he said. 'I think we could cheer her up with a very special treat.' He smiled at me. 'Watch this,' he said.

He took Maria's hand. 'Maria?' he said, mimicking the falsetto of a condescending adult. 'Would you like me to give you something very special? Something . . . pink?' Maria sniffed. 'You'd like that, wouldn't you? Is that what you'd like? Something nice and round and pink that tastes like candy?' She nodded with a half-smile, then bared her teeth. 'OK, then. I'll get you some. But only if you're quiet. Hear?'

I watched, aghast, as he returned to the canvas carrier bag and fished out a bottle of aspirin.

Yes, you heard me right this time, too. I said aspirin. Not Tylenol. Not acetaminophen. But aspirin. In other words, the substance that gives your children Reyes syndrome if they happen to have the flu. I'm telling you. I could not believe my eyes. I was too shocked to move. I watched aghast as Jesse walked over to Maria and asked her, 'How old are you now, Maria? Two? Or three?'

'Three,' Maria said.

'Three? You're three already? I remember when you were a teeny tiny little baby. You were only *this* big. I never thought you would grow up to be such a *lovely, big, beautiful* girl. Did I?' Maria smiled and shook her head.

'I'm big,' she said. 'I'm three.'

'That's right,' he said. 'You're three. And you know what *that* means, don't you? *That* means you can have *three* lovely little fat pink aspirins! Doesn't it?'

Maria nodded. I myself was too shocked to move.

'Put out your hand then. Put out your hand, you little rascalette.'

I honestly didn't expect him to be able to open the bottle. After all, it had a child-proof cap. But whoever had used it last had not closed it right. Because Jesse was able to open it without any trouble. I'm telling you. I could not believe my eyes. I just stood there staring at him as he pushed his forefinger past the cotton.

'That's the thing that's so nice about Eluisa,' he told me. 'She always gives us aspirin for dessert.'

Extract from Sea Pictures

ALAN BROWNJOHN

One day, nostalgically, in a hidden

Envelope, a man came across a photograph
Of his grandparents paddling from Margate to Ramsgate
Hand-in-hand with his father, the grandmother's left hand
Hanging on to a spade, while grandfather, farthest out,
Exhorts the trio forward through the ripples.
He knew his grandfather was a photographer
By those sepia pictures in the envelope
Hidden in a personal drawer; and yet he must
Have that day leased the camera to someone else
To take this picture, there has to be another
To capture those ancient people, and that girl.
In 1907 you were not supposed

34

To move an inch, a fraction, especially ladies:
Photographs were a posed phenomenon,
And these three relations strolling the tideline foam
Eighty years ago had managed to hold the pose,
The boy's disconsolate look, grandfather's look,
And the movement of their ankles and their shins
Through the ridges of the incoming wet.
So they all slosh through a gentle undertow
Out of their early century, moving on
To assume their immortality somewhere else;
And grandfather gets a picture of the girl.
The grandmother's face in all these photographs

SEA PICTURES

35

Is the indulgence of her husband's whim
Of trapping into a box the garden scenes,
The family groups, the walkers breasting tapes,
And the impending sea storms, lots of those,
Even though the very moment a lens cap
Is back in place, and the camera stored away,
The sunlit poses are turning sepia.
Photographs watch and watch the changes caused
By time, and trace them happening as surely
As the hour hand on the clock can be seen to move
If you follow it with sufficient concentration.
One night in a landlocked country, the owner of

36

A camera waits for the orange light to gleam
To tell him he can use the flash. He stands
In a city in a distant mountain province
Where the sea is rarely invoked in metaphor,
But where his inherited disposition
(A grandfather's whim) removes a lens cap in
A snow-filled street, and a woman in furs, in seconds,
Turns round on the ice, and balances, and smiles in the dark:
A set of images dangerous to put
In a hidden envelope found in the morning post;
And the smile and the darkness are both permanent.
The woman on the sundeck would have taken

37

A photograph of the single bicycle's tracks,
Inexplicable to walking families,
Who might grasp footprints or even horses' hoofs,
But can't see people ever *cycling* here,
Let alone applying the brakes to stop
And watch a ferry pass, as the man does now,

ALAN BROWNJOHN

A prince at a ruined castle and some initials
Attaching to a girl by Lake Balaton,
Remembering a dog on a Black Sea strand
Unchained by death, and pausing here for breath
Before he jogs towards the one seagull rock.
When they stop looking, the man and the woman

38

With their boot full of blackberries on the clifftop
Whose living dog gazes out between the bars,
The cyclist stops, with less than the certainty
Of someone who has cycled before today,
And more with the insecurity of someone
Who has rarely achieved a balance on his ride,
And is glad to be getting one foot firmly down
On the sand, and the other down beside it, and lean
On the handles of the vehicle, and keep
The twangling instrument upright while he stares,
While he stares far out to sea at the fixed clouds.
He is *all the daughters of his father's house*

39

And all the . . . He sees boys who write initials
Where only the waves will come across them
Grow into lovers bargaining on sundecks,
Losing their lens caps in Hungarian snow,
And turning round from clifftops to where the broughams
Have changed into hearses. Now I've reached the end
Of its interlacing tracks, I hold the bicycle
Cleverly upright with one steadying hand,
And space my feet for balance, and watch the sea:
The clouds, having settled where to rest, will not
Be moving again for the rest of the still day,
The waters have become an off-blue curtain

SEA PICTURES

40

Let down by the horizon, and behind
This fabric something impels it, sways it . . .
The tide smooths down its shifting folds and layers
To touch me only as a small grey hem
Criss-crossing against the wheel I point at it,
And turning over into colourless,
Amenable ripples; but the wider air,
A huger, superseding element,
Fills everything with its roar, I can't make out
One wave or breeze to listen to for itself
In the general outcry, where I now observe
The boat sail out of sight, to vast applause.

Doctor in the House

A. ALVAREZ

Twenty-two years ago, when my wife was expecting our first child, we bought a house in Flask Walk in Hampstead. It is a narrow, white-faced, square-windowed building on three floors, built around 1770, with a semi-basement at the rear and a small garden front and back, and it was badly run-down when we bought it. But we had the place painted and gussied up, central heating put in and a downstairs dividing wall taken out to make a drawing-room. We also built a two-storey addition on to the back of the house: a kitchen and dining-room below, a bathroom and a study for my wife above. But, because we did not want to spoil the atmosphere of the place, we made no attempt to straighten the bulging panels and crazily-angled floor in the hall.

Twenty years and two children later, the house was warmer but almost as run-down as when we first moved in. Every so often we called in two amiable Irishmen, Jimmy the Painter and his boozy cousin, who lashed about indiscriminately with brushfuls of white paint. But the cousin had grown drunker and more indiscriminate over the years, until the mess he made balanced out the fresh paint and it no longer seemed worthwhile to pay good money merely to break even. So the paintwork chipped and yellowed, the panels cracked in the heat, and every month my wife would say, 'We've got to do something about it.'

Yet it was my wife who was preventing us redecorating. She is a child psychotherapist, the semi-basement is her consulting room, and the rules of her curious profession state that patients must be spared the details of their therapist's private life. Of all details, decorating is the least deniable.

We found the solution to our problem living around the corner a hundred yards away. John Williamson is a short, compact man in his middle fifties. He has white hair, a white beard and a lively mind, and he is court painter and builder to Hampstead village. Like me, he works on his own, and I got to know him because – also like me – he is always around. At first, we nodded to each other, then we said hello, then we stopped and chatted. When he mentioned that he was interested in rock climbing, I took him off to an outcrop south of London where he struggled and dangled and cursed and seemed to enjoy himself. At the

237

end of this devious courtship, he agreed to slot us into his very full timetable, partly out of friendship, partly because he is full of intellectual curiosity: he was intrigued by the idea of fitting his own work around my wife's. Hampstead has plenty of eccentrics but, for him, a steady procession of disturbed children would be a first.

We went away for a week while he started on the drawing-room and when we got back we realised the benefit of using a builder who understood the idiosyncrasies of these old Hampstead houses. Some of the walls are panelled and one of the largest panels had cracked and caved-in on one side. John had literally fished out the edge of the panel – he used fish hooks and string – packed it from below and glued it. He also discovered a whole wall of panelling that had been covered up a century ago with a kind of glorified cardboard. The room was not simply redecorated, it was transformed. Uneven, crumbling areas of wall had been stripped and replastered, cracked door panels filled, edges sharpened, details clarified. It was not just a question of new wallpaper and fresh paint, although there was plenty of both; it was more like the refitting of an old ship for an ocean voyage. The whole structure felt sounder, trimmer, more likely to weather the next decade or two of abuse.

John then moved to the top of the staircase and began slowly to work his way down, 'making good' as he came. When he stripped away our old William Morris wallpaper he found walls that were crumbling away, wood that was cracked and rotting. He ripped off the worn carpet and discovered that the risers of the eighteenth-century stairs were sagging and broken. Without carpets, the stairwell was like a loudspeaker, amplifying his hammering and scraping and unexpectedly tuneful singing. Every so often he would call me down from my study at the top of the house to show me some fresh marvel of Georgian jerry-building – a stair or a section of wall patched together from whatever odds and ends of wood the builder happened to have at hand two centuries ago, and still miraculously in place. 'Always been cowboys in this trade,' he announced. 'If I tried that on, the district surveyor would string me up by my bleeding thumbs.' I now understood why the staircase had shifted and creaked when we thundered up and down it, and why the ceiling below had consistently disintegrated no matter how often it was replastered.

There were places, however, where even John's nerve failed: an ominous bulge in a landing wall, for instance, which he tapped and probed and finally said, 'Strip that away and God knows what we'll find.' But there were other bulges that he cut away without hesitation, knowing they contained nothing he couldn't cope with, and others still that he insisted we leave be for aesthetic reasons. 'It's like an old lady,' he said. 'Take away the bulges and she won't be the same.' It was as though he and the house had some kind of secret understanding, like a sympathetic doctor with a truculent old patient.

He had reckoned the work would take him four to six weeks. Naturally, it took three months, and by the end John had become part of the family. He is a man who likes to talk and at first he was put out to find there were times and places (namely, downstairs when my wife had patients) when talking wasn't allowed. Each morning, while my wife was seeing her early patient and I was drinking coffee in the kitchen above her consulting room, he would tiptoe in like Sebastian the Cat and launch into an elaborate pantomime that became wilder and more unbuttoned as the weeks went by. Even so, he obeyed the crazy rules and didn't actually speak – to his surprise, I suspect, as much as to ours. Later in the day, he and my wife would chat together over tea and biscuits, and in the evening we would all have a drink and admire the day's progress. He would fill us in on local gossip, but mostly he talked about our house, about how it was responding to treatment, about his diagnosis of the latest ailment and his general prognosis of the patients' health. I had been raised in a family with two older sisters; now I began to discover belatedly what it must be like to have a lively kid brother with a passion for fixing things.

Oddly enough, all three of us were enjoying ourselves, although it seemed as if the house would never be right again, the chaos would never end. In the garden the snowdrops came and went, then the crocuses appeared, vivid splinters of colour in the dank air. John sanded and smoothed and plastered and hammered, and the dust sifted down through the echoing house, coating the furniture, filling the air, filling our lives. Then one day he stopped banging and began to sing in a slightly abstracted way, as though his mind were on something else entirely. Within a week, the ceilings were painted, then the dados, the banisters, finally the hall itself. Order was emerging from chaos, after all. Then John appeared with a collapsible table and slowly, meticulously, the wallpaper went up. Then the carpeting firm arrived, the echoes ceased, the house was finished. We drank together in celebration, we toasted John's labour and skill, we toasted the house and its resurrection. We put a record on the hi-fi and John, who is a jazz buff, sang along with Charlie Parker, passionately blowing into an imaginary saxophone. When he finally left to practise his magic elsewhere, I felt the family was diminished – despite his bill.

One Yellow Chicken

HELEN DUNMORE

One yellow chicken
she picks up expertly and not untenderly
from the fragile stir of the chickens,

its soft beak gobbles feverishly
at a clear liquid which may be
a dose of sugar-drenched serum,

the beak's flexible brown membrane
seems to engulf the chicken
as it tries to fix on the dropper's glass tip.

Clear yellow juice gulps through the tube
and a few drops, suddenly colourless,
swill round a gape wide as the brim of a glass,

but the chicken doesn't seem afraid,
or only this much, only for this long
until the lab assistant flicks it back on
to the slowly-moving conveyor of chickens

and it tumbles, catches itself,
then buoyed up by the rest
reels out of sight, cheeping.

" Here's your problem pal.....
an anchovy in the distributor. "

Lesson of the Master

JOHN FULLER

His vision was titanic: the little we enact
Of comic calamity is at his whim,
Every misunderstanding, lack of tact,
Miraculous obtuseness, foretold by him.

Here are the maps of transatlantic drift
And dangerous friendship; the calculated stealth
Of evil, where culture is power and the gift
Of beauty a disaster, like ill-health.

He knew, as we do, how the physical
Acquires significance from our attention to it:
The wet boot held towards the fire, the full
Black hair. We come to see his meaning through it.

Fiction for him was, as for God, like playing
With the helpless questors of Eden. His face the face
Of Mrs Assingham, or Mrs Tristram saying,
'I should like to put you in a difficult place.'

If a charming vulgarian intended to strike
Some bargain with a snob, he would insist,
'You say you are civilised? Very well. I should like
To make you prove it.' He was an empiricist.

If pleasure beckoned, we could never follow.
If ghosts should appear behind the protective glass,
They too would prove our conversations hollow
And, like desire, would never come to pass.

JOHN FULLER

Innocence is always shocking. It resembles
A clumsiness to which our heart goes out.
And we are stupefied. The hand trembles.
It is, we suppose, what love is all about.

Surely we realise that we have lost,
Way back, the path that might have led to joy?
Behind us is a threshold we have crossed;
Before us, other simpler lives we must destroy.

For after all, his humour comes down to this:
Betrayal is licensed by Bradshaw, and the sexed
Admirer foreshortens his future with a kiss
That leads, alas, to the closure of the text.

Marion and James Clapp, in the late thirties

Marion and Norman King, fifty years later

Reader, I Married Them

SUSANNAH CLAPP

Three years ago, after forty-six years of marriage, my mother became a widow. A year later, at the age of seventy-four, she took a second husband and became a second wife. Her marriages have both been happy ones – 'equally happy' in her opinion. Her second wedding did not involve a break with her past but an adjustment, a repatterning of her memories. I have known my stepfather all my life; my mother has known him for over fifty years.

They first met in 1936, on a boat going to Russia. My mother had graduated in classics and was about to go to work in a corset factory, leaving the West Country for the East End of London. My stepfather, a would-be architect turned designer, was living on Shadwell Basin opposite the Prospect of Whitby, and working in advertising: he was paid £7 a week; the three-week trip cost £21. My mother wore a side parting, strappy shoes, and a cotton dress in French blue with a frill neck and diagonal fastening; my stepfather sported Donegal tweeds and a fob watch. They were both members of the Labour Party, who were to become – and unbecome – Communists.

Out of Hay's Wharf, the Soviet captain mooched about in a cloth cap and tattered coat – though he dressed up to go saluting through the Kiel Canal. The crew of comrades, worried that the boat wasn't moving quickly enough, sent it round in circles for two days while they took equal turns at dismantling the engine – and the passengers bought tots of vodka for 4d.

On the train to Moscow, Tartars hacked alarmingly at their lunch with huge knives. In the city, the guests baked in heat, and dined every day on chicken and stewed fruit. My stepfather, visiting friends in an apartment block, was faced with a set of doors sealed after a visit from the KGB; my mother was taken to admire the people's parks, but thought it a pity for the people that they were so gravelly.

They chatted to a future minister of agriculture, and to a Richmond bookseller with very long nails, and they chatted up each other. But my stepfather also fell for a dainty art-teacher. She had fine fair hair and clothes bought, on principle, from Woolworth's. She was the group leader, a dispenser of comradely treats, such as trips inside the Kremlin; and she married my stepfather.

READER, I MARRIED THEM

And my mother married my father. He had appeared at a meeting of the National Organisation of Unemployed Workers in Bath – a dark chap with over-length hair and a terrible overcoat; my mother assumed he was one of the unemployed workers. This was at a time when Henry Moore and Eric Gill were coming to the Propaganda Art Centre that my stepfather helped to run in the East End; a time when it was, he claims, easy to fill halls in Wapping by advertising lectures on dialectical materialism. Even the golden streets of England's most sedately seductive city had contained processions of hunger marchers.

As far as his family was concerned, my father might as well have been jobless: he was banned from driving the family car, not because he was dangerous, which he was, but because reading books wasn't proper work. He was a teacher in a family of farmers, a thin boy with sturdy siblings, a pupil who set himself to win scholarships – the only one ever from his village school to grammar school – because he hated cold farmhouses, butter-churning, and being kicked by cows. Like many loquacious men, he was a stammerer. The elocution lessons he had attended to cure his stutters had wiped out his family burr – the Bristolian elisions which create a new vocabulary, making a looking-glass a 'myrrh' – and he worried that he sounded like a parson. He was anxious and romantic, tender-hearted and absent-minded.

And he was very impractical. My stepfather – an ex-soldier and the son of a tailor – can turn his own shirt collars and make teas fit for a vicarage; my father's notion of domesticity was using his pyjamas as a tea cosy. My father spent forty years helping schoolchildren to put the right verbs in their sentences; my stepfather – a designer of logos, a sketcher and cherisher of cornices and architraves – is, like most visual people, a bad speller, who likes his *Pocket Gem Dictionary* at his side when writing a letter. My father was untidy and soft-spoken; my stepfather is a dandy and hot-tempered. My mother has acknowledged these differences by burning more saucepans and using more words in her second marriage than in her first.

During the war my stepfather became a Desert Rat and lectured to his regiment on the importance of the Russian Front. My father taught and firewatched in Bath, seeing the city's hills blaze under the unexpected blitz, shepherding evacuees into his school, and later laying out their bodies in the bombed playground.

After the war each couple symmetrically sprouted one child – a boy and a girl. There were joint picnics, and visits at Christmas, teas in the garden, and encounters on Aldermaston Marches. When, in their seventies, my parents decided to leave the suburbs, they chose not Bournemouth but King's Cross, and settled ten minutes away from my stepfather's house.

They moved at a time when greenness seemed about to creep over the area. There were fewer prostitutes under the arches; there were bicycles and window boxes in the tenement blocks. At the back of the station, overlooked by two huge gas-holders, a small wild park was created by the GLC – a park which is likely soon to be destroyed by developers. It has a pool with minnows in it; it has cowslips and borage and a kingfisher. Through the trees pokes the red and white tower of St Pancras. My father, the reluctant countryman, liked to go to this park, and went there with my mother on a sunny day in August 1986: it was the day before he died. She photographed him sitting in the long grass; he told her that he was happier than he had been for years.

My mother took to her bed for a time; she retired into herself for longer. But she never did what agony aunts described as 'letting oneself go'. She didn't stop going to the hairdresser, and she didn't stop buying new clothes. On her first serious shopping expedition, she belted herself into a black shiny mac with a yellow lining – and was pursued through Russell Square by an unknown man asking eagerly, 'Are you an artist?'

He was not her only follower. A few weeks after my father died, my stepfather became a widower. He and my mother sat together in the evenings, watched *EastEnders* and talked about their partners and their politics. Outings were proposed, meetings jointly attended, his blue Lada was as often as not outside her flat. But the real breakthrough came in the New Year. My mother wanted to go to the Chinese New Year Lion Dance in Soho, and she didn't want to go alone. I couldn't go with her, and suggested she summon her escort. She hesitated; I pressed; he responded with enthusiasm, 'At last I feel I'm getting somewhere.'

He was. A couple of months after the Lion Dance, a Bath schoolteacher was stunned to see my father's widow strolling through the streets of the city arm in arm with Another Man. A month later my mother and I walked through an exhibition of maps at the British Museum talking about her engagement. Three months on, she had sold her flat and most of her furniture and was giggling her way through a registry office service in Finsbury Town Hall.

Most friends were enthusiastic about my mother's new arrangements – and fell to wondering which of the people they'd known when they were twenty-four might end up by their side at seventy-four. But Gertrude has given remarriage a bad name: there were those who expected me to behave like Hamlet. There were fathers who, scenting the possibility of being replaced in the future, looked wistful on their own account. There were women who gazed at me with compassion, sure that I was nursing a secret grief. 'Don't you *really* mind?'

I didn't mind. I was pleased. I was pleased for my mother, who was full of beams and bustle. And I was pleased for me. I couldn't rise to the sense of betrayal which was being pressed upon me. I didn't believe in it. For one thing, my mother hadn't done a straight swap. In her first marriage she was an artistic and practical woman married to a man who was full of words. Married to a practical artist, she has demonstrated her verbal acuity — and become slightly less organised. For another thing, I like my stepfather. My mother knew she was on safe ground when, in answer to a query of my stepfather's, she gave a composed and frank reply, the kind of response which has earned her the title 'the duchess'.

'What would you do if your daughter objected to our marrying?' my stepfather asked her.

'I'd find out if she had a particular reason for disapproving of you,' said the rational woman. 'If she knew that you beat women, for example. If it turned out that that wasn't the case, that it was just that she didn't like you — well, we wouldn't see much of her.'

But they do see a lot of me, as they do of the rest of their past. On the wall of their house is a photograph, taken forty years ago in their small back garden. It shows two women, each holding a baby. One baby is looking plaintive and interesting and has a full head of hair. The other baby is hairless, gurgling, and seems to be making a pass at its contemporary. The two women are my stepfather's two wives. The plaintive baby is my stepbrother. I am the bald one.

Echolocation

STEPHEN AMIDON

Henry Keating was late getting home. He had worked detention duty at his school, two hours of keeping surly students with torn jeans and heavy metal T-shirts in their cafeteria seats, trying to be patient as they swore beneath their breaths or snapped pencils. By the time he returned to his townhouse it was nearly dark and he had lost his usual parking place. He was forced to park at the far end of the complex, near the colony of overflowing dumpsters. Henry hated parking here. The reeking green boxes, lit only by a flickering street light, always seemed to be besieged by dogs and raucous birds. They were emptied only sporadically, with violent slams that would shock him upright in bed at four in the morning. Henry made his wife take out the trash, even on nights she worked overtime.

After checking that all four doors of his car were locked, Henry buried his mouth and nose in his coat collar and walked quickly by the dumpsters. He was just clear of them when he heard the voice. A child's voice, tinny and echoed. Henry stopped and looked around. There was a moment's silence. Then, the voice. 'OK, you guys. No joke. Tommy? Listen up.'

It came from within the nearest dumpster. Henry approached it. The door was wedged shut with a rusted exhaust pipe. 'No joke, you guys.'

Henry removed the pipe, careful not to cut his hand. He pulled the door open. In the pulsing sodium light he could see a young boy, no more than eight years old, sitting on a bag of garbage. 'What are you doing in here?' Henry asked in his teacher's voice.

'What am I doing in here?' the boy repeated, blinking at the wan light.

'I mean . . . what's going on?'

'I'm in here is what.'

Henry held out his hands. The boy stood, allowing Henry to grab him under the armpits and lift him through the door. He brushed some coffee grounds from his clothes, then kicked the dumpster ferociously.

'Who put you in there?' Henry asked. 'How long have you been here? Who are you?'

The boy stared at him. His lower lip seemed to quiver. Henry reached out, touching him reassuringly on the shoulder. The boy lunged forward, poking

Henry's chest with a claw-stiff hand. Henry could see that he wasn't crying, but smiling. 'Now you're it!' he sang, before racing off. 'Sucker!'

Henry found a solitary letter on the hallway's polished floor when he shouldered open his front door. Familiar handwriting on the envelope froze him in the threshold. It was from his father. Henry squatted near the letter for several seconds, examining it without touching it. There was a North Carolina postmark but no return address. His wife walked in through the still-open door. She had to perform a small hop to keep from stepping on his outstretched hand.

'What?' she asked.

'From my father.'

'Your father.'

They stared at it for a moment, then she told him to go ahead and open it. It was a short letter, just a few lines, inviting him to come visit. Any time. No explanation, no news. Just an invitation, written on a torn segment of gridded computer paper. On the bottom of the page was a hand-drawn map, showing how to get to the house from the regional airport. He appeared to live in a sparsely populated area. He described his home's location physically, giving no address. Nor was there a phone number. Henry gave the letter to his wife to read. She handed it back to him.

'I guess you'd better go, don't you think?' she said, looping her limp hair behind her ear, like she did.

Henry looked at the letter again. It had been eleven years since he had heard from Henry Sr., who had vanished after announcing one evening that he was going on a business trip. All he took with him was a suitcase and a paperback. No mementoes or personal papers, not even the leather briefcase the family had given him the previous Christmas. A few days later a man from the US Attorney's office came to explain that Henry Sr., a patent lawyer, was a key witness in a big sweep against organised patent fraud. He was going to be out of touch for a while. There was no real danger, he claimed, but there were people involved in the case who might try to 'influence' him. Henry remembered that the man had dense hair coming out of his ears, but when his pants rode above his socks, his shins were waxy and hairless. The man didn't know when Henry Sr. would be able to return home but said that they would soon be able to speak with him by phone. Yet he never called. Never wrote or sent word. A police car passed the house every hour, and Henry and his sister were driven to school by two black men in an LTD. They stopped abruptly after a few weeks, claiming that Henry Sr. should be able to return within a year. But he never did.

At first, Henry had suspected that his mother knew where he was, that her pained silence was merely discretion. But by the time she died of cancer five years later he knew that she was just as much in the dark as he. The only contact with Henry Sr. was the monthly cheques, drawn on a bank in Washington and signed in his meticulous hand. Twice Henry had travelled to DC to enquire at the bank, scour the phone book and bother the authorities. But that was in the early days, during summer breaks from college. He had long since given up trying to find out.

Much had happened to Henry since his father's disappearance. He had finished high school, lettering in cross-country and serving as vice-president of the History Club. He had delayed entering college for a year to back-pack through Europe, but came home after two months to spend the rest of the year as a night manager at Swensen's. He had attended Rutgers, taken a position teaching high school, married a paralegal he met at a Bicentennial party, lost a child to late miscarriage. He broke his arm on a bicycling trip in the Catskills, then had it rebroken when it didn't set properly. He had learned about money, real estate and job politics. And, gradually, he had stopped thinking about his father.

Henry folded the letter back in the envelope.

'Yes,' he said. 'I think I better.'

He waited three days before setting out so that he could finish grading final exams. He decided to drive, since school was over and he had no firm plans for the summer. Having a car would enable him to make a quick exit. He left before dawn on a Sunday morning, borrowing his wife's Volvo for the cruise control. He drove I-95 nearly all the way, stopping to top off the tank at the Vince Lombardi service area and later for lunch at a Stuckey's in Virginia.

He tried to think about his father as he drove. It was difficult – he had to actively retrieve the fading images, the scattered information. He recalled a painstaking, reserved man who seemed to have to think for a moment before laughing or growing angry. A man who tore all the postcard advertisements from a magazine before reading it. A man whose favourite saying was 'Take your time, do it right'. As he was growing up, Henry believed this caution to be the key to his father's character. His identity. Henry Keating Sr. – a cautious man. At the time, this readily explained his blowing the whistle on his colleagues, his going into hiding. Yet, in light of it, his failure to contact his family made no sense. Even if he were still afraid, Henry thought, he should at least have called or written an explanation. But there was nothing. Nothing. Henry could never understand that.

ECHOLOCATION

When, below Petersburg, he passed a billboard that advertised tours through a system of caverns, Henry was struck by another forgotten incident – visiting the caves with his family when he was nine. They were returning from an exhausting vacation in Florida, tormented by residual sand and peeling skin. Only his father wanted to stop. His mother and Beth petulantly stayed in the car. Henry wanted to remain with them, but his father insisted he come along. There were about twenty others on the tour, mostly travelling families. At the caves' mouth, Henry and his father were given a small plastic flashlight and told to keep close. The guide was a middle-aged black man with wire-rim glasses. He smelt of the same after-shave that Henry Sr. wore.

The tour moved through the caverns along a path lit by strings of naked bulbs. The guard stopped often, explaining in a softly echoing voice the difference between stalactites and stalagmites, showing the nooks where runaway slaves or Confederate raiders had hidden, inviting them to touch the cool waters of underground streams. After about fifteen minutes Henry felt his father's hand on his shoulder.

'We wait here,' he whispered.

Henry watched with growing fear as the group moved around the next corner. His father's grip was firm.

'Follow me,' Henry Sr. said when they were on their own.

'But Dad . . .'

'Do as you're told, Hank.'

He led him down an ancillary corridor, lit only by widely spaced floor lanterns that gave off pale, sinking light. A few times, their flashlight illumined thin, deep crevices which they had to hop over. They twice ducked beneath strings that held 'No Entry' placards. The walls gleamed with slimy water. Henry Sr. stopped when they came to a junction.

'Dad . . .' Henry pleaded.

'Quiet,' his father said, cocking his head to listen. After several seconds he nodded down the left corridor. 'This way.'

They walked a hundred feet. His father stopped, again cocking his head. 'OK. In here.'

He led him through a brief, low passage, turning out the flashlight before they reached the end. He had to stoop, though Henry could walk upright. They entered a dark room, recoiling at the sharp sulphuric stink. Henry sensed great space but couldn't be sure. It seemed as if the air were humming, like an idling machine ready to trip into action. He waited for his father to switch on his flashlight.

258

'Go ahead,' Henry Sr. said, keeping them in darkness.

'Where?'

'Walk in.'

'Dad . . .'

'Do it, Hank.'

'You come too.'

'Do what you're told.'

Something in his father's voice made Henry step into the cave. The ground was layered in small, slick steppes. He walked slowly, his arms outstretched, feeling for some resistance. Yet there was only the strange humming that seemed to by-pass his hearing to connect directly with his muscles and nerves. He stopped after a few steps.

'Is this O K?' he asked in a small voice.

'Further,' Henry Sr. said.

He walked a dozen or more steps. The humming grew more intense.

'I'm coming back now, Dad.'

'All right,' he said. 'Head toward my voice.'

Yet Henry had moved so far in that the voice echoed confusingly around him. He walked in one direction, then another.

'I'm lost, Dad.'

There was a long silence. For an instant, he suspected that he'd been left on his own.

'All right,' his father said eventually. 'Look for the light, then.'

The light flared on, a blood-red glow. Henry Sr. had cupped his palm over the end. As Henry walked towards it, he could see the bones and veins in his father's hand. He could also hear that his father's breath was as rapid as his.

'Look, Hank,' he said. He removed his hand from the flashlight and let the beam play around the cave. It wasn't that large at all, no bigger than his school gym. What seemed to be an infinity of small black stalactites covered the roof. Henry was about to ask what they were when the strange hum gave way to the frantic flutter of wings as the bats scattered to avoid the painful light.

It was dusk when Henry arrived in the county where his father lived, a sparsely-populated rectangle in the north-central section of the state. The landscape was a succession of sunscorched tobacco fields, cow pastures and dense clusters of pine. Paint-chipped shacks and billboards, some of them faceless, lined the road. Once he saw a prison work-gang ripping brush from a gulley. No one seemed to be guarding them. Occasionally, set back from the road, there were squat, windowless modern buildings surrounded by security fences. Their signs murmured names like 'Zytex' and 'CZB Industries'. Henry had to abandon the cruise control here – the roads were too winding.

He hit the dog as he neared his father's property. He saw it cross his path several hundred feet ahead, but let the brake go when it reached the other side of the road. It stopped upon noticing him, however, looking directly at the windshield, its ears pricked, its left-front leg elevated. When the car was less than fifty feet away it bounded back into the road, ears back, running straight for him. Henry swerved only slightly for fear of going into a skid. The edge of his bumper clipped the dog's hindquarters. He looked in his side mirror as he pulled over to the soft shoulder to see the dog spinning on the pavement. He reversed, then got out of his car. The dog was on its feet now, turning tight circles as it frantically licked the spot where it had been struck. It was a mongrel, with some sort of hound predominant. Henry watched it collapse on the shoulder, its sides heaving.

He found a milk-coloured section of tarp in the weeds by the side of the road, which he gradually worked beneath the dog. It watched him but made no effort to co-operate or resist. It was breathing with long sighs now, reminding Henry of the way his grandfather used to snore as he slumped in front of the television. He opened the trunk and, with great difficulty, lifted the dog into it by clutching the edges of the tarp. He closed the hood on to the latch and drove off slowly towards his father's house. The entrance was only a hundred yards away.

The driveway was a long, pot-holed dirt road that snaked through pine trees. One side sloped into a small gulley littered with rusting appliances and ruptured trash bags. Yellowed 'No Trespassing' signs were affixed high on stripped trunks, having grown far above eye-level. Henry had to manoeuvre slowly to straddle the drive's deeper holes. Each time he miscalculated he could hear the dog whimper.

The drive eventually opened into an expanse of thin grass that surrounded a double-wide trailer-home resting on cinder blocks. To one side of it was a padlocked corrugated shed. To the other was a satellite dish, about twelve feet in diameter, perched on an aluminium tripod that elevated it above the home's roof. A powder-blue pick-up truck was parked near the woods. Electric and telephone cables swooped in from the forest behind the house. The yard was littered with unsurprising garbage – food wrappers, flattened cans, sodden newspapers. Henry pulled as close to the front door as he could. He set the emergency brake, then walked quickly to the trunk. The dog was still alive, sighing occasionally in its milk-coloured shroud. Blood now smeared the plastic. Henry wasn't sure what to do. He heard the screen door slam and looked up to see his father standing above him.

He was wearing a beige terrycloth robe, open to the waist, exposing a bump of a gut that hadn't been there eleven years earlier. His face seemed fleshier too, the brown eyes sunken a bit, the small chin doubled. His unkempt brown hair was longer and thinner, but not grey. He leaned on a crutch beneath his right arm.

'Hello, Hank,' he said tonelessly, using the nickname Henry hadn't heard in eleven years. 'Need some help with your stuff?'

Henry noticed that his tongue was black.

'You'd better look at this,' he said.

His father hobbled down the three steps, keeping his right knee straight. They looked in the trunk for a moment. Henry Sr. pulled back an edge of the plastic to get a better view, then replaced it.

'That's my dog,' he said, his voice still toneless. 'Where'd you find him?'

'Out on the road. Not far from here.'

'Did you see who got him?'

Henry looked at the dog as he shook his head.

'Ah well,' Henry Sr. said, 'I only had him to bark if anybody came up the drive. Let's take him around the back to die.'

Henry shook the plastic gently. 'I think he already has.'

Henry Sr. bent closer. 'So he has.'

They buried it at the edge of the woods behind the trailer. They worked in silence, with Henry digging a shallow grave while his father wrapped the tarp tightly around the corpse with black electrical tape. Henry was glad for the work – it somehow removed the awkwardness from their meeting, focusing it on an intermediary object. It was dark when they finished. They went into the trailer by the back door, passing through a small kitchen and a hallway panelled with simulated wood. The main room contained a small wet bar, a tatty sofa, several stuffed chairs and a large television set. There was also a stereo and a glass table covered with ring-shaped stains and worn magazines. *Playboy*, *Popular Mechanics*, *Scientific American*. A floor-to-ceiling bookshelf covered one wall. In the far corner there was a card table which held a computer, a phone, and stacks of stuffed manilla folders. Track lights flared on.

'Wanna drink?' Henry Sr. asked from the doorway. 'Beer, for instance?'

'Beer,' Henry said. 'Sure.'

As his father hobbled to the wet bar, Henry looked at the books. Most were duplicates of those in Henry Sr.'s old home library – purple and blue collections of patent laws, technical manuals, Mimeographed specifications bound in ring notebooks. In a bottom corner he noticed different books, a cluster of biographies and memoirs. Howard Hughes. Elvis. J. D. Salinger. Hess. Boëthius. Thomas Merton.

'Take a seat,' his father said, handing him a beer in a tall glass. He held a similar glass, topped with blackish wine. Henry sat on the edge of a stuffed chair, careful not to spill his drink. Henry Sr. sprawled on the couch, his slightly bowed legs jutting from his loosening robe. A few drops spilled from his glass, disappearing into the terrycloth.

'So. Here you are.'

Henry nodded impatiently, making a show of waiting for his father to speak.

'Wanna watch some TV?' Henry Sr. asked, fishing a remote control panel from between the cushions.

'We really don't do that, Dad.'

He nodded once, swinging the panel, pendulum-like. 'So how was your trip?'

'Long,' Henry said. 'But Carol's Volvo makes it easy. Cruise control.'

'Who's Carol?'

'My wife.'

Henry Sr. nodded noncommitally. 'You have kids?'

Henry shook his head.

'How about your sister?'

'What, kids, or married?'

'Both.'

'Neither.'

There was a long silence.

'Do you know about Mom?' Henry asked, making a show of controlling his bitterness.

Henry Sr. looked out the door. Giant mosquitoes clicked against the screen. 'Yes, I do, Hank. That's the one thing I do know about.'

Henry took his first sip of beer.

'So what do you do to make a buck?' his father asked.

'I teach high school.'

'Really? What subject?'

'History. Twentieth-century American.'

Henry Sr.'s eyes widened. 'What, Sacco and Vanzetti? The Black Sox scandal? Tailgunner Joe McCarthy? Leopold and Loeb? Lee Harvey's lost years?' He leaned closer. 'Elvis's midnight drug flights? My Lai? Gerald A. K. Smith?'

'Well, those things, too. I usually try to keep a bit more to the beaten path.'

There was a long silence.

'It's ironic,' Henry Sr. said, looking at the blank television screen, 'but I've been doing some reading about history myself. I find myself speculating about what life would be like if certain key events had happened differently. Like if Hitler had been assassinated before the war. Or, conversely, if Kennedy hadn't been assassinated. Do you ever teach these sort of thoughts?'

Henry gave a short laugh. 'Not really.'

'You should, though, Hank.'

'And what sort of conclusions have you reached?' Henry asked with a vague smile.

Henry Sr. shrugged. 'Mostly that things would be the same. That things have a habit of coming to a head, to a junction, no matter what happens on the way. I mean, Grant and Lee were gonna have it out, if not at Gettysburg, then at Harrisburg or Terre Haute or in, well, wherever. Don't you think?'

Henry spread his hands to indicate he had no answer. There was another long silence.

'Are you sure you don't want to watch some television, Hank? I get sixty channels with this dish.'

They watched a kick-boxing match on ESPN. Henry continued to maintain a distant, expectant silence. After the match ended in controversy from a low kick, Henry Sr. limped to the kitchen and put two Cornish game hens in the oven. He also microwaved two potatoes and a plastic pouch of oriental-style vegetables. He offered Henry a glass of the blackish wine, which he explained he made from kits he bought at K-Mart. Henry took an experimental sip. He recoiled, wiping the black film from his lips.

'Can I have another beer?' he said hoarsely, handing back the glass.

As they ate Henry Sr. explained the details of his case. It had begun when he accidentally uncovered evidence of a plot within his firm to defraud the Pentagon by falsifying patents. He worked on his own for over two months putting together evidence. He described the series of midnight arrests on the night he disappeared, how he'd spent three months in a motor lodge not far from the house, how they'd settled him in Puerto Rico for two years before moving him to North Carolina. His voice was impassive as he told his story, as if he were relating the plot of a movie he'd seen the previous night. 'They made me start working for my money after they moved me here, the bastards. That's what all this is,' he said, gesturing with a half-eaten hen leg to the books and the computer.

'What do you do?' Henry asked.

'Investigate patents pending for fraud and so forth. I rarely find anything, though. I make a lot of mistakes. I skip pages. I don't follow leads. No one checks my work. No one seems to care.'

Henry gave his plate a short, sharp push away from him. He plucked the paper towel from his lap, wiped his mouth, then crunched it into a ball and tossed it violently on the plate. 'So what's going on here, Dad? What are you doing in this place?'

Henry Sr. took a sip of his drink, watching the towel uncurl on his son's plate. 'Yeah, well, I suppose I have some explaining to do, as they say. Where would you like for me to start?'

'Why you never called or came back would be good.'

Henry Sr. took another sip. The inside rim of his lips were black with the thick wine. 'There's a momentum to isolation.'

Henry stared at his father, waiting for him to continue. 'What's that supposed to mean?' he asked after a minute. 'Can't you come back?'

'Where to, Hank? You asking me to come live with you and Carol?'

Henry looked at his plate. 'But what about years ago? Couldn't you have come back then?'

'Maybe.'

'Maybe?' He met his father's gaze. 'You know, if you keep up with all this evasive bullshit I might as well turn around and drive home.'

'You won't, though,' Henry Sr. said.

'So why have you sent for me then?' he asked softly, picking charred skin from a miniature wing.

'Hard to say, Hank. No real reason.' He swirled the dregs of his wine in the glass. 'Don't hold your breath for an apology, though.'

They were silent for a long time.

'Let's watch some TV,' Henry said.

The eleven o'clock news led with a story about a local girl who had gone missing. Prudence Atwater, aged seven. She was last seen early that morning on the way to church school. They showed a hazy colour photo of her – pigtails and a toothless grin. It was followed by an appeal from her parents, a couple in their mid-twenties. The mother's eyes were puffy. The father wore a baseball cap and had a thin blond moustache. The report ended with a policeman asking the public to call a toll-free number.

'Have you ever noticed,' Henry Sr. asked from the sofa, 'how people in times of sorrow or stress tend to express themselves in clichés? I've been watching a lot of TV in the past few years, as you've probably figured out, and I've noticed this. For example, the victims of tornadoes or floods always, and I mean always, say, "Well, at least we're still alive. I guess all we can do is pick up the pieces and start rebuilding." And when a young person dies people always speak of the waste, of potential nipped in the bud, as if it were inconceivable that this kid could have grown up without becoming an Eichmann or a Speck. The term happy-go-lucky is often used. And people like these,' he nodded at the screen, 'always ask that their loved one just be returned unharmed, claiming that they're not interested in pressing charges. As if the creep who has their kid is going to say, Oh well, in that case. I often wonder if camera crews haven't got these disaster cue cards which they carry around for use in these circumstances.' He faced his son. 'What these people never realise is that things usually don't work out the way you plan. If they were smart, they'd be glad the kid is gone. Because then they'll be able to imagine a life which will be infinitely more satisfying than any actual one could have been.'

Henry couldn't think of anything to say. They watched the sports and the farming weather. When the news ended he looked at his father, wanting to ask him what he meant. But he had fallen asleep.

Henry awoke the next morning to the microwave's beep. It took him a moment to get his bearings – he was in a bedroom, lying atop a shabby quilt, staring at a calendar decorated with photos of circuitry. He slipped into his pants and walked through the simulated wood hallway to the kitchen. His father was taking a cup of steaming coffee from the microwave.

'Morning,' he said. 'You want some Java?'

Henry nodded. His father handed him the mug, then prepared another, filling it with cold tap water and a heaping teaspoon of instant granules before putting it in the oven.

'What did you do to your leg?' Henry asked, gesturing to the crutch his father leaned on.

'Oh, I twisted my knee falling into a ditch,' Henry Sr. said as he punched in the code. 'This place is full of ravines and rabbit holes. Warrens, is the right word.' He looked at his son. ''Member the time you fell off your bike into that ditch and impaled your knee on a broken bottle?'

'The blood.'

'Incredible.'

'I didn't cry, though.'

'You were in shock, Hank. You couldn't have cried.'

'You say.'

'Eleven stitches, right?'

'Still have the scar.' Henry looked at his father. 'You were teaching me.'

'You got away from me.'

The oven's klaxon sounded. Henry Sr. removed his mug, puffing at the steaming surface of the coffee. Bits of foam flew off, splattering the oven door.

'You know how they say you're supposed to get right back on your bike after a fall like that?' Henry asked.

Henry Sr. nodded imperceptibly.

'Well, I've always wondered why you didn't let me. I mean, I wanted to. But you said no.'

'Where would you have gone, Hank?'

There was a long silence.

'So what's on the agenda?' Henry asked.

'A tour in the pick-up.'

'Did they find that little girl?'

Henry Sr. scowled after taking a sip. 'Not yet.'

They set out a half hour later, driving towards the interstate. Henry Sr. explained the function of the windowless modern buildings set back from the road as they went. Most were microchip manufacturers, although there was one complex where PCBs were recycled and another where personal tear gas canisters, for self-defence use, were made.

'This county has one of the lowest per capita incomes in the States,' Henry Sr. explained. 'You take what you can get.'

They were stopped at a roadblock just before the access ramp to the highway by a state trooper holding a clipboard. 'Do you live around here, sir?' he asked.

'Sure do. Just back up the state road,' Henry Sr. said, jerking his thumb over his shoulder.

'Have you see this girl in the past twenty-four hours?' the trooper asked, handing him a reproduction of the Polaroid they had seen on the news.

'Just on the news,' Henry Sr. said, making to hand it back.

'Would you care to look at it, sir,' the trooper said, ducking his head and looking at Henry.

Henry took the photo. 'Sorry,' he said, handing it back.

'Thank you,' the trooper said, moving off to wave down the next car.

They travelled two stops west along the interstate. Before the end of the exit ramp, they turned on to a dirt road that led to a whitewashed cinderblock building. There were four cars parked in its gravel lot, as well as a squat billboard trailer that read 'Girls' and 'Miller Longnecks 99c'. As they walked towards the building a man in a plaid sports coat emerged, walked quickly to his car and drove off. Henry stopped abruptly twenty feet from the door, his feet scraping on the gravel. His father stopped and pivoted on his crutch to face him.

'Let me guess what's inside,' Henry said. 'There'll be a bartender, maybe he's a Vietnam vet with crude tattoos and wise eyes, who'll blandly say your name and nod hello as we enter, in memory of those 3 a.m. pseudo-profound conversations you two've had. He'll serve you your favourite beer without having to be told which it is. Then there'll be a washed-out blonde dancer leaning against the juke box — it's her break — and she'll narrow her eyes and slowly exhale cigarette smoke through her nostrils like some dragon lady as she remembers a recent insult or infidelity you've perpetrated against her. The men at the tables, lay-over truckers or unemployed textile workers, men who know the feel of tools and weapons and have cruel senses of humour, will mutter to each other how you're all right, recalling some heroic stand you made in this very place against a guy who got to the final round of a Tough Man contest. And after we sit at the best table, the g-string dancer, she's the washed-out blonde's cousin, will sidle on over, thrusting a gartered thigh forward in the well-practised knowledge you'll fold in a five with a little bit of a tickle to her beacon-like clit. This is a place you've made into yours, Dad, and you're taking me in here to show me that I'm a stranger now, that our family is dead and gone.'

They were silent for a while, watching the trucks as they raced by on the interstate with Dopplered groans.

'Actually,' Henry Sr. said, 'I brought you here because it has the only ping-pong table in the county.'

Despite the cars in the parking lot, the club was empty of customers. There was a bar along one wall and, at the back of the room, a square stage backed by mirrors and surrounded by three long tables. There were also about a dozen four-seat tables scattered throughout the club. The oriental man behind the bar was reading a newspaper. When he saw Henry Sr. and Henry he called out over his shoulder. A young oriental woman with short legs appeared in the door behind the bar. She wore a US army shirt with the nameplate blacked out. It was open to the waist, exposing small breasts and lacy panties.

'Not necessary,' Henry Sr. said to her. He made a swatting motion with his left hand to the bar tender.

The girl disappeared.

'Spongy or hard?' the bartender asked.

ECHOLOCATION

'Spongy,' Henry said.

'Hard,' said his father.

After collecting their paddles, they passed through an open archway covered by hanging beads to the room with the table. Its walls were lined with stacks of empty bottles, broken chairs and dented beer kegs. There was a gashed stereo speaker beneath the single, barred window. Without a word, Henry and his father began to warm up.

They had played ping-pong at least once a week through most of Henry's teens. Silent, pitched pre-dinner battles in the finished basement. It was the only thing they did together with any regularity. They were evenly matched for the first few years, splitting games that often went past 21. In the months leading up to Henry Sr.'s departure, Henry had begun to get the upper hand, winning nearly every match, occasionally shutting out his father.

After trying unsuccessfully to play while leaning on his crutch, Henry Sr. placed it against the wall and hopped back to the table. 'I'm going to have to play with a hand on the table,' he said.

Henry conceded this breach of the rules with a terse nod.

'You serve,' his father said.

The first game was tentative, with most points coming on unforced errors. Henry, who hadn't played in eleven years, had difficulty finding his distance. He was too cautious – many of his shots hit the net. Henry Sr. had obviously kept in practice, yet his injured leg disturbed his balance, causing him occasionally to lurch forward and overhit. Twice, attempted slams sailed high above the table, hitting Henry in the chest and in the neck. Yet Henry Sr.'s power and accuracy allowed him eventually to win the first game by 4 points. As they changed ends music filtered in from the next room. Customers had arrived. The girl was dancing.

Henry changed tactics in the second game. He played defensively, returning everything soft and deep, waiting for his father to falter on his bad leg. Although Henry Sr. was able to hit several winners off his son's feeble shots, he missed more often, including a few which again slammed into Henry's body. One struck him just below the eye. His father never apologised or acknowledged the blows, but simply readied to play on. Henry evened the match with a 21–14 win.

Henry Sr. soon figured out his son's strategy. He played more conservatively in the rubber game. They had several long rallies, each waiting for the other to make an error. The tempo would gradually increase until one would try a slam. After fifteen minutes they were tied at 21. Henry had the serve. He spun one wide to his father's backhand, hoping to drive him away from the table so he could pass him on the opposite side. Henry Sr. anticipated him, however, catching the ball early, then moving across the table. Henry still tried to go down the right side, but caught the ball on the edge of his racket. It shot off at a forty-five degree angle, bouncing behind his father, a clean winner.

'Lucky shot,' Henry Sr. said as he hobbled after the ball. They were the first words spoken in the match.

Henry still had the serve. He aimed one into his father's body. Henry Sr. moved around it, hitting a fast, flat return to his son's backhand. Henry could only manage to return a weak lob. Henry Sr. took two steps to his left in preparation for a forehand smash. Yet his leg gave way as he swung, causing him to hit the ball too late. It sailed in a direct line across the table, striking Henry in the left eye. He dropped his racket and cupped his hands over his eye, which immediately began to water. He rubbed it for several seconds, then looked at his hand in front of his face. It was a blur. He looked to the other side of the table. His father was gone. The beads in the doorway swayed.

He picked up his racket and walked into the main room. Henry Sr. stood near the door, watching the stage. Henry joined him, his left eye still watering, his vision blurred. There were three bikers sitting at the long table that bordered the stage, watching impassively as the oriental girl danced above them. She was completely naked except for a garter and heels. Her shaved crotch was dotted with stubble. One of the bikers produced a pack of cigarettes and passed it around. He then tossed a box of matches to the girl, who caught it without looking at him. Still dancing, she took two wooden matches from the box and inserted them into her nipples. She then struck a match, which she used to light the other two. She stood over the bikers now, slowly working down to her knees and thrusting her torso towards the men. One by one, they lit their cigarettes on the two burning matches. The girl then leapt to her feet, turning rapid pirouettes that extinguished the flames and left a double-helix of metal-grey smoke around her naked body.

'I won,' Henry said.

His father looked him over. 'Funny. You don't look like it.'

They had lunch at a nearby diner called Poor Boyz BBQ. Henry ordered the Barbecue Special in the belief that it would be the smothered spare ribs that he and Carol ate at the family restaurant in New Jersey. Instead, he was served a clay-coloured mound of shredded pork, a matching lump of mashed potatoes, a pile of cigarette-butt-sized green beans, and a pleated paper cup soggy with coleslaw. The food came on a multi-ply paper plate, with a short plastic fork and a chemically moistened towel in a foil wrapper. Henry could only eat a few mouthfuls, washing them down with large gulps of over-sweetened iced tea. His father ate greedily. He still wasn't speaking. Henry's eye had stopped watering, although the bulbous welt that had come up on the bottom lid now throbbed. And his vision was still blurred, giving everything a fuzzy patina. Henry scooped some ice from his drink, folding it into his moistened towel. The chemical sting its juices caused when he applied the compress to his eye was strangely pleasing.

They headed home after eating. The same state trooper stopped them.

'Any luck?' Henry Sr. asked.

The trooper tapped his clipboard against his leg. 'Just heard on the radio that they found her shoes at the edge of the woods behind the Free Will Baptist Church. They're trying to scrounge up a search line. You should head on over there if you got the time.'

Henry Sr. nodded as he pulled off.

'We gonna do that?' Henry asked. He was surprised by how boyish his voice sounded.

His father looked over at him, smiling and nodding. 'That's a hell of shiner you got there, son.'

The Free Will Baptist Church was a massive brick building with four white-washed Ionic colonnades and a gleaming steeple. There were about twenty vehicles in its football-field-sized parking lot – police cruisers, pick-ups with jumbo wheels, rusting Datsuns and Impalas, a remote TV van with a small dish on the roof. Henry Sr. parked near the crowd which had gathered around a long folding table at the back end of the lot. Two women with blue windbreakers arranged food and drink on it. Beyond the table, some thirty men were listening to a deputy sheriff with long sideburns and a SWAT-style baseball cap. A camera crew stood to one side, filming the speaker. Henry and his father joined the crowd. Some of the men gave them quick, nervous smiles before averting their eyes. Henry thought of the other times he'd shared that look of guilty complicity – with frat brothers while initiating freshmen, with his sister while listening to their parents argue or make love, with his wife after the miscarriage. Henry looked at his father. His eyes were lively, thrilled.

'What you have to be cognisant of,' the deputy was saying, 'is that we are searching for a little girl, a little alive girl is what we're gonna presume, who is in some way injured or incapacitated. So don't go stomping through the woods like a one-legged man in an ass-kicking contest, all right?' The group's nervous laughter stopped quickly, self-consciously. 'And use your pole only to move aside brush. Do not, I repeat, do not, go jamming that boy into the ground like you're throwing seed. The other thing is that you must maintain the line. Keep about ten feet apart from the next fella and keep up with him. Don't go wandering on up ahead or lollygagging behind. OK,' he said, standing on his toes for a moment to gauge the size of the crowd, 'looks like we got sufficient personnel for a line. Grab yourself a stick and form up at the edge of the woods. If you wanna get a cup of coffee or one of them butter biscuits grab it now 'cause we ain't gonna be stopping for no grub till we come out to Diley Creek.'

They took three-foot sections of dowel and fluorescent armbands from another deputy. Henry Sr. left his crutch at the table, using the search stick for support. He led Henry up the sprawling lawn to the edge of the thick wood of pine and scrub. Silently, the men formed the line. To Henry Sr.'s left was a fat man in a Century 21 blazer. To Henry's right was a young man with a shirt emblazoned with a chest X-ray design. He had a dusting of flour over the hair on his forearms and carried a Swiss army knife in a small sheath on his belt. The sideburned deputy weaved among them for a minute, positioning them at ten-foot intervals. The camera crew would follow closely. He tried to launch the line with a blast from his whistle, yet the pea caught in the aperture, causing the whistle to give a reedy screech. He shook it to loosen the pea, but by then the searchers had moved off.

They walked in slow silence, stumbling over tangled roots or in animal dens hidden by pine needles. It took them five minutes to cover a hundred yards. The only sounds they made were the snap of dry wood beneath their feet and the muted squelch of the deputies' radios. Henry's still-blurred vision made it hard for him to keep with the line. The woods appeared to him as one amorphous, looming growth. He wasn't sure where to step. He would get caught up or wander ahead, only to be quickly restored to the line by the hovering deputies.

They found unrelated items as they moved deeper into the woods – an unopened package of hot dog buns, a waterlogged hymnal, a car radio, a condom that had been nailed to a tree. After a half hour the camera crew decided to return to the church, where they'd wait for news. Men began to carry on conversations with those next to them, nervous, bland talk to dispel the enormity of what they were trying to find. A flat bottle of Jack Black passed surreptitiously down the line. Henry looked at his father. He was moving well with his stick, better than with the crutch. He spoke at length to the man in the Century 21 blazer, who listened with a reddened, befuddled face. At one point Henry wandered close enough to overhear his father.

'So I suppose that next you'll be telling me you'd rather watch a documentary about Coolidge than one about Jim Jones . . .'

ECHOLOCATION

One hour into the search, someone found a human-sized mound covered by disturbed leaves and a section of chicken wire. Fabric was visible beneath the surface. The searchers gathered around in a loose circle as the sideburned deputy spoke into his radio. When he finished, he stepped up and gingerly picked through the debris, his free hand reflexively balanced on his gun.

'Nah,' he said to nobody in particular. 'It's just nothing.'

The men seemed uncertain of whether to be relieved or disappointed. Henry looked at his father. A slight, contemptuous smile bent his mouth. They re-formed the line and moved on. Henry caught the teen with the X-ray shirt staring at him.

'What you call a boomerang that don't come back?' the boy asked.

Henry shrugged.

'A stick.'

Henry laughed indulgently, but the boy just turned away.

They reached the creek. It was small and slow moving, dammed with heaps of rusty metal that created whirlpools of industrial froth.

'Listen up,' the sideburned deputy said as the men formed a cluster on the bank. 'I ain't authorised to take nobody further than this here creek. If any of y'all wanna keep on looking on your own, that's fine. If not, just follow the creek up that way a stretch and you'll come out on the state road. There's a bus waiting to take you back to the church.'

Nobody seemed to want to keep on searching. They began to shuffle along the path above the creek. Henry made to join them, but felt his father tug on his sleeve.

'What do you say we keep on, Hank?' he asked.

'How's your leg?'

'It'll hold.'

Henry looked into the dirty water. His vision still hadn't completely focused. 'All right.'

They found a place to cross the creek several hundred feet downstream. The woods soon grew thicker, hastening the dusk. Cicadas revved, a noise Henry had heard only in movies. Sourceless smoke hovered in some of the depressed coves.

'Nothing like this in Allendale, eh?' Henry Sr. asked.

'No way.'

'I walk through the woods around the trailer sometimes. Just randomly. I love their emptiness. The isolation. Some people walk through the woods and see God but I think that's a crock of shit. Because, the thing is you're on your own, Hank. Once I saw a couple making love and other times I've seen hunters waiting to ambush deer, but that's all. That's all.' They walked in silence for a minute. 'What's amazing is how your mind can just go blank out here. That's the real awe of it. Once I got lost, really lost, and ended up walking until dawn, when I came to the interstate. I sat there watching the trucks bombing down to Raleigh. Beautiful, beautiful.'

He stopped and faced his son. His features sagged a little, making him look older.

'I guess that's why I wanted you to come down here,' he said softly. 'To tell you . . . Tell you you're on your own, Hank. I could never bring myself to tell you that when you were a boy.'

'Is this why you didn't come back?' Henry asked, trying in vain to see his father's expression through the dusk and the blur of his swollen eye.

'My leaving had nothing to do with being a witness or a hero or anything other than the fact that I simply wanted to get out. There was no danger, Hank. I just wanted out. I'd wanted to go for years but didn't have the opportunity or the guts. This witness protection thing was the way. The way out. They didn't even want me in the programme, but I insisted, and they needed my testimony. There was never any threat to my life.'

They listened to the insects for a moment.

'The thing is that I believed I could change everything,' Henry Sr. said, his voice softening. 'That with one move I could break free. Erase the tapes. Get a new life.' He looked at his feet. 'And now you can see how well . . . ' His voice caught. He pinched the bridge of his nose and shook his head once. 'How well I've succeeded.'

Henry reached out to touch his father, but didn't complete the gesture. He felt an inexplicable swell of energy. 'Let's find this little bitch,' he said, charging off into the brush. He could hear his father limping after him.

They worked furiously, ripping away brush, upturning mounds of loose earth. They took turns leading the way. They had no set course. They followed hunches. After an hour of this, near dark, they came upon a clearing, a circle of knee-high grass a hundred yards in diameter. At its opposite edge was an unnatural mass. Henry couldn't make out what it was. He set off towards it, parting the high grass with his prodding stick. His father followed as quickly as he could.

Near the middle of the clearing Henry felt a powerful shock across his legs, just above his knees. As if he'd been struck by a whip. A hot pulse rippled through his groin and viscera as he fell into a sitting position. He rubbed at the flesh of his thighs, which tingled with residual pain. Henry Sr. passed him and cleared away the high grass with his stick, exposing a section of silver wire eighteen inches off the ground.

'It's a pasture marker,' he explained. 'To keep in cows. It's electrified, but I guess you know that.'

Henry struggled to his feet and looked around. The shock had refocused his eyesight. He could now see that the mass was an abandoned car. A fifties Chevy or Buick, with rounded roof and long fins. It had no tyres or windows. Moss and vine punctured the rusted-through doors. His father held down the electric wire with his prodding stick, allowing Henry to step over it. Henry did the same for him. They walked quickly towards the car.

They stopped abruptly twenty feet away, as if there were another electric barrier. The cicadas screamed at the darkness.

'Jesus God,' Henry said.

'Do you feel it?' Henry Sr. asked.

'Yes.'

'She's in there, Hank.' He took a step closer.

'Let's get somebody,' Henry said, staying back.

'No. We have to look, Henry. Come on.'

'Dad . . . '

'Come on.'

They walked slowly to the car. Henry Sr. stopped a few steps from it and looked at his son, nodding almost imperceptibly. Henry looked at the car for a moment. The cicadas swelled to a crescendo, like blood pressure through his ears. He strode quickly to the front door, jerking it open so hard that it fell to the ground. He had to dance away to keep it from cracking into his shins. He looked in. The leather had rotted from the seats, exposing metal springs. He looked under the gutted dashboard, then searched the back seat area. Nothing.

'Hank.'

He joined his father at the back of the car. He was moving his hands through the standing water which filled the trunk, clearing away squirming tadpoles and cumuli of light-green scum. It, too, was empty. Henry looked at his father. They shook their heads in unison when their eyes met.

'Nothing,' said Henry.

'Yes,' his father replied. 'I mean no.'

It was after ten o'clock by the time they returned to the mobile home. They said nothing. Henry Sr. put two large potatoes and a tray of frozen lasagne in the microwave, then poured two glasses of blackish wine. Henry took his without a word and drank it down, nodding approval as he swallowed the dregs. After they finished eating Henry Sr. flicked on the television. They watched from the table, not bothering to clear the dirty dishes. The eleven o'clock news came on. Breathlessly, the young newsreader reported that Prudence Atwater had just been found alive in the back of a van in South Carolina. A man and a woman were under arrest. Initial reports described them as drifters with histories of mental illness. Prudence was confused and tired, but unharmed. After the report there was a piece on local efforts to find her. There was a brief segment on the search line at the church, including a shot containing Henry and his father. Henry was surprised how small and old his father looked as he leaned on his prodding stick.

'So what's the plan?' Henry Sr. asked after clicking off the television.

Henry finished the dregs of a glass of the blackish wine. 'Maybe I'll stay here a while,' he said, staring into the empty glass. 'That all right?'

Henry Sr. picked the gallon plastic jug from the floor. 'Stay as long as you like,' he said, refilling Henry's glass. 'Stay all summer if you want.'

'Maybe I will,' Henry said, returning his father's black smile. 'Maybe I will.'

Elsewhere

DAVID HARSENT

With him gone, her mind's-
eye view of the dock
was coiled rope, hanks of chain,
tarps, and a rat's arse
slipping between pallets.

The steep along Belstone Tor
seemed a welter of foxholes.
She would sleepwalk
with the night-patrols and litter
the map with tank-traps.

By the time she had ticked
six months off, her daydreams
were all of housewifery;
buffed floors, Kilner jars
in ranks of three, the weight

of a pound of cookers
in a string bag with wooden handles.
She dressed herself in dirndls
and nodded to the slow,
formal music of recipes.

She was as lonely
as a woman with two husbands.
On the trip from cellar to kitchen
she went lightly, thinking
some guilt might be raised with the dust,

DAVID HARSENT

driftless, no more than a guest
like the rafter's pipistrelle
or the toad, stock-still
beside the flour keg,
stunned by its diamond solitaire.

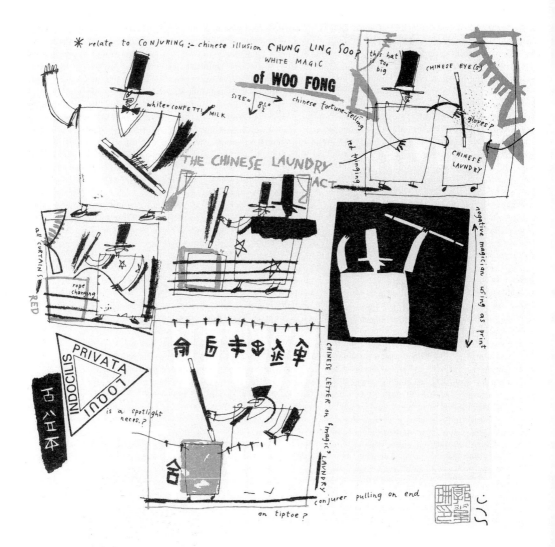

Head in the Sand

JONATHAN TREITEL

His wife was in his arms again. He accepted the weight of her, the warmth of her, her musky aroma, her hair tickling his neck . . . then he became aware that she could not possibly be in his arms because she had died of tuberculosis in the laager. He knew he was dreaming: ascending through tissued layers of sleep towards wakefulness. He wanted to swoop back down.

But his eyes opened. He saw the honeycomb mesh of a wire fence; beyond that: an expanse of dusty veld with a pink dawn at the bottom. He rolled on to his side. Bulky objects tumbled off his chest, croaking and mumbling. An orange thing jumped on to a crossbeam beneath the low rafters. It tilted its head back to emit a repetitive racket: halfway between a human sob and the clatter of a Gattling.

The night before last he had escaped from the laager. The actual break-out had been easy enough: he had just got one of those stupid red-faced English guards drunk on a bottle of maize spirit; then slipped away through a gap in the paling. But what good did freedom do? All his friends had warned him he was safer inside. They had said (using the laager English-Afrikaans argot) that the *bloodies* were sure to *nab* him: he would not survive twenty-four hours out there. Otto had drawled in his Transvaal yokel accent the old adage: Better the devil you know than . . . And Dirk had interrupted Otto with one of his city-slicker cynical remarks that the laager was the most luxurious place to be during the *pacification* – if only because (Dirk had added) the English had destroyed everything outside.

But certainly there was nothing for him inside the laager. His only son, Louis, had been reported missing-believed-dead while besieging Mafeking. And his wife, Marie, had died in the women's section of the laager less than a week ago. They had not let him see her at the end, not let him hold her . . .

He rolled a white egg between his palms. Bits of straw and a downy feather clung to the shell: he blew them away. A hen jumped on his shoulder, nagging him: he ignored it. He rubbed his thumbtip in a spiral on the egg's blunter end. He considered his farm. A few hundred acres near Rustenburg. His father had homesteaded there. Nothing grand or special about it – just half a dozen fields of tobacco, maize; a shed with some pigs and goats in it (he had tried keeping chickens but they had never survived) – yet it was where he belonged. The house had been built by his father: it was wooden, painted a clear white. How often he had stood on the verandah at sunset, watching his workers carry in the hanks of raw tobacco, and felt at peace.

He was hungry. He smashed the egg against his kneecap, and sucked its insides. It tasted bad. He ate another five eggs.

He rose to his feet, brushed away the screeching hens (a yellow one with white blotches; a brown one; a black one with a wound on its throat), bowed to avoid bumping his head on the rafters, and opened the wire mesh gate. He stepped out into the yard. A few dazed chickens hopped after him. He glanced around. This farm was evidently owned by a soft-living Uitlander: nobody was up yet.

Then it occurred to him it would be wise to conceal his presence in the coop: he would have to give the impression the eggs had been stolen by a hyena. He went back inside and kicked the straw about. He knocked the remaining eggs on to the floor and stomped on most of them. He scraped the yolk off his soles against the fence. And what about the birds? Surely the hyena would have ravaged them too? He picked up the nearest hen with both hands, clutching it firmly. Its soft body squirmed. He opened his mouth. He pushed a wing between his teeth. He felt an itchy flutter against palate and tongue. The feathers tasted like rancid grease. He bit hard. A bone crunched. A blurred loud cluck. The stupid rooster sat on its rafter and did nothing. He threw the hen down in a corner, on top of a mess of shattered eggshells and oozing fluids.

He stood in the shade of a spinney. It was noon. He was making good progress. If he just followed the river Amstel until it met the Avon, then walked true east, he would be home by nightfall. The call of an unseen songbird. He turned and glanced behind. He gazed into the blue distance at the mountains of Delft. How soft they looked, and how fragile.

This is the seeming paradox: a barbed wire fence surrounded where his farm had been, but when he peered through it he could see no occupants or sign of cultivation. The fence itself looked like a kind of vegetation: its iron spikes were lush and curly. Marie and he had gone for endless walks here, long ago in their courting days.

The fence was too high to jump over and too thick to crawl under. He followed it round. A sign in English: 'TRESPASSERS WILL BE PROSECUTED'.

At last he found a spot where a giant eucalyptus (he remembered planting it about the time of Louis's birth) had toppled across the wire. Its roots stuck out. He climbed along the trunk – balancing carefully on the slippery grey bark.

He jumped down. At first sight his farm looked abandoned. The land was not irrigated. He kicked a clod: it crumbled to dust. He passed his maize field: the husky cobs sprawled on the earth, desiccated and useless. The tobacco plants were flopped over: the leaves were curing themselves under the sun. He chewed a leaf thoughtfully; then spat it out.

Here had stood his pig shed. There his goat pen. Over there the quarters of the farm workers. Nothing but a few charred beams, now. He bent and stroked a lump of blackened wood. He dug his fingernail into a niche filled with soft greasy-feeling ash . . . It seemed the English had burned everything. So be it. He realised he was content, in a way, that his farm should pass away at the same time as his wife and son. A kind of symmetry and purity.

And at last he arrived at his house. Two exterior walls were still erect. The roof had collapsed. He advanced cautiously through what had been the vegetable garden. He had heard many stories in the laager about the cowardice and treachery of the English. Otto had said some cousins of his had come home only to be murdered by a platoon of *bloodies* who had hidden in the bedroom. And Dirk had explained this was quite a common tactic. But there was no human track here. A patch of grass had been cropped by some animal; a mound of strange pale droppings had accumulated on the verandah. Once upon a time, Louis had played here with his pet goat. He had chanted songs in the native language to his favourite servant. Then the goat had become too smelly, and Marie had insisted it was slaughtered. Off-white paint was flaking from what remained of the verandah railing, ugly red in the light of sunset.

He stepped inside his old home. An acrid smell like in the chicken coop. Or perhaps this was emanating from his own clothes and body? A few broken chairs and tables; bits of glass and china; plaster from the fallen-in ceiling. Nothing much besides: the place had been thoroughly looted. He rapped the air where the dining-table had stood. He patted the 'sideboard', the 'display cabinet', the niche that had been filled with Marie's dowry of fine blue-and-white Dutch china . . . A door-frame was still in existence, though – unattached to anything. He chose to walk round it, through the 'wall'.

A bedroom with no bed. The heavy cast-iron bedstead had been stolen – perhaps melted down to make munitions. But the mattress, the dear old cream-and-brown mattress stuffed with straw, on which Marie and himself had made love and dreamed, lay on the floor at a slight angle. Three white ellipsoids rested on it. What the hell were they doing here? He was outraged; he remembered telling Louis the story of Goldilocks, putting on a special gruff voice to say what Daddy Bear has to say. They were each the size of a baby or a small tombstone. Could they be some kind of bomb . . . a booby trap? But they were surely too abstract: too uncomplicated to be dangerous. What they most resembled (the comparison was involuntary) was giant eggs.

For an instant, he supposed the chickens were having their revenge. This thought was so absurd (he realised) that he concluded he must be in a dream. But he was not. He knew he was not.

So these three items were actual. Tentatively, he crawled across the mattress, stretched out his hand and tapped the biggest one. It was smooth and warm. He banged it quite firmly: it wobbled as if some liquid were swirling in its middle. He took off his boot, and raised it, about to hammer its heel on the thing as hard as he damn well could.

The full moon shone through the 'window' and the 'wall'. Something made Piet look round. He saw the solid moon, the stars, the shadowy veld, and, charging towards him across his farmland, a score of creatures with a head and two legs – but taller than a man, and faster, and hissing, and winged. They bounded through the vegetable garden and sprang up on to the verandah.

So this is what the *bloodies* have done to me, he thought. Marie and Louis are gone. My maize, my tobacco, my goats, my Blacks, my pigs, my sanity – all gone. He buried his head beneath the mattress.

And, somewhere else, the largest crowd of Englishmen and Englishwomen that had ever gathered in one place had gathered. The uncrowned king marched to the front of the podium. He declared, '*The siege of Mafeking has been broken!*' And everybody cheered. Everybody kissed and hugged. Men tipped their top hats or tossed their caps in the air. A million women raised their magnificent hats, each ornamented with a dyed plume, and waved them. A million ostrich feathers swayed on high.

Contributors' Notes

Fleur Adcock was born in New Zealand but has lived in England since 1963. *Selected Poems* was published in 1983 and *The Incident Book* in 1986, both by Oxford University Press, who published her translations of the Romanian poet Grete Tartler in 1989. She is also editor of the *Faber Book of 20th Century Poetry* (1987).

A. Alvarez was born in London in 1929. He has written several books of literary criticism and his selected poems, *Autumn to Autumn*, was published by Macmillan in 1978. He is the author of two novels, and has also written books on suicide, divorce, gambling, North Sea oil, and mountaineering: *Feeding the Rat* (Bloomsbury, 1988).

Stephen Amidon was born in Chicago. He writes for the *Literary Review* and the *Financial Times*, and Bloomsbury are publishing his novel next year. He lives in London with his wife and his daughter Clementine.

Martin Amis's novels include *The Rachel Papers* (1973), *Success* (1978) and *Money* (1984) (all Cape). His new novel, *London Fields* (Cape), was published in 1989. He has also published *The Moronic Inferno* (essays) (1986) and *Einstein's Monsters* (short stories) (1987) (both Cape).

Paul Bailey is the author of six novels. His first, *At the Jerusalem* (Cape, 1967), won the Somerset Maugham Award and his last, *Gabriel's Lament* (Cape, 1986), was shortlisted for the Booker Prize. He is working on a new novel to be published by Bloomsbury.

Cathy Bowman was born in El Paso, Texas, and now lives in New York City. Her work has appeared in *Kingfisher*, *The Paris Review* and *River Styx*. She is currently working on a collection of poetry entitled *Texas, Then*.

Scott Bradfield is thirty-four years old and the author of a collection of short stories, *The Secret Life of Houses* (Unwin Hyman, 1988), and a novel, *The History of Luminous Motion* (Bloomsbury, 1989). Born in California, he now lives in London. He is at work on a second novel.

Alan Brownjohn was born in London. In 1979 he gave up his teaching career to become a full-time writer. His latest collection of poetry, *The Observation Car* (Century Hutchinson), will be published in 1990, as will his first novel, *The Way You Tell Them* (André Deutsch). He also reviews and edits poetry, and in 1979 received the Cholmondeley Award for Poetry.

Angus Calder supports Dundee United. He is founder member of two curling clubs and once, long ago, playing for *Tribune* against the *New Statesman*, threw in to run Paul Johnson for a duck. In less exalted moments he wrote *The People's War* (1969) and *Revolutionary Empire* (1981) (both Cape), and was first Convenor of the Scottish Poetry Library.

Susannah Clapp is deputy editor of the *London Review of Books*.

Peter Dale is the co-editor with William Cookson of the poetry quarterly *Agenda*. His most recent books are *The Poems of Jules Laforgue* (Anvil, 1987) and *Narrow Straits* (Hippopotamus Press, 1987). Penguin republished his verse translation of François Villon in 1988.

Helen Dunmore was born in Yorkshire in 1952. Her published poetry includes *The Apple Fall* (1983), *The Sea Skater* (1986) and *The Raw Garden* (1988) (all Bloodaxe).

Gavin Ewart was born in London in 1916. He has worked in publishing, for the British Council, as a salesman, and as an advertising copywriter, with War Service, 1940–46. His published poetry includes *The Collected Ewart, 1933–1980* (1982) and *The New Ewart* (1982), *Late Pickings* (1987) and *Penultimate Poems* (1989) (all Century Hutchinson).

James Fenton's most recent book of poems, *Manilla Envelope*, appeared this year. He is a foreign correspondent for the *Independent* newspaper.

Jeff Fisher, an Australian, lives and works in London.

Maureen Freely was born in Neptune, New Jersey, grew up in Istanbul, Turkey, and now lives in a village in South Oxfordshire. She is the author of two novels, *Mother's Helper* (1979), and *The Life of the Party* (1985) (both Cape), and reviews fiction for the *Observer*. 'The Babysitter' is an extract from her novel in progress, *The Stork Club*.

John Fuller has published eleven collections of poetry, most recently *The Grey Among the Green* (Chatto, 1988). His fourth book of fiction, *The Burning Boys* (Chatto), appeared in the spring of 1989. He lives in Oxford and Wales.

Simon Gray's plays include *Otherwise Engaged*, *Quartermaine's Terms* and

Melon. He has also published novels and memoirs. His essay 'Still Trying' is adapted from his contribution to The Contemporary Authors Autobiography Series, Volume 3.

David Harsent's *Selected Poems* was published by the Oxford University Press in 1989. More recently, he has been working on an opera with the composer Harrison Birtwistle.

David Holden is an American writer living in London.

Dan Jacobson was born in Johannesburg in 1929. He is the author of many novels, short stories and critical essays. He is also professor of English at University College, London. These are his first published poems.

Benoît Jacques, a Belgian, lives in London. 'Play it by Ear' is taken from his book of the same title.

James Lasdun was born in London and now lives in New York. His collection of short stories, *The Silver Age*, was published by Cape in 1985 and a volume of poetry, *A Jump Start*, by Secker & Warburg in 1987.

Michael Leunig contributes cartoons and drawings to the Melbourne *Age* and is responsible for a number of books, including *The Penguin Leunig*, *The Second Leunig*, *A Bag of Roosters* and *Ramming the Shears*.

Malcom Lowry's filmscript of *Tender is the Night* was written between 1949 and 1950. The film was never made. He is the author of *Ultramarine* (1933) and *Under the Volcano* (1947). His posthumous publications include *Hear Us O Lord From Heaven They Dwelling Place* (1961), *Dark as the Grave Wherein my Friend is Laid* (1968) and *October Ferry to Gabriola* (1970) (all Cape).

David Mamet has written many plays, including *Speed-the-Plow*, *American Buffalo* and *Glengarry Glen Ross* (for which he received a Pulitzer Prize). His screenwriting credits include *The Verdict* (nominated for an Oscar), *The Postman Always Rings Twice*, *The Untouchables*, *House of Games* and *Things Change*.

Ian McEwan is the author of the short story collection *First Love, Last Rites* (1975) and *In Between the Sheets* (1978); the novels *The Cement Garden* (1978), *The Comfort of Strangers* (1981) and *A Child in Time* (1987); *Imitation Game: Three Plays for Television* (1981); and *Or Shall We Die: Liberetto for Oratorio by Michael Berkeley* (1983) (all Cape). 'Berlin' is an extract from his forthcoming novel.

John McGahern was born in 1934 in the West of Ireland, where he lives now.

His books include *The Barracks* (1963), *Nightlines* (1970), *The Pornographer* (1985), and *High Ground* (1979) (all Faber). 'Monaghan Day' is an extract from a novel which Faber will publish next year.

Candia McWilliam was born in 1955 in Edinburgh and now lives in Oxford. Her first novel, *A Case of Knives* (Bloomsbury, 1988), was the joint winner of the 1988 Betty Trask Award. Her second novel, *A Little Stranger*, was published by Bloomsbury in 1989.

Andrew Motion's most recent collection of poems, *Natural Causes* (Chatto, 1987), won the 1987 Dylan Thomas Memorial Award. He is at work on a biography of Philip Larkin as well as a series of novels.

Julie O'Callaghan was born in Chicago in 1954 and now lives in Dublin. Her poetry collection *Edible Anecdotes* (Dolmen) was published in 1983, and she has recently completed a second. A volume of poems for older children, *Taking My Pen For a Walk* (Orchard Books), was published in 1988.

Nigel Parry is a photographer and designer living in London.

Harold Pinter's plays include *The Caretaker*, *The Homecoming* and *Betrayal*. His *Collected Poems and Prose* (Methuen) appeared in 1986.

Peter Porter has lived in London since 1951, when he arrived from Brisbane, Australia. He is a poet and freelance journalist and broadcaster. His *Collected Poems* (1983) was published by Oxford University Press, as was *Fast Forward* (1984) and *The Automatic Oracle* (1987).

Craig Raine's books of poetry include *The Onion, Memory* (1978), *Postcard Home* (1979) (both Oxford University Press) and *Rich* (Faber, 1984). His book of essays, *Haydn and the Valve Trumpet* (Faber) will appear in 1990.

Christopher Reid has published three books of poetry: *Arcadia* (1979), *Pea Soup* (1982) (both Oxford University Press) and *Katherine Brac* (Faber, 1985). He is currently at work on a play.

Carol Rumens was born in South London. She has published six volumes of poetry, including *Selected Poems* (Chatto, 1987) and *The Greening of the Snow Beach* (Bloodaxe, 1988). She has also written a novel, *Plato Park* (Flamingo, 1987), and several short stories.

Dyan Sheldon was born in New York. Since the early seventies she has lived in England. Her novels include *Victim of Love* (1982) and *Dreams of an Average*

Man (1985) (both Heinemann). She is working on a new novel, and her short stories have appeared in many anthologies.

Mary Sullivan is a reviewer and a writer of short fiction and poetry. She also writes about walking.

D. J. Taylor was born in Norwich in 1960. *A Vain Conceit*, his study of contemporary British fiction, was published by Bloomsbury in 1989. He is also the author of a novel, *Great Eastern Land* (Secker & Warburg, 1986).

Jonathan Treitel was born in London in 1959. He has worked as a physicist and lived in San Francisco and Tokyo. Next year, his poems will appear in *Faber's Poetry Introduction 7* and Bloomsbury will be publishing his novel.

Stephen Wall lives in Oxford when he is teaching at the University, and on the borders of Wales when he is not. He is the author of *Trollope and Character* (Faber, 1988).

Nigel Williams was born in 1948 and lives in London. He has written four novels and his plays include *Class Enemy*, *Country Dancing*, *Nativity*, *Charlie* (for Central Television) and *Breaking Up* (for the BBC). For the last twenty years he has worked as an arts documentary film maker, and is at present the editor of BBC 2's *Bookmark*. He is the son of David Williams, the writer and critic.

The illustrations by Ian Beck, Guy Billout, Debbie Cook, Susan Curtis, George Hardie, Clifford Harper, Andrew Kulman, Paul Leith, Pierre Le-Tan, Sarah Maxey, and Philip Wiesbecker first appeared in the Trickett & Webb Calendar for 1983, 1986, 1988 and 1989.

Ian Hamilton, formerly editor of the *New Review* (1974–9) and author of *Fifty Poems, Robert Lowell: A Biography* and *In Search of J. D. Salinger*.